The Islamic State

Dear Junaid,

Best wishes,

Dean A[...]

The Islamic State

Combating the Caliphate Without Borders

Yonah Alexander and Dean Alexander

LEXINGTON BOOKS
Lanham • Boulder • New York • London

Published by Lexington Books
An imprint of The Rowman & Littlefield Publishing Group, Inc.
4501 Forbes Boulevard, Suite 200, Lanham, Maryland 20706
www.rowman.com

Unit A, Whitacre Mews, 26-34 Stannary Street, London SE11 4AB

British Library Cataloguing in Publication Information Available

Library of Congress Cataloging-in-Publication Data Available

Includes bibliographical references and index.
ISBN 978-1-4985-2511-4 (cloth : alk. paper)
ISBN 978-1-4985-2513-8 (paper : alk. paper)
ISBN 978-1-4985-2512-1 (electronic)

∞ ™ The paper used in this publication meets the minimum requirements of American
National Standard for Information Sciences Permanence of Paper for Printed Library
Materials, ANSI/NISO Z39.48-1992.

Printed in the United States of America

Contents

Abbreviations and Key Terms

AQ	Al-Qa'ida/Al-Qa'ida Central
AQAP	Al-Qa'ida in the Arabian Peninsula
AQI	Al-Qa'ida in Iraq
AQIM	Al-Qa'ida in the Islamic Maghreb
Caliph	The political and religious leader of the Muslim community. The Ottoman Empire's Abdul Mejid II was the last official Caliph.
Caliphate	An Islamic empire ruled by a Caliph. Mustafa Kemal Ataturk, President of the Turkish Republic, abolished the last Caliphate in 1924.
Da'esh	Islamic State of Iraq and al-Sham
FTO	Foreign Terrorist Organization
IS	Islamic State
ISI	Islamic State of Iraq
ISIL	Islamic State of Iraq and the Levant
ISIS	Islamic State of Iraq and Greater Syria; Islamic State of Iraq and al-Sham
Kurdistan	A region that is majority Kurdish, encompassing territories in Iraq, Syria, Iran, and Turkey.
Kurds	An ethnic minority group in the Middle East, the majority of whom are Sunni Muslims although others follow disparate religions.

Mujahideen	Muslim holy warriors or fighters
NATO	North Atlantic Treaty Organization
Peshmerga	Armed forces of the Kurdistan Regional Government (KRG), which covers part of Iraq. The term has been used more broadly to define Kurdish fighters.
PKK	Kurdish Workers Party
PUK	Patriotic Union of Kurdistan
Qur'an/ Koran	Islamic holy text
Sharia	Islamic law
Shaheed	Martyr
Shia/Shiite	The smaller of the two main branches of Islam. Shiites believe that the Caliph should be a direct descendant of the Prophet Muhammad. Bahrain, Iraq, Iran, and Lebanon are countries with a Shia/Shiite majority.
Sunni	The predominant of the two main branches of Islam. They believe that the Caliph should be designated by the religious leaders of the Islamic community and not based on lineage to the Prophet Muhammad.
UAE	United Arab Emirates
UK	United Kingdom
UN	United Nations
Yazidi	Ethno-religious minority group in the Middle East, Armenia, and the Caucasus regions.
YPG	People's Protection Units (Kurdish militia in Syria)

Maps

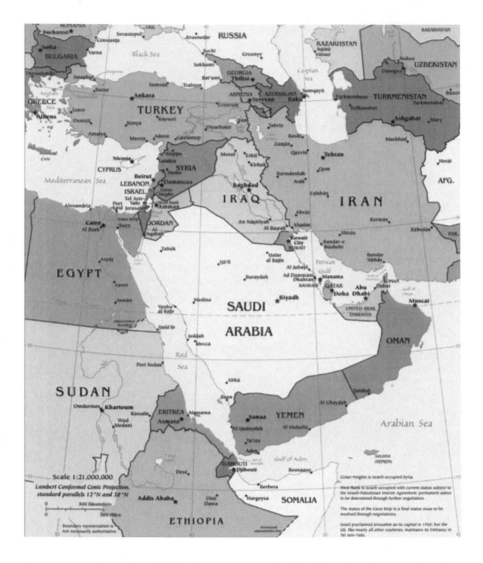

Figure 0.1. Map of the Middle East. *Source: The World Factbook, Central Intelligence Agency (undated).*

Figure 0.2. Map of Iraq. *Source: The World Factbook, Central Intelligence Agency (undated).*

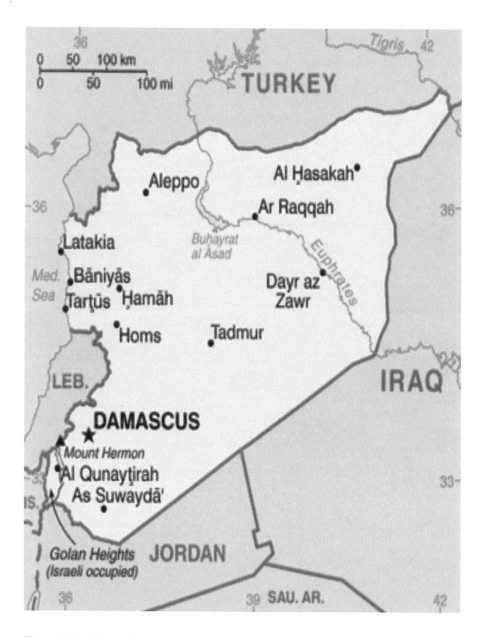

Figure 0.3. Map of Syria. *Source: The World Factbook, Central Intelligence Agency (undated).*

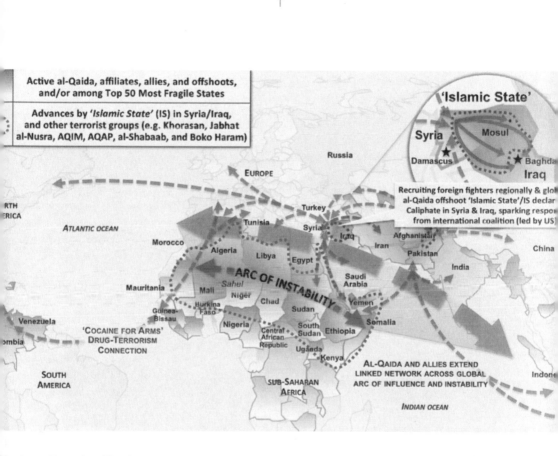

Figure 0.4. Terrorism Hot Spots: "Islamic State" Expands Arc of Instability Globally. *Source: Yonah Alexander-University Center for Terrorism Studies (April 2015).*

Preface

The so-called "Islamic State" (IS) that has swept into power in parts of Syria and Iraq presents an imminent danger to the global community, with its capacity as an effective, ideologically motivated, and bloodthirsty fighting force, coupled with its expanding territorial reach, on the ground and online. The Islamic State has taken on a quasi-state form that mixes modernity with ancient rites, and aggressively promotes sectarian violence and religious extremism with a decidedly apocalyptic bent.

By April 2015, it had established affiliate terror organizations that have claimed responsibility for deadly attacks in Afghanistan, Algeria, Egypt, Libya, Saudi Arabia, Tunisia, and Yemen. Likewise, the IS has won the allegiance of terror groups from as far away as Indonesia, Pakistan, the Philippines, and Nigeria, where Boko Haram's leaders pledged fealty to the IS self-declared caliphate. Also worrisome, the IS has been successfully radicalizing and recruiting fighters worldwide through its sophisticated social media tactics and aggressive offline actions. The Islamic State purveys an extremist, violence-infused ideology with an expansive outlook to match, as articulated by its widely uttered slogan, *baqiyya wa tatamaddad,* which essentially implies that the Islamic State is here to stay and will continue expanding.

For the international community, the Islamic State's savage yet partly successful record so far, as occupiers and killers, combined with its designs for the Levant and beyond, warrants very close scrutiny. Indeed, the Islamic State has introduced to the Middle East a new level of extremism and brutality, marked by volatile fluidity, with far-reaching, dangerously destabilizing effects on state and non-state actors, regionally and globally. In fact, General John Allen, Special Presidential Envoy for the Global Coalition to Counter the Islamic State, described the Islamic State as "one of the darkest forces that any country has ever had to deal with" as well as "a truly unparalleled threat to the region that we have not seen before."[1]

Similar sentiments were shared during a January 2015 joint press conference of U.S. President Barack Obama and British Prime Minister David Cameron. Prime Minister Cameron said, "We face a poisonous and fanatical ideology that wants to pervert one of the world's major religions, Islam, and create conflict, terror and death. With our allies, we will confront it wherever it appears."[2] In turn, President Obama expressed the need to develop "strategies to counter violent extremism that radicalizes recruits and mobilizes people, especially young people, to engage in terrorism."[3]

JIHADIST MARCH ON BAGHDAD

In early June 2014, the "Islamic State of Iraq and al Sham" (ISIS), a jihadist group controlling areas straddling the borders of Iraq and Syria, launched its offensive drive in Iraq with breathtaking pace and fanatical levels of violence. The Iraqi army, although greatly outnumbering the terrorists, crumbled before its foe. In doing so, the Iraqi army surrendered wide expanses of urban and rural territory, and fled in defection and full retreat. Although the speed of this conquest shocked the global community, in hindsight it should not have come as a surprise, given the sectarianism, belligerency, and mistrust that increasingly plagued Iraqi society during the eight years of Shiite Iraqi Prime Minister Nouri al-Maliki's ascendancy, from 2006–2014. This fragile hold on power manifested itself fully on the battlefield, as the allegiance of the Iraqi army in the face of death proved to be fleeting. Ultimately, ISIS drove to within striking distance of Baghdad and largely precipitated the collapse of al-Maliki's rule. He was replaced by a more broadly based Iraqi leadership.

By the end of June 2014, ISIS renamed itself the Islamic State and projected its claims of "sovereignty" over an occupied territory in Iraq and Syria that measured about the size of Belgium, with a population of eight million inhabitants. At the Grand Mosque in Mosul in July 2014, Abu Bakr al-Baghdadi proclaimed himself Caliph Ibrahim of the Islamic State.

Even prior to this declaration, Iraq, which had been viewed as a case study for effective counter-insurgency after the American-Iraqi successes in 2007 (though some political violence and instability remained), had fallen headlong into chaos and violence. From 2013 onward, Iraq experienced a marked rise in political violence, exacerbated by the Islamic State's antecedents, Shiite militias, and Iraqi government forces. In 2014, 12,282 persons were killed in Iraq, some two-thirds died since the expanded efforts against the IS in the second half of the year.[4]

Meanwhile, Syria was in the midst of a civil war that by spring 2015 had resulted in more than 210,000 deaths, while millions more became internally displaced persons and transnational refugees. The Syrian Observatory for Human Rights reported that 76,021 people were killed in 2014 during the Syrian conflict, of which 33,278 were civilians.[5]

The Islamic State and its progenitors aggravated and opportunistically took advantage of the de facto unraveling of these two states in the preceding years and today. The IS quasi-state now rests on a large swath of territory subsuming eastern Syria and western Iraq, with Raqqa, Syria, as its declared capital, and in possession of the second-largest city in Iraq, Mosul. As such, this newly declared Islamic State is not a "traditional" terrorist organization, but a transnational variant of a more dangerous degree.

And yet, by the end of March 2015, the IS lost some 25 percent of the land (13,000 square kilometers) it controlled at its zenith, thousands of IS fighters had been killed as well as about half of its top leadership, its funding sources have weakened, declining services in areas under its control have been noted, and internal strife has expanded.[6] The seemingly invincibility of IS perceived in summer 2014 was shattered by spring 2015. And still, the quasi-state's broad aspirations and inherent capabilities—due to control of land, thousands of fighters, ample funding, and otherwise—merit careful and dedicated efforts to ensure their demise.

REACTION: SHOCK AND DISMAY

In many parts of the world, especially in Muslim countries and the West, there was collective disbelief on several fronts. Where had these uncompromising, apocalyptically oriented fighters come from? How did the IS become so powerful so quickly? And, why did the international community fail to foresee and respond to its rise? Indeed, while the emergence of the terrorist group as a quasi-state actor seemed dramatic and surprising, its antecedents had been lurking and gaining strength in the region for more than a decade.

By summer 2014, even the most casual observer understood that the declaration of the Islamic State as a new caliphate warranted an immediate international response. The Islamic State achieved its weighty milestones in a short period through aggressive efforts, while eliciting widespread fear and finger pointing regarding its causes, and considerable perplexity as to viable solutions.

The purpose of this book is to provide an in-depth look at and analysis of these and related issues. In doing so, the work strives to offer insights into the nature of the IS and what the international community can do to combat it. In order to achieve this objective, the origins, intentions, leadership, capabilities, and operations of the IS are explored. The Islamic State's multifaceted efforts and effects in the region and beyond are described. Also, national, regional, and global strategies that are being pursued to address the new threat are examined. To this end, a range of recommendations are offered on specific steps that governmental, intergovernmental, and non-governmental bodies can take to counter the IS menace. Lastly, additional insights are presented relevant to combating the IS and undermining its potential future capabilities.

IS BACKGROUND AND CONTEXT

A brief historical and strategic context is in order. The Islamic State evolved out of a predecessor of the former al-Qa'ida in Iraq (AQI). Steadily, it had become a major actor in the Syrian civil war since its initial escalation during the uprising in 2011. Its terrorist predecessors were always on the brutal fringes of organizations like al-Qa'ida. AQI and IS leaders, from Abu Musab al-Zarqawi to Abu Bakr al-Baghdadi, were often denounced by other jihadists for their overly aggressive tactics and indiscriminate killing. In particular, these groups often targeted fellow Muslim civilians as well as religious and ethnic minorities with unusual brutality, including highly publicized beheadings.

The Islamic State's radical ideologies of Salafism-Jihadism-Takfirism, its fervent focus on Islamic eschatology, global ambitions, and harsh actions have served to recruit members worldwide to its cause. Concurrently, the IS has sought to intimidate individuals, communities, and countries across the globe. These threats and widespread IS massacres of Sunni, Shiite, and non-Muslim victims were often recorded and broadcasted through online social networks and the Islamic State's own propaganda outlets.

The United Nations has characterized some Islamic State massacres as violations of international law, accusing the group of committing acts of genocide, crimes against humanity, and war crimes. Increasingly, governments, non-profits, non-governmental organizations worldwide—non-Muslims and Muslim-alike—have harshly criticized the ideology and actions of the IS.

Apparently taking their cues on cruelty from the Assad regime as well as from ancient practices, IS's jihadists now seem to view the most horrific tactics as acceptable and almost passé. The Islamic State's frequent beheadings, amputations, crucifixions, mass executions, stonings, throwing people off buildings, and ease with burying—and even burning—people alive mark a new level of evil. With each passing day, new lows in the annals of human depravity are straddled: from organ harvesting to fund operations to the proposed sale of the bodies of dead opposition fighters.

The Islamic State's often-issued ultimatums requiring non-Sunni believers in its territories to convert, pay a *jizya* (tax), or be killed, have inflamed sectarian sentiments as well as accelerated internal and external displacement of refugees. The savage practices of the Islamic State have contributed to an alarming humanitarian crisis while further undermining any chance of reconciliation in the region for many years to come.

It is critical to distinguish the mindset and activities of the Islamic State from traditional Islam. As U.S. Secretary of State John Kerry aptly put it in January 2015, "The biggest error that we could make would be to blame Muslims collectively for crimes not committed by Muslims alone—crimes that the overwhelming majority of Muslims oppose, crimes that their faith utterly rejects, and that Muslim leaders themselves have the greatest ability to address."[7]

In January 2015, French Prime Minister Manuel Valls said, "France is at war against terrorism, jihadism, and radical Islamism. France is not at war against Islam."[8] France is participating in airstrikes in Iraq against the IS.

Likewise, Turkish Foreign Minister Mevlüt Çavuşoğlu noted in January 2015 that while the IS is a "merciless terrorist organization," [9] the group does not represent Islam.[10] Analogously, in September 2014, Australian Prime Minister Tony Abbott said the IS has "declared war on the world," but, "it can never be right to kill in the name of God."[11]

RADICAL RECRUITS AND VICTIMS: NO CHILD LEFT BEHIND

For the Islamic State, no child is too young for radicalization and recruitment at its schools and training camps. Additionally, older children are being mobilized for combat in high-risk areas. These actions grossly violate international law's prohibition against the use of child fighters.

In December 2014, Usaid Barho, a fourteen-year-old Syrian national, was forced into joining the IS. Barho was instructed to become a suicide bomber, but surrendered to Iraqi security forces while wearing a suicide-bomber belt, and approaching the targeted mosque. This case illustrates the IS's use of children as so.[12]

At the same time, no victim is too young or old to be exploited or punished, in the most horrific of manners, including torture, crucifixion, and rape. Clearly, the IS regime and these kinds of heinous practices have no place in modern society.

In Syria, the IS and its supporters regularly ignore any compunction against opportunistic attacks and looting of possessions of other jihadist groups. In response, opposition jihadist fighters, such as Jabhat al-Nusra, pushed the IS out of parts of Aleppo in 2014. The next year, collaboration between the two was witnessed in a few instances, such as during the IS's attack on Yarmouk.

The Islamic State's vision and practices have attracted many recruits from other Sunni and anti-Assad groups. Ultimately, the IS has been able to acquire substantial territory, assets, and spoils from rebel forces and from the Syrian and Iraqi militaries. These acquisitions have significantly buttressed the fortunes and capabilities of the IS. Still, by the first quarter of 2015, the IS has experienced some military setbacks—including the losses in Kobani (Syria) as well as Tikrit and the Sinjar mountain range (Iraq)—as well as political and social failings.

Even so, the Islamic State has been especially cunning in looting banks, conducting extortion, and engaging in commerce such as oil trading and smuggling. Also, it has raised funds from other criminal activities to enhance its revenue streams. As a result, the Islamic State has amassed unprecedented assets to fund its regime. The confluence of this newly acquired wealth, various dramatic military successes, and police-state rule have made the IS a formidable threat to security in the Middle East and beyond.

While playing the role of conqueror, the Islamic State has attempted to provide some semblance of governance as it provides administrative and service-oriented support, although, of late, of poorer quality. In territories that it controls, the IS collects taxes, administers courts, and runs schools. The organization has an elaborate hierarchy, comprised of al-Baghdadi as caliph, two deputies, twelve governors each for Syria and Iraq, the Shura council, and various councils overseeing disparate issues, such as finance, the military, and security. The IS has also afforded its operatives some autonomy in their operations, injecting elements of decentralization.

Reports that al-Baghdadi was killed during U.S. airstrikes in Syria in November 2014 turned out to be incorrect. Several times in 2015, it was reported that al-Baghdadi was wounded during U.S. airstrikes. Ultimately, al-Baghdadi's death, when it occurs, would not decimate the Islamic State. After all, the group developed a hierarchical framework with seasoned leaders to take his place. Yet, U.S.-led coalition airstrikes have reportedly killed about half of the IS top leadership.

IS EXPLOITS REGIONAL DEMOGRAPHICS

In Iraq, Shiites comprise about 64 percent of the population, while Sunnis and Christians (and other minorities) account for some 33 percent and 3 percent, respectively. Other diverse constituencies that exist in Iraq include Kurds, neo-Baathist, tribes, religious and ethnic minorities, refugees, and diverse militias, among others.

Former Iraqi Prime Minister al-Maliki's exclusionary policies, marginalization and brutalization of Sunnis, arrest of Sunni political leaders, and attempts to consolidate his own Shiite-oriented power base led to growing and widespread Sunni disillusionment and discontent in Iraq. In particular, during 2012–2014, Sunnis viewed themselves as regularly excluded from the political, social, and economic power base of Iraq. Lest we forget, though, under Saddam Hussein's regime, the Shiites and Kurds were often ostracized and victimized.

Within Iraq, some Sunnis—comprised of urban and rural men, tribesmen, and ex-Baathists, who met while being held in Iraqi prisons after the U.S. invasion—ultimately forged an alliance or outright enlisted with ISIS. Others resisted ISIS's appeals and supported the Iraqi army. Allegiance to the Iraqi regime worked to the detriment of those insurgents when the ISIS discovered who had collaborated. A case in point, in fall 2014 over 500 members of the Sunni Albu Nimr tribe in Iraq were massacred by the IS for fighting the group. Likewise, in November 2014, the IS killed over twenty-five unarmed Sunni Albu Fahd tribesmen near Ramadi.

In Syria, as in Iraq, ISIS has exploited Sunni disenchantment to secure recruits and collaborators in a country that is 75 percent Sunni, 13 percent Shiite/Alawite/Ismaili, and 10 percent Christian. The policies of Syrian President Bashar al-Assad, an Alawite, and his apparatus, have led Syria down the path of division and extreme civil conflict. As a result, much of the country has become ungovernable and provided an opportune environment from which ISIS could recruit. Soon, ISIS's newly-acquired manpower, plus weapons gained through fighting against Assad regime and rebel groups, enabled them to project power, conquer land, and govern parts of Syria with some degree of administrative efficiency buttressed by ample intimidation. The group's experience coming to power in Syria was critical as it launched its bloody conquest in Iraq.

By fall 2014, the Islamic State had attracted some 21,000 to 31,500 fighters, and millions of supporters—many through duress—in areas under its rule, across the region, and globally. Some estimates place the number of IS fighters to be above 100,000. There are more than 20,000 foreign fighters recruited from over ninety countries—some 3,400 from Western nations—who have traveled to Syria.[13] Thousands of them have been thrilled by the chance to fight for and live in the IS caliphate and reclaim Sunni honor, among other reasons.

INTERNATIONAL RESPONSE

The Islamic State has also garnered (some would say it has sought) many enemies, including countries, other terrorist organizations, rebel groups, dissenters, and more. From Saudi Arabia to Iran, from the United States to Australia, from European to Asian countries, and from Hezbollah to Hamas, there is widespread disdain for and fear of the Islamic State. Whether this animus is effectively transformed into a steady and forceful response by these entities, militarily and otherwise, will determine the future of the Islamic State.

Presently, the Islamic State is characterized as a hybrid pseudo-sovereign terrorist group, and an organized criminal entity. Ultimately, the goal must be to weaken and, over the long term, defeat the Islamic State.

Fortunately, the global community is taking note. It is crafting policies that will best serve each country's own interests, as expected, given the often divergent and competing needs and perspectives. Still, some decisions, such as authorization of airstrikes on Iraqi and Syrian targets of the Islamic State, have proven fairly positive. Since then, Islamic State's footprint in Iraq has shrunk, although some consolidation—if not advancement—has occurred in Syria.

Concurrently, there appears to be fervent acceleration of IS affiliates or franchises—for lack of a better term—in an increasing number of countries. So, too, lone wolves and cabals from Australia, Belgium, Canada, Denmark, France, United Kingdom, and the United States have attempted to or successfully carried out terrorist attacks on behalf of or aligned with the Islamic State.

The sixty-plus member countries of the coalition aligned against the Islamic State provide a solid basis from which to counter this de-facto jihadist state. The question is whether or not the coalition will pursue additional effective strategies to decimate the IS, as the entity experienced some military setbacks in fall 2014 through spring 2015. According to U.S. Central Command, "Operation Inherent Resolve [is], the operation to eliminate the ISIL terrorist group and the threat they pose to Iraq, Syria, the region, and the wider international community. The destruction of ISIL targets in Syria and Iraq further limits the terrorist group's ability to project terror and conduct operations."[14]

U.S.-led airstrikes initiated in August 2014 against IS-controlled territories in Iraq (and September 2014 in Syria) were conducted mainly in response to the widespread massacre of the Yazidi minority group, the beheadings of two U.S. journalists (James Foley and Steven Sotloff), the capture of Mosul Dam, and threats to Erbil, Iraq, where the U.S. maintains a consulate and advisors. Moreover, as a superpower with a long history and interests in the region, especially in Iraq, the United States could not ignore the enveloping chaos there.

As the international coalition was mobilized, U.S. and coalition forces—including Muslim countries—have expanded their attacks on various targets in Iraq and Syria. For instance, numerous IS command and control centers, training camps, and weapons facilities have been struck. In addition, the coalition conducted airstrikes against Jabhat al-Nusra and the Khorasan Group, both affiliates of al-Qa'ida.

In November 2014 and subsequently, coalition airstrikes escalated, and rapidly targeted other Sunni jihadist groups besides the Islamic State. These actions, in conjunction with U.S. plans to authorize additional military trainers and allocate more funding to combating the Islamic State, were steps in the right direction.

Also, Turkey's decision in November 2014 to train Kurdish fighters in northern Iraq and Iraq's National Guard troops against IS was a positive development. Still, the United States and other forces, including the Kurds, have made it clear that Turkey could do more to stop the flow of foreign fighters into Syria and Iraq, and to use ground forces against the IS.

As of November 2014, U.S.-led coalition airstrikes in Syria had resulted in the deaths of 785 IS fighters and 72 members of Jabhat al-Nusra. In January 2015, Stuart Jones, U.S. ambassador to Iraq, stated that some 6,000 IS militants had been killed by coalition forces. The Pentagon did not confirm this figure, but U.S. Defense Secretary Chuck Hagel suggested that thousands had been killed. In March 2015, Army Gen. Lloyd Austin, the commander of U.S. Central Command, estimated more than 8,500 Islamic State fighters have been killed, and that the IS is no longer able to acquire and hold new territory. [15]

Overall, by early December 2014, there had been some 1,200 airstrikes against IS targets in Iraq and Syria, which aided Iraqi and Kurdish efforts (and, indirectly, Syrian government offenses) fighting the group. The Islamic State's momentum has been undermined to some degree in Iraq, while also impacting "ISIL's command-and-control nodes, supply lines, fighters and leaders, and military and economic infrastructure and resources in Syria." [16]

By January 6, 2015, "U.S. and coalition air forces had conducted a total of 1,676 air strikes against Islamic State militants in Iraq and Syria since Aug. 8, and had used some 4,775 munitions." [17] During the airstrikes "3,222 targets" [18] were hit. [19] Among the "targets damaged or destroyed included:

- 58 tanks;
- 184 HMMWVs, the highly mobile multi-purpose wheeled vehicles known as Humvees;
- 26 armored personnel vehicles;
- 303 technical vehicles;
- 394 other vehicles;
- 79 artillery, anti-aircraft weapons or mortars;
- 41 staging areas;
- 11 improvised explosive device positions;
- 16 command posts;

- 92 checkpoints;
- 17 guard shacks;
- 980 other buildings or barracks;
- 673 fighting positions;
- 52 bunkers;
- 14 boats;
- 23 stockpiles;
- 259 oil infrastructure sites."[20]

By February 2015, the number of coalition airstrikes reached over 2,800.[21] As of March 29, 2015, "Coalition nations conducting airstrikes in Iraq include the United States, Australia, Belgium, Canada, Denmark, France, Jordan, the Netherlands, and the United Kingdom. Coalition nations conducting airstrikes in Syria include the United States, Bahrain, Jordan, Saudi Arabia, and the United Arab Emirates."[22] By March 12, 2015, "the total cost of operations related to ISIL since kinetic operations started on Aug. 8, 2014, is $1.83 billion and the average daily cost is $8.5 million."[23]

According to U.S. Central Command, from August 2014 to March 2015, ISIL lost between 20–25 percent of populated areas in Iraq that it once controlled. That area translates to about 4,100–5,200 square miles.[24] Still, since 2014, IS "has controlled 85 percent of Anbar, the largest province in Iraq, including parts of its capital, Ramadi, as well as the entire city of Fallujah and many other cities and towns."[25] The Islamic State's control in Syria as of March 2015 is mostly the same as in August 2014 except "its withdrawal from 'Ayn al 'Arab [Kobani] and Tall Hamis."[26] In April 2015, the IS made some advances towards Damascus, as the group gained control of Yarmouk.[27]

Also, as of March 18, 2015, coalition forces damaged or destroyed 5,314 ISIL targets, including:

- "Tanks 73
- Humvees 282
- Staging areas 408
- Buildings 1,652
- Fighting positions 1,003
- Oil collection points and refineries 151
- Other targets 1,745."[28]

In December 2014, the United Arab Emirates suspended its participation in such airstrikes, pointing to limited rescue capabilities for its pilots should they encounter difficulties during sorties. Two months later, after the IS's immolation of a Jordanian pilot who was captured in Syria, the United Arab Emirates resumed participation in airstrikes against the IS. Also, Jordan accelerated the frequency of its airstrikes against the IS targets. Following the February 2015 decapitation of twenty-one Egyptian Coptic Christians in Libya by the self-declared Tripoli Province of the Islamic State, Egypt conducted airstrikes against IS strongholds in Libya,[29] as well as IS-linked militants in that country.[30]

In March 2015, the Iraqi army and Shiite-comprised militias, guided by Iranian advisers and volunteer fighters, launched attacks to recapture the IS-controlled city of Tikrit, the birthplace of Saddam Hussein, and a Sunni-majority enclave. Along with the defeat of the IS in Tikrit, there is concern about a possible massacre of Sunnis at the hands of the largely Shiite forces. If so, it will deepen Sunni-Shiite rifts in Iraq and regionally. Concurrently, Kurdish Peshmerga forces, in coordination with Iraqi Shiite militias, are attacking IS-held areas west of Kirkuk. Their objective is to free those areas from the IS, so as to ease their prospective launch against Mosul, Iraq's second largest city and the most important location held by the IS in Iraq.[31]

To some degree, the predictions of Professor Samuel Huntington in his book, *The Clash of Civilizations*—"the fault lines between civilizations will be the battle lines of the future"—appear to have taken form between some elements of the West and Muslim world, spurred by the Islamic State's activities and tentacles in its region and beyond.[32]

TIMETABLE FOR THE DEFEAT OF THE IS

Despite these advances against the IS, Lieutenant General James Terry, who leads U.S. forces against the IS in Syria and Iraq, predicted in December 2014 that defeating the IS would "at least take a minimum of three years."[33] In January 2015, General Martin Dempsey, Chairman of the U.S. Joint Chiefs of Staff, expressed doubts about the readiness of Iraqi troops to fight IS forces. Also, General Dempsey indicated it was unknown when Iraqi forces would be ready to launch a counteroffensive against IS militants, but added that U.S. forces would assist in those efforts.[34]

Meanwhile, in January 2015, Iraqi Prime Minister Haider al-Abadi argued that the U.S.-led coalition against the IS has been "very slow in its support and training of the [Iraqi] army." As such, he added, the coalition needs to accelerate its assistance.[35] Prime Minister al-Abadi conceded that the Iraqi army "could need three years to rebuild and restructure its military."[36]

The lack of "formal" U.S. and coalition ground combat forces—at least as of April 15, 2015—has limited the effectiveness of the campaign against some of these terrorists. Still, the U.S.-organized coalition efforts have proven somewhat more effective against Islamic State forces in Kobani, Tikrit, and the Sinjar mountains region. According to U.S. Navy Rear Adm. John

Kirby, there were several reasons for the defeat of the IS in Kobani in January 2015, including airstrikes, a reliable partner in the Kurdish fighters, and Turkey's allowing the "resupply through Turkey to Kurdish forces inside."[37] Also, further extending American participation by embedding U.S. advisers/trainers in Iraqi army units would raise the likelihood of direct military engagement by U.S. soldiers on-the-ground with IS fighters.

Ultimately, the sixty-plus member coalition aligned against the Islamic State provides a solid basis from which to counter this de facto jihadist state. The open question is whether or not the coalition can pursue additional effective strategies to further degrade, if not destroy, the IS in the near term. Even with the military defeat of the Islamic State, it is possible that the "matter of rebuilding governments in the Arab world—[is] a task that will take decades."[38]

POSING THE RIGHT QUESTIONS, RECOMMENDATIONS FOR THE MOST EFFECTIVE SOLUTIONS

To that end, this book seeks to address the current gap in realistic assessments regarding the IS threat, the risks it poses, and its broader implications at national, regional, and global levels. Worst case, the Islamic State could present a serious challenge to the three-centuries-old state system. This book seeks to shed light on the critical questions posed by the IS, including:

- First, how are terrorist groups defeated, and what are the implications for the Islamic State?
- Second, should the IS be viewed as a threat equal to or greater than al-Qa'ida for the United States and the international community?
- Third, will the IS and its foreign fighters export terrorism to their home countries?
- Fourth, is the assistance of Assad's regime and Iran needed to defeat the IS, and what are the implications of an approach to these governments?
- Fifth, would military support, including airstrikes, by the United States and its allies against the IS in Syria strengthen Assad's regime, and, if this is unavoidable, what can the United States do to undermine the Syrian government?
- Sixth, will non-Islamic countries such as Russia and China join the international coalition that is fighting the IS?
- And seventh, can the IS be destroyed or will its successes on and off the battlefields in the Middle East ultimately expand its influence into other regions, particularly Europe and North America, at least in the form of terrorist incidents?

This book is organized into seven sections. The first chapter provides historical context on the evolution of the IS from its early origins in 1999 as a progenitor of al-Qa'ida in Iraq to the declaration of a caliphate in 2014. The second chapter deals with the movement's intentions and capabilities, namely: its ideology, strategy, current posture, headquarters, training, tactics, weapons, targets, financing, radicalization and recruitment, publicity, and use of execution videos. The third chapter discusses membership and structure of the IS as well as its leadership and hierarchy. The backgrounds of Abu Bakr al-Baghdadi, its self-proclaimed caliph, and his key associates are examined. Profiles of leaders arrested and killed are also provided.

The Islamic State's plans and actions to establish a caliphate in Iraq, Syria, and beyond are analyzed in chapter 4. The fifth chapter details the phenomenon of foreign fighters in Syria and Iraq, IS supporters elsewhere, and the role of women in the IS. National, regional, and global responses to confront the IS are detailed in chapter 6. Special attention is paid to the policies of Muslim and Western countries and international bodies such as the United Nations and NATO. Chapter 7 provides conclusions and recommendations for combating the Islamic State. A selected bibliography and an index are provided at the end of the book.

NOTES

1. Rago, Joseph. "Inside the war against the Islamic State." *Wall Street Journal*, December 26, 2014. Accessed December 27, 2014. http://www.wsj.com/articles/joe-rago-inside-the-war-against-islamic-state-1419636790.

2. Holland, Steve and Roberta Rampton. "Obama, Cameron vow to take on 'poisonous ideology' of radical Islam." *Reuters*, January 16, 2015. Accessed February 13, 2015. http://uk.reuters.com/article/2015/01/16/uk-britain-usa-idUKKBN0KP2BB20150116.

3. Ibid.

4. Rasheed, Ahmed and Ralph Boulton. "2014 Deadliest Year in Iraq for Civilians since 2006–7 Bloodshed—U.N." *Reuters*, January 3, 2015. Accessed February 6, 2015. http://in.mobile.reuters.com/article/idINKBN0KB0JP20150102?irpc=932.

5. "Syria's War Killed 76,021 in 2014: Monitor." *Times of India*. January 1, 2015. Accessed February 6, 2015. http://m.timesofindia.com/world/middle-east/Syrias-war-killed-76021-in-2014-Monitor/articleshow/45717659.cms.

6. "The caliphate cracks." *The Economist*, March 21, 2015. Accessed March 23, 2015. http://www.economist.com/news/leaders/21646750-though-islamic-state-still-spreading-terror-its-weaknesses-are-becoming-apparent."The pushback." *Economist*, March 21, 2015. Accessed March 23, 2015. http://www.economist.com/news/briefing/21646752-sustaining-caliphate-turns-out-be-much-harder-declaring-one-islamic-state-not.

7. "Remarks at the World Economic Forum." *U.S. Department of State*, January 23, 2015. Accessed February 13, 2015. http://www.state.gov/secretary/remarks/2015/01/236254.htm.

8. "Valls: France will face more threats." *Connexion*, January 14, 2015. Accessed January 17, 2015. http://www.connexionfrance.com/news_articles.php?id=6542.

9. Zeyrek, Deniz. "Turkey concerned by return of Turkish ISIL fighters." *Hürriyet Daily News*, January 15, 2015. Accessed February 13, 2015. http://www.hurriyetdailynews.com/turkey-concerned-by-return-of-turkish-isil-fighters-.aspx?pageID=238&nID=76945&NewsCatID=338.

10. Ibid.

11. Hurst, Daniel. "Tony Abbott tells UN Isis has 'declared war on the world." *Guardian*, September 24, 2014. Accessed February 4, 2015. http://www.theguardian.com/world/2014/sep/25/tony-abbott-un-isis-declared-war-on-world.

12. Arango, Tim. "A Boy in ISIS. A Suicide Vest. A Hope to Live." *NY Times,* December 26, 2014. Accessed February 4, 2015. http://www.nytimes.com/2014/12/27/world/middleeast/syria-isis-recruits-teenagers-as-suicide-bombers.html?_r=1.

13. Rasmussen, Nicholas. "Current Terrorist Threat to the United States." Testimony before the Senate Select Committee on Intelligence, February 12, 2015. Accessed February 15, 2015. http://www.nctc.gov/docs/Current_Terrorist_Threat_to_the_United_States.pdf.

14. Mar. 15: Military Airstrikes Continue Against ISIL in Syria and Iraq." CJTF—Operation Inherent Resolve News Release, U.S. Department of Defense. March 15, 2015. Accessed March 20, 2015. http://www.centcom.mil/en/news/articles/mar.-15-military-airstrikes-continue-against-isil-in-syria-and-iraq.

15. Starr, Barbara. "U.S. officials say 6,000 ISIS fighters killed in battles." *CNN*, January 22, 2015. Accessed February 13, 2015. http://edition.cnn.com/2015/01/22/politics/us-officials-say-6000-isis-fighters-killed-in-battles/index.html?iid=ob_article_organicsidebar_expansion&iref=obnetwork. Burns, Robert. "Dempsey says Iranian hand in Iraq could turn out well." *Charlotte Observer,* March 3, 2015. Accessed March 6, 2015. http://www.charlotteobserver.com/news/politics-government/article12218762.html.

16. Allen, John. "Degrading and defeating ISIL." *Defense News*, December 29, 2014. Accessed December 31, 2014. http://www.state.gov/s/seci/235545.htm.

17. Alexander, David. "U.S.-led air strikes have hit 3,222 Islamic State targets: Pentagon." *Reuters*, January 7, 2015. Accessed February 13, 2015. http://www.reuters.com/article/2015/01/07/us-mideast-crisis-strikes-damage-idUSKBN0KG1ZM20150107.

18. Ibid.

19. Ibid.

20. Ibid.

21. Redfield, John. "ISIL strategy is working, but will take time, admiral says." United States Central Command, March 13, 2015. Accessed March 14, 2015. http://www.centcom.mil/en/news/articles/isil-strategy-working-but-will-take-time-admiral-says.

22. "Airstrikes hit ISIL in Syria, Iraq." CJTF—Operation Inherent Resolve News Release. U.S. Department of Defense, March 29, 2015. Accessed March 29, 2015. http://www.defense.gov/news/newsarticle.aspx?id=128485.

23. "Airstrikes in Iraq and Syria." U.S. Department of Defense, undated. Accessed March 25, 2015. http://www.defense.gov/home/features/2014/0814_iraq/.

24. "Iraq and Syria: ISIL's reduced operating areas as of March 2015." U.S. Department of Defense, undated. Accessed March 28, 2015. http://www.defense.gov/home/features/2014/0814_iraq/ReducedOperatingAreas0315.pdf.

25. Mohammed, Riyad. "How ISIS regained momentum in Iraq." *Business Insider*, April 19, 2015. Accessed April 19, 2015. http://www.businessinsider.com/how-isis-regained-momentum-in-iraq-2015-4.

26. Ibid.

27. Westall, Sylvia and Mariam Karouny. "Islamic State expands in Damascus, al Qaeda vows sharia for city." *MSNBC.com*, April 1, 2015. Accessed April 2, 2015. http://www.msn.com/en-ca/news/world/islamic-state-expands-in-damascus-al-qaeda-vows-sharia-for-city/ar-AAajtWI.

28. "Targets damaged/destroyed as of March 2015." Department of Defense, March 18, 2015. Accessed March 21, 2015. http://www.defense.gov/home/features/2014/0814_iraq/.

29. Welch, William. "Egypt launches airstrikes against ISIL in Libya." *USA Today*, February 16, 2015. Accessed February 23, 2015. http://www.usatoday.com/story/news/world/2015/02/16/egypt-airstrikes-isil-libya/23482049/.

30. Kirkpatrick, David D. "Egypt Launches Airstrike in Libya Against ISIS Branch." *NY Times*, February 16, 2015. Accessed February 23, 2015. http://www.nytimes.com/2015/02/17/world/middleeast/isis-egypt-libya-airstrikes.html.

31. Rasheed, Ahmed and Dominic Evans. "Iraqi forces try to seal off Islamic State around Tikrit." *Reuters*, March 3, 2015. Accessed March 14, 2015. http://www.reuters.com/article/2015/03/03/us-mideast-crisis-iraq-idUSKBN0LZ10Q20150303.

32. Arens, Moshe. "Like it or not, Israel is Europe's outpost in the war on the west." *Haaretz*, January 12, 2015. Accessed February 13, 2015. http://www.haaretz.com/opinion/.premium-1.636486.

33. Stewart, Philip and David Alexander, "Islamic State fight to take at least 3 years, U.S. general says." *Huffington Post*, December 18, 2014. Accessed December 20, 2014. http://www.huffingtonpost.com/2014/12/18/james-terry-islamic-state-fight_n_6348282.html?ncid=txtlnkusaolp00000592.

34. "Top U.S. Officer Seeks To Increase Military Aid To Iraq." *Radio Free Europe Radio Liberty*, January 9, 2015. Accessed February 13, 2015. http://www.rferl.org/content/us-wants-to-increase-military-aid-to-iraq/26783979.html.

35. "Iraqi PM criticises 'slowness' of US-led coalition." *Sydney Morning Herald*, January 12, 2015. Accessed February 13, 2015. http://www.smh.com.au/world/iraqi-pm-criticises-slowness-of-usled-coalition-20150112-12medb.html.

36. "Iraq May Need Three Years To Rebuild Military." *Radio Free Europe Radio Liberty*, January 12, 2015. Accessed February 13, 2015. http://www.rferl.org/content/iraq/26788341.html.

37. Roulo, Claudette. "Competent, Willing Partnerships Result in Gains Against ISIL." *U.S. Department of Defense*, January 27, 2015. Accessed February 13, 2015. http://www.defense.gov/news/newsarticle.aspx?id=128052.

38. "The caliphate cracks." *Economist*, March 21, 2015. Accessed March 23, 2015. http://www.economist.com/news/leaders/21646750-though-islamic-state-still-spreading-terror-its-weaknesses-are-becoming-apparent.

Acknowledgements

The co-authors of this book did not begin their academic work on terrorism in 2015. Collectively, they have accumulated more than seventy years of experience in this field as students, professors, and advisors to private and public bodies worldwide. Their extensive field research, for example, in the Middle East (particularly in Syria, Turkey, Lebanon, Jordan, Egypt, Israel, Morocco, and Cyprus) has afforded them with critical insights on this complex topic. They have jointly collaborated in numerous academic efforts over several decades, including the publication of the book *Terrorism and Business: The Impact of September 11, 2001* (Transnational Publishers: Ardsley, NY, 2002). Dean Alexander expanded his work in this area with the publication of his book *Business Confronts Terrorism: Risks and Responses* (University of Wisconsin Press: Madison, WI, 2004). He presented his research findings on the Islamic State and foreign fighters at the Terrorism Experts Conference organized by NATO's Centre of Excellence-Defence Against Terrorism (COE-DAT) in Ankara, Turkey, in October 2014.

Yonah Alexander wishes to thank Michael S. Swetnam (CEO, Potomac Institute for Policy Studies) for his research collaboration in producing *Usama bin Ladin's al-Qa'ida: Profile of a Terrorist Network* (Transnational Publishers: Ardsley, NY, published in February 2001, some six months before 9/11), as well as the subsequent volume *al-Qa'ida: Ten Years After 9/11 and Beyond* (Potomac Institute Press: Arlington, VA, 2012). These volumes have been translated into many languages, including Turkish, Greek, Dutch, Polish, and Korean.

Special gratitude is also due to General Alfred Gray, USMC (Ret.), Chairman, Board of Regents, Potomac Institute for Policy Studies, and to Professor Don Wallace, Jr., Chairman, the International Law Institute, for their encouragement of our work over the years.

Both of these institutions co-sponsored with the Inter-University Center for Terrorism Studies (IUCTS) and the Center for National Security Law (the University of Virginia School of Law) a seminar on "ISIS: An Emerging Global Sunni Caliphate?" held on August 28, 2014, at the Potomac Institute for Policy Studies. A report of this event, moderated by Professor Yonah Alexander, with the participation of Professor Ruth Wedgwood (the Johns Hopkins University), Dr. Wayne H. Zaideman (former FBI), Ambassador (Ret.) Edward Marks (former U.S. Department of State), and Dan Raviv (CBS News), was published by the IUCTS in October 2014. Mr. Swetnam and General (Ret.) Gray also contributed to the seminar's deliberations. This event was broadcasted domestically and internationally. It may be viewed at: http://www.c-span.org/video/?321173-1/policy-experts-expansion-isil.

Western Illinois University's Homeland Security Research Program, which Professor Dean Alexander directs, organized a seminar, "ISIL/Islamic State and Law Enforcement Responses to Terrorism." The event was held on April 15, 2015, featuring Professor Alexander and Professor Thomas Meloni. Dean Alexander wishes to thank Dr. Terry Mors, Professor and Director, the School of Law Enforcement and Justice Administration, Western Illinois University, for his continued support, particularly during fall 2014.

Dr. Patrick Murphy, Garth Neuffer, Dr. Mir Sadat, Dr. Robert Turner, Dr. Terry Mors, and Dr. Jack Schafer, also deserve our gratitude for their useful suggestions on the manuscript. Those who chose to stay anonymous have provided other valuable insights. Sharon Layani (University of Michigan), as a Research Associate at the Inter-University Center for Terrorism Studies, has contributed extraordinarily to the timely production of the book. Uri Lerner (American University) and David Daoud (Suffolk University Law School) also assisted in coordinating the work of selected interns consisting of Andrew DuBois (Trinity University), Christopher Hartnett (George Washington University), Vijay Randhawa (George Mason University), Susanna Seltzer (Carnegie Mellon University), and Addison Winger (University of Wisconsin).

Additional support during the production phase of the book was provided by the following researchers and interns: Benjamin Schaefer (Hofstra University), Andrew Jackson Coley (Quinnipiac University), Dan Layman (Georgetown University), Laura Blackerby (American University), Genevieve Boutilier (University of Maryland Baltimore County), Julie Byrne (The Catholic University of America), Dor Cohen (Brandeis University), Elinoam Hafner (University of Maryland), Elizabeth Howard (University of Mary Washington), Julia Johnson (Johns Hopkins University), Ethan Kannel (Cornell University), Eric Pons (Emory University), Andrew Tabas (Georgetown University), Rohit P. Tallapragada (Georgetown University), and Richard Veliz (George Mason University).

In light of the fact that there is a wide variety of transliterations from Arabic and other Middle Eastern and Asian languages, we have used spellings of terms, concepts, and names that either are commonly accepted in the literature or those which may be most convenient for readers. Against this backdrop, it must also be stated that in preparing this work the authors relied upon the most credible information available during the research process. Although they are solely responsible for the contents and views expressed in the book, the authors cannot accept liability for any errors, omissions, or future actions that may be effected by any persons or entity based on the materials contained in this publication. Nevertheless, it is hoped that this book will encourage further scholarship in this important field of global security concerns.

April 2015

Chapter One

Historical Context

EVOLUTION OF A MONIKER

The organization that is now known as the Islamic State (IS) went through several permutations of its name through the course of its history. Its guiding concept, however, was always political, coupled with violence.

Jama'at al Tawhid wal Jihad (JTJ) or "The Group of Unification and Jihad," was established in 1999. The first name change to Tanzim Qaidat al-Jihad fi Bilad al-Rafidain or "The Organization of the Base [al-Qa'ida] of Jihad in the Land of the Two Rivers," (Mesopotamia, modern-day Iraq) reflected the group's merger with al-Qa'ida in 2004. This incarnation was commonly referred to as al-Qa'ida in Iraq (AQI).[1] In 2006, the second name change, to "Islamic State of Iraq," (ISI) was meant to emphasize the group's Iraqi leadership at a time when American and Iraqi security forces were highlighting the non-Iraqi contingent among al-Qa'ida fighters, hoping to convince Iraqi Sunni tribes to abandon their ties with AQI.[2]

In 2013, the third name change, to al-Dawla al-Islamiya fil-Iraq wal-Sham or "Islamic State in Iraq and Greater Syria" (ISIS) came about during the struggle between ISI and Jabhat al-Nusrah li-Ahl ash-Shām or the "Support Front for the People of al-Sham," (shortened to Jabhat al-Nusra, al-Nusra Front, or JN) for leadership of al-Qa'ida forces in Iraq and Syria.[3] Al-Sham is a geographical designation commonly used to the territory comprising modern-day Syria, Lebanon, Israel, the Palestinian Authority, and Jordan.

The final declared name change came in June 2014, after a string of victories for ISIS. These victories comprised conquering and administering considerable territory on both sides of the Iraq-Syria border. Coinciding with the first day of Ramadan, ISIS issued a statement declaring it to be "the

1

Islamic State"—the caliphate—without any consideration for modern borders and boundaries.

It should be noted that many of these acronyms are linguistically dubious. AQI, for example, transliterates: al-Qa'ida, an Arabic phrase meaning "the base," and the initial "I" for "Iraq," a modern English name for the region referred to in the original Arabic organization name as Bilad al-Rafidain ("land of the two rivers"). Similarly, the full Arabic name of the Islamic State before June 2014 was al-Dawla al-Islamiya fil-Iraq wal-Sham. Al-Sham, as mentioned, can also be referred to as just Syria. On the other hand, this name may have been a reference to Bilad al-Sham, which refers to the seventh-century name for what would become Syria, Lebanon, Jordan, Israel, and parts of Sinai and Turkey.[4]

Variations on this area would later be called "the Levant," an imperialist-era term, and "Greater Syria." But "Greater Syria" uses the Hellenistic name for the region, which was revived during the Arab nationalism of the early twentieth century. Meanwhile, the Arabic al-Sham is a name given to the region by the series of caliphates that ruled over it (the Umayyad and Abbasid) until the Ottoman Empire split the region down further. Thus, a modern English translation of the group's name would be "Islamic State of Iraq and Greater Syria." "Islamic State of Iraq and the Levant," is also correct, if outdated. "Islamic State of Iraq and Syria," may be correct but misses the point of using al-Sham instead of "Syria," to begin with: evoking the broader Islamic caliphates of old.[5]

The Arab and Israeli presses use a permutation of the "Islamic State of Iraq and Syria," with the acronym DAAISH (Da'ash, Da'ish, Da'esh), which is shorthand for the Arabic name.[6] Da'esh "also speaks to another name that means 'to crush underneath your foot.'"[7] The IS considers the term Da'esh to be an insult.[8] Towards the end of 2014, several Obama administration officials, including Secretary of State John Kerry and Secretary of Defense Chuck Hagel, began to use "Da'esh" in an attempt to malign the group and distinguish that entity from the Muslim faith.[9] Meanwhile, the Associated Press and Reuters use the ISIL acronym in their style guides and the U.S. Government largely does the same.

Despite the most recent name change to the Islamic State, the acronyms ISIS and ISIL are also used in the book. As much as possible, the book references the group and its antecedents with the appropriate term, although some quoted text may reference other names. However, the "Islamic State" and "IS" will be used interchangeably.

FOUNDATION THROUGH AWAKENING

Abu Musab al-Zarqawi was a fringe figure in the global jihad movement for much of the 1990s, who originally tried to join the mujahedeen in Afghanistan in 1989. There are several differing accounts of his activities before joining al-Qa'ida. But, a rough pattern of repeated false starts and narrow escapes emerges. Born in Jordan in 1966, in his youth he had frequent run-ins with police, labeling him a thug and common criminal, aggravated by his alcohol and drug abuse. Following exposure to Salafist preachers in Jordan, in 1989, he left for Afghanistan with the goal of participating in the jihad against the Soviets, although their withdrawal began that year. While in Afghanistan at that time, he is alleged to have worked as a journalist for an Islamist publication, attended a terror training camp along the Afghani-Pakistani border, and met militant Jordanian Salafist cleric, Sheikh Abu Muhammad al-Maqdisi. [10]

Al-Zarqawi returned to Jordan in 1993. In Jordan, he regrouped with a former jihadi contact in Afghanistan, Abu Muntassir Bilah Muhammad. Al-Zarqawi, al-Maqdisi, and Muhammad formed al-Tawhid, and later Bayat al-Imam, with the goal of removing the monarchy and establishing an Islamic state. [11] In 1994, al-Zarqawi was imprisoned for having weapons in his home, and sentenced to 15 years in prison. [12] At the Sawaqa prison, al-Zarqawi further embraced jihadi tenets as taught by al-Maqdisi and other Salafists. [13] The two recruited for their group, Bayat al-Imam, inside and outside of prison. [14]

Al-Zarqawi was released in King Abdullah's 1999 amnesty program, which sought to soften the Muslim Brotherhood's position on parliamentary reforms. After his so-called millennium plot was discovered later that year, al-Zarqawi fled to Pakistan. There, al-Zarqawi was briefly imprisoned, and then went to Afghanistan. [15]

In Afghanistan, al-Zarqawi met with Osama bin Laden but did not join al-Qa'ida due to ideological differences. Al-Zarqawi felt bin Laden did not focus enough on Israel and was too lenient on non-Salafists. Bin Laden was weary of al-Zarqawi, concerned that he was a mole of the Jordanian government. Also, bin Laden found al-Zarqawi's animus against the Shiites and his aggressive nature to be problematic. Al-Zarqawi intended to form his own training camp for jihadists from Jordan and neighboring countries. [16]

In 2000, al-Zarqawi established a terror training camp in Herat, Afghanistan, with $5,000 in front capital from bin Laden. There, al-Zarqawi formed "Jund al-Sham, or Soldiers of the Levant," which had many Syrians in leadership positions, and actively recruited fighters from there. [17] The base in Herat enabled al-Zarqawi to sneak in foreign jihadists through Iran, without having to transverse Pakistan. [18]

In late 2001, al-Zarqawi fled to Iran to receive medical attention after being wounded in combat in Afghanistan against coalition forces in Operation Enduring Freedom. Traveling with him to Iran were about 300 fighters. However, al-Zarqawi was expelled by Iranian authorities and relocated to Iraq in March 2002.[19] From Iraq, al-Zarqawi also traveled to Lebanon and Syria where he "expanded his network, recruited and trained new fighters, and set up bases, safe houses, and military training camps."[20] Following the U.S. invasion of Iraq in March 2003, al-Zarqawi's focus coalesced, and following a request by al Qa'ida, he assisted foreign fighters to enter Iraq through Syria.[21]

By August 2003, his group conducted attacks against the Jordanian embassy in Iraq, the United Nations headquarters, and a suicide car bomb against the Shiite sacred shrine in Najaf.[22] In April 2004, al-Zarqawi is believed to have been the perpetrator in the beheading of American Nicholas Berg in Iraq.[23] The killing was videotaped and distributed widely, featuring the group's "trademark black banner of al-Zarqawi's newest group: al-Tawhid wa al-Jihad, or Monotheism and Jihad."[24] Additional foreigners, including Americans, were kidnapped and beheaded by Zarqawi's group; some of them included Eugene Armstrong (U.S.), Jack Hensley (U.S.), Kenneth Bigley (UK), and Shosei Koda (Japan).[25]

Al-Zarqawi merged his group with several other jihadists under the new Jama'at al-Tawhid w'al-Jihad (JTJ) banner. Al-Zarqawi led the training of militants at JTJ. His group became known for being less organized, but more violent, than al-Qa'ida.[26] During the Iraqi insurgency, JTJ largely targeted Shiite Muslims, considered heretics by Salafi jihadists. The Shiite community was much easier to target than coalition forces. JTJ's approach to attacking civilians led to a high death toll.[27] Additionally, under al-Zarqawi's leadership attacks against Iraqi police stations, army recruiting stations, and politicians were prevalent.[28]

In essence, al-Zarqawi's targeting of foreign governmental (embassies) and non-governmental agencies (UN), Iraqi security services and government officials, foreign contractors and humanitarian workers, and Shiite religious institutions and civilians was done to: persuade foreigners to leave Iraq and thereby eliminate their influence; undermine the capabilities of counter-Zarqawi forces; and exacerbate the Sunni-Shiite rift in Iraq, so that Sunnis would join his cause.[29]

JTJ was made up of predominantly foreign fighters. As noted, al-Zarqawi was Jordanian. His campaign against Shiites exploited Sunni resentment. It soon earned him the endorsement of al-Qa'ida. In December 2004, al-Zarqawi pledged *bay'ah* (allegiance) to bin Laden, who named him emir of the newly formed al-Qa'ida in the Land of the Two Rivers (al-Qa'ida in Iraq, or AQI).[30]

Ultimately, al-Zarqawi's emphasis on targeting civilians became a major concern for al-Qa'ida leadership. Ayman al-Zawahiri, Bin Laden's lieutenant, sent al-Zarqawi a letter dated July 9, 2005, urging him to refocus his efforts on American forces rather than on Shiite civilians.[31] Al-Zarqawi ignored this admonition. For instance, in February 2006 the bombing of a revered Shiite shrine in Samarra by al-Qa'ida in Iraq dramatically increased sectarian tensions and violence,[32] while alienating other Iraqi insurgents and otherwise sympathetic Sunnis.

Elsewhere, al-Zarqawi's group was involved in the assassination of U.S. Agency for International Development representative in Jordan, Laurence Foley, in 2002, as well as the 2004 prospective plot to use truck and chemicals in Jordan to kill some 80,000 people.[33] In November 2005, Zarqawi's group, al-Qa'ida in Iraq, conducted three nearly simultaneous suicide bombings at prominent hotels—Radisson SAS, Grand Hyatt, and Days Inn—in Amman, Jordan, that resulted in over 60 deaths and wounding about 115 people. The suicide bombers were all Iraqi, including one failed perpetrator—Sajida Rishawi, the wife of the bomber at the Radisson SAS, whose belt did not explode.[34] Rishawi was hanged in February 2015, after the release of a video showing the immolation of Jordanian pilot, Muath al-Kasasbeh, by the Islamic State.[35]

Al-Zarqawi was killed in a U.S. airstrike on a safe house near Baquoba, Iraq, in June 2006.[36] He was succeeded by Abu Ayyub al-Masri, also known as Abu Hamza al-Muhajir.[37] The new leader created the Islamic State of Iraq (ISI) in 2006. ISI was placed under the control of Abu Umar al-Baghdadi. This was an attempt to put an Iraqi face on a group that had been derided for its foreign leadership and ranks.[38]

This attempt to inject an Iraqi facade onto ISI was unsuccessful. Oppressed Sunni tribes began to break away from AQI's iron-fisted sharia dominion. Instead, they allied with coalition forces in what is now called the Anbar (or Sunni) Awakening. These "Sons of Iraq," a name chosen to emphasize the foreignness of AQI commanders, hoped to gain pardons for their earlier fighting against Iraqi and coalition forces. Too, they sought local development contracts and power in the Iraqi central government. Their realignment coincided with the "surge" of U.S. troops and helped break the back of the insurgency.[39]

ASSASSINATIONS AND ASSUMPTION OF POWER BY ABU BAKR AL-BAGHDADI

In 2010, Abu Ayyub al-Masri and Abu Umar al-Baghdadi were killed during a joint U.S.-Iraqi raid on an ISI safe house.[40] Abu Bakr al-Baghdadi then gained control of ISI.[41] At that point, ISI was mostly made up of Iraqi fighters. Their main targets were still Shiites but al-Baghdadi also attacked the mostly Shiite security forces. Many of the former Sons of Iraq joined up with ISI.[42] The ISI was also comprised of Baathists and other individuals—including hard-core jihadists—who were held at Bucca and other detention facilities in Iraq. Al-Baghdadi inherited the group after it was significantly weakened by military attacks initiated by Iraqi government and tribal forces since the Anbar Awakening in 2007.

A RETURN TO FORM

Abu Bakr al-Baghdadi capitalized on the chaos arising during the inception of the 2011 uprising in Syria. He, too, began operating across the Iraqi border against President Bashar al-Assad's Alawite regime. Alawites are a sub-sect of Shiite Islam. ISI, in conjunction with Ayman al-Zawahiri, created Jabhat al-Nusra in Syria in late 2011. Jabhat al-Nusra, with Muhammad al-Jawlani as its leader, was to serve as a front for al-Qa'ida's activities in Syria.[43] Jabhat al-Nusra first took credit for an attack in March 2012.[44] Jabhat al-Nusra rose to become the most effective rebel fighting force in Syria. Jabhat al-Nusra's success inspired al-Baghdadi to extend his own organization across the border.[45]

ISI grew in strength in Iraq when al-Baghdadi announced the "Breaking Walls" campaign in Iraq in July 2012. The plan focused on regaining territory formerly held by ISI, and attacking the al-Maliki regime. In April 2013, al-Baghdadi stated that the group's aim would not only be to attack the existing Iraq government but also to establish its own Islamic state in Iraq and the Levant region.[46]

In April 2013, al-Baghdadi released a statement claiming that ISI and al-Qa'ida had created Jabhat al-Nusra. Also, he said that they were now merging with ISI into the Islamic State of Iraq and al-Sham.[47] Abu Muhammad al-Jawlani, the leader of Jabhat al-Nusra, disputed the claim and reiterated his allegiance to al-Qa'ida and al-Zawahiri.[48] In contrast, al-Baghdadi never made such pledges.[49] As these tensions unfolded, many Jabhat al-Nusra fighters defected to al-Baghdadi's organization.[50]

In May 2013, al-Zawahiri rebuked al-Baghdadi and ordered ISI to return to Iraq and leave Syria to Jabhat al-Nusra.[51] More specifically, al-Zawahiri released a letter officially canceling the supposed merger between the Islamic State of Iraq and Jabhat al-Nusra. Al-Zawahiri called on both groups to cease infighting. Also, he chastised al-Baghdadi for attempting to expand without his permission.[52]

In response, in June 2013, the ISI leader released an audio message defying and challenging al-Zawahiri. Also, al-Baghdadi asserted that he commanded the Islamic State of Iraq and al Sham.[53] In addition, al-Baghdadi expressed his refusal to adhere to the boundaries put in place by the 1916 Sykes-Picot Agreement (Asia Minor Agreement)—crafted in secret by France and Great Britian with assent of Russia as a framework to carve up the Ottoman Empire.[54] Never before had al-Qa'ida's internal disputes been aired in such a public fashion.[55] Thus, the attempted merger actually resulted in a permanent split between the ISIS and al-Qa'ida. Nevertheless, the groups continued to fight side by side in Syria on occasion.[56]

Al-Zawahiri was forced to intervene again after the January 2014 coordinated revolt against ISIL's excesses by other Syrian rebel groups. The ISI became powerful, in part, by taking territory and resources from other groups, including both mainstream and Islamist.[57] In February 2014, however, al-Zawahiri disowned ISIL, declaring that al-Qa'ida was no longer responsible for the actions of ISIS.[58] ISIL's spokesman, Abu Mohammed al-Adnani, retorted that al-Zawahiri should pledge allegiance to al-Baghdadi, the true emir, if he set foot in the Islamic State.[59]

Other al-Qa'ida affiliates started to weigh in on the leadership dispute. At first, al-Qa'ida in the Islamic Maghreb (AQIM) and al-Qa'ida in the Arabian Peninsula (AQAP) were neutral and encouraged reconciliation. However, the so-called "central region" of AQIM as well as some AQAP fighters came out in support of ISIL[60] Relations between ISIL and other al-Qa'ida affiliates continued to improve as ISIL expanded its activities in Iraq. On June 29, 2014, ISIL rebranded itself as the Islamic State (IS) claiming that al-Baghdadi is the caliph of its newly established caliphate.[61]

U.S. and coalition airstrikes against ISIS, Jabhat al-Nusra, and the Khorasan Group initiated in 2014 could affect collaboration among the three groups. There are reports that Jabhat al-Nusra fighters are leaving the group and joining ISIS, as many as seventy in one day in September 2014.[62] Also, it is projected that the groups will downplay the tensions among them in favor of focusing their efforts on combating U.S. and coalition forces. The Islamic fighters view this fight as a new Crusade against Muslims.[63] Al-Qa'ida's leader Zawahiri called coalition attacks a "war on Islam."[64] Jabhat al-Nusra spokesman, Abu Firas al-Suri, predicted, "This war will not end in months nor years, this war could last for decades."[65]

IN PARALLEL — THE MISSTEPS OF NOURI AL-MALIKI, POLITICAL STRIFE AND ELECTION VIOLENCE IN IRAQ, AND THE ASCENDANCY OF HAIDER AL-ABADI

Nouri al-Maliki

The government of Iraqi Prime Minister Nouri al-Maliki undermined the contributions and aspirations of the Sons of Iraq. The expected development contracts never materialized, and their wages remained unpaid. Further still,

Sunnis were politically marginalized under al-Maliki's majority-Shiite government.[66] Al-Maliki used "de-Baathification" laws—created to keep members of Saddam Hussein's regime out of office—selectively against his Sunni rivals. He brought former Shiite militants into the armed forces and purged high-ranking Sunni officers.

As Maliki expelled Sunni political rivals from the military in conjunction with consolidating political power, corruption increased. The 2010 Iraqi elections granted secular rival and former Prime Minister Ayad Allawi's coalition a plurality in the parliament. But al-Maliki demanded a recount,[67] and forced the resignation of anti-corruption officials. The corruption-penetrated Iraqi government precipitated popular protests in 2011, which were brutally put down by al-Maliki's government. Al-Maliki soon began the practice of circumventing the military chain of command and directly ordering officers to carry out dubious arrests.[68] Exacerbating Sunni-Shiite tensions were accusations that Sunni Vice President Tariq al-Hashemi was involved in acts of terrorism. He was later sentenced to death in absentia.[69]

Likewise, in December 2012, Iraqi security forces raided the home of Iraqi Finance Minister Rafie al-Issawi, a Sunni, and arrested ten of his bodyguards.[70] These activities precipitated mass protests by Iraqi protestors throughout the country from late December 2012 through 2013.

In December 2013, Iraqi security forces violently dismantled a 300–400-person Sunni protest camp in Ramadi, leading to the deaths of seventeen people.[71] Previously, an April 2013 attack by Iraqi security forces on another Sunni protest camp in Hawija killed forty-five people.[72] These incidents further fueled dissension within the Iraqi Sunni community, and, in turn, setting the groundwork for appeal of ISIS to this constituency.

Al-Maliki's Shiite-dominated government was tainted by years of Sunni accusations of oppression, including mass killings, extralegal detentions, and the arrest and removal of Sunni leadership. Moderate Iraqi Sunnis had been marginalized and repressed, making them relatively easy prey for Sunni extremist groups, such as ISIS and its progenitors. ISIS and its antecedents capitalized on such sectarian tensions, arguing that they could protect Sunnis against the Shiites' onslaught.[73]

In June 2013, leading Sunni cleric Sheikh Youssef al-Qaradawi "called on all those able to undertake jihad and fighting to head to Syria to stand by the Syrian people who are being killed at the hands of the regime and are now being killed at the hands of what he called the party of Satan." In particular, al-Qaradawi was referring to Hezbollah, and its leader Hassan Nasrallah, who in the previous month publicly acknowledged that Hezbollah was fighting in Syria on behalf of the Assad regime.[74] Nasrallah's pronouncement further polarized Sunni-Shiite tensions in Iraq, Lebanon, and Syria, as did the November 2013 declaration Nasrallah made that Hezbollah troops were present in Syria, supporting the Assad regime.[75]

Political Strife and Election Violence

By February 2014, Iraqi Parliament Speaker Usama Nujaifi warned of a civil war between the people and the army if the Anbar crisis continued without a political solution.[76] The following month, the United Nations expressed concern about the rising violence in Iraq, as 703 people died in February 2014. That figure was significantly higher than the previous year.[77]

In March 2014, a series of bombings in Baghdad, concentrated in a largely Sunni neighborhood in the northern part of the city, killed thirty-three people and wounded a dozen.[78]

By April 2014, the Iraqi election campaign began with no single bloc expected to win a majority.[79] The U.N.'s envoy to Iraq warned that Iraq's election campaign would be "highly divisive" amid a yearlong surge in bloodshed.[80] Also, that month saw car bombs in Shiite neighborhoods of Baghdad that killed thirty-four people and wounded dozens more.[81] Elsewhere in Iraq, in one day alone, April 21, 2014, suicide bombings and other attacks across Iraq killed thirty-three people and wounded eighty others.[82]

Among the political rallies targeted by violence during April 2014 were:

- A campaign rally for a militant Shiite group where bombings killed at least thirty-three people. The attacks unleashed a further series of sectarian attacks.[83]
- A Kurdish political rally in northeastern Iraq, where a suicide bombing killed thirty people and wounded fifty others.[84]

By late April 2014, voting in Iraq's elections began.[85] Iraq's election saw a 60 percent turnout. It was relatively peaceful, with only fourteen deaths across the country.[86] Iraq's death toll in April 2014 exceeded 1,000.[87]

Iraq lacked a fully functional government from April to August 2014, significantly impeding its ability to respond to the IS threat. Parliamentary elections were held in late April[88] and, in the initial results announced in May 2014, Maliki's State of Law party won 92 of 328 parliamentary seats.[89] However, this figure was not a majority.[90] Unfortunately, political violence did not let up, as bombings and other acts targeting various religious and ethnic groups continued, including some one hundred deaths alone in attacks across Iraq during May 27–29, 2014.[91]

The Iraqi Independent High Electoral Commission (IHEC) received 854 complaints, which had to be considered before the official results were announced.[92] The Iraqi Supreme Court certified the election results on June 16, 2014, without making significant changes to the preliminary results.[93] Despite significant complaints, Nouri al-Maliki insisted on accepting his party's nomination for a third term as prime minister.[94]

As the Islamic State made gains in Samarra, Mosul, and Tikrit by June 2014, it became clear that a new unity government would be necessary to try to prevent Iraq from fracturing further. Initial attempts at forming a government failed as Sunni and Kurdish members of parliament walked out of the first meeting of the Iraqi Parliament. This deadlock, in turn, postponed the naming of a speaker of parliament for two weeks.[95] Parliament finally elected a moderate Sunni, Salim al-Jubouri, as speaker of parliament on July 15th after two failed votes.[96] Fouad Massoum, a Kurdish politician, was elected president on July 24th.[97]

Massoum appointed Haider al-Abadi, a moderate Shiite member of the State of Law Coalition and deputy prime minister, to replace al-Maliki as prime minister on August 11th.[98] Upon being appointed, Prime Minister al-Abadi was responsible for forming a coalition government. However, the process was hampered by al-Maliki's refusal to relinquish his post as prime minister.[99] On August 14th, Prime Minister al-Maliki finally agreed to step down under considerable U.S. and Iranian pressure on August 14th.[100]

In late August 2014, several Sunni politicians abandoned negotiations to form a government. This decision arose after a Shiite militia shot and killed seventy-three people at a Sunni mosque in the eastern Iraqi village of Bani Wais while Iraqi security forces prevented rescue teams from accessing the mosque. (The attack at the Sunni mosque was apparently carried out in response to roadside bombs against Shiite targets).[101]

Al-Abadi Reign

However, by September 8, 2014, the parliament approved a power-sharing plan that would allow for three vice presidents, including al-Maliki and former Prime Minister Ayad Allawi.[102] Kurdish members of parliament returned to the legislature in Baghdad on October 13th, shoring up the legitimacy of al-Abadi's government.[103]

The new Iraqi government of al-Abadi took several steps to stabilize the country and build an inclusive coalition, which would simultaneously undermine the interests of the Islamic State. Newly elected Oil Minister Adel Abdul Mahdi made conciliatory gestures to Iraqi Kurdistan on oil production.[104] Al-Abadi retired two high-level al-Maliki-allied military commanders for their failure to hold ground against the IS and for their earlier association with discriminatory practices against Sunni Iraqis.[105]

The new government also made efforts to shift power and security authority to the provincial levels of government, to appease Sunni interests. Al-Abadi expressed interest in establishing a national guard, where locally-recruited soldiers would serve local populations.[106] This last initiative could go a long way in attracting Sunni "hearts and minds," while spurring greater participation in local security as their efforts would protect their own locales and not areas of Iraq where they otherwise have no affinity or interest.

Unfortunately, al-Maliki and his allies continued to make things difficult for the new government, blocking two crucial cabinet appointments, the Ministers of the Interior and of the Military, for months.[107] When the Iraqi Parliament finally voted to approve an Interior Minister, they chose Mohammed Ghabban, a candidate closely tied to the Badr Organization, which ran several Shiite death squads and coordinated attacks on Sunnis. Al-Abadi had tried to placate Sunni and Kurdish opposition by keeping Badr-linked politicians out of power. The appointment of Ghabban threatened to derail the push for unity.[108]

As 2014 marked its end in Iraq, new statistics quickly confirmed a bloody and frightful year. According to the UN office in Iraq, between January and November 2014, approximately 12,000 people were killed and about another 22,000 were injured there in acts of terrorism and other violence. In light of this extensive carnage, Special Representative of the Secretary General for Iraq and Head of UN Assistance Mission in Iraq Nickolay Mladenov appealed to "the Iraqi political, religious and social leaders to act decisively to rise above their differences in order to resolve the pending political, social and economic problems, and restore confidence among Iraq's communities, more particularly those disaffected groups, as part of consolidating the democratic process."[109]

In 2015, things started on a positive note as al-Abadi met with representatives of Iraq's al-Anbar province to discuss plans to liberate it from IS control. Al-Abadi underscored the importance of having refugees return to the province.[110] Al-Abadi said that a "tribal revolution" was needed to effectuate the defeat of the Islamic State.[111]

Sunni-Shiite reconciliation on the political front faced a setback in February 2015, when Iraq's two primary Sunni political parties suspended their activities in parliament following the assassination of a high ranking Sunni tribal leader and the abduction of a Sunni member of parliament.[112]

ISIS EVOLUTION TO IS AND SELECTED TERRITORIAL SUCCESSES AND DEFEATS

Background

ISIS's path and transformation to the Islamic State, exemplified by some military successes and setbacks, will be highlighted next. Coalition force activities and countermeasures by Iraqi, Kurdish, and Syrian government forces are addressed here and with a different emphasis in chapter 6.

In March 2013, ISIS forces took Raqqa, its first provincial capital captured in Syria.[113] In July 2013, ISIS forces attacked prisons in Abu Ghraib and Taji in Iraq, liberating numerous prisoners. At Abu Ghraib, between 500–1,000 inmates escaped, many linked to al-Qa'ida.[114] These escapees subsequently contributed to the successes of the group as it rampaged through parts of Iraq and Syria. In January 2014, ISIS acquired control of Fallujah, Iraq.[115]

June 2014

In a remarkable success, ISIS forces gained control of Mosul after four days of intermittent attacks in June 2014. Many Iraqi soldiers simply abandoned their posts.[116] In light of the loss of Mosul, Iraq's then-Prime Minister Nuri al-Maliki asked parliament to declare a state of emergency.[117] Meanwhile, the United States condemned the seizure of Mosul by ISIS, calling the situation "extremely serious," and urging fractious political groups to fight Iraq's enemies together.[118] ISIS's success in Mosul meant that it controlled "large parts of eastern Syria and western Iraq, a vast cross-border haven for militants in the Sunni Muslim core of the Middle East."[119]

During their onslaught on Mosul, ISIS militants also captured eighty Turkish citizens who were seized in two separate incidents. In fearing for the well-being of its citizens, Turkey's interactions vis-à-vis ISIS and its successors became somewhat muted for a period.[120]

Also in June 2014, ISIS forces overran Tikrit and closed in on the biggest oil refinery in the country.[121] In addition, ISIS forces captured the predominantly Turkmen city of Tal Afar.[122] ISIS claimed they massacred 1,700 captive Shiite members of Iraq's security forces. The group posted grisly pictures of a mass execution in Tikrit as evidence of the killings and warnings of more devastation to come.[123]

Yet, June 2014 also resulted in some setbacks to ISIS. For instance, Iraqi Army infantry units, bolstered by Shiite militias, pushed back against Sunni militants north of Baghdad and near Samarra.[124] Meanwhile, Iraqi Kurdish forces took advantage of the chaos elsewhere in Iraq and seized control of disputed oil hub of city of Kirkuk and oil fields of Bai Hassan in summer 2014.[125] According to analyst Dr. Marwan Kabalan, the instability undermining Iraq is simultaneously aiding the Kurdistan Regional Government (KRG) to keep control of Kirkuk. Too, Dr. Kabalan noted, "[t]hanks to Daesh, the fragmentation and disintegration of Iraq has become more real and possible today than any time in the past."[126]

Elsewhere, Iraqi troops abandoned posts, alarming the Iraqi government and its allies worldwide. Meanwhile, Iraq's parliament failed to reach a quorum for a vote on declaring a nationwide state of emergency as ISIS insurgents advanced on Baghdad.[127]

At the end of June 2014, ISIS renamed itself "The Islamic State." The group declared the establishment of an Islamic Caliphate, with its capital in

Raqqa, Syria.[128] Around this time, the Islamic State published a "Five-Year Plan," outlining its projected territorial holdings, which include Spain, North Africa, the Sahel, the Balkans, and the Middle East.[129] Some analysts deem the authenticity of this plan questionable.

July 2014

In early July 2014, Abu Bakr al-Baghdadi, the caliph of the Islamic State, delivered a significant sermon in the Great Mosque of Mosul (Great Mosque of al-Nuri), that was widely touted by the entity and its followers.[130] Also that month, the Islamic State paraded captured tanks, armored personnel carriers, and a Scud missile through Raqqa.[131] The IS demanded that other rebel groups swear their loyalty to the IS and give up their weapons.[132] Subsequently, the IS captured several towns and the largest oil field in Syria. Jabhat al-Nusra ceded control of the al-Omar oil field to IS without a fight.[133]

In addition, the IS expelled rival factions from Deiz al-Zor, Syria. The Islamic State was then in control of the city and the majority of the province.[134] Islamic State fighters were not only engaging the Iraqi and Syrian militaries during summer 2014, they also continued to target civilians, including car bombings and suicide bombings in Baghdad and elsewhere.[135]

As an aside, in January 2015, the Hazzm movement, a secular rebel group, announced that it would be joining Jabhat al-Shamiyya, an umbrella organization comprised of several Islamist rebel groups in Syria. With this move, few secular rebel groups remain in northern Syria.[136]

In other troubling developments, the IS seized a former chemical weapon depot and looted the equipment and supplies in the Muthanna facility north of Baghdad in July 2014.[137] Also, IS seized eighty-eight pounds of nuclear material from Mosul University.[138]

August–September 2014

In August 2014, IS fighters took control of Iraq's biggest dam (the Mosul Dam), an oilfield, and over a dozen cities. The capture of the electricity generating Mosul Dam gave the Sunni militants the ability to flood major Iraqi cities and withhold water.[139] Later that month, Iraqi and Kurdish forces, with the help of U.S. airstrikes, recaptured the Mosul Dam.[140]

In addition, IS militants surged across northern Iraq toward the capital of the Kurdish region, Erbil. This IS advancement led to tens of thousands of Christians' fleeing for their lives. This latest offensive prompted additional discussions of Western military action against the IS.[141]

Furthermore, IS fighters encircled and threatened the Yazidi people who were trapped on Iraq's Sinjar Mountains. In doing so, the IS fighters killed hundreds—if not more—of Yazidis. Also, the IS took hundreds of Yazidi women and children as slaves.[142]

So too, July 2014 gave IS militants a mixed record of success. For instance, U.S. airstrikes helped Kurdish Peshmerga forces regain control of several towns (e.g., Gwer, Mahmour, and Teleskof) and some nearby villages in Iraq.[143] After weeks of clashes with Kurdish fighters, Islamic State militants captured the town of Jalawla, northeast of Baghdad.[144] Also, IS fighters gained control of several towns in the Aleppo province of Syria. Previously, other Islamist groups controlled those towns.[145] Also, IS militants captured the Tabqa air base in northeast Syria.[146]

Furthermore, IS militants attacked the Lebanese town of Arsal and engaged with Lebanese armed forces.[147] During the fighting between the forces, IS killed at least nineteen Lebanese soldiers.[148] Also, ISIS captured twenty-seven Lebanese soldiers and Internal Security Force members.[149]

In September 2014, Kurdish forces halted some IS advances in the Kobani region of Syria.[150] Iraqi forces suffered losses against IS fighters in Saqlawiya, an hour outside Baghdad. IS militants overran an Iraqi armed forces camp.[151]

October 2014

Islamic State fighters captured the town of Kubaisa in western Iraq. Meanwhile, the IS continued to pressure Kurdish forces in Kobani.[152] Islamic State forces entered Kobani and took several neighborhoods in the eastern part of the city. Control of Kobani would give IS a strategic stretch of land along the Turkish border.[153] In opposition, U.S.-led coalition airstrikes and Kurdish ground forces undermined some IS advances.[154]

Elsewhere, IS militants successfully shot down several Iraqi military helicopters.[155] IS forces surrounded Haditha, Iraq, with possible plans to attack the city.[156] Also, the IS seized an Iraqi Army base in Hit, in Anbar province, some eighty-five miles from Baghdad. In contrast to previous retreats by Iraqi soldiers, they took their weaponry before abandoning the base.[157]

In addition, the IS acquired three Syrian fighter jets from government military bases that were overrun. Iraqi pilots who have joined the IS are apparently teaching other militants how to fly the planes.[158] Ultimately, two of three fighter jets stolen by IS were shot down by the Syrian military.[159]

Also, IS militants conducted nearly fifteen attacks on Kurdish forces in northern Iraq. The group also focused attacks on Mosul Dam and the Sinjar mountain range.[160] Moreover, IS terrorists targeted Baghdad with car bombs and mortar attacks, with over 150 people killed in several attacks.[161] In October 2014, the IS lost control of Zumar to Kurdish Peshmerga forces and Jurf al-Sakhar to the Iraqi army.[162]

November–December 2014

In November 2014, the IS claimed responsibility for a car bombing in Baghdad, which targeted Shiites, killing ten and injuring more than twenty.[163] By December 2014, Kurdish Peshmerga forces freed about 70 percent of the Sinjar Mountains in northern Iraq from Islamic State control. Aided by U.S. air support, the Kurds were able to provide a safe haven to several hundred Yazidis who were under threat from the IS. In their offensive, the Kurds also liberated the towns of Zumar and Sunoni.[164]

January 2015

By the end of January 2015, Kurdish forces recaptured some 90 percent of Kobani from IS fighters. This marked an important defeat of the IS. Also, it was a positive development for the coalition. Some 100,000 locals fled Kobani once the city was controlled by IS fighters. During the conflict about 1,800 people were killed.[165] Thousands of refugees cannot return to their homes because much of Kobani was devastated during the conflict.[166]

In light of the Islamic State's defeat in Kobani, IS supporters tweeted the hashtag #PrayForTheBrothersInKobaniCampaign. Also, the IS was losing some ground in Mosul and Diyala.[167] The Syrian Observatory for Human Rights reported that IS was relocating troops from areas firmly under its control in Syria to the north of the city of Al-Hasakah where clashes continued against Kurdish YPG forces.[168]

Despite the successes of Kurdish forces in Kobani in January 2015, U.S. officials stressed that the battle for Mosul would be a more difficult challenge, but strategy to retake the city was being crafted.[169] Incidentally, as Kurdish Peshmerga forces pushed towards Mosul, mistrust and wariness loomed between the Kurds and the liberated Sunni population. The Kurds viewed the Sunni civilians with suspicion as they remained in the region despite it being controlled by the IS.[170]

After Kurdish Peshmerga forces launched an artillery barrage against IS-controlled Mosul in January 2015, the IS released a video in which the group threatened Western nations, including the United States. The IS militants stated that they would kill President Obama in the White House and make the United States a Muslim country. Also, at the end of the video, a captured Kurdish soldier was executed.[171]

IS fighters continued their attacks against Kirkuk in northern Iraq. The attacks appeared to be aimed at capturing the key oil-rich city or to diverting Kurdish troops from trying to capture the IS stronghold in Mosul.[172] During this offensive, IS militants took over Maktab Khalid, an area about twelve miles southwest of Kirkuk.[173]

Elsewhere, Iraqi security forces took back five villages from the IS in the province of Salah il-Din, killing twenty-six IS fighters.[174] On January 12, 2015, more than seventy IS fighters were killed in fighting with Iraqi and Kurdish forces in Sultan Abdullah, a village in northern Iraq. The previous day, in Gwer, a town some sixty kilometers from Kurdistan's capital, Erbil, twenty-eight IS and twenty-three Kurdish forces were killed during fighting.[175]

In January 2015, Ammar al-Hakim of the Supreme Iraqi Islamic Council stated that Iraqi security forces and allied Shiite militias were capable of defeating ISIS.[176] Likewise, Kurdish Peshmerga forces announced that, after regaining 500 square kilometers from IS, its forces had cut off a major supply route between Mosul and the rest of ISIS controlled territory.[177] Subsequently, Kurdish Peshmerga forces continued their advance against ISIS, capturing four villages north of Mosul.[178] Also, Kurdish Peshmerga forces retook the Khabbaz oilfield near Kirkuk, but stated that fifteen workers had been abducted.[179]

Masoud Barzani, president of Iraqi Kurdistan, expressed discontent over the fact that Kurdish representatives were not invited to a meeting held between the U.S.-led coalition and Iraqi officials in London in January 2015.[180] Kurdish Prime Minister Nechirvan Barzani stated that the fight against ISIS would be drawn out and that Mosul would not be retaken until, at the earliest, autumn 2015.[181] In advance of an impending invasion of Mosul, in January 2015, IS militants were taking steps to fortify and defend the city of Mosul, including digging trenches, blowing bridges, and sealing off streets with concrete walls.[182]

February 2015

Kurdish YPG forces had seized 163 villages around Kobani from IS fighters.[183] Elsewhere in Syria, YPG forces captured, from IS fighters, twenty villages, farmland, and buildings in the Abo Qasayeb area.[184] Also, IS forces pulled out a large portion of its fighters and military hardware from areas near Aleppo.[185] In addition, YPG forces captured several villages in Raqqa province and seized a major road between Aleppo and Al-Hasakah.[186]

The Syrian Observatory for Human Rights reported that the IS had relocated over 1,000 fighters from Syria to Iraq.[187] In Iraq, IS militants captured the town of Al-Baghdadi, a town located in Anbar Province, Iraq.[188]

Iraqi forces pushed back an assault on Al-Asad airbase and the nearby town of Al-Baghdadi in Anbar province. U.S. Marines are stationed at the Al-Asad airbase where they are conducting training operations.[189] The United States announced plans to open a military airbase in Iraqi Kurdistan in order to aid in the eventual assault on Mosul.[190]

U.S. military officials stated that IS would be greatly weakened if the Iraqi government made efforts to mend the rift with the Sunni population.[191] Also, the United States announced plans to speed up arms supplies to Jordan.[192]

March and April 2015

In March 2015, "Peshmerga Fighters supported by Combined Joint Task Force—Operation Inherent Resolve, seized a key ridgeline in Northern Iraq west of Kirkuk."[193] More specifically, "Peshmerga forces were able to seize critical portions of Route 80 in Iraq. Coalition forces conducted supporting air strikes, resulting in the destruction of ten enemy fighting positions, five tactical units and ten ISIL weapons systems."[194]

Also, during March 2015, IS forces made advances against Assad regime forces in the provinces of Hama, Homs, and Damascus. In Hama province, IS forces killed over seventy regime soldiers. Meanwhile, the Syrian government killed nineteen IS fighters in the group's stronghold, Deir al-Zor, in eastern Syria.[195]

In an important development in late March, Jabhat al-Nusra forces, in combination with four other groups—Ahrar al Sham, Jund al Aqsa, Jaish al Sunnah, and Failaq al Sham—dislodged the Syrian army from the provincial capital Idlib. Besides killing at least fifty Syrian soldiers, the opposition forces who created a 6,000-man force called the Fateh Army, acquired four tanks during the military offensive. As a result of this effort, "[t]he capture of Idlib [capital of Idlib province, which had a population of about 100,000] leaves Nusra and its allies in control of an area the size of Lebanon in northern Syria, stretching from Aleppo to the province of Latakia in the west. The only major town remaining under government control in the area is Jisr al Shugur."[196] Upon the control of Idlib, Abu Mohamad al-Golani, Jabhat al-Nusra leader, said that sharia law would be established there.[197]

Also in March 2015, Iraqi security forces repulsed an IS attack on a section of Ramadi, although later the IS captured other portions of the city. In another operation, "anti-ISIL forces were able to seize critical portions of Route 47 in Syria, a key ISIL communications and supply line leading into Iraq. In addition, key terrain was seized in the Jazera region and 94 nearby villages were liberated."[198]

In addition, ISIL was denied "access to primary travel routes historically used to move its personnel and materials into Iraq—namely Tal Afar and Mosul."[199] Elsewhere, by March 2015, the IS was dislodged from the town of Al-Baghdadi as well as "from seven villages northwest of Al Baghdadi on the road to Hadithah."[200]

In late March 2015 the United States provided air support to Iraqi security forces and Popular Mobilization Forces battling the Islamic State in Tikrit.

This assistance occurred after the withdrawal of some Iranian-linked Shiite militias, which the United States was reticent about collaborating with in the campaign. Despite the apparent success of the air campaign against IS forces, control of Tikrit was expected to be time-consuming, difficult, and costly. [201]

Yet, by early April 2015, the Iraqi government declared a "magnificent victory" in Tikrit. [202] The defeat of the IS "involved some 30,000 personnel, two thirds of them from the Popular Mobilisation (Hashid Shaabi), a force comprising dozens of Iranian-backed Shia militia." [203] Additionally, while "Iranian military advisers, led by Gen. Qasem Soleimani of the Revolutionary Guards' Quds Force, initially co-ordinated the operation," U.S. airstrikes made the difference once efforts against the IS stalled. [204]

Still, there were reports of pockets of the IS resistance in Tikrit, coupled with portions of the city being mined and booby-trapped. Moreover, there was substantial devastation in the birthplace of Saddam Hussein as a result of numerous battles there over the years. Too, in an ironic twist, in Tikrit, the United States was essentially facing two de facto but different enemies: IS forces and Iran. The former was Sunni and the latter Shiite (which concomitantly was also allied with U.S. anti-IS coalition partner, Iraq). Each entity—the IS and Iran—with their disparate actions and aspirations, are all ultimately antithetical to U.S. interests. [205]

Nevertheless, the aforementioned selected victories over the Islamic State reflect a segment of the new reality on the ground, whereby, as of March 2015, "the group's advance in Iraq has been halted by Iraqi security forces, Kurdish Peshmerga, and tribal elements, with the support of U.S. and Coalition air operations." [206] As such, the IS "can no longer do what he did at the outset, which is to seize and to hold new territory. He has assumed a defense crouch in Iraq," said U.S. Central Command Commander Gen. Lloyd J. Austin III. [207]

More broadly, General John Allen asserted, that by March 2015, coalition forces have "achieved the first phase of our campaign: we have blunted ISIL's organization's strategic, operational, and tactical momentum in Iraq." [208] General Allen also highlighted ISIL's missteps in attacking Erbil, and its loss in Kobani, as demonstrating that the group is far from invincible, and is suffering from a weakened morale. [209]

Yet, in Syria in early April 2015, the IS had taken control of the Yarmouk Palestinian refugee camp, several kilometers outside of Damascus, and 90 percent of Yarmouk. Control of the refugee camp pitted anti-Assad regime Palestinian fighters, Aknaf Beit al-Maqdis, against the IS. Meanwhile, the Assad regime targeted the refugee camp with shelling and barrel bombs. In relation to the capture of Yarmouk, Jabhat al-Nusra allegedly aided the Islamic State against other rebel groups. [210] The advance by the IS at Yarmouk marked the closest the group has come to the Syrian capital. [211]

In sum, while the Islamic State seemed invincible in June 2014, some nine months later, its potency in terms of military capabilities in Iraq—at the very least—have waned, although the group appears to have maintained some constancy, if not strengthening, in Syria.

NOTES

1. Zelin, Aaron Y. "The War between ISIS and al-Qaeda for Supremacy of the Global Jihadist Movement." Washington Institute for Near East Policy, June 2014. Accessed October 20, 2014. http://www.washingtoninstitute.org/uploads/Documents/pubs/ResearchNote_20_Zelin.pdf.

2. Ghosh, Bobby. "ISIS: A Short History." *Atlantic*, August 14, 2014. Accessed October 20, 2014. http://www.theatlantic.com/international/archive/2014/08/isis-a-short-history/376030/. Zelin, Aaron Y. "The War between ISIS and al-Qaeda for Supremacy of the Global Jihadist Movement." Washington Institute for Near East Policy, June 2014. Accessed October 20, 2014. http://www.washingtoninstitute.org/uploads/Documents/pubs/ResearchNote_20_Zelin.pdf.

3. Sommer, Allison Kaplan. "What's in a name? A guide to the subtle but serious implications of choosing, ISIS, ISIL, Islamic State or Da'ash." *Haaretz*, September 11, 2014. Accessed October 20, 2014. http://www.haaretz.com/blogs/routine-emergencies/.premium-1.615126. Zelin, Aaron Y. "The War between ISIS and al-Qaeda for Supremacy of the Global Jihadist Movement." Washington Institute for Near East Policy, June 2014. Accessed October 20, 2014. http://www.washingtoninstitute.org/uploads/Documents/pubs/ResearchNote_20_Zelin.pdf.

4. Ghosh, Bobby. "ISIS: A Short History." *Atlantic*, August 14, 2014. Accessed October 20, 2014. http://www.theatlantic.com/international/archive/2014/08/isis-a-short-history/376030/.

5. Tharoor, Ishaan. "ISIS or ISIL? The debate over what to call Iraq's terror group." *Washington Post*, June 18, 2014. Accessed October 20, 2014. http://www.washingtonpost.com/blogs/worldviews/wp/2014/06/18/isis-or-isil-the-debate-over-what-to-call-iraqs-terror-group/.

6. Sommer, Allison Kaplan. "What's in a name? A guide to the subtle but serious implications of choosing, ISIS, ISIL, Islamic State or Da'ash." *Haaretz*, September 11, 2014. Accessed October 20, 2014. http://www.haaretz.com/blogs/routine-emergencies/.premium-1.615126.

7. Sommers, Chloe. "The Pentagon has a new name for ISIS." *CNN*, December 19, 2014. Accessed December 21, 2014. http://www.cnn.com/2014/12/18/politics/pentagon-now-calls-isis-daesh/index.html?iid=article_sidebar.

8. Ibid.

9. Ibid.

10. Gettleman, Jeffrey. "Abu Musab al-Zarqawi Lived a Brief, Shadowy Life Replete With Contradictions." *NY Times*, June 9, 2006. Accessed February 23, 2015. http://www.nytimes.com/2006/06/09/world/middleeast/09zarqawi.html?_r=0. Weaver, Mary Anne. "The Short, Violent Life of Abu Musab al-Zarqawi." *Atlantic*, June 8, 2006. Accessed February 23, 2015. http://www.theatlantic.com/magazine/archive/2006/07/the-short-violent-life-of-abu-musab-al-zarqawi/304983/2/.

Gambill, Gary. "Abu Musab al-Zarqawi: A biographical sketch." *Jamestown Terrorism Monitor*, Vol. 2, Iss. 24, December 15, 2004. Accessed February 15, 2015. http://www.jamestown.org/single/?tx_ttnews%5Btt_news%5D=27304#.VOc06MY8c2e.

11. Weaver, Mary Anne. "The Short, Violent Life of Abu Musab al-Zarqawi." *Atlantic*, June 8, 2006. Accessed February 23, 2015. http://www.theatlantic.com/magazine/archive/2006/07/the-short-violent-life-of-abu-musab-al-zarqawi/304983/2/.

12. Ibid.

13. Whitlock, Craig. "Al-Zarqawi's Biography." *Washington Post*, June 8, 2006. Accessed February 23, 2015. http://www.washingtonpost.com/wp-dyn/content/article/2006/06/08/AR2006060800299.html. Weaver, Mary Anne. "The Short, Violent Life of Abu Musab al-

Zarqawi." *Atlantic*, June 8, 2006. Accessed February 23, 2015. http://www.theatlantic.com/magazine/archive/2006/07/the-short-violent-life-of-abu-musab-al-zarqawi/304983/.

14. Ibid.

15. "Abu Musab al-Zarqawi." *Independent*, June 9, 2006. Accessed October 20, 2014. http://www.independent.co.uk/news/obituaries/abu-musab-alzarqawi-481622.html. Chehab, Zaki. "Iraq Ablaze: Inside the Insurgency." 2006. Accessed October 20, 2014. http://books.google.com/books?id=vZv6Pmb-KVoC&printsec=frontcover&dq=Iraq+Ablaze:+Inside+the+Insurgency&hl=en&sa=X&ei=1EIXVNTrNsiZsQTJ3ILwAw&ved=0CB8Q6AEwAA#v=onepage&q=Zarqawi.

Whitlock, Craig. "Al-Zarqawi's Biography." *Washington Post*, June 8, 2006. Accessed October 20, 2014. http://www.washingtonpost.com/wp-dyn/content/article/2006/06/08/AR2006060800299_2.html?nav=rss_world/africa.

16. Napoleani, Loretta. "The Myth of Zarqawi." *Antiwar*, November 11, 2005. Accessed October 20, 2014. http://www.antiwar.com/orig/napoleoni.php?articleid=7988. Weaver, Mary Ann. "The Short, Violent Life of Abu Musab al-Zarqawi." *Atlantic*, July 1, 2006. Accessed November 25, 2014. http://www.theatlantic.com/magazine/archive/2006/07/the-short-violent-life-of-abu-musab-al-zarqawi/304983/.

17. Weaver, Mary Ann. "The Short, Violent Life of Abu Musab al-Zarqawi." *Atlantic*, July 1, 2006. Accessed November 25, 2014. http://www.theatlantic.com/magazine/archive/2006/07/the-short-violent-life-of-abu-musab-al-zarqawi/304983/.

18. Gambill, Gary. "Abu Musab al-Zarqawi: A biographical sketch." *Jamestown Terrorism Monitor*, Vol. 2, Iss. 24, December 15, 2004. Accessed February 15, 2015. http://www.jamestown.org/single/?tx_ttnews%5Btt_news%5D=27304#.VOc06MY8c2e.

19. Zelin, Aaron Y. "The War between ISIS and al-Qaeda for Supremacy of the Global Jihadist Movement." Washington Institute for Near East Policy, June 2014. Accessed October 20, 2014. http://www.washingtoninstitute.org/uploads/Documents/pubs/ResearchNote_20_Zelin.pdf. Weaver, Mary Ann. "The Short, Violent Life of Abu Musab al-Zarqawi." *Atlantic*, June 8, 2006. Accessed November 25, 2014. http://www.theatlantic.com/magazine/archive/2006/07/the-short-violent-life-of-abu-musab-al-zarqawi/304983/.

Whitlock, Craig. "Al-Zarqawi's Biography." *Washington Post*, June 8, 2006. Accessed October 20, 2014. http://www.washingtonpost.com/wp-dyn/content/article/2006/06/08/AR2006060800299_2.html?nav=rss_world/africa.

20. Weaver, Mary Anne. "The Short, Violent Life of Abu Musab al-Zarqawi." *Atlantic*, June 8, 2006. Accessed February 23, 2015. http://www.theatlantic.com/magazine/archive/2006/07/the-short-violent-life-of-abu-musab-al-zarqawi/304983/4/.

21. Gambill, Gary. "Abu Musab al-Zarqawi: A biographical sketch." *Jamestown Terrorism Monitor*, Vol. 2, Iss. 24, December 15, 2004. Accessed February 15, 2015. http://www.jamestown.org/single/?tx_ttnews%5Btt_news%5D=27304#.VOc06MY8c2e.

22. Weaver, Mary Ann. "The Short, Violent Life of Abu Musab al-Zarqawi." *Atlantic*, June 8, 2006. Accessed February 23, 2015. http://www.theatlantic.com/magazine/archive/2006/07/the-short-violent-life-of-abu-musab-al-zarqawi/304983/4/.

23. Ross, Brian. "Abu Musab al-Zarqawi: Life of Brutality." *ABC News*, June 8, 2006. Accessed February 23, 2015. http://abcnews.go.com/blogs/headlines/2006/06/abu_musab_alzar/.

24. Weaver, Mary Anne. "The Short, Violent Life of Abu Musab al-Zarqawi." *Atlantic*, June 8, 2006. Accessed February 23, 2015. http://www.theatlantic.com/magazine/archive/2006/07/the-short-violent-life-of-abu-musab-al-zarqawi/304983/4/.

25. Wong, Edward. "British hostage is beheaded in Iraq." *NY Times*, October 8, 2004. Accessed February 19, 2015. http://www.nytimes.com/2004/10/08/international/middleeast/08CND-IRAQ.html?_r=0. "American hostage is beheaded." *CBC News*, September 20, 2004. Accessed Februay 19, 2015. http://www.cbc.ca/news/world/american-hostage-beheaded-video-1.473228.

"Beheaded Japanese to be flown home." *CNN.com*, October 31, 2004. Accessed February 19, 2015. http://www.cnn.com/2004/WORLD/meast/10/31/japan.hostage/index.html.

"Hostage's wife devastated." *NBC News*, September 22, 2004. Accessed February 19, 2015. http://www.nbcnews.com/id/6070324/ns/world_news-mideast_n_africa/t/hostages-wife-devastated/#.VOdWWcY8c2c.

26. Ould Mohamedou, Dr. Mohammad-Mahmoud. "ISIS and the Deceptive Rebooting of Al Qaeda." Geneva Centre for Security Policy, August 2014. Accessed October 20, 2014. http://www.gcsp.ch/Regional-Development/Publications/GCSP-Publications/Policy-Papers/GCSP-Policy-Paper-ISIS-and-the-Deceptive-Rebooting-of-Al-Qaeda.

27. Ghosh, Bobby. "ISIS: A Short History." *Atlantic*, August 14, 2014. Accessed October 20, 2014. http://www.theatlantic.com/international/archive/2014/08/isis-a-short-history/376030/.

28. Gambill, Gary. "Abu Musab al-Zarqawi: A biographical sketch." *Jamestown Terrorism Monitor*, Vol. 2, Iss. 24, December 15, 2004. Accessed February 15, 2015. http://www.jamestown.org/single/?tx_ttnews%5Btt_news%5D=27304#.VOc06MY8c2e.

29. Ibid.

30. Ould Mohamedou, Dr Mohammad-Mahmoud. "ISIS and the Deceptive Rebooting of Al Qaeda." Geneva Centre for Security Policy, August 2014. Accessed October 20, 2014. http://www.gcsp.ch/Regional-Development/Publications/GCSP-Publications/Policy-Papers/GCSP-Policy-Paper-ISIS-and-the-Deceptive-Rebooting-of-Al-Qaeda. Barrett, Richard. "Foreign Fighters in Syria." The Soufan Group, June 2014. Accessed June 23, 2014. http://soufangroup.com/wp-content/uploads/2014/06/TSG-Foreign-Fighters-in-Syria.pdf.

Charles River Editors, The Islamic State of Iraq and Syria: The History of ISIS/ISIL, (July 8, 2014) ISBN13: 9781500443429; ISBN10: 1500443425.

31. "English Translation of Ayman al-Zawahiri's letter to Abu Musab al-Zarqawi." *Weekly Standard*, October 12, 2005. Accessed October 20, 2014. http://www.weeklystandard.com/Content/Public/Articles/000/000/006/203gpuul.asp?page=2. Bloom, Mia. "Even al Qaeda denounced beheading videos. Why the Islamic State brought them back." *Washington Post*, August 22, 2014. Accessed October 20, 2014. http://www.washingtonpost.com/posteverything/wp/2014/08/22/even-al-qaeda-denounced-beheading-videos-why-the-islamic-state-brought-them-back/.

32. DeYoung, Karen and Walter Pincus. "Al-Qaeda in Iraq May Not Be Threat Here." *Washington Post*, March 18, 2007. Accessed October 20, 2014. http://www.washingtonpost.com/wp-dyn/content/article/2007/03/17/AR2007031701373_pf.html. Gambill, Gary. "Abu Musab al-Zarqawi: A biographical sketch." *Jamestown Terrorism Monitor*, Vol. 2, Iss. 24, December 15, 2004. Accessed February 15, 2015. http://www.jamestown.org/single/?tx_ttnews%5D=27304#.VOc06MY8c2e.

33. Weaver, Mary Anne. "The Short, Violent Life of Abu Musab al-Zarqawi." *Atlantic*, June 8, 2006. Accessed February 23, 2015. http://www.theatlantic.com/magazine/archive/2006/07/the-short-violent-life-of-abu-musab-al-zarqawi/304983/4/.

34. "Jordan remembers victims of 2005 hotel bombings." *Jordan Times*, November 8, 2014. Accessed February 23, 2015. http://jordantimes.com/jordan-remembers-victims-of-2005-hotel-bombings.

35. Michaels, Jim and John Bacon. "Jordan executes two in response to pilot's slaying." *USA Today*, February 3, 2015. Accessed February 23, 2015. http://www.usatoday.com/story/news/world/2015/02/03/islamic-state-jordanian-pilot/22798055/.

36. Roberts, Joel. "What's Next After Zarqawi's Death?" *CBS News*, June 8, 2006. Accessed October 20, 2014. http://www.cbsnews.com/news/whats-next-after-zarqawis-death/.

37. Kaplan, Eben. "Abu Hamza al-Muhajir, Zarqawi's Mysterious Successor (aka Abu Ayub al-Masri)." Council on Foreign Relations. June 13, 2006. Accessed October 20, 2014. http://www.cfr.org/iraq/abu-hamza-al-muhajir-zarqawis-mysterious-successor-aka-abu-ayub-al-masri/p10894.

38. "Al-Qa'ida in Iraq (AQI)." The National Counterterrorism Center. Accessed October 20, 2014. http://www.nctc.gov/site/groups/aqi.html.

39. Ghosh, Bobby. "ISIS: A Short History." *Atlantic*, August 14, 2014. Accessed October 20, 2014. http://www.theatlantic.com/international/archive/2014/08/isis-a-short-history/376030/.

40. Ibrahim, Waleed. "Al Qaeda's two top Iraq leaders killed in raid." *Reuters*, April 19, 2010. Accessed October 20, 2014. http://www.reuters.com/article/2010/04/19/us-iraq-violence-alqaeda-idUSTRE63I3CL20100419. Roggio, Bill. "U.S. and Iraqi forces kill Al Masri and Baghdadi, al Qaeda in Iraq's top two leaders." *Long War Journal*, April 19, 2010. Accessed October 20, 2014. http://www.longwarjournal.org/archives/2010/04/al_qaeda_in_iraqs_to.php.

41. Roggio, Bill. "U.S. and Iraqi forces kill Al Masri and Baghdadi, al Qaeda in Iraq's top two leaders." *Long War Journal*, April 19, 2010. Accessed October 20, 2014. http://www. longwarjournal.org/archives/2010/04/al_qaeda_in_iraqs_to.php. Zelin, Aaron. "Abu Bakr al-Baghdadi: Islamic State's Driving Force." Washington Institute for Near East Policy, July 30, 2014. Accessed October 20, 2014. http://www.washingtoninstitute.org/policy-analysis/view/abu-bakr-al-baghdadi-islamic-states-driving-force.

42. Ghosh, Bobby. "ISIS: A Short History." *Atlantic*, August 14, 2014. Accessed October 20, 2014. http://www.theatlantic.com/international/archive/2014/08/isis-a-short-history/376030/.

43. "Terrorist Designation of Al-Nusrah Front Leader Muhammad Al-Jawlani." U.S. Department of State, May 16, 2013. Accessed October 20, 2013. http://www.state.gov/r/pa/prs/ps/2013/05/209499.htm.

44. "Islamist group claims Syria bombs 'to avenge Sunnis.'" *Al-Arabiya* News, March 21, 2012. Accessed October 20, 2014. http://english.alarabiya.net/articles/2012/03/21/202177.html.

45. Crompton, Paul. "The rise of the new 'caliph,' ISIS chief Abu Bakr al-Baghdadi." *Al Arabiya News*, June 30, 2014. Accessed September 24, 2014. http://english.alarabiya.net/en/perspective/profiles/2014/06/30/The-rise-of-the-new-caliph-ISIS-chief-Abu-Bakr-al-Baghdadi.html.

46. Arraf, Jane, "Al Qaeda in Iraq faces serious financial crunch," *Christian Science Monitor,* July 2, 2010. Accessed October 20, 2014. http://web.stanford.edu/group/mappingmilitants/cgi-bin/groups/view/1#note27. Lewis, Jessica. "Al Qaeda in Iraq resurgent: The breaking the walls campaign, part I." *Middle East Security Report 14*. Institute for the Study of War, September 2013. Accessed October 20, 2014. http://www.understandingwar.org/sites/default/files/AQI-Resurgent-10Sept_0.pdf.

47. Joscelyn, Thomas. "Al Qaeda in Iraq, Al Nusrah Front emerge as rebranded single entity." *Long War Journal*, April 9, 2013. Accessed October 20, 2013. http://www. longwarjournal.org/archives/2013/04/the_emir_of_al_qaeda.php.

48. Ibid.

49. Zelin, Aaron Y. "The War between ISIS and al-Qaeda for Supremacy of the Global Jihadist Movement." Washington Institute for Near East Policy, June 2014. Accessed October 20, 2014. http://www.washingtoninstitute.org/uploads/Documents/pubs/ResearchNote_20_Zelin.pdf.

50. Atassi, Basma. "Qaeda chief annuls Syrian-Iraqi jihad merger." *Al-Jazeera*, June 9, 2013. Accessed October 20, 2014. http://www.aljazeera.com/news/middleeast/2013/06/2013699425657882.html.

51. Ibid.

52. Ibid.

53. Joscelyn, Thomas. "Islamic State of Iraq leader defies Zawahiri in alleged audio message." *Long War Journal*, June 15, 2013. Accessed October 20, 2014. http://www. longwarjournal.org/archives/2013/06/islamic_state_of_ira_3.php.

54. Osman, Tarek. "Why border lines drawn with a ruler in WW1 still rock the Middle East." *BBC*, December 13, 2013. Accessed October 25, 2014. http://www.bbc.com/news/world-middle-east-25299553.

55. Ould Mohamedou, Dr Mohammad-Mahmoud. "ISIS and the Deceptive Rebooting of Al Qaeda." Geneva Centre for Security Policy, August 2014. Accessed October 20, 2014. http://www.gcsp.ch/Regional-Development/Publications/GCSP-Publications/Policy-Papers/GCSP-Policy-Paper-ISIS-and-the-Deceptive-Rebooting-of-Al-Qaeda.

56. Joscelyn, Thomas. "Islamic State of Iraq leader defies Zawahiri in alleged audio message." *Long War Journal*, April 15, 2013. Accessed October 20, 2013. http://www. longwarjournal.org/archives/2013/06/islamic_state_of_ira_3.php.

57. Zelin, Aaron. "Inside Baseball on Syrian Rebel Infighting." *War on the Rocks*, February 7, 2014. Accessed October 20, 2014. http://warontherocks.com/2014/02/inside-baseball-on-syrian-rebel-infighting/.

58. Zelin, Aaron. "As-Saḥāb Media presents a new statement from al-Qā'idah: "On the Relationship of Qā'idat al-Jihād and the Islamic State of Iraq and al-Shām." *Jihadology*, February 2, 2014. Accessed October 20, 2014. http://jihadology.net/2014/02/02/as-sa%E1%B8%A5ab-media-presents-a-new-statement-from-al-qaidah-on-the-relationship-of-qaidat-al-jihad-and-the-islamic-state-of-iraq-and-al-sham/.

59. Zelin, Aaron Y. "The War between ISIS and al-Qaeda for Supremacy of the Global Jihadist Movement." Washington Institute for Near East Policy, June 2014. Accessed October 20, 2014. http://www.washingtoninstitute.org/uploads/Documents/pubs/ResearchNote_20_Zelin.pdf. Zelin, Aaron. "Al-Qaeda Disaffiliates with the Islamic State of Iraq and al-Sham." The Washington Institute for Near East Policy, February 4, 2014. Accessed October 20, 2014. http://www.washingtoninstitute.org/policy-analysis/view/al-qaeda-disaffiliates-with-the-islamic-state-of-iraq-and-al-sham.

60. Zelin, Aaron. "New statement from the Central Region of al-Qā'idah in the Islamic Maghrib: Advocacy From the Islamic Maghrib For the Islamic State of Iraq and al-Shām." *Jihadology*, February 2, 2014. Accessed October 20, 2014. http://jihadology.net/2014/03/22/new-statement-from-the-central-region-of-al-qaidah-in-the-islamic-maghrib-advocacy-from-the-islamic-maghrib-for-the-islamic-state-of-iraq-and-al-sham/. Zelin, Aaron Y. "The War between ISIS and al-Qaeda for Supremacy of the Global Jihadist Movement." Washington Institute for Neat East Policy, June 2014. Accessed October 20, 2014. http://www.washingtoninstitute.org/uploads/Documents/pubs/ResearchNote_20_Zelin.pdf.

61. Cassman, Daniel. "Islamic State In Iraq And Syria | Mapping Militant Organizations." *Stanford: Mapping Militant Organizations*. Accessed November 4, 2014. http://web.stanford.edu/group/mappingmilitants/cgi-bin/groups/view/1#note52. Barrett, Richard. "Foreign Fighters in Syria." The Soufan Group, June 2014, Accessed October 20, 2014. http://soufangroup.com/wp-content/uploads/2014/06/TSG-Foreign-Fighters-in-Syria.pdf.

62. Chulov, Martin. "Isis reconciles with al-Qaida group as Syria air strikes continue." *Guardian*, September 28, 2014. Accessed November 20, 2014. http://www.theguardian.com/world/2014/sep/28/isis-al-qaida-air-strikes-syria.

63. Karouny, Mariam. "U.S.-led strikes pressure al-Nusra Front to join with ISIS." *Al-Arabiya*, September 26, 2014. Accessed October 20, 2014. http://english.alarabiya.net/en/perspective/analysis/2014/09/26/U-S-led-strikes-pressure-al-Nusra-Front-to-join-with-ISIS-.html.

64. Ibid.

65. Ibid.

66. Ghosh, Bobby. "ISIS: A Short History." *Atlantic*, August 14, 2014. Accessed October 20, 2014. http://www.theatlantic.com/international/archive/2014/08/isis-a-short-history/376030/.

67. Fadel, Leila and Karen DeYoung. "Ayad Allawi's bloc wins most seats in Iraqi parliamentary elections." *Washington Post*, March 27, 2010. Accessed October 20, 2014. http://www.washingtonpost.com/wp-dyn/content/article/2010/03/26/AR2010032602196.html.

68. Al-Ali, Zaid. "How Maliki ruined Iraq." *Foreign Policy*, June 19, 2014. Accessed October 20, 2014. http://www.foreignpolicy.com/articles/2014/06/19/how_maliki_ruined_iraq_armed_forces_isis.

69. Salaheddin, Sinan. "Tariq al-Hashemi, Sunni Vice President Of Iraq, Sentenced To Death In Absentia." *World Post*, September 9, 2012. Accessed October 20, 2014. http://www.huffingtonpost.com/2012/09/09/tariq-al-hashemi-vice-president-death-sentence_n_1868347.html.

70. Hauser, Christine. "Iraq: Maliki demands that protesters step down." *NY Times*, January 3, 2013. Accessed July 19, 2014. http://www.nytimes.com/2013/01/03/world/middleeast/iraq-maliki-demands-that-protesters-stand-down.html?_r=1.

71. "Iraq: Investigate Violence at Protest Camp." Human Rights Watch. January 3, 2014. Accessed July 15, 2014. http://www.hrw.org/news/2014/01/03/iraq-investigate-violence-protest-camp.

72. "Iraq: Parliament Report Alleges Officials Ordered Raid." Human Rights Watch. May 4, 2013. Accessed July 15, 2014. http://www.hrw.org/news/2013/05/04/iraq-parliament-report-alleges-officials-ordered-raid.

73. "Iraq" The World Factbook, Central Intelligence Agency, undated. https://www.cia.gov/library/publications/the-world-factbook/geos/print/country/countrypdf_iz.pdf.

74. "Leading Sunni Muslim cleric calls for 'jihad' in Syria." *Reuters*, June 1, 2013. Accessed June 22, 2014. http://www.reuters.com/article/2013/06/01/us-syria-crisis-qaradawi-idUSBRE9500CQ20130601.

75. Black, Ian. "Hezbollah will carry on backing Bashar al-Assad, says leader Nasrallah." *Guardian*, November 14, 2013. Accessed June 19, 2014. http://www.theguardian.com/world/2013/nov/14/hezbollah-assad-syria-nasrallah-lebanon.

76. "Nujaifi warns against civil war." *Aswat al-Iraq*, February 24, 2014. Accessed October 20, 2014. http://en.aswataliraq.info/(S(npkr3345qzfzyj55ufclkcft))/Default1.aspx?page=article_page&id=155419&l=1.

77. "United Nations reports 703 deaths in Iraq during February." *Daily News*, March 1, 2014. Accessed October 20, 2014. http://www.nydailynews.com/news/world/united-nations-reports-703-deaths-iraq-february-article-1.1707566.

78. Adnan, Duraid. "Iraq: Bombs Kill at Least 33 in Baghdad." *NY Times*, March 27, 2014. Accessed October 20, 2014. http://www.nytimes.com/2014/03/28/world/middleeast/iraq-bombs-kill-at-least-33-in-baghdad.html?_r=0.

79. "Iraq general election campaign begins." *BBC News*, April 1, 2014. Accessed October 20, 2014. http://www.bbc.com/news/world-middle-east-26838755.

80. Rao, Prashant. "Iraq suicide bomb kills six as U.N. warns of 'divisive' polls." *Daily Star*, April 2, 2014. Accessed October 20, 2014. http://www.dailystar.com.lb/News/Middle-East/2014/Apr-02/252051-suicide-bombing-in-iraq-kills-5-army-recruits.ashx#axzz33VOhE7Oi.

81. "Iraq attacks kill 34 on anniversary of Baghdad fall." *Daily Star*, April 8, 2014. Accessed October 20, 2014. http://www.dailystar.com.lb/News/Middle-East/2014/Apr-08/252682-iraq-attacks-kill-12-as-soldiers-ambush-militants.ashx#axzz33VOhE7Oi.

82. "Dozens killed in Iraq attacks and bombings." *Al-Jazeera*, April 21, 2014. Accessed October 20, 2014. http://www.aljazeera.com/news/middleeast/2014/04/dozens-killed-iraq-attacks-bombings-201442120818144322.html.

83. Hendawi, Hamza and Sameer N. Yacoub. "Shiite rally bombing sparks reprisals in Iraq." *Yahoo News*, April 26, 2014. Accessed October 20, 2014. http://news.yahoo.com/shiite-rally-bombing-sparks-reprisals-iraq-094458412.html.

84. "Iraq suicide bomb at Kurdish political rally kills 30." *BBC News*, April 28, 2014. Accessed October 20, 2014. http://www.bbc.com/news/world-middle-east-27198219.

85. "Iraq elections kick off amid threat of bomb attacks, huge security presence." *CBS News*, April 30, 2014. Acessed October 20, 2014. http://www.cbsnews.com/news/iraq-elections-kick-off-amid-threat-of-bomb-attacks-huge-security/.

86. Vick, Karl. "Iraq Votes in Relative Peace, But Governing Remains a Challenge." *Time*, May 2, 2014. Accessed October 20, 2014. http://time.com/86033/iraq-elections-maliki/.

87. "Iraq's April death toll exceeds1,000—officials." *RT*, May 2, 2014. Accessed October 20, 2014. http://rt.com/news/156396-iraq-death-terrorism-violence/.

88. "Iraq electoral commission says it received 854 violation complaints." *Al Arabiya*, May 4, 2014. Accessed October 9, 2014. http://english.alarabiya.net/en/special-reports/iraq-elections/2014/05/04/Iraq-electoral-commission-says-it-received-854-violation-complaints.html.

89. Otten, Cathy and Suadad al-Salhy. "Uncertainty as Iraq election results revealed." *Al Jazeera*, May 26, 2014. Accessed October 10, 2014. http://www.aljazeera.com/news/middleeast/2014/05/uncertainty-as-iraq-election-results-revealed-201452611145311548.html.

90. "Iraq's Maliki 'set to win elections.'" *Al-Jazeera*, May 19, 2014. Accessed October 20, 2014. http://www.aljazeera.com/news/middleeast/2014/05/iraq-maliki-set-win-elections-201451913511590643.html.

91. "Violence across Iraq claims 54 lives." *RT*, May 29, 2014. Accessed October 20, 2014. http://rt.com/news/162132-iraq-violence-dead-bombing/. "Suicide bombing at Baghdad

mosque kills 20." *CNN*, May 27, 2014. Accessed October 20, 2014. http://www.cnn.com/2014/05/27/world/meast/iraq-violence/index.html.

Zhongxi, Ren. "35 people killed in bomb attacks across Iraq." *CCTV*, May 28, 2014. Accessed October 20, 2014. http://english.cntv.cn/2014/05/28/ARTI1401235814649289.shtml.

92. "Iraq electoral commission says it received 854 violation complaints." *Al Arabiya*, May 4, 2014. Accessed October 10, 2014. http://english.alarabiya.net/en/special-reports/iraq-elections/2014/05/04/Iraq-electoral-commission-says-it-received-854-violation-complaints.html.

93. Abi-Habib, Maria and Ali A. Nabhan. "Iraq Parliament to Elect New Government." *Wall Street Journal*, June 26, 2014. Accessed October 10, 2014. http://blogs.wsj.com/frontiers/2014/06/26/iraq-parliament-to-elect-new-government/.

94. Rubin, Alissa. "Iraqi Premier to Run for a Third Term." *NY Times*, July 4, 2014. Accessed October 10, 2014. http://www.nytimes.com/2014/07/05/world/middleeast/iraqs-maliki-to-run-again-rejecting-pressure-to-step-down.html.

95. Lee, John. "New Parliamentary Session Abandoned." *Iraq Business News*, July 1, 2014. Accessed October 10, 2014. http://www.iraq-businessnews.com/2014/07/01/new-parliamentary-session-abandoned/. Lee, John. "New Delay in Forming Govt." *Iraq Business News*, July 14, 2014. Accessed October 10, 2014. http://www.iraq-businessnews.com/2014/07/14/new-delay-in-forming-govt/.

96. Rubin, Alissa and Suadad Al-Salhy. "Iraqi Parliament Elects Speaker in Effort to Form New Government." *NY Times*, July 15, 2014. Accessed October 10, 2014. http://www.nytimes.com/2014/07/16/world/middleeast/iraq.html.

97. Morris, Loveday. "Veteran Kurdish politician elected president of Iraq." *Washington Post*, July 24, 2014. Accessed October 10, 2014. http://www.washingtonpost.com/world/middle_east/veteran-kurdish-politician-elected-president-of-iraq/2014/07/24/28448523-487b-4091-a4f1-fb7eefb87899_story.html.

98. Taylor, Adam. "Meet Haider al-Abadi, the man named Iraq's new prime minister." *Washington Post*, August 11, 2014. Accessed October 10, 2014. http://www.washingtonpost.com/blogs/worldviews/wp/2014/08/11/meet-haider-al-abadi-the-man-named-iraqs-new-prime-minister/.

99. Hammoudi, Laith. "New PM Named to End Maliki's Rule." *Iraq Business News*, August 12, 2014. Accessed October 10, 2014. http://www.iraq-businessnews.com/2014/08/12/new-pm-named-to-end-malikis-rule/.

100. Michaels, Jim. "Iraqi Prime Minister al-Maliki agrees to step down." *USA Today*, August 17, 2014. Accessed October 10, 2014. http://www.usatoday.com/story/news/world/2014/08/14/al-maliki-iraq/14066619/.

101. Sabah, Zaid, Khalid Al-Ansary and Aziz Alwan. "Sunnis Quit Iraq Government Talks After 73 Shot Dead at Mosque." *Bloomberg*, August 22, 2014. Accessed October 10, 2014. http://www.bloomberg.com/news/2014-08-22/dozens-killed-as-iraqi-militia-gunmen-attack-sunni-mosque-1-.html. Bengali, Shashank. "Shiite militiamen in Iraq kill scores of Sunni worshipers at mosque." *LA Times*, August 22, 2014. Accessed November 4, 2014. http://www.latimes.com/world/middleeast/la-fg-iraq-violence-20140823-story.html.

102. Fahim, Kareem and Azam Ahmed. "Lawmakers Approve Cabinet in Iraq, but 2 Posts are Empty." *International NY Times,* September 8, 2014. Accessed November 3, 2014. http://www.nytimes.com/2014/09/09/world/middleeast/iraq.html.

103. Ibid.

104. El Gamal, Rania. "New Iraq oil minister faces security challenge, Kurdish dispute." *Reuters,* September 9, 2014. Accessed November 3, 2014. http://www.reuters.com/article/2014/09/09/us-iraq-crisis-oil-idUSKBN0H414120140909.

105. Parker, Ned and Mark Heinrich. "Iraq PM Abadi retires two top generals after Islamic State conquests. *Reuters,* September 23, 2014. Accessed November 3, 2014. http://www.reuters.com/article/2014/09/23/us-iraq-crisis-army-idUSKCN0HI1K320140923.

106. Yacoub, Sameer N. "To stem extremism, Iraqi leaders mull reducing Baghdad's power." *Daily Star*, October 11, 2014. Accessed November 3, 2014. http://www.dailystar.com.lb/News/Middle-East/2014/Oct-11/273714-to-stem-extremism-iraqi-leaders-mull-reducing-baghdads-power.ashx#axzz3G8QG6cMz.

107. Semple, Kirk. "At War Against IS, Iraqi Premier is Facing Battles Closer to Home." *International NY Times,* October 15, 2014. Accessed November 3, 2014. http://www.nytimes.com/2014/10/16/world/middleeast/at-war-against-isis-iraqi-premier-is-facing-battles-closer-to-home.html?ref=world.

108. Morris, Loveday. "Appointment of Iraq's new interior minister opens door to militia and Iranian influence." *Washington Post*, October 18, 2014. Accessed November 3, 2014. http://www.washingtonpost.com/world/appointment-of-iraqs-new-interior-minister-opens-door-to-militia-and-iranian-influence/2014/10/18/f6f2a347-d38c-4743-902a-254a169ca274_story.html.

109. "Casualty figures for November 2014." *UN Iraq*, December 1, 2014. Accessed December 4, 2014. http://www.uniraq.org/index.php?option=com_k2&view=item&id=2963:casualty-figures-for-november-2014&Itemid=633&lang=en.

110. Hussein, Ahmed. "Abadi, Anbar delegation discuss confronting ISIL." *Iraqi News*, January 10, 2015. Accessed March 31, 2015. http://www.iraqinews.com/baghdad-politics/abadi-anbar-delegation-discuss-confronting-isil/.

111. Sarhan, Amre. "Iraq needs 'tribal revolution' against ISIS, says Iraqi PM." *Iraqi News*, January 7, 2015. Accessed March 31, 2015. http://www.iraqinews.com/baghdad-politics/iraq-needs-tribal-revolution-isis-says-iraqi-pm/.

112. Kalin, Stephen. "Iraq's Sunni blocs halt parliament activities after sheikh's killing." *Reuters*, February 14, 2015. Accessed March 31, 2015. http://www.reuters.com/article/2015/02/14/us-mideast-crisis-iraq-killing-idUSKBN0LI0N120150214.

113. "U.S. drops arms to Kurds battling IS." *BBC News*, August 2, 2014. Accessed October 20, 2014. http://www.bbc.com/news/world-middle-east-24179084.

114. "Iraq gunmen launch deadly attack on Abu Ghraib and Taji prisons." *Al-Arabiya*, July 22, 2013. Accessed October 20, 2014. http://english.alarabiya.net/en/News/middle-east/2013/07/22/Iraqi-security-forces-foil-attack-on-Abu-Ghraib-and-Taji-prisons.html.

115. "Iraqi Army launches assault on al Qaeda allies in Fallujah." *France 24*, January 6, 2014. Accessed October 20, 2014. http://www.france24.com/en/20140105-iraq-promises-crush-terrorists-who-control-fallujah/.

116. Chulov, Martin. "Isis insurgents seize control of Iraqi city of Mosul." *The Guardian*, June 10, 2014. Accessed October 20, 2014. http://www.theguardian.com/world/2014/jun/10/iraq-sunni-insurgents-islamic-militants-seize-control-mosul. Al-Sinjary, Ziad. "Insurgents in Iraq overrun Mosul provincial government headquarters." *Reuters*, June 9, 2014. Accessed October 20, 2014. http://www.reuters.com/article/2014/06/09/us-iraq-security-idUSKBN0EK22V20140609.

117. Salman, Raheem, Ashmed Rasheed and Isabel Coles. "Iraqi PM asks parliament to declare state of emergency after insurgents seize Mosu." *Reuters*, June 10, 2014. October 20, 2014. http://www.reuters.com/article/2014/06/10/us-iraq-security-mosul-idUSKBN0EL11V20140610.

118. Dunham, Will. "U.S. condemns Mosul attack, calls Iraq situation 'extremely serious.'" *Reuters*, June 10, 2014. Accessed October 20, 2014. http://www.reuters.com/article/2014/06/10/us-iraq-security-usa-idUSKBN0EL1TN20140610.

119. Karouny, Mariam. "Iraqi insurgent commander is jihad's rising leader." *Reuters*, June 11, 2014. Accessed October 20, 2014. http://www.reuters.com/article/2014/06/11/us-iraq-security-baghdadi-insight-idUSKBN0EM1TI20140611.

120. Karadeniz, Tulay and Nick Tattersall. "Turkey says militants hold 80 Turks hostage in Iraq's Mosul." *Reuters*, June 11, 2014. Accessed October 20, 2014. http://www.reuters.com/article/2014/06/11/us-iraq-security-turkey-hostages-idUSKBN0EM1X820140611.

121. Hassan, Ghazwan. "Iraq insurgents take Saddam's home town in lightning advance." *Reuters*, June 11, 2014. Accessed October 20, 2014. http://www.reuters.com/article/2014/06/12/us-iraq-security-idUSKBN0EM11U20140612.

122. Al-Sanjary, Ziad and Ahmed Rasheed. "Advancing Iraq rebels seize northwest town in heavy battle." *Reuters*, June 15, 2014. Accessed October 20, 2014. http://www.reuters.com/article/2014/06/15/us-iraq-security-idUSKBN0EP0KJ20140615.

123. Nordland, Rod and Alissa J. Rubin. "Massacre Claim Shakes Iraq." *NY Times*, June 15, 2014. Accessed October 20, 2014. http://www.nytimes.com/2014/06/16/world/middleeast/iraq. html.

124. "Iraqi Forces Push Back Against Rebels." *Stratfor Global Intelligence*, June 16, 2014. Accessed October 20, 2014. http://us4.campaign-archive1.com/?u= 74786417f9554984d314d06bd&id=0d7a2277a9&e=e928e08e1d.

125. Mahmoud, Mustafa and Raheem Salman. "Kurdish forces take over two oilfields in north Iraq." *Reuters*, July 11, 2014. Accessed October 20, 2014. http://www.reuters.com/ article/2014/07/11/us-iraq-security-oilfields-idUSKBN0FG0V920140711.

126. Kabalan, Marwan. "Kurds stand to gain the most from the turmoil." *Gulf News*, December 25, 2014. Accessed December 27, 2014.http://gulfnews.com/opinions/columnists/kurds-stand-to-gain-most-from-the-turmoil-1.1431953.

127. Coles, Isabel. "Iraq parliament fails to convene for vote on state of emergency." *Reuters*, June 12, 2014. Accessed October 20, 2014. http://www.reuters.com/article/2014/06/12/us-iraq-security-parliament-idUSKBN0EN11U20140612.

128. "ISIS changes name, declares Islamic 'caliphate.'" *Haaretz*, June 29, 2014. Accessed October 20, 2014. http://www.haaretz.com/news/middle-east/1.602008.

129. Curry, Colleen. "See the Terrifying ISIS Map Showing Its 5-Year Expansion Plan." *ABC News*, July 3, 2014. Accessed October 20, 2014. https://abcnews.go.com/International/ terrifying-isis-map-showing-year-expansion-plan/story?id=24366850.

130. Chulov, Martin. "Abu Bakr al-Baghdadi emerges from shadows to rally Islamist followers." *Guardian*, July 6, 2014. Accessed October 20, 2014. http://www.theguardian.com/world/ 2014/jul/06/abu-bakr-al-baghdadi-isis.

131. "ISIS parades ballistic Scud missile in Syrian town." *Al-Arabiya*, July 2, 2014. Accessed October 20, 2014. http://english.alarabiya.net/en/News/2014/07/02/ISIS-parades-ballistic-Scud-missile-in-Syrian-town.html.

132. Muir, Jim. "Iraq militant groups ordered to swear Isis allegiance." *BBC News*, July 2, 2014. Accessed October 20, 2014. http://www.bbc.com/news/world-middle-east-28123258.

133. Surk, Barbara. "Extremist group takes Syrian towns, key oil field." *Associated Press*, July 3, 2014. Accessed October 20, 2014. http://bigstory.ap.org/article/tribe-syria-border-town-allies-jihadis.

134. Diadosz, Alexander. "Islamic State expels rivals from Syria's Deir al-Zor: activists." *Reuters*, July 14, 2014. Accessed October 20, 2014. http://www.reuters.com/article/2014/07/ 14/us-syria-crisis-east-idUSKBN0FJ1HD20140714.

135. Evans, Dominic. "Islamic State says carried out Baghdad suicide bombing." *Reuters*, July 23, 2014. Accessed October 20, 2014. http://www.reuters.com/article/2014/07/23/us-iraq-security-idUSKBN0FS0QZ20140723. "Islamic State Claims Wave of Baghdad Bombings." *Voice of America*, July 20, 2014. Accessed October 20, 2014. http://www.voanews.com/ content/reu-islamic-state-claims-wave-of-baghdad-bombing/1961322.html.

136. "Western-Backed Rebels Join Aleppo Alliance: Syria Monitor." *NDTV,* January 31, 2015. Accessed February 5, 2015. http://www.ndtv.com/world-news/western-backed-rebels-join-aleppo-alliance-syria-monitor-736029.

137. Nichols, Michelle and Missy Ryan. "Iraq tells U.N. 'terrorist groups' seized former chemical weapons depot." *Reuters*, July 8, 2014. Accessed October 20, 2014. http://www. reuters.com/article/2014/07/09/us-iraq-security-chemicalweapons-idUSKBN0FD26K20140709.

138. Nichols, Michelle. "Exclusive: Iraq tells U.N. that 'terrorist groups' seized nuclear materials." *Reuters*, July 9, 2014. Accessed October 20, 2014. http://www.reuters.com/article/2014/ 07/09/us-iraq-security-nuclear-idUSKBN0FE2KT20140709.

139. Georgy, Michael. "Islamic State says captured 15 Iraqi towns, Mosul dam and military base." *Reuters*, August 7, 2014. Accessed October 20, 2014. http://www.reuters.com/article/ 2014/08/07/us-iraq-security-islamicstate-idUSKBN0G710S20140807. Rasheed, Ahmed Raheem Salman. "Islamic State grabs Iraqi dam and oilfield in victory over Kurds." *Reuters*, August 3, 2014. Accessed October 20, 2014. http://www.reuters.com/article/2014/08/03/us-iraq-security-idUSKBN0G20FU20140803.

140. "Iraq says ISIS no longer in control of key dam." *CBS*, August 18, 2014. Accessed August 22, 2014. http://www.cbsnews.com/news/iraq-isis-no-longer-in-control-of-mosul-dam/.
141. Coles, Isabel. "Islamic State surges in North Iraq, near Kurdistan border." *Reuters*, August 7, 2014. Accessed October 20, 2014. http://www.reuters.com/article/2014/08/07/us-iraq-security-idUSKBN0G70LO20140807.
142. Georgy, Michael and Ahmed Rasheed. "Islamic State killed 500 Yazidis, buried some victims alive: Iraq." *Reuters*, August 10, 2014. Accessed October 20, 2014. http://www.reuters.com/article/2014/08/10/us-iraq-security-yazidis-killings-idUSKBN0GA0DQ20140810.
143. Cooper, Helene and Rod Nordland. "Capitalizing on U.S. Bombing, Kurds Retake Iraqi Towns." *NY Times*, August 10, 2014. Accessed October 20, 2014. http://www.nytimes.com/2014/08/11/world/middleeast/iraq.html. Palkot, Greg and Jennifer Griffin. "US air strikes helping Kurdish, Iraqi forces retake Mosul dam from Islamic State." *Fox News*, August 17, 2014. Accessed October 20, 2014. http://www.foxnews.com/politics/2014/08/17/us-air-strikes-helping-kurdish-iraqi-forces-retake-mosul-dam-for-islamic-state/.
144. Georgy, Michael and Ahmed Rasheed. "Islamic State defeats Kurds in town of Jalawla northeast of Baghdad." *Reuters*, August 11, 2014. Accessed October 20, 2014. http://www.reuters.com/article/2014/08/11/us-iraq-security-jalawla-idUSKBN0GB0OV20140811.
145. Fahmy, Omar and Tom Perry. "Islamic State seizes more territory in Syria: monitor." *Reuters*, August 13, 2014. Accessed October 20, 2014. http://www.reuters.com/article/2014/08/13/us-syria-crisis-islamicstate-idUSKBN0GD18C20140813.
146. Westall, Sylvia. "Hundreds dead as Islamic State seizes Syrian air base: monitor." *Reuters*, August 25, 2014. Accessed October 20, 2014. http://www.reuters.com/article/2014/08/25/us-syria-crisis-idUSKBN0GO0C520140825.
147. "Ceasefire in Lebanon border town extended." *Al-Arabiya*, August 6, 2014. Accessed October 20, 2014. http://english.alarabiya.net/en/News/middle-east/2014/08/06/Ceasefire-in-Lebanon-border-town-extended.html.
148. "Kahwagi: Army will do utmost to free hostages." *Daily Star*, August 12, 2014. Accessed October 20, 2014. http://www.dailystar.com.lb/News/Lebanon.
149. "ISIS executes second Lebanese soldier." *Daily Star*, September 6, 2014. Accessed October 20, 2014. http://www.dailystar.com.lb/News/Lebanon-News/2014/Sep-06/269801-isis-executes-second-lebanese-soldier.ashx#axzz3DmNCUNaq.
150. "Kurds say halted ISIS advance on Syrian town." *Daily Star*, September 22, 2014. Accessed November 20, 2014. http://dailystar.com.lb/News/Middle-East/2014/Sep-22/271492-syrian-kurdish-fighters-halt-advance-by-isis-east-of-kobani-kurdish-forces-spokesman.ashx#axzz3DEnuDIKa.
151. Rasheed, Ahmed and Saif Sameer Hameed. "Iraqi soldiers describe heavy losses as Islamic State overruns camp." *Reuters*, September 22, 2014. Accessed November 20, 2014. http://www.reuters.com/article/2014/09/22/us-iraq-crisis-saqlawiya-idUSKCN0HH2LT20140922.
152. "US jets attack Isis as Biden apologises to Turkish president for remarks about foreign fighters." *Guardian,* October 4, 2014. Accessed November 20, 2014. http://www.theguardian.com/world/2014/oct/04/us-jets-attack-isis-syrian-town-turkish-leader-rebukes-biden.
153. Regan, Helen. "ISIS Has Entered the Key Syrian Border Town of Kobani." *Time*, October 7, 2014. Accessed November 20, 2014. http://time.com/3476929/isis-syria-kobani-is-isil/.
154. Shoichet, Catherine, Josh Levs and Mohammed Tawfeeq. "U.N. envoy on Kobani: Don't let another city fall to ISIS." *CNN*, October 7, 2014. Accessed November 20, 2014. http://www.cnn.com/2014/10/07/world/meast/isis-airstrikes/. Fantz, Ashley and Susanna Capelouto. "Coalition hits ISIS hard in Kobani; militants keep pushing." *CNN*, October 14, 2014. Accessed November 20, 2014. http://www.cnn.com/2014/10/14/world/meast/isis-threat/.
155. Semple, Kirk and Omar Al-Jawoshy. "ISIS Militants Shoot Down Iraqi Helicopter, Killing 2." *NY Times*, October 8, 2014. Accessed November 20, 2014. http://www.nytimes.com/2014/10/09/world/middleeast/isis-iraq-violence.html.
156. Smith-Spark, Laura, Ben Wedeman, and Greg Botelho. "Leaders of Iraq's Anbar province call for U.S. ground forces to stop ISIS." *CNN,* October 11, 2014. Accessed November 20, 2014. http://www.cnn.com/2014/10/11/world/meast/isis-threat/.

157. Jamieson, Alastair. "ISIS Seizes Anbar Base After Iraqi Army's 'Tactical' Retreat." *NBC News,* October 13, 2014. Accessed November 20, 2014. http://www.nbcnews.com/storyline/isis-terror/isis-seizes-anbar-base-after-iraqi-armys-tactical-retreat-n224671.

158. Westall, Sylvia. "Islamic State flying three jets in Syria: monitor." *Reuters,* October 18, 2014. Accessed November 20, 2014. http://www.reuters.com/article/2014/10/18/us-mideast-crisis-jets-idUSKCN0I60TM20141018.

159. "ISIS' alleged fighter jet fleet dwindling?" *CBS News,* October 22, 2014. Accessed November 20, 2014. http://www.cbsnews.com/news/isis-alleged-fighter-jet-fleet-dwindling/.

160. Walker, Brian. "ISIS forces launch multiple attacks on Kurdish territory in Iraq, officials say." *CNN,* October 21, 2014. Accessed November 20, 2014. http://www.cnn.com/2014/10/20/world/meast/isis-airstrikes/.

161. James, Catherine and Luke Harding. "Isis targets Baghdad with wave of car bombs and mortar attacks killing 150." *Guardian,* October 16, 2014. Accessed November 20, 2014. http://www.theguardian.com/world/2014/oct/16/isis-targets-baghdad-car-bombs-mortar-attacks.

162. Cronk, Terri Moon. "ISIL loses control over once-dominated Iraq territory." *DoD News,* April 13, 2015. Accessed April 14, 2015. http://www.defense.gov/news/newsarticle.aspx?id=128576. Bryant, Christian. "ISIS loses two Iraqi towns to Kurdish Iraqi forces." *NewsNet5,* October 25, 2014. Accessed April 14, 2015. http://www.newsnet5.com/newsy/isis-loses-two-iraqi-towns-to-kurdish-iraqi-offensives.

163. "Iraq blast targeting Shiites kills at least 10." *Al Arabiya,* November 2, 2014. Accessed November 20, 2014. http://english.alarabiya.net/en/News/middle-east/2014/11/02/Iraq-blast-targeting-Shiites-kills-at-least-10-.html.

164. "Kurds free large part of Iraq's Sinjar town from IS." *IANS,* December 22, 2014. Accessed December 24, 2014. https://in.news.yahoo.com/kurds-free-large-part-iraqs-sinjar-town-202403593.html. "Peshmerga Fighters Free Yazidis Besieged by ISIS on Iraq's Sinjar Mountain." *NBC News,* December 19, 2014. Accessed December 22, 2014. http://www.nbcnews.com/storyline/isis-terror/peshmerga-fighters-free-yazidis-besieged-isis-iraqs-sinjar-mountain-n271536.

Zehari, Abdelhamid. "Iraq Kurds press fightback as top jihadi reported killed." *Daily Star,* December 19, 2014. Accessed December 22, 2014. http://www.dailystar.com.lb/News/Middle-East/2014/Dec-19/281651-iraq-kurds-press-fightback-as-top-jihadi-reported-killed.ashx#sthash.Z1CbDZAP.dpuf.

165. Naylor, Hugh and Karen DeYoung. "Kurds drive Islamic State fighters from strategic town of Kobane." *Washington Post.* January 26, 2015. Accessed February 6, 2015. http://www.washingtonpost.com/world/assad-is-defiant-ahead-of-peace-discussion-scheduled-monday-in-moscow/2015/01/26/55d0ea22-a564-11e4-a2b2-776095f393b2_story.html. Daou, Rita. "Kurds Expel ISIS from Syria's Kobani." *Daily Star,* January 26, 2015. Accessed February 2, 2015. http://www.dailystar.com.lb/News/Middle-East/2015/Jan-26/285356-kurds-expel-isis-from-syrias-kobani-monitor.ashx.

"ISIS handed huge symbolic defeat in Kobani." *CBS News,* January 26, 2015. Accessed February 6, 2015. http://www.cbsnews.com/news/syria-border-town-kobani-taken-back-from-isis-kurdish-fighters-say/

166. "This is what Kobane looks like after Kurds drove out Islamic State." *News.com.au,* January 30, 2015. Accessed February 4, 2015. http://mobile.news.com.au/world/asia/this-is-what-kobane-looks-like-after-kurds-drove-out-islamic-state/story-fnh81fz8-1227201572933.

167. Shiloach, Gilad. "ISIS Morale Slipping After Multiple Losses." *Vocativ,* January 27, 2015. Accessed February 13, 2015. http://www.vocativ.com/world/isis-2/isis-kobani/.

168. "IS sends military reinforcement to the northern countryside of al-Hasakah." *Syrian Observatory for Human Rights,* January 12, 2015. Accessed February 23, 2015. http://syriahr.com/en/2015/01/is-send-military-reinforcement-to-the-northern-countryside-of-al-hasakah/.

169. Klapper, Bradley. "Ain al-Arab seen as key win, Mosul may require new tactics." *Daily Star,* January 29, 2015. Accessed February 3, 2015. http://www.dailystar.com.lb/News/Middle-East/2015/Jan-29/285655-ain-al-arab-seen-as-key-win-mosul-may-require-new-tactics.ashx.

170. Salama, Vivian. "Iraqi Kurds gain ground from ISIS, local Sunnis wary." *Daily Star,* January 29, 2015. Accessed February 4, 2015. http://www.dailystar.com.lb/News/Middle-East/2015/Jan-29/285690-iraqi-kurds-gain-ground-from-isis-local-sunnis-wary.ashx.

171. Bender, Jeremy. "ISIS To Obama: We Will Cut Off Your Head In The White House." *Yahoo News,* January 28, 2015. Accessed February 3, 2015. http://finance.yahoo.com/news/isis-obama-cut-off-head-184200336.html.

172. Yeranian, Edward. "Battles Intensify Near Kirkuk; Twin Blasts Rock Baghdad." *Voice of America,* January 30, 2015. Accessed February 5, 2015. http://www.voanews.com/content/eight-killed-baghdad-blasts/2620333.html. Basil, Yousuf, Jomana Karadsheh, and Laura Smith-Spark. "ISIS launches attack on oil-rich northern Iraqi city of Kirkuk." *CNN,* January 30, 2015. Accessed February 5, 2015. http://www.cnn.com/2015/01/30/middleeast/isis-attack/.

173. McDonnell, Patrick J. and Nabih Bulos. "Islamic State attacks Iraq's oil-rich northern city of Kirkuk." *Chicago Tribune,* January 30, 2015. Accessed February 5, 2015. http://www.chicagotribune.com/news/nationworld/la-fg-iraq-kirkuk-islamic-state-20150130-story.html.

174. Hussein, Ahmed. "5 villages liberated, 26 ISIL terrorists killed southern Salah il-Din." *Iraqi News,* January 3, 2015. Accessed March 31, 2015. http://www.iraqinews.com/features/villages-liberated-isil-terrorists-killed-southern-salah-il-din/.

175. "Over 70 IS militants killed in northern Iraq." *Business Standard,* January 12, 2015. Accessed February 13, 2015. http://www.business-standard.com/article/news-ians/over-70-is-militants-killed-in-northern-iraq-115011200072_1.html. "23 Kurdish soldiers killed in IS attack." *Times of India,* January 10, 2015. Accessed February 13, 2015. http://timesofindia.indiatimes.com/world/middle-east/23-Kurdish-soldiers-killed-in-IS-attack/articleshow/45835224.cms.

176. Hussein, Ahmed. "Hakim to British Ambassador: Iraqis capable to liberate their territories from ISIL." *Iraqi News,* January 16, 2015. Accessed February 23, 2015. http://www.iraqinews.com/features/hakim-to-british-ambassador-iraqis-capable-to-liberate-their-territories-from-isil/.

177. Coles, Isabel. "Kurdish forces squeeze Islamic State supply line in northern Iraq." *Reuters,* January 21, 2015. Accessed February 23, 2015. http://www.reuters.com/article/2015/01/21/us-mideast-crisis-iraq-mosul-idUSKBN0KU2ET20150121.

178. Mamoun, Abdelhak. "Peshmerga forces liberate 4 villages north of Mosul, killing 28 ISIS elements." *Iraqi News,* January 21, 2015. Accessed February 23, 2015. http://www.iraqinews.com/iraq-war/peshmerga-forces-liberate-4-villages-north-mosul-killing-28-isis-elements/.

179. Mahmoud, Mustafa. "Kurds retake oil facility in north Iraq, 15 workers still missing." *Reuters,* January 31, 2015. Accessed February 23, 2015. http://www.reuters.com/article/2015/01/31/us-mideast-crisis-iraq-oil-idUSKBN0L406N20150131.

180. Kalin, Stephen. "Kurds criticize exclusion from U.S.-led coalition meeting." *Reuters,* January 23, 2015. Accessed February 23, 2015. http://www.reuters.com/article/2015/01/23/us-mideast-crisis-coalition-kurds-idUSKBN0KW0WW20150123.

181. Nakhoul, Samia, Ned Parker, and Isabel Coles. "Kurdish PM says U.S.-led coalition against Islamic State faces long war." *Reuters,* January 30, 2015. Accessed February 23, 2015. http://www.reuters.com/article/2015/01/30/iraq-kurdistan-idUSKBN0L315S20150130.

182. Rasheed, Ahmed and Ned Parker. "In Mosul, Islamic State turns captured city into fortress." *Reuters,* January 22, 2015. Accessed February 23, 2015. http://www.reuters.com/article/2015/01/22/us-mideast-crisis-iraq-mosul-idUSKBN0KV13320150122.

183. Westall, Sylvia, "Kurds regain Syrian villages from Islamic State: monitor." *Reuters,* February 14, 2015. Accessed February 23, 2015. http://www.reuters.com/article/2015/02/14/us-mideast-crisis-syria-kobani-idUSKBN0LI0EV20150214.

184. "YPG takes control over 20 villages and farmlands in al- Hasakah." Syrian Observatory for Human Rights, February 22, 2015. Accessed February 23, 2015. http://syriahr.com/en/2015/02/ypg-takes-control-over-20-villages-and-farmlands-in-al-hasakah/.

185. Al-Khalidi, Suleiman. "Islamic State pulls forces and hardware from Syria's Aleppo: rebels." *Reuters,* February 9, 2015. Accessed February 23, 2015. http://www.reuters.com/article/2015/02/09/us-mideast-crisis-syria-islamicstate-idUSKBN0LD1L920150209.

186. "YPG and supported factions take control over the road of Aleppo- al- Hasakah and 7 villages in al- Raqqa." Syrian Observatory for Human Rights, February 17, 2015. Accessed February 23, 2015. http://syriahr.com/en/2015/02/ypg-and-supported-factions-take-control-over-the-road-of-aleppo-al-hasakah-and-7-villages-in-al-raqqa/.

187. "ISIS isolates one of its Islamist judges after his objection on the execution way of the Jordanian pilot." Syrian Observatory for Human Rights, February 6, 2015. Accessed February 23, 2015. http://syriahr.com/en/2015/02/isis-executes-one-of-its-islamist-judges-after-his-objection-on-the-execution-way-of-the-jordanian-pilot/.

188. Hameed, Saif, David Alexander, and Stephen Kalin. "Islamic State fighters seize western Iraqi town: officials." *Reuters*, February 12, 2015. Accessed February 23, 2015. http://www.reuters.com/article/2015/02/12/us-mideast-crisis-iraq-anbar-idUSKBN0LG23120150212.

189. Hameed, Saif, Stephen Kalin, and David Alexander. "Iraqi army repels attack on base hosting U.S. Marines: officials." *Reuters*, February 13, 2015. Accessed February 23, 2015. http://www.reuters.com/article/2015/02/13/us-mideast-crisis-iraq-anbar-idUSKBN0LH1JD20150213.

190. Berwani, Hawar. "US 'eyeing new air base' in Iraq amid talk of major offensive on ISIS." *Iraqi News*, February 15, 2015. Accessed February 23, 2015. http://www.iraqinews.com/iraq-war/us-eyeing-new-air-base-in-iraq-amid-talk-of-major-offensive-on-isis/.

191. Alexander, David. "Iraq reconciliation would help counter Islamic State—U.S. military." *Reuters*, February 3, 2015. Accessed February 23, 2015. http://www.reuters.com/article/2015/02/03/us-mideast-crisis-usa-iraq-idUSKBN0L72FL20150203.

192. Stewart, Phil and Suleiman Al-Khalidi. "U.S. moving to resupply Jordan's military with munitions: officials." *Reuters*, February 13, 2015. Accessed February 23, 2015. http://www.reuters.com/article/2015/02/13/us-usa-jordan-arms-idUSKBN0LH2GP20150213.

193. "Peshmerga fighters take key ridgeline." CJTF—Operation Inherent Resolve News Release. U.S. Central Command, March 12, 2015. Accessed March 15, 2015. http://www.centcom.mil/en/news/articles/mar.-12-peshmerga-fighters-take-key-ridgeline.

194. Ibid.

195. Holmes, Oliver and Mariam Karouny, "Islamic State moves west to attack Syrian army in Homs: monitor." *Reuters*, March 23, 2015. Accessed March 24, 2015. http://www.reuters.com/article/2015/03/23/us-mideast-crisis-syria-islamic-state-idUSKBN0MJ0X920150323.

196. Alhamadee, Mousab and Roy Gutman. "Al Qaida affiliate seizes major city in northern Syria." *McClatchy News Service*, March 28, 2015. Accessed March 28, 2015. http://www.mcclatchydc.com/news/nation-world/world/middle-east/article24782413.html.

197. Westall, Sylvia and Mariam Karouny. "Islamic State seizes vast Damascus refugee camp." *Reuters*, April 1, 2015. Accessed April 2, 2015. http://www.mcclatchydc.com/news/nation-world/world/middle-east/article24782413.html.

198. "March 10: Anti-ISIL Fighters Retake Key Terrain." CJTF—Operation Inherent Resolve News Release. U.S. Central Command, U.S. Department of Defense, March 10, 2015. Accessed March 15, 2015. http://www.centcom.mil/en/news/articles/mar.-10-anti-isil-fighters-retake-key-terrain.

199. Ibid.

200. Redfield, John. "With ISIL in 'defensive crouch,' Iraqi forces re-take town from terrorist control." U.S. Central Command Public Affairs, March 6, 2015. Accessed March 15, 2015. http://www.centcom.mil/en/news/articles/with-isil-in-defensive-crouch-iraqi-forces-re-take-town-from-terrorist-cont.

201. Roulo, Claudette. "Coalition of airstrikes enable renewal of Tikrit ground offensive." *DOD News*, U.S. Department of Defense, March 27, 2015, Accessed March 28, 2015. http://www.defense.gov/news/newsarticle.aspx?id=128480.

202. "Islamic State conflict: Iraq declares Tikrit 'victory.'" *BBC*, April 1, 2015. Accessed April 1, 2015. http://www.bbc.com/news/world-middle-east-32153836.

203. Ibid.

204. Ibid.

205. Morris, Loveday. "In fight for Tikrit, U.S. finds enemies on both sides of the battle lines." *Washington Post*, March 27, 2015. Accessed March 28, 2015. http://www.washingtonpost.com/world/iraqi-cleric-urges-unity-amid-tension-over-us-strikes/2015/03/27/75bb4f5a-d40b-11e4-8b1e-274d670aa9c9_story.html?hpid=z9.

206. Redfield, John. "With ISIL in 'defensive crouch,' Iraqi forces re-take town from terrorist control." U.S. Central Command Public Affairs, U.S. Department of Defense, March 6, 2015.

Accessed March 15, 2015. http://www.centcom.mil/en/news/articles/with-isil-in-defensive-crouch-iraqi-forces-re-take-town-from-terrorist-cont.

207. Ibid.

208. Allen, John. Special Presidential Envoy for the Global Coalition to Counter ISIL. "Remarks at the Atlantic Council." U.S. Department of State, March 2, 2015. Accessed March 9, 2015. http://www.state.gov/s/seci/238108.htm.

209. Ibid.

210. "Islamic State-controlled Yarmouk refugee camp conditions 'beyond inhumane.'" *Daily Telegraph*, April 7, 2015. Accessed April 7, 2015. http://www.telegraph.co.uk/news/worldnews/islamic-state/11519106/Islamic-State-controlled-Yarmouk-refugee-camp-conditions-beyond-inhumane.html.

211. Dick, Marlin. "ISIS storms Damascus suburb of Yarmouk." *Daily Star*, April 2, 2015. Accessed April 2, 2015. http://www.dailystar.com.lb/News/Middle-East/2015/Apr-02/293055-isis-storms-damascus-suburbof-yarmouk.ashx.

Chapter Two

Intentions and Capabilities

This chapter discusses the intentions and capabilities of the Islamic State. In doing so, the following topics are addressed: the group's ideology, current posture, strategy, headquarters, training, tactics, weapons, targets, financing, radicalization and recruitment, publicity, and execution videos. Given the broad nature of these topics, there is, invariably, some overlap in the discussion of some themes.

IDEOLOGY

Prior to delving into the Islamic State's ideology, definitions of several key terms—Takfirism, Islamism, Salafism, Jihadism, and Wahhabism—are necessary. Hassan Mncimneh of the German Marshall Fund of the United States offers the following insights: "Takfirism may be viewed as the ultimate expression of unconstrained Islamism. Islamism is the ideological proposition that the legitimacy of the political order be derived from Islam. Salafism is an institutionalized form of Islamism professing the conviction that such legitimacy resides solely in the emulation of the precedents of early Islamic history. Jihadism is the belief that the use of force is permissible (and/or obligatory) and governed by Islamic jurisprudence, as reinterpreted by Islamism."[1]

Wahhabism, named after Muhammad ibn Abd al-Wahhab, is a radical, exclusionist, puritanical form of Sunni Islam, notes former MI-6 agent Alastair Cooke. More particularly, Wahhabism holds "that the period of the Prophet Muhammad's stay in Medina was the ideal of Muslim society (the 'best of times'), to which all Muslims should aspire to emulate."[2]

The Islamic State (IS) is a Sunni Salafist jihadist organization that seeks to establish a transnational caliphate based on its strict interpretation of sharia. The IS traces its ideological lineage back from the inception of Islam to fourteenth century Muslim philosopher Ibn Taymiyyah, through Saudi Arabian-linked Wahhabism and, more recently, to some aspects of the Muslim Brotherhood's Sayyid Qutb. Too, Takfirism, which calls for the designation of fellow Muslims as apostates, meriting excommunication, and even death, is woven into the Islamic State's ideology. The IS longs to bring about a world like the one inhabited by the Prophet Mohammad and his initial successors or *caliphs* (followers) in the seventh century, utilizing acts of violence (e.g., beheadings and crucifixions) and *jizya* (requiring non-Muslims who do not convert to pay a tax) cited in the Koran.[3]

The caliphate soon emerged following Mohammad's death, during which the Rashidun Caliphate (632–661 C.E.) grew through the sword, encompassing Arabia and areas that now include the Levant, Egypt, Iran, and Armenia. Subsequent caliphates of varied lengths and successes spanned nearly 1,300 years, ending with the Ottoman Caliphate in 1924.[4] Others argue that the caliphate was not "an enduring institution, central to Islam and Islamic thought," but rather, "a political or religious idea whose relevance has waxed and waned according to circumstance."[5]

Against that backdrop, Princeton University's Bernard Haykel characterizes the Islamic State's ideology as "a kind of untamed Wahhabism. Wahhabism is the closest religious cognate."[6] Additionally, the *New York Times* reports that Islamic State fighters "are open and clear about their almost exclusive commitment to the Wahhabi movement of Sunni Islam. The group circulates images of Wahhabi religious textbooks from Saudi Arabia in the schools it controls."[7]

According to Ed Husain, a former UK Islamist now with the Council of Foreign Relations, "For five decades, Saudi Arabia has been the official sponsor of Sunni Salafism across the globe."[8] Saudi Arabia has joined the coalition against the IS as it now perceives that group as a threat to the monarchy. Also, Husain estimates that "Salafi adherents and other fundamentalists represent 3 percent of the world's Muslims."[9] Using this percentage vis-à-vis the estimated 1.6 billion Muslims in the world, Salafists number some forty-eight million people worldwide.[10]

Yale lecturer Graeme Wood argues, "The reality is that the Islamic State is Islamic. Very Islamic. Yes, it has attracted psychopaths and adventure seekers, drawn largely from the disaffected populations of the Middle East and Europe. But the religion preached by its most ardent followers derives from coherent and even learned interpretations of Islam."[11] Moreover, he states, "Muslims can reject the Islamic State; nearly all do. But pretending that it isn't actually a religious, millenarian group, with theology that must be understood to be combated, has already led the United States to underestimate it and back foolish schemes to counter it."[12] Likewise, Haykel explains, "Slavery, crucifixion, and beheadings are not something that freakish [jihadists] are cherry-picking from the medieval tradition," but rather, "are smack in the middle of the medieval tradition and [Islamic State fighters] are bringing it wholesale into the present day."[13]

Besides their viewpoint that it is an obligation to establish a caliphate and implement strict sharia law, some analysts point to the Islamic State's ideological focus on the eschatology or End Times. More particularly, in an Islamic State's bloody-infused apocalypse, there is "the belief that there will be only 12 legitimate caliphs, and Baghdadi is the eighth; that the armies of Rome will mass to meet the armies of Islam in northern Syria [Dabiq, which IS now controls]; and that Islam's final showdown with an anti-Messiah will occur in Jerusalem after a period of renewed Islamic conquest."[14]

As such, and in conjunction with their doctrinal emphasis and attraction to martyrdom, IS ideologues and fighters embrace and seek to accelerate conditions to hasten the End Times. This is further evidenced by Musa Cerantonio, an Australian convert to Islam and reported IS-recruiter who—according to Graeme Wood—believes, "it is foretold that the caliphate will sack Istanbul [Cerantonio's interpretation of what city Rome stands for] before it is beaten back by an army led by the anti-Messiah, whose eventual death—when just a few thousand jihadists remain—will usher in the apocalypse."[15]

Also, IS-linked imams in western Iraq and eastern Syria preach about "tawhid (strict monotheism), bida'a (deviation in religious matters) and wala wal baraa (loyalty to Islam and disloyalty to anything un-Islamic)."[16] IS ideologues characterize the current traditional practice of Islam as "invented Islam," distinct from their perception of Islam and Islamic history.[17]

The Islamic State's bloodthirsty tactics seem to have been influenced by a work of jihadist Abu Bakr Naji, *The Management of Savagery*.[18] Naji warned, "If we are not violent in our jihad and if softness seizes us, that will be a major factor in the loss of the element of strength."[19] Additionally, Naji encouraged jihadists "to expose the weakness of America's centralized power by pushing it to abandon the media psychological war and the war by proxy until it fights directly."[20] Likewise, Islamic State leadership has referenced the book, "which argues that extreme violence is necessary as psychological leverage to achieve power."[21]

Sheikh Ali Al-Khudair's book, *The Essence of Islam: Tawheed and the Message*,[22] was used at Islamic State organized seminars that trained prospective imams and *khateebs* (person who delivers sermons at a mosque) in 2014.[23] "This book is originally based on a study of Sheikh Muhammad Ibn Abdul-Wahhab's treatise entitled 'The Essence and Foundation of Islam.'"[24] The Raqqa-based Islamic State seminars were highlighted in the first issue of the group's *Islamic State Report*.[25]

The IS calls itself a caliphate with Abu Bakr al-Baghdadi, the leader of the organization, named Caliph Ibrahim, of this ostensible super-state. Al-

Baghdadi demands that all Muslims swear allegiance to him. In doing so, he seeks to supersede the authority of the religious and secular leadership in the Muslim world and beyond. The title of caliph is meant to hold authority over emirs, imams, and other subjects.[26]

Al-Baghdadi wrote in the first edition of *Dabiq*—an IS online publication—that the world is split into "the camp of Muslims and the mujahidin everywhere, and the camp of the Jews, the crusaders, their allies, and with them the rest of the nations and religions . . . all being led by America and Russia and mobilized by the Jews."[27] This outlook is essentially an articulation of the viewpoint—including that of Ibn Taymiyyah, mentioned above—that the world is divided into two spheres: the House of Islam (*Dar al-Islam*) and the House of War (*Dar al-Harb*). In the former, Muslim-indoctrinated governments enforce Islamic law. In the latter, predominately Muslim countries do not enforce Islamic law or these are areas that have not been subjugated by Muslims. In either case, in the House of War a perpetual jihad exists until there is conversion to or subjugation by Islam.[28]

Unmasking the ideological components of the IS is critical to its ultimate defeat. As General John Allen, U.S. envoy countering the Islamic State, assessed very well, "We're not just fighting a force, you know, we're fighting an idea."[29] It is "an image that it is an Islamic proto-state, in essence, the Islamic caliphate." Moreover, he noted, the Islamic State tries to portray an "image of invincibility and image of an advocate on behalf of the faith of Islam."[30]

Within that context, the Islamic State is categorically and violently opposed to many Muslim and non-Muslim ethnic and religious groups (e.g., Yazidis). It considers Shiite Muslims to be apostates who abandoned the faith, worse than heretics or infidels. In addition, the IS targets certain Sunni groups, like the Surooris. The Surooris are a group formed by Mohammed Suroor Zain al-Abedin, who refuted traditional Salafism while supporting religious rebellion.[31] Moreover, the IS conducted attacks against Sahawat forces—Arab Sunni Muslims who rose against al-Qa'ida forces in 2006 during the Sunni Tribal Awakening—and against anyone affiliated with the Iraqi and Syrian governments. In some instances, the IS allowed individuals associated with governmental bodies, which it refers to as apostates, to repent for their past crimes.

The IS does not recognize modern regional boundaries in the Middle East, which were established by the Sykes-Picot Agreement after World War I. Rather, it aims to establish a state based on sharia, on whatever territory it can acquire.[32]

It is critical to note that the vast majority of Muslims and their leaders globally oppose and condemn the tenets and actions of the IS. The critics vehemently argue that the group does not represent or understand traditional Islam. More specifically, in August 2014, Saudi Arabia's Grand Mufti

Sheikh Abdulaziz al-Sheikh denounced the Islamic State and al-Qa'ida, claiming that the groups are "enemy number one of Islam, and Muslims are their first victims."[33] Also, al-Sheikh said, "the ideas of extremism, radicalism and terrorism do not belong to Islam in any way."[34]

That same month, Egypt's top religious authority, Grand Mufti Shawqi Allam, condemned the IS.[35] Also, in January 2015, Egyptian President al-Sisi said, "Religious discourse is the greatest battle and challenge facing the Egyptian people. We need a modern, comprehensive understanding of the religion of Islam"[36] and not "relying on a discourse that has not changed for 800 years."[37]

Vocal rejection of IS ideology and actions is increasing worldwide, through numerous outlets and instrumentalities. For instance, the first issue of the anti-Muslim-extremist magazine, *Haqiqah*—which was launched in London in March 2015—characterized members of the Islamic State (and others) as "individuals who study Islam from a superficial point of view and emerge with their own ideas and imaginary interpretations, which often diverge greatly from established Islamic principles. We can see that many of the characteristics found in these young men and women are similar to those identified as the Khawarij (Extremist/Dissenters) by the Prophet Muhammad (PBUH). They have no grounding in Islamic sciences or jurisprudence and yet want to establish an 'Islamic state'/'Islamic System.' In the pursuit of their ill-intended aim, they are prepared to bulldoze the fundamental teachings of Islam."[38]

CURRENT POSTURE

As of April 2015, the IS holds territory in parts of Iraq and Syria, with aspirations to gain additional territory in the region, including Lebanon and beyond.[39] The Islamic State's areas of control have shifted as its military operations—in offensive and defensive modes—have ensued.

The IS's highest priorities appear to be fighting its apostate enemies and state-building in the areas it controls.[40] Still, the IS's goals also include interest in attacking Western and other nations, to punish and coerce them into withdrawing support for the fight against it.[41] Along those lines, in a November 2014 audio release, al-Baghdadi called for his supporters to "erupt volcanoes of jihad" as coalition airstrikes escalated, including killing Islamic State operatives near Mosul and elsewhere.[42] These priorities have shifted even further—for the Islamic State's very survival—given coalition efforts to use air power and related military resources against the IS. Also, in November 2014, al-Baghdadi announced that the IS would be expanding to five countries: Algeria, Egypt, Libya, Saudi Arabia, and Yemen.[43]

Manpower associated with the IS grew very rapidly during 2014. In September 2014, the CIA estimated that the IS had between 20,000 and 31,500 fighters. The previous month, when American-led air strikes against the organization began, the CIA put the group's strength at 10,000 militants.[44]

In November 2014, "Fuad Hussein, the chief of staff of Kurdish President Massoud Barzani," projected that the Islamic State had an army of "at least 200,000 fighters."[45] After all, Hussein argued, this figure is more accurate given the Islamic State's activities in the region, including IS attacks at ten sites in Kurdistan during October 2014.[46]

The Islamic State's supporters and operatives come from all over the world. Yet, it is critical to note "the pervasive role played by members of Iraq's former Baathist army in an organization more typically associated with flamboyant foreign jihadists and the gruesome videos in which they star."[47] More specifically, "almost all of the leaders of the Islamic State are former Iraqi officers, including the members of its shadowy military and security committees, and the majority of its emirs and princes."[48]

Still, in an attempt to eliminate rivals, after the Islamic State captured Mosul, between twenty-five to sixty former Baathists aligned with the IS were killed. An Iraqi parliamentarian explained the basis of the killings, "ISIL knows very well they can't stay if these groups move against them. They are not giving them the opportunity."[49]

The Baathists include a faction led by Izzat Ibrahim al-Douri, a former Saddam operative who heads up the Naqshbandi Army (or JRTN). In April 2015, it was reported that al-Douri was killed near Tikrit.[50]

The Islamic State and Baathists "had a marriage of convenience at the start of the takeover of Mosul. Baathists got muscle from ISIS, and ISIS got local legitimacy through the Baathists," Letta Tayler of Human Rights Watch explained.[51]

The IS originally relied on donations from wealthy investors in Saudi Arabia and Kuwait to counter Assad's Alawite regime in Syria.[52] Additionally, the popularity of the Islamic State's ideology has caused an influx of foreign fighters into the conflict in Syria and Iraq. Regional neighbors and even Western nations have dark premonitions that such fighters could return to their home countries and launch terrorist attacks.[53]

By late December 2014, reports surfaced that conditions in some cities under IS control, namely Raqqa and Mosul, had deteriorated. Thus, "Isis's vaunted exercise in state-building appears to be crumbling" as "[r]esidents say services are collapsing, prices are soaring and medicines are scarce."[54] Other failings include the lack of drinking water and flour, limited water and electricity supplies, widespread disease, inadequate doctors and medical supplies, and differences in benefits between IS local and foreign fighters.[55] These shortcomings undermine the legitimacy of IS as a sovereign both internally and externally, although no open rebellion of its citizenry has been manifested at this point. [56]

STRATEGY

Similarities and Differences with Other Groups

The IS grew quickly largely because it took advantage of a situation which it did not create. Al-Qa'ida capitalized on instability in Afghanistan, al-Qa'ida in the Islamic Maghreb (AQIM) took advantage of chaos in Algeria, al-Qa'ida in the Arabian Peninsula (AQAP) profited from lawlessness in Yemen, and al-Shabaab benefited from the failed state of Somalia. The Islamic State's antecedents used the civil war in Syria and disunity in Iraq as springboards to serve as agents of disorder in these respective countries. However, none of these groups—aside from the IS—were able to establish a proto-state, although some quasi-control of territory appended to a number of groups. Nevertheless, while these terror groups did not succeed in that realm—statehood—they are still all active agents in undermining stability in their regions. Analogously, while the IS has already lost some territory, it is probable that the group will be operating—in one form or another—for many years. [57]

The IS and al-Qa'ida likewise evolved amidst tensions between regional actors and local insurgencies, combined with their efforts against foreign intervention. [58] The principal differentiation between the two terror groups has been in their focus. Although evolving, the Islamic State initially focused mostly inward, seeking in fact to build an Islamic state. In contrast, al-Qa'ida and its affiliates sought to push jihad globally, outside its respective bases of operation. Additionally, bin Laden sought to unify Muslims against the West and secular Muslim leadership. IS perceives its role more in the creation of an Islamic state, with a strong Sunni identity and regional focus. [59]

While there have been some recent examples in the United States, Australia, Canada, and Europe by IS-linked or -inspired operatives conducting attacks in those areas, the IS also propagates a strong call to arms, including for foreign fighters to assist in Syria and Iraq. Increasingly, there has been a push by IS to establish affiliates globally, most prominently in the Middle East and South Asia.

The primary strategic differences that led to the split between the IS and Jabhat al-Nusra (backed by al-Qa'ida) boil down to medium-term goals. Both seek to establish the reign of sharia in the long term and depose secular regimes in Iraq and Syria. Jabhat al-Nusra, however, supports a gradual approach of enforcing sharia and cooperating with other rebel groups.

The IS perceives itself as a strictly Islamic sovereign. Thus, all territories and people that fall under its control are immediately forced to accept sharia.

Likewise, the IS fights against all groups that are not the "legitimate Islamic State," including Jabhat al-Nusra and al-Qa'ida under al-Zawahiri. Al-Baghdadi and his organization see themselves as the true successors to bin Laden.[60] Armed conflict between Jabhat al-Nusra and IS continued as recently as February 2015, although some collaboration continued on a case-by-case basis, as in Yarmouk in April 2015.[61]

Natural Resources and Basic Necessities: Water, Electricity, and Food

The Islamic State's leadership appreciates the complexities and multifaceted nature of trying to serve as a sovereign state. IS leadership knows that a state needs resources and thus prioritized the capture of oil. It understands that people need water, irrigation, electricity, and food to live. Moreover, distribution of these necessities is the main interaction most people have with their government. Thus, the IS set out to capture important resources and make clear that it is in charge of administering these benefits for the populace under its control.

The Islamic State's rapid expansion and consolidation of power in the territories it controls is, in part, a result of its strategic focus on resources. Its militants captured oil fields in Syria and set up makeshift refineries to process crude oil.[62] This allowed them to make millions of dollars selling oil on the black market at just $30 per barrel, at the time about a third of market prices. King Abdullah II of Jordan stated that IS can produce oil and oil by-products valued at just under $1 billion per year.[63] Yet, with declining oil prices during fall 2014 and beyond, the IS's capacity to garner funds from this resource, along with coalition airstrikes against petroleum facilities, has been hindered.

Islamic State leadership comprehends the potency of withholding water, irrigation, electricity, and food from its subjects and enemies. The IS has focused on capturing hydroelectric dams for control over water. In February 2014, it took Fallujah Dam, which is situated on the Euphrates River. The IS blackmailed the skilled workers at the dam to continue working, a policy repeated at oil refineries and other dams.

In late April 2014, the Islamic State closed eight of the ten floodgates of the Fallujah Dam, which left the cities of Karbala, Najaf, Babylon, and Nasiriyah with little drinking water. Also, this tactic affected farms, making it impossible for them to meet their needs.

The IS's goal was to create a drought in Shiite holy cities further south on the river, and disrupt parliamentary elections. This manipulation of water supplies threatened up to ten million people with drought, thirst, and famine. The Iraqi government responded by opening up the floodgates of the Haditha Dam, further up the Euphrates. This caused massive flooding around Fallujah and along the canals between the two dams, displacing up to 40,000 people. The Islamic State relented and opened another of the Fallujah gates. [64]

The IS has also used other dams as tactical weapons against its enemies. In April 2014, IS militants took hold of the Nuaimiyah Dam, which is on the Euphrates, "and deliberately diverted its water to deluge government forces in the surrounding area." [65] The situation was only reversed when Iraqi forces staged an attack that was to trap militants between them and the floodwaters, forcing IS to reopen the floodgates. [66]

The IS presented an even bigger threat when it captured Mosul Dam on the Tigris River in August 2014. The dam, Iraq's largest, can produce 1,010 megawatts of electricity and holds twelve billion cubic meters of water in its reservoir. This accounts for most of the electricity and water for Iraq and the irrigation lifeblood of Iraqi Kurdistan. [67] What is more, the Mosul Dam's poor placement on unstable soil means it requires constant repairs. If the dam were to fail for any reason, Mosul would be under sixty-four feet of water within hours [68] and a fifteen-foot wave would come crashing into Baghdad. An estimated half million people were threatened by the capture of this strategic location. [69]

Another element of the IS's resource strategy is wheat. During the American sanctions on Iraq and the UN food-for-oil program in the 1990s, Saddam Hussein set up a national system of subsidized wheat collection and distribution. This system continued after the U.S. invasion in 2003. The U.S. Department of Agriculture estimated that up to 25 percent of rural Iraqis were dependent on it while another 25 percent used it to round out their supplies. Whether by design or through sheer luck, the IS's military campaign coincided with the collection season. Militants were able to defraud the Iraqi government by forcing other farmers to sell wheat from areas controlled by the Islamic State. Iraqi officials did not check the source of wheat that was submitted to the program. Thereby, many Iraqi government payments benefited the Islamic State. [70]

During summer 2014, the IS was able to capture government storage silos that were full of wheat. "The United Nations estimates land under IS control accounts for as much as 40 percent of Iraq's annual production of wheat, one of the country's most important food staples alongside barley and rice." [71] The IS also controls flour mills silos and grain stockpiles in Iraq. [72]

The IS uses wheat as a commodity, handing it out to supporters or Sunni populations it wants mollified. Likewise, the IS withholds wheat from minorities and other groups it considers enemies. Many farmers who fled IS advances were invited back to make sure their businesses kept running, as long as they converted to Islam and paid a tax. Those that refused simply had their land, produce, and livestock confiscated. [73]

Yet, it seems that all is not well with farming under IS control. In fact, in January 2015, it was reported that there is growing nervousness among farmers under IS control in Iraq and Syria due to poorly planted and maintained crops for the spring 2015 harvest.[74]

Going International

In addition to recruiting fighters from overseas, IS has other plans for those who stay in their native lands. Since coalition airstrikes commenced in August 2014 (Iraq) and September 2014 (Syria), senior IS leaders as well as IS operatives and their media instrumentalities have voiced support for attack in a respective jihadist's home country. In particular, in September 2014, Abu Mohammed al-Adnani, IS spokesman, issued a fatwa supporting lone-wolf attacks by the group's adherents abroad.[75] These activities are enabled by complementing the Islamic State's identity as a regional military force with significant publicity and global outreach for its cause.

During 2014, there were "at least 18 ISIL-linked attacks against western interests in the past year, resulting in 24 deaths and 11 injuries," said National Counterterrorism Center director Nicholas Rasmussen.[76] In 2014–15, IS-inspired or linked terror attacks and plots occurred in the United States, UK, Canada, Australia, France, Libya, Tunisia, Saudi Arabia, Yemen, and elsewhere.

United States

Islamic State-connected or inspired plots in the United States include civilian, military, and law enforcement targets. In September 2014 in Oklahoma, a black convert to Islam, Alton Nolen, beheaded a female co-worker and attempted to behead another woman, before he was shot and taken into custody. Prior to the incident, Nolen apparently tried to get his co-workers to convert to Islam. Nolen's Facebook page had photos and commentary on jihadi beheadings as well as photos of jihadi fighters. While further investigation will continue in this case, one can presume that Nolen was inspired by the recent publicity on IS beheadings.[77]

Also, several U.S. cases targeting law enforcement are set out below. In September 2014, Mufid A. Elfgeeh, 30, of Rochester, New York, was charged with "three counts of attempting to provide material support and resources"[78] to ISIS, "one count of attempted murder of current and former members of the United States military, one count of possessing firearms equipped with silencers in furtherance of a crime of violence, and two counts of receipt and possession of unregistered firearm silencers."[79] Elfgeeh faces over one hundred years in prison in relation to these charges.[80]

In New York City in October 2014, Zale Thompson, a black convert to Islam, attacked several police officers with an axe, before he was shot and killed. Thompson is believed to have been inspired by jihadist groups, including the Islamic State.[81]

In January 2015, "Christopher Lee Cornell, 20, of Green Township, OH, was charged with attempting to kill officers and employees of the United States and possession of a firearm in furtherance of a crime of violence."[82] Cornell had planned to use pipe bombs to attack the U.S. Capitol, and subsequently use semi-automatic M-15 rifles to kill individuals there. Cornell was a recent convert to Islam who became exposed to radical tenets of the Islamic State. He claimed to be inspired by the group to undertake the attack. Cornell's efforts were undermined as he interacted with a confidential informant, after articulating pro-IS perspectives on Twitter, using an "alias 'Raheel Mahrus Ubaydah.'"[83] Subsequently, the indictment added a charge of solicitation to commit a crime of violence. All three charges have maximum penalty of twenty years. Cornell pled not guilty to the charges.[84]

Cornell told the informant that he thought, "We should just wage jihad under our own orders and plan attacks and everything. I believe we should meet up and make our own group in alliance with the Islamic State here and plan operations ourselves."[85] Cornell stated that he received approval for the attack from Anwar al-Awlaki, a dual U.S.-Yemeni cleric and senior al-Qa'ida in the Arabian Peninsula operative, who was killed in a drone strike in 2011. There appear to be doubts to this allegation as Cornell converted to Islam subsequent to Awlaki's death.[86]

In April 2015, "John T. Booker Jr., 20, of Topeka, Kansas, was charged" with "one count of attempting to use a weapon of mass destruction (explosives), one count of attempting to damage property by means of an explosive and one count of attempting to provide material support" ISIL.[87] Booker was arrested in a sting operation as he was about to breach Fort Riley Military Base in a vehicle he believed contained a bomb. His goal was to conduct a suicide bomb at the site. Booker faces a maximum life prison sentence.[88]

In light of terrorists targeting police globally, the New York Police Department warned its officers in January 2014 to "Pay close attention to people as they approach and look for their hands as they approach you."[89] Similarly, an October 17, 2014, U.S. Department of Homeland Security report forewarned, "the most likely perpetrators of a potential ISIL-directed or inspired Homeland attack include individuals acting under the direction of foreign-based terrorists, returning foreign fighters, and those who are inspired by the ongoing conflict in Syria and Iraq but who cannot or will not travel overseas."[90] Such perpetrators are most probably going to "employ tactics involving edged weapons, small arms, or improvised explosive devices (IEDs)."[91]

Also, in March 2015, the Islamic State's Hacking Division disclosed the names, photos, ranks, and home addresses of one hundred U.S. military members—"pilots, airmen, sailors and commanders involved in the U.S.-led airstrikes against the group in Iraq and Syria"—that the group called to be attacked.[92] The Hacking Division, in a Web posting, made a call for violent action, "We made it easy for you by giving you addresses, all you need to do is to take the final step, so what are you waiting for?"[93]

While the group claimed the information was obtained through hacking U.S. government websites, the content appears to have been gathered through the use of publicly available information on the Internet, such as Facebook. In response to this threat, the U.S. military announced, "our Criminal Investigation Division is working with the Federal Bureau of Investigation and has provided the information to local units and, as always, we encourage soldiers to take prudent measures to limit the sharing of personal information online."[94]

Europe

Several European cases are worth highlighting. An ISIS-linked European who traveled to Syria, then returned to the continent to undertake an attack, is noteworthy. Mehdi Nemmouche, a French citizen, has been in custody in France since his arrest for a May 2014 shooting at the Jewish Museum of Belgium in Brussels, which killed four persons. Nemmouche served with ISIS in Syria as a captor and torturer of its hostages.[95] The brutality and deviancy of Nemmouche is illustrated by an account of ISIS French hostage in Syria, Nicolas Hénin. Hénin said that Nemmouche bragged about "raping a woman before slitting her throat and killing her baby[,]" whom he subsequently beheaded.[96]

In January 2015, Belgium police killed two men and arrested another person in Verviers. The two who were killed apparently fought with IS in Syria. The cabal had precursors for explosives, Kalashnikovs, handguns, and grenades, as well as police uniforms. The two men are believed to have been part of an IS node "with organized structures, a logistical support network and links back to Syria and Iraq."[97]

Additionally, Belgian authorities conducted raids elsewhere in Belgium, arrested some dozen individuals, in efforts to stymie a prospective, imminent "plot to kill Belgian police in streets and stations."[98] Belgian police also arrested an IS-linked suspected arms trafficker, Neetin Karasular. He apparently sold weapons to Amedy Coulibaly, who in January 2015 attacked a Paris kosher supermarket, killing four people before being killed by police. Coulibaly claimed to have been acting on behalf of the Islamic State. Concurrently, Belgium is launching airstrikes against the IS in Iraq, as part of the U.S.-led coalition.[99]

In January 2015, Said and Cherif Kouachi, French brothers of Algerian extraction, undertook a bold armed attack at the offices of the satiric magazine *Charlie Hebdo* in Paris, killing twelve persons and injuring eleven. The

brothers undertook the attack on behalf of al-Qa
la.[100] Within days, Amedy Coulibaly, as referenc
attack against a kosher supermarket in Paris, killing f
French policewoman. Coulibaly claimed affiliation with th

In January 2015, Gilles de Kerchove, the European Uni
rorism chief, acknowledged that it was impossible to prevent l
attacks like the incidents at the Charlie Hebdo and kosher super
Paris that same month. He frowned upon the option of imprisoning
who return to their home countries from Iraq and Syria, suggesting
prisons are "massive incubators" for extremism.[102]

Likewise, in January 2015, the director-general of MI5, Andrew Parker,
warned that core al-Qa'ida in Syria, principally the Khorasan Group, were
planning large-scale terror attacks against Western targets. Parker acknowledged, that, unfortunately, not all plots would be disrupted. Moreover, Parker
lamented that there is a "growing gap between the increasingly challenging
threat and the decreasingly availability of capabilities to address it."[103]

Parker's concerns stem from cases such as the November 2014 incident in
which three British Muslim extremists—Haseeb Hamayoon, Nadir Sayed,
his cousin, Yousaf Syed—were arrested in relation to a plot to behead a
British citizen in a public place in the UK.[104] Subsequently, in March 2015,
Brusthom Ziamani, a 19-year-old from south London, was sentenced to
twenty-two years in prison for his plan to undertake a terrorist act. In particular, Ziamani intended to behead a soldier in the UK, similar to the 2013
murder of Lee Rigby. At the time of his arrest, Ziamani possessed a ten-inch
kitchen knife, hammer, and a black flag used by jihadi groups worldwide.[105]

In February 2015, an IS-inspired, former gang member, Omar Abdel
Hamid el-Hussein, undertook two attacks in Copenhagen, Denmark, at a café
that was sponsoring a free speech seminar featuring Lars Vilks (the Danish
cartoonist who drew the controversial cartoon featuring the Prophet Mohammed) and a synagogue. The incidents resulted in two deaths and five
injuries. The same day as the attacks, el-Hussein was shot and killed outside
his home following an exchange of gunfire with Danish police.[106]

Elsewhere

The Islamic State supporters in Australia were planning on performing a
public execution there, while draping the victim in the black IS flag.[107] In
September 2014, fifteen people were arrested during police raids in Sydney
and Brisbane in connection to the plot. Among them, a 22-year-old named
Omarjan Azari was detained and charged with conspiracy to commit a terrorist act. Australia is among the countries with the highest per capita number of
people traveling to the Middle East to fight with extremist groups such as
Jabhat al-Nusra and the Islamic State.[108]

ida in the Arabian Peninsu-
ed above, carried out an
ur, and assassinated a
e Islamic State. [101]
on's counterter-
00 percent of
market in
ihadis
hat

rne, two Australian police offi-
;-inspired man, Numan Haider.
In April 2015, Australian police
<e a terror attack in Melbourne
alian and New Zealand Armed
nong those arrested were Sevdet
: associated with Haider. [110]
ominent attacks took place in the
5, such as in Tunisia, Libya, and
dertook an armed attack on the
wenty-two foreign tourists and a
e Okba Ibn Nafaa Brigade for the
lity for the incident. [112] Later that
month, Tunisian security forces arrested and killed various members of the
Okba Ibn Nafaa Brigade, including the perceived leader of the attack, Lok-
man Abu Sakhra, an Algerian. [113]

The attack on the Bardo Museum undermined Tunisian attempts at fostering stability in the first country to experience the Arab Spring, particularly in
relation to generating revenue in the country's tourism industry. By April
2015, another group in Tunisia, calling itself the Soldiers of the Caliphate
(Jund al-Khilafah), pledged allegiance to the Islamic State and al-Baghdadi.
Moreover, it claimed responsibility for the Bardo Museum attack. [114]

In January 2015, two terrorists with the Libyan branch of IS—Abu Ibraheem Al-Tunsi and Abu Sulaiman Al-Sudani—used gunfire and a car bomb
to attack the Corinthia Hotel in Tripoli, Libya. At least ten persons, including
five foreigners—among them American security contractor David Berry—
were killed during the attack. The head of the self-declared Libyan government, Omar al-Hassi, resided at the hotel. [115]

In February 2015, the IS affiliate decapitated twenty-one Egyptian Coptic
Christians in Libya in the self-declared Tripoli Province of the Islamic State.
A videotape of the incident was broadcast globally. [116] In April 2015, the IS
affiliate in Libya bombed the gate of the Moroccan Embassy and conducted
shootings at the South Korean Embassy. [117] Also that month, the IS released a
video through a media arm, al-Furqan, showing Ethiopian Christians being
killed by IS affiliates in eastern and southern Libya. One group of victims in
eastern Libya—deemed Barka Province—were beheaded. The other set of
victims in southern Libya—called Fazzan Province—were shot in the
head. [118]

In March 2015, the Sanaa branch of the Islamic State claimed responsibility for two suicide bombings that struck the Badr mosque in south Sanaa—
predominantly attended by Houthi (Shiite) Muslims—as well as another suicide bombing at the Al-Hashush mosque in northern Sanaa. The attacks at
the two mosques killed over 142 people, and injured more than 350. Accord-

ing to the IS-linked statement, "Infidel Huthis should know that the soldiers of the Islamic State will not rest until they eradicate them . . . and cut off the arm of the Safavid (Iranian) plan in Yemen."[119] The incidents severely aggravated the crisis in Yemen exemplified by Sunni-Shiite tensions. Within the country, Houthi rebels targeted the forces loyal to President Abdo Rabbo Mansour Hadi. The strife in Yemen also entangles the interests of Sunni nations such as Saudi Arabia and Egypt with Shiite Iran. In fact, Saudi Arabia is leading a coalition of Sunni countries in airstrikes against Houthi targets in Yemen, while Iran has attempted to supply weapons, among other assistance.[120]

HEADQUARTERS

The province and city of Raqqa in northern Syria are undeniably the heart of the Islamic State. Raqqa is the fledgling caliphate capital. Raqqa was initially taken over by various al-Qa'ida affiliates in March 2013, including Ahrar al-Sham and Jabhat al-Nusra. Raqqa came under control of the ISIS in 2013. While the IS was not officially an entity at that point, the groundwork for its control of the region was set forth. Around this time, the idea of creating an Islamic state—initially based in Raqqa—started to circulate.[121]

Key components for laying the groundwork of this state were the control and distribution of the supply of bread and electricity, the provision of services, and the use of selective violence. Kurdish civilians and minorities were either driven out or persecuted. Non-compliant Sunnis with the al-Qa'ida affiliate members were also subject to violence. Tactics used by the IS against its foes included the imprisonment of adults and children, torture, and public execution.[122]

As the IS has complete control there, it focuses its energies on other activities, such as nation- and institution-building activities. Certain levels of normalcy and stability have been attained. Food is available to some, although bread supplies are insufficient in the former breadbasket of Syria. Resources are lacking at hospitals run under IS supervision. Schools are open and operate but pupils are indoctrinated with IS dogma. Non-Islamic subjects, such as science and history, are no longer taught. Traditional crime in the area has declined, which may be due to fear of sharia punishments, including cutting off the hand of a thief.[123] In February 2014, ISIS live-tweeted the amputation of a thief in Maskanah, Syria.[124]

A few examples of the difficult conditions in Raqqa are worth noting. Na'eem Square, formerly a pleasant place to gather, is now where decapitated heads are left on spikes. Traffic lights do not work, so armed traffic police, who do not have whistles, try to instill order on the roads. Among things that are deemed *haram* (forbidden) are "smoking tobacco, improper dressing, and swearing."[125]

The Islamic State's interpretation of sharia law is very strict. Also, churches have been shut down and some turned into IS recruitment centers. Islamic State harshness is not inflicted solely on the non-Sunni. Those deemed to be involved in plotting against the IS can face public crucifixions. At times, there is a semblance of administrative efficiency, enhanced by brutal intimidation. Administratively, this theocratic police state has been something of a success, assuming one ignores externalities such as the ever-present viciousness of the regime.[126]

The IS maintains compliance with the population it controls through public executions and other punishments. These acts serve the purpose of garnering worldwide media attention, which attracts supporters to the Islamic State and leads other militant groups to pledge their support.[127]

TRAINING

Some of the Islamic State's training seems to trace back to Abu Musab al-Zarqawi, the founder of al-Qa'ida in Iraq. Trained in Afghanistan, al-Zarqawi claimed to have been in direct contact with bin Laden. Al-Zarqawi, who was killed in 2006, set the groundwork for the IS in many ways. His strategy included the deliberate targeting of civilian populations. His influence on the group's training practices likely remains strong.[128]

A second source of military training comes from the Chechen members of IS leadership. The fighters often gained experience fighting Russian security forces. For example, IS military leader Abu Omar al-Shishani and his cohort come from the Pankisi Gorge region of Georgia, characterized as a training ground for various terrorist organizations.[129]

Many of the IS's local leaders are former officers in the Iraqi army. They augmented their military credentials with years of terrorist and insurgent tactics during the Iraqi insurgency.[130] One of these individuals is Abu al-Sweidawi, the IS governor of Anbar. Al-Sweidawi was a lieutenant in the Iraqi army under Saddam Hussein. His military experience, and that of his fellow former soldiers, help them make largely good decisions on the ground. Abu Abdul Rahman al-Bilawi, a deceased cabinet member, was also a former member of the Iraqi army.[131]

IS fighters do not distinguish between combatants and non-combatants in their treatment. In some cases, IS fighters "killed civilians with merciless glee, and didn't have to be ordered to do so."[132]

The Islamic State runs training camps in Syria and Iraq geared to adults and children. The training encompasses doctrinal matters, the importance of martyrdom, and military-type training.[133] There are over thirty terrorist training camps run by the Islamic State and other jihadist groups. A number of them were targeted by coalition airstrikes since fall 2014. [134]

New IS fighters, even those who had previous training with other groups, such as the Free Syrian Army and Jabhat al-Nusra, were required to attend a forty-day training camp, comprised of doctrinal and weapons training. At one training camp, Afghan and Chechen fighters led the training, and recruits were given a *nom de guerre* plus $150 per month. [135]

Thousands of foreign fighters are believed to have joined the Islamic State. These individuals come with varying levels of military-type training and experience, which is leveraged by the IS against its enemies.

At a Mayadeen camp in eastern Syria, recruits are initially tested on their knowledge of the Koran. Subsequently, the trainers denigrate the Syrian regime, Free Syrian Army, and other groups. [136]

Sharia training varies on the recruits' perceived value or allegiance. It often comprises insulting the recruit's existing interpretations of Islam and replacing it with Salafist tenets. Also, recruits are taught Arabic. Overall training ranges from two weeks to a year. Following graduation, recruits are observed to assess their suitability for assignments. [137]

The Islamic State has set up training camps for children, so that they can continue the fight in the next generation. The IS instructs these children in its extremist beliefs and hatred of the West. Many of these children are exposed first hand to the violence carried out by the group. The children are encouraged to actively participate by informing on traitors and even giving blood transfusions to wounded fighters. [138]

Noteworthy, too, the group's training is not without its mishaps. For instance, in February 2014, twenty-two ISIS members were killed when an Iraq-based suicide bombing instructor accidentally detonated himself and his class during a training exercise. [139]

For those unable to travel to the caliphate to undertake training, the Islamic State issued an electronic book, *How to Survive in the West: A Mujahid Guide*, in March 2015. By reading the book, one "will be taught how to lead a double-life, how to keep your Secret life private, how to survive in a threatening land, how you can Arm and strengthen the Muslims when the time for Jihad comes to your country, and neighborhood. In simple terms, from this guide book—you will learn how to be a Sleeper-cell which activates at the right time when the Ummah needs you." [140] The book, published without a named author, is somewhat lacking in tradecraft still provides some insights as well as allows for additional publicity for the Islamic State. [141]

TACTICS

Military and Guerrilla Tactics

The terror tactics that the IS has used are manifold, including suicide bombings, car bombings, improvised explosive devices, sniper attacks, public executions, and mass executions.[142] According to one account, the tactics used by the IS varies depending on who is leading the unit of fighters. For instance, Libyan-led "fighters tended to be much tougher and involved hand-to-hand combat" while "[r]aids led by Chechens . . . [the] Islamic State's best fighters, tended to be well-planned and tactical. Both utilized an initial wave of suicide bombers, and ended with conquered territory littered with mines and IEDs."[143]

Some evidence of IS tactics can be found in the training they are providing to the Muslim Brotherhood members in Egypt. One methodology is having cells, isolated in teams of five, where only one of the five people is in contact with any other group. An Egyptian militant elaborated on other training, "They told us to plant bombs then wait 12 hours so that the man planting the device has enough time to escape from the town he is in."[144]

More importantly, though, former Brig. Gen. Hassan Dulaimi of the Iraqi army, suggests the success of the Islamic State stems from the fact that, "[t]he people in charge of military operations in the Islamic State were the best officers in the former Iraqi army, and that is why the Islamic State beats us in intelligence and on the battlefield."[145]

The Islamic State's record of ferocious violence should have come as no surprise when the tactics of its antecedents are recalled. In June 2013, the group undertook two simultaneous attacks against al-Taji and Abu Ghraib prisons, killing about thirty persons and freeing hundreds of prisoners, some who now have prominent roles in the Islamic State.[146] During August 2013, ISIS bombings in Baghdad killed over fifty people. Two months later, several vehicle-borne improvised explosive devices (VBIEDs) in Ninwea (Nineveh) Province, including one near a school, took fourteen lives and caused over 140 injuries.[147] In October and December 2013, the group undertook several suicide bombings against Shabaks in Mosul and a television complex in Tikrit, respectively.[148]

Likewise, the Islamic State's potency rests with its military "planning and foresight and a sophisticated tactical and strategic command,"[149] exhibited as well by its predecessor. The July 2012 "Breaking the Walls"[150] campaign, which "involved a growing wave of high-explosive truck bombings designed to provoke Shia [Shiite] unrest and soften key striking points," is a case in point.[151] Additionally, the July 2013 "Soldiers Harvest"[152] efforts, which involved "a more targeted campaign of assassinations and bombings against the security forces," proved to be a tactic that would be replicated by the

IS.[153] The goals of these two campaigns "were a carefully honed mix of psychological warfare and targeted strikes intended to weaken military command structures."[154] Here too, the group achieved its goals.

Also, during June 2014, the Islamic State occupied and withdrew from cities in order to: "(1) to degrade the security capabilities in these cities, to widen the gaps there, and to openly intermingle with the local population, especially ISIS sympathizers or those predisposed to being sympathetic to ISIS, to push them to revolt against the government, and, (2) to weaken confidence in the government's security services."[155]

In light of its expanding its size, influence, and newly developed skills in combat, the IS can be characterized more as a militia or army than a terrorist group.[156] Moreover, its annual reports reveal a metrics-driven military command that is "a strong indication of a unified, coherent leadership structure that commands from the top down."[157]

Similarly, U.S. officials have characterized the Islamic State's tactics as more akin to an army than insurgents, as it holds captured land territory and coordinates its attacks well.[158] The Islamic State is highly skilled in urban guerrilla warfare.[159] Some IS fighters use special operations tactics, techniques, and procedures.[160] In August 2014, U.S. Secretary of Defense Chuck Hagel described the IS as, "They're beyond just a terrorist group. They marry ideology, a sophistication of strategic and tactical military prowess."[161]

Other modes of operations[162] include conducting surprise attacks, and then withdrawing before suffering serious casualties.[163] In line with previous actions to release operatives and sympathizers from prison, in July 2014, IS militants used roadside bombs and gunfire to attack a prisoner transfer convoy from Taji en route to Baghdad. Fifty-one prisoners and nine guards were killed.[164]

Savagery Perfected

The IS has also been responsible for numerous—and increasingly savage—massacres, including ordinary civilians, Yazidis, Shiites, Kurds, and Syrian rebels as well as Syrian, Iraqi, and Lebanese army members. For instance, in July 2014, fifty-three handcuffed and blindfolded corpses were found outside the mostly Shiite village of Khamissiya, killed by IS forces.[165]

The following month, IS fighters demanded that Yazidis in the village of Kocho convert to Islam or die. The militants killed over eight men and captured at least 300 women.[166] Elsewhere, IS militants executed up to 700 tribesmen in eastern Syria in revenge for their leading an uprising against IS. Many of those killed were civilians.[167] In November 2014, IS executed another several hundred members of the Albu Nimr tribe in Iraq's Anbar province.[168]

The Islamic State has conducted other atrocities, such as beheadings, mass executions, burning and burying people alive, stonings, and amputations.[169] For example, in July 2014, IS fighters beheaded several captured Syrian soldiers and displayed their heads on spikes across Raqqa.[170]

Group members stoned a man to death in Mosul after he was convicted of adultery.[171] Analogously, some "15 people, nine of them women, have been executed by extremists in Syria, since July [2014] for alleged adultery and homosexuality."[172] In two instances in January 2015, homosexuals were thrown off of roofs in order to show the public the penalty for such behavior.[173]

In Bujaq, Syria, the IS punished several musicians with ninety lashes for playing "non-Islamic" music on a "non-Islamic" electronic keyboard in January 2015.[174] Other entertainment is also met with harsh punishment, as in the execution of thirteen teenagers in Mosul for watching a televised soccer match.[175]

The IS has become notorious for the gruesome and heinous practice of beheading its captives, whether they are civilians or combatants. Regarding this issue, Sheikh Husayn Bin Mahmud, a prominent online jihadist scholar, issued a statement entitled, "The Question of Beheadings," in which he lauded the beheading of American journalist James Foley and condemned Muslim leaders who said that the beheading was contrary to Islamic teachings. Sheikh Mahmud then discussed the permissibility beheadings those like Foley under Islamic law, while stressing that killing other Muslims is absolutely forbidden.[176] Some IS members have become disillusioned with the group's killing of other Muslims as a violation of Islamic law.[177]

Besides Foley, the IS beheaded and released the videos of fellow journalist, American-Israeli Steven Sotloff in September 2014, and former U.S. soldier and aid worker Peter Kassig—who converted to Islam while a hostage and used the name Abdul-Rahman—in November 2014.[178] The Islamic State beheaded two British citizens and fellow aid workers David Haines and Alan Henning during September 2014 and October 2014, respectively.[179] In January 2015, the IS beheaded Japanese hostages Haruna Yukawa and Kenji Goto.[180]

The Islamic State uses beheadings to instill fear and attract new members. Also, the IS has undertaken mass killings of Iraqi and Syrian soldiers—from beheadings and gunfire to burying soldiers alive—who were kidnapped or surrendered.[181]

In Saudi Arabia, beheadings are very much in practice. More specifically, in August 2014, Saudi Arabia beheaded some criminals, including for other crimes such as "drug trafficking, adultery, apostasy and 'sorcery.'"[182] While government-sanctioned beheadings have taken place throughout history, it is rare in modernity. Still seventy-nine decapitations took place in Saudi Arabia in 2013.[183] In 2014, there were eight-seven beheadings in Saudi Arabia. During the first half of January 2015, eleven such punishments took place.[184]

During January 2015, Saudi Interior Ministry spokesman Maj. Gen. Mansour al-Turki differentiated between beheadings done in Saudi Arabia, which he said were judicially sanctioned punishments, and ISIL beheadings. Al-Turki asserted, "ISIS has no legitimate way to decide to kill people... the difference is clear."[185] Meanwhile, the UN characterizes beheadings as always a violation of international law.[186]

Also, in January 2015, Saudi blogger Raif Badawi received his initial twenty lashings for criticizing that nation's religious establishment. Overall, Badawi's punishment is "1000 lashes, 10 years in jail and a fine of more than $US260,000."[187] Subsequent lashings were postponed during subsequent weeks due to Badawi's illness and global outrage about his sentence.

Exploitation of Women and Children as Policy

The Islamic State's exploitation of the spoils of war include the kidnapping, slavery, and sale of captured women and girls. According to a Yazidi advocacy group, Sinjar Crisis Management Team, some 6,000 Yazidi women and girls were captured and sold to IS fighters, who haggled over prices for this "human commodity." Some of the harms these females endure include forced marriages and rape.[188]

In one of the most sickening examples in the annals of IS savagery, it was reported in April 2015 that a nine-year-old Yazidi girl was raped by ten IS fighters, and impregnated. The unnamed girl, who will likely die if she gives birth, was among some 200 Yazidi women, elderly, and children ultimately released by the group. Some of the released prisoners detailed their experiences of brutal sexual abuse at the hands of the IS militants during their detention in northern Iraq.[189]

According to an Islamic State video, and noted in its publication *Dabiq*, a "slave market day" exists in the Islamic State, whereby women and girls, including Yazidis and Christians, are sold for cash and weapons. Market participants manifest further deviancy, as younger females fetch a higher price than their elders.[190] The Islamic State slave markets include price lists that include costs for "Yazidi and Christian girls as young as one to nine years of age [sold] for a price of $172 in Iraq."[191] Moreover, "[t]he price for the girls between one- and nine-years is the highest, followed by Yazidi or Christian girls between the ages of 10 and 20, priced at $130. Women between the ages of 20 and 30 were being sold for $86; a 30 to 40 year was being sold for $75 and 40 to 50 year old women were listed for sale at a price of $43."[192]

The IS also targets civilians as detailed in a July 2014 UN report. More specifically, the report accused Islamic State fighters in Iraq of executions, rape, and forced recruitment of children during its campaign in northern Iraq. [193]

The IS's exploitation of children is not limited to Iraq. For instance, UNICEF reported that IS's closing of schools has affected 670,000 children in Syria. [194] The effects of the lack of formal education will negatively affect multiple generations.

Effects of Coalition Airstrikes

Once allied airstrikes on IS targets in Iraq began, the Islamic State changed tactics accordingly. Reports indicate that the IS has fallen back on more traditional terrorist and insurgent tactics, such as hiding among the population, focusing on dense urban areas, emptying arms depots, leaving command and control centers for private homes, and moving in small groups rather than in large columns. [195]

Airstrikes have succeeded in driving the militants from some of the territory they conquered, including valuable resources such as oil fields. However, the IS still poses a threat, as its members often blend into population centers to avoid targeting and increase civilian casualties. [196] In light of coalition efforts, the IS tended to abandon the use of convoys for motorcycles, reduced the number of checkpoints, moved checkpoints to side streets, placed large IS flags on abandoned civilian homes, and increased the number of headquarters to 20. [197]

Islamic State's Options for Non-Muslims and Shiites

In areas it has conquered, the IS provides non-Muslims with few options: conversion to Islam, pay the *jizya* (tax), or death. [198] As it amassed more territory, the IS killed and threatened thousands of Yazidis, an ancient ethnoreligious community whose beliefs are rooted in Zoroastrianism. [199] Likewise, Christians who have come under IS control are given the choices of conversion, paying the *jizya,* or being killed. [200] The systematic attacks against Yazidis and Christians have been characterized by some, including the United Nations, as genocide. [201] The IS has inflicted innumerable punishments on minorities and others, including beheadings, burying people alive, and crucifixions. [202]

Furthermore, the Islamic State appears to be supporting the use of its tactics, particularly beheadings, by affiliated members, such as in Europe, Australia, and the Middle East, as well as inspiring unaffiliated jihadists around the global to undertake attacks on behalf (or in support of) the group. [203] Also, the IS and other Islamist groups have methodically destroyed the holy sites, statues, and places of worship of Shiites and minority groups such as Christians and Jews, as well as such historical sites of utmost significance as the ancient city of Niniveh.[204]

New Media

Besides its kinetic activities, widespread savagery, and territorial gains, the Islamic State benefits from its prodigious publicity output, which takes the form of photos, websites, social media, music, videos, and even video games.[205] More specifically, the IS "has proved fluent in YouTube, Twitter, Instagram, Tumblr, internet memes (see: #catsofjihad) and other social media. Amateur videos and images are also being uploaded daily by its footsoldiers."[206] The importance of getting its message to a global audience was demonstrated by the translation of a speech by "IS spokesman Abu Mohammad al-Adnani al-Shami into English, Turkish, Dutch, French, German, Indonesian and Russian."[207]

Many of these social media efforts require technical skills not commonly found among Syrian and Iraqi IS operatives. Therefore, foreigners with familiarity with social media and other technical capacities are particularly important IS recruits.[208] A former Taliban recruiter observed, "Look at the videos they're making. You think those people were trained in Syria and Iraq? Those people were trained in the West."[209]

As discussed below, a critical component of the IS strategy and success thus far has been extensive efforts to radicalize and recruit prospective followers, particularly using social media. Additionally, the IS utilizes new media to propagate its message, intimidate its adversaries, and otherwise undertake strategic communications, often in multiple languages, along varied online instrumentalities.

In January 2015, the IS released photos on social media featuring an eight-man sniper team posing with "long-range Russian-made Dragunov sniper rifles."[210] The unit is based with the "Ninewa Division of northern Iraq."[211] In December 2014, an IS sniper killed "Iranian Revolutionary Guard Brigadier General Hamid Taqavi," who was among other Iranian soldiers advising Shiite militias in Iraq.[212]

WEAPONS

The Islamic State possesses a formidable arsenal beyond the usual terrorist assortment of small arms, grenades, and improvised explosive devices. Most of its advanced weaponry was captured from Iraqi or Syrian forces.[213] The IS has acquired tanks, reconnaissance drones, howitzers, rocket launchers, anti-aircraft and anti-gun weapons, body armor, Man Portable Air Defense Systems (MANPADS), and armored personnel carriers.[214] More specifically, the IS's heavy weapon arsenal includes:[215] SA-7 and Stinger shoulder-fired surface-to-air missiles; M79 Osa, HJ-8, and AT-4 Spigot anti-tank weapons; Type 59 field guns and M198 howitzers; Humvees;[216] T-54/55 and T-72 main battle tanks; truck-mounted DShK guns; ZU-23-2 anti-aircraft guns; BM-21 Grad multiple rocket launchers; at least one Scud missile; and a M-1 Abrams tank.[217]

When the IS captured Mosul Airport in June 2014, it seized a number of helicopters and cargo planes that were stationed there.[218] While reports surfaced that its fighters had captured UH-60 Blackhawk helicopters, this was denied by Pentagon spokesman Cmdr. Bill Speaks who said, "We do know that they made false claims . . . particularly with Blackhawk helicopters, which have never been sold to Iraq."[219] It is also rumored that three Russian-made Mi-17 helicopters used by the Iraqi Special Forces were seized at Mosul Airport.[220] It is believed that the IS currently does not possess pilots or the knowledge of how to fly the aircraft. Thus, the organization probably cannot deploy them, although two IS aircraft were apparently shot down.[221]

Still, in July 2013 a Jordanian air force pilot, Ahmad Majali, defected and joined Jabhat al-Nusra, at that time an IS ally.[222] One report has also indicated that among the tanks seized in Mosul was an M-1 Abrams tank noted above.[223]

More disturbing, IS members are attempting to build biological weapons for potential attacks. The production of biological weapons is rather inexpensive relative to other weapons of mass destruction, but can still inflict physical and psychological damage if used.[224] Likewise, reports of the IS gaining access to nuclear materials in Mosul are troubling.[225]

Analogously, the United Nations is concerned about the possibility that IS extremists could obtain any undeclared chemical weapons in Syria. Sigrid Kaag, the head of the UN mission that is monitoring the destruction of Syria's chemical weapons program, said that 96 percent of the chemical weapons stockpile has been destroyed. Yet, Ms. Kaag was skeptical whether the Syrian government reported the accurate amount of chemical weaponry in the first place.[226] Also, Human Rights Watch claimed that the IS has utilized ground-fired cluster munitions in at least one location in Syria.[227]

TARGETS

The Islamic State targets nations, regimes, groups, and persons who do not support them: from secular Sunni Muslims and Shiites and fellow Islamists who oppose the IS worldview, to Christians, Yazidis, Sahawat members, and inhabitants of lands IS conquered or it seeks to acquire. Among regional players, the IS designates al-Qa'ida, the Turkish government, and the Iranian government—to name a few—among its adversaries.[228]

In the past, IS predecessors ISI and AQI largely targeted Shiites. AQI even bombed the holy Shiite Askariyah Shrine in Samarra, Iraq, which deepened sectarian tensions and violence.[229]

Journalists and Foreigners

Westerners have become a major target for the IS, which it exploits further through publicity-fueling beheadings. During summer 2014, two American journalists, James Foley and Steven Sotloff, and British aid worker David Haines were beheaded. The Islamic State beheaded two British citizens and fellow aid workers David Haines and Alan Henning during September 2014 and October 2014, respectively.[230] In October 2014, Frenchman Herve Gourdel was beheaded by an IS-linked Jund al-Khilafah—Soldiers of the Caliphate in Algeria.[231] In January 2015, IS beheaded Japanese hostages Haruna Yukawa and Kenji Goto.[232]

The beheadings were recorded and distributed worldwide. This vivid carnage further buttressed the IS as an intimidating and potent player in the region. The IS has kidnapped at least two other Americans in Syria.[233]

James Foley's story has unfortunately become a pattern for Western hostages of the Islamic State. In November 2012, unknown militants kidnapped Foley, an American journalist working in Syria.[234] Ultimately, the IS gained control of Foley and demanded a $132 million ransom for his release. While the U.S. government refused to pay the ransom, it attempted to rescue Foley and the other Americans the IS held. Regrettably, the American hostages were not at the location the U.S. forces targeted.[235]

In August 2014, a video of Foley's beheading was posted online. Prior to his beheading, Foley was forced to denounce the U.S. Also, he was scripted to urge his family to fight against the IS's true enemy, the American government.[236]

In the video, the IS claimed to hold three other Americans and multiple UK citizens. The UK, like the United States, refuses to pay ransoms, although other European countries, notably France, have paid captors for the release of their citizenry. As the United States and UK do not pay ransoms to kidnappers, their citizens have a difficult time getting released.[237]

In August 2014, Qatar played a role in the release of U.S. hostage, writer Peter Theo Curtis, who was being held by Jabhat al-Nusra. Qatar, which has connections with jihadi groups in Syria, is increasingly engaged in weakening accusations that it is actually funding and otherwise supporting Sunni jihadi groups in Syria.[238]

The IS militant who beheaded Foley and Sotloff spoke English with a London accent in the respective videos. The UK foreign minister stated that the killer was likely British.[239] The UK and other governments are trying to identify the killer, as the campaign of beheadings of Western hostages appears to expand.[240] It was subsequently concluded that the assassin is dual UK-Kuwaiti national Mohammed Emwazi, otherwise known as "Jihadi John."

In August 2014, IS militants also beheaded a Sunni Lebanese soldier, Ali al-Sayyed, who they kidnapped after raiding the Lebanese town of Arsal.[241] The jihadists are holding hostage an additional twenty-three Lebanese soldiers and policemen.[242] The IS and Jabhat al-Nusra proposed that the Lebanon government release Islamist prisoners in exchange for the Lebanese prisoners.[243]

U.S. President Barack Obama proclaimed that the murders of two American journalists only increased the country's resolve to combat the Islamic State (he used the term ISIL, as is customary of the Obama administration).[244] Representatives of the Qatari government stated that the beheadings are a "crime against the principles of Islam."[245]

In January 2015, the Islamic State killed Japanese hostage Haruna Yukawa. The other Japanese hostage, Kenji Goto, was holding a photo of Yukawa's decapitated body. Also, the IS released an audio recording blaming the Japanese government for the death of Yukawa, for not paying the $200 million ransom that the group demanded.[246] By the end of that month, Goto was beheaded by the IS, as discussion to trade Goto for Sajida al-Rishawi, a failed female Iraqi suicide bomber who targeted a Jordanian hotel, never materialized. The Jordanians also proposed that their pilot, Moaz al-Kasasbeh, who is also being held by the IS, be included in any swap.[247]

In response, Jordanian government spokesman, Mohammad al-Momani, said, "Jordan is ready to release prisoner Sajida al-Rishawi if the Jordanian pilot Lieutenant [Maaz] al-Kasaesbeh was released and his life spared."[248] The three-person hostage trade ended up being too difficult to forge, particularly as the Jordanians sought proof-of-life on their pilot. By the end of January 2015, a video was released indicating that Goto was purportedly beheaded.

The effect of individuals in high-risk areas—such as Syria—and ultimately being kidnapped by terror groups, inevitably affects the home country of these citizens. For instance, Japan, which was largely a contributor of humanitarian aid in the Middle East and limited from foreign military operations by its constitution, found it was enmeshed in international crisis and media hysteria.

In February 2015, the IS released a video purportedly showing al-Kasasbeh being burned alive in a metal cage. The viciousness and vulgarity of the act led to admonitions and increased air attacks from Jordan and condemnation of the civilized world community.

Treatment of Christians, Yazidis, and Others

Ms. Flavia Pansieri, United Nations Deputy High Commissioner for Human Rights to the Human Rights Council's Special Session on Iraq, reported in September 2014 that the IS and associated forces in Iraq undertook "targeted killings, forced conversions, abductions, slavery, sexual and physical abuse and torture, and the besieging of entire communities on the basis of ethnic, religious, or sectarian affiliation. Mosques, shrines, churches, and other religious sites and places of cultural significance have also been deliberately destroyed."[249] Additionally, she noted that "Christian, Yezidi, Turkmen, Shabak, Kaka'e, Sabaeans and Shi'a communities have been targeted through particularly brutal persecution, as ISIL has ruthlessly carried out what may amount to ethnic and religious cleansing in areas under its control."[250] At the Badouch Prison in Mosul in July 2014, some 650 prisoners of religious and ethnic minorities, including Shiites, were summarily executed.[251]

According to a December 2014 report by Amnesty International, "hundreds and possibly thousands of Yazidi women and girls who have been forcibly married, 'sold' or given as 'gifts' to IS fighters or their supporters. Often, captives were forced to convert to Islam."[252] This phenomenon in the Sinjar region of Iraq instilled so much fear that some captives committed suicide in order to avoid or end their abuse. "The majority of the perpetrators are Iraqi and Syrian men; many of them are IS fighters but others are believed to be supporters of the group. Several former captives said they had been held in family homes where they lived with their captors' wives and children."[253] Amnesty International designates such activities as war crimes and crimes against humanity.[254]

The treatment of Yazidi women and girls is in line with the rules set out in an IS pamphlet, "Question and Answers on Female Slaves and their Freedom," that was distributed online. In this document, Islamic State claims that the Koran permits "taking non-Muslim women and girls captive."[255]

The IS merciless persecution of the Yazidis in Iraq spurred U.S. bombing campaign against IS in Iraq, as thousands of members of this minority were threatened with death. Islamic State forces surrounded 35,000–50,000 Yazidis in Sinjar. The U.S. intervened with airstrikes while the Iraqi army and Kurdish forces broke the siege.[256] The IS killed hundreds of Yazidis as it captured cities in Iraq.[257]

The Islamic State also released a video showing its military forcing Yazidis to convert to Islam.[258] As in that video, most Yazidis are given the option to convert to Islam or face death, as was the case of 300 Yazidis in northern Iraq who were offered this choice.[259]

In December 2014, Iraq's Ministry of Human Rights reported that over "150 females, including pregnant women, were executed in Fallujah by a militant [from the Islamic State] named Abu Anas Al-Libi after they refused to accept jihad marriage."[260] "Many families were also forced to migrate from the province's northern town of Al-Wafa after hundreds of residents received death threats."[261]

Christian minorities have become one of the most prominent targets of the IS violence. Christians living in areas occupied by the IS are required to pay the *jizya*, a tax on non-Muslims for those who do not convert or leave the area.[262] Under a February 2014 Dhimmi Agreement between the IS and the Christian residents of Raqqa, Syria, each Christian is required to pay between $178 and $715 each year, depending on the individual's income.[263]

In 2004, Mosul had some 60,000 Christians out of a population of two million residents. When the IS took over Mosul in June 2014, it initially provided Christians with three options: "convert to Islam, pay a tax, or face execution. They later revoked the tax as an option."[264] In July 2014, the last Christians in Mosul were expelled from the city, rather than killed, after their Muslim neighbors intervened. And with that, Mosul was devoid of Christians for the first time in 2,000 years.[265] In total, tens of thousands of people have fled Mosul, the largest city under IS control, for fear of the regime's ideology and savagery.[266]

During the expulsion of Christians from its territory, the IS often takes all possessions with monetary value from Christian families. The Christians are forced to leave with nothing.[267]

In keeping with its viewpoint of differentiating Muslims from non-Muslims, the IS identifies and publicly designates all Christians living in their territories. The IS marks the homes of Christians with the Arabic letter "N" for Nasara (Arabic for Christian).[268] In order to demonstrate its dominance over Christians in the region, the IS has burned down several churches, converted other churches to mosques, and placed IS flags on top of those buildings.[269] The IS has carried out other atrocities including killing of Christians and Yazidi men in areas the group has conquered, while women and girls have been sold as slaves.[270]

Treatment of Combatants and Non-Combatants

The IS has also treated Iraqi and Syrian prisoners of war with particular cruelty.[271] Islamic State fighters massacred 250 Syrian soldiers after their capture at the Tabqa air base.[272] After taking over a city or military base, the militants often performed mass executions of hundreds of Iraqi soldiers who surrendered or were captured.[273] The IS then posted photos on the Internet. The IS claimed that it executed approximately 1,700 soldiers in one killing spree.[274]

The Islamic State's killing of combatants and non-combatants in areas it has acquired through force and elsewhere can be characterized as comprising war crimes, crimes against humanity, genocide, and crimes of aggression. These violations of international law could ultimately be brought before the International Criminal Court in the Netherlands, should that possibility arise.[275] Also, as universal jurisdiction attaches to such crimes, sovereign courts—including the Iraqi and Syrian judiciary—could be the frameworks for such prosecutions.[276]

In addition, civil suits against the Islamic State and its members could take hold as civil litigation against state-sponsors of terrorism, terrorist groups, terrorists/extremists, and their abettors are succeeding with greater frequency worldwide.[277] Still, it would be very naïve to suggest that any of the prospective measures will deter the Islamic State, its leaderships, members, and supporters from their brutality now and in the future.

The Syrian Observatory for Human Rights (SOHR) reports that the Islamic State killed some 2,000 people in Syria during June 28–December 27, 2014, as follows: 1,175 civilians, of which eight and four were women and children, respectively. Of that total, 930 came "from al-Shaitaat tribe in the eastern countryside of Deir Ezzor."[278] The remaining 800 persons or so killed were as follows:

- 502 Syrian government soldiers and officers.[279]
- "81 fighters of the Nusra Front, rebel and Islamic battalions."[280]
- 120 of its members for "exceeding the limits in religion."[281]

SOHR adds that the overall numbers of persons killed by the Islamic State during that time is "higher than the number documented by SOHR because there are hundreds of missing and detainees inside the IS jails, loss of communication with about a thousand men of al-Shaitaat tribe as well as because there are dozens of Kurds who have still been missing since the beginning of IS attack on the countryside of Ayn al-Arab 'Kobani' in September 16."[282]

Kurdish civilians, among other minority groups such as Yazidis, have been attacked and driven out of their homes. The IS has established detention centers for adults and children.[283]

Treatment of IS Subjects

The Islamic State's terror tactics have left even compliant and ordinary civilians under threat. The IS has carried out mass kidnappings in Iraq after invading cities, towns, and villages.[284] Thousands of civilians have been abducted from northern Iraqi villages despite not exercising any form of resistance against the extremist group.[285] Those associated with the Iraqi regime, including government officials and civil servants, have been kidnapped and executed.[286]

Likewise, the IS targets individuals who dare to criticize the regime. For instance, in September 2014, the IS tortured and then publicly assassinated human rights lawyer Samira Salih al-Nuaimi in the Mosul district. Al-Nuaimi was tried and convicted of apostasy in a sharia court, and sentenced with death for condemning—via Facebook—the IS destruction of religious sites in Mosul.[287]

Insubordination and cowardice is treated harshly by the IS. In February 2015, it was revealed that the IS "executed three of its most prominent leaders, known as Abu Nazar al-Obeidi, Qais Abu Mohamed and al-Ansari, after accused them of cowardice in the face of the security forces during clashes in the villages of al-Nay in the area of al-Hawd al-Azim, located 65 km north of Baqubah."[288]

FINANCING

Overview

The Islamic State's net worth is estimated at $2 billion, making it the richest jihadist organization in the world. It is rapidly becoming independent of wealthy donors in the Persian Gulf and other funding sources. As the group has gained control of more territory, it has been able to sustain its operations through a combination of oil revenues, extortion, border tolls, bank seizures, and granary sales, among others. According to some estimates, about $1.5 billion was acquired from sources in Mosul alone.[289]

In January 2015, it was announced that the Islamic State had approved a 2015 budget in the amount of $2 billion, with an expected surplus of $250 million. There are some doubts to the accuracy of this information, some characterizing the announcement as merely another IS propaganda effort.[290]

On October 23, 2014, David Cohen, the Under Secretary for Terrorism and Financial Intelligence at the U.S. Department of Treasury, said, the Islamic State's "primary funding tactics enable it today to generate tens of millions of dollars per month. Those tactics include the sale of stolen oil, the ransoming of kidnap victims, theft and extortion from the people it currently dominates, and, to a lesser extent, donations from supporters outside of Syria and Iraq."[291]

In March 2015, the Financial Action Task Force projected that the IS garners funds from five main methodologies, in order of size: "(1) illegal proceeds from occupation of territory, such as bank looting, extortion, control of oil fields and refineries, and robbery of economic assets and illicit taxation of goods and cash that transit territory where ISIL operates; (2) kidnapping for ransom; (3) donations including by and through non-profit organizations; (4) material support such as support associated with FTFs [foreign terrorist fighters] and (5) fundraising through modern communication networks."[292] The levels arising from these sources are inconsistent, affected by various factors, including coalition military efforts against ISIL.[293]

The IS has been extensively involved in organized crime, including smuggling, extortion, kidnapping for ransom, and theft. The IS smuggles raw materials from Syria, especially crude oil.[294]

The IS has issued annual reports giving numerical data on its operations and accomplishments, aiding it too, in obtaining further donations and support.[295] In the past, the IS received donations from various resources. Based on a study of 200 documents captured from al-Qa'ida and the IS, the RAND Corporation determined that from 2005 to 2010, less than 5 percent of the group's operating budget came from outside donations, with the majority originating from Iraq.[296]

Interestingly enough, the expenditures that the IS must outlay monthly are in the millions of dollars. For instance, the IS pays foreign fighters between $350–$500 per month while its skilled and unskilled other employees can earn 1,500 Euros and 50 Euros monthly, respectively.[297]

Donations

Private supporters in the region, including those based in Jordan, Syria, and Saudi Arabia, are believed to have provided the bulk of more recent funding, until the capture of Mosul.[298] Kuwait was a source of donations as well: "[A]lthough impossible to quantify the value of private Kuwaiti assistance to the rebels, it almost certainly reaches into the hundreds of millions of dollars."[299] Kuwait has served as a hub for IS donations, collecting money from other Gulf countries, and then sending the money indirectly to Syria by way of Turkey or Jordan.[300] Other examples of government acquiesce of private support include the "Qatari government has done less to stop the flow than its neighbors in Saudi Arabia and the United Arab Emirates."[301]

Former Iraqi Prime Minister al-Maliki accused the Qatari and Saudi governments of funding the IS. However, he did not produce any evidence at the time.[302] On August 22, 2014, a German minister also accused Qatar of funding the IS. However, a few days later, the German government announced that it has no evidence of this, and apologized for the accusation.[303]

Iran's Ministry of Intelligence and Security previously provided funding and arms to the precursor of the IS, al-Qa'ida in Iraq.[304] In a reversal of this policy, in early 2014, Iran offered to provide assistance to the United States and Iraq fighting al-Qa'ida advances.[305]

In September 2014, an ISIL official was reported to have obtained $2 million from individuals based in the Gulf states. Non-profit organizations, including charitable institutions across the globe which serve Syrian refugees, could be used as conduits for funds to the IS. Additionally, bulk cash are susceptible for smuggling across borders as well as cash donations provided to the IS, and IS-aligned intermediaries. Also, material support arising from the vast number of foreign fighters in Syria and Iraq, including IS-aligned operatives, includes both financial and other assistance (e.g., military supplies and equipment to clothing and first aid kits), which benefits the group.[306]

Oil

As noted previously, the group sells crude and refined oil to smugglers. These criminals transport it outside of IS controlled areas. The oil products are sold at a substantial discount in Turkey, to Kurds in Iraq, and the Assad regime, earning the IS about $1 million per day. Coalition airstrikes and the tightening of border crossings by Turkey and Iraqi Kurdistan, have hampered the IS's oil production, refinement, and distribution.[307]

Since 2012, when the group captured oil fields in Syria, oil has been sold back to the Syrian regime as well as electricity from power plants.[308] In the eastern province of Deir al-Zor, the IS seized the Koniko gas field from Jabhat al-Nusra and other Islamist terrorists, who had controlled it for several weeks after acquiring it from tribal gunmen. Koniko is one of the largest gas plants in Syria. "A fighter from a rebel group that has clashed with ISIL said the gas field was worth hundreds of thousands of dollars a week in output."[309] Other estimates suggest that the IS earns up to $3 million a day from selling oil and gas.[310] To counter the IS's reliance on illicit oil trade, coalition forces have bombed "modular refineries and tanker trucks."[311]

In light of declining global oil prices, IS operatives are involved in generating funds through a newly established, "highly-sophisticated organ-smuggling division whose operatives sell human hearts, livers and kidneys within the international black market."[312] This new revenue stream is made possible by the participation of "foreign doctors to harvest kidneys, livers, hearts and other body parts not only from fighters killed in combat but also from living prisoners including children abducted from the Shi'ite Muslim or Christian populations in both Iraq and Syria."[313]

Extortion

The group has extorted or imposed taxes on businesses and individuals, netting some $8 million a month. The extortion encompasses individuals who reside in their territory, conduct commerce there, or those simply passing through their territory. Extortion payments can run 10 percent of revenue, and religious minorities—who are not killed—are forced to pay the *jiyza* tax.[314]

Kidnapping

According to the U.S. Department of Treasury, kidnapping for ransom is now the second most lucrative source of funding for terrorists, after the financial support provided by state sponsors.[315] The IS earned some $20 million from kidnapping (mostly foreigners) during the first eight months or so of 2014. Although funding from kidnapping is irregular, this revenue-generating tactic is used as opportunities for exploiting captured victims allow.[316] Other estimates suggest that the IS has earned up to $45 million in kidnapping activities.[317]

U.S. journalist James Foley was reportedly held for a ransom of $132 million before ultimately beheaded. The U.S. government declined to provide this sum, as part of a policy to discourage the payment of ransoms.[318] The kidnapping of Westerners has been a good source of revenue for terrorists and organized criminals.[319] For instance, in January 2015, two female Italian aid workers, Vanessa Marzullo and Greta Ramelli, were released by the captors, Jabhat al-Nusra, following the payment of an alleged ransom of $15 million.[320]

The United States and UK have a no ransom policy, although other countries, including France, have paid kidnapping ransoms to terrorists and organized crime syndicates.[321] During the 2014–2015 hostage negotiations over two Japanese nationals who were ultimately beheaded by the IS, the Japanese government ultimately declined paying the $200 million ransom for release of its citizens.[322]

Following the release of a video in which Japanese hostage Kenji Goto's decapitated body was shown, Japan's Prime Minister Shinzo Abe stated that Japan "would not give in to terrorism." Abe also pledged to increase his country's role in the U.S.-led coalition against the IS. Goto's execution occurred less than one week after Haruna Yukawa, another Japanese national, was also killed by the IS.[323]

Kayla Mueller, a Northern Arizona University graduate, was kidnapped in August 2013 after leaving her job at the Doctors Without Borders hospital in Aleppo, Syria. She was held by the Islamic State, and killed in February 2015. The IS claimed her death was due to Jordanian airstrikes in Syria. After Mueller's death her parents questioned U.S. policy which forbids the payment of ransoms in relation to terrorist kidnappings.[324] In July 2014 the IS wrote Mueller's family stating that she "would be executed in 30 days if Pakistani neuroscientist Aafia Siddiqui were not released or the American's family did not pay a ransom of 5 million euros ($6.6 million)." Following appeals to commute the death sentence, including by activist Mauri Saalakhan, who leads a U.S. campaign to free the Pakistani," Mueller was not killed in that timeframe.[325]

Terror cells of the IS are required to send up to 20 percent of the income generated from kidnapping, extortion, and other activities to the next level of the group's leadership. Higher-ranking commanders then redistribute these monies to provincial or local cells that are in difficulties or need money to conduct attacks.[326]

Bank Robberies

In terms of theft, IS forces stole up to $429 million from the Central Bank in Mosul on June 13, 2014 (although some media outlets say that the sum could be anywhere from $65 to $400 million).[327] "Before Mosul, their total cash and assets were $875m [£515m]. Afterwards, with the money they robbed from banks and the value of the military supplies they looted, they could add another $1.5bn to that."[328] However, U.S. intelligence raised doubts about the veracity of this claim, questioning whether such sums could be looted from a bank and whether the robbery had even occurred.[329]

Additional monies valued in the millions of dollars and gold bullion were also stolen from other banks.[330] Overall, the Islamic State "seized cash from 62 government and non-government banks upon taking Mosul, Tikrit, Fallujah, and 13 other cities."[331]

Other Funding Schemes

Also, the IS stole priceless antiquities from archeological digs and sold them on the black market.[332] Other revenue sources include the sale and extortion of agricultural products, such as wheat, as well as payments arising from electricity production and water supplies.[333] Additionally, "ISIS is behind the sale of Syrian women and girls for forced marriages and to be used by sexual predators as unpaid prostitutes or concubines. One of the lucrative ISIS enterprises is the sale of young girls, as young as 10-years-old, to wealthy Arab businessmen and government officials from different Middle East countries."[334]

In February 2015, it was reported that the IS offered to exchange the bodies of Kurdish fighters killed in Kobani for $10,000–$20,000. There are suggestions that this tactic indicates that the group has funding difficulties.[335]

Also, Iraqi government employees who reside in IS-territory, but receive their salaries elsewhere (e.g., Kirkuk), are taxed up to 50 percent by the IS. In a similar, but less onerous scheme, the IS forces individuals who withdraw funds from their bank accounts must provide alms of 5 percent.[336]

Analogously, in another attempt at demonstrating the attributes of a sovereign, in November 2014, the Islamic State announced that it was planning on issuing its own currency—Islamic dinar gold, silver, and copper coins. The "gold [coins] will have two denominations, silver three and copper two."[337] However, the coins are unlikely to be accepted as a legitimate form of exchange outside of Islamic State territory.[338]

Government Responses

The U.S. Treasury Department's plans to degrade the Islamic State's financial strengths encompass: reducing its revenue streams, undermining its access to domestic and international financial systems, and imposing sanctions on its leadership and financial facilitators. Financial sanctions are imposed on anyone conducting business with the IS in relation to oil sales, Also, the U.S. government seeks to discourage other countries from paying ransom payments on behalf of their citizens who are kidnapped.

As of fall 2014, over twenty-four external donors and their networks have been stopped, with more to be pursued. Attempts are being made to reduce the Islamic State's capability to use Syrian, Iraqi, and the international banking system for fundraising and distributing funds. Lastly, the U.S. government has placed sanctions on and seized the assets of the Islamic State, its operatives and supporters, and abettor organizations.[339]

In a March 2015 report, the Financial Action Task Force proposed several steps to undermine IS funding, such as: targeted financial sanctions, e.g., on those who facilitate foreign fighter networks and firms that import commodities from the IS; impeding kidnapping for ransom payments; limiting the use of the Internet to raise and transfer funds; undermining support schemes for and by foreign fighters and purveyors of material support to the IS; and preventing the abuse of various sectors, such as finance and cultural artifacts. Additionally, countries and other actors in combating IS financing should be cognizant of the humanitarian needs in Syria, which should not be undermined during efforts to weaken IS funding opportunities.[340] These and other efforts to undermine IS are undertaken at national, regional, and international levels.

RADICALIZATION AND RECRUITMENT

Introduction

In relation to extremist and terror groups, individuals are radicalized, and later recruited due to various triggers. Among the diverse reasons for embracing radical concepts are: ideological motivations; revenge for real or perceived victimization; socio-economic marginalization and alienation; political marginalization and alienation; to obtain protection against perceived oppressors; to seek acceptance, respect, status through affiliation with the group, pressure from family, friends, and community (participation in the group is expected); to expunge dishonor to family due to moral indiscretion (e.g., adultery, sexual deviancy); to seek purpose or excitement in life; and as an alternative to failures or setbacks in education, job, and/or personal life.

Although estimates vary widely, by February 2015, some 3,400 Westerners—out of over 20,000 foreign fighters—have traveled abroad to fight in Syria from over 90 countries. Among this group is an estimated 180 Americans, as of March 2015.[341] Attracting foreign fighters is an especially high priority for the IS. The group uses diverse and advanced recruitment tactics, with distinct tailored messages for different demographics in diverse locations.

The Islamic State has attained a high level of success recruiting foreign members to join its cause, compared to many other terrorist networks. Its success of recruiting foreigners is due, in part, to the "media-savvy western militants."[342] The IS and other groups have engaged in various methods of propaganda to recruit prospective jihadists worldwide to join their causes.[343]

Religious Institutions and Schools

Some individuals working for the IS spread the terrorist network's ideologies through various institutions, including mosques and schools. At some mosques, religious figures voice ideas of Muslim superiority, inferiority of ethnic and religious minorities, and the danger these groups pose to the Muslim religion. Imams who have specific goals of recruiting new members to join IS may make anti-Zionist remarks and reference Koran text degrading non-Muslims. Furthermore, they emphasize the fragility of the Muslim population in the Middle East due to alleged "treacherous and war-mongering"[344] actions taken by Israel and other Western nations.

In Tunisia, for instance, "the radicalization process usually starts in mosques. Many mosques fell under extremist control during the turmoil that followed the 2011 uprising (a period marked by a general lack of security). Mosques were used to propagate an extremist religious discourse."[345]

A Syrian former IS terrorist, Abu Almouthanna, explained that he joined the Islamic State after his unit in Jabhat al-Nusra was defeated in a battle with the IS. His quench for killing IS opponents arose from the fact that he was imprisoned and tortured by the Syrian regime shortly after the start of the Syrian conflict.[346]

Besides mosques in the Middle East and elsewhere, the IS has another methodology to disseminate the organization's rhetoric globally, particularly Westerners.[347] Social media has been a major tool in the Islamic State's recruitment activities.[348] The terrorist group utilizes online social media in multiple languages to attract individuals worldwide to support its cause. The terrorist network established various Twitter accounts and Facebook pages to share its ideology, entice followers, denigrate its enemies, and showcase its successes.

Besides social media, the IS created the Al-Hayat Media Center, a multilingual media source that distributes modern-style videos and online magazines globally. The IS disseminates its content in multiple languages, with subtitles offered in additional languages so as to amplify its message widely.

The *Islamic State Report* is an online magazine that provides updates to jihadists globally about its activities. By only highlighting its successes, the *Islamic State Report* leads its readers to the conclusion that it is winning against its enemies.[349]

In January 2015, an allegedly IS-linked website, khilafalive.info, claimed that an "Islamic State TV channel"[350] would be launched. The IS has established several "regional broadcasters, including the FM radio station Al-Bayan in Mosul, Iraq and a satellite TV station,"[351] based in Libya.[352]

Face-to-Face

Another method by which the IS proliferates its brand is through merchandising, whether online or face-to-face. This is generally more appealing to young recruits than other approaches. The Islamic States and other entities worldwide market IS clothing, flags, toys, and souvenirs, including maps. Some of the funds earned from these sales are forwarded to IS, its members, or other supporters.[353]

Online

These social media efforts have aided in the radicalization and recruitment of foreigners —both men and women (including children)—to the Islamic State. As of spring 2014, the leading countries in terms of supplying foreign fighters in the Syrian conflict—although not all to the IS—include Tunisia (3,000 fighters), Saudi Arabia (2,500), Morocco (1,500), Jordan (1,000), Russian Federation (over 800), France (over 700), and Turkey (over 400).[354] The message of participating in the Syrian civil war—on whatever side—has materialized in bringing nationals from across the globe to the conflict.[355]

In areas with limited Internet access, the IS resorts to distributing pamphlets, other low-tech methods, and face-to-face recruitment.[356] Often, initial online communication is text-based, both to ensure proper translation and to keep detailed records on all interactions.[357]

Recruitment of members from other Islamic countries seems to be more stringent and careful than elsewhere. Some prospective members have to first demonstrate their abilities while fighting for other groups before being nominated to join the IS.[358] In Malaysia, Saudi Arabia, and Turkey, the IS targets prospective devotees through Facebook, YouTube, Twitter, blogs, and online forums. Also, the Islamic State uses face-to-face methodologies, including recruitment centers, leafleting, and spray-painting militant slogans, to attract other disciples.[359]

The IS has also resorted to flashy forms of recruitment intended to target younger audiences. In September 2014, the IS released its own video game, a modification of the Grand Theft Auto series. The game, "Grand Theft Auto: Salil al-Sawarem [sound of swords]," features attacks on soldiers and military convoys, allowing players to attack and immediately kill them, with characters yelling "Allahu Akbar" [God is Great] after carrying out killings or terrorist attacks. An IS official said that the goal of the game was to "raise the morale of the mujahedin and to train children and youth how to battle the West and to strike terror into the hearts of those who oppose the Islamic State."[360]

Interestingly enough, the IS has also sought the participation of deaf and mute recruits from Europe. More specifically, in March 2015, the IS released a video featuring a pair of deaf and mute fighters using sign language to interact between them. In doing so, the video seeks to portray the caliphate as a place where those impaired can live otherwise normal lives, like the two men who serve as heavily-armed traffic police.[361]

Recruiting Women

There are some 5,000 women serving the IS in Syria.[362] Recruiting women has become an essential part of the group's recruitment strategy.[363] Women operatives can more thoroughly examine women (or men dressed as women) passing through checkpoints than men. These women try to ensure that their husband-fighters will stay in their assigned regions. Also, women are essential for procreation, and to indoctrinate the children they raise in IS's ideals.[364]

In addition, women function as matchmakers between male and female recruits. The promise of a wife is often included in recruitment strategies aimed at male fighters.[365] In al-Bab, Syria, single women and widows can sign up to marry an IS member, who will subsequently propose to the woman.[366]

Malaysian intelligence officials have confirmed that British, Australian, and Malaysian women have volunteered to participate in jihad al-nikah (marriage jihad) or sexual jihad while serving IS fighters. Apparently, based on a 2013 Wahhabi edict, the practice basically calls upon Muslim women to serve as sexual comfort for jihadi fighters.[367] Other women in areas conquered by IS are coerced into marriages.[368] Some Western women have been recruited to serve as wives to IS fighters.[369]

Women-only units, such as Islamic State's al-Khansaa brigade, enforce a strict interpretation of sharia law, including ensuring that women dress modestly. Of note, some sixty women traveled to Syria to join the al-Khansaa brigade.[370] Jihadi publications geared towards women, like al-Qa'ida's *Al-Shamikha*, offer women tips on beauty, fund-raising for jihadists, and convincing the men in their lives to join the jihad.[371] Likewise, IS media operations gear some of their propaganda to Western women. This IS outreach had some success, as women from the United States, UK, Austria, and Australia have attempted to or successfully joined the Islamic State.[372]

Recruiting Children

The IS also views children as legitimate recruits for the cause. In al-Bab, Syria, children aged 14 to 15 receive doctrinal and weapons training.[373] Likewise, the IS runs summer camps to expose children to its ideology, including reverence for the IS leader Abu Bakr al-Baghdadi.[374] In Mosul, teenagers may enroll in training camps lasting over three weeks, with studies highlighting the Quran, jihadist doctrine, the importance of martyrdom, and weapons training.[375] Also, at IS training camps, children handle automatic weapons as well as observe beheading and stoning incidents.[376]

A June 2014 Human Rights Watch report revealed that various militant groups—the Free Syrian Army, Jabhat al-Nusra, and IS, among others—have encouraged children to fight "on the frontlines."[377] Children have "spied on hostile forces, acted as snipers, treated the wounded on battlefields, and ferried ammunition and other supplies to battles while fighting raged."[378]

The report found that boys joined the respective groups for various reasons, such as that they: followed their friends or family, had few other options as schools were closed, or suffered at the hands of the Syrian government.[379] Meanwhile, the IS has "more aggressively targeted children for recruitment, providing free lectures and schooling that included weapons and other military training."[380] Too, the IS has kidnapped and brainwashed children living in areas it has conquered.[381]

According to the Syrian Observatory for Human Rights, the IS recruited 400 children during the first three months of 2015. The IS provided the children with weapons and doctrinal training.[382] The children "were recruited near schools and mosques and in public areas where Islamic State carries out killings and brutal punishments on local people."[383]

In addition to text-based tweets, the Islamic State also uses social media to radicalize and recruit children. Photos of children, ranging from toddlers to teens, include them holding various weapons and, often standing in front of the Islamic State flag. There are also photos of children in classrooms adorned with the flag, and being instructed in IS's version of Islam.[384]

Some children have even posed with the heads of individuals that the IS beheaded, as in the case of a seven-year-old child, the son of Australian jihadist Khaled Sharouff who joined IS, who posed with a decapitated head in Raqqa.[385]

Another example is the January 2015 video showing a young boy associated with the IS executing two individuals who confessed to working for
Russia's Federal Security Branch.[386] Also, in March 2015, a video was released showing a child shoot and kill an Israeli citizen of Palestinian descent,
Mohamed Said Ismail Musallam, who was accused of spying for Israel.[387]

PUBLICITY

Overview

The IS employs social media exceptionally well. The extent of IS's political
and media outreach aimed at garnering support is unprecedented in the history of global jihadist movements.[388] The Al-Furqaan Institute for Media,
founded in November 2006, produces CDs, DVDs, posters, pamphlets, and
Web-related propaganda products.[389] But the Islamic State's main media
outlet is the I'tisaam Media Foundation, which was formed in March 2013. It
distributes through the Global Islamic Media Front (GIMF). The Foundation
produces HD-quality photographs and professionally edited propaganda
films for online distribution.[390]

In 2014, the IS established a subsidiary, Al-Hayat Media Center, which
targets a Western audience and produces materials in English, German, Russian, and French.[391] One of its videos showed IS fighter Abu Abdullah al-
Habashi, a 20-year-old British national originally from Eritrea, stating he has
"no sympathy" for those executed by the IS.[392] Al-Habashi posed in front of
a Syrian soldier who was strung up and decapitated. He later told the BBC
Newsnight program, "People love to see heads on spikes. I feel no sympathy
for them because they are all enemies of Allah."[393] With such a perspective,
it is not surprising that by 2015, the IS resorted to burning alive their hostages, as in the case of Jordanian captured pilot, Lt. Muath al-Kasasbeh.[394]

In a recruitment video, al-Habashi urged others from the UK to fight in
the Middle East. Also, the recruitment video featured fighters from the UK,
Finland, and the United States. Al-Habashi asserted, "We don't need any
democracy, we don't need any communism, we don't need anything like
that."[395] Rather, all that is required, he explained, is sharia law.[396]

Interesting enough, the IS uses "family imagery in its aggressive and
highly polished online recruiting on social media, including videos showing
fighters pushing children on swings and passing out toys, and children playing on bouncy castles and bumper cars, riding ponies, and eating pink cotton
candy. Those images are designed to reassure mothers that their children will
be safe in a place racked by fighting and regular bombing."[397]

Even in defeat and setbacks, the IS propaganda machine continues at full
force. For example, a pro-IS news agency released a video of IS fighters
acknowledging that the group had pulled out of Kobani. The video stated that

the U.S.-led coalition efforts were the primary reason for the group's defeat there.[398]

Twitter

The IS also runs an extensive Twitter campaign.[399] The organization distributes its message by organizing hashtag campaigns and encouraging tweets on popular hashtags. On June 24, 2014, IS launched the social media campaign, "Warning to the American People," centered on the hashtag #CalamityWill-BefallUS. This propaganda mode of the Islamic State encouraged participants to retweet official propaganda and slogans to discourage American intervention in Iraq. Its supporters also retweet propaganda with trending hashtags to increase exposure, such as #worldcup or to popular users like Oprah.[400]

In June 2014, Twitter began deleting IS-affiliated accounts, citing breaches of their terms of service. As a result, the IS reduced its use of Twitter. The Islamic State migrated to Friendica, then Diaspora, and ultimately to VK, a Russian media site.[401] Since then, IS communicates through private accounts that are deleted after their use. Its members use software applications that enable IS propaganda to be distributed directly from its supporters' accounts. There are now an estimated 27,000 pro-IS accounts, down from the 50,000 users on the Al-I'tisam page.[402]

In September 2014, the IS released the video of the beheading of British aid worker David Haines on Twitter, before it was subsequently removed.[403] Likewise, that month, a Twitter account aligned with a Gaza-based group that pledged loyalty to IS called for the assassination of Twitter employees in the United States and Europe. This threat arose due to Twitter's recent steps to shut down IS-affiliated Twitter accounts.[404]

In December 2014, a leading disseminator of jihadist content through a Twitter account, Shami Witness, was discovered to be a Bangalore, India-based technology executive, Mehdi Masroor Biswas. Shami Witness, now suspended, had some 18,000 followers, among the most for pro-Islamic State Twitter account.[405]

In one tweet, Biswas wrote, "If I had a chance to leave everything and join them I might have . . . my family needs me here."[406] While the elimination of the "Shami Witness account is a setback for ISIS and raises red flags and unease among fellow jihadists" it will not mark the end of advocacy for the group online.[407]

On Twitter and elsewhere online, English-speaking militants claiming to be based in Syria and aligned with the IS advocated support for the attacks in Paris in January 2015. For instance, British female national Umm Jafar Britaniyah, a Syrian-based IS member, tweeted, "ALLAHU AKBAR!!!!!! OUR brothers in France!!! May Allah reward them abundantly and grant them VICTORY AMEEN!!"[408]

Multilingual

The IS publishes information about itself in several languages to spread its message. The Islamic State has accounts on websites like Tumblr and Instagram in addition to its campaigns on Twitter. This allows the IS to create a disproportionately large online presence.[409]

Dabiq

The Islamic State is also producing a magazine called *Dabiq*, including an English version online.[410] *Dabiq* is published in German, Russian, and Arabic as well.[411] This publication is used to promote the IS's ideology, which includes that violence is required to implement those views. The inclusion of the group's military successes, religious commentary, call to arms, and other propaganda comprise the content of *Dabiq*.

Dabiq encourages pious Sunni Muslims outside the region to immigrate to the Islamic State. The publication utilizes religious rhetoric to discredit other jihadi groups, makes IS successes look like the divine will of God, denigrates the West, and predicts the IS's ultimate triumph. The magazine is named after a small Syrian town, where it is prophesized that the West and Islam will eventually clash. As well, the town was the site of a historic Ottoman battle, which cemented the old caliphate. The magazine has published multiple issues, with the first released on July 5, 2014.[412]

In the December 2014, Issue 6 of *Dabiq* magazine, the Islamic State writes, "This month, an attack was carried out in Sydney by Man Haron Monis, a Muslim who resolved to join the mujāhidīn of the Islamic State in their war against the crusader coalition . . . He did not do so by undertaking the journey to the lands of the Khilāfah [caliphate] and fighting side-by-side with his brothers but rather, by acting alone and striking the kuffār [nonbelievers] where it would hurt them most—in their own lands and on the very streets that they presumptively walk in safety."[413]

In doing so, *Dabiq* strongly encouraged others to adopt lone-wolf attacks on behalf of the IS, by explaining how relatively simple it was for Monis to get a weapon and cause havoc: "It didn't take much. He got hold of a gun and stormed a cafe taking everyone inside hostage . . . he prompted mass panic, brought terror to the entire nation, and triggered an evacuation of parts of Sydney's central business district."[414]

Monis was killed as Australian security forces ended the hostage siege, during which two hostages also died. A week before the incident Monis converted to Sunnism from Shiism, and declared allegiance to the Islamic

State. It is important to note that Monis had a long criminal record—including allegations of involvement in the killing of his former wife and sexual crimes—as well as exhibitions of mental instability. He can be classified as a lone wolf, who embraced IS ideology, and acted upon it in targeting individuals in Australia.[415]

Al-Zarqawi's former plan for a caliphate is among other topics included in a *Dabiq* issue. In doing so, the messages of the Islamic State are clear and cohesive. The steps toward establishing a caliphate are listed as emigration (*hijrah*), congregation (*jama'ah*), destabilizing idolatry (*taghut*), consolidation (*tamkin*), and culminating in creation of the caliphate (*Khilafah*).[416]

Kidnapping

As noted, an additional media tactic that the IS utilizes is to distribute online videos of individuals it has kidnapped. More specifically, the captives are required to read statements admonishing their respective governments (e.g., the United States, in the cases of James Foley and Steve Sotloff) and adulating IS. A new entry in this strategy is the propaganda video for IS by captured British journalist John Cantlie.[417]

"Positive" Messaging

A component of IS publicity is to ensure that a negative depiction of the group is prevented. To ensure this outcome—the IS uses, among other things, coercion of the population. For instance, in summer 2014, IS leadership informed activists in Syria's Deir al-Zor province that they must swear allegiance to it and submit to censorship. The IS also banned activists from working with television stations. They were told that any videos, pictures, or written reports needed to be reviewed by the Islamic State's Information Office before distribution.[418]

EXECUTION VIDEOS

Introduction

While video messages containing graphic beheadings of hostages—whether civilians or military—have been used by various terror groups, including al-Qa'ida in Iraq, this methodology has become a hallmark of the Islamic State. Several prominent beheadings took place during 2014 and 2015. These killings were videotaped and IS propaganda containing these beheadings were distributed globally, including with nearly ceaseless frequency on some media outlets.

Foley

The beheading of James Foley, an American journalist kidnapped in Syria in 2012, took place in August 2014. A video of the beheading was disseminated through YouTube, although forensics experts suggest Foley was killed off-camera.[419]

The Islamic State demanded $132 million in ransom for Foley's release. But, as negotiating with terrorists is against U.S. policy, that proposal was rejected.[420] A U.S. military rescue mission was attempted for Foley and other hostages, but they were not at the predicted site.[421] In the video made just before he was murdered, Foley was forced to make statements blaming his own death on the actions of the American government and military, including his brother, John Foley, who is a U.S. Air Force pilot. Foley's executioner (known as "Jihadi John") also claimed that Steven Sotloff, another American journalist, would be the next victim if U.S. airstrikes did not cease.[422] The British-accented killer—later determined to be Mohammed Emwazi—made good on that promise in September 2014.[423]

Sotloff

In the video execution-style of Steven Sotloff, who was later revealed to have held an Israeli passport (a fact that was hidden from his captors until after his death),[424] the executioner claimed the death was in retaliation for the continued U.S. airstrikes in northern Iraq. More specifically, the killer (Mohammed Emwazi) remarked:

> You, Obama, have but to gain from your actions but another American citizen. So just as your missiles continue to strike our people, our knife will continue to strike the necks of your people.[425]

Haines

David Haines was forced to address the camera on his knees and make statements blaming the U.S. government for his death.[426] The killer, apparently the same man who murdered Foley and Sotloff, is believed to be Mohammed Emwazi.[427] The video of Haines's execution included naming the next victim, Alan Henning, another British aid worker. This video was released in September 2014.[428]

Henning

Another victim of the Islamic State's bloody tactics was British aid worker Alan Henning, who was a taxicab driver. Henning was captured in the Syrian city of al-Dana in December 2013 while aiding in humanitarian relief efforts for Syrian refugees.[429] A former cellmate of Henning's said that he was in good spirits while in captivity. Henning expected to be released soon.[430] In October 2014, IS released a video of Henning's murder at the hands of Mohammed Emwazi. The murder was claimed to have occurred to punish the UK's decision to join the U.S.-led bombing campaign against the group.[431]

The murder evoked the anger and condemnation of the British Muslim community, with the spokesman of the Manchester Central Mosque saying this marked the "beginning of the end" for the IS.[432] In the wake of Henning's murder, Prime Minister David Cameron reportedly tasked the British intelligence community to find "Jihadi John," so that he could be captured or killed.[433] As noted, "Jihadi John" was later identified as a former London-based university graduate Mohammed Emwazi.[434]

Kassig

As with other of its former victims, the video of Alan Henning's murder ended with the Islamic State's next prospective beheading victim, the 26-year-old American Peter Kassig. Kassig was a former Army Ranger who served in Iraq in 2007.[435] After his discharge from the army, he returned to the Middle East in 2012. Kassig founded the Special Emergency Response and Assistance (SERA) aid organization in Lebanon to provide aid to Syrian refugees. In October 2013, he disappeared on his way to Deir Ezzor in Syria, while on a SERA relief effort.[436] Kassig reportedly voluntarily converted to Islam while in captivity. Kassig changed his name to Abdul Rahman and prayed five times a day.[437] In November 2014, the Islamic State issued a video showing Kassig's severed head as well as the decapitations of over twelve Syrian soldiers.[438]

Iraqi Soldiers

This spate of Western victims is only one part of a campaign of recorded summary execution-style murders that has been a part of ISIS's strategy. In June 2014, ISIS conquered Mosul. Shortly thereafter, the IS released a video, The Sound of Swords Clashing. The video is an hour-long depiction of several executions of Iraqi soldiers.

Five days after the fall of Tikrit to the ISIS, the group claimed to have killed an additional 1,700 soldiers. To inculcate fear and advance interest by ISIS recruits, several photos of those killings were made available on its Twitter account. The photos showed Iraqi soldiers in civilian clothes, bound and lying in a shallow mass grave, across from a firing squad armed with what seemed to be the soldiers' own guns. The caption proclaimed the "liquidation of the herds of the Safavid arm."[439] This reference to a Persian dynasty and, by inference, to all Shiites, was made in an attempt to exacerbate sectarian conflict.[440]

Syrian Soldiers

Videos of other soldier beheadings were issued by IS during summer 2014. In July 2014, after conquering a Syrian army base in Raqqa, IS militants decapitated captured soldiers and displayed their headless bodies as a warning.[441]

Kurdish and Lebanese Soldiers

In August 2014, the Islamic State posted videos online showing the beheadings of Kurdish and Lebanese soldiers.[442] For example, IS beheaded Lebanese Army Sergeant Ali al-Sayyed, who was captured by the terrorist organization in Arsal.[443] Islamic State member Abu Musaab Hafid al-Baghdadi posted pictures of the beheading on Twitter.[444] Reports indicate that Al-Sayyed was a Sunni Muslim[445] from the town of Fneidiq, near Akkar.[446]

Likewise, in September 2014, the IS beheaded a second Lebanese soldier, who was captured in Arsal. The soldier, Abbas Medlej, from Baalbek, was a Shiite. The IS claimed it beheaded Medlej because he attempted to escape.[447] In March 2015, the IS released a video purporting to show the beheading of four Kurdish (Peshmerga) forces in northern Iraq.[448]

Other Shiites

In late March 2015, the IS released a video showing the execution of eight men claimed to be Shiites. The executioners were shown handed knives by a black-clad boy. The killings allegedly took place in Syria's Hama province. A portion of the audio accompanying the video includes an IS fighter bragging that current military efforts against the IS would strengthen the group. Additionally, the victims were derided as "impure infidels" and that "[o]ur swords will soon, God willing, reach the Nuseiries and their allies like Bashar and his party."[449] The release of the video will only enflame Shiite-Sunni tensions in Syria and beyond. Moreover, the incident, once again, underscores the IS viewpoint of Shiites as apostates.

NOTES

1. Mneimneh, Hassan. "Takfirism." *AEI Critical Threats*. October 1, 2009. Accessed October 31, 2014. http://www.criticalthreats.org/al-qaeda/basics/takfirism.

2. Cooke, Alastair. "You cannot understand ISIS if you do not know the history of Wahhabism in Saudi Arabia." *Huffington Post*, August 24, 2014. Accessed September 1, 2014. http://www.huffingtonpost.com/alastair-crooke/isis-wahhabism-saudi-arabia_b_5717157.html.

3. Husain, Ed. "Saudis must stop exporting extremism." *NY Times*, August 4, 2014. Accessed August 30, 2014. http://www.nytimes.com/2014/08/23/opinion/isis-atrocities-started-with-saudi-support-for-salafi-hate.html. Gee, Alison. "Crucifixion from ancient Rome to modern Syria." *BBC News Magazine*, May 7, 2014. Accessed October 26, 2014. http://www.bbc.com/news/magazine-27245852.

Joshi, Shashank. "Where does the Islamic State's fetish with beheading people come from?" *Telegraph*. September 14, 2014. Accessed October 25, 2014. http://www.telegraph.co.uk/news/worldnews/middleeast/syria/11071276/Where-does-the-Islamic-States-fetish-with-beheading-people-come-from.html.

Kirkpatrick, David. "ISIS' harsh brand of Islam is rooted in austere creed." *NY Times*, September 24, 2014. Accessed October 24, 2014. http://www.nytimes.com/2014/09/25/world/middleeast/isis-abu-bakr-baghdadi-caliph-wahhabi.html?_r=0.

Massie, Christopher. "Is ISIS a faith-based terrorist group?" *Columbia Journalism Review*, September 17, 2014. Accessed October 24, 2014. http://www.cjr.org/behind_the_news/is_isis_a_faith-based_terroris.php?page=all.

Coker, Margaret. "The new Jihad." *Wall Street Journal*, July 11, 2014. Accessed October 24, 2014. http://online.wsj.com/articles/why-the-new-jihadists-in-iraq-and-syria-see-al-qaeda-as-too-passive-1405096590.

Wood, Graeme. "What ISIS's leader really wants." *New Republic*, September 1, 2014. Accessed October 26, 2014. http://www.newrepublic.com/article/119259/isis-history-islamic-states-new-caliphate-syria-and-iraq.

Shazad, Syed Saleem. "Takfirism: a messianic ideology." *Le Monde diplomatique*, July 3, 2007. Accessed October 25, 2014. http://mondediplo.com/2007/07/03takfirism.

Al Jifri, Habib Ali. "Taking on takfirism will require more than a quick fix." *National*, August 24, 2014. Accessed October 26, 2014. http://www.thenational.ae/opinion/comment/taking-on-takfirism-will-require-more-than-a-quick-fix.

Sowerwine, James E. "Caliph and caliphate." Oxford Bibliographies, December 14, 2009. Accessed October 26, 2014. http://www.oxfordbibliographies.com/view/document/obo-9780195390155/obo-9780195390155-0013.xml.

Luttwak, Edward. "Caliphate Redivivus? Why a careful look at the 7th century can predict how the new caliphate will end." *Strategica*, Issue 17, August 1, 2014, Hoover Institution. Accessed October 26, 2014. http://www.hoover.org/research/caliphate-redivivus-why-careful-look-7th-century-can-predict-how-new-caliphate-will-end.

4. Al-Tamimi, Aymenn Jaweed. "The Dawn of the Islamic State of Iraq and Ash-Sham." Hudson Institute, March 11, 2014. Accessed October 21, 2014. http://www.hudson.org/research/10169-the-dawn-of-the-islamic-state-of-iraq-and-ash-sham. Kirkpatrick, David. "ISIS' harsh brand of Islam is rooted in austere creed." *NY Times*, September 24, 2014. Accessed October 24, 2014. http://www.nytimes.com/2014/09/25/world/middleeast/isis-abu-bakr-baghdadi-caliph-wahhabi.html?_r=0.

Coker, Margaret. "The new Jihad." *Wall Street Journal*, July 11, 2014. Accessed October 24, 2014. http://online.wsj.com/articles/why-the-new-jihadists-in-iraq-and-syria-see-al-qaeda-as-too-passive-1405096590.

Shazad, Syed Saleem. "Takfirism: a messianic ideology." *Le Monde diplomatique*, July 3, 2007. Accessed October 25, 2014. http://mondediplo.com/2007/07/03takfirism.

Al Jifri, Habib Ali. "Taking on takfirism will require more than a quick fix." *National*, August 24, 2014. Accessed October 26, 2014. http://www.thenational.ae/opinion/comment/taking-on-takfirism-will-require-more-than-a-quick-fix.

Sowerwine, James E. "Caliph and caliphate." Oxford Bibliographies, December 14, 2009. Accessed October 26, 2014. http://www.oxfordbibliographies.com/view/document/obo-9780195390155/obo-9780195390155-0013.xml.

Luttwak, Edward. "Caliphate Redivivus? Why a careful look at the 7th century can predict how the new caliphate will end." *Strategica*, Issue 17, August 1, 2014, Hoover Institution. Accessed October 26, 2014. http://www.hoover.org/research/caliphate-redivivus-why-careful-look-7th-century-can-predict-how-new-caliphate-will-end.

"The abolition of the caliphate." *Economist*, March 8, 1924. Accessed October 26, 2014. http://www.economist.com/node/11829711.

Wood, Graeme. "What ISIS's leader really wants." *New Republic*, September 1, 2014. Accessed October 26, 2014. http://www.newrepublic.com/article/119259/isis-history-islamic-states-new-caliphate-syria-and-iraq.

5. Danforth, Nick. "The Myth of the Caliphate." *Foreign Affairs*, November 19, 2014. Accessed December 1, 2014. http://www.foreignaffairs.com/articles/142379/nick-danforth/the-myth-of-the-caliphate.

6. Kirkpatrick, David. "ISIS' harsh brand of Islam is rooted in austere Saudi creed." *NY Times*, September 24, 2014. Accessed October 1, 2014. http://www.nytimes.com/2014/09/25/world/middleeast/isis-abu-bakr-baghdadi-caliph-wahhabi.html?_r=0.

7. Ibid.

8. Husain, Ed. "Saudis must stop exporting extremism." *NY Times*, August 23, 2014. Accessed August 30, 2014. http://www.nytimes.com/2014/08/23/opinion/isis-atrocities-started-with-saudi-support-for-salafi-hate.html.

9. Ibid.

10. Desilver, Drew. "World's Muslim population more widespread than you think." *Fact-Tank*, June 7, 2014. Accessed November 15, 2014. http://www.pewresearch.org/fact-tank/2013/06/07/worlds-muslim-population-more-widespread-than-you-might-think/.

11. Wood, Graeme. "What ISIS really wants." *Atlantic*, March 2015. Accessed March 3, 2015. http://www.theatlantic.com/features/archive/2015/02/what-isis-really-wants/384980/.

12. Ibid.

13. Ibid.

14. Ibid.

15. Ibid.

16. Hassan, Hassan, "The secret world of Isis training camps—ruled by sacred texts and the sword." *Guardian*, January 24, 2015. Accessed February 4, 2015. http://www.theguardian.com/world/2015/jan/25/inside-isis-training-camps.

17. Ibid.

18. Arango, Tim and Eric Schmitt, "U.S. actions in Iraq fueled the actions of a rebel." *NY Times*, August 10, 2014. Accessed October 20, 2014. http://www.nytimes.com/2014/08/11/world/middleeast/us-actions-in-iraq-fueled-rise-of-a-rebel.html?_r=2.

19. Ignatius, David. "The manual that chillingly foreshadows the Islamic State." *Washington Post*, September 25, 2014. Accessed October 20, 2014. http://www.washingtonpost.com/opinions/david-ignatius-the-mein-kampf-of-jihad/2014/09/25/4adbfc1a-44e8-11e4-9a15-137aa0153527_story.html.

20. Ibid.

21. Ibid.

22. "Propagating the correct manhaj." Islamic State Report: An Insight into the Islamic State, Issue 1, Page 1, Shaban 1435, Al-Hayat Media Center. https://azelin.files.wordpress.com/2014/06/islamic-state-of-iraq-and-al-shc481m-22islamic-state-report-122.pdf.

23. Ibid.

24. Ibid.

25. Ibid.

26. Pizzi, Michael. "In declaring a caliphate, Islamic State draws a line in the sand." *Al-Jazeera*, June 30, 2014. Accessed October 21, 2014. http://america.aljazeera.com/articles/2014/6/30/islamic-state-caliphate.html.

27. Seib, Gerald. "Why the Islamic State represents a dangerous turn in the terror threat." *Wall Street Journal*, August 18, 2014. Accessed October 21, 2014. http://online.wsj.com/articles/capital-journal-why-isis-represents-a-dangerous-threat-1408382052.

28. Lewis, Bernard. *The Multiple Identities of the Middle East*. Schocken Books, New York, 1998, pp. 121–122. "Dar al-Harb." Oxford Islamic Studies Online. Accessed October 29, 2014. http://www.oxfordislamicstudies.com/article/opr/t125/e490.

"Dar al-Islam." Oxford Islamic Studies Online. Accessed October 29, 2014. http://www.oxfordislamicstudies.com/article/opr/t125/e491.

Zaheer, Kalid. "Is the west Darul-Harb for Muslims?" *Express Tribune*, April 13th, 2014. Accessed October 21, 2014. http://tribune.com.pk/story/144205/is-the-west-darul-harb-for-muslims/.

29. Rago, Joseph. "Inside the war against the Islamic State." *Wall Street Journal*, December 26, 2014. Accessed December 27, 2014. http://www.wsj.com/articles/joe-rago-inside-the-war-against-islamic-state-1419636790.

30. Ibid.

31. Al-Rashed, Abdulrahman. "ISIS is now chasing the Surooris." *Al-Arabiya*, August 22, 2014. Accessed October 21, 2014. http://english.alarabiya.net/en/views/2014/08/22/ISIS-is-now-chasing-the-Surooris.html.

32. Gordon, Jennifer Thea. "ISIS' desire to erase Sykes-Picot is rooted in fiction, not history." *National Interest*, September 17, 2014. Accessed October 30, 2014. http://nationalinterest.org/feature/isis%E2%80%99-desire-erase-sykes-picot-rooted-fiction-not-history-11293. Koch, Martin. "Sykes-Picot drew Middle East's arbitrary borders." *Deutsche Welle*, June 25, 2014. Accessed October 30, 2014. http://www.dw.de/sykes-picot-drew-middle-easts-arbitrary-borders/a-17734768.

33. "Saudi Arabia's grand mufti denounces Iraq's Islamic State group." *Daily Times*, August 20, 2014. Access November 17, 2014. http://www.dailytimes.com.pk/foreign/20-Aug-2014/saudi-arabia-s-grand-mufti-denounces-iraq-s-islamic-state-group.

34. Kirkpatrick, David. "ISIS' harsh brand of Islam is rooted in austere Saudi creed." *NY Times*, September 24, 2014. Accessed October 1, 2014. http://www.nytimes.com/2014/09/25/world/middleeast/isis-abu-bakr-baghdadi-caliph-wahhabi.html?_r=0.

35. Alsharif, Asma. "Egypt's top religious authority condemns Islamic State." *Reuters*, August 12, 2014. Accessed October 20, 2014. http://www.reuters.com/article/2014/08/12/us-iraq-security-egypt-mufti-idUSKBN0GC1BN20140812.

36. Ahmed, Qanta. "How to save Islam from the Islamists." *Spectator*, January 17, 2015. Accessed February 18, 2015. http://www.spectator.co.uk/features/9416462/how-to-save-islam-from-the-islamists/.

37. Ibid.

38. Sieczkowski, Cavan. "ISIS ideology is not true Islam, and these Imams are fighting back." *Huffington Post*, March 27, 2015. Accessed March 28, 2015. http://www.huffingtonpost.com/2015/03/27/imam-isis-haqiqah-magazine_n_6956028.html.

39. "Hezbollah: ISIS wants Lebanon." *Daily Star*, August 31, 2014. Accessed October 21, 2014. http://www.dailystar.com.lb/News/Lebanon-News/2014/Aug-31/269106-hezbollah-isis-wants-lebanon.ashx#axzz3GmuaaoXh.

40. Carmon, Y., Y. Yehoshua, and A. Leone. "Understanding Abu Bakr Al-Baghdadi And The Phenomenon Of The Islamic Caliphate State." MEMRI, September 14, 2014. Accessed October 21, 2014. http://www.memri.org/report/en/0/0/0/0/0/0/8147.htm.

41. Hundal, Sunny. "The real threat from the Islamic State is to Muslims, not the West." *Al-Jazeera*, August 26, 2014. Accessed October 21, 2014. http://www.aljazeera.com/indepth/opinion/2014/08/real-threat-from-islamic-state--201482316357532975.html.

42. Ernst, Douglas. "Islamic State releases tape of Iraqi leader calling for jihad." *Washington Times*, November 13, 2014. Accessed November 13, 2014. http://www.washingtontimes.com/news/2014/nov/13/islamic-state-releases-al-baghdadi-audio-erupt-vol/. "US officials say ISIS leader survived airstrike, audio tape emerges." *Fox News*, November 13, 2014. Accessed November 13, 2014. http://www.foxnews.com/politics/2014/11/13/us-officials-say-isis-leader-survived-airstrike-audio-tape-emerges/.

Ellis, Ralph and Mohammed Tawfeeq, "Warplanes hit convoy near Mosul in attempt to kill ISIS members." *CNN*, November 10, 2014. Accessed November 11, 2014. http://edition.cnn.com/2014/11/08/world/meast/iraq-violence/.

43. "Islamic State leader urges attacks in Saudi Arabia: speech." *Reuters*, November 13, 2014. Accessed November 15, 2015. http://www.reuters.com/article/2014/11/13/us-mideast-crisis-baghdadi-idUSKCN0IX1Y120141113.

44. "CIA: As Many as 31,000 Islamic State Fighters in Iraq, Syria." *Voice of America*, September 11, 2014. Accessed October 21, 2014. http://www.voanews.com/content/kerry-secures-arab-backing-for-push-against-islamic-state/2446934.html.

45. "IS is seven times bigger than Western estimates." *Business Standard*, November 16, 2014. Accessed November 16, 2014. http://www.business-standard.com/article/news-ians/is-seven-times-bigger-than-western-estimates-114111600180_1.html.

46. Ibid.

47. Sly, Liz. "The hidden hand behind the Islamic State's militants? Saddam Hussein's." *Washington Post*. April 4, 2015. Accessed April 4, 2015. http://www.washingtonpost.com/world/middle_east/the-hidden-hand-behind-the-islamic-state-militants-saddam-husseins/2015/04/04/aa97676c-cc32-11e4-8730-4f473416e759_story.html?hpid=z1.

48. Ibid.

49. "Islamic State rounds up ex-Baathists to eliminate potential rivals in Iraq's Mosul." *Reuters*, July 8, 2014. Accessed August 28, 2014. http://www.reuters.com/article/2014/07/08/us-iraq-security-mosul-idUSKBN0FD1AE20140708.

50. Loveday, Morris and Brian Murphy. "Iraqi officials: Top Saddam Hussein aide killed by anti-insurgent forces." *Washington Post*, April 17, 2015. Accessed April 18, 2015. http://www.washingtonpost.com/world/middle_east/iraqi-officials-top-saddam-hussein-aide-killed-by-anti-insurgent-forces/2015/04/17/0c6497a2-e50c-11e4-b510-962fcfabc310_story.html.

51. Ibid.

52. Simcox, Robin. "Understanding the Islamic State." The Henry Jackson Society, September 4, 2014. Accessed October 21, 2014. http://henryjacksonsociety.org/wp-content/uploads/2014/09/UnderstandingIslamicStateEd2014.pdf.

53. "Saudi king warns of terror threat to the world." *Al-Arabiya*, August 29, 2014. Accessed October 21, 2014. http://english.alarabiya.net/en/News/middle-east/2014/08/30/Saudi-king-warns-of-terror-threat-to-the-world.html.

54. Sly, Liz. "Islam's Dysfunctional State: In Isis-controlled Syria and Iraq everyday life is falling apart." *Independent*. December 26, 2014. Accessed December 27, 2014. http://www.independent.co.uk/news/world/middle-east/islams-dysfunctional-state-in-isiscontrolled-syria-and-iraq-everyday-life-is-falling-apart-9945774.html.

55. Ibid.

56. Ibid.

57. Ould Mohamedou, Mohammad-Mahmoud. "ISIS and the deceptive rebooting of al-Qaeda." Geneva Centre for Security Policy, May 2014. Accessed October 21, 2014. http://www.gcsp.ch/Regional-Development/Publications/GCSP-Publications/Policy-Papers/GCSP-Policy-Paper-ISIS-and-the-Deceptive-Rebooting-of-Al-Qaeda.

58. Ibid.

59. Ibid.

60. Zelin, Aaron Y. "The war between ISIS and al-Qaeda for supremacy of the global jihadist movement." Washington Institute, June 2014. Accessed October 20, 2014. http://www.washingtoninstitute.org/uploads/Documents/pubs/ResearchNote_20_Zelin.pdf.

61. "Jabhat al-Nusra and Islamic battalions clashes with ISIS and regime forces in Aleppo." *Syrian Observatory for Human Rights*, February 3, 2015. Accessed February 23, 2015. http://syriahr.com/en/2015/02/jabhat-al-nusra-and-islamic-battalions-clashes-with-isis-and-regime-forces-in-aleppo/.

62. "US-led forces hit ISIL oil targets in Syria." *Al-Jazeera*, September 29, 2014. Accessed October 21, 2014. http://www.aljazeera.com/news/middleeast/2014/09/us-led-forces-hit-isil-oil-targets-syria-2014928141921406915.html.

63. Pelley, Scott. "The Islamic State: Repercussions." *CBS News*, September 21, 2014. Accessed October 21, 2014. http://www.cbsnews.com/news/isis-islamic-state-repercussion-leon-panetta-king-abdullah-jordan/.

64. Scensson, Birgit. "Water as an instrument of war." *Qantara*, June 13, 2014. Accessed October 21, 2014. http://en.qantara.de/content/flood-disaster-in-iraq-water-as-an-instrument-of-war. Milner, Alex. "Mosul Damn: Why the battle for water matters in Iraq." *BBC News*, August 18, 2014. Accessed October 21, 2014. http://www.bbc.com/news/world-middle-east-28772478.

65. Johnson, Keith. "Water wars in the land of two rivers." *Foreign Policy*, July 2, 2014. Accessed October 21, 2014. http://www.foreignpolicy.com/articles/2014/07/02/water_wars_in_the_land_of_two_rivers. Vidal, John. "Water supply key to outcome of conflicts in Iraq and Syria, experts warn." *Guardian*, July 2, 2014. Accessed October 21, 2014. http://www.theguardian.com/environment/2014/jul/02/water-key-conflict-iraq-syria-isis.

66. Mustafa, Hamza. "Iraqi government forces say ISIS water supply sabotage foiled." *Asharq Al-Awsat*, April 9, 2014. Accessed October 21, 2014. http://www.aawsat.net/2014/04/article55330975.

67. Milner, Alex. "Mosul Damn: Why the battle for water matters in Iraq." *BBC News*, August 18, 2014. Accessed October 21, 2014. http://www.bbc.com/news/world-middle-east-28772478.

68. Ibid.

69. Gibbons-Neff, Thomas. "This is what could happen if the Islamic State destroys the Mosul Dam." *Washington Post*, August 8, 2014. Accessed October 21, 2014. http://www.washingtonpost.com/news/checkpoint/wp/2014/08/08/this-is-what-could-happen-if-the-islamic-state-destroys-the-mosul-dam/.

70. Fick, Maggie. "Special Report—Wheat warfare: Islamic State uses grain to tighten grip in Iraq." *Reuters*, September 30, 2014. Accessed October 21, 2014. http://uk.mobile.reuters.com/article/idUKKCN0HP12N20140930?irpc=932.

71. Ibid.

72. Ibid.

73. Ibid.

74. Fick, Maggie. "Special Report: For Islamic State, wheat season sows seeds of discontent." *Reuters*, January 20, 2015. Accessed February 23, 2015. http://www.reuters.com/article/2015/01/20/us-mideast-crisis-planting-specialreport-idUSKBN0KT0W420150120.

75. Ferrigno, Lorenzo, Laurie Segall and Evan Perez. "NYPD, other law enforcement on alert after ISIS threat resurfaces." *CNN*, January 12, 2015. Accessed February 18, 2015. http://edition.cnn.com/2015/01/11/us/nypd-law-enforcement-isis-threat/.

76. Rasmussen, Nicholas. "Current threats against the United States." Statement before the Senate Select Committee on Intelligence. *National Counterterrorism Center*, February 12, 2015. Accessed February 15, 2015. http://www.nctc.gov/docs/Current_Terrorist_Threat_to_the_United_States.pdf.

77. Daly, Michael. "The Muslim convert behind America's first workplace beheading." *Daily Beast*, September 27, 2014. Accessed October 21, 2014. http://www.thedailybeast.com/articles/2014/09/27/the-muslim-convert-behind-america-s-first-workplace-beheading.html.
Anderson, Evan. "Moore attack suspect has criminal history and concerning Facebook page." *News 9*, September 26, 2014. Accessed October 21, 2014. http://www.news9.com/story/26641141/moore-attack-suspect-has-criminal-history-and-concerning-facebook-page.
Keneally, Meghan. "Here cop who shot Okla. beheading suspect was also company exec." *ABC News*, September 26, 2014. Accessed October 21, 2014. http://abcnews.go.com/US/hero-cop-shot-attacker-beheaded-colleague-company-exec/story?id=25790102.

78. "Rochester man indicted on charges of attempting to provide material support to ISIS, attempting to kill U.S. soldiers and possession of firearms and silencers." United States Department of Justice, September 16, 2014. Accessed October 21, 2014. http://www.justice.gov/nsd/pr/rochester-man-indicted-charges-attempting-provide-material-support-isis-attempting-kill-us.

79. Ibid.

80. Ibid.

81. Mooney, Mark. "Ax attack against New York City cops was inspired by terrorists, police say." *ABC News*, October 24, 2014. Accessed October 26, 2014. http://abcnews.go.com/US/ax-attack-york-city-cops-inspired-terrorists-police/story?id=26436991.

82. "Cincinnati-area man arrested in plot to attack U.S. government officers." *FBI Cincinnati Division*, January 14, 2015. Accessed February 18, 2015. http://www.fbi.gov/cincinnati/press-releases/2015/cincinnati-area-man-arrested-in-plot-to-attack-u.s.-government-officers.

83. Thomas, Pierre, Jack Date, Mike Levine, and Jack Cloherty. "Ohio man arrested for alleged ISIS-inspired plot on US capitol, FBI says." *ABC News*, January 14, 2015. Accessed February 18, 2015. http://abcnews.go.com/Politics/ohio-man-arrested-alleged-isis-inspired-attack-us/story?id=28227724. Williams, Pete and M. Alex Johnson. "Ohio man charged with plotting to attack U.S. capitol." *NBC News*, January 14, 2015. Accessed February 18, 2015. http://www.nbcnews.com/news/us-news/ohio-man-charged-plotting-attack-u-s-capitol-n286326.

84. Perry, Kimball. "Accused Ohio terrorist pleads not guilty in Capitol plot." *USA Today*, January 22, 2015. Accessed February 18, 2015. http://www.usatoday.com/story/news/nation/2015/01/22/terror-suspect-plea/22184235/.

85. Thomas, Pierre, Jack Date, Mike Levine, and Jack Cloherty. "Ohio man arrested for alleged ISIS-inspired plot on US capitol, FBI says." *ABC News*, January 14, 2015. Accessed February 18, 2015. http://abcnews.go.com/Politics/ohio-man-arrested-alleged-isis-inspired-attack-us/story?id=28227724.

86. Ibid.

87. "Topeka, Kansas, man charged in plot to explode car bomb at military base." Office of Public Affairs. U.S. Department of Justice. April 10, 2015. Accessed April 10, 2015. http://www.justice.gov/opa/pr/topeka-kansas-man-charged-plot-explode-car-bomb-military-base.

88. Ibid.

89. Parascandola, Rocco and Thomas Tracy. "NYPD alerted to ISIS threat against cops, soldiers, civilians." *NYY Daily News*, January 11, 2015. Accessed February 18, 2015. http://www.nydailynews.com/new-york/nyc-crime/nypd-alerted-isis-threat-cops-civilians-article-1.2073649.

90. "DHS analysis finds ISIL most likely to conduct IED, small arms attacks in Western countries." *Public Intelligence*, December 5, 2015. Accessed February 18, 2015. https://publicintelligence.net/dhs-analysis-isil-attack-tactics/.

91. Ibid.

92. Vanden Brook, Tom. "Troops notified their names are on the Islamic State kill list." *Detroit Free Press*, March 23, 2015. Accessed March 30, 2015. http://www.freep.com/story/news/nation/2015/03/23/pentagon-response-islamic-state-kill-list/70335810/.

93. Schmidt, Michael and Helene Cooper. "ISIS urges sympathizers to kill U.S. service members it identifies on website." *NY Times*, March 21, 2015. Accessed March 21, 2015. http://www.nytimes.com/2015/03/22/world/middleeast/isis-urges-sympathizers-to-kill-us-service-members-it-identifies-on-website.html?_r=0.

94. Vanden Brook, Tom. "Troops notified their names are on the Islamic State kill list." *Detroit Free Press*, March 23, 2015. Accessed March 30, 2015. http://www.freep.com/story/news/nation/2015/03/23/pentagon-response-islamic-state-kill-list/70335810/.

95. "Brussels Jewish Museum killings: Suspect 'admitted attack.'" *BBC News*, June 1, 2014. Accessed October 21, 2014. http://www.bbc.com/news/world-europe-27654505. Corbet, Sylvie and Lori Hinnant. "French ex-hostage says tortured in Syria by Brussels shooting suspect Mehdi Nemmouche." *Huffington Post,* September 6, 2014. Accessed October 21, 2014. http://www.huffingtonpost.com/2014/09/06/mehdi-nemmouche-syria_n_5777064.html.
Dickey, Christopher. "French Jihadi Mehdi Nemmouche is the shape of terror to come." *Daily Beast*, September 9, 2014. Accessed October 21, 2014. http://www.thedailybeast.com/articles/2014/09/09/the-face-of-isis-terror-to-come.html.

96. Chazan, David. "Brussels museum shooting suspect 'beheaded baby.'" *Telegraph*, September 7, 2014. Accessed October 21, 2014. http://www.telegraph.co.uk/news/worldnews/middleeast/syria/11080079/Brussels-museum-shooting-suspect-beheaded-baby.html.

97. Cruickshank, Paul, Steve Almasy and Deborah Feyerick. "Source: Belgium terror cell has links to ISIS, some members still at large." *CNN*, January 16, 2015. Accessed February 18, 2015. http://www.cnn.com/2015/01/16/world/belgium-anti-terror-operation/index.html.

98. Ibid.

99. Cruickshank, Paul, Steve Almasy and Deborah Feyerick. "Source: Belgium terror cell has links to ISIS, some members still at large." *CNN*, January 16, 2015. Accessed February 18, 2015. http://www.cnn.com/2015/01/16/world/belgium-anti-terror-operation/index.html.; Martinez, Michael, Dominique Debucquoy-Dodley and Ray Sanchez. "Vignettes: More about the 17 killed in French terror attacks." *CNN*, Janaury 11, 2015. Accessed February 18, 2015. http://www.cnn.com/2015/01/10/world/france-paris-who-were-terror-victims/index.html

100. Smith-Spark, Laura, Margot Haddad and Sandrine Amiel. "Suspects detained in Paris over attacks as Kerry visits." *CNN*, January 17, 2015. Accessed February 18, 2015. http://www.cnn.com/2015/01/16/europe/france-charlie-hebdo-attacks/index.html.

101. Witte, Griff. "In a kosher grocery store in Paris, terror takes a deadly toll." *Washington Post*, January 9, 2015. Accessed February 18, 2015. http://www.washingtonpost.com/world/

europe/paris-kosher-market-seized-in-second-hostage-drama-in-nervous-france/2015/01/09/
f171b97e-97ff-11e4-8005-1924ede3e54a_story.html. Birnbaum, Michael. "Who is kosher market suspect Amedy Coulibaly?" *Washington Post*, January 9, 2015. Accessed February 18, 2015. http://www.washingtonpost.com/blogs/worldviews/wp/2015/01/09/who-is-kosher-market-suspect-amedy-coulibaly/.

102. "European Union anti-terror chief says new attacks can't be prevented." *DNA*, January 14, 2015. Accessed February 18, 2015. http://www.dnaindia.com/world/report-european-union-anti-terror-chief-says-new-attacks-can-t-be-prevented-2052346.

103. Ritchie, Alice. "West facing mass casualty attacks: MI5." *Daily Star*, January 10, 2015. Accessed February 18, 2015. http://www.dailystar.com.lb/News/World/2015/Jan-10/283641-west-facing-mass-casualty-attacks-mi5.ashx#sthash.3cdb59TJ.dpuf.

104. Evans, Martin. "Terror suspects plotted to behead member of the public, court hears." *Telegraph*, November 20, 2014. Accessed November 20, 2014. http://www.telegraph.co.uk/news/uknews/terrorism-in-the-uk/11243712/Terror-suspects-plotted-to-behead-a-member-of-the-public-at-a-Remembrance-Day-parade-court-hears.html.

105. "Soldier beheading plan teenager Brusthom Ziamani jailed." *BBC News*, March 20, 2015. Accessed March 23, 2015. http://m.bbc.com/news/uk-31987242.

106. Olsen, Jan. "Denmark shooting highlight links between gangs and radicals." *AP*, February 21, 2015. Accessed February 25, 2015. http://news.yahoo.com/denmark-shooting-highlight-links-between-gangs-radicals-101057480.html.

107. Siegel, Matt. "Australian PM says police raids follow IS linked beheading plot." *Reuters*, September 18, 2014. Accessed October 21, 2014. http://www.reuters.com/article/2014/09/18/us-australia-security-raids-idUSKBN0HC2FJ20140918.

108. Taylor, Rob. "Australia foils alleged beheading plot linked to Islamic State." *Wall Street Journal*, September 18, 2014. Accessed October 29, 2014. http://online.wsj.com/articles/australia-detains-suspects-in-terrorism-probe-1411008044?tesla=y&mg=reno64-wsj&url=http://online.wsj.com/article/SB10772401218227423777504580160872924652534.html.

109. Di Stefano, Mark. "ISIS supporter shot dead after allegedly attempting to behead police officers." *BuzzFeed*, September 24, 2014. Accessed October 21, 2014. http://www.buzzfeed.com/markdistefano/aussie-teen-terror-plot#tt92hk.

110. Maiden, Samantha et al. "Melbourne terror plot: raids live coverage." *Herald Sun*, April 18, 2015. Accessed April 19, 2015. http://www.heraldsun.com.au/news/law-order/melbourne-terror-plot-raids-live-coverage/story-fni0fee2-1227309151268.

111. "Woman wounded in Tunisia museum attack dies." *SkyNews*, March 29, 2015. Accessed March 29, 2015. http://news.sky.com/story/1454732/woman-wounded-in-tunisia-museum-attack-dies.

112. "Tunisian forces kill nine from militant group behind Bardo Museum attack." *AFP*, March 29, 2015. Accessed March 29, 2015. http://english.alarabiya.net/en/News/middle-east/2015/03/29/Tunisian-forces-kill-nine-from-militant-group-behind-Bardo-Museum-attack-.html.

113. "Tunis Bardo Museum attack: Thousands join protest march." *BBC*, March 29, 2015. Accessed March 29, 2015. http://www.bbc.com/news/world-africa-32105232.

114. Gall, Carlotta. "Group linked to the Islamic State claims responsibility for the Tunisia attack." *NY Times*, April 1, 2015. Accessed April 1, 2015. http://www.nytimes.com/2015/04/01/world/africa/group-linked-to-islamic-state-claims-responsibility-for-tunisia-attack.html?src=recg.

115. "Gunmen attack Corinthia Hotel in Libya." *WDSU.com*, January 28. 2015. Accessed February 4, 2015. http://www.wdsu.com/national/gunmen-attack-corinthia-hotel-in-libya/30938752. "Father of American killed in Libya speaks out." *CNN*, January 28, 2015. Accessed February 3, 2015. http://www.cnn.com/videos/us/2015/01/28/lead-intv-berry-father-american-killed-libya.cnn.

Lamothe, Dan. "Security contractor David Berry, killed in Libya, leaves a legacy of U.S. military service." *Washington Post*, January 28, 2015. Accessed February 3, 2015. http://www.washingtonpost.com/news/checkpoint/wp/2015/01/28/security-contractor-david-berry-killed-in-libya-leaves-a-legacy-of-u-s-military-service/.

"Nine dead in Libya hotel attack." *iAfrica*, January 28, 2015. Accessed February 9, 2015. http://news.iafrica.com/worldnews/980374.html.

Jha, Supriya. "Islamic State raid on luxury Libya hotel: American among 10 killed, FBI to investigate." *ZNews*, January 28, 2015. Accessed February 4, 2015. http://zeenews.india.com/news/world/islamic-state-raid-on-luxury-libya-hotel-american-among-10-killed-fbi-to-investigate_1537514.html.

116. Welch, William M. "Egypt launches airstrikes against ISIL in Libya." *USA Today*, February 16, 2015. Accessed February 23, 2015. http://www.usatoday.com/story/news/world/2015/02/16/egypt-airstrikes-isil-libya/23482049/.

117. "Islamic State militants claim attack on embassies in Libya." *Reuters*, April 13, 2015. Accessed April 14, 2015. http://uk.reuters.com/article/2015/04/13/uk-libya-bomb-idUKKBN0N401R20150413.

118. Gambrell, Jon and Merrit Kennedy. "Video: Islamic State kills Ethiopian Christians in Libya." *Miami Herald*, April 19, 2015. Accessed April 19, 2015. http://www.miamiherald.com/news/nation-world/world/article18908868.html.

119. "142 dead in Yemen mosque bombings claimed by the Islamic State." *AFP*, March 21, 2015. Accessed March 23, 2015. http://www.ndtv.com/world-news/142-dead-in-yemen-mosque-bombings-claimed-by-islamic-state-748392.

120. Ibid. "More fighting, air strikes in Yemen, civilian death toll exceeds 500." *Egypt Independent*, April 24, 2015. Accessed April 25, 2015. http://www.egyptindependent.com/news/more-fighting-air-strikes-yemen-civilian-death-toll-exceeds-550.

121. Kajjo, Sirwan. "The fight for Raqqa." *Syria in Crisis*, June 3, 2014. Accessed October 28, 2014. http://carnegieendowment.org/syriaincrisis/?fa=55782. Paraszczuk, Joanna. "Syria: How did Raqqa fall to the Islamic State & ash-Sham? (Syria Untold)." *EA Worldwide*. January 14, 2014. Accessed October 30, 2014. http://eaworldview.com/2014/01/raqqa-fall-islamic-state-iraq-ash-sham-syria-untold/.

Balkiz, Ghazi and Alexander Smith. "What life is like inside ISIS' capital city of Raqqa, Syria." *NBC News*. September 25, 2014. Accessed October 30, 2014. http://www.nbcnews.com/storyline/isis-terror/what-life-inside-isis-capital-city-raqqa-syria-n211206.

122. Balkiz, Ghazi and Alexander Smith. "What life is like inside ISIS' capital city of Raqqa, Syria." *NBC News*, September 25, 2014. Accessed October 30, 2014. http://www.nbcnews.com/storyline/isis-terror/what-life-inside-isis-capital-city-raqqa-syria-n211206. Aarja, Hadill. "ISIS enforces strict religious law in Raqqa." *Al-Monitor*, March 21, 2014. Accessed October 30, 2014. http://www.al-monitor.com/pulse/security/2014/03/isis-enforces-islamic-law-raqqa-syria.html.

"Scenes from daily life in the defacto capital of Isis." *Vanity Fair*, October 6, 2014. Accessed October 15, 2014. http://www.vanityfair.com/politics/2014/10/raqqa-syria-isis-daily-life.

123. Pizzi, Michael. "Syrian rebels hold a cautionary tale as ISIL rises in Iraq." *Al Jazeera America*, June 28, 2014. Accessed October 26, 2014. http://america.aljazeera.com/articles/2014/6/26/isil-iraq-syria.html. Dark, Edward. "US strikes in Syria won't turn locals against Islamic State." *Al Monitor*, September 16, 2014. Accessed October 26, 2014. http://www.al-monitor.com/pulse/ru/originals/2014/09/syrians-support-islamic-state-refuse-us-strike.html.

Al Fares, Ziad. "Frontline Isis: How the Islamic State is brainwashing children with Stone Age school curriculum." *International Business Times*, September 1, 2014. Accessed October 16, 2014. http://www.ibtimes.co.uk/frontline-isis-how-islamic-state-brainwashing-children-stone-age-school-curriculum-1463474.

"Iran cuts off man's hand for stealing." *Guardian*, October 24, 2014. Accessed November 3, 2014. http://www.theguardian.com/world/2010/oct/24/iran-thief-hand-cut-off.

124. Kuruvilla, Carol. "Syrian extremists reportedly live-tweeted the amputation of a thief's hand." *NY Daily News*, February 28, 2014. Accessed November 10, 2014. http://www.nydailynews.com/news/world/syrian-extremists-reportedly-live-tweeted-amputation-thief-hand-article-1.1706824.

125. "Scenes from daily life in the defacto capital of isis." *Vanity Fair*. October 6, 2014. Accessed October 15, 2014. http://www.vanityfair.com/politics/2014/10/raqqa-syria-isis-daily-life.

126. "Sunni rebels declare new 'Islamic caliphate.'" *Al-Jazeera*, June 30, 2014. Accessed October 21, 2014. http://www.aljazeera.com/news/middleeast/2014/06/isil-declares-new-islamic-caliphate-201462917326669749.html. Tran, Mark. "Who are Isis? A terror group too extreme even for al-Qaida." *Guardian*, June 11, 2014. Accessed October 21, 2014. http://www.theguardian.com/world/2014/jun/11/isis-too-extreme-al-qaida-terror-jihadi

Siegel, Jacob. "Islamic extremists are now crucifying peole in Syria—and tweeing out the pictures." *Daily Beast,* April 30, 2014. Accessed October 30, 2014. http://www.thedailybeast.com/articles/2014/04/30/islamic-extremists-now-crucifying-people-in-syria-and-tweeting-out-the-pictures.html.

127. "Islamic State: Can its savagery be explained?" *BBC News,* September 9, 2014. Accessed February 4, 2015. http://www.bbc.com/news/world-middle-east-29123528.

128. Weaver, Mary Anne. "The short, violent life of Abu Musab al-Zarqawi." *Atlantic*, July 1, 2006. Accessed October 21, 2014. http://www.theatlantic.com/magazine/archive/2006/07/the-short-violent-life-of-abu-musab-al-zarqawi/304983/2/.

129. McClam, Erin. "Rising star of ISIS has Chechen background and fierce reputation." *NBC News*, July 2, 2014. Accessed October 21, 2014. http://www.nbcnews.com/storyline/iraq-turmoil/rising-star-isis-has-chechen-background-fierce-reputation-n146466.

130. Burgess, Joe, Gregor Aisch, C.J. Chivers, Alicia Parlapiano, Sergio Peçanha, Archie Tse, Derek Watkins, and Karen Yourish. "How ISIS works." *NY Times*, September 15, 2014. Accessed October 19, 2014. http://www.nytimes.com/interactive/2014/09/16/world/middleeast/how-isis-works.html.

131. Al-Hashimi, Hisham. "Revealed: The Islamic State 'cabinet,' from finance minister to suicide bomb deployer." *Telegraph*, July 9, 2014. Accessed October 21, 2014. http://www.telegraph.co.uk/news/worldnews/middleeast/iraq/10956193/Revealed-the-Islamic-State-cabinet-from-finance-minister-to-suicide-bomb-deployer.html.

132. Hall, Benjamin. "'You want to kill': ISIS deserter recounts training, torture and terror." *Foxnews.com*, November 6, 2014. Accessed November 26, 2014. http://www.foxnews.com/world/2014/11/06/want-to-kill-isis-deserter-recounts-training-torture-and-terror/.

133. "Boys of war: ISIS recruit, kidnap children as young as 10." *RT*, July 2, 2014. Accessed October 21, 2014. http://rt.com/news/170052-isis-kidnap-recruit-children/.

134. Roggio, Bill and Caleb Weiss, "Jihadist training camps proliferate in Iraq and Syria." *Long War Journal*, October 24, 2014. Accessed October 27, 2014. http://www.longwarjournal.org/archives/2014/10/jihadist_training_ca.php.

135. Hall, Benjamin. "'You want to kill': ISIS deserter recounts training, torture and terror." *Foxnews.com*, November 6, 2014. Accessed November 26, 2014. http://www.foxnews.com/world/2014/11/06/want-to-kill-isis-deserter-recounts-training-torture-and-terror/.

136. Hassan, Hassan, "The secret world of Isis training camps—ruled by sacred texts and the sword." *Guardian*, January 24, 2015. Accessed February 4, 2015. http://www.theguardian.com/world/2015/jan/25/inside-isis-training-camps.

137. Ibid.

138. Brannen, Kate. "Children of the Caliphate." *Foreign Policy*, October 24, 2014. Accessed February 6, 2015. http://foreignpolicy.com/2014/10/24/children-of-the-caliphate/.

139. Adnan, Duraid and Tim Arango. "Suicide bomb trainer in Iraq accidentally blows up his class." *New York Times*, February 10, 2014. Accessed October 20, 2014. http://www.nytimes.com/2014/02/11/world/middleeast/suicide-bomb-instructor-accidentally-kills-iraqi-pupils.html?_r=1.

140. Altman, Howard. "Jihadi e-book advises sleeper cells." *Tampa Bay Tribune,* March 30, 2015. http://tbo.com/list/military-news/jihadi-ebook-advises-sleeper-cells-20150330/.

141. Ibid.

142. "Iraq." Conflict Encyclopedia. Uppsala Universitet. Accessed October 29, 2014. http://www.ucdp.uu.se/gpdatabase/gpcountry.php?id=77&regionSelect=10-Middle East#.

143. Hall, Benjamin. "'You want to kill': ISIS deserter recounts training, torture and terror." *Foxnews.com*, November 6, 2014. Accessed November 26, 2014. http://www.foxnews.com/world/2014/11/06/want-to-kill-isis-deserter-recounts-training-torture-and-terror/.

144. "Exclusive: Islamic State guides Egyptian militants, expanding its influence." *Reuters*, September 5, 2014. Accessed October 21, 2014. http://www.reuters.com/article/2014/09/05/us-egypt-islamicstate-idUSKBN0H018F20140905.

145. Sly, Liz. "The hidden hand behind the Islamic State's militants? Saddam Hussein's." *Washington Post*. April 4, 2015. Accessed April 4, 2015. http://www.washingtonpost.com/world/middle_east/the-hidden-hand-behind-the-islamic-state-militants-saddam-husseins/2015/04/04/aa97676c-cc32-11e4-8730-4f473416e759_story.html?hpid=z1.

146. U.S. State Department, "Chapter 6, Foreign Terrorist Organizations." *Country Reports on Terrorism 2013*, April 2014. Accessed September 20, 2014. http://www.state.gov/j/ct/rls/crt/2013/224829.htm.

147. Ibid.

148. Ibid.

149. Jones, Sam. "Iraq crisis: Sophisticated tactics key to Isis strength." *Financial Times*. June 26, 2014. Accessed November 2, 2014. http://www.ft.com/intl/cms/s/0/6436f754-fd18-11e3-bc93-00144feab7de.html#axzz3Ii2TcyLC.

150. Ibid.

151. Ibid.

152. Ibid.

153. Ibid.

154. Ibid.

155. Abbas, Mushreq. "ISIS 'hit and run' tactics reveal Iraqi security weaknesses." *Al Monitor*, June 9, 2014. Accessed October 6, 2014. http://www.al-monitor.com/pulse/originals/2014/06/iraq-isis-new-tactic-mosul.html#ixzz3JJ7ub66F.

156. Bilger, Alex. "Annual reports reveal a metrics-drive military command." Institute for the Study of War, May 22, 2014. Accessed October 21, 2014. http://www.understandingwar.org/sites/default/files/ISWBackgrounder_ISIS_Annual_Reports_0.pdf. Vick, Karl and Aryn Baker. "Extremists in Iraq continue march towards Baghdad." *Time*, June 11, 2014. Accessed October 21, 2014. http://time.com/2859454/iraq-tikrit-isis-baghdad-mosul/.

157. Bilger, Alex. "Annual reports reveal a metrics-drive military command." Institute for the Study of War, May 22, 2014. Accessed October 21, 2014. http://www.understandingwar.org/sites/default/files/ISWBackgrounder_ISIS_Annual_Reports_0.pdf.

158. MacKenzie, Drew. "How ragtag ISIS became military machine." *Newsmax*, August 28, 2014. Accessed November 11, 2014. http://www.newsmax.com/Newsfront/ISIS-military-tactics-resources/2014/08/28/id/591385/.

159. Vick, Karl and Aryn Baker. "Extremists in Iraq continue march towards Baghdad." *Time*, June 11, 2014. Accessed October 21, 2014. http://time.com/2859454/iraq-tikrit-isis-baghdad-mosul/.

160. Meek, James Gordon. "ISIS an 'incredible' fighting force, US special ops sources say." *ABC News*, August 25, 2014. Accessed November 10, 2014. http://abcnews.go.com/Blotter/isis-incredible-fighting-force-us-special-ops-sources/story?id=25116463.

161. Ibid.

162. Hall, Benjamin. "'You want to kill': ISIS deserter recounts training, torture and terror." *Foxnews.com*, November 6, 2014. Accessed November 26, 2014. http://www.foxnews.com/world/2014/11/06/want-to-kill-isis-deserter-recounts-training-torture-and-terror/.

163. Cockburn, Patrick. "Battle to establish Islamic state across Iraq and Syria." *Independent*, June 9, 2014. Accessed October 21, 2014. http://www.independent.co.uk/news/world/middle-east/battle-to-establish-islamic-state-across-iraq-and-syria-9510044.html.

164. "Militants 'kill 60' in ambush on Iraq prison convoy." *BBC News*, July 24, 2014. Accessed October 20, 2014. http://www.bbc.com/news/world-middle-east-28459360.

165. Salman, Raheem and Isra' Al-Rubei'i. "Fifty-three blindfolded bodies found in Iraq as political leaders bicker." *Reuters*, July 9, 2014. Accessed October 20, 2014. http://www.reuters.com/article/2014/07/09/us-iraq-security-idUSKBN0FE1UE20140709.

166. Sly, Liz. "Islamic State fighters kill dozens of Yazidi villagers." *Washington Post*, August 16, 2014. Accessed October 20, 2014. http://www.washingtonpost.com/world/middle_east/yazidis-killed-in-kocho-near-sinjar-after-obama-calls-off-rescue-mission/2014/08/15/31478a3c-e46e-4c4c-8406-d0f27073a308_story.html .

167. "Activists: Jihadis Close to North Syria Army Base." *Epoch Times*, August 18, 2014. Accessed October 29, 2014. http://m.theepochtimes.com/n3/887702-activists-jihadis-close-to-north-syria-army-base/. "Islamic State group 'executes 700' in Syria." *Al-Jazeera*, August 17, 2014. Accessed October 20, 2014. http://www.aljazeera.com/news/middleeast/2014/08/islamic-state-group-executes-700-syria-2014816123945662121.html.

168. "Iraq blast targeting Shiites kills at least 10." *Al Arabiya*, November 2, 2014. Accessed November 20, 2014. http://english.alarabiya.net/en/News/middle-east/2014/11/01/Islamic-State-kills-85-more-members-of-Iraqi-tribe.html. Georgy, Micahel. "Iraq says 322 tribe members killed, many bodies dumped in well." *Reuters*, November 2, 2014. Accessed November 20, 2014. http://www.reuters.com/article/2014/11/02/us-mideast-crisis-iraq-idUSKBN0IM0I920141102.

169. Pamuk, Humeyra. "Yazidis haunted by cries for help as militants bury victims alive." *Reuters*, August 18, 2014. Accessed October 21, 2014. http://www.reuters.com/article/2014/08/18/us-iraq-security-yazidis-idUSKBN0GI1QK20140818. Cockburn, Patrick. "Playing with Fire: Why Private Gulf Financing for Syria's Extremist Rebels Risk Igniting Sectarian Conflict at Home." The Brookings Project on U.S Relations with the Islamic World, December, 2013. Accessed October 21, 2014. http://www.brookings.edu/~/media/research/files/papers/2013/12/06%20private%20gulf%20financing%20syria%20extremist%20rebels%20sectarian%20conflict%20dickinson/private%20gulf%20financing%20syria%20extremist%20rebels%20sectarian%20conflict%20dickinson.pdf.

170. Abdulrahim, Raja. "Islamic State fighters capture military base in Syria, behead soldiers." *LA Times*, July 25, 2014. Accessed October 20, 2014. http://www.latimes.com/world/middleeast/la-fg-islamic-state-military-base-syria-20140725-story.html.

171. Salman, Raheem. "Islamic State militants stone man to death in Iraq: witness." *Reuters*, August 22, 2014. Accessed October 20, 2014. http://www.reuters.com/article/2014/08/22/us-iraq-security-stoning-idUSKBN0GM0Q820140822.

172. "Miraculous survival of Syrian woman 'stoned for adultery'." *TVNZ*, January 31, 2015. Accessed February 18, 2015. http://tvnz.co.nz/world-news/miraculous-survival-syrian-woman-stoned-adultery-6226609.

173. "Islamic State group reportedly throws homosexuals off roof as punishment." *Ynet*, January 18, 2015. Accessed February 4, 2015. http://www.ynetnews.com/articles/0,7340,L-4616171,00.html.

174. Pleasance, Chris. "ISIS police sentence musicians to 90 lashes because they were playing an 'un-Islamic' electronic keyboard." *Daily Mail*, January 20, 2015. Accessed February 6, 2015. http://www.dailymail.co.uk/news/article-2918061/ISIS-police-sentence-musicians-lashes-playing-Islamic-electonic-keyboard.html.

175. Mamoun, Abdelhak. "ISIS executes 13 Iraqis for watching football game between Iraq and Jordan in Mosul." *Iraqi News*, January 22, 2015. Accessed February 23, 2015. http://www.iraqinews.com/iraq-war/isis-executes-13-iraqis-watching-football-game-iraq-jordan-mosul/.

176. bin Mahmud, Shaykh Hussayn. "The question of beheadings." Jihadology, August 19, 2013. Accessed October 21, 2014. http://jihadology.net/2014/08/20/new-article-from-shaykh-%E1%B8%A5ussayn-bin-ma%E1%B8%A5mud-the-question-of-beheadings/.

177. Ward, Clarissa. "ISIS too extreme for the extremists?" *CBS News*, September 5, 2014. Accessed October 21, 2014. http://www.cbsnews.com/news/isis-european-jihadist-tells-clarissa-ward-why-he-left-syria/.

178. "New ISIS video shows beheading of American hostage Peter Kassig." *Fox News*, November 16, 2014. Accessed November 16, 2014. http://www.foxnews.com/world/2014/11/16/new-isis-video-purportedly-shows-beheading-american-hostage-peter-kassig/.

179. "Profile of British hostage David Haines." *BBC News*, September 14, 2014. Accessed September 15, 2014. http://www.bbc.com/news/uk-29086517. "Alan Henning 'killed by the Islamic State.'" *BBC News*, October 4, 2014. Accessed October 15, 2014. http://www.bbc.com/news/uk-29485405.

180. Ryall, Julian. "Japan PM says photo released by Isil shows dead hostage Haruna Yukawa." *Telegraph*, January 25, 2015. Accessed February 18, 2015. http://www.telegraph.co.uk/news/worldnews/islamic-state/11368118/Japan-PM-says-photo-released-by-Isil-shows-dead-hostage-Haruna-Yukawa.html.

181. Baker, Aryn. "Isis claims massacre of 1,700 Iraqi soldiers." *Time,* June 15, 2014. Accessed October 18, 2014. http://time.com/2878718/isis-claims-massacre-of-1700-iraqis/. Greene, Leonard. "Syrian soldiers march to their death in ISIS massacre." *NY Post*, August 28, 2014. Accessed October 17, 2014. http://nypost.com/2014/08/28/syrian-soldiers-march-to-their-death-in-isis-massacre/.

182. Tharoor, Ishaan. "Saudi Arabia, key to Obama's strategy, beheaded at least 8 people last month." *Washington Post*. September 11, 2014. Accessed September 16, 2014. http://www.washingtonpost.com/blogs/worldviews/wp/2014/09/11/saudi-arabia-key-to-obamas-strategy-beheaded-at-least-8-people-last-m. Joshi, Shashank. "Where does the Islamic State's fetish with beheading people come from?" *Telegraph*. September 14, 2014. Accessed October 25, 2014. http://www.telegraph.co.uk/news/worldnews/middleeast/syria/11071276/Where-does-the-Islamic-States-fetish-with-beheading-people-come-from.html.

183. Zimmerman, Jonathan. "Practice of beheading not limited to the Islamic State." *LA Times,* September 28, 2014. Accessed October 25, 2014. http://www.latimes.com/opinion/op-ed/la-oe-zimmerman-beheading-history-20140929-story.html. Tharoor, Ishaan. "Saudi Arabia, key to Obama's strategy, beheaded at least 8 people last month." *Washington Post*. September 11, 2014. Accessed September 16, 2014. http://www.washingtonpost.com/blogs/worldviews/wp/2014/09/11/saudi-arabia-key-to-obamas-strategy-beheaded-at-least-8-people-last-month/.

Di Giovanni, Janine. "When it comes to beheadings, ISIS has nothing over Saudi Arabia." *Newsweek*, October 14, 2014. Accessed October 25, 2014. http://www.newsweek.com/2014/10/24/when-it-comes-beheadings-isis-has-nothing-over-saudi-arabia-277385.html.

184. McGeough, Paul. "The Saudis are every bit as sickening as Islamic State." *Sydney Morning Herald*, January 22, 2015. Accessed February 18, 2015. http://www.smh.com.au/world/the-saudis-are-every-bit-as-sickening-as-islamic-state-20150122-12v32g.html.

185. Gubash, Charlene and Alexander Smith. "ISIS beheadings and Saudi punishments: 'difference is clear.'" *NBC News*, February 2, 2015. Accessed February 18, 2015. http://www.nbcnews.com/news/world/isis-beheadings-saudi-punishments-difference-clear-n296876.

186. Ibid.

187. McGeough, Paul. "The Saudis are every bit as sickening as Islamic State." *Sydney Morning Herald*, January 22, 2015. Accessed February 13, 2015. http://www.smh.com.au/world/the-saudis-are-every-bit-as-sickening-as-islamic-state-20150122-12v32g.html.

188. Semple, Kirk. Yazidi girls seized by ISIS speak out after escape. *NY Times*, November 14, 2014. Accessed November 16, 2014. http://www.nytimes.com/2014/11/15/world/middleeast/yazidi-girls-seized-by-isis-speak-out-after-escape.html?google_editors_picks=true&_r=0.

189. Malm, Sara. "Nine-year-old sex slave is pregnant by 10 ISIS militants raping her, says aid worker." *Daily Mail*, April 12, 2015. Accessed April 13, 2015. http://www.dailymail.co.uk/news/article-3035577/Nine-year-old-sex-slave-pregnant-10-ISIS-militants-raping-says-aid-worker.html.

190. Buchanan, Rose Troup. "Isis fighters barter over Yazidi girls on 'slave market day'—the shocking video." *Independent*, November 3, 2014. Accessed November 4, 2014. http://www.independent.co.uk/news/world/middle-east/isis-fighters-barter-over-yazidi-girls-on-slave-market-day--the-shocking-video-9836589.html. Varghese, Johnlee. "Shocking: ISIS official 'slave' price list shows Yazidi, Christian girls aged '1 to 9' being sold for $172." *International Business Times*, November 5, 2014. Accessed November 7, 2014. http://www.ibtimes.co.in/shocking-isis-official-slave-price-list-shows-yazidi-christian-girls-aged-1-9-being-sold-613160.

191. Varghese, Johnlee. "Shocking: ISIS official 'slave' price list shows Yazidi, Christian girls aged '1 to 9' being sold for $172." *International Business Times*, November 5, 2014. Accessed November 7, 2014. http://www.ibtimes.co.in/shocking-isis-official-slave-price-list-shows-yazidi-christian-girls-aged-1-9-being-sold-613160.

192. Ibid.

193. Evans, Dominic and Maggie Fick. "U.N. accuses Islamic State of executions, rape, forced child recruitment in Iraq." *Reuters*, July 18, 2014. Accessed October 20, 2014. http://www.reuters.com/article/2014/07/18/us-iraq-security-idUSKBN0FN27N20140718.

194. "Islamic State school closures in Syria affect 670,000: U.N." *Reuters*, January 6, 2015. Accessed February 23, 2015. http://www.reuters.com/article/2015/01/06/us-mideast-crisis-syria-unicef-idUSKBN0KF13720150106.

195. Griffin, Jennifer. "Iraq militants changing tactics, complication US aitrstrike mission." *Fox News*, August 12, 2014. Accessed October 21, 2014. http://www.foxnews.com/politics/2014/08/12/iraq-militants-changing-tactics-complicating-us-airstrike-mission/.

196. "Will air strikes spell change in Islamic State's tactics?" *First Post*, September 19, 2014. Accessed October 21, 2014. http://www.firstpost.com/world/will-air-strikes-spell-change-in-islamic-states-tactics-1720839.html.

197. Salman, Raheem and Yara Bayoumy. "Wary of air strikes, ISIS militants change tactics." *Al-Arabiya*, September 27, 2014. Accessed October 21, 2014. http://english.alarabiya.net/en/perspective/analysis/2014/09/27/Wary-of-air-strikes-ISIS-militants-change-tactics.html.

198. Piggot, Mark. "Isis tells Iraqi Christians: convert, pay 'jihad tax' or face death." *International Business Times,* July 19, 2014. Accessed October 21, 2014. http://www.ibtimes.co.uk/isis-tells-iraqi-christians-convert-pay-jihad-tax-face-death-1457376.

199. Jalabi, Raya. "Who are the Yazidis and why is Isis hunting them?" *Guardian*, August 11, 2014. Accessed October 21, 2014. http://www.theguardian.com/world/2014/aug/07/who-yazidi-isis-iraq-religion-ethnicity-mountains.

200. Kokab, Farshori. "UN: Minorities in Iraq Threatened by Islamic State." *Voice of America*, August 6, 2014. Accessed October 21, 2014. http://www.voanews.com/content/un-says-minorities-in-iraq-threatened-by-islamic-state/1973195.html. Jones, Sam and Owen Bowcott. "Religious leaders say Isis persecution of Iraqi Christians has become genocide." *Guardian*, August 8, 2014. Accessed October 21, 2014. http://www.theguardian.com/world/2014/aug/08/isis-persecution-iraqi-christians-genocide-asylum.

Chulov, Martin. "Iraq's largest Christian town abandoned as Isis advance continues." *Guardian*, August 7, 2014. Accessed October 21, 2014. http://www.theguardian.com/world/2014/aug/07/isis-offensive-iraq-christian-exodus.

201. Jones, Sam and Owen Bowcott "Religious leaders say Isis persecution of Iraqi Christians has become genocide." *Guardian*, August 8, 2014. Accessed October 21, 2014. http://www.theguardian.com/world/2014/aug/08/isis-persecution-iraqi-christians-genocide-asylum. Arraf, Jane. "Islamic State persecution of Yazidi minority amounts to genocide, UN says." *Christian Science Monitor*, August 7, 2014. Accessed October 21, 2014. http://www.csmonitor.com/World/Middle-East/2014/0807/Islamic-State-persecution-of-Yazidi-minority-amounts-to-genocide-UN-says-video.

202. Doyle, Chris. "ISIS wants a five-star ticket to pulicity. It gets it. *Al-Arabiya*, August 27, 2014. Accessed October 21, 2014. http://english.alarabiya.net/en/views/news/middle-east/2014/08/27/ISIS-wants-a-five-star-ticket-to-publicity-It-gets-it-.html.

203. Keneally, Meghan. "Here cop who shot Okla. beheading suspect was also company exec." *ABC News*, September 26, 2014. Accessed October 21, 2014. http://abcnews.go.com/US/hero-cop-shot-attacker-beheaded-colleague-company-exec/story?id=25790102. "Australia raids over 'Islamic State plot to behead.'" *BBC News*, September 18, 2014. Accessed October 21, 2014. http://www.bbc.com/news/world-asia-29245611.

204. Mozes, N. "Syrian Heritage Sites, Holy Places Destroyed In Civil War." Memri, January 14, 2014. Accessed October 21, 2014. http://www.memri.org/report/en/print7747.htm.

205. Crompton, Paul. "Grand Theft Auto: ISIS? Militants reveal video game." *Al-Arabiya*, September 20, 2014. Accessed October 21, 2014. http://english.alarabiya.net/en/variety/2014/09/20/Grand-Theft-Auto-ISIS-Militants-reveal-video-game.html. Yan, Holly. "Showing off its crimes: How ISIS flaunts its brutality as propaganda." *CNN*, September 4, 2014. Accessed October 21, 2014. http://www.cnn.com/2014/09/04/world/meast/isis-terror-as-propaganda/.

Hubbard, Ben and Shane Scott."ISIS Displaying a Deft Command of Varied Media" *NY Times*, August 30, 2014. Accessed October 21, 2014. http://www.nytimes.com/2014/08/31/world/middleeast/isis-displaying-a-deft-command-of-varied-media.html.

206. Rose, Steve. "The Isis propaganda machine: hi-tech media jihad." *Guardian*, October 7, 2014. Accessed October 9, 2014. http://www.theguardian.com/world/2014/oct/07/isis-media-machine-propaganda-war.

207. Ajballi, Mustapha. "How ISIS conquered social media." *Al Arabiya News*, June 24, 2014. Accessed October 9, 2014. http://english.alarabiya.net/en/media/digital/2014/06/24/How-has-ISIS-conquered-social-media-.html.

208. Abramson, Daniel. "Islamic State Online: Jihadist Propaganda 2.0." *Geopolitical Monitor*, September 23, 2014. Accessed October 21, 2014. http://www.geopoliticalmonitor.com/islamic-state-online-jihadist-propaganda-2-0/. Schmidt, Michael. "Canadian killed in Syria lives On as pitchman for jihadis." *NY Times*, July 15, 2014. Accessed October 21, 2014. http://www.nytimes.com/2014/07/16/world/middleeast/isis-uses-andre-poulin-a-canadian-convert-to-islam-in-recruitment-video.html.

209. Masi, Alessandria. "ISIS recruiting Westerners: How the 'Islamic State' goes after non-Muslims and recent converts in the West" *International Business Times*. September 8, 2014. Accessed October 21, 2014. http://www.ibtimes.com/isis-recruiting-westerners-how-islamic-state-goes-after-non-muslims-recent-converts-west-1680076.

210. Verkaik, Robert. "Islamic State sniper: ISIS sets up sharp-shooter battalion inspired by infamous Iraqi killer who took out 40 Americans in Baghdad." *Daily Mail*, January 28, 2015. Accessed February 4, 2015. http://www.dailymail.co.uk/news/article-2928652/Iraqi-Sniper-ISIS-posts-pictures-sniper-battalion-inspired-Chris-Kyle-s-notorious-insurgent-rival-Juba-killed-40-Americans-Baghdad.html?utm_content=bufferb9a04&utm_medium=social&utm_source=twitter.com&utm_campaign=buffer.

211. Ibid.

212. Ibid.

213. Gibbons-Neff, Thomas. "ISIS propaganda videos show their weapons, skills in Iraq." *Washington Post*, June 18, 2014. Accessed October 21, 2014. http://www.washingtonpost.com/news/checkpoint/wp/2014/06/18/isis-propaganda-videos-show-their-weapons-skills-in-iraq/.

214. Simcox, Robin. "Understanding the Islamic State." Henry Jackson Society, September 4, 2014. Accessed October 21, 2014. http://henryjacksonsociety.org/wp-content/uploads/2014/10/Understanding-the-Islamic-State.pdf.

215. Bender, Jeremy. "As ISIS routes the Iraqi army, here's a look at what the jihadists have in their arsenal." *Business Insider,* July 8, 2014. Accessed October 21, 2014. http://www.businessinsider.com/isis-military-equipment-breakdown-2014-7?op=1#t-55-tanks-1. Gibbons-Neff, Thomas. "ISIS propaganda videos show their weapons, skills in Iraq." *Washington Post*, June 18, 2014. Accessed October 21, 2014. http://www.washingtonpost.com/news/checkpoint/wp/2014/06/18/isis-propaganda-videos-show-their-weapons-skills-in-iraq/.

Tilghman, Andrew and Jeff Schogol. "How did 800 ISIS fighters rout 2 Iraqi divisions?" *Military Times*, June 12, 2014. Accessed October 21, 2014. http://www.militarytimes.com/article/20140612/NEWS08/306120062/How-did-800-ISIS-fighters-rout-2-Iraqi-divisions-.

216. Kreiter, Marcy. "ISIS-captured U.S. humvees being shipped to al Qaeda rebels in Syria." *International Business Times*, June 22, 2014. Accessed October 21, 2014. http://www.ibtimes.com/isis-captured-us-humvees-being-shipped-al-qaeda-rebels-syria-1608432.

217. Gertz, Bill. "ISIL moving seized U.S. tanks, humvees to Syria." *Free Beacon*, June 17, 2014. Accessed October 21, 2014. http://freebeacon.com/national-security/isil-moving-seized-u-s-tanks-humvees-to-syria/.

218. Yacoub, Sameer N and Adam Schreck. "Militants overrun most of major Iraqi city." *Associated Press*, June 10, 2014. Accessed October 21, 2014. http://bigstory.ap.org/article/iraq-militants-seize-provincial-hq-mosul-city.

219. Gertz, Bill. "ISIL moving seized U.S. tanks, humvees to Syria." *Free Beacon*, June 17, 2014. Accessed October 21, 2014. http://freebeacon.com/national-security/isil-moving-seized-u-s-tanks-humvees-to-syria/.

220. Ibid.

221. Beaumont, Peter. "How effective is Isis compared with the Iraqi Army and Kurdish peshmerga?." *Guardian*, June 12, 2014. Accessed October 21, 2014. http://www.theguardian.com/world/2014/jun/12/how-battle-ready-isis-iraqi-army-peshmerga.

222. Ibid.

223. Gertz, Bill. "ISIL moving seized U.S. tanks, humvees to Syria." *Free Beacon*, June 17, 2014. Accessed October 21, 2014. http://freebeacon.com/national-security/isil-moving-seized-u-s-tanks-humvees-to-syria/.

224. Doornbos, Harald and Jenan Moussa. "Found: The Islamic State's terror laptop of doom." *Foreign Policy Magazine*, August 28, 2014. Accessed October 21, 2014. http://www.foreignpolicy.com/articles/2014/08/28/found_the_islamic_state_terror_laptop_of_doom_bubonic_plague_weapons_of_mass_destruction_exclusive.

225. Rush, James. "'Terrorist groups' in Iraq have seized nuclear materials from university, U.N. is warned." *Daily Mail*, July 10, 2014. Accessed October 21, 2014. http://www.dailymail.co.uk/news/article-2687290/Militants-seize-nuclear-materials-university-Iraq-United-Nations-warned.html. "Iraq rebels 'seize nuclear materials.'" *BBC News*, July 10, 2014. Accessed October 21, 2014. http://www.bbc.com/news/world-middle-east-28240140.

226. "US concerned extremists could get undeclared Syrian chemical weapons." *Voice of America News*, September 4, 2014. Accessed October 21, 2014. http://www.voanews.com/content/us-concerned-extremists-could-get-undeclared-syrian-chemical-weapons/2439343.html.

227. "A look at dangers posed by ISIS." *Al-Arabiya*, September 2, 2014. Accessed October 21, 2014. http://english.alarabiya.net/en/perspective/features/2014/09/02/A-look-at-dangers-posed-by-ISIS-.html.

228. "Why the Islamic State represents a dangerous turn in the terror threat." *Wall Street Journal*, August 18, 2014. Accessed October 21, 2014. http://online.wsj.com/articles/capital-journal-why-isis-represents-a-dangerous-threat-1408382052.

229. "Islamic State in Iraq and Syria." Mapping Militant Organizations. Stanford University. Accessed October 29, 2014. http://web.stanford.edu/group/mappingmilitants/cgi-bin/groups/view/1#note71.

230. "Profile of British hostage David Haines." *BBC News*, September 14, 2014. Accessed September 15, 2014. http://www.bbc.com/news/uk-29086517. "Alan Henning 'killed by the Islamic State.'" *BBC News*, October 4, 2014. Accessed October 15, 2014. http://www.bbc.com/news/uk-29485405.

231. "ISIS-linked Algeria group beheads Frenchman" *Al-Arabiya*, September 24, 2014. Accessed October 21, 2014. http://english.alarabiya.net/en/News/middle-east/2014/09/24/ISIS-linked-group-beheads-Frenchman-Gourdel-Video.html. Walt, Vivienne. "Frenchman's beheading raises fears of wider fight against ISIS." *Time*, September 25, 2014. Accessed November 4, 2014. http://time.com/3429815/france-isis-beheading/.

232. Ryall, Julian. "Japan PM says photo released by Isil shows dead hostage Haruna Yukawa." *Telegraph*, January 25, 2015. Accessed February 18, 2015. http://www.telegraph.co.uk/news/worldnews/islamic-state/11368118/Japan-PM-says-photo-released-by-Isil-shows-dead-hostage-Haruna-Yukawa.html.

233. Landler, Mark and Eric Schmitt. "ISIS says it killed Steven Sotloff after U.S. strikes in northern Iraq." *NY Times*, September 2, 2014. Accessed October 22, 2014. http://www.nytimes.com/2014/09/03/world/middleeast/steven-sotloff-isis-execution.html.

234. Rasheed, Ahmed and Michael Georgy. "Islamic State video purports to show beheading of U.S. journalist." *Reuters*, August 19, 2014. Accessed October 22, 2014. http://www.reuters.com/article/2014/08/19/us-iraq-security-idUSKBN0GH0JL20140819.

235. "Pentagon provides statement on rescue operation." U.S. Department of Defense, August 20, 2014. Accessed October 22, 2014. http://www.defense.gov/news/newsarticle.aspx?id=122974.

236. Allen, Nick and Philip Sherwell. "Hunt for 'British' Islamic State killer of US journalist James Foley." *Telegraph*, August 20, 2014. Accessed October 21, 2014. http://www.telegraph.co.uk/news/worldnews/middleeast/iraq/11044977/Hunt-for-British-Islamic-State-killer-of-US-journalist-James-Foley.html.

237. Callimachi, Rukmini. "Before killing James Foley, ISIS demanded ransom from U.S." *NY Times*, August 20, 2014. Accessed October 21, 2014. http://www.nytimes.com/2014/08/21/world/middleeast/isis-pressed-for-ransom-before-killing-james-foley.html.

238. Bakr, Amena. "Qatar seeks to free more U.S. hostages in Syria: source." *Reuters*, August 26, 2014. Accessed October 21, 2014. http://www.reuters.com/article/2014/08/26/us-syria-crisis-qatar-usa-idUSKBN0GQ0JW20140826. Goldman, Adam and Karen DeYoung. "Qatar played now-familiar role in helping to broker U.S. hostage's release." *Washington Post*, August 25, 2014. Accessed October 21, 2014. http://www.washingtonpost.com/world/national-

security/american-executive-former-fbi-agent-and-qataris-sought-to-free-peter-theo-curtis/
2014/08/25/43d24bac-2c85-11e4-9b98-848790384093_story.html.

239. "Militants use British killer as propaganda." *Boston Herald*, August 20, 2014. Accessed October 21, 2014. http://bostonherald.com/news_opinion/international/europe/2014/08/british_fighter_appears_to_have_role_in_beheading.

240. Maclean, William. "Islamic State issues video of beheading of U.S. hostage." *Reuters*, September 2, 2014. Accessed October 21, 2014. http://www.reuters.com/article/2014/09/02/us-iraq-crisis-islamicstate-video-idUSKBN0GX20R20140902.

241. "ISIS militants behead captive Lebanese soldier, video shows." *Al-Arabiya*, August 30, 2014. Accessed October 21, 2014. http://english.alarabiya.net/en/News/middle-east/2014/08/30/ISIS-militants-behead-captive-Lebanese-soldier-video.html. Karouny, Mariam. "Islamic State militants behead captive Lebanese soldier: video." *Reuters*, August 30, 2014. Accessed October 21, 2014. http://www.reuters.com/article/2014/08/30/us-syria-crisis-beheading-idUSKBN0GU0J020140830.

242. Amrieh, Antoine. "Thousands mourn beheaded Lebanese soldier." *Daily Star*, September 3, 2014. Accessed October 21, 2014. http://www.dailystar.com.lb/News/Lebanon-News/2014/Sep-03/269411-gunfire-in-nlebanon-after-beheaded-soldier-identified.ashx#axzz3E99kNDfM.

243. Ibid.

244. "Obama says beheadings will not intimidate US." *Al-Jazeera*, September 3, 2014. Accessed October 21, 2014. http://www.aljazeera.com/news/middleeast/2014/09/obama-says-beheadings-will-not-intimidate-us-201493104158626440.html.

245. "Qatar: Foley beheading 'crime' against Islam's principles." *Al-Arabiya*, August 21, 2014. Accessed October 21, 2014. http://english.alarabiya.net/en/News/middle-east/2014/08/21/Qatar-Foley-beheading-crime-against-Islam-s-principles.html.

246. Ryall, Julian. "Japan PM says photo released by Isil shows dead hostage Haruna Yukawa." *Telegraph*, January 25, 2015. Accessed February 18, 2015. http://www.telegraph.co.uk/news/worldnews/islamic-state/11368118/Japan-PM-says-photo-released-by-Isil-shows-dead-hostage-Haruna-Yukawa.html.

247. Sherlock, Ruth. "Isil hostage murder casts doubts on prisoner swap." *Irish Independent*, February 2, 2015. Accessed February 18, 2015. http://www.independent.ie/world-news/asia-pacific/isil-hostage-murder-casts-doubts-on-prisoner-swap-30955845.html.

248. "Jordan says ready to release Iraqi militant if pilot released." *Al Arabiya*, January 28, 2015. Accessed February 18, 2015. http://english.alarabiya.net/en/News/middle-east/2015/01/28/Jordan-says-ready-to-release-Iraqi-militant-if-pilot-released.html.

249. Pansieri, Flavia. "Address by Ms. Flavia Pansieri, United Nations Deputy High Commissioner for Human Rights to the Human Rights Council's Special Session on Iraq." UN Human Rights, September 1, 2014. Accessed October 21, 2014. http://www.ohchr.org/EN/NewsEvents/Pages/DisplayNews.aspx?NewsID=14980&LangID=E#sthash.mzsi4qsZ.dpuf.

250. Ibid.

251. Ibid.

252. "Escape from Hell—Torture, Sexual Slavery in Islamic State Captivity in Iraq." *Amnesty International*, December 22, 2014. Accessed December 27, 2014. http://www.amnestyusa.org/research/reports/escape-from-hell-torture-sexual-slavery-in-islamic-state-captivity-in-iraq.

253. Ibid.

254. Ibid.

255. Botelho, Greg. "ISIS: Enslaving, having sex with 'unbelieving' women, girls is OK." *CNN*, December 13, 2014. Accessed December 15, 2014. http://www.cnn.com/2014/12/12/world/meast/isis-justification-female-slaves/.

256. Salih, Mohammed A. and Wladimir van Wigenburg. "Iraqi Yazidis: 'If we move they will kill us.'" Al-Jazeera, August 5, 2014. Accessed October 21, 2014. http://www.aljazeera.com/news/middleeast/2014/08/iraqi-yazidis-if-move-they-will-kill-us-20148513656188206.html.

257. Lockhart, Keely. "Islamic State video shows conversion of Yazidi men to Islam." *Telegraph*, August 21, 2014. Accessed October 21, 2014. http://www.telegraph.co.uk/news/

worldnews/middleeast/iraq/11048298/Islamic-State-video-shows-conversion-of-Yazidi-men-to-Islam.html.

258. Ibid.

259. Salih, Mohammed A. and Wladimir van Wigenburg. "Iraqi Yazidis: 'If we move they will kill us.'" *Al-Jazeera*, August 5, 2014. Accessed October 21, 2014. http://www.aljazeera.com/news/middleeast/2014/08/iraqi-yazidis-if-move-they-will-kill-us-20148513656188206.html. "ISIS militants tell 300 Yazidi families to convert or die." *Huffington Post*, August 9, 2014. Accessed October 21, 2014. http://www.huffingtonpost.com/2014/08/09/isis-yazidis_n_5664586.html.

260. "Iraq: 150 women executed after refusing to marry ISIL militants." Anadolu Agency, December 16, 2014. Accessed December 18, 2014. http://www.turkishpress.com/news/415983/.

261. Ibid.

262. Ibrahim, Raymond. "Islamic jizya: 'protection' from whom?" *American Thinker*, August 3, 2014. Accessed October 21, 2014. http://www.americanthinker.com/2014/08/islamic_jizya_protection_from_whom.html. Phillips Erb, Kelly. "Islamic State warns Christians: convert, pay tax, leave or die." *Forbes*, July 19, 2014. Accessed October 21, 2014. http://www.forbes.com/sites/kellyphillipserb/2014/07/19/islamic-state-warns-christians-convert-pay-tax-leave-or-die/.

263. Khayat, M. "The Islamic State's treatment of Christians." MEMRI, August 14, 2014. Accessed October 21, 2014. http://www.memrijttm.org/the-islamic-states-iss-treatment-of-christians.html.

264. Cousins, Sophie. "Christians flee Mosul amid threats to convert or die." *USA Today*, July 29, 2014. Accessed October 21, 2014. http://www.usatoday.com/story/news/world/2014/07/29/mosul-iraq-christians/13238013/.

265. Krohn, Jonathan. "Has last Christian left Iraqi city of Mosul after 2,000 years?" *NBC News*, July 27, 2014. Accessed October 21, 2014. http://www.nbcnews.com/storyline/iraq-turmoil/has-last-christian-left-iraqi-city-mosul-after-2-000-n164856. Otten, Cathy. "Last remaining Christians flee Iraq's Mosul." *Al-Jazeera*, July 22, 2014. Accessed October 21, 2014. http://www.aljazeera.com/news/middleeast/2014/07/last-remaining-christians-flee-iraq-mosul-201472118235739663.html.

266. Salama, Vivian. "Islamic State militants execute female Iraqi human rights activist." *Huffington Post*, September 25, 2014. Accessed October 21, 2014. http://www.huffingtonpost.com/2014/09/25/samira-nuaimi-killed_n_5880900.html?cps=gravity.

267. Cousins, Sophie. "Christians flee Mosul amid threats to convert or die." *USA Today*, July 29, 2014. Accessed October 21, 2014. http://www.usatoday.com/story/news/world/2014/07/29/mosul-iraq-christians/13238013/.

268. Khayat, M. "The Islamic State's treatment of Christians." MEMRI, August 14, 2014. Accessed October 21, 2014. http://www.memrijttm.org/the-islamic-states-iss-treatment-of-christians.html. Cousins, Sophie. "Christians flee Mosul amid threats to convert or die." *USA Today*, July 29, 2014. Accessed October 21, 2014. http://www.usatoday.com/story/news/world/2014/07/29/mosul-iraq-christians/13238013/.

269. Khayat, M. "The Islamic State's Treatment Of Christians." MEMRI, August 14, 2014. Accessed October 21, 2014. http://www.memrijttm.org/the-islamic-states-iss-treatment-of-christians.html.

270. Ibid. Cousins, Sophie. "Christians flee Mosul amid threats to convert or die." *USA Today*, July 29, 2014. Accessed October 21, 2014. http://www.usatoday.com/story/news/world/2014/07/29/mosul-iraq-christians/13238013/.

271. Wagner, Meg. "'I had a great will to live': Lone survivor of ISIS massacre that killed as many as 560 played dead to escape terrorists." *NY Daily*, September 4, 2014. Accessed October 21, 2014. http://www.nydailynews.com/news/world/lone-survivor-isis-massacre-played-dead-report-article-1.1927471. Moore, Jack. "Iraqi soldier survives Isis' Tikrit massacre by pretending to be dead." *International Business Times*, September 4, 2014. Accessed October 21, 2014. http://www.ibtimes.co.uk/iraqi-soldier-survives-isis-tikrit-massacre-by-pretending-be-dead-1463992.

Chapter 2

Greene, Leonard. "Syrian soldiers march to their death in ISIS massacre." *New York Post,* August 28, 2014. Accessed November 4, 2014. http://nypost.com/2014/08/28/syrian-soldiers-march-to-their-death-in-isis-massacre/.

272. Greene, Leonard. "Syrian soldiers march to their death in ISIS massacre." *New York Post*, August 28, 2014. Accessed October 21, 2014. http://nypost.com/2014/08/28/syrian-soldiers-march-to-their-death-in-isis-massacre/. Bloom, Dan. "Marched to their deaths: Sickening ISIS slaughter continues as 250 soldiers captured at Syrian airbase are stripped then led to the desert for mass execution." *Daily Mail*, August 28, 2014. Accessed October 21, 2014. http://www.dailymail.co.uk/news/article-2736764/Marched-deaths-Sickening-ISIS-slaughter-continues-250-soldiers-captured-Syrian-airbase-stripped-led-desert-mass-execution.html.

273. Salaheddin, Sinan. "HRW: ISIS killed 770 Iraqi troops." *Daily Star*, September 3, 2014. Accessed October 21, 2014. http://www.dailystar.com.lb/ArticlePrint.aspx?id=269417&mode=print.

274. Ibid.

275. "ICC at a glance." ICC Online. International Criminal Court. Accessed October 29, 2014. http://www.icc-cpi.int/en_menus/icc/about%20the%20court/icc%20at%20a%20glance/Pages/icc%20at%20a%20glance.aspx. "Frequently asked questions." ICC Online. International Criminal Court. Accessed October 29, 2014. http://www.icc-cpi.int/en_menus/icc/about%20the%20court/frequently%20asked%20questions/pages/faq.aspx.

276. "Universal jurisdiction." International Justice Resource Center. Accessed October 21, 2014. http://www.ijrcenter.org/cases-before-national-courts/domestic-exercise-of-universal-jurisdiction. "Universal Jurisdiction." Learn About Human Rights. Amnesty International. Accessed October 29, 2014. http://www.amnesty.org/en/international-justice/issues/universal-jurisdiction.

277. Elsea, Jennifer K. "Suits against terrorist states by victims of terrorism." CRS Report for Congress, August 8, 2008. Accessed October 21, 2014. http://fas.org/sgp/crs/terror/RL31258.pdf. Goldsmith, Jack and Ryan Goodman. "U.S Civil Litigation and International Terrorism." Civil Litigation Against Terrorism. Edited by John Norton Moore. Carolina Academic Press. 2004. Accessed October 21, 2014. http://www.law.harvard.edu/faculty/rgoodman/pdfs/US_Civil_Litigation_n_International_Terrorism.pdf.

Schupack, Adam N. "The Arab-Israeli conflict and civil litigation against terrorism." 60 *Duke Law Journal* 207 (2000). Accessed October 21, 2014. http://scholarship.law.duke.edu/cgi/viewcontent.cgi?article=1475&context=dlj.

Savage, Charlie. "Terror suit against Jordanian bank tests U.S. diplomacy and secrecy laws." *NY Times*, April 1, 2014. Accessed October 21, 2014. http://www.nytimes.com/2014/04/02/us/terror-suit-against-jordanian-bank-tests-us-diplomacy-and-secrecy-laws.html?_r=0.

"Case docket: Hate and extremism cases." Southern Poverty Law Center. Accessed October 21, 2014. http://www.splcenter.org/get-informed/case-docket?keys=&agenda=21&landmark=All.

278. "About 2000 people killed by Islamic State since the establishment of 'Caliphate.'" Syrian Observatory for Human Rights. December 28, 2014. Accessed December 29, 2014. http://syriahr.com/en/2014/12/about-2000-people-killed-by-islamic-state-since-the-establishment-of-caliphate/.

279. Ibid.

280. Ibid.

281. Ibid.

282. Ibid.

283. Aarja, Hadil. "ISIS enforces strict religious law in Raqqa." *Al Monitor,* March 21, 2014. Accessed October 30, 2014. http://www.al-monitor.com/pulse/security/2014/03/isis-enforces-islamic-law-raqqa-syria.html#.

284. "ISIS kidnaps 50 men in Iraq's Kirkuk region." *Daily Star*, May 9, 2014. Accessed October 21, 2014. http://www.dailystar.com.lb/ArticlePrint.aspx?id=269633&mode=print.; "'ISIS commits mass murder, advertises it': Iraq executions detailed." *RT*, June 27, 2014. http://rt.com/news/168916-isis-iraq-war-crimes/.

285. "ISIS kidnaps 50 men in Iraq's Kirkuk region." *Daily Star*, May 9, 2014. Accessed October 21, 2014. http://www.dailystar.com.lb/ArticlePrint.aspx?id=269633&mode=print.

286. Pansieri, Flavia. "Address by Ms. Flavia Pansieri, United Nations Deputy High Commissioner for Human Rights to the Human Rights Council's Special Session on Iraq." UN Human Rights, September 1, 2014. Accessed October 21, 2014. http://www.ohchr.org/EN/NewsEvents/Pages/DisplayNews.aspx?NewsID=14980&LangID=E.

287. Salama, Vivian. "Islamic State militants execute female Iraqi human rights activist." *Huffington Post*, September 25, 2014. Accessed October 21, 2014. http://www.huffingtonpost.com/2014/09/25/samira-nuaimi-killed_n_5880900.html?cps=gravity.

288. Sarhan, Amre. "ISIS executes three of its leaders for cowardice in Diyali" *Iraqi News*, February 23, 2013. Accessed February 24, 2015. www.iraqinews.com/iraq-war/isis_executes_three_leaders_cowardice_diyali./.

289. Chulov, Martin. "How an arrest in Iraq revealed Isis's $2bn jihadist network." *Guardian*, June 15, 2014. Accessed October 21, 2014. http://www.theguardian.com/world/2014/jun/15/iraq-isis-arrest-jihadists-wealth-power.

290. "Islamic State group sets out first budget, worth $2bn." *Al-Araby*, January 4, 2015. Accessed January 11, 2015. http://www.alaraby.co.uk/english/news/2015/1/4/islamic-state-group-sets-out-first-budget-worth-2bn.

291. "Attacking ISIL's financial foundation." Remarks of Under Secretary for Terrorism and Financial Intelligence David S. Cohen at the Carnegie Endowment for International Peace, October 23, 2014. Accessed October 28, 2014. http://www.treasury.gov/press-center/press-releases/Pages/jl2672.aspx.

292. Financial Action Task Force. *Financing of the terrorist organization Islamic State of Iraq and the Levant (ISIL)*, Financial Action Task Force, February 2015, Accessed March 15, 2015. http://www.fatf-gafi.org/media/fatf/documents/reports/Financing-of-the-terrorist-organisation-ISIL.pdf.

293. Ibid.

294. Chuvlov, Martin. "How an arrest in Iraq revealed Isis's $2bn jihadist network." *Guardian*, June 15, 2014. Accessed October 21, 2014. http://www.theguardian.com/world/2014/jun/15/iraq-isis-arrest-jihadists-wealth-power.

295. Khalaf, Roula and Sam Jones. "Selling terror: how Isis details its brutality." *Financial Times*, June 17, 2014. Accessed October 21, 2014. http://www.ft.com/intl/cms/s/2/69e70954-f639-11e3-a038-00144feabdc0.html?—ftcamp=crm/email/2014617/nbe/AsiaMorningHeadlines/product#axzz3AIZZptiX.

296. Laub, Zachary. "Islamic State in Iraq and Syria." Council on Foreign Relations, August 8, 2014. Accessed October 21, 2014. http://www.cfr.org/iraq/islamic-state-iraq-syria/p14811.

297. Financial Action Task Force. "Financing of the terrorist organization Islamic State of Iraq and the Levant (ISIL)." February 2015. Accessed March 15, 2015. http://www.fatf-gafi.org/media/fatf/documents/reports/Financing-of-the-terrorist-organisation-ISIL.pdf.

298. Ibid.Cockburn, Patrick. "Iraq crisis: How Saudi Arabia helped Isis take over the north of the country." *Independent*, July 13, 2014. Accessed October 21, 2014. http://www.independent.co.uk/voices/comment/iraq-crisis-how-saudi-arabia-helped-isis-take-over-the-north-of-the-country-9602312.html.

299. Cockburn, Patrick. "Playing with fire: Why private gulf financing for Syria's extremist rebels risk igniting sectarian conflict at home." The Brookings Project on U.S Relations with the Islamic World, December, 2013. Accessed October 21, 2014. http://www.brookings.edu/~/media/research/files/papers/2013/12/06%20private%20gulf%20financing%20syria%20extremist%20rebels%20sectarian%20conflict%20dickinson/private%20gulf%20financing%20syria%20extremist%20rebels%20sectarian%20conflict%20dickinson.pdf.

300. Rogin, Josh. "America's allies are funding ISIS." *Daily Beast*, June 14, 2014. Accessed October 21, 2014. http://www.thedailybeast.com/articles/2014/06/14/america-s-allies-are-funding-isis.html.

301. Windrem, Robert. "Who is funding ISIS? Wealthy Gulf 'angel investors,' officials say." *NBC News*, September 21, 2014. Accessed November 10, 2014. http://www.nbcnews.com/storyline/isis-terror/whos-funding-isis-wealthy-gulf-angel-investors-officials-say-n208006.

302. Cary, Glenn and Deema Almashabi. "Jihadi recruitment in Riyadh revives Saudi Arabia's greatest fear." *Bloomberg*, June 16, 2014. Accessed October 21, 2014. http://www.

bloomberg.com/news/2014-06-15/jihadis-recruitment-drive-in-riyadh-revives-biggest-saudi-threat.html.

303. "Qatar financing ISIS jihadists: German minister." *Daily Star*, August 20, 2014. Accessed October 21, 2014. http://www.dailystar.com.lb/News/Middle-East/2014/Aug-20/267815-qatar-financing-isis-jihadists-german-minister.ashx#axzz3AwfNltC2. "Germany says regrets any offense caused by Qatar-IS link comments." *Reuters*, August 22, 2014. Accessed October 21, 2014. http://www.reuters.com/article/2014/08/22/us-iraq-security-germany-qatar-idUSKBN0GM0SX20140822.

304. "Treasury designates Iranian Ministry of Intelligence and Security for Human Rights Abuses and Support for Terrorism." The United States Department of Treasury, February 6, 2012. Accessed October 21, 2014. http://www.treasury.gov/press-center/press-releases/Pages/tg1424.aspx.

305. Laub, Zachary and Jonathon Masters. "Islamic State in Iraq and Syria." Council on Foreign Relations, August 8, 2014. Accessed October 21, 2014. http://www.cfr.org/iraq/islamic-state-iraq-syria/p14811.

306. Financial Action Task Force. "Financing of the terrorist organization Islamic State of Iraq and the Levant (ISIL)." February 2015. Accessed March 15, 2015. http://www.fatf-gafi.org/media/fatf/documents/reports/Financing-of-the-terrorist-organisation-ISIL.pdf.

307. "Attacking ISIL's financial foundation." Remarks of Under Secretary for Terrorism and Financial Intelligence David S. Cohen at The Carnegie Endowment For International Peace, October 23, 2014. Accessed October 28, 2014. http://www.treasury.gov/press-center/press-releases/Pages/jl2672.aspx .

308. Ibid.

309. Holmes, Oliver. "Al Qaeda breaks link with Syrian militant group ISIL." *Reuters*, February 3, 2014. Accessed October 21, 2014. http://www.reuters.com/article/2014/02/03/us-syria-crisis-qaeda-idUSBREA120NS20140203.

310. Davidson, Janine. "In Iraq/Syria conflict, the Islamic State leverages international community's self-imposed boundaries." Council on Foreign Relations, August 12, 2014. Accessed October 21, 2014. http://blogs.cfr.org/davidson/2014/08/12/in-iraqsyria-conflict-the-islamic-state-leverages-international-communitys-self-imposed-boundaries/.

311. Rago, Joseph. "Inside the war against the Islamic State." *Wall Street Journal*, December 26, 2014. Accessed December 27, 2014. http://www.wsj.com/articles/joe-rago-inside-the-war-against-islamic-state-1419636790.

312. Kouri, Jim. "ISIS harvesting, selling human organs to fund terrorist operations." Examiner.com, December 20, 2014. Accessed December 26, 2014. http://www.examiner.com/article/isis-harvesting-selling-human-organs-to-fund-terrorist-operations.

313. Ibid.

314. Laub, Zachary and Jonathon Masters. "Islamic State in Iraq and Syria." Council on Foreign Relations, August 8, 2014. Accessed October 21, 2014. http://www.cfr.org/iraq/islamic-state-iraq-syria/p14811. "Attacking ISIL's Financial Foundation." Remarks of Under Secretary for Terrorism and Financial Intelligence David S. Cohen at The Carnegie Endowment For International Peace, October 23, 2014. Accessed October 28, 2014. http://www.treasury.gov/press-center/press-releases/Pages/jl2672.aspx.

315. Dreazen, Yochi. "Isis uses mafia tactics to fund its own operations without help from the Persian Gulf." *Foreign Policy*, June 23, 2014. Accessed October 21, 2014. http://complex.foreignpolicy.com/posts/2014/06/16/isis_uses_mafia_tactics_to_fund_its_own_operations_without_help_from_persian_gulf_d. "Remarks of Under Secretary Cohen at CSIS." US Department of the Treasury, June 2, 2014. Accessed October 21, 2014. http://www.treasury.gov/press-center/press-releases/Pages/jl2415.aspx.

316. "Attacking ISIL's Financial Foundation." Remarks of Under Secretary for Terrorism and Financial Intelligence David S. Cohen at The Carnegie Endowment For International Peace, October 23, 2014. Accessed October 28, 2014. http://www.treasury.gov/press-center/press-releases/Pages/jl2672.aspx.

317. Financial Action Task Force. "Financing of the terrorist organization Islamic State of Iraq and the Levant (ISIL)." February 2015, Accessed March 15, 2015. http://www.fatf-gafi.org/media/fatf/documents/reports/Financing-of-the-terrorist-organisation-ISIL.pdf.

318. "Islamic State sought $132 million ransom for journalist." *Voice of America*, August 21, 2014. Accessed October 21, 2014. http://www.voanews.com/content/islamic-state-sought-ransom-for-journalist/2423730.html.

319. Bello, Marisol. "Kidnapping Westerners is big business." *USA Today*, August 21, 2014. Accessed October 21, 2014. http://www.usatoday.com/story/news/world/2014/08/20/james-foley-islamic-state-kidnapping/14350483/.

320. "Two Italian aid workers abducted in Syria freed." *DNA*, January 16, 2015. Accessed February 18, 2015. http://www.dnaindia.com/world/report-two-italian-aid-workers-abducted-in-syria-freed-2053076.

321. "'No ransom' hostage policy: Our view." *USA Today*, September 3, 2014. Accessed October 21, 2014. http://www.usatoday.com/story/opinion/2014/09/02/isis-hostage-ransom-beheading-kidnapping-editorials-debates/14986203/. Black, Ian and Julian Borger. "British government faces dilemma by refusing to pay hostage ransoms to Isis." *Guardian*, September 2, 2014. Accessed October 21, 2014. http://www.theguardian.com/world/2014/sep/02/british-government-dilemma-refusing-pay-hostage-ransom-isis.

Taylor, Adam. "The logic of not paying ransoms." *Washington Post*, August 21, 2014. Accessed October 21, 2014. http://www.washingtonpost.com/blogs/worldviews/wp/2014/08/21/the-logic-of-not-paying-ransoms/.

322. "Japan considers ransom as IS threatens 2 hostages." *News & Record*, January 21, 2015. Accessed February 18, 2015. http://www.news-record.com/japan-considers-ransom-as-is-threatens-hostages/article_89100889-4011-56ee-b249-e47c5ae2a2f3.html. "Fate of two Japanese held hostage by IS uncertain after ransom deadline expires." *South China Morning Post*, January 23, 2015. Accessed February 18, 2015. http://www.scmp.com/news/asia/article/1689791/mother-japanese-captive-asks-islamic-state-his-release-ransom-deadline.

323. "Japan outraged at IS 'beheading' of hostage Kenji Goto." *BBC News*, February 1, 2015. Accessed February 4, 2015. http://www.bbc.com/news/world-middle-east-31075769.

324. "Kayla Mueller's dad tells 'Today' show: Policy trumped lives." *Townhall*, February 22, 2015. Accessed Februay 22, 2015. http://townhall.com/news/politics-elections/2015/02/22/kayla-muellers-dad-tells-today-show-policy-trumped-lives-n1960703.

325. Bell, Alistair. "Islamic State 'sentenced' U.S. hostage to death last year: activist." *Reuters*, February 7, 2015. Accessed February 21, 2015. http://www.reuters.com/article/2015/02/07/us-mideast-crisis-hostage-idUSKBN0LA1YQ20150207.

326. Allam, Hannah. "Records show how Iraqi extremists withstood U.S. anti-terror efforts." *McClatchy DC*, June 23, 2014. Accessed October 21, 2014. http://www.mcclatchydc.com/2014/06/23/231223/records-show-how-iraqi-extremists.html.

327. Caulderwood, Kathleen. "Mosul bank robbery isn't the only thing funding ISIS." *International Business Times*, June 13, 2014. Accessed October 21, 2014. http://www.ibtimes.com/mosul-bank-robbery-isnt-only-thing-funding-isis-1601124. Arraf, Jane. "Al Qaeda in Iraq faces serious financial crunch." *Christian Science Monitor*, July 2, 2010. Accessed October 21, 2014. http://web.stanford.edu/group/mappingmilitants/cgi-bin/groups/view/1#note27.

328. Chuvlov, Martin. "How an arrest in Iraq revealed Isis's $2bn jihadist network." *Guardian*, June 15, 2014. Accessed October 21, 2014. http://www.theguardian.com/world/2014/jun/15/iraq-isis-arrest-jihadists-wealth-power.

329. "U.S. official doubts ISIS Mosul bank heist windfall." *NBC News*, June 24, 2014. Accessed October 21, 2014. http://www.nbcnews.com/storyline/iraq-turmoil/u-s-official-doubts-isis-mosul-bank-heist-windfall-n139846.

330. Moore, Jack. "Mosul seized: Jihadis loot $429m from city's Central Bank to make Isis world's richest terror force." *International Business Times*, June 11, 2014. Accessed October 21, 2014. http://www.ibtimes.co.uk/mosul-seized-jihadis-loot-429m-citys-central-bank-make-isis-worlds-richest-terror-force-1452190.

331. "Islamic State group sets out first budget, worth $2bn." *Al-Araby*, January 4, 2015. Accessed January 11, 2015. http://www.alaraby.co.uk/english/news/2015/1/4/islamic-state-group-sets-out-first-budget-worth-2bn.

332. Chuvlov, Martin. "How an arrest in Iraq revealed Isis's $2bn jihadist network." *Guardian*, June 15, 2014. Accessed October 21, 2014. http://www.theguardian.com/world/2014/jun/15/iraq-isis-arrest-jihadists-wealth-power.

333. Macias, Amanda and Jeremy Bender. "Here is how the world's richest terrorist group makes millions every day." *Business Insider,* August 27, 2014. Accessed October 26, 2014. http://www.businessinsider.com/isis-worlds-richest-terrorist-group-2014-8.

Financial Action Task Force. "Financing of the terrorist organization Islamic State of Iraq and the Levant (ISIL)." February 2015, Accessed March 15, 2015. http://www.fatf-gafi.org/media/fatf/documents/reports/Financing-of-the-terrorist-organisation-ISIL.pdf.

334. Kouri, Jim. "ISIS harvesting, selling human organs to fund terrorist operations." *Examiner.com*, December 20, 2014. Accessed December 26, 2014. http://www.examiner.com/article/isis-harvesting-selling-human-organs-to-fund-terrorist-operations.

335. Mamoun, Abdelhak. "ISIS offers to hand over Kurdish fighters bodies in exchange for $20,000 for each." *Iraqi News*, February 23, 2015. Accessed February 22, 2015. http://www.iraqinews.com/features/isis-offers-hand-kurdish-fighters-bodies-exchange-20000/.

336. Financial Action Task Force. "Financing of the terrorist organization Islamic State of Iraq and the Levant (ISIL)." February 2015. Accessed March 15, 2015. http://www.fatf-gafi.org/media/fatf/documents/reports/Financing-of-the-terrorist-organisation-ISIL.pdf.

337. Chulov, Martin. "Isis to mint own Islamic dinar coins in gold, silver and copper." *Guardian*, November 14, 2014. Accessed November 15, 2014. http://www.theguardian.com/world/2014/nov/14/isis-gold-silver-copper-islamic-dinar-coins.

338. Ibid.

339. "Attacking ISIL's Financial Foundation." Remarks of Under Secretary for Terrorism and Financial Intelligence David S. Cohen at The Carnegie Endowment For International Peace, October 23, 2014. Accessed October 28, 2014. http://www.treasury.gov/press-center/press-releases/Pages/jl2672.aspx.

340. Financial Action Task Force. "Financing of the terrorist organization Islamic State of Iraq and the Levant (ISIL)." February 2015. Accessed March 15, 2015. http://www.fatf-gafi.org/media/fatf/documents/reports/Financing-of-the-terrorist-organisation-ISIL.pdf.

341. "ISIS recruits fighters through powerful online campaign." *CBS News*, August 29, 2014. Accessed October 21, 2014. http://www.cbsnews.com/news/isis-uses-social-media-to-recruit-western-allies/. Herridge, Catherine. "US official: Number of foreign fighters in Syria spikes." *Fox News*, July 25, 2014. Accessed October 21, 2014. http://www.foxnews.com/politics/2014/07/25/us-intelligence-officials-situation-in-syria-greater-and-more-complex/.

Miller, Jake. "U.S. officials estimate over 20,000 foreign fighters are aiding extremists." *CBS News*, February 11, 2015. Accessed February 19, 2015. http://www.cbsnews.com/news/u-s-officials-estimate-over-20000-foreign-fighters-aiding-extremists/.

342. Hennigan, W.J. "Islamic State's media-savvy mlitants spread message with ease." *Los Angeles Times*, August 30, 2014. Accessed October 21, 2014. http://www.latimes.com/world/middleeast/la-fg-isis-propaganda-20140831-story.html.

343. Karadsheh, Jomana, Jim Sciutoo and Laura Smith-Spark. "How foreign fighters are swelling ISIS ranks." *CNN*, September 14, 2014. Accessed October 21, 2014. http://www.cnn.com/2014/09/12/world/meast/isis-numbers/."Foreign fighters still flowing to Syria, U.S. intelligence says." *Reuters*, February 10, 2015. Accessed February 19, 2015. http://uk.reuters.com/article/2015/02/10/uk-mideast-crisis-fighters-idUKKBN0LE2YF20150210.

344. "Friday Sermon in Spain: 'Allah, Destroy the Plundering Jews, Do Not Spare a Single One.'" MEMRI TV. Middle East Media Institute TV Monitoring Project. August 25, 2014. Accessed October 29, 2014. http://www.memritv.org/clip/en/4448.htm.

345. Ghribi, Asma. "Tunisia struggles to cope with returnees from Syrian jihad." *Foreign Policy*, September 12, 2014. Accessed September 28, 2014. http://foreignpolicy.com/2014/09/12/tunisia-struggles-to-cope-with-returnees-from-syrian-jihad/.

346. Hall, Benjamin. "'You want to kill': ISIS deserter recounts training, torture and terror." *Foxnews.com*, November 6, 2014. Accessed November 26, 2014. http://www.foxnews.com/world/2014/11/06/want-to-kill-isis-deserter-recounts-training-torture-and-terror/.

347. Masi, Alessandria. "ISIS Recruiting Westerners: How The 'Islamic State' Goes After Non-Muslims And Recent Converts In The West." *International Business Times,* September 8, 2014. Accessed October 21, 2014. http://www.ibtimes.com/isis-recruiting-westerners-how-islamic-state-goes-after-non-muslims-recent-converts-west-1680076.

348. Trowbridge, Alexander. "Jihadists on the move in Iraq with weapons, hashtags." *CBS News*, June 16, 2014. Accessed October 21, 2014. http://www.cbsnews.com/news/isis-jihadists-on-move-in-iraq-using-weapons-and-twitter-hashtags/.

349. Hall, John. "ISIS militants produce slick weekly magazine packed with English language Islamist propaganda designed to recruit and radicalize would-be extremists in the West." *Daily Mail*, June 25, 2014. Accessed October 21, 2014. http://www.dailymail.co.uk/news/article-2668912/ISIS-militants-produce-slick-weekly-magazine-packed-English-language-Islamist-propaganda-designed-recruit-radicalise-extremists-West.html.

350. Taylor, Adam. "Mysterious 'Islamic State TV channel' appears online." *Washington Post*, January 16, 2015. Accessed February 18, 2015. http://www.washingtonpost.com/blogs/worldviews/wp/2015/01/16/mysterious-islamic-state-tv-channel-appears-online/?tid=hpModule_04941f10-8a79-11e2-98d9-3012c1cd8d1e&hpid=z11.

351. Ibid.

352. Ibid.

353. "The ISIS gift shop: T-shirts and hoodies sold online." *Al-Arabiya*, June 24, 2014. Accessed October 21, 2014. http://english.alarabiya.net/en/variety/2014/06/24/The-ISIS-gift-shop-T-shirts-and-hoodies-now-sold-online.html.Dana, Joseph. "The Jihadi Gift Show." *Slate*, August 8, 2014. Accessed October 21, 2014. http://www.slate.com/articles/news_and_politics/roads/2014/08/need_an_isis_hoodie_the_world_s_most_notorious_terrorist_group_has_a_gift.html.

Culzac, Natasha. "Dress like a jihadist: Isis and terror-related merchandise flogged online and in Indonesian stores." *Independent*, June 24, 2014. Accessed October 21, 2014. http://www.independent.co.uk/news/world/middle-east/dress-like-a-jihadist-isis-and-terrorrelated-merchandise-flogged-online-and-in-indonesian-stores-9560230.html.

354. Barrett, Richard. "Foreign Fighters in Syria." The Soufan Group, June 2014. Accessed October 21, 2014. http://soufangroup.com/wp-content/uploads/2014/06/TSG-Foreign-Fighters-in-Syria.pdf.

355. Ibid.

356. Dehn, Sharon. "ISIS Militants Use 'Jihadi Cool' to Recruit Globally." *Voice of America*, September 5, 2014. October 21, 2014. http://www.voanews.com/content/isis-militants-use-jihadi-cool-to-recruit-globally/2440430.html.

357. Walsh, Nick. "Syrian jihadists using Twitter to recruit foreign fighters." *CNN*, June 4, 2014. Accessed October 21, 2014. http://www.cnn.com/2014/06/03/world/meast/syria-defector-recruits-westerners/.

358. "The path to jihad and the Islamic State." *Jerusalem Post*, September 6, 2014. Accessed October 21, 2014. http://www.jpost.com/Middle-East/The-path-to-jihad-374571.

359. Shi-Ian, Lee. "Malaysian Militants for ISIS Recruited through Social Media." *Malaysian Insider*, September 22, 2014. Accessed October 29, 2014. http://www.themalaysianinsider.com/malaysia/article/malaysian-militants-for-isis-recruited-through-social-media-says-source. Scott, Alev and Christie-Miller, Alexander. "Exclusive: ISIS starts recruiting in Istanbul's vulnerable suburbs." *Newsweek*, September 12, 2014. Accessed October 21, 2014. http://www.newsweek.com/2014/09/19/exclusive-how-istanbul-became-recruiting-ground-islamic-state-269247.html.

Carey, Glen and Almashabi, Deema. "Jihadi recruitment in Riyadh revives Saudi Arabia's greatest fear." *Bloomberg*, June 16, 2014. Accessed October 21, 2014. http://www.bloomberg.com/news/2014-06-15/jihadis-recruitment-drive-in-riyadh-revives-biggest-saudi-threat.html.

Yeginsusept, Ceylan. "ISIS Draws a Steady Stream of Recruits From Turkey." *NY Times*, September 15, 2014. Accessed October 21, 2014. http://www.nytimes.com/2014/09/16/world/europe/turkey-is-a-steady-source-of-isis-recruits.html.

360. Grossman, Michelle. "WATCH: Islamic State's terror video game." *Jerusalem Post*, September 21, 2014. Accessed October 21, 2014. http://www.jpost.com/Middle-East/IS-claims-it-created-a-terror-video-game-375935.

361. "Sign-language ISIS video looks to snare deaf, mute recruits in Europe." *NBC News*, March 8, 2015. Accessed March12, 2015. http://www.nbcnews.com/storyline/isis-terror/sign-language-isis-video-recruits-deaf-mute-europe-n319631.

362. Hickey, Jennifer. "ISIS Targeting of Western Women May Signal New Role of Female Jihadist." *Newsmax*. August 7, 2014. Accessed October 21, 2014. http://www.newsmax.com/Newsfront/ISIS-jihad-recruitment-Western/2014/08/07/id/587508/.

363. Tanzeem, Ayesha. "Islamic State Recruits Women to Support Its Fight." *Voice of America*. August 27, 2014. Accessed October 21, 2014. http://www.voanews.com/content/islamic-state-recruits-women-to-support-its-fight/2429629.html.

364. Dettmer, Jamie. "The ISIS Online Campaign Luring Western Girls to Jihad." *Daily Beast*, August 6, 2014. Accessed October 21, 2014. http://www.thedailybeast.com/articles/2014/08/06/the-isis-online-campaign-luring-western-girls-to-jihad.html. "ISIS forcing Raqqa women to wed its fighters, say activists." *Asharq Al-Awsat*, February 17, 2014. Accessed October 21, 2014. http://www.aawsat.net/2014/02/article55329041.

365. Dettmer, Jamie. "The ISIS Online Campaign Luring Western Girls to Jihad." *Daily Beast*, August 6, 2014. Accessed October 21, 2014. http://www.thedailybeast.com/articles/2014/08/06/the-isis-online-campaign-luring-western-girls-to-jihad.html. "ISIS forcing Raqqa women to wed its fighters, say activists." *Asharq Al-Awsat*, February 17, 2014. Accessed October 21, 2014. http://www.aawsat.net/2014/02/article55329041.

366. Chastain, Mary. "ISIS Opens Official 'Marriage' Office in Syria, Offers Honeymoons to Jihadist Couples." *Brietbart*. July 28, 2014. Accessed October 21, 2014. http://www.breitbart.com/Big-Peace/2014/07/28/ISIS-Opens-Official-Marriage-Office-in-Syria-Offers-Honeymoons-to-Jihadist-Couples.

367. Shei-Ian, Lee. "Malaysian women join Middle East jihadists as 'comfort women,' reveals intelligence report." *Malaysian Insider*, August 27, 2014. Accessed October 21, 2014. http://www.themalaysianinsider.com/malaysia/article/malaysian-women-join-middle-east-jihadists-as-comfort-women-reveals-intelli. Sridharan, Vasudevan. "'Sexual Jihad': British, Australian and Malaysian Women Going to Iraq as 'Comfort Women' for Isis." *Yahoo News*, August 27, 2014. Accessed October 21, 2014. https://uk.news.yahoo.com/sexual-jihad-british-australian-malaysian-women-going-iraq-100826538.html#LULQNrD.

368. "Islamic State militants open office for potential wives: monitor." *Reuters*, July 28, 2014. Accessed October 21, 2014. http://www.reuters.com/article/2014/07/28/us-syria-crisis-women-idUSKBN0FX1C420140728.

369. Bell, Alistair. "Islamic State attracts female jihadis from U.S. heartland." *Reuters*, September 14, 2014. Accessed October 21, 2014. http://www.reuters.com/article/2014/09/14/us-iraq-crisis-usa-women-idUSKBN0H90DE20140914.

370. Grossman, Michelle. "Report: 60 British women now in Syria in all-female Islamic State brigade." *Jerusalem Post*, September 8, 2014. Accessed October 21, 2014. http://www.jpost.com/Middle-East/Report-60-UK-women-fighting-in-Syria-with-all-female-Islamic-State-police-374761.

371. "Al-Qaeda's new magazine for woman mixes beauty and bomb tips." *Fox News*, March 14, 2011. Accessed October 21, 2014. http://www.foxnews.com/world/2011/03/14/al-qaedas-new-magazine-women-mixes-beauty-bomb-tips/. "Al-Shamikha, Al Qaeda Women's Magazine, Launches: Report" *Huffington Post*, March 14, 2011. Accessed October 21, 2014. http://www.huffingtonpost.com/2011/03/14/al-shamikha-al-qaeda-womens-magazine_n_835572.html.

372. "American teen wears hijab in court as she pleads guilty to charges she tried to join ISIS in Syria." *Daily Mail*, September 10, 2014. Accessed October 21, 2014. http://www.dailymail.co.uk/news/article-2750264/Colorado-woman-set-plead-guilty-terror-case.html. Deam, Jenny. "Colorado woman's quest for jihad baffles neighbors." *LA Times*, July 25, 2014. Accessed October 21, 2014. http://www.latimes.com/nation/la-na-high-school-jihadi-20140726-story.html#page=1.

Charlton, Corey. "Teenage girl jihadists hunted by Interpol inspire first copycats as two more Austrian children try to run away to Syria to join ISIS." *Daily Mail*, September 10, 2014. Accessed October 21, 2014. http://www.dailymail.co.uk/news/article-2750637/Teenage-girl-jihadists-inspire-copycats-try-run-away-Syria-join-ISIS.html.

Squire, Nick. "Austrian teenage girl jihadist 'killed in Syria.'" *Telegraph*, September 15, 2014. Accessed October 21, 2014. http://www.telegraph.co.uk/news/worldnews/europe/austria/11098039/Austrian-teenage-girl-jihadist-killed-in-Syria.html.

Bacchi, Umberto. "Austrian Teenage Jihadi Brides Samra Kesinovic and Sabina Selimovic 'Alive.'" *International Business Times*, September 16, 2014. Accessed October 21, 2014. http://www.ibtimes.co.uk/austrian-teenage-jihadi-brides-samra-kesinovic-sabina-selimovic-alive-1465725.

Yeatman, Dominic. "Meet the British women jihadis fighting for IS." *Metro*, September 7, 2014. Accessed October 21, 2014. http://metro.co.uk/2014/09/07/meet-the-british-women-jihadis-fighting-for-is-4860074/.

"British rocker mom joins ISIS, vows to 'behead Christians with blunt knife.'" *RT*, September 1, 2014. Accessed October 21, 2014. http://rt.com/uk/184212-british-mother-isis-christians/.

Gillman, Ollie. "New picture emerges of British jihadist Sally Jones with partner and new-born baby taken ten years before she joined ISIS." *Daily Mail*, September 12, 2014. Accessed October 21, 2014. http://www.dailymail.co.uk/news/article-2753864/New-picture-emerges-British-jihadist-Sally-Jones-partner-new-born-baby-taken-ten-years-joined-ISIS.html.

Hunter, Chris. "'Why I joined Islamic State': Chatham mum Sally Jones speaks of jihadist mission after moving to Syria with husband Junaid Hussain." *Kent Online*, September 8, 2014. Accessed October 21, 2014. http://www.kentonline.co.uk/medway/news/jihadist-sally-jones-23110/.

Gadher, Dipesh. "'My son and I love life with the beheaders.'" *Sunday Times*, September 7, 2014. Accessed October 21, 2014. http://www.thesundaytimes.co.uk/sto/news/uk_news/National/Terrorism/article1455900.ece.

"White British girl who's now a 'celebrity jihadi': Mother-of-two a 'top priority' for MI6 and she calls on Muslims to join the terror group." *Daily Mail*. September 1, 2014. Accessed October 21, 2014. http://www.dailymail.co.uk/news/article-2739705/White-British-girl-s-celebrity-jihadi-Mother-two-priority-MI6-calls-Muslims-join-terror-group.html.

Herrman, Joshi. "INVESTIGATION: the chilling tale of how a typical Lewisham teen became an Isis bride in Syria." *London Evening Standard*, July 25, 2014. Accessed October 21, 2014. http://www.standard.co.uk/lifestyle/london-life/investigation-the-chilling-tale-of-how-a-typical-lewisham-teen-became-an-isis-bride-in-syria-9628523.html.

373. Banco, Erin. "ISIS Is recruiting child soldiers, committing war crime, as it gains ground in Aleppo," *International Business Times*. August 27, 2014. Accessed October 21, 2014. http://www.ibtimes.com/isis-recruiting-child-soldiers-committing-war-crime-it-gains-ground-aleppo-1671414.

374. "Watch: Bosnian children attend 'ISIS summer camp' in Syria." *Jerusalem Post*, September 16, 2014. Accessed October 21, 2014. http://www.jpost.com/Middle-East/Watch-Bosnian-children-attend-ISIS-summer-camp-in-Syria-375467.

375. "Boys of war: ISIS recruit, kidnap children as young as 10." *RT*, July 2, 2014. Accessed October 21, 2014. http://rt.com/news/170052-isis-kidnap-recruit-children/.

376. Hastings, Deborah. "ISIS recruits children to perform beheadings, shoot rifles, carry out terrorist attacks." *NY Daily News*, August 29, 2014. Accessed October 21, 2014. http://www.nydailynews.com/news/world/isis-training-children-behead-launch-terrorist-attacks-article-1.1921995.

377. "Maybe We Live and Maybe We Die." Human Rights Watch, July 23, 2014. Accessed October 21, 2014. http://www.hrw.org/node/126059/section/2.

378. Ibid.

379. Ibid.

380. Ibid.

381. "Boys of war: ISIS recruit, kidnap children as young as 10." *RT*, July 2, 2014. Accessed October 21, 2014. http://rt.com/news/170052-isis-kidnap-recruit-children/.

382. "Islamic State recruits 400 children since January: Syria monitor." *Reuters*, March 24, 2015. Accessed March 25, 2015. http://wxerfm.com/news/articles/2015/mar/24/islamic-state-recruits-400-children-since-january-syria-monitor/.

383. "ISIS recruits 400 children since January: Report." *Times of India*. March 24, 2015. Accessed March 26, 2015. http://timesofindia.indiatimes.com/world/middle-east/ISIS-recruits-400-children-since-January-Report/articleshow/46675202.cms.

384. Siegel, Jacob. "ISIS is using social media to reach You, its new audience." *Daily Beast*, August 31, 2014. Accessed October 29, 2014. http://www.thedailybeast.com/articles/2014/08/31/isis-s-use-of-social-media-to-reach-you-its-new-audience.html. Bernard, Doug. "ISIL Wages Skilled Social Media War." *Voice of America*, June 18, 2014. Accessed October 21, 2014. http://www.voanews.com/content/isil-wages-skilled-social-media-war/1939505.html.

"The inside story of a Canadian ISIS suicide bomber, as told by Tumblr." *Motherboard*, June 12, 2014. Accessed October 21, 2014. http://motherboard.vice.com/read/the-story-of-a-canadian-isis-suicide-bomber-brought-to-you-by-tumblr.

"Hashtag Terror: How ISIS Manipulates Social Media." Anti-Defamation League. July 11, 2014. Accessed October 21, 2014. http://www.adl.org/combating-hate/international-extremism-terrorism/c/isis-islamic-state-social-media.html.

385. Crane, Emily, Louise Cheer, and Sally Lee. "Terror boss praises convicted terrorist Khaled Sharrouf as 'good, loveable kid' . . . while his 7-year-old holds a severed head." *Daily Mail*, August 11, 2014. Accessed October 21, 2014. http://www.dailymail.co.uk/news/article-2721230/Thats-boy-Australian.

386. "ISIS video shows boy executing alleged Russian spies in Syria." *Syrian Observatory for Human Rights*, January 14, 2015. Accessed February 23, 2015. http://syriahr.com/en/2015/01/isis-video-shows-boy-executing-alleged-russian-spies-in-syria/.

387. Talbott, Elise and Abeer Salman. "New ISIS video claims to show child killing a Palestinian captive." *CNN*, March 11, 2015. Accessed March 14, 2015. http://edition.cnn.com/2015/03/10/middleeast/isis-video-israeli-killed/.

388. Al-Tamimi, Aymenn. "The Dawn of the Islamic State of Iraq and ash-Sham." Current Trends in Islamic Ideology, March 11, 2014. Accessed October 21, 2014. http://www.hudson.org/research/10169-the-dawn-of-the-islamic-state-of-iraq-and-ash-sham.

389. Roggio, Bill. "US targets al Qaeda's al Furqan media wing in Iraq." *Long War Journal*, October 28, 2007. Accessed October 21, 2014. http://www.longwarjournal.org/archives/2007/10/us_targets_al_qaedas.php#.

390. Stone, Jeff. "ISIS attacks Twitter streams, hacks accounts to make jihadi message go viral." *International Business Times*, June 17, 2014. Accessed October 21, 2014. http://www.ibtimes.com/isis-attacks-twitter-streams-hacks-accounts-make-jihadi-message-go-viral-1603842.

391. "ISIS declares Islamic Caliphate, appoints Abu Bakr Al-Baghdadi as 'Caliph,' declares all Muslims must pledge allegiance to him." MEMRI, June 30, 2014. Accessed October 21, 2014. http://www.memri.org/report/en/0/0/0/0/0/0/8049.htm.

392. Robinson, Martin. "Shocking moment British jihadi fighting with Isis in Syria and Iraq stands in front of beheaded man and boasts 'it's what people want to see.'" *Daily Mail*, August 7, 2014. Accessed October 21, 2014. http://www.dailymail.co.uk/news/article-2718816/Shocking-moment-British-jihadi-fighting-Isis-Iraq-stands-beheaded-man-boasts-s-people-want-see.html.

393. Ibid.

394. Luck, Taylor and William Booth. "Islamic State's killing of pilot, depicted in video, spurs calls for revenge in Jordan." *Washington Post*, February 3, 2015. Accessed February 18, 2015. http://www.washingtonpost.com/world/islamic-state-video-purports-to-show-captured-jordanian-pilot-being-burned-to-death/2015/02/03/b5021462-abcc-11e4-ad71-7b9eba0f87d6_story.html.

395. Ibid.

396. Ibid.

397. Sullivan, Kevin and Karla Adam. "Hoping to create a new society, the Islamic State recruits entire families." *Washington Post*. December 24, 2014. Accessed December 30, 2014. http://www.washingtonpost.com/world/national-security/hoping-to-create-a-new-homeland-the-islamic-state-recruits-entire-families/2014/12/24/dbffceec-8917-11e4-8ff4-fb93129c9c8b_story.html?hpid=z3.

398. Mroue, Bassam. "Islamic State fighters admit defeat in Syrian town of Kobani." *Houston Chronicle,* January 31, 2015. Accessed February 4, 2015. http://www.chron.com/news/nation-world/world/article/Islamic-State-fighters-admit-defeat-in-Syrian-6054657.php.

399. "ISIS Propaganda Campaign Threatens U.S.." *Anti-Defamation League Blog*, June 27, 2014. Accessed October 21, 2014. http://blog.adl.org/extremism/isis-propaganda-campaign-threatens-u-s.

400. Macias, Amanda. "ISIS Has A New Twitter Hashtag For Threats Against Americans." *Business Insider*, June 27, 2014. Accessed October 21, 2014. http://www.businessinsider.com/isis-is-using-twitter-to-make-threats-to-us-2014-6. Siegel, David. "ISIS is Using Social Media to Reach YOU, Its New Audience." *Daily Beast*, August 31, 2014. Accessed October 21, 2014. http://www.thedailybeast.com/articles/2014/08/31/isis-s-use-of-social-media-to-reach-you-its-new-audience.html.

Malik, Shiv, Sandra Laville, Elena Cresci and Aisha Gani. "Isis in duel with Twitter and YouTube to spread extremist propaganda." *Guardian*, September 24, 2014. Accessed October 21, 2014. http://www.theguardian.com/world/2014/sep/24/isis-twitter-youtube-message-social-media-jihadi.

401. Tucker, Patrick. "The Islamic State Is Losing the Twitter War." *Defense One*, September 12, 2014. Accessed October 21, 2014. http://www.defenseone.com/technology/2014/09/islamic-state-losing-twitter-war/94031/. "Islamic State shifts to new platforms after Twitter block." *BBC News*, August 21, 2014. Accessed October 21, 2014. http://www.bbc.com/news/world-middle-east-28843350.

402. Tucker, Patrick. "The Islamic State is losing the Twitter war." *Defense One*, September 12, 2014. Accessed October 21, 2014. http://cdn.defenseone.com/defenseone/interstitial.html?v=2.1.1&rf=http%3A%2F%2Fwww.defenseone.com%2Ftechnology%2F2014%2F09%2Fislamic-state-losing-twitter-war%2F94031%2F.

403. Ibid.

404. "ISIS threatens Twitter employees in U.S. and Europe." *Week*, September 9, 2014. Accessed October 21, 2014. http://theweek.com/speedreads/index/267831/speedreads-isis-threatens-twitter-employees-in-us-and-europe.

405. Karam, Joyce. "Shami Witness arrest rattles ISIS' cages on Twitter." *Al-Arabiya*, December 14, 2014. Accessed December 15, 2014. http://english.alarabiya.net/en/perspective/features/2014/12/14/Shami-Witness-arrest-rattles-ISIS-cages-on-Twitter.html. "Unmasked: the man behind top Islamic State Twitter account." *Channel 4 News*, December 11, 2014. Accessed December 12, 2014. http://www.channel4.com/news/unmasked-the-man-behind-top-islamic-state-twitter-account-shami-witness-mehdi.

406. "Unmasked: the man behind top Islamic State Twitter account." *Channel 4 News*, December 11, 2014. Accessed December 12, 2014. http://www.channel4.com/news/unmasked-the-man-behind-top-islamic-state-twitter-account-shami-witness-mehdi.

407. Karam, Joyce. "Shami Witness arrest rattles ISIS' cages on Twitter." *Al-Arabiya*, December 14, 2014. Accessed December 15, 2014. http://english.alarabiya.net/en/perspective/features/2014/12/14/Shami-Witness-arrest-rattles-ISIS-cages-on-Twitter.html.

408. Paraszczuk, Joanna. "English-speaking IS militants laud Charlie Hebdo attackers." *Radio Free Europe Radio Liberty*, January 9, 2015. Accessed February 18, 2015. http://www.rferl.org/content/charlie-hebdo-islamic-state-praise/26785047.html.

409. Macias, Amanda. "ISIS has a new Twitter hashtag for threats against Americans." *Business Insider*, June 27, 2014. Accessed October 21, 2014. http://www.businessinsider.com/isis-is-using-twitter-to-make-threats-to-us-2014-6. Siegel, Jacob. "ISIS is using social media to reach you, its new audience." *Daily Beast*, August 31, 2014. Accessed October 21, 2014. http://www.thedailybeast.com/articles/2014/08/31/isis-s-use-of-social-media-to-reach-you-its-new-audience.html.

Malik, Shiv, Sandra Laville, Elena Cresci and Aisha Gani. "Isis in duel with Twitter and YouTube to spread extremist propaganda." *Guardian*, September 24, 2014. Accessed October 21, 2014. http://www.theguardian.com/world/2014/sep/24/isis-twitter-youtube-message-social-media-jihadi.

410. "Why the Islamic State represents a dangerous turn in the terror threat." *Wall Street Journal*, August 18, 2014. Accessed October 21, 2014. http://online.wsj.com/articles/capital-journal-why-isis-represents-a-dangerous-threat-1408382052. Berger, J.M. "How ISIS games Twitter." *Atlantic*, June 16, 2014. Accessed October 21, 2014. http://www.theatlantic.com/international/archive/2014/06/isis-iraq-twitter-social-media-strategy/372856/.

411. Mullen, Jethro and Brian Todd. "Battling 'crusaders': ISIS turns to glossy magazine for propaganda." *CNN*, September 17, 2014. Accessed October 21, 2014. http://edition.cnn.com/2014/09/17/world/meast/isis-magazine/. McCoy, Terrance. "Dabiq: The apocalyptic magazine the Islamic State uses to recruit and radicalise foreigners." *Sydney Morning Herald*, September 17, 2014. Accessed October 21, 2014. http://www.smh.com.au/world/dabiq-the-apocalyptic-magazine-the-islamic-state-uses-to-recruit-and-radicalise-foreigners-20140917-10hwrm.html.

Kovensky, Josh. "ISIS's new mag looks like a New York glossy—with pictures of mutilated bodies." *New Republic*, September 25, 2014. Accessed October 21, 2014. http://www.newrepublic.com/article/119203/isiss-dabiq-vs-al-qaedas-inspire-comparing-two-extremist-magazines.

412. Gambhir, Harleen K. "Dabiq: The strategic messaging of the Islamic State." Understanding War, August 15, 2014. Accessed October 21, 2014. https://www.understandingwar.org/backgrounder/dabiq-strategic-messaging-islamic-state.

413. Safi, Michael. "Sydney siege gunman Man Haron Monis praised in Isis publication." *Guardian*, December 29, 2014. Accessed December 30, 2014. http://www.theguardian.com/world/2014/dec/30/sydney-siege-gunman-man-haron-monis-praised-in-isis-publication.

414. Ibid.

415. Safi, Michael and Ben Quinn, "Man Haron Monis: fringe figure whose crime record and erratic behaviour made him notorious." *Guardian*, December 15, 2014. Accessed December 16, 2014. http://www.theguardian.com/australia-news/2014/dec/15/man-haron-monis-sydney-siege-suspect. Macdonald, Hamish et al. "Sydney hostage taker Man Haron Monis had history of 'mental instability.'" *ABC News*, December 15, 2014. Accessed December 16, 2014. http://abcnews.go.com/International/sydney-hostage-taker-identified-man-haron-monis/story?id=27607179.

416. Ibid.

417. Whitehead, Tom. "New Isil video tactic may give glimmer of hope for hostage Alan Henning." *Telegraph*, September 19, 2014. Accessed October 21, 2014. http://www.telegraph.co.uk/news/uknews/terrorism-in-the-uk/11109404/New-Isil-video-tactic-may-give-glimmer-of-hope-for-hostage-Alan-Henning.html.

418. Westall, Sylvia. "Islamic State imposes media controls in Syrian province." *Reuters*, August 1, 2014. Accessed October 20, 2014. http://www.reuters.com/article/2014/08/01/us-syria-crisis-media-idUSKBN0G13SV20140801.

419. "U.S. identifies ISIS militant who killed journalist James Foley." *Fox6 Now*, September 25, 2014. Accessed October 21, 2014. http://fox6now.com/2014/09/25/u-s-identifies-isis-militant-who-killed-journalist-james-foley/. Caulfield, Phillip. "James Foley's beheading video may have been staged separately from his death: expert." *NY Daily News*, August 25, 2014. Accessed October 21, 2014. http://www.nydailynews.com/news/national/james-foley-killed-off-camera-expert-article-1.1915845.

420. Callimachi, Rukmini. "Before killing James Foley, ISIS demanded ransom from U.S." *NY Times*, August 20, 2014. Accessed October 21, 2014. http://www.nytimes.com/2014/08/21/world/middleeast/isis-pressed-for-ransom-before-killing-james-foley.html.

421. "Pentagon Provides Statement on Rescue Operation." Department of Defense, August 20, 2014. Accessed October 21, 2014. http://www.defense.gov/news/newsarticle.aspx?id=122974.

422. Sherwell, Philip and Nick Allen. "Hunt for 'British' Islamic State killer of US journalist James Foley." *Telegraph*, August 20, 2014. Accessed October 21, 2014. http://www.telegraph.co.uk/news/worldnews/middleeast/iraq/11044977/Hunt-for-British-Islamic-State-killer-of-US-journalist-James-Foley.html.

423. Maclean, William. "Islamic State issues video of beheading of U.S. hostage." *Reuters*, September 2, 2014. Accessed October 21, 2014. http://www.reuters.com/article/2014/09/02/us-iraq-crisis-islamicstate-video-idUSKBN0GX20R20140902.

424. Rayner, Gordon. "Steven Sotloff hid Jewish faith and Israeli citizenship from Isil kidnappers." *Telegraph*, September 4, 2014. Accessed October 21, 2014. http://www.telegraph.co.uk/news/worldnews/middleeast/11075575/Steven-Sotloff-hid-Jewish-faith-and-Israeli-citizenship-from-Isil-kidnappers.html.

425. Lamothe, Dan. "Here's the transcript of the video showing Steven Sotloff's reported execution." *Washington Post*, September 2, 2014. Accessed October 21, 2014. http://www. washingtonpost.com/news/checkpoint/wp/2014/09/02/heres-the-transcript-of-the-video-showing-steven-sotloffs-reported-execution/.

426. Landler, Mark and Eric Schmitt. "ISIS says it killed Steven Sotloff after U.S. strikes in northern Iraq." *NY Times*, September 2, 2014. Accessed October 21, 2014. http://www.nytimes.com/2014/09/03/world/middleeast/steven-sotloff-isis-execution.html.

427. "Profile: David Haines." *BBC News*, September 4, 2014. Accessed October 21, 2014. http://www.bbc.com/news/uk-29068550.

428. "David Haines killing: Hostage rescue options limited—UK." *BBC News*, September 15, 2014. Accessed October 21, 2014. http://www.bbc.com/news/uk-29201765. Levs, Josh and Jethro Mullen. "Britain vows to 'confront' the ISIS 'menace' after killing of David Haines." *CNN*, September 14, 2014. Accessed October 21, 2014. http://www.cnn.com/2014/09/14/world/meast/isis-david-haines-beheading/index.html?hpt=hp_t1.

429. Wright, Oliver and Tom Harper. "Alan Henning: Second British hostage in Isis beheading video named as 'kind and funny' aid worker from Salford." *Independent*, September 15, 2014. Accessed October 21, 2014. http://www.independent.co.uk/news/uk/home-news/alan-henning-second-british-hostage-in-isis-beheading-video-named-as-kind-and-funny-aid-worker-9732162.html.

430. Glanfield, Emma. "Alan Henning 'was certain he was going to be freed': Hostage held with him reveals how Briton 'laughed and joked' with other detainees when he was first kidnapped." *Daily Mail*, October 5, 2014. Accessed October 21, 2014. http://www.dailymail.co.uk/news/article-2781811/Alan-Henning-certain-going-freed-Hostage-held-reveals-Briton-laughed-joked-detainees-kidnapped.html.

431. "British hostage Alan Henning 'killed by Islamic State.'" *BBC News*, October 3, 2014. Accessed October 21, 2014. http://www.bbc.com/news/uk-29484718.

432. Saul, Heather. "Alan Henning beheading: British Muslims say aid worker's death marks the 'beginning of the end' for Isis." *Independent*, October 4, 2014. Accessed October 21, 2014. http://www.independent.co.uk/news/uk/home-news/alan-henning-beheading-british-muslims-warn-aid-workers-death-marks-the-beginning-of-the-end-for-isis-9774528.html.

433. "British Prime Minister David Cameron orders spy chiefs to hunt down 'Jihadi John.'" *Times of India*, October 5, 2014. Accessed October 21, 2014. http://timesofindia.indiatimes.com/world/uk/British-Prime-Minister-David-Cameron-orders-spy-chiefs-to-hunt-down-Jihadi-John/articleshow/44405700.cms.

434. Mekhennet, Souad and Adam Goldman. "'Jihadi John': Islamic State killer is identified as Londoner Mohammed Emwazi." *Washington Post*, February 26, 2015. Accessed February 27, 2015. http://www.washingtonpost.com/world/national-security/jihadi-john-the-islamic-state-killer-behind-the-mask-is-a-young-londoner/2015/02/25/d6dbab16-bc43-11e4-bdfa-b8e8f594e6ee_story.html.

435. "US hostage Kassig letter: 'I am scared to die.'" *BBC News*, October 6, 2014. Accessed October 21, 2014. http://www.bbc.com/news/world-us-canada-29501837.

436. Golgowski, Nina. "Peter Kassig, former U.S. soldier and current aid worker, threatened as next ISIS victim." *Daily News*, October 4, 2014. Accessed October 21, 2014. http://www.nydailynews.com/news/national/peter-kassig-u-s-soldier-current-aid-worker-threatened-isis-victim-article-1.1962652.

437. De Graff, Mia. "How American captive Peter Kassig converted to Islam in ISIS captivity and now prays five times a day under the new name Abdul-Rahman." *Daily Mail*, October 6, 2014. Accessed October 21, 2014. http://www.dailymail.co.uk/news/article-2782441/How-American-captive-Peter-Kassig-converted-Islam-ISIS-captivity-prays-five-times-day-new-Abdul-Rahman.html.

438. "New ISIS video shows beheading of American hostage Peter Kassig." *Fox News*, November 16, 2014. Accessed November 16, 2014. http://www.foxnews.com/world/2014/11/16/new-isis-video-purportedly-shows-beheading-american-hostage-peter-kassig/.

439. Baker, Aryn. "ISIS Claims Massacre of 1,700 Iraqi Soldiers." *Time*, June 15, 2014. Accesseed October 21, 2014. http://time.com/2878718/isis-claims-massacre-of-1700-iraqis/.

440. Ibid.

441. Abdulrahim, Raja. "Islamic State fighters capture military base in Syria, behead soldiers." *LA Times*, July 25, 2014. Accessed October 21, 2014. http://www.latimes.com/world/middleeast/la-fg-islamic-state-military-base-syria-20140725-story.html.

442. Mamoun, Abdelhak. "Urgent Video: ISIS beheads Kurdish soldiers, broadcasts video from downtown Mosul." *Iraqi News*, August 29, 2014. Accessed October 29, 2014. http://www.iraqinews.com/iraq-war/urgent-isis-beheads-kurdish-soliders-broadcasts-video-downtown-mosul/. "ISIS Militants Behead Lebanese Soldier and Hold 18 More Hostage." *NY Times*, August 30, 2014. Accessed October 21, 2014. http://www.nytimes.com/2014/08/31/world/middleeast/isis-militants-behead-lebanese-soldier-and-hold-more.html.

443. "Islamic State Fighters Behead Captive Lebanese Soldier in Video." *Newsweek*, August 30, 2014. Accessed October 20, 2014. http://www.newsweek.com/islamic-state-fighters-behead-captive-lebanese-soldier-video-267727.

444. "Lebanon/IS: Soldier Beheading a War Crime if Confirmed." Human Rights Watch, September 1, 2014. Accessed October 20, 2014. http://www.hrw.org/news/2014/09/01/lebanonis-soldier-beheading-war-crime-if-confirmed.

445. "Islamic State Militants Behead Captive Lebanese Soldier." *Newsloop Top News*, August 31, 2014. Accessed October 20, 2014. https://www.youtube.com/watch?v=TbQFvVm1w2U .

446. "Funeral of Lebanese soldier beheaded by IS militants." *Free Malaysia Today*, September 4, 2014. Accessed October 20, 2014. http://www.freemalaysiatoday.com/category/videos/2014/09/04/funeral-of-lebanese-soldier-beheaded-by-is-militants/.

447. Smith, Jennifer. "'My son's been slaughtered': Mother's agony as she learns of Lebanese soldier son's beheading by IS militants on Twitter after he tried to escape captivity." *Daily Mail*, September 6, 2014. Accessed October 20, 2014. http://www.dailymail.co.uk/news/article-2746431/My-son-s-slaughtered-Mother-s-agony-learns-Lebanese-soldier-son-s-beheading-IS-militants-Twitter-tried-escape-captivity.html.

448. "Islamic State video purports to show Kurdish peshmerga forces." *Reuters*, March 20, 2015. Accessed March 23, 2015. http://www.reuters.com/article/2015/03/20/us-mideast-crisis-islamicstate-beheading-idUSKBN0MG0VH20150320.

449. "Islamic State group beheads 8 Shiites in Syria's Hama." *Washington Post*, March 29, 2015. Accessed March 29, 2015. http://www.washingtonpost.com/world/middle_east/islamic-state-group-beheads-8-shiites-in-syrias-hama/2015/03/29/fd3d3a06-d631-11e4-bf0b-f648b95a6488_story.html.

Chapter Three

Membership, Structure, and Leadership

This chapter discusses the membership, structure, and leadership of the Islamic State. To the extent that they are relevant, these issues are addressed tangentially in other sections of the book.

MEMBERSHIP

Islamic State supporters include Iraqi Sunnis, who feel that they have been marginalized by Iraq's government under former Prime Minister al-Maliki. Among the Iraqi Sunnis are former Baathists, who embrace the IS for mostly practical—not ideological—reasons. The entry of the Islamic State's progenitors into Syria led to a swell of Syrian Sunni support as well. Also, as the IS controls swaths of territory in both Syria and Iraq, some of the populace under its control lend their support to the pseudo-sovereign. In addition, foreign recruits numbering in the thousands also comprise IS membership.

The IS experienced its largest recruitment gain to date in July 2014 as 6,300 new fighters joined its ranks, 1,000 of whom were foreigners.[1] This information suggests that previous estimates that the IS only had 7,000 to 10,000 fighters[2] was an underestimation. In September 2014, the CIA estimated that the Islamic State had attracted some 20,000 to 31,500 fighters.[3] There are purportedly millions of more IS supporters—many through duress—in areas under its rule, across the region, and globally.

According to the Syrian Observatory for Human Rights, there are currently 50,000 IS fighters in Syria, 20,000 of whom are not Syrian.[4] In November 2014, Fuad Hussein, the chief of staff of Kurdish President Masoud Barzani, projected that the Islamic State had an army of "at least 200,000 fighters."[5]

After all, Hussein argued, this figure is more accurate given the Islamic State's activities in the region, including IS attacks at sites in Kurdistan during October 2014. [6]

It is worth noting, too, that the Islamic State has received mixed levels of support from some jihadi terrorist groups, such as al-Qa'ida in the Arabian Peninsula, al-Qa'ida in the Islamic Maghreb, and Ansar Bait al-Maqdis (Egypt). Stronger levels of support, including swearing allegiance to the Islamic State and al-Baghdadi, have been proclaimed by Boko Haram (Nigeria), al-Sharia Tunisia, Tehreek-e-Khilafat (Pakistan), Jund al-Khilafa (Algeria), Abu Sayyaf (Philippines), Supporters of the Islamic State in the Arabian Peninsula (Yemen), and Mujahidin of Indonesia Timur. [7] Factions of other jihadi groups, such as al-Shabaab in Somalia, have declared fealty to al-Baghdadi and the Islamic State.

Also, in 2014, a group in Libya declared the city of Darna as the Barka Province of the Islamic State's caliphate. [8] This IS-affiliate was formed in Libya by former fighters in Syria called the al-Battar Brigade. They took control of Darna by killing government officials and rival militiamen. In September 2014, an IS emir, Mohammed Abdullah, a Yemeni, arrived in Darna. The following month, several hundred Darna residents pledged fealty to al-Baghdadi. [9]

During 2015, the IS-aligned operatives are trying to run Darna in line with IS administrative and ideological modes in Syria and Iraq. As such, they are taxing property, establishing schools, police, and court systems, while enforcing strict sharia law with "public lashings and executions." [10]

Other growing pockets of strong support for the Islamic State include parts of Tunisia—the origin of the Arab Spring—and from where the largest number of foreign fighters, some 3,000, went to fight in the Syrian civil war. [11] It was reported that the IS has an affiliate as well in Saudi Arabia, among other countries.

A less than complimentary account of Islamic State supporters notes that the "followers include tribes by the United States, foreign fighters from Muslim communities in Europe, united by their sense of victimisation, but also fanatics who seem to believe Islam is a religion of war, psychotics and mass murderers who are only looking for the thrill of the kill." [12]

STRUCTURE AND HIERARCHY

The IS has a condensed hierarchical organizational structure, with clear command chains. [13] Concurrently, by allowing for so many different elements within the organization, one can argue that some autonomy also exists. Besides the role of caliph or the commander-in-chief, which is held by al-Baghdadi, IS has two deputies: one for Iraq (formerly, Abu Muslim al-

Turkmani, who was killed in December 2014) and another for Syria (Abu Ali al-Anbari).[14] Also, al-Baghdadi has a cabinet of advisers.[15] The executive branch of IS (or al-Imara) includes al-Baghdadi, formerly al-Turkmani, al-Anbari, and the cabinet.[16]

The Islamic State's cabinet is comprised of: Abu Abdul Kadr ("general management official"), Bashar Ismail al-Hamdani ("In charge of prisoners and detainees"), Abu Louay ("General security official"), Abu Salah ("In charge of general finance for the Iraqi provinces of the emirate"), Abu Hajar al-Assafi ("General coordinator between the Islamic state's provinces— transports messagepost across the territory"), Abu Kassem ("Charged with managing the arrival of foreign and Arab jihadists, including overseeing the running of guesthouses for them. He is also reportedly a 'transporter of suicide bombers.'"), and Abu Adbul Rahman al-Bilwali ("Chief of the general military council for the Iraqi provinces of the Islamic state, and a captain in the Iraqi military under ousted dictator Saddam Hussein. He was killed on 5th June 2014 in Mosul").[17]

Within the IS's hierarchical structure are twelve governors each for Iraq and Syria.[18] Six of the governors include: Abu Nabil ("Salaheddin state governor"), Nene Abed Naif al-Jubouri ("Kirkuk state governor"), Ahmed Mohsin Khalal al-Jihaishi ("Governor of the south and middle Euphrates of the Islamic state"), Abu Jurnas ("Governor of provinces close to the borders of the state"), Abu Abdul Salem AKA Abu Mohammed al-Sweidawi ("Anbar governor and member of the Islamic State military council"), and Abu Maysara ("Baghdad state governor").[19] Also, the organization has various councils that relate to disparate issues: Financial Council (weapons, oil transactions), Leadership Council (crafting laws, key policies), Military Council (defending IS), Legal Council (determinations on executions and recruitment), Fighters Assistance Council (assisting foreign fighters), Security Council (law enforcement, executions), Intelligence Council (content on IS's enemies), and Media Council (oversees social and traditional media).[20] The War Council consists of Abu Shema ("Guardian of warehouses"), Abu Suja ("General coordinator for the affairs of martyrs and women"), and Abu Kifah ("In charge of operations using improvised explosive devices (IEDs) and rigging bombs").[21]

In addition, there exists a Shura Council, which governs religious and military affairs of the IS.[22] Moreover, the Shura Council "reports directly to al-Baghdadi and ensures the state's various local councils and governors are adhering to the caliphate's version of Islamic law."[23] Also, the Shura Council also has authority to remove the caliph.[24]

Another analysis of the framework of the Islamic State provides, "there is also a parallel command structure: elite units next to normal troops; additional commanders alongside nominal military head Omar al-Shishani; power brokers who transfer or demote provincial and town emirs or even make them disappear at will. Furthermore, decisions are not, as a rule, made in Shura Councils, nominally the highest decision-making body. Instead, they are being made by the 'people who loosen and bind' (*ahl al-hall wa-l-aqd*), a clandestine circle whose name is taken from the Islam of medieval times."[25]

It is important to emphasize the key roles and influence that former Saddam Hussein Baathist officers play in the senior leadership and decision-making processes of the Islamic State. In bringing their military knowhow and networks, the Iraqi Baathists perform indispensable functions. For instance, the Baathists who form part of the IS regime are adept at using "fear to secure the submission of the people under" their control.[26] While formerly secular, the Baathist leadership comprising the Islamic State leadership is outwardly devout, although its religious devotion may mask pragmatic posturing.[27] Ultimately, "[t]he secret of IS' success lies in the combination of opposites, the fanatical beliefs of one group [jihadists]and the strategic calculations of the other [secular Baathist]."[28]

The purposeful inclusion of former Baathist officers resulted in the expansive presence of these former Saddam loyalists in the progenitors of the IS, and ultimately, the current iteration of the entity.[29] Still, one could characterize the participation of Baathists in the Iraqi jihadist milieu in terms of a continuum: Abu Musab al-Zarqawi (viewed the Baathists with askance, but permitted their membership); Abu Omar al-Baghdadi (an Iraqi officer, expanded their involvement); and Abu Bakr al-Baghdadi (a Muslim scholar who recruits Baathists rather actively).[30]

More broadly, in order to cushion itself from internal or external threats, IS leadership tends to use intermediaries and go-betweens.[31] Likewise, there appears to be an Iraqi leadership and operative overlay and presence even in IS-controlled areas of Syria, let alone in Iraq.[32]

Furthermore, while there is a definite hierarchical element in IS's structure, Western analysts often do "not take into account a reality where tribal, regional, cultural and historical ties often take precedence."[33]

In the areas under its control, the IS has built a multi-tiered "holistic system of governance that includes religious, educational, security, humanitarian, and infrastructure projects."[34] The Islamic State, as its name implies, intends to and does act as a *de facto* state in the areas it controls, even if it has not obtained *de jure* recognition. One instrumentality of state-issued services is the work of the Islamic State's Office of Consumer Protection in Raqqa, where its head, Abu Salih al-Ansari, explained that "It's an office that's concerned with protecting shoppers by inspecting the goods being sold in shops, markets, shopping centers and wholesale outlets, discovering goods that are spoiled or not suitable for sale and taking those responsible to account. Likewise, we inspect restaurants and sweet-shops, and monitor slaughterhouses, so we can keep people from getting sick and guard against harmful substances."[35]

Concurrently, the IS seeks to attract Muslims from across the globe to relocate to the territory under its control. The IS, like al-Qa'ida, is an organization that inspires individuals to act locally, while the groups themselves are based elsewhere. The IS has tentacles abroad, as witnessed in Australia in September 2014, when authorities arrested an IS-linked cabal allegedly planning beheadings there.[36] Also in September 2014, Jund al-Khilafa, a new group that pledged allegiance to the Islamic State, beheaded French hiker Herve Gourdel in response to French collaboration in Western airstrikes against IS targets in Iraq.[37] In December 2014, Algerian military forces killed Abdelmalek Gouri, the leader of the Jund al-Khilafah (Soldiers of the Caliphate), a group that claimed allegiance to the IS and decapitated Gourdel in September 2014.[38] In December 2014, a possible IS-planned or -inspired plot to publicly kill a member of the Queen's Guard in the UK was revealed. As such, security measures to protect these targets were revised, including the addition of armed police and modifying the activities of the Queen's Guard.[39]

The structure of the IS differs greatly from that of al-Qa'ida. While al-Qa'ida still has remnants of a hierarchal structure, its named affiliates—al-Qa'ida in the Arabian Peninsula (AQAP), al-Qa'ida in the Islamic Maghreb (AQIM), and Jabhat al-Nusra—are afforded, and claim, significant autonomy. Additionally, other terror groups, including al-Shabaah in Somalia, have claimed allegiance to al-Qa'ida, although some al-Shabaab members are supporting the IS. In the wake of the suicide bombings in London in 2005, British Metropolitan Police Commissioner Ian Blair observed, "Al Qaeda is not an organization. Al Qaeda is a way of working," whereby the entity provides "training . . . [and] expertise"[40] to disparate groups and individuals located around the globe, who are then tasked with carrying out attacks.

LEADERSHIP

This section discusses the IS leadership hierarchy, from Abu Bakr al-Baghdadi, its self-proclaimed caliph, to his key associates. Profiles of selected leaders arrested and killed are also included. More extensive entries are provided for al-Baghdadi, given his importance to the Islamic State. In January 2015, U.S. Secretary of State John Kerry stated that U.S.-led coalition airstrikes had killed nearly half of the Islamic State's leadership.[41]

Abu Bakr al-Baghdadi

As there are varying perspectives about al-Baghdadi's background, two extended versions are provided: an accolade-filled biography taken from a jihadi forum user and another made up from press accounts.

Pro-al-Baghdadi Biography

In July 2013, a jihadi forum user released a biography of the Abu Bakr al-Baghdadi "(AKA Abu Du'a, Ibrahim bin Awwad bin Ibrahim al-Badri al-Radhwi al-Husseini al-Samarrai),"[42] which is deemed mostly accurate.[43] Referring to al-Baghdadi as "the Emir of the Islamic State of Iraq and the Levant,"[44] the biography states that he is a descendent of various "honorable tribes[,]" including the "Hashimite" and "Qurashiyah."[45]

Al-Baghdadi is further described as a "professor, teacher, former educator, recognized preacher, and a graduate of the Islamic University in Baghdad, where he finished his academic studies (BA, MA and PhD). He is known as a preacher and a person of knowledge in Islamic culture, Shariah knowledge, and jurisprudence, and possessing vast knowledge of history and lineage."[46]

In relation to his family life, al-Baghdadi is said to be married, coming "from a religious family. His brothers and uncles include preachers and teachers in Arabic, eloquence and logic. Their religious creed is Salafist."[47]

The jihadi forum biography states that al-Baghdadi's "security and military expertise on the ground developed in the last eight years. This security and military expertise crystallized clearly and it matured when it was applied on the ground, when he was exposed to its hardships and sacrifices through practical application in the last eight and a half years of fighting and hit-and-run strikes."[48]

Al-Baghdadi is then said to have established the group "Jeish Ahl al-Sunnah wal Jama'a, which was active in particular in Diyala, Samarra, and Baghdad. Afterwards, he took over the Shariah Committee in it when the emir of the Shariah Committee took the leadership position of the group. Subsequently, this group, Jeish Ahl al-Sunnah wal Jama'a, pledged allegiance and joined the Mujahideen Shura Council."[49] Al-Baghdadi then joined the Council's Shariah Committee and served as a member of the Shura Council, until the declaration of the Islamic State of Iraq. Then, he assumed the position of general supervisor of the State's Shariah Committee and became a member in the State's Shura Council."[50] After several years, "Abu Omar al-Baghdadi al-Husseini al-Qurashi (Hamid Daoud)" brought "him in to be his successor."[51]

Media accounts of al-Baghdadi

Al-Baghdadi was born in 1971 in Samarra, Iraq.[52] He has claimed "to be a direct descendant of the prophet Muhammad."[53] Al-Baghdadi earned a doctorate from the Islamic University in Baghdad. He served as a cleric in Samarra until the U.S. invasion of Iraq.[54]

Others have characterized him also as a street thug, who was arrested in Fallujah in 2004 along with Sunni "hard-core militants"[55] during the "Iraqi Sunni insurgency."[56] Between 1994–2004, al-Baghdadi rented a room near a mosque in Tobchi, a mixed Sunni-Shiite neighborhood on the western side of Baghdad.[57] By some accounts, al-Baghdadi was a jihadist during Saddam Hussein's regime, particularly after moving to Baghdad in the 1990s. Others say that he embraced jihadism while captive at a U.S. prison in Iraq, Camp Bucca. Purportedly, he was held there for five years or less, depending on the account that suggests his arrest took place in 2004 or 2005. In 2009, al-Baghdadi was transferred into Iraqi control. The following year, al-Baghdadi was released from prison.[58]

At Camp Bucca, al-Baghdadi met various jihadists (including al-Qa'ida) and Baathists, who would later collaborate with him in various groups.[59] At least a dozen top IS leaders were imprisoned in Camp Bucca at one point. Later al-Baghdadi joined the Islamic State of Iraq (ISI), and became close to Abu Musab al-Zarqawi. Al-Zarqawi was killed in 2006, as was his successor, Abu Omar al-Baghdadi in 2010.[60] After the latter's death, al-Baghdadi became ISI's leader.[61]

There are varying accounts about whether al-Baghdadi ever left Iraq and Syria, and worked with al-Zarqawi in Afghanistan.[62] Following the inception of the Syrian revolution and civil war erupted in 2011 and 2012, respectively, al-Baghdadi sought to expand his group, and sent an operative—Abu Mohammed al-Golani—to establish Jabhat al-Nusra in Syria. The success of Jabhat al-Nusra led al-Baghdadi to propose a merger to form the Islamic State of Iraq and Syria (ISIS). The subsequent chasm between al-Baghdadi and al-Golani/al-Qa'ida led to al-Qa'ida to disassociating itself from al-Baghdadi. In late June 2014, the Islamic State was declared when al-Baghdadi designated himself as Caliph Ibrahim. On July 5, 2014, al-Baghdadi gave his first public speech at the Great Mosque of al-Nuri in Mosul, where he underscored his role as caliph, and called for all Muslims to embrace jihad and support the Islamic State.[63]

In November 2014, some twenty Islamic State operatives, including a close aide to al-Baghdadi (Auf Abdulrahman Elefery, code name Abu Suja), were killed in coalition airstrikes on a convoy of Islamic State members near Mosul. Although initially thought to have been killed or injured in the attack, al-Baghdadi survived (either not present in the convoy or just injured). In fact, later that month, al-Baghdadi called for his supporters to "erupt volcanoes of jihad" as coalition airstrikes escalated.[64] In subsequent accounts during 2014 and 2015, al-Baghdadi was reported to have been injured or killed in coalition airstrikes.

Al-Baghdadi's meteoric rise to power is partly due to the deaths of various leaders who headed antecedents of the Islamic State. In addition, al-Baghdadi was fortunate to have the chance to take advantage of the chaos in

Syria during its civil war, and Sunni dissatisfaction with Shiite and Alawite-led governments in Iraq and Syria, respectively. [65]

Still, al-Baghdadi achievements with regard to the Islamic State due to his own skills should not be dismissed. He is viewed as a "shrewd strategist, a prolific fundraiser and a ruthless killer," by some. [66] Too, his credibility rests with the fact that he leads an organization that has attained significant military victories and has acquired territory and wealth. [67]

With the successes of the Islamic State, al-Baghdadi could be viewed as Usama bin Laden's true heir to jihadists worldwide rather than Ayman al-Zawahiri, al Qa'ida's current head. In comparing the two, al-Baghdadi has helped create the Islamic State, while al-Zawahiri has largely been ineffective, practically limited to hiding on the Afghanistan-Pakistani border. [68]

Al-Baghdadi is considered to be a commander and tactician. In contrast, al-Qa'ida's leader, Ayman al-Zawahiri, is perceived more as an ideologue. By some accounts, it is the image of al-Baghdadi as a fighter and strategist that appeals to prospective IS recruits. [69]

The U.S. State Department's Rewards for Justice offers up to $10 million for information that leads to the capture ("arrest or conviction") of al-Baghdadi, listed as Abu Du'a. [70] The only other person whose capture offers a higher reward—$25 million—is al-Zawahiri. [71]

Streamlined biographies of other IS leaders are set out below.

Abu Omar al-Shishani [72]

- Position: IS military commander in Syria. He may have been promoted to the overall commander of IS forces.
- Alias: His real name is Tarkhan Batirashvili.
- Origin: Ethnic Chechen. He served in the Georgian army where he excelled.
- He left Georgia in early 2012 after being released from prison. He became committed to the jihad while being held for harboring weapons illegally.
- He has been featured in several IS videos.
- Some news sources reported that he was killed in May 2014. However, since then, he has appeared in several videos and pictures.

Al Nasir Li Din Allah Abu Sulayman [73]

- Position: IS Minister of War since May 2010.
- Alias: His real name is Neaman Salman Mansour al Zaidi.
- Origin: He is from Morocco. He might also be a Syrian citizen.
- Potentially trained in Afghanistan and studied with senior aides to Osama bin Laden.

- It has been claimed that the war ministry is responsible for organizing the majority of the IS terrorist activities.
- Iraqi forces claimed to have killed Sulayman in 2011. However, the IS has denied that he is dead. He is still listed as the Minister of War. [74]

Abu Mohammed al-Adnani [75]

- Position: IS official spokesman.
- Alias: It is believed that his real name is Taha Sobhi Falaha.
- Origin: He was born in Syria in 1987.
- Some Iraqi sources have stated that al-Baghdadi appointed him as an emir, although Western sources have yet to confirm this development.
- He was among the first non-Iraqis to join the campaign against U.S. forces when they invaded Iraq.
- In an audio message he posted online on September 21, 2014, he called on all Muslims in the West to kill non-Muslims, be they civilian or military, specifically in those countries which had joined the alliance against the Islamic State. When a Muslim encountered an "infidel," he called on him or her to "Smash his head in with a rock, slit his throat with a knife, run him over with your car, throw him to his death from a great height, strangle him, or poison him." Addressing Americans and Europeans, he warned: "You will pay dearly as you walk down your own streets, looking back over your shoulder in fear of the Muslims."

Abu Ayman al-Iraqi [76]

- Position: Member of the IS military council. He commands troops in the Syrian cities of Adlib and Aleppo, and in the mountains of Latakia.
- Origin: He was a colonel in the Iraqi air defense intelligence during Saddam Hussein's regime.
- He was in prison from 2007 to 2010. He traveled to Syria after being released from prison.

Abu Ahmad al-Alwani [77]

- Position: Member of the IS military council.
- Alias: His real name is Waleed Jassem al-Alwani.
- Background: He served in the military under Saddam Hussein.

Abu Fatima al-Jaheishi[78]

- Position: Previously, he oversaw all IS operations in the southern portion of Iraq. He has since relocated to Kirkuk.
- Alias: His real name is Ni'ma Abd Nayef al-Jabouri.

Abu Abdullah al-Husseini al-Qurashi[79]

- Position: He was named the deputy and prime minister of ISI in 2010. He has not been mentioned since and not much else is known about him.

Abu Waheeb[80]

- Position: Leader of ISIS forces in Anbar, Iraq.[81]
- Alias: Real Name: Shaker Wahib Al-Fahdawi.[82]
- Aliases: Desert Lion,[83] Nusayri Hunter, Teacher of the Nusayris.[84]
- Origin: Born in 1986, likely in Iraq.
- Education: He never completed his studies in Computer Science at University of Anbar. He was captured by U.S. forces in 2006 and held on charges of belonging to al-Qa'ida.[85]
- Incarcerated at Bucca Prison in southern Iraq until 2009, when he was transferred to Tikrit Prison.[86] He escaped in 2012 during an attack on that prison. Upon his escape, he became an ISIS field commander. His years of experience planning, training, and preparation inside Bucca and Tikrit prisons helped in that role.
- Iraqi security forces announced his death in January 2014.[87] However, these reports have been denied by ISIS, which began publishing new pictures of him online.[88]

Sheikh Omar Gharba[89]

- Position: Cleric of Idlib-based Free Syrian Army brigade. He switched allegiance and later joined ISIS.
- Alias: Omar Gharba' Al-Khojji.

ARRESTED AND DECEASED LEADERS

Coalition airstrikes have resulted in the deaths of various IS officials, including "Abu Muslim al-Turkmani, who was Baghdadi's deputy in charge of Iraq and would be the most senior ISIS leader to fall this year."[90] Among others killed in mid-December 2014 coalition airstrikes were "Abd al (or Abdul) Basit, the military chief; and Radwin Talib."[91] Haji Bakr, a former Iraqi military officer and close adviser to Abu Bakr al-Baghdadi, was also killed in 2014.[92] More broadly, in order to cushion itself from internal or external threats, IS leadership tends to use intermediaries and go-betweens.[93]

In January 2015, Abu Malik, an IS chemical weapons expert, was killed in a coalition airstrike near Mosul. While it is not believed that the group possesses major supplies of chemical weapons, it has used chlorine gas in the past. Previously, Malik was linked to al-Qa'ida and the Saddam Hussein regime.[94] Also that month, Raqqa governor, Abu Luqman, was apparently killed by the IS over fears that he would be participating in a coup against al-Baghdadi.[95]

In February 2015, General John Allen stated that 50 percent of the Islamic State's leadership in Iraq has been killed.[96] Likewise, that month, U.S. Secretary of State John Kerry said, "We've disrupted their command structure, undermined its propaganda, taken out half of their senior leadership."[97]

Still, some have questioned whether coalition airstrikes and other military efforts have truly weakened the Islamic State's leadership and structure. After all, they argue, "the Islamic State's Shura and Sharia councils, the advisory bodies that help inform the major decisions of the group's leader Abu Bakr al-Baghdadi, remain intact."[98] Moreover, it is suggested that the Islamic State's command-and-control capabilities have been maintained with fallen regional and other administrators being readily replaced.[99]

Samir Abd Muhammad al-Khlifawi (also known as Haji Bakr)[100]

According to an April 2015 report in *Der Spiegel* based on internal Islamic State documents, Haji Bakr, was a "former colonel in the intelligence service of Saddam Hussein's air defense force [who] had been secretly pulling the strings at IS for years."[101] Haji Bakr "sketched out the structure of the Islamic State, all the way down to the local level, compiled lists relating to the gradual infiltration of villages and determined who would oversee whom."[102] Bakr's blueprint for the Islamic State was such that it included "plans also include areas like finance, schools, daycare, the media and transportation. But there is a constantly recurring, core theme, which is meticulously addressed in organizational charts and lists of responsibilities and reporting requirements: surveillance, espionage, murder and kidnapping."[103] Moreover, from its inception, the object of the organization "was to have everyone keeping an eye on everyone else."[104]

Between 2006–2008, Bakr was imprisoned in Camp Bucca and Abu Ghraib. There, Bakr and other former Saddam loyalists networked to establish a broad base of contacts, from which they would subsequently call upon in forging the Islamic State.[105] "In 2010, Bakr and a small group of former Iraqi intelligence officers made Abu Bakr al-Baghdadi, the emir and later 'caliph,' the official leader of the Islamic State. They reasoned that Baghda-di, an educated cleric, would give the group a religious face."[106]

As a leading strategist for ISIS, Bakr planned the structures and plans of the organization, such as his travels in late 2012 from Iraq to Tal Rifaat, in Aleppo Province. There he served as part of an advance team that intended to acquire territory in Syria, and subsequently undertake attacks in Iraq. By late 2012, terror training camps were established, catering primarily to foreign fighters. By 2013, ISIS had several hundred fighters in Tal Rifaat.[107]

By 2013, missionary or "dawah," offices were established in northern Syria and elsewhere. However, they soon were revealed to be fronts for the recruitment of foreign fighters that had entered the region and would ulti-mately align with the group. Among the northern Syrian cities and towns where the dawahs were formed included: Raqqa, Manbij, al-Bab, Atarib, Azaz, Sermada, Atmeh, Kafr Takharim, al-Dana and Salqin.[108] By "fall 2013, IS books listed 2,650 foreign fighters in the Province of Aleppo alone. Tunisians represented a third of the total, followed by Saudi Arabians, Turks, Egyptians and, in smaller numbers, Chechens, Europeans and Indone-sians."[109]

In March 2013, when Raqqa fell, ISIS killed various prospective politi-cians and leaders in hopes of removing potential rivals. So too, in October 2013, ISIS called for a reconciliation meeting, but, instead, the group killed opposition leaders. These acts of intimidation led to various clan leaders taking an oath to Abu Bakr al-Baghdadi. During 2013, ISIS acquired exten-sive territory in northern Syria. Then, in late 2013, the group tortured to death an important rebel leader and doctor, triggering attacks from numerous rebel groups, including Jabhat al-Nusra. In January 2014, Bakr, still based in Tal Rifaat, was killed by "a local commander named Abdelmalik Hadbe."[110]

Abu Abdul Rahman al-Bilawi[111]

- Position: He was a member of the IS military council.
- His real name was Adnan Ismael Najm.
- Origin: He was born in Anbar province, Iraq.
- He was arrested by U.S. forces in 2005.
- He was killed in Anbar province by U.S. forces in June 2014.

Abu Hajjar[112]

- Position: Was IS's most trusted messenger.
- He was captured in Mosul a few days before IS troops took the city in June 2014.

- He told his interrogators that Mosul would be captured. After two weeks of interrogation Hajjar talked.
- Iraqi intelligence officers collected over 160 flash drives from Hajjar and a messenger for Abdulrahman al-Bilawi. Hajjar told Iraqi intelligence officers where Abdulrahman al-Bilawi was located.

Abu Ayyub al-Masri [113]

- Position: He was the head of al-Qa'ida in Iraq following Abu Musab al-Zarqawi. He worked closely with al-Baghdadi. He was also referred to as the ISIS Minister of War.
- Origin: He was Egyptian.
- In 2010, he was killed by Iraqi troops, who were backed by U.S. forces.

Abu Musab al-Zarqawi [114]

- Position: He was the leader of al-Qa'ida in Iraq.
- Previously, he was known as Ahmad Fadhil Nazzal al-Khalaylah.
- Origin: He was a Bedouin from Jordan. He was killed by U.S. air strikes in 2006.
- In 2003, he was mistakenly identified by then Secretary of State Colin Powell as the key link between Saddam Hussein and al-Qa'ida.

Abu Alaa al-Iraqi [115]

- Position: He was head of the ISIS military council in the city of Tal Afar.
- He was killed in September 2014.

Amru Al-Absi [116]

- Also known as Abu al-Arthir, Abu Al-Asir. [117]
- Selected as ISIS's provincial leader for Homs, Syria in the Aleppo (Halab) region.
- As one of the principal leaders of ISIS in Syria, he has been in charge of kidnappings.

Imad Ahmad Jomaa [118]

- Position: He was considered the leader of the Fajr Al-Islam Brigade, which was originally part of the Homs-based Farouk Brigades.
- Aliases: Abu Ahmad Jomaa, Mahmoud Jomaa.
- Origin: Currently in his late 20s, he hails from Qusair

- He came from a poor family which was not religious. He used to sell milk out of a Suzuki van before the Syrian revolution. He has two brothers and three sisters. He was divorced, but subsequently remarried.
- He was heavily involved in the battle for the Qalamoun region.
- Recently, he and his brigade were living in Arsal, a predominantly Sunni Lebanese town close to the Syrian border. Arsal is hosting some 100,000 Syrian refugees.
- After ISIS successes in July 2014, Fajr Al-Islam released a YouTube video pledging allegiance to Abu Bakr Al-Baghdadi. [119]
- He was arrested by the Lebanese Army in August 2014.

ASSOCIATED GROUPS

Al-Qa'ida/Al-Qa'ida Central (AQC)

On February 3, 2014, AQC disavowed ISIS: "Al-Qaeda has no connection with the group called the ISIS, as it was not informed or consulted about its establishment. It was not pleased with it and thus ordered its suspension. Therefore, it is not affiliated with al-Qaeda and has no organizational relationship with it." [120] On July 13, 2014, As Sahab, al-Qa'ida's media production arm, tweeted out an old Osama bin Laden video, followed by a Zawahiri video denouncing the caliphate.

Al-Qa'ida in the Arabian Peninsula (AQAP)

In August 2014, AQAP announced its support for IS. [121] AQAP later modified its approach to IS, and released the following statement:

> Based on our experience with drones, we advise our brothers in Iraq to be cautious about spies among them because they are a key factor in setting goals; be cautious about dealing with cell phones and internet networks; do not gather in large numbers or move in large convoys; spread in farms or hide under trees in the case of loud humming of warplanes; and dig sophisticated trenches because they reduce the impact of shelling. [122]

Furthermore, there are allegations of AQAP fighters training in Iraq and IS fighters in Yemen. Analogously, in August 2014, AQAP's main ideologue, Ibrahim al-Rubaish, released a statement supporting the IS:

> I congratulate all the Mujahideen on all battlefronts and all Muslims on the victories that our brothers in Iraq have achieved against the puppets of the [Iranians] . . . The Sunnis of Iraq have realized that co-existence in Iraq is not possible . . . and that fighting the rejectionists [Shiites] is a legally binding

duty. The same situation is being repeated in Yemen and the Gulf. Will Sunnis learn the lesson of Iraq and take the initiative?[123]

AQAP appears to have adopted some of IS's tactics. In September 2014, AQAP beheaded in a public execution fourteen unarmed Yemeni soldiers. Jalal Baleedi, an influential field commander in the group who supports ISIS, ordered the decapitations.[124] Likewise, AQAP declared its intention to establish an Islamic emirate in the remote eastern Hadramout province. The terror group also ordered the public to obey its strict interpretation of Islamic law.[125]

AQAP's leader, Nasser al-Wuhayshi, has not commented on ISIS. But Abdul Majid al-Raymi, an AQAP spiritual leader, pledged allegiance to Abu Bakir al-Baghdadi. Al Raymi also asked all of his Yemeni followers to do so. Other AQAP leaders have indicated support for ISIS.[126]

In February 2015, a group of fighters formerly with AQAP pledged that their allegiance to the IS, stating in a video:

- "We announce the formation of armed brigades specialized in pounding the apostates in Sanaa and Dhamar" [two central provinces in Yemen][127]
- "We announce breaking the pledge of allegiance to the sheikh, the holy warrior and scholar Sheikh Ayman al-Zawahiri . . . We pledge to the caliph of the believers Ibrahim bin Awad al-Baghdadi to listen and obey."[128]

U.S. Attorney General Eric Holder articulated his deep concerns about an AQAP-IS alliance. Holder argued that the prevalence of Westerners joining IS, coupled with AQAP's expertise, poses a significant danger to U.S. security.[129]

Al-Qa'ida in the Islamic Maghreb (AQIM)

AQIM tried to help heal the Jabhat al-Nusra and IS rift prior to the break between the two entities. AQIM publicly rejected the caliphate and IS, stating:

> [We] confirm that we still adhere to our pledge of allegiance to our sheikh and emir, Ayman al Zawahiri, since it is a Sharia-accorded pledge of allegiance that remains hanging on our necks, and we do not see what requires use to break it . . . It is obvious for the Muslims and all jihadi organizations that follow the correct method, that the announcement of such a serious step (meaning the establishment of the Caliphate), will not happen but after the expansion of consultation.[130]

Yet some AQIM leaders, including Sheikh Abdullah Othman al-Assimi, publicly supported and swore fealty to the IS. These AQIM leaders also criticized al-Qa'ida for not doing so.[131]

The Algerian government arrested dozens of AQIM defectors who pledged allegiance to Abu Bakr al-Baghdadi. Those arrested are working to establish their own branch of the IS in North Africa.[132] These AQIM defectors benefit from ISIS fighters who return to North Africa.[133]

Al-Sharia Tunisia

The spokesman of al-Sharia Tunisia, Seifeddine Rais, declared loyalty to IS leader Abu Bakr al-Baghdadi.[134] The group has posted pro-IS propaganda on its websites and social media.[135]

Tehreek-e-Khilafat

In July 2014, Pakistani terror group Tehreek-e-Khilafat became the first non-Middle Eastern terror group to swear allegiance to IS. The group's leader vowed to raise the Islamic State flag in Pakistan and Afghanistan.[136]

Jund al-Khilafa in Algeria

Jund al-Khilafa in Algeria is not to be confused with the al-Qa'ida-linked group of the same name based along the Pakistan/Afghanistan border, which is responsible for attacks in Kazakhstan and France.[137] Jund al-Khilafa in Algeria was formed out of the al-Huda Battalion and Algerian jihadi groups. The group pledged its allegiance to al-Baghdadi hours after it released a hostage video of a captured French hiker Herve Gourdel on September 23, 2014.[138] It demanded an end to French collaboration in Western airstrikes against ISIS targets in Iraq. The French government rejected that demand and promised to do everything possible to rescue the hostage.[139] On September 24, 2014, Jund al-Khilafa released a video showing that it had decapitated Herve Gourdel.[140]

Ansar Bait Al-Maqdis

The influence of IS tactics spread to Egypt, where Ansar Bait al-Maqdis beheaded four people in the Sinai in August 2014.[141] A commander of al-Maqdis confirmed that IS is training its members, "They (IS) teach us how to carry out operations."[142] Also, the Egyptian government confirmed that IS and al-Maqdis are collaborating.[143]

Abu Sayyaf

An al-Qa'ida-linked Filipino group, Abu Sayyaf, pledged allegiance to IS in a video posted in July 2014. Abu Sayyaf has been kidnapping, ransoming, and executing Western and East Asian hostages since 2000. Currently, the group holds about ten hostages in the Sulu jungles. Abu Sayyaf is still considered a major threat in the Philippines and in neighboring Malaysia. [144]

On September 24, 2014, Abu Sayyaf released a statement threatening to execute two German hostages, Dr. Stefan Viktor Okonek and Henrite Dielen, unless a ransom was paid and Germany withdrew cooperation with anti-IS operations. [145]

Jordanian Jihadist Figures

There is a lack of unanimity among leading Jordanian jihadist figures relative to IS and its self-appointed caliph, al-Baghdadi. For instance, the former right hand man of bin Laden, Abu Qatada, rejects the caliphate, and states "No emir should be considered caliph or the like. And those who don't realize that are the most corrupt." [146] Subsequently, Abu Qatada claimed that the ISIS beheadings are against Islam. [147] Also, Abu Mohammad al-Maqdisi, one of the most influential jihadi theologians, denounced ISIS. [148] Omar Mahdi Zeidan, a Salafist jihadist leader based in Irbid, issued a statement criticizing both Abu Qatada and al-Maqdisi. Also, he called on al-Zawahiri to pledge allegiance to al-Baghdadi. [149]

Influence of ISIS in Southeast Asia

Through online social media, ISIS militants have actively reached out to Malaysian Muslims, asking them to join ISIS. Meanwhile, four organizations—identified by the acronyms BKAW, BAJ, and ADI, plus "Dimzia"—are said to have strong links with similar groups active in the Southeast Asia region, the Islamic State, and Abu Sayyaf. [150]

ISIS in India

ISIS seeks to add adherents in India, the country with the third largest Islamic population. [151] However, support for ISIS in India appears to be thin, limited largely to pro-ISIS graffiti in Srinagar in divided Kashmir.

In September 2014, al-Qa'ida announced it was opening a branch in India. Al-Qa'ida leader al-Zawahiri believes that the Indian subcontinent, including Bangladesh, Myanmar, and Pakistan, are susceptible to jihadi influences. Likewise, as support for ISIS grows outside of India, it could likely positively affect the group's supporters and funding in India. [152]

Boko Haram

Both ISIS and Boko Haram seek to establish an "Islamic Caliphate." ISIS has assisted Boko Haram in its efforts to conquer northern Nigeria. Previously, Boko Haram faced challenges in conquering cities. In 2015, Boko Haram was able to hold onto territory. [153]

In March 2015, Boko Haram's leader, Abubakar Shekau, claimed allegiance to al-Baghdadi. He said the group had joined the caliphate. The impetus for this shift could include intentions to globalize Boko Haram's posture, a manner to buttress support from abroad, and instill energy into a group that was increasingly threatened by Nigerian and foreign armies. [154]

Jaysh Rijal al-Tariqa al-Naqshbandia [155]

A prominent Sufi Islamist group in Iraq, [156] Jaysh Rijal al-Tariqa al-Naqshbandia (JRTN), is allegedly assisting ISIS forces in maintaining control over the city of Mosul.

Mujahidin of Indonesia Timur [157]

Sheikh Abu Wardah, the leader of the Mujahidin of Indonesia Timur, declared his allegiance to the Islamic State in an audio file posted online, July 1, 2014.

The Khorasan Group

This group is comprised of former al-Qa'ida operatives throughout the Middle East and beyond, including Pakistan and Afghanistan. Their exclusive motive appears to be to attack the United States. Khorasan refers to a region in Iran. The United States has been tracking this group intensely since July 2014, but did not confirm its existence until the American airstrike campaign in Syria began. [158]

In 2014, the United States increased airport security again due to the expertise that members of this group possess in relation to liquid and other difficult-to-detect explosives. The recruitment of Western individuals is also a key aspect of this group besides attacking Western nations. [159] The organization is believed to have been close to executing an attack on the American mainland.

The Khorasan Group, which is based in Syria, is affiliated with Jabhat al-Nusra. Khorasan's leader was Muhsin al-Fadhli, before he was reportedly killed in coalition airstrikes in September 2014. A 33-year-old male Kuwaiti, al-Suri spent part of his life in Iran, where he operated the al-Qa'ida Iranian branch after Yasin al-Suri was detained. Once al-Suri reclaimed his position upon release, [160] al-Fadhli was reassigned to Syria. [161]

In addition, the Khorasan Group is linked to al-Qa'ida in the Arabian Peninsula's Ibrahim al-Asiri, who is on the U.S. most wanted terrorist list. Al-Asiri is accused of trying to bring down flights from Europe to the United States through the shipment of printer cartridges packed with explosives. He is also implicated as an accomplice to the infamous and unsuccessful "underwear bomber," Umar Farouk Abdulmutallab in 2009.[162] The Transportation Security Administration's July 2014 move to ban uncharged laptops and cell phones from certain flights was apparently prompted by the Khorasan Group. U.S. officials claim that the group had been testing explosives in camps located in Syria.[163]

NOTES

1. Perry, Tom. "Islamic State recruits at record pace in Syria: monitor" *Reuters*, August 19, 2014. Accessed October 23, 2014. http://www.reuters.com/article/2014/08/19/us-syria-crisis-islamicstate-idUSKBN0GJ0W420140819.

2. Abouzeid, Rania, Mark Tran, Ian Black, Roger Tooth, Shiraz Maher, and Martin Chulov. "The Terrifying Rise of Isis: $2bn in Loot, Online Killings and an Army on the Run." *Guardian,* June 16, 2014. Accessed October 23, 2014. http://www.theguardian.com/world/2014/jun/16/terrifying-rise-of-isis-iraq-executions.

3. Sciutto, Jim et al, "ISIS can 'muster' between 20,000 and 31,500 fighters, CIA says." *CNN*, September 12, 2014. Accessed September 13, 2014. http://www.cnn.com/2014/09/11/world/meast/isis-syria-iraq/.

4. "Islamic State 'has 50,000 fighters in Syria'" *Al-Jazeera*, August 19, 2014. Accessed October 23, 2014. http://www.aljazeera.com/news/middleeast/2014/08/islamic-state-50000-fighters-syria-2014819184258421392.html.

5. "IS is seven times bigger than Western estimates." *Business Standard*, November 16, 2014. Accessed November 16, 2014. http://www.business-standard.com/article/news-ians/is-seven-times-bigger-than-western-estimates-114111600180_1.html.

6. Ibid.

7. "Libyan city becomes the first outside Iraq, Syria to join Islamic State group's 'caliphate.'" *Fox News*, November 9, 2014. Accessed November 10, 2014. http://www.foxnews.com/world/2014/11/09/libyan-city-becomes-first-outside-iraq-syria-to-join-islamic-state-group/.

8. Ibid.

9. Keilberth, Mirco et al. "The 'Caliphate's' colonies: Islamic State's gradual expansion into North Africa." *Spiegel Online International*, November 18, 2014. Accessed November 19, 2014. http://www.spiegel.de/international/world/islamic-state-expanding-into-north-africa-a-1003525.html.

10. Eljarh, Mohamed. "A snapshot of the Islamic State's Libyan stronghold." *Foreign Policy*, April 1, 2015. Accessed April 7, 2015. http://foreignpolicy.com/2015/04/01/a-snapshot-of-the-islamic-states-libyan-stronghold-derna-libya-isis/.

11. Ibid.

12. Ibrahim, Osman Rifat. "Why Abu Bakr al-Baghdadi is an imposter." *Al-Jazeera*, July 14, 2014. Accessed July 21, 2014. http://www.aljazeera.com/indepth/opinion/2014/07/baghdadi-impostor-20147991513785260.html.

13. Green, R. "The Rift In The Global Jihad Movement." MEMRI, February 20, 2014. Accessed October 21, 2014. http://www.memri.org/report/en/0/0/0/0/0/0/7841.htm.

14. "Leadership structure of the Islamic State." Terrorism Research and Analyst Consortium. Accessed October 21, 2014. http://www.trackingterrorism.org/chatter/leadership-structure-islamic-state. Thompson, Nick and Shubert, Atika. "The anatomy of ISIS: How the 'Islamic State' is run, from oil to beheadings" *CNN*, October 7, 2014. Accessed October 21,

2014. http://www.cnn.com/2014/09/18/world/meast/isis-syria-iraq-hierarchy/index.html?hpt=
hp_t1.

"Abu Muslim al-Turkmani: From Iraqi officer to slain ISIS deputy." *Al-Arabiya*, December 19, 2014. Accessed December 22, 2014. http://english.alarabiya.net/en/perspective/profiles/
2014/12/19/Abu-Muslim-al-Turkmani-From-Iraqi-officer-to-slain-ISIS-deputy.html.

15. "Leadership Structure of the Islamic State." Terrorism Research and Analyst Consortium. Accessed October 21, 2014. http://www.trackingterrorism.org/chatter/leadership-structure-islamic-state. Thompson, Nick and Shubert, Atika. "The anatomy of ISIS: How the 'Islamic State' is run, from oil to beheadings." *CNN*, October 7, 2014. Accessed October 21, 2014. http://www.cnn.com/2014/09/18/world/meast/isis-syria-iraq-hierarchy/index.html?hpt=
hp_t1.

16. Ibid.

17. "Revealed: the Islamic State 'cabinet,' from finance minister to suicide bomb deployer." *Telegraph*. July 9, 2014. Accessed November 1, 2014. http://www.telegraph.co.uk/news/
worldnews/middleeast/iraq/10956193/Revealed-the-Islamic-State-cabinet-from-finance-minister-to-suicide-bomb-deployer.html.

18. "Leadership Structure of the Islamic State." Terrorism Research and Analyst Consortium, No date. Accessed October 21, 2014. http://www.telegraph.co.uk/news/worldnews/
middleeast/iraq/10956193/Revealed-the-Islamic-State-cabinet-from-finance-minister-to-suicide-bomb-deployer.html. Thompson, Nick and Shubert, Atika. "The anatomy of ISIS: How the 'Islamic State' is run, from oil to beheadings." *CNN*, October 7, 2014. Accessed October 21, 2014. http://www.cnn.com/2014/09/18/world/meast/isis-syria-iraq-hierarchy/index.html?
hpt=hp_t1.

19. Sherlock, Ruth. "Inside the leadership of the Islamic State: how the new 'caliphate' is run." *Telegraph*, July 9, 2014. Accessed November 1, 2014. http://www.telegraph.co.uk/news/
worldnews/middleeast/iraq/10956280/Inside-the-leadership-of-Islamic-State-how-the-new-caliphate-is-run.html.

20. "Leadership Structure of the Islamic State." Terrorism Research and Analyst Consortium, No date. Accessed October 21, 2014. http://www.trackingterrorism.org/chatter/
leadership-structure-islamic-state. Thompson, Nick and Shubert, Atika. "The anatomy of ISIS: How the 'Islamic State' is run, from oil to beheadings." *CNN*, October 7, 2014. Accessed October 21, 2014. http://www.cnn.com/2014/09/18/world/meast/isis-syria-iraq-hierarchy/
index.html?hpt=hp_t1.

21. "Revealed: the Islamic State 'cabinet,' from finance minister to suicide bomb deployer." *Telegraph*. July 9, 2014. Accessed November 9, 2014. http://www.telegraph.co.uk/news/
worldnews/middleeast/iraq/10956193/Revealed-the-Islamic-State-cabinet-from-finance-minister-to-suicide-bomb-deployer.html.

22. "Leadership Structure of the Islamic State." Terrorism Research and Analyst Consortium. Accessed October 21, 2014. http://www.trackingterrorism.org/chatter/leadership-structure-islamic-state. Thompson, Nick and Shubert, Atika. "The anatomy of ISIS: How the 'Islamic State' is run, from oil to beheadings." *CNN*, October 7, 2014. Accessed October 21, 2014. http://www.cnn.com/2014/09/18/world/meast/isis-syria-iraq-hierarchy/index.html?hpt=
hp_t1.

23. "Inside the hierarchy of the Islamic State." *YNet News*, September 20, 2014. Accessed October 21, 2014. http://www.ynetnews.com/articles/0,7340,L-4573040,00.html.

24. "Leadership Structure of the Islamic State." Terrorism Research and Analyst Consortium, No date. Accessed October 21, 2014. http://www.trackingterrorism.org/chatter/
leadership-structure-islamic-state. Thompson, Nick and Shubert, Atika. "The anatomy of ISIS: How the 'Islamic State' is run, from oil to beheadings." *CNN*, October 7, 2014. Accessed October 21, 2014. http://www.cnn.com/2014/09/18/world/meast/isis-syria-iraq-hierarchy/
index.html?hpt=hp_t1.

25. Reuter, Christoph. "The terror strategist: Secret files reveal the structure of the Islamic State." *Der Spiegel*, April 18, 2015. Accessed April 19, 2015. http://www.spiegel.de/
international/world/islamic-state-files-show-structure-of-islamist-terror-group-a-1029274.html.

26. Sly, Liz. "The hidden hand behind the Islamic State's militants? Saddam Hussein's." *Washington Post*. April 4, 2015. Accessed April 4, 2015. http://www.washingtonpost.com/

world/middle_east/the-hidden-hand-behind-the-islamic-state-militants-saddam-husseins/2015/04/04/aa97676c-cc32-11e4-8730-4f473416e759_story.html?hpid=z1.

27. Ibid.

28. Reuter, Christoph. "The terror strategist: Secret files reveal the structure of the Islamic State." *Der Spiegel,* April 18, 2015. Accessed April 19, 2015. http://www.spiegel.de/international/world/islamic-state-files-show-structure-of-islamist-terror-group-a-1029274.html.

29. Ibid.

30. "Most of the Islamic State's leaders were officers in Saddam Hussein's Iraq." *Washington Post,* April 4, 2015. Accessed April 4, 2015. http://www.washingtonpost.com/world/most-of-islamic-states-leaders-were-officers-in-saddam-husseins-iraq/2015/04/04/f3d2da00-db24-11e4-b3f2-607bd612aeac_graphic.html.

31. Sly, Liz. "The hidden hand behind the Islamic State's militants? Saddam Hussein's." *Washington Post.* April 4, 2015. Accessed April 4, 2015. http://www.washingtonpost.com/world/middle_east/the-hidden-hand-behind-the-islamic-state-militants-saddam-husseins/2015/04/04/aa97676c-cc32-11e4-8730-4f473416e759_story.html?hpid=z1.

32. Ibid.

33. "Killing top ISIS leaders won't cripple group: experts." *Daily Star,* December 20, 2014. Accessed December 24, 2014. http://www.dailystar.com.lb/News/Middle-East/2014/Dec-20/281742-killing-top-isis-leaders-wont-cripple-group-experts.ashx#sthash.Z3q55qc4.dpuf.

34. Caris, Charles C. and Samuel Reynolds. "ISIS Governance in Syria." Institute for the Study of War, July 2014. Accessed October 21, 2014. http://www.understandingwar.org/sites/default/files/ISIS_Governance.pdf.

35. Al-Hayat Media Center. "On patrol with the Office of Consumer Protection." *Islamic State Report: An Insight into the Islamic State,* Issue 1, Page 5, Shaban 1435. https://azelin.files.wordpress.com/2014/06/islamic-state-of-iraq-and-al-shc481m-22islamic-state-report-122.pdf.

36. "Cops in Australia: We thwarted grisly ISIS plot." *CBS News,* September 18, 2014. Accessed October 21, 2014. http://www.cbsnews.com/news/australian-officials-isis-plot-to-behead-random-person-in-sydney-thwarted/."Australian Leader Warns of Planned Random Attack." *Associated Press,* September 18, 2014. Accessed October 29, 2014. http://bigstory.ap.org/article/56314454376943a0b2c9fdbcaed18177/arrests-made-australian-counterterrorism-raids.

37. "'Jund al-Khilafah in Algeria' Renews Pledge to IS, Abu Bakr al-Baghdadi." *Site Monitoring Service Jihadist Threat,* September 22, 2014. Accessed October 23, 2014. https://news.siteintelgroup.com/Jihadist-News/jund-al-khilafah-in-algeria-renews-pledge-to-is-abu-bakr-al-baghdadi.html.

38. Ouali, Aomar. "Algerian Army Kills Man Behind French Beheading." *AP,* December 23, 2014. Accessed December 25, 2014. http://abcnews.go.com/International/wireStory/algeria-army-kills-man-french-beheading-27784460.

39. Dorman, Nick. "ISIS plot to kill The Queen's Guards: Lee Rigby-style murder fears." *Daily Mirror,* December 27, 2014. Accessed December 27, 2014. http://www.mirror.co.uk/news/uk-news/isis-plot-kill-queens-guards-4882079#rlabs=1.

40. "Cops: London Attacks Were Homicide Blasts." *Fox News,* July 15, 2005. Accessed October 21, 2014. http://www.foxnews.com/story/2005/07/15/cops-london-attacks-were-homicide-blasts/.

41. Sarhan, Amre. "50 percent of ISIS leadership killed, says U.S. Secretary of State." *Iraqi News,* January 23, 2015. Accessed April 8, 2015. http://www.iraqinews.com/iraq-war/50-isis-leadership-killed-says-u-s-secretary-state/.

42. "A biography of Abu Bakr al-Baghdadi." *Siteintelgroup.com,* August 12, 2014. Accessed September 20, 2014. http://news.siteintelgroup.com/blog/index.php/entry/226-the-story-behind-abu-bakr-al-baghdadi.

43. Ibid.

44. Ibid.

45. Ibid.

46. Ibid.

47. Ibid.

48. Ibid.

49. Ibid.

50. Ibid.

51. Ibid.

52. Crompton, Paul. "The rise of the new 'caliph,' ISIS chief Abu Bakr al-Baghdadi." *Al Arabiya News*, June 30, 2014. Accessed September 25, 2014. http://english.alarabiya.net/en/perspective/profiles/2014/06/30/The-rise-of-the-new-caliph-ISIS-chief-Abu-Bakr-al-Baghdadi.html.

53. McCoy, Terrence. "How ISIS leader Abu Bakr al-Baghdadi became the world's most powerful jihadist leader." *Washington Post*, June 11, 2014. Accessed June 25, 2014. http://www.washingtonpost.com/news/morning-mix/wp/2014/06/11/how-isis-leader-abu-bakr-al-baghdadi-became-the-worlds-most-powerful-jihadi-leader/.

54. Crompton, Paul. "The rise of the new 'caliph,' ISIS chief Abu Bakr al-Baghdadi." *Al Arabiya News*, June 30, 2014. Accessed September 25, 2014. http://english.alarabiya.net/en/perspective/profiles/2014/06/30/The-rise-of-the-new-caliph-ISIS-chief-Abu-Bakr-al-Baghdadi.

55. Arango, Tim and Eric Schmitt. "U.S. actions in Iraq fueled rise of a rebel." *NY Times*, August 10, 2014. Accessed August 20, 2014. http://www.nytimes.com/2014/08/11/world/middleeast/us-actions-in-iraq-fueled-rise-of-a-rebel.html?_r=1.

56. Ibid.

57. Sherlock, Ruth, "How a talented footballer became world's most wanted man." *Telegraph*. November 11, 2014. Accessed November 14, 2014. http://www.telegraph.co.uk/news/worldnews/middleeast/iraq/10948846/How-a-talented-footballer-became-worlds-most-wanted-man-Abu-Bakr-al-Baghdadi.

58. Crompton, Paul. "The rise of the new 'caliph,' ISIS chief Abu Bakr al-Baghdadi." *Al Arabiya News*, June 30, 2014. Accessed September 25, 2014. http://english.alarabiya.net/en/perspective/profiles/2014/06/30/The-rise-of-the-new-caliph-ISIS-chief-Abu-Bakr-al-Baghdadi.html. Arango, Tim and Eric Schmitt. "U.S. actions in Iraq fueled rise of a rebel." *NY Times*, August 10, 2014. Accessed August 20, 2014. http://www.nytimes.com/2014/08/11/world/middleeast/us-actions-in-iraq-fueled-rise-of-a-rebel.html?_r=1.

Sherlock, Ruth, "How a talented footballer became world's most wanted man." *Telegraph*, November 11, 2014. Accessed November 14, 2014. http://www.telegraph.co.uk/news/worldnews/middleeast/iraq/10948846/How-a-talented-footballer-became-worlds-most-wanted-man-Abu-Bakr-al-Baghdadi.

Eichelberger, Erika. "How the top Iraqi terrorist was helped by a Bush-signed agreement." *Mother Jones*, June 18, 2014. Accessed August 20, 2014. http://www.motherjones.com/politics/2014/06/abu-bakr-al-baghdadi-release-george-bush.

59. Sherlock, Ruth, "How a talented footballer became world's most wanted man." *Telegraph*, November 11, 2014. Accessed November 14, 2014. http://www.telegraph.co.uk/news/worldnews/middleeast/iraq/10948846/How-a-talented-footballer-became-worlds-most-wanted-man-Abu-Bakr-al-Baghdadi.

60. Crompton, Paul. "The rise of the new 'caliph,' ISIS chief Abu Bakr al-Baghdadi." *Al Arabiya News*, June 30, 2014. Accessed September 25, 2014. http://english.alarabiya.net/en/perspective/profiles/2014/06/30/The-rise-of-the-new-caliph-ISIS-chief-Abu-Bakr-al-Baghdadi.html. Sherlock, Ruth, "How a talented footballer became world's most wanted man." *Telegraph*, November 11, 2014. Accessed November 14, 2014. http://www.telegraph.co.uk/news/worldnews/middleeast/iraq/10948846/How-a-talented-footballer-became-worlds-most-wanted-man-Abu-Bakr-al-Baghdadi.

Ward, Clarissa. "The origins of ISIS: Finding the birthplace of jihad." *CBS News*, November 4, 2014. Accessed November 5, 2014. http://www.cbsnews.com/news/the-origins-of-isis-finding-the-birthplace-of-jihad/.

61. Sherlock, Ruth, "How a talented footballer became world's most wanted man." *Telegraph*, November 11, 2014. Accessed November 14, 2014. http://www.telegraph.co.uk/news/worldnews/middleeast/iraq/10948846/How-a-talented-footballer-became-worlds-most-wanted-man-Abu-Bakr-al-Baghdadi.

62. Arango, Tim and Eric Schmitt. "U.S. actions in Iraq fueled rise of a rebel." *NY Times*, August 10, 2014. Accessed August 20, 2014. http://www.nytimes.com/2014/08/11/world/middleeast/us-actions-in-iraq-fueled-rise-of-a-rebel.html?_r=1.

63. "Islamic State's caliph lauds Iraq rebellion." *Al Jazeera*, July 6, 2014. Accessed July 7, 2014. http://www.aljazeera.com/news/middleeast/2014/07/islamic-state-caliph-lauds-iraq-rebellion-20147512574517772.html. Crompton, Paul. "The rise of the new 'caliph,' ISIS chief Abu Bakr al-Baghdadi." *Al Arabiya News*, June 30, 2014. Accessed September 25, 2014. http://english.alarabiya.net/en/perspective/profiles/2014/06/30/The-rise-of-the-new-caliph-ISIS-chief-Abu-Bakr-al-Baghdadi.html.

Sherlock, Ruth, "How a talented footballer became world's most wanted man." *Telegraph*, November 11, 2014. Accessed November 14, 2014. http://www.telegraph.co.uk/news/worldnews/middleeast/iraq/10948846/How-a-talented-footballer-became-worlds-most-wanted-man-Abu-Bakr-al-Baghdadi.

64. Ernst, Douglas. "Islamic State releases tape of Iraqi leader calling for jihad." *Washington Times*, November 13, 2014. Accessed November 13, 2014. http://www.washingtontimes.com/news/2014/nov/13/islamic-state-releases-al-baghdadi-audio-erupt-vol/. Sherlock, Ruth and Magdy Samaan. "Islamic State leader Abu Bakr al-Baghdadi's close aide killed in US air strike." *Daily Telegraph*, November 9, 2014. Accessed November 9, 2014. http://www.telegraph.co.uk/news/worldnews/islamic-state/11219630/Islamic-State-leader-Abu-Bakr-al-Baghdadis-close-aide-killed-in-US-air-strike.html.

65. McCoy, Terrence. "How ISIS leader Abu Bakr al-Baghdadi became the world's most powerful jihadist leader." *Washington Post*, June 11, 2014. Accessed June 25, 2014.http://www.washingtonpost.com/news/morning-mix/wp/2014/06/11/how-isis-leader-abu-bakr-al-baghdadi-became-the-worlds-most-powerful-jihadi-leader/.

66. Ibid.

67. Arango, Tim and Eric Schmitt. "U.S. actions in Iraq fueled rise of a rebel." *NY Times*, August 10, 2014. Accessed August 20, 2014. http://www.nytimes.com/2014/08/11/world/middleeast/us-actions-in-iraq-fueled-rise-of-a-rebel.html?_r=1.

68. McCoy, Terrence. "How ISIS leader Abu Bakr al-Baghdadi became the world's most powerful jihadist leader." *Washington Post*, June 11, 2014. Accessed June 25, 2014. http://www.washingtonpost.com/news/morning-mix/wp/2014/06/11/how-isis-leader-abu-bakr-al-baghdadi-became-the-worlds-most-powerful-jihadi-leader/.

69. "Syria Iraq: The Islamic State militant group." *BBC News*, August 2, 2014. Accessed October 21, 2014. http://www.bbc.com/news/world-middle-east-24179084.

70. "Abu Du'a." U.S. Department of State, No date. Accessed November 15, 2014. http://www.rewardsforjustice.net/english/abu_dua.html. "Program overview: Rewards for justice." U.S. Department of State, No date. Accessed November 15, 2014. http://www.rewardsforjustice.net/english/about-rfj/program-overview.html.

71. "Ayman al-Zawahiri." U.S. Department of State, No date. Accessed November 15, 2014. http://www.rewardsforjustice.net/english/ayman_zawahiri.html.

72. Mroue, Bassem. "Chechen in Syria a rising star in extremist group" *AP*, July 2, 2014. Accessed October 23, 2014. http://bigstory.ap.org/article/chechen-syria-rising-star-extremist-group. Cullinson, Allen. "Meet the Rebel Commander in Syria That Assad, Russia and the U.S. All Fear." *Wall Street Journal*, November 19, 2013. Accessed October 23, 2014. http://online.wsj.com/news/articles/SB10001424052702303309504579181962177007316.

73. Joscelyn, Thomas. "The Islamic State of Iraq and the Sham's quiet war minister." *Long War Journal*, June 16, 2014. Accessed October 23, 2014. http://www.longwarjournal.org/archives/2014/06/the_islamic_states_q.php. "Review of the Listing of Al-Qa'ida in the Arabian Peninsula (AQAP) and the re-listing of 6 Terrorist Organisations." Parliamentary of Australia Joint Committee on Intelligence and Security, August 22, 2011. Appendix H. Accessed October 30, 2014. http://www.aph.gov.au/parliamentary_business/committees/house_of_representatives_committees?url=pjcis/aqap_6%20terrorist%20orgs/report.htm.

74. "Al-Qaeda Iraq "war minister" killed in raid." *Al-Arabiya*, February 25, 2011. Accessed October 23, 2014. http://www.alarabiya.net/articles/2011/02/25/139188.html.

75. Anjarini, Suhaib. "Syria: Jihadist factions close to civil war." *Al-Akhbar*, March 8, 2014. September 21, 2014. http://english.al-akhbar.com/node/18940.

76. "Exclusive: Top ISIS leaders revealed." *Al-Arabiya*, February 13, 2014. Accessed October 23, 2014. http://english.alarabiya.net/en/News/2014/02/13/Exclusive-Top-ISIS-leaders-revealed.html.

77. Ibid.

78. Ibid.

79. Shadid, Anthony. "Iraqi Insurgent Group Names New Leaders." *NY Times,* May 16, 2010. Accessed October 23 2014. http://atwar.blogs.nytimes.com/2010/05/16/iraqi-insurgent-group-names-new-leaders/.

80. Abbas, Mushreq. "Has al-Qaeda found Zarqawi's successor?" *Al-Monitor*, January 15, 2014. Accessed October 23, 2014. http://www.al-monitor.com/pulse/originals/2014/01/iraq-isis-shaker-wahib-zarqawi.html#.

81. "Al Qaeda is taking over whole cities in Iraq." *Vice News*, January 16, 2014. Accessed October 23, 2014. http://www.vice.com/read/al-qaeda-are-taking-over-whole-cities-in-iraq.

82. Abbas, Mushreq. "Has al-Qaeda found Zarqawi's successor?" *Al-Monitor*, January 15, 2014. Accessed October 23, 2014. http://www.al-monitor.com/pulse/originals/2014/01/iraq-isis-shaker-wahib-zarqawi.html#.

83. Ibid.

84. Van Ostaeyen, Pieter. "Who is Shaker Wahib al-Fahdawi aka Abu Waheebaka aka Nusayri Hunter aka Teacher of the Nausayris?" *Terrorism Research & Analysis Consortium*, No date. Accessed October 23, 2014. http://www.trackingterrorism.org/article/rising-star-isis-sunni-terrorist-abu-wahib-shakir-al-fahdawi-leader-ussud-al-anbar-brigade.

85. Younes, Amima. "Collective Escape from Tikrit Prison." *Sky News Arabic*, September 28, 2012. Accessed October 30, 2014. http://www.skynewsarabia.com/web/article/47628/%D9%81%D8%B1%D8%A7%D8%B1-%D8%AC%D9%85%D8%A7%D8%B9%D9%8A-%D8%B3%D8%AC%D9%86-%D8%AA%D9%83%D8%B1%D9%8A%D8%AA.

86. "Iraq Retakes Tikrit Prison." *Al-Jazeera Arabic,* September 28, 2012. Accessed October 30, 2014. http://www.aljazeera.net/news/arabic/2012/9/28/%D8%A7%D9%84%D9%82%D9%88%D8%A7%D8%AA-%D8%A7%D9%84%D8%B9%D8%B1%D8%A7%D9%82%D9%8A%D8%A9-%D8%AA%D8%B3%D8%AA%D8%B9%D9%8A%D8%AF-%D8%B3%D8%AC%D9%86-%D8%AA%D9%83%D8%B1%D9%8A%D8%AA.

87. "Counter-Terrorism Agency: The Snipers of the Golden Team Killed Shaker Wahib East of Ramadi." *Al-Sumaria TV Arabic,* January 2, 2014. Accessed October 30, 2014. http://www.alsumaria.tv/news/89651/%D8%AC%D9%87%D8%A7%D8%B2-%D9%85%D9%83%D8%A7%D9%81%D8%AD%D8%A9-%D8%A7%D9%84%D8%A7%D8%B1%D9%87%D8%A7%D8%A8-%D9%82%D9%86%D8%A7%D8%B5%D9%88-%D8%A7%D9%84%D9%81%D8%B1%D9%82%D8%A9-%D8%A7%D9%84%D8%B0%D9%87%D8%A8%D9%8A%D8%A9/ar.

88. HH. "ISIS denies the death of Shaker Wahib and publishes pictures of him inside the security center in Al-Ramadi while he wears a police helmet." *Al-Mada Press Arabic,* January 4, 2014. Accessed October 3, 2014. http://almadapress.com/ar/news/23854/%D8%AF%D8%A7%D8%B9%D8%B4-%D9%8A%D9%86%D9%81%D9%8A-%D9%85%D9%82%D8%AA%D9%84-%D8%B4%D8%A7%D9%83%D8%B1-%D9%88%D9%87%D9%8A%D8%A8-%D9%88%D9%8A%D9%86%D8%B4%D8%B1-%D8%B5%D9%88%D8%B1%D8%A7.

89. "Syaikh Omar Gharda From FSA join to Islamic State IS ISIS." YouTube video, 2:02. Posted by "Juund Shawal," September 4, 2014. Accessed October 30, 2014. https://www.youtube.com/watch?v=KvH6jaQSV48.

90. Zebari, Abdelhamid. "Iraq Kurds press fightback as top jihadi reported killed." *Daily Star*, December 19, 2014. Accessed December 22, 2014. http://www.dailystar.com.lb/News/Middle-East/2014/Dec-19/281651-iraq-kurds-press-fightback-as-top-jihadi-reported-killed.ashx#sthash.Z1CbDZAP.dpuf.

91. "Top ISIS militants killed in airstrikes; more U.S. troops going to Iraq." *NY Daily News*, December 18, 2014. Accessed December 23, 2014. http://www.nydailynews.com/news/world/top-isis-militants-killed-troops-iraq-article-1.2050316#bmb=1.

92. "Most of the Islamic State's leaders were officers in Saddam Hussein's Iraq." *Washington Post*, April 4, 2015. Accessed April 4, 2015. http://www.washingtonpost.com/world/most-

of-islamic-states-leaders-were-officers-in-saddam-husseins-iraq/2015/04/04/f3d2da00-db24-11e4-b3f2-607bd612aeac_graphic.html.

93. Sly, Liz. "The hidden hand behind the Islamic State's militants? Saddam Hussein's." *Washington Post.* April 4, 2015. Accessed April 4, 2015. http://www.washingtonpost.com/world/middle_east/the-hidden-hand-behind-the-islamic-state-militants-saddam-husseins/2015/04/04/aa97676c-cc32-11e4-8730-4f473416e759_story.html?hpid=z1.

94. "IS toxic terrorist killed in Iraq." *Irish Independent*, January 31, 2015. Accessed February 5, 2015. http://www.independent.ie/world-news/is-toxic-terrorist-killed-in-iraq-30952634.html. Drury, Flora. "Islamic State chemical weapons expert who trained under Saddam killed in airstrike near Mosul, says US central command." *Daily Mail*, January 31, 2015. Accessed February 5, 2015. http://www.dailymail.co.uk/news/article-2934130/ISIS-chemical-weapons-expert-trained-Saddam-killed-airstrike-near-Mosul-says-central-command.html.

"Air strike kills IS 'chemical weapons expert': US." *Times of India*, January 31, 2015. Accessed February 5, 2015. http://timesofindia.indiatimes.com/world/us/Air-strike-kills-IS-chemical-weapons-expert-US/articleshow/46073733.cms.

95. Masi, Alexandria. "ISIS Raqqa 'Governor' alledgedly executed, prompting wave of arrests for defection." *International Business Times*. February 2, 2015. Accessed February 4, 2015. http://www.ibtimes.com/isis-raqqa-governor-allegedly-executed-prompting-wave-arrests-defection-1802820 .

96. Lamothe, Dan. "Gen. John Allen: Islamic State has lost half of its leaders in Iraq." *Washington Post*, February 25, 2015. http://www.washingtonpost.com/news/checkpoint/wp/2015/02/25/gen-john-allen-islamic-state-has-lost-half-of-its-leaders-in-iraq/.

97. Kerry, John. "Remarks at the Munich Security Conference Panel Discussion." U.S. Department of State, February 8, 2015. Accessed March 10, 2015. http://www.state.gov/secretary/remarks/2015/02/237298.htm.

98. Lake, Eli and Josh Rogin, "U.S. exaggerates Islamic State casualties." *Bloomberg View*, March 13, 2015. Accessed April 7, 2015. http://www.bloombergview.com/articles/2015-03-13/did-kerry-exaggerate-islamic-state-casualties-.

99. Ibid.

100. Roggio, Bill. "ISIS confirms death of senior leader in Syria." *Long War Journal*, February 5, 2014. Accessed October 23, 2014. http://www.longwarjournal.org/archives/2014/02/isis_confirms_death.php. "Exclusive: Top ISIS leaders revealed." *Al-Arabiya*, February 13, 2014. Accessed October 23, 2014. http://english.alarabiya.net/en/News/2014/02/13/Exclusive-Top-ISIS-leaders-revealed.html.

101. Reuter, Christoph. "The terror strategist: Secret files reveal the structure of the Islamic State." *Der Spiegel*, April 18, 2015. Accessed April 19, 2015. http://www.spiegel.de/international/world/islamic-state-files-show-structure-of-islamist-terror-group-a-1029274.html.

102. Ibid.

103. Ibid.

104. Ibid.

105. Ibid.

106. Ibid.

107. Ibid.

108. Ibid.

109. Ibid.

110. Ibid.

111. Chulov, Martin. "How an arrest in Iraq revealed Isis's $2bn jihadist network." *Guardian*, June 15, 2014. Accessed October 23, 2014. http://www.theguardian.com/world/2014/jun/15/iraq-isis-arrest-jihadists-wealth-power. "Exclusive: Top ISIS leaders revealed." *Al-Arabiya*, February 13, 2014. Accessed October 23, 2014. http://english.alarabiya.net/en/News/2014/02/13/Exclusive-Top-ISIS-leaders-revealed.html.

112. Chulov, Martin. "How an arrest in Iraq revealed Isis's $2bn jihadist network." *Guardian*, June 15, 2014. Accessed October 23, 2014. http://www.theguardian.com/world/2014/jun/15/iraq-isis-arrest-jihadists-wealth-power.

113. Pincus, Walter and Karen DeYoung. "Al-Qaeda in Iraq May Not Be Threat Here." *Washington Post*, March 17, 2007. Accessed October 23, 2014. http://www.washingtonpost.

com/wp-dyn/content/article/2007/03/17/AR2007031701373_pf.html. Bazinet, Kenneth and Gordon-Meek, James. "Top two Al Qaeda operatives in Iraq, Abu Ayyub al-Masri and Abu Umar al-Baghdadi, killed: U.S." *NY Daily News*, April 19, 2010. Accessed October 23, 2014. http://www.nydailynews.com/news/world/top-al-qaeda-operatives-iraq-abu-ayyub-al-masri-abu-umar-al-baghdadi-killed-u-s-article-1.165110.

"Review of the Listing of Al-Qa'ida in the Arabian Peninsula (AQAP) and the re-listing of 6 Terrorist Organisations." Parliamentary of Australia Joint Committee on Intelligence and Security, Appendix H, August 22, 2011. Accessed October 30, 2014. http://www.aph.gov.au/parliamentary_business/committees/house_of_representatives_committees?url=pjcis/aqap_6%20terrorist%20orgs/report.htm.

114. Burns, John. "U.S. Strike Hits Insurgent at Safehouse." *NY Times*, June 8, 2006. Accessed October 23, 2014. http://www.nytimes.com/2006/06/08/world/middleeast/08cnd-iraq.html?pagewanted=all&_r=0. Weaver, Mary Anne. "The Short, Violent Life of Abu Musab al-Zarqawi." *Atlantic*, June 8, 2006. Accessed October 23, 2014. http://www.theatlantic.com/magazine/archive/2006/07/the-short-violent-life-of-abu-musab-al-zarqawi/304983/.

115. "Iraq air strikes 'kill senior Islamic State members.'" *BBC*, September 4, 2014. Accessed October 23, 2014. http://www.bbc.com/news/world-middle-east-29068416.

116. "Designations of Foreign Terrorist Fighters" *U.S. Department of State*. September 24, 2014. Accessed on November 4, 2014. www.state.gov/r/pa/prs/ps/2014/09/232067.htm.

117. "In the Matter of the Designation of Amru al-Absi, Also Known as Abu al-Arthir, Also Known as Abu al-Asir as a Specially Designated Global Terrorist Pursuant to Section 1(b) of Executive Order 13224, as Ammended." *U.S. Department of State [Public Notice 8903]. Federal Register.* Vol. 79, No. 194. October 7, 2014. Accessed November 4, 2014. http://docs.regulations.justia.com/entries/2014-10-07/2014-23937.pdf .

118. Rainey, Venetia. "Who is Imad Ahmad Jomaa?" *Daily Star*. August 4, 2014. Accessed October 30, 2014. http://www.dailystar.com.lb/News/Lebanon.

119. "Pledging of Allegiance to the Islamic State by Liwa' Fajr Al Islam." YouTube. July 28, 2014. Accessed October 30, 2014. https://www.youtube.com/watch?v=BDYPcuc2ZB0.

120. "Al-Qaeda disavows ISIS militants in Syria." *BBC*, February 3, 2014. Accessed October 23, 2014. http://www.bbc.com/news/world-middle-east-26016318.

121. Wong, Kristina. "Al Qaeda in Yemen declares support for ISIS." *Hill*, August 19, 2014. Accessed October 23, 2014. http://thehill.com/business-a-lobbying/215480-al-qaeda-in-yemen-declares-support-for-isis.

122. Al-Moshki, Ali Ibrahim. "AQAP announces support for ISIL." *Yemen Times*, August 19, 2014. Accessed October 23, 2014. http://www.yementimes.com/en/1808/news/4216/AQAP-announces-support-for-ISIL.htm.

123. "Yemeni Al-Qaeda leader hails ISIS gains in Iraq." *Al-Arabiya*, August 13, 2014. Accessed October 23, 2014. http://english.alarabiya.net/en/News/middle-east/2014/08/13/Yemeni-Al-Qaeda-leader-hails-ISIS-gains-in-Iraq.html.

124. Wong, Kristina. "ISIS is spreading, experts warn." *Hill*, September 9, 2014. Accessed October 23, 2014. http://thehill.com/policy/defense/217032-isis-is-spreading-experts-warn.

125. "Al-Qaida Wing Announces Plans for Islamic Emirate in Yemen." *Voice of America*, July 22, 2014. Acessed October 23, 2014. http://www.voanews.com/content/al-qaida-wing-announces-plan-for-islamic-emirate-in-yemen/1962901.html.

126. Wong, Kristina. "ISIS is spreading, experts warn." *Hill*, September 9, 2014. Accessed October 23, 2014. http://thehill.com/policy/defense/217032-isis-is-spreading-experts-warn.

127. Browning, Noah. "Al Qaeda supporters in Yemen pledge allegiance to the Islamic State: group." *Reuters*, February 11, 2015. Accessed February 23, 2015. http://www.reuters.com/article/2015/02/11/us-yemen-security-qaeda-idUSKBN0LF0E720150211.

128. Ibid.

129. Calabresi, Massimo. "Understanding the ISIS Threat to Americans at Home." *Time*, September 9, 2014. Accessed October 23, 2014. http://time.com/3313613/isis-barack-obama-terrorism-threat/.

130. Joscelyn, Thomas. "AQIM rejects Islamic State's caliphate, reaffirms allegiance to Zawahiri." *Long War Journal*, July 14, 2014. Accessed October 30, 2014. http://www.longwarjournal.org/archives/2014/07/aqim_rejects_islamic.php#ixzz3D8O8cNoW.

131. Yess, Hamid. "Al-Qaeda in Islamic Maghreb backs ISIS." *Al-Monitor*, July 2, 2014. Accessed October 23, 2014. http://www.al-monitor.com/pulse/security/2014/07/aqim-declaration-support-isis-syria-maghreb.html#.

132. Shabbi, Omar. "AQIM defectors raise fears of IS branch in North Africa." *Al-Monitor*, September 9, 2014. Accessed October 23, 2014. http://www.al-monitor.com/pulse/originals/2014/09/north-africa-algeria-aqim-establish-islamic-state.html#.

133. Oumar, Jemal. "North Africa: Maghreb Al-Qaeda Torn Apart By ISIS." *allAfrica*, August 15, 2014. Accessed October 23, 2014. http://allafrica.com/stories/201408160016.html?page=2.

134. Arfaoui, Jamel. "Tunisia: Ansar Al-Sharia Tunisia Spokesman Backs Isis." *allAfrica*, July 8, 2014. Accessed October 23, 2014. http://allafrica.com/stories/201407090299.html.

135. Zelin, Aaron. "Shabāb al-Tawḥīd Media presents a new video message from Anṣār al-Sharī'ah in Tunisia's Shaykh Kamāl Zarūq: 'Appeal To Support the Islamic State of Iraq and al-Shām'" *Jihadology* June 4, 2014. Accessed October 23, 2014. http://jihadology.net/2014/06/04/shabab-al-taw%e1%b8%a5id-media-presents-a-new-video-message-from-an%e1%b9%a3ar-al-shariah-in-tunisias-shaykh-kamal-zaruq-appeal-to-support-the-islamic-state-of-iraq-and-al-sham/.

136. Crilly, Rob and Saleem Mehsud. "Pakistani terror group swears allegiance to Islamic State." *Telegraph*, July 9, 2014. Accessed October 23, 2014. http://www.telegraph.co.uk/news/worldnews/asia/pakistan/10955563/Pakistani-terror-group-swears-allegiance-to-Islamic-State.html.

137. "Jund al-Khilafah." *Terrorism Research & Analysis Consortium*, 2014. Accessed October 23, 2014. http://www.trackingterrorism.org/group/jund-al-khilafah-jak. "Jund al-Khilafah Claims France Shootings." *SITE Monitoring Service Enterprise*, March 22, 2012. Accessed October 23, 2014. http://ent.siteintelgroup.com/Jihadist. Roggio, Bill. "Jund al Khilafah claims attack in Kazakhstan." *Long War Journal*, November 16, 2011. Accessed October 23, 2014. http://www.longwarjournal.org/archives/2011/11/jund_al_khilafah_cla.php.

138. "'Jund al-Khilafah in Algeria' Renews Pledge to IS, Abu Bakr al-Baghdadi." *Site Monitoring Service Jihadist Threat*, September 22, 2014. Accessed October 23, 2014. https://news.siteintelgroup.com/Jihadist-News/jund-al-khilafah-in-algeria-renews-pledge-to-is-abu-bakr-al-baghdadi.html. "Islamist Group Threatens French Hostage In Video." *Sky News*, September 22, 2014. Accessed October 23, 2014. http://news.sky.com/story/1340339/islamist-group-threatens-french-hostage-in-video. "ISIL ally abducts Frenchman in Algeria." *Al Jazeera*, September 23, 2014. Accessed October 23, 2014. http://m.aljazeera.com/story/201492219175850454.

139. Callimachi, Rukmini. "Group Backing Islamic State Vows to Kill French Citizen." *NY Times*, September 22, 2014. Accessed October 23, 2014. http://www.nytimes.com/2014/09/23/world/africa/group-backing-islamic-state-vows-to-kill-french-citizen.html.

140. Callimachi, Rukmini. "French Hostage in Algeria Is Beheaded in Video Released by Militants." *NY Times*, September 24, 2014. Accessed October 23, 2014. http://www.nytimes.com/2014/09/25/world/africa/herve-gourdel-french-hostage-beheaded-algeria.html?gwh=2FA51B436454B7D837344C9F9E77B3E0&gwt=pay&assetType=nyt_now&_r=0.

141. "Video shows beheading of four Egyptians in Sinai." *Al Arabiya*, August 28, 2014. Accessed October 23, 2014. http://english.alarabiya.net/en/News/middle-east/2014/08/28/Sinai-militants-claim-beheading-of-4-Egyptians.html.

142. Georgy, Michael. "Exclusive: Islamic State guides Egyptian militants, expanding its influence." *Reuters*, September 5, 2014. Accessed October 23, 2014. http://www.reuters.com/article/2014/09/05/us-egypt-islamicstate-idUSKBN0H018F20140905.

143. Szep, Jason and Shadi Bushra. "Egypt says coalition must battle ISIS and other terrorists." *Daily Star*, September 14, 2014. Accessed October 23, 2014. http://www.dailystar.com.lb/News/Middle-East/2014/Sep-14/270602-egypt-says-coalition-must-battle-isis-and-other-terrorists.ashx#axzz3DUeSH4oB.

144. Moore, Jack. "Malaysia Declares 'Red Alert' in Sabah as Filipino Terror Group Abu Sayyaf Pledge Allegiance to Isis." *International Business Times*, September 22, 2014. Ac-

cessed October 23, 2014. http://www.ibtimes.co.uk/malaysia-declares-red-alert-sabah-filipino-terror-group-abu-sayyaf-pledge-allegiance-isis-1466647?utm_medium=social.

145. Mezzofiore, Gianluca. "Philippines: Abu Sayyaf Terror Group Threatens to Kill Two German Hostages Over Isis Airstrikes and Ransom." *International Business Times,* September 24, 2014. Accessed October 23, 2014. http://www.ibtimes.co.uk/philippines-abu-sayyaf-terror-group-threatens-kill-two-german-hostages-over-isis-airstrikes-1466969.

146. Al-Samadi, Tamer. "Rift grows between Jabhat al-Nusra and ISIS." *Al Monitor,* November 15, 2013. Accessed October 23, 2014. http://www.almonitor.com/pulse/security/2013/11/isis-jabhat-nusra-rift-syria-jordan-1.html##ixzz3DUgz0Qyl.

147. Su, Alice. "Isis beheadings of journalists are against Islam, says Abu Qatada." *Guardian,* September 7, 2014. Accessed October 23, 2014. http://www.theguardian.com/world/2014/sep/07/isis-beheadings-islam-abu-qatada.

148. "Top Jordan jihadist denounces ISIS caliphate." *Al Arabiya,* July 2, 2014. Accessed October 23, 2014. http://english.alarabiya.net/en/News/middle-east/2014/07/02/Top-Jordan-jihadist-denounces-ISIS-caliphate-.html.

149. Al-Samadi, Tamer. "Rift grows between Jabhat al-Nusra and ISIS." *Al Monitor,* November 15, 2013. Accessed October 23, 2014. http://www.al-monitor.com/pulse/security/2013/11/isis-jabhat-nusra-rift-syria-jordan-1.html##ixzz3DUhQrUZE.

150. "Influence of ISIS felt in China, Southeast Asia." *Want China Times,* September 9, 2014. Accessed October 23, 2014. http://www.wantchinatimes.com/news-subclass-cnt.aspx?id=20140909000105&cid=1101.

151. "ISIS makes inroads into India, Pakistan." *The Tribune: India,* September 7, 2014. Accessed October 23, 2014. http://www.tribuneindia.com/2014/20140908/main5.htm.

152. Park, Madison. "Al Qaeda says it's opening new branch in India." *CNN,* September 4, 2014. Accessed October 23, 2014. http://www.cnn.com/2014/09/04/world/asia/al-qaeda-india/.

153. Moore, Jack. "Boko Haram Receives Strategic Advice From Isis as Caliphate Dream Grows." *International Business Times,* September 9, 2014. Accessed October 23, 2014. http://www.ibtimes.co.uk/boko-haram-receives-strategic-advice-isis-caliphate-dream-grows-1464639.

154. "What the evil alliance between Boko Haram, ISIS means for Nigeria." *News Nigeria,* March 8, 2015. Accessed March 12, 2015. http://thenewsnigeria.com.ng/2015/03/08/what-the-evil-alliance-between-boko-haram-isis-means-for-nigeria/.

155. Wong, Kristina. "Al Qaeda in Yemen declares support for ISIS." *Hill,* August 19, 2014. Accessed October 23, 2014. http://thehill.com/business-a-lobbying/215480-al-qaeda-in-yemen-declares-support-for-isis.

156. "Jaysh Rijal al-Tariqa al-Naqshbandia." *Mapping Militant Organizations,* July 15, 2014. Accessed October 23, 2014. http://web.stanford.edu/group/mappingmilitants/cgi-bin/groups/view/75.

157. Zelin, Aaron. "MIT Press presents a new video message from Mujāhidīn of Indonesia Timur's Shaykh Abū Wardah: "Swearing Allegiance To the Caliphate State." *Jihadology,* June 30, 2014. Accessed October 23, 2014. http://jihadology.net/2014/06/30/mit-press-presents-a-new-video-message-from-mujahidin-of-indonesia-timurs-shaykh-abu-wardah-swearing-allegiance-to-the-caliphate-state/.

158. Korte, Gregory. "What is Khorasan Group, and why are we at war with it?" *USA Today,* September 23, 2014. Accessed October 23, 2014. http://www.usatoday.com/story/news/politics/2014/09/23/khorasan-group-in-syria-what-is-it/16105605/.

159. Miller, Greg and Karen DeYoung. "Airstrikes Mark a Dramatic Shift." *High Beam Research,* September 24, 2014. Accessed October 23, 2014. http://www.highbeam.com/doc/1P2-37210384.html.

160. "Wanted Information leading to the location of Yasin al-Suri Up to $10 Million Reward." *Rewards for Justice,* 2014. Accessed October 23, 2014. http://web.archive.org/web/20120106223319/http://www.rewardsforjustice.net/index.cfm?page=suri&language=english.

161. Poladian, Charles. "Muhsin Al-Fadhli, Khorasan Leader, Killed By US-Led Airstrike: Report." *International Business Times,* September 28, 2014. Accessed October 23, 2014. http://www.ibtimes.com/muhsin-al-fadhli-khorasan-leader-killed-us-led-airstrike-report-1696029.

162. Motta, Mary. "Who are the Khorasan?" *Voice of America*, September 23, 2014. Accessed October 23, 2014. http://www.voanews.com/content/who-are-the-khorasan/2459854. html. "Profile: Umar Farouk Abdulmutallab." *BBC,* October 12, 2011. Accessed October 23, 2014. http://www.bbc.com/news/world-us-canada-11545509.

163. Victor, Philip J. "What is the Khorasan group." *Al Jazeera,* September 23, 2014. Accessed October 23, 2014. http://america.aljazeera.com/articles/2014/9/23/syria-khorasan-airstrikes.html.

Chapter Four

Establishing a Caliphate

From a State to an Empire

During its summer offensive in 2014, ISIS adopted a strategy known as the "Baghdad Belt," which prioritized gaining control of the territory surrounding Baghdad. The goal was to cut off access to the capital, and besiege the city. U.S. forces discovered plans for a similar strategy within intelligence recovered following the 2006 airstrike that killed Abu Musab al-Zarqawi.[1]

Territorial conquest has always been a goal of the Islamic State and its predecessor organizations. By early June 2014, ISIS forces had reached within thirty-seven miles of Baghdad.[2] The Islamic State's summer 2014 offensive in Iraq stunned the West and humiliated the Iraqi government. By September 30, 2014, they were within six miles of the capital.[3]

By fall 2014 and winter 2015, the IS experienced some losses, including control of the Sinjar mountains, Tikrit, and elsewhere (Iraq) and Kobani (Syria). In particular, by spring 2015, the IS lost some 25–30 percent of the territory it once held in Iraq.[4] Still, IS fighters launched renewed attacks in Ramadi and elsewhere, as well as in Syria, demonstrating that its defeat will require significant time and effort. For instance, in Syria in April 2015, the IS was also in control of Yarmouk, a town several miles from Damascus.

How was the Islamic State able to rise from the ruins of al-Qa'ida in Iraq, all but defeated by the American troop surge and the Anbar Awakening of Sunni militias, and rebound from its leadership crisis to directly threaten the capital? The answers lie in part in the chaos just across the border with Syria, and continued fragmentation of the political and sectarian scene in Iraq. Likewise, how could the IS gain control over large swaths of lands in Syria? Its successes in Syria are partly rooted in the chaos that developed there since the Arab Spring.

SYRIA

The IS, then known as the Islamic State of Iraq (ISI), joined the fight against the Assad regime shortly after the Syrian crisis began in spring 2011. By June 2012, a civil war was designated as such by the International Committee of the Red Cross.[5] The ISI forces captured the city of Raqqa in March 2013. In doing so, ISI became the first rebel group to capture a provincial capital. The group has been more attractive to foreign fighters than other jihadist organizations (such as al-Qa'ida) due, in part, to al-Baghdadi's reputation as a talented military tactician as well as its online social presence, which fuels the radicalization and recruitment of foreign fighters.[6]

The ISI worked closely with Jabhat al-Nusra, another al-Qa'ida affiliate that al-Baghdadi claims was created by ISI, during the beginning of the Syrian conflict. Relations soured as al-Baghdadi attempted to take over the leadership of both organizations. In early 2014, the ISI, now calling itself the Islamic State of Iraq and Greater Syria (ISIS), ignored al-Qa'ida's orders to redirect its efforts to Iraq and denounced Jabhat al-Nusra. ISIS accused al-Qa'ida and Jabhat al-Nusra of adhering to the Western-imposed Sykes-Picot borders. In turn, those two groups disassociated themselves from al-Baghdadi's organization shortly thereafter. The former jihadi allies became violent enemies, as exemplified by various battles between ISIS and Jabhat al-Nusra.[7] However, there have been reports that relations between the IS and JN have improved since coalition airstrikes targeted both groups in fall 2014, particularly in collaboration in capturing Yarmouk, Syria, in April 2015.

ISIS has not been popular with other rebel groups in Syria for several reasons. ISIS has many foreign fighters, divergent and often conflicting goals and implementations, and a strategy of attacking other groups for territory and supplies. Baghdadi's primary goal has been to establish a sovereign state, not just to oust President Assad from power. Interestingly enough, as the IS raises funds from various means, it does not refrain from selling oil to the regime in Damascus.[8]

By regularly attacking other insurgents for weapons, supplies, and territory, ISIS embodies organized crime characteristics with its interests in pecuniary and tangible gains. In other words, its interest in ideological goals sometimes becomes secondary.

Despite being invited into Aleppo by other rebel forces, ISIS used the safe haven to extort or threaten residents and steal from other insurgents in an attempt to gain control. In January 2014, a coalition of rebel forces pushed ISIS out of Aleppo. This falling out with other rebel groups contributed to al-Qa'ida's distancing itself from and denouncing ISIS in February 2014.[9]

When its bloody campaign in Iraq began, ISIS used its consolidated territory in Syria as a secure staging area. Before allied airstrikes in Iraq and Syria, ISIS was able to employ these regions as a safe haven for falling back and regrouping. ISIS installed its own leadership in these cities and towns. In doing so, ISIS forced its ideology upon citizens there, and ruled with an iron fist, publicly executing dissidents and minorities. [10]

ISIS's harshness against civilians has its costs to the organization and movement. By some accounts, ISIS faces more significant resistance from Syrian civilians than any other rebel or extremist group. [11] In August 2013, people in Raqqa protested against ISIS, demanding the release of prisoners and victims of kidnapping by ISIS. [12] Some even called upon ISIS to leave their city. [13] At one point, there were forty-one known civil organizations in Raqqa holding protests against ISIS. [14] Yet, as discussed elsewhere, ISIS has still managed to maintain its capital there.

In Raqqa and elsewhere, the Islamic State organized militias to violently end protests, dispersing crowds with gunfire, and sentencing individuals to torture or death. [15] The more moderate players in the Syrian conflict have turned popular animosity against ISIS into a public relations tool. By January 2014, the majority of those living in ISIS-controlled areas believed that ISIS operates to advance Western interests and suppress the removal of the Assad regime. [16]

The Islamic State continued to make some gains in Syria, even after its advances there and in Iraq faced U.S.-led airstrikes. [17] By September 30, 2014, Islamic State forces were three miles from Kobani, a Kurdish city of perhaps 50,000 on the Syrian side of the Syrian-Turkish border. This prompted Turkey to station tanks and armored personnel carriers on its side of the border. Also, Turkey considered further deployment of troops to create a buffer zone. [18]

By October 21, 2014, allied airstrikes, coupled with Kurdish Peshmerga and other forces, had gained some momentum against the IS in Kobani. Around this time, the United States dropped weapons and supplies to Iraqi (Kurdish) Peshmerga forces in Kobani, while Turkey allowed Kurdish fighters to travel to Kobani. [19] Ultimately, the IS was defeated in Kobani.

Also, allied airstrikes in Syria have been effective in their targeting of the Islamic State's makeshift oil refineries. The refineries have helped the IS militants fund up to $3 million per month from black market oil sales. [20]

IRAQ

Fallujah, the first major Iraqi city to fall to ISIS in January 2014, held a particularly traumatic significance for the United States. Just over forty miles west of Baghdad, Fallujah was the site of a very difficult and brutal conflict that occurred between U.S. forces and al-Qa'ida. [21] After several years of struggle, Fallujah experienced a short period of hard-won relative stability. By January 2014, that was no longer the case. After three-way fighting among IS militants, Iraqi military troops, and tribal militias, the IS gained control of most of the city.

Skirmishes continued after the IS announced its victory in Fallujah. Some tribes in the Anbar province temporarily cooperated with Iraqi government forces to counter the IS, although tensions between them remained high.[22] Iraqi government forces launched an attack to retake the area but failed.[23] Periodic assaults from Iraqi forces and tribal fighters continued for months. By summer 2014, the IS appeared to have less control over Fallujah than over the more recently captured city of Mosul.[24]

ISIS made its most significant gains in June 2014, when it started a southward offensive. That month, ISIS seized Mosul, the province of Nineveh, as well as the Salahuddin and Kirkuk provinces.[25]

Mosul is the second largest city in Iraq with an estimated 1.5 million. The majority of Mosul's population is Sunni Muslim. Islamic State forces gained control of the city on June 10, 2014, after four days of intermittent attacks. Many Iraqi soldiers simply abandoned their posts, presenting little resistance to the militants.[26] The victorious IS fighters were reportedly met with cheers and victory parades from the people of Mosul.[27] However, as many as 500,000 people fled the city after it was attacked by ISIS. Also, ISIS was successful in capturing the chief of the Turkish mission in Mosul and fifty consular staff, taking them as hostages. They were released in September 2014.[28] By October 2014, the Islamic State was in control of a number of cities in the northern "Baghdad Belt," including Balad, Dhululiyah, Dojama, Dujail, Ishaqi, Khalis, Taji, and Tarmiyah.[29]

Yet, there are still many residents who oppose the Islamic State's rule. These opponents are frequently killed for defying the IS.[30] When the IS took over Nineveh, its surrounding villages of Shiite Muslims from the Shabak and Turkmen minority ethnic groups were purged.[31]

Analogously, some Iraq- and Syria-based foreign fighters who joined the Islamic State were not allowed to leave the organization, after having a change of heart. Among such individuals are reportedly thirty Britons. In fact, IS leadership has threatened those seeking to depart the group with death.[32] For those who participate in fighting with IS or other jihadi groups, their ultimate fate is often death.[33]

In addition, the IS undertook repressive violence against ethnic and religious minorities in the cities it conquered. Christians, in particular, were targeted. On July 18, 2014, the IS issued an ultimatum that Christians of Mosul and other towns that must convert to Islam, pay a "protection tax" (*jizya*), or leave the city immediately.[34] If the Christians refused to follow the demands of IS, they were killed.[35]

On August 7, 2014, the IS militants captured the Mosul Dam, which was previously protected by Kurdish forces. This development raised considerable concern in the Iraqi government and its allies. After all, the Mosul Dam is the largest dam in Iraq. It provides electricity and water for most of northern Iraq. However, the Mosul Dam is poorly constructed and requires constant repairs. If the dam were to break, due to sabotage or otherwise, a sixty-five-foot tall wave would flood Mosul, while Baghdad would be hit by a fifteen-foot wall of water. If such a scenario were to unfold, up to half a million people would be killed.[36]

U.S. airstrikes focused on the region around the Mosul Dam during August 16–17, 2014.[37] These efforts enabled Kurdish troops to retake control of the dam by August 18.[38] Fighting and airstrikes continued around the dam through September 2014.[39] By September 22, 2014, Kurdish forces were able to bring the dam and adjacent plant back online.[40]

Additionally, the IS conquered the city of Bayij in the Salahuddin province. Bayij hosts Iraq's largest oil refinery. ISIS units entered Bayij in early June 2014. The group torched several government buildings, including courts and police headquarters. Soon, ISIS militants surrounded the oil refinery. There, they were able to convince Iraqi governmental security forces to withdraw from the refinery complex. Thus, ISIS was in control of Iraq's largest oil refinery, a key revenue source for the jihadist group.[41]

Next, ISIS proceeded to take over Tikrit, about eighty miles north of Baghdad. Tikrit, the capital of the Salahuddin province with a large Sunni population, is Saddam Hussein's birthplace and hometown.[42] In early June 2014, ISIS captured the city as part of its southward lightning offensive that stopped just short of Baghdad. Iraqi army forces offered little or no resistance to the ISIS onslaught.[43]

ISIS reportedly captured the provincial governor, Ahmad Abdallah.[44] The Iraqi army has attempted to retake Tikrit on a number of occasions. In late August 2014, after retaking the Mosul Dam, the Iraqi army tried to retake Tikrit a third time. Despite attacking with helicopter gunships, mortar, and artillery fire, the Iraqi army was unsuccessful against ISIS machine gun and mortar fire. As a result, the Iraqi army was forced to withdraw.[45]

The ISIS June 2014 blitzkrieg from Mosul to Tikrit covered nearly 250 miles. During that time, Iraqi security forces abandoned their posts, leaving American and Soviet-made military hardware, weapons, and equipment to be captured by ISIS. Consequently, ISIS controlled almost one-third of Iraqi territory. ISIS had already conquered most of western Al-Anbar province, except for Ramadi, the province's capital, and other minor pockets.[46]

In early August 2014, the IS conquered Iraq's largest Christian town, Qaraqosh. Located between Mosul and the Kurdish capital of Erbil, Qaraqosh fell to the IS after Kurdish Peshmerga troops withdrew from the area. Qaraqosh's population of about 50,000 was predominantly Christian, as in the nearby town of Tal Kayf. Both towns were abandoned overnight in the face of the IS onslaught. These IS victories proved troublesome to Kurds, as IS was only some twenty-four miles away from Erbil.[47]

EXPANSION

There are numerous signs that the IS is looking to expand its influence beyond its current areas of operations. For example, the second edition of its *Dabiq* magazine featured a message to the IS and its supporters: "You will invade the Arabian Peninsula, and Allah will enable you to conquer it. You will then invade Persia, and Allah will enable you to conquer it. You will then invade Rome, and Allah will enable you to conquer it."[48] Furthermore, American intelligence officials have stated that the IS is actively working on establishing cells across the globe, including in Europe. This news only added to Western governments' fears of terrorism and instability due to the expanding reach of the IS.[49]

The Islamic State has been increasing the pace and ferocity of its social media campaign, in Europe, North America, and elsewhere. The Islamic State seeks to retake the parts of Spain, Portugal, and France—known as al-Andalus—which were once controlled by the Moors. The IS frequently spreads propaganda via Twitter, aimed at intimidating Westerners and inspiring Muslims living in that region to aid the movement.[50]

ISIS has also had success in recruiting people within the city of Melilla, a Spanish enclave in Morocco. In 2014, nine individuals were arrested in the enclave on suspicion of being involved in a terror cell with ties to ISIS. Spanish and Moroccan authorities moved in and dismantled the cell, which was active at recruiting fighters for the Islamic State. The leader of the cell was a Spaniard and brother of a former Spanish soldier who is now fighting with ISIS, according to Spain's Interior Ministry. The other eight militants are Moroccan. They were trained in the use of explosives and firearms, and had traveled to Mali and other parts of western Africa to gain recruits.[51]

Sources disagree on whether the IS intends to expand into Jordan. One pro-IS militant in Jordan said, "[ISIS] . . . ha[s] no interest in targeting Jordan. When I have not consolidated my presence firmly enough in Iraq and Syria I cannot move to Jordan." Others see IS influence seeping into Jordan. Moreover, they think that IS attempts at expansion are imminent.[52]

Other examples of the expansion of the Islamic State and its message include the establishment of IS affiliates globally, terror groups worldwide claiming support for the group, as well as lone wolves and cabals carrying out terrorist attacks internationally on behalf of the Islamic State. These themes are covered in more detail elsewhere in the book, including later in this chapter.

CULTURAL ANNIHILATION

Additionally, the IS destroyed many priceless artifacts in museums, monuments, religious shrines, and ancient cities in Iraq and Syria, arguing that those figures and objects were prohibited under Islam. Likewise, this destruction was carried out to extinguish the cultural heritage of other faiths and people. Among some of the principal sites damaged by the IS were:

- Assyrian cities of Nimrud and Khorsabad along with the Khorsabad Palace, Mosul Museum and Mosul Library, Jonah's Tomb, and ancient city of Hatra in Iraq, and
- Great Mosque of Aleppo, the ancient city of Bosra, and a Crusader castle Crac des Chevaliers.[53]

Also, Islamic State militants destroyed statues of religious and cultural figures, including the Virgin Mary and Saladin. Other places succumbing to the IS path were the tomb of a twelfth century philosopher, several ancient churches, and some Shiite mosques.[54]

ELSEWHERE

Pakistan-Afghanistan

Since January 2015, there appears to be growing support for the Islamic State among some former Taliban, Pakistani Taliban, and other jihadists in Afghanistan and Pakistan.[55] As noted by Gen. John Campbell, commander of the Resolute Support mission, "There have been reports of people trying to recruit both in Afghanistan and Pakistan." Additionally, Gen. Campbell said, "Potentially, there are people who are disgruntled with the Taliban, they haven't seen [Taliban commander] Mullah Omar in years, or they want to go a different way. So there are people vulnerable to the Daesh message, and so we're looking at it very hard."[56]

Also, in January 2015, IS spokesman, Abu Mohammed al-Adnani, issued a statement announcing the expansion of the Caliphate, "We bring the mujahideen the good news of the Islamic State's expansion to Khorasan (a region encompassing Afghanistan, Pakistan, and other nearby lands). Therefore, we call upon all the mujahideen in Khorasan to join the caravan of the Khilafah [caliphate] and abandon disunity and factionalism."[57] Moreover, al-Adnani announced the appointment of former Pakistani Taliban "commander Hafez Saeed Khan will serve as the 'governor of this new geographic province of the Islamic State.'"[58] Also, al-Adnani requested, "We call upon all the soldiers of the Islamic State who are in Khorasan to listen and to obey the Wali, Hafez Saeed Khan, and his deputy (may Allah preserve them both), and to prepare for the great tribulations they will face. The factions will assemble against you and the rifles and bayonets will multiply against you. But you are up to it, with Allah's permission."[59]

Pakistan

Beyond conquering physical territory and recruiting followers in the West, the IS has also gained allies among jihadi groups around the world. Among those embracing the IS are some Pakistani militants.

With reference to Pakistan, D. Suba Chandran of the Institute of Peace and Conflict Studies argues that there are three reasons why the IS message could be enticing in Pakistan:

> First, the split within the Pakistani Taliban pushes the multiple groups to look beyond the Afghan Taliban and the al Qaeda, hence a section within the TTP looks at the ISIL... Second, a section of the militants consider the existing organizations including the Afghan Taliban and the al Qaeda are spent forces and do not have a coherent road map; on the other hand they see the ISIL as a credible alternative . . . Third, a section looks at the ISIL as a credible option and the future of international jihad. From establishing edicts to managing local administration, the ISIL is running day to day affairs of the Caliphate, while the old jihadi orders in Pakistan are on the run or hiding elsewhere.[60]

Still, Chandran continues, the IS success among the Pakistani and Afghani Taliban and al Qa'ida members might be limited, as these groups already have a strong presence in Pakistan. Also, at this point, the IS does not appear to have an organizational structure in Pakistan.[61] Pakistani groups that might align with the Islamic State, Chandran notes, include elements of "the Punjabi Taliban. The sectarian militants (belonging to the erstwhile Lashkar-e-Jhangvi) and others such as the Jaish-e-Mohammad, who have been fighting along with the TTP in the FATA, may be tempted to replicate the IS strategy in Punjab, especially in targeting the Shias, Ahmediayas and other minority communities."[62]

At Pakistan's Lal Mosque in Islamabad, Chief Cleric Maulana Abdul Aziz, expressed support for the goals of IS. Also, at an adjacent madrassa, students pledged support for IS and its leader, al-Baghdadi.[63] By some accounts, other followers of the Islamic State are based in northwest Pakistan, possibly numbering some "12,000 followers."[64] According to the Pak Institute for Peace Studies, the Islamic State is a "real and emerging threat for Pakistan."[65]

Meanwhile, various Pakistani jihadis have made videos voicing their support for the IS. In October 2014, Tehreek-e-Taliban Pakistan (the Pakistani Taliban), through its spokesman, Shahidullah Shahid announced, "Oh our brothers, we are proud of you in your victories. We are with you in your happiness and your sorrow. . . . We are with you, we will provide you with Mujahideen (fighters) and with every possible support."[66] Pakistan has several unstable regions ideal for fostering satellite groups there for the IS. Still, there are other Sunni jihadi groups that would compete for support in that region.[67]

In January 2015, a Pakistani soldier was beheaded in a video by Pakistani and Afghan militants after they pledged loyalty to the IS.[68] Later that month, Pakistani officials announced that they had arrested Yousaf al-Salafi, who was the commander of IS's Pakistani cell. He was responsible for sending locals to fight for the IS.[69]

In April 2015, Hafiz Muhammad Saeed, the leader of the IS in Pakistan, and two other fighters, were killed when an explosive they were handling exploded prematurely in Tirah Valley, Pakistan. Saeed was the founder of Laskar-e-Taiba and Jamaat-ud-Dawa, both designated by the United States as foreign terrorist organizations.[70]

Afghanistan

As reported in January 2015, a former Guantanamo Bay prisoner, Afghani Mullah Abdul Rauf, is attempting to establish a base for the IS in the southern part of Afghanistan. Rauf, who appears to be based in Zamin Dawar area of north Helmand, apparently pays "recruits up to $500 (£330) per month to fight for IS."[71]

While trying to show the Islamic State as a model for Afghanistan—and the world—in January 2015, Abu Bakr al-Baghdadi was quoted as stating that Afghan Taliban leader Mullah Omar was "demented," and that "Mullah Omar does not deserve any spiritual or political credibility . . . The organization has achieved in two years what Taliban could not achieve in its campaign in ten years."[72]

In March 2015, Afghani President Ashraf Ghani said that "[ISIL] is already sending advance guards to southern and western Afghanistan to test our vulnerabilities." Therefore, he urged that the United States consider slowing down its planned withdrawal of troops from Afghanistan; otherwise ISIL could threaten Afghanistan from within.[73]

The IS claimed responsibility for an April 2015 suicide bombing outside a bank in Jalalabad, Afghanistan, which killed over thirty-five persons and injured at least 100. This marked the first IS attack in Afghanistan. The Afghan Taliban, led by Mullah Omar, and Lashkar-i-Islam, condemned the attack.[74]

Yemen

In October 2014, a new group supporting the Islamic State was allegedly established in Yemen. Calling itself the "Supporters of the Islamic State in the Arabian Peninsula," the group issued a press release through Twitter and elsewhere vowing to support the IS against coalition airstrikes. Also, the group made clear its animus towards Yemeni President Abdo Rabbo Mansour Hadi, for accommodating Houthi (Shiite) interests in a new government coalition.[75] Still, there is some doubt about the authenticity of the press release and validity of the group. With the fall of the Hadi regime in January 2015, and the closure of the U.S. embassy during the following month, U.S. intelligence gathering and counterterrorism efforts in Yemen have been severely undermined.[76]

The downfall of the Hadi regime underscores the disintegration of sovereign states in the region along, mostly, Sunni-Shiite lines and power-based interests.[77] The continued fracturing of Yemen, coupled with growing control by the Houthis (Zaidi Shiite rebels), will create further chaos in that country, lending opportunities for al-Qa'ida in the Arabian Peninsula and the Islamic State to establish firmer bases there than previously.

The March 2015 introduction of Saudi Arabian-led airstrikes against Houthi interests, coupled with support from other Sunni majority countries, further complicated the already highly tenuous reality in Yemen. Additionally, it further pitted various sub-state, national, and regional powers over influence in Yemen, while enflaming Sunni-Shiite strife there and beyond.[78] The Saudis and other Sunni countries—"five Gulf Arab states and Jordan, Egypt, Morocco, Pakistan and Sudan"—are seeking to reinstate Yemeni President Abdo Rabbo Mansour Hadi, who was forced to flee the capital, Sanaa, and then, Aden, as Houthi forces advanced.[79] Former Yemeni President Ali Abdullah Saleh opposes Hadi's ascendency to power.

Saleh is purportedly now aligned with the Houthis. As elsewhere in the region, Iran is viewed as supporting Shiite interests—in the form of the Houthi rebels—with financial and military aid, including weapons and advisers.[80] Moreover, the Saudi Ambassador to the United States, Adel Al-Jubeir, claimed, "We have reports of Hezbollah operatives being in Yemen."[81]

Libya

As discussed earlier, in October 2014, a small Sunni jihadi group in Darna, Libya, the Islamic Youth Shura Council (Majlis Shura Shabab al-Islam), proclaimed that city to be part of the Islamic State's caliphate. Although other groups vie for control of its citizenry, the Islamic Youth Shura Council's contingent there includes fighters who organized a forum at the al-Sahaba Mosque, and conduct "Islamic police" activities.[82] Also, in June

2014, the group issued a statement supporting IS leader Abu Bakr al-Baghda-di stating, "It is incumbent on us to support this oppressed Islamic State that is taken as an enemy by those near and those far, among the kuffar (infidels) or the munafeqin (hypocrites) or those with marda al-nafous (deceased souls) alike."[83]

In 2014–2015 IS affiliates in Libya launched several terror attacks, including at the Corinthian Hotel, the beheadings of twenty-one Egyptian Cop-tic Christians, and the murders of thirty Ethiopian Christians—fifteen were beheaded while the other half were shot in the head.[84]

Turkey

The southeastern Turkish town of Sanliurfa (or Urfa), close to the Islamic State's de facto capital of Raqqa, Syria, is home to well-armed IS sleeper cells and operatives. Moreover, the IS has outsourced some of its activities, such as kidnappings, to the Turkish mafia. This was the case in the failed kidnapping of a Syrian rebel commander, Abu Issa, his *nom de guerre*.[85] Islamic State operatives visit Sanliurfa "to rest, visit their families, secure supplies—and now, many Syrians fear, to extend their campaign of persecu-tion against activists and more-moderate rebels."[86]

Islamic State operatives in Turkey have also established recruitment cen-ters in the country, including in Istanbul.[87] Moreover, the October 2014 discovery of "150 Kilograms of C4 explosives, 20 vests for suicide attacks, and a number of guns and bullets"[88] in the southeastern province of Gazian-tep portends expanded efforts by the Islamic State in Turkey.[89] Also, an Istanbul-based store, Islami Giyim, sells jihadi clothes, including IS-branded merchandise such as shirts, sweatshirts, and pants.[90]

The magazine, *Admilar*, that issued a pro-IS article is published in Istan-bul. The magazine's editor, Ali Osman Zor, is a convicted terrorist and self-designated "Islamic revolutionary." Ali supports the methods and goals of the Islamic State, explaining that the entity is a natural reaction to alleged Western transgressions and the persecution of Sunni Muslims. The publica-tion was the object of a bombing in March 2015. In that incident, Ali's brother, Unsal Zor, was killed. Ali suggests that the CIA and Mossad were involved in the bombing.[91]

Simultaneously, the U.S. government has increased pressure on Turkey to stem the flow of foreign fighters from Turkey as well as terrorists traveling through Turkey to reach Syria and Iraq.[92] According to Mohammed, a hu-man smuggler in Kilis, Turkey, the Turkish government's actions along this end are insufficient, "For example, someone comes from Tunisia. He flies to the international airport wearing jihadi clothes and a jihadi beard and he has jihadi songs on his mobile. If the Turkish government wants to prevent them coming into the country, it would do so, but they don't."[93] Since 2015,

Turkey has increased its efforts and successes in stopping foreign fighters trying to enter the country, en route to neighboring war zones.

To a degree, any individual who claims support for the Islamic State outside of its current "jurisdiction" is a success for the group, affording it a quasi-presence abroad. This affinity with the Islamic State, whether comprised of operatives who radicalize and recruit others, raise funds for IS activities, plan terrorist attacks on behalf of IS (coordinated or otherwise), or provide online and offline strategic communications, aids the group in pushing its reach outside of Syria and Iraq. Efforts and activities that are directly linked and coordinated with Islamic State operatives in Syria and Iraq demonstrate a higher level of complexity and threat than unaffiliated, self-selected adherents.

Cabals and Lone Wolves Worldwide

As referenced earlier, IS-affiliated or inspired operatives in the United States, UK, and Australia, and elsewhere, have been involved in planning terrorist attacks in their home countries.[94] More specifically, in October 2014, British authorities arrested four men in London believed to be planning an ISIS-linked terror attack, such as a public beheading or other public killing.[95] One operative, Tarik Hassane of Saudi Arabian and Moroccan descent, was studying medicine in Sudan but earlier lived in the UK. Hassane apparently traveled to Syria to meet with IS and craft the UK-based plot.[96]

In September 2014, in Oklahoma, Alton Nolen, a black convert to Islam who expressed support for jihad and ISIS, beheaded one woman and repeatedly stabbed another woman, before he was shot and taken into custody.[97] Similarly, in October 2014, Martin Couture-Rouleau, a Canadian convert to Islam who embraced jihadi and IS tenets, purposely ran over two Canadian soldiers in Quebec, killing one. Following a police chase, the suspect was shot and killed. Two days later in Ottawa, Canada, announced it would participate in allied strikes against IS in Iraq, which Couture-Rouleau condemned.[98] That same week, another Canadian convert to Islam in Ottawa, Michael Zehaf-Bibeau, shot and killed an honor guard Canadian soldier at the National War Memorial. Zehaf-Bibeau also fired numerous rounds at the Canadian parliament, Parliament Hill, before he was shot and killed. Zehaf-Bibeau appears to have undertaken the attack in disagreement over Canadian policy against the Islamic State.[99]

In September 2014, authorities in Spain and Morocco arrested nine men believed to be linked with the Islamic State, who were planning to undertake a terror attack in Spain. The cabal included eight Moroccans and one Spaniard.[100] Also in June 2014, in Melilla, Spain, six Spaniards were arrested for recruiting Islamist fighters to Libya, Mali, and Syria.[101]

In August 2014, it was reported that the Islamic State planned to kill Pope Francis for "bearing false witness against Islam."[102] The existence of the plot, let alone the prospect that it might be successful, exacerbates Muslim-Christian tensions, which, too, is part of the Islamic State's goals.

Elsewhere in Europe, the Ardennes region in Belgium witnessed the existence of jihadist training after Abd Al-Wadoud Abu Daoud listed photos of combat and weapons training on his Facebook page. Daoud is believed to be linked to a prominent family of Belgian-based jihadists, Elouassaki, some of whom joined Islamist groups trying to oust Syrian President Bashar al-Assad. In particular, Houssien Elouassaki, who led Sharia4Belgium in Vilvoorde, Belgium, was killed fighting in Syria in August 2014.[103]

In January 2015, IS spokesman, Abu Mohammed al-Adnani, issued a statement calling for lone-wolf attacks by European Muslims: "We renew our call to the mujahideen in Europe and the disbelieving West and everywhere else, to target the crusaders in their own lands and wherever they are found. We will argue, before Allah, against any Muslim who has the ability to shed a single drop of crusader blood but does not do so, whether with an explosive device, a bullet, a knife, a car, a rock or even a boot or a fist."[104]

Additionally, al-Adnani praised IS-inspired attacks during fall 2014–winter 2015, "Indeed, you saw what a single Muslim did with Canada and its parliament of shirk, and what our brothers in France, Australia, and Belgium did . . . And there were many others who killed, ran others over, threatened, frightened, and terrorized people, to the extent that we saw the crusader armies deployed on the streets in Australia, Canada, France, Belgium, and other strongholds of the cross to whom we promise—by Allah's permission—a continuation of their state of alert, terror, fear, and loss of security."[105]

The foregoing examples of Islamic State-linked or -inspired terror plots, including some reaching fruition, and IS encroachment abroad, demonstrate that the movement's reach spans the globe even if it has not conquered such overseas lands. This is somewhat reminiscent of the scope and reach of al-Qa'ida, which, while based in Afghanistan, was able to launch attacks and inspire adherents worldwide. Next, we turn to Islamic State's attempts to govern parts of Syria and Iraq.

RUNNING A STATE

The Islamic State as a sovereign state and caliphate arose at the end of June 2014.[106] For all its bloody tactics, violent ideology, and aggressive expansion, the Islamic State also has an abhorrent strategy for ruling in areas it conquers—statism through intimidation. This is particularly so in Raqqa, Syria, deemed the Islamic State's capital.[107]

In March 2013, several al-Qa'ida affiliates conquered Raqqa from Assad forces. Ahrar al-Sham and al-Nusra Front fighters were the original groups to claim the region. At the time, the two cooperated with ISIS members and shared control of the region. Stories of attempted order and sharia restrictions surfaced from this time period.[108]

From June 2013, the ISIS began "using a mix of intimidation and organization," to establish governmental legitimacy in Raqqa. ISIS chief Abu Bakr al-Baghdadi took only a year to set up the necessary institutions.[109] Disloyal activists and rebels were allowed to live in peace if they later repented by pledging loyalty to al-Baghdadi.[110]

A July 2014 Institute for the Study of War report on ISIS governance states, "ISIS has built a holistic system of governance that includes religious, educational, judicial, security, humanitarian, and infrastructure projects, among others."[111] Furthermore, ISIS governance can be delineated along "two broad categories: administrative and service-oriented. Administrative offices are responsible for managing religious outreach and enforcement, courts and punishments, educational programming, and public relations."[112] Meanwhile, "service-oriented offices manage humanitarian aid, bakeries, and key infrastructure such as water and electricity lines."[113]

Moreover, the IS strategy for control of the populace includes public outreach, affordable food, and administering utilities and public necessities. The organization engages in public outreach programs to bolster its hold on towns and cities. Too, it encourages others to join the cause while inspiring fear in its enemies and dissidents. Also, the IS held *da'wah* (proselytizing) meetings with local populations in order to promote its ideology, build ties to the community, and expand its political power. Other forms of *da'wah* outreach include the distribution of pamphlets outlining the IS ideology and establishing *da'wah* offices.[114] Many of these outreach programs target children specifically, to enhance multi-generational commitment to the IS.[115] Other efforts at radicalizing and recruiting children are dealt with elsewhere.

Additionally, ISIS-run bakeries provide bread at a price lower than what both the government and black markets offer.[116] To complement basic state services, the IS set up various social services: an office for orphans, food kitchens for the poor, and vaccination campaigns. For those within the state deemed "good Muslims," additional beneficial services are available.[117] Other terror groups, such as Hamas and Hezbollah, also offer social services, including education and health care.

The IS collects taxes, administers courts, and runs schools in territories that it controls. Its fighters provide security services for the local populace so that normal services such as garbage collection can be provided. The IS even established a regulatory agency to ensure food standards are met.[118] Thus, at this point, the Islamic State offers some government services.

A snapshot of some of the services that the Islamic State promises to provide, as in the case of the province of Aleppo, is noteworthy. Aleppo, with 1.2 million inhabitants, was officially declared to be controlled by the Islamic State.[119] There, the Islamic State is involved in mandating *zakat*, or charity, which has a Zakat Chamber.[120] In addition, a Department of Public Relations and Tribal Affairs provides information and gains insight from the public, while reaching out to tribes to ensure strong ties with the regime.[121] Likewise, the Islamic State promises to provide drinking water to the inhabitants, while also allowing for the irrigation of farms. Furthermore, the municipality endeavors to provide clean and landscaped streets and sidewalks.[122] The Department of Transport and Traffic allows for smooth transport and traffic conditions, aided by traffic police.[123]

By late December 2014, reports surfaced that conditions in some cities under IS control, namely Raqqa and Mosul, had deteriorated. Put it another way, "Isis's vaunted exercise in state-building appears to be crumbling" as "[r]esidents say services are collapsing, prices are soaring and medicines are scarce."[124] Other failings include the lack of drinking water and flour, limited water and electricity supplies, widespread disease, inadequate doctors and medical supplies, and differences in benefits between IS local and foreign fighters.[125] These shortcomings undermine the legitimacy of IS as a sovereign both internally and externally, although no open rebellion of its citizenry has been manifested at this point.[126]

Along those lines, in January 2015, the IS released a video showing the group seizing UN aid shipments and placing IS insignia on the boxes. The group then distributed this assistance in Aleppo.[127] In doing so, the IS sought to show that it was providing assistance to its citizenry, even if it arises from theft.

In areas outside of Aleppo and Raqqa, IS's governance is much less developed, particularly in small towns and rural areas. Still, IS does manage to have some services, such as humanitarian aid and recruitment services, in those areas, as well as in places outside its control, although to a far lesser degree.[128]

The Islamic State has extended its legitimacy strategy to Iraq. In September 2014, the IS created a police force in Nineveh, in northwestern Iraq, with the goal of implementing "the orders of the religious judiciary."[129] The force's stated purpose is to "maintain order and arrest culprits and the corrupt."[130] ISIS claimed it would not be used as "a tool to suppress dissent."[131] Yet, Nineveh's residents reported that the main duty of the police appears to be detaining people opposed to the IS cause. The police have set up checkpoints on the roads, conducted house raids, and arrested many residents.[132]

By spring 2015, government services within the Islamic State were in decline, pressured by coalition airstrikes, shortages, and widespread dissatisfaction with the offerings.

Recruitment

The Islamic State recruits internationally for skilled Muslim workers, such as doctors and engineers, trying to convince them to move to the caliphate.[133] At institutions such as hospitals, skilled workers, even those who belong to minority groups, have been permitted to remain while the Islamic State management oversees operations.[134]

The Islamic State's recruitment efforts are manifold. Besides online efforts that have been discussed elsewhere, the IS has recruitment centers in Syria.[135] Among terror training camps run by the Islamic State is one based in Eastern Ghouta, not far from Damascus. There, "fighters running through obstacle courses; engaging in target practices and gun firing exercises, kidnapping, disarming, and maneuvering; and participating in hand-to-hand combat drills"[136] also gain instruction in IS ideology and religion.[137]

An October 2014 IS video, "The Blood of Jihad in Nineveh," features an IS terror training camp (Sheikh Abu Azzam Al-Ansari camp) in northern Iraq. The video shows individuals receiving hand-to-hand combat and weapons training, religious and ideological instruction, and first-aid training for a wounded fighter. There are an estimated one hundred recruits filmed at this terror training camp.[138]

At another IS training camp in Kilis, Syria, ideological indoctrination was followed by military-type instruction, which lasted thirty days in total, with instructors from Yemen and Saudi Arabia. The training was described as difficult, and trainees hailed from across the globe, including the West.[139]

Besides training camps for adults, IS offers ideological and military-type training to children through its "Zarqawi's Cubs Camp" program.[140] In 2014, at one summer camp for children in Raqqa, the IS gave children dolls with blond hair and blue eyes, dressed in an orange jumpsuit, with instructions to behead the dolls. The orange-garbed dolls were supposed to depict Westerners in Guantanamo and Abu Ghraib prison uniforms.[141] Besides learning to fire weapons at the training camps for children, youths read and recite passages from the Quran, and watch gruesome videos, including "heads cut off, lashings or stonings."[142]

However, the relative stability in Raqqa during summer 2014 came at a high cost for those the IS considers heathens or apostates. Three churches in Raqqa were closed, with the largest converted into a recruitment center. Women must have their hair and faces covered in public, and smoking in public has been banned.[143]

Reports and videos have portrayed brutal public executions in IS lands. Anti-IS activists have covertly recorded such incidents, as it is one of the few ways the outside world can see what is happening there. The regime conducts house-to-house searches for the dissenters, which may result in capture and execution.[144]

By spring 2015, some fracturing of leadership in Raqqa took hold whereby Raqqa governor Abu Luqman was apparently killed by the IS over fears that he would be participating in a coup against al-Baghdadi.[145] Should further dissatisfaction with IS central leadership continue in Raqqa—both the capital city and province—and elsewhere, control over its citizenry will likely suffer as well.

Islamic State Guidelines

Of relevance, the "Media Office of the Ninawa [Nineveh] Province" issued a "Contract of the City," which includes 16 notes or guidelines to the citizenry there, namely:[146]

- "All Muslims will be treated well, unless they are allied with oppressors or help criminals.
- Money taken from the government is now public. Whoever steals or loots faces amputations. Anyone who threatens or blackmails will face severe punishment (This section also quotes a verse from the Quran (Al-Ma'idah: 33) that says that criminals may be killed or crucified).
- All Muslims are encouraged to perform their prayers with the group.
- Drugs, alcohol, and cigarettes are banned.
- Rival political or armed groups are not tolerated.
- Police and military officers can repent, but anyone who insists upon apostasy faces death.
- Sharia law is implemented.
- Graves and shrines are not allowed, and will be destroyed.
- [Women] are told that stability is at home and they should not go outside unless necessary. They should be covered, in full Islamic dress.
- Be happy to live in an Islamic land."[147]

One Analysis of Islamic State Governance

An apologetic and rosy, although otherwise informative, account of the IS's capacity to govern and its social incubation—transforming hostile communities into supportive populations—is worth sharing. The IS governance has characteristics and facets that can be grouped along the following: the "Nice Guy Act," "Law and Order Party," "Free Market Jihadis," and "Great Communicators."[148] In the "Nice Guy Act," the Islamic State provides Islamic education to children, disburses cash to the population, foments religiosity, and shows respect to local elders.[149] As the "Law and Order Party," the IS establishes sharia courts that allow predictability, are backed up by force, and with efficiency. Under this paradigm, all family and commercial services are addressed that engender stability, although with some brutality. Additionally, this consistency in the judiciary has allowed for some popularity among those governed. [150]

In December 2014, the Islamic State released photographs of a convicted thief having his hand cut off in accordance with sharia law, as practiced by IS in the Syrian city of al-Bab in Aleppo province. Also that month, the IS publicly whipped three men in the Iraqi city of Kirkuk for consumption of alcohol. Previously, the IS disseminated photos of a crucifixion of an alleged Assad regime spy. [151]

Abu Riad of the town of Al-Bab, Syria, in IS territory, echoed this glowing account in September 2014, "They [IS] brought law and order; they went after the criminals and bandits and cleaned up the town. Under the rebels, it was chaos and lawlessness. Now I can be sure my merchandise is safe and I can transport it safely as no one dares steal here anymore." [152] Also, press reports state, "some of Aleppo's industrialists and factory owners opted to move their machinery from the Sheikh Najjar industrial zone into IS territory in Al-Bab, as they knew it would be safe from looting there." [153]

Under "Free Market Jihadis," a small-government approach exists, allowing local councils to perform without much interference. Commerce and trade are encouraged, although proceeds are split among the population, with the IS taking its share. The influx of foreign fighters appears to have invigorated some local economies, even making IS-controlled areas more prosperous than elsewhere in Syria. [154]

As "Great Communicators," the IS has focused extensively on strategic communications and utilizing social media at every opportunity. The IS holds open-air gatherings during which IS ideology and services are discussed. The Islamic State uses the media very well, particularly in terms of projecting power. [155] Also, the IS slogan, "will remain and spread," implies that the entity continues to exist despite opposition, and grows with more potency across boundaries. [156] This in turn makes a listener to the IS propaganda believe that the Islamic State is always successful in its military operations and other activities.

How has IS been able to govern and garner support in Syria among some segments of the populations—those that were not killed, driven out of their homes, or otherwise living in terror? According to a journalist who traveled to Syria in September 2014, IS popularity "seems to have more to do with the failings of the Syrian opposition and the fractious rebel factions than with the Islamic State's own strength. For almost three years, the opposition and the local rebels had failed to provide any semblance of civil administration or public services to the vast areas they controlled. This lawless chaos added to the people's misery, already exacerbated by the horrors of war. In the end, they rallied around the only group that managed to give them what they wanted: the Islamic State." [157] Moreover, the journalist adds, U.S. and allied air strikes and efforts against the IS will likely not undermine support for IS, but rather buttress the Islamic State while instilling greater disdain for the West.[158]

Another report suggests that the Islamic State's capacity to govern rests principally on the support of local militias and tribes that aid the organization. Such collaboration is fickle and rests on economic benefits and fear.[159] This potential malleability will allow potential schisms between the Islamic State and its temporary benefactors, making the organization ultimately vulnerable.

In sum, leaving the IS to spread across Iraq and Syria, with its designs abroad, is certainly not a solution. Both in terms of military and civilian governance, the IS has serious weaknesses and flaws that are susceptible to internal and external pressures. Some of these deficiencies were already in display in late 2014 and early 2015. The fierce brutality and subjugation that the Islamic State imposes in areas under its control are unsustainable. In the near and long term, the Islamic State's apparatus, structures, fighters, and operatives, as well as its leadership, must be dealt with swiftly, aggressively, and adeptly. Otherwise, the Islamic State's ruinous ways—anchored in militancy and some degree of competence in governance—will gain further traction in the region, and ultimately spread its deadly tentacles throughout the globe.

NOTES

1. Roggio, Bill. "Analysis: ISIS, allies reviving 'Baghdad belts' battle plan." *Long War Journal*, June 14, 2014. Accessed October 30, 2014. http://www.longwarjournal.org/archives/2014/06/analysis_isis_allies.php.

2. White, Jeffrey. "ISIS, Iraq, and the War in Syria: Military Outlook." The Washington Institute for Policy Studies, June 19, 2014. Accessed October 30, 2014. http://www.washingtoninstitute.org/policy-analysis/view/isis-iraq-and-the-war-in-syria-military-outlook.

3. Sherlock, Ruth and Robert Tait. "Isil fighters advance to within six miles of Baghdad." *Telegraph*, September 29, 2014. Accessed October 30, 2014. http://www.telegraph.co.uk/news/worldnews/middleeast/iraq/11129512/Isil-fighters-advance-to-within-six-miles-of-Baghdad.html.

4. Mackay, Mairi. "U.S.: ISIS loses over quarter of the territory in Iraq—three things you need to know." *CNN*, April 15, 2015. Access April 15, 2015. http://www.cnn.com/2015/04/15/middleeast/isis-loses-territory-iraq/

5. Chulov, Martin and Julian Borger. "Bashar al-Assad could face prosecution as Red Cross rules Syria is in civil war." *Guardian*, July 15, 2014. Accessed October 30, 2014. http://www.theguardian.com/world/2012/jul/15/syria-civil-war-red-cross.

6. "US drops arms to Kurds battling IS." *BBC*, August 2, 2014. Accessed October 30, 2014. http://www.bbc.com/news/world-middle-east-24179084.

7. Fishman, Brian. "Welcome to the Islamic State of Syria." *Foreign Policy*, April 10, 2013. Accessed October 30, 2014. http://foreignpolicy.com/2013/04/10/welcome-to-the-islamic-state-of-syria/. "US drops arms to Kurds battling IS." *BBC*, August, 2014. Accessed October 30, 2014. http://www.bbc.com/news/world-middle-east-24179084.

8. Ibid.

9. Ibid.

10. Barkan, L. "Life Under The Shadow Of The Islamists In Syria—Part IV: The Resistance Of The Residents." MEMRI, January 17, 2014. Accessed October 30, 2014. http://www.memri.org/report/en/print7767.htm.

11. Ibid.

12. Ibid.

13. Ibid.

14. Ibid.

15. Ibid.

16. Ibid.

17. "US-led forces hit ISIL oil targets in Syria." *Al-Jazeera*, September 29, 2014. Accessed October 30, 2014. http://www.aljazeera.com/news/middleeast/2014/09/us-led-forces-hit-isil-oil-targets-syria-2014928141921406915.html.

18. Sherlock, Ruth and Tait, Robert. "Isil fighters advance to within six miles of Baghdad." *Telegraph*, September 29, 2014. Accessed October 30, 2014. http://www.telegraph.co.uk/news/worldnews/middleeast/iraq/11129512/Isil-fighters-advance-to-within-six-miles-of-Baghdad.html. Abbas, Thair. "Turkish parliament to consider "buffer zone" against ISIS." *Asharq Al-Awsat*, September 30, 2014. Accessed October 30, 2014. http://www.aawsat.net/2014/09/article55337076.

19. Solaker, Gulsen and Perry, Tom. "Turkey to let Iraqi Kurds reinforce Kobani as U.S. drops arms to defenders." *Reuters*, October 20, 2014. Accessed October 30, 2014. http://www.reuters.com/article/2014/10/20/us-mideast-crisis-usa-airdrops-idUSKCN0I904X20141020. "Iraq's Peshmerga to Send Fighters to Kobani." *Voice of America*, October 22, 2014. Accessed October 30, 2014. http://www.voanews.com/content/us-kurdish-forces-still-control-most-of-kobani/2491917.html.

Watson, Ivan and Holly Yan. "U.S. airdrops give much needed aid in Kobani, but did ISIS get some?" *CNN*, October 22, 2014. Accessed November 3, 2014. http://www.cnn.com/2014/10/22/world/meast/isis-threat/index.html.

20. "US-led forces hit ISIL oil targets in Syria." *Al-Jazeera*, September 29, 2014. Accessed October 30, 2014. http://www.aljazeera.com/news/middleeast/2014/09/us-led-forces-hit-isil-oil-targets-syria-2014928141921406915.html.

21. Ghazi, Yasir and Tim Arango. "Iraq Fighters, Qaeda Allies, Claim Falluja as New State." *NY Times*, January 3, 2014. Accessed October 30, 2014. http://www.nytimes.com/2014/01/04/world/middleeast/fighting-in-falluja-and-ramadi.html.

22. Sly, Liz. "Al-Qaeda force captures Fallujah amid rise in violence in Iraq." *Washington Post*, January 3, 2014. Accessed October 30, 2014. http://www.washingtonpost.com/world/al-qaeda-force-captures-fallujah-amid-rise-in-violence-in-iraq/2014/01/03/8abaeb2a-74aa-11e3-8def-a33011492df2_story.html.

23. "Iraqi Army launches assault on al Qaeda allies in Fallujah." *France 24*, January 6, 2014. Accessed October 30, 2014. http://www.france24.com/en/20140105-iraq-promises-crush-terrorists-who-control-fallujah/.

24. Abbas, Mushreq. "Fallujah key to defeating Islamic State." *Al Monitor*, July 9, 2014. Accessed October 30, 2014. http://www.al-monitor.com/pulse/originals/2014/07/iraq-fall-fallujah-isis-baghdadi-crisis.html#.

25. Adaki, Oren. "ISIS updates on Iraqi operations from social media." *Long War Journal*, June 11, 2014. Accessed October 30, 2014. http://www.longwarjournal.org/archives/2014/06/isis_updates_in_iraq_from_soci.php.

26. Chulov, Martin. "Isis insurgents seize control of Iraqi city of Mosul." *Guardian*, June 10, 2014. Accessed October 30, 2014. http://www.theguardian.com/world/2014/jun/10/iraq-sunni-insurgents-islamic-militants-seize-control-mosul.

27. "Photos Document ISIS Victories In Iraq: Victory Parades And Warm Welcome By Locals Alongside Massacres of Shi'ite Soldiers." MEMRI, June 16, 2014. Accessed October 30, 2014. http://www.memri.org/report/en/print8031.htm.

28. "Iraq crisis: Militants 'seize Tikri' after taking Mosul." *BBC*, June 11, 2014. Accessed October 30, 2014. http://www.bbc.com/news/world-middle-east-27800319.

29. Roggio, Bill. "Analysis: ISIS, allies reviving 'Baghdad belts' battle plan." *Long War Journal*, June 14, 2014. Accessed October 30, 2014. http://www.longwarjournal.org/archives/2014/06/analysis_isis_allies.php.

30. Williams, Holly. "In captured Iraqi city of Mosul, residents welcome ISIS." *CBS News*, June 17, 2014. Accessed October 30, 2014. http://www.cbsnews.com/news/in-captured-iraqi-city-of-mosul-residents-welcome-isis/.

31. Menezes, Alroy. "ISIS Caputres Largest Christian Town In Iraq And Several Others, Thousands Of Minorities Flee." *International Business Times*, August 7, 2014. Accessed October 30, 2014. http://www.ibtimes.com/isis-captures-largest-christian-town-iraq-several-others-thousands-minorities-flee-1651618.

32. Townsend, Mark. "Isis threatens to kill British jihadis wanting to come home." *Guardian*, October 25, 2014. Accessed October 30, 2014. http://www.theguardian.com/world/2014/oct/25/isis-threatens-kill-british-jihadis-wanting-to-come-home.

33. "Study: 23 British jihadis have already died in Syria, Iraq." *Haaretz*, October 25, 2014. Accessed October 30, 2014. http://www.haaretz.com/news/middle-east/1.622671.

34. Pandey, Avaneesh. "ISIS Asks Iraqi Christians To Convert, Pay Up Or Die, Sparks Mass Exodus From Mosul." *International Business Times*, July 19, 2014. Accessed October 30, 2014. http://www.ibtimes.com/isis-asks-iraqi-christians-convert-pay-or-die-sparks-mass-exodus-mosul-1633404.

35. "Iraqi Christians flee after Isis issue Mosul ultimatum." *BBC*, July 18, 2014. Accessed October 30, 2014. http://www.bbc.com/news/world-middle-east-28381455.

36. Malas, Nour. "Mosul Dam's Takeover by ISIS Raises Risk of Flooding." *Wall Street Journal*, August 11, 2014. Accessed October 30, 2014. http://online.wsj.com/articles/mosul-dams-takeover-by-isis-raises-risk-of-flooding-1407799954.

37. "Aug. 17: U.S. Military Conducts Airstrikes Against ISIL Near the Mosul Dam." *United States Central Command*, August 17, 2014. Accessed October 30, 2014. http://www.centcom.mil/en/news/articles/aug.-17-u.s.-military-conducts-airstrikes-against-isil-near-the-mosul-dam.

38. Malas, Nour and Tamer El-Ghobashy. "Iraq Crisis: Islamic State Militants Driven From Mosul Dam." *Wall Street Journal*, August 19, 2014. Accessed October 30, 2014. http://online.wsj.com/articles/iraq-crisis-islamic-state-militants-driven-from-mosul-dam-1408363291?tesla=y.

39. "Airstrikes Hit ISIL Near Mosul Dam." U.S. Department of Defense, September 13, 2014. Accessed October 30, 2014. http://www.defense.gov/news/newsarticle.aspx?id=123156.

40. Sadiq, Hosmand. "Peshmerga Bring Mosul Dam Back Online." *Bas News*, September 22, 2014. Accessed November 3, 2014. http://basnews.com/en/News/Details/Peshmerga-Bring-Mosul-Dam-Back-Online/35017.

41. Roggio, Bill. "ISIS takes control of Bayji, Tikirit in lightning southward advance." *Long War Journal*, June 11, 2014. Accessed October 30, 2014. http://www.longwarjournal.org/archives/2014/06/isis_take_control_of_1.php.

42. Ibid.

43. "Iraq crisis: Militants 'seize Tikri' after taking Mosul." *BBC*, June 11, 2014. Accessed October 30, 2014. http://www.bbc.com/news/world-middle-east-27800319.

44. Roggio, Bill. "ISIS takes control of Bayji, Tikrit in lightning southward advance." *Long War Journal*, June 11, 2014. Accessed October 30, 2014. http://www.longwarjournal.org/archives/2014/06/isis_take_control_of_1.php.

45. Weaver, Matthew. "Isis fighters show strength as they repel Iraqi Army's attempt to retake Tikrit." *Guardian*, August 19, 2014. Accessed October 30, 2014. http://www.theguardian.com/world/2014/aug/19/isis-fighters-iraq-army-fails-tikrit.

46. Roggio, Bill. "ISIS takes control of Bayji, Tikirit in lightning southward advance." *Long War Journal*, June 11, 2014. Accessed October 30, 2014. http://www.longwarjournal.org/archives/2014/06/isis_take_control_of_1.php.

47. Castillo, Mariano. "ISIS overtakes Iraq's largest Christan city." *CNN*, August 8, 2014. Accessed August 9, 2014. http://www.cnn.com/2014/08/07/world/meast/iraq-isis-christian-city/index.html.

48. "Why the Islamic State Represents a Dangerous Turn in the Terror Threat." *Wall Street Journal*, August 18, 2014. Accessed October 30, 2014. http://online.wsj.com/articles/capital-journal-why-isis-represents-a-dangerous-threat-1408382052.

49. Miller, Greg. "Islamic State working to establish cells outside Middle East, U.S. says." *Washington Post*, August 14, 2014. Acessed October 30, 2014. http://www.washingtonpost.com/world/national-security/islamic-state-working-to-establish-cells-outside-iraq-and-syria-us-says/2014/08/14/639c32b0-23f5-11e4-8593-da634b334390_story.html.

50. Kern, Soeren. "Islamic State: "We Will Take Spain Back." Gatestone Institute, August 17, 2014. Accessed October 30, 2014. http://www.gatestoneinstitute.org/4616/islamic-state-spain.

51. Koplowitz,Howard. "ISIS Recruitment: Spain, Morocco Arrest Terror Cell With Links To Islamic State." *International Business Times*, September 26, 2014. Accessed October 30, 2014. http://www.ibtimes.com/isis-recruitment-spain-morocco-arrest-terror-cell-links-islamic-state-1695414.

52. "ISIS' appeal presents Jordan with new test." *Al-Arabiya*, August 31, 2014. Accessed October 30, 2014. http://english.alarabiya.net/en/perspective/analysis/2014/08/31/ISIS-appeal-presents-Jordan-with-new-test.html.

53. Cullinane, Susannah, Hamdi Alkhshali and Mohammed Tawfeeq. "Tracking a trail of historical obliteration: ISIS trumpets destruction of Nimrud." *CNN*, April 13, 2015. Accessed April 15, 2015. http://www.cnn.com/2015/03/09/world/iraq-isis-heritage/index.html.

54. "As euphoria fades, Mosul wonders what ISIL rule will bring." *National*, June 25, 2014. Accessed October 30, 2014. http://www.thenational.ae/world/middle-east/as-euphoria-fades-mosul-wonders-what-isil-rule-will-bring#full. Dolamari, Mewan. "IS Militants Destroy Oldest Church in Iraq." *BasNews*, September 25, 2014. Accessed October 30, 2014. http://basnews.com/en/News/Details/IS-Militants-Destroy-Oldest-Church-in-Iraq/35382.

55. "Islamic State group reaches for Afghanistan and Pakistan." *Daily Mail*, January 16, 2015. Accessed April 30, 2015. http://www.dailymail.co.uk/wires/ap/article-2914009/Islamic-State-group-reaches-Afghanistan-Pakistan.html.

56. Tan, Michelle. "4-star: ISIS recruiting in Afghanistan, Pakistan." *Army Times*, January 15, 2015. Accessed February 18, 2015. http://www.armytimes.com/story/military/2015/01/15/islamic-state-recruiting-afghanistan/21818909/.

57. Nolan, Markham and Gilad Shiloach. "ISIS Statement Urges Attacks, Announces Khorasan State." *Vocativ*, January 26, 2015. Accessed February 18, 2015. http://www.vocativ.com/world/isis-2/isis-khorasan/.

58. Ibid.

59. Panda, Ankit. "Meet the 'Khorasan Shura': The Islamic State's Leaders for South Asia." *Diplomat*, January 29, 2015. Accessed February 18, 2015. http://thediplomat.com/2015/01/meet-the-khorasan-shura-the-islamic-states-leaders-for-south-asia/.

60. Chandran, D. Suba. "Pakistan's Militant Groups in 2015." *Institute for Peace and Conflict Studies*, January 2015. Accessed February 18, 2015. http://www.ipcs.org/pdf_file/issue/SR174-Forecasts-MilitantGroupsPak-Suba.pdf.

61. Ibid.

62. Ibid.

63. Khan, Azam. "No regret over supporting IS, says Lal Masjid cleric." *Express Tribune*, December 15, 2015. Accessed February 18, 2015. http://tribune.com.pk/story/806711/no-regret-over-supporting-is-says-lal-masjid-cleric/.

64. "Islamic State group reaches for Afghanistan and Pakistan." *Daily Mail*, January 16, 2015. Accessed April 30, 2015. http://www.dailymail.co.uk/wires/ap/article-2914009/Islamic-State-group-reaches-Afghanistan-Pakistan.html.

65. Ibid.

66. "Joining forces: TTP declares allegiance to Islamic State." *Express Tribune*, October 5, 2014. Accessed October 30, 2014. http://tribune.com.pk/story/771622/joining-forces-ttp-declares-allegiance-to-islamic-state/.

67. Ahmad, Tufail. "Pakistani Jihadi Groups Swear Oath Of Fealty To Abu Bakr Al-Baghdadi, The Rise Of Tahreek-e-Khilafat Wa Jihad (TKJ)" MEMRI Jihad and Terror Monitor, July

11, 2014. Accessed October 30, 2014. http://www.memrijttm.org/pakistani-jihadi-groups-swear-oath-of-fealty-to-abu-bakr-al-baghdadi-the-rise-of-tahreek-e-khilafat-wa-jihad-tkj.html.

68. Mehsud, Saud. "Pakistani soldier beheaded by Afghan, Pakistani IS supporters: video." *Reuters*, January 11, 2015. Accessed February 23, 2015. http://www.reuters.com/article/2015/01/11/us-pakistan-is-idUSKBN0KK0HA20150111.

69. "Pakistan arrests local Islamic State commander: sources." *Reuters*, January 21, 2015. Accessed February 23, 2015. http://www.reuters.com/article/2015/01/21/us-pakistan-is-idUSKBN0KU1E720150121.

70. Wright, Bruce. "ISIS Pakistan leader killed: Hafiz Muhammad Saeed dies from his own Islamic State bomb explosion." *International Business Times*, April 17, 2015. Accessed April 17, 2015. http://www.ibtimes.com/isis-pakistan-leader-killed-hafiz-muhammad-saeed-dies-own-islamic-state-bomb-1886190.

71. "Islamic State forces target Afghanistan's Helmand province." *Channel 4 News*, January 14, 2015. Accessed February 18, 2015. http://www.channel4.co/news/is-target-afghanistans-helmand-province.

72. Mamoun, Abdelhak. "ISIS leader al-Baghdadi describes Taliban leader as 'demented' and "ignorant Prince of war." *Iraqi-News*, January 29, 2015. Accessed February 23, 2015. http://www.iraqinews.com/iraq-war/isis-leader-al-baghdadi-describes-taliban-leader-demented-ignorant-prince-war/.

73. Sanchez, Raf. "Isil is already sending 'advanced guards' to Afghanistan, Ashraf Ghani warns." *Telegraph*, March 25, 2015. Accessed March 26, 2015. http://www.telegraph.co.uk/news/worldnews/northamerica/usa/11495078/Isil-is-already-sending-advance-guards-to-Afghanistan-Ashraf-Ghani-warns.html.

74. "First-ever suicide attack in Afghanistan kills 35." *The News*, April 19, 2015. Accessed April 19, 2015. http://www.thenews.com.pk/Todays-News-13-37072-First-ever-IS-suicide-attack-in-Afghanistan-kills-35.

75. Saeed, Ali. "Email declares pro-Islamic State group in Yemen." *Yemen Times*, October 15, 2014. Accessed October 30, 2014. http://www.yementimes.com/en/1824/news/4435/Email-declares-pro-Islamic-State-group-in-Yemen.htm.

76. "ISIS claims credit for twin suicide attacks in Yemen that reportedly killed more than 100." *Fox News*, March 20, 2015. Accessed March 21, 2015. http://www.foxnews.com/world/2015/03/20/dozens-dead-in-twin-suicide-attacks-in-yemen/.

77. Rampton, Roberta. "Obama defends U.S. counterterrorism strategy in Yemen." *Daily Mail*, January 25, 2015. Accessed February 18, 2015. http://www.dailymail.co.uk/wires/reuters/article-2925472/Obama-defends-U-S-counter-terrorism-strategy-Yemen.html#ixzz3QFBG3f8l.

78. Sly, Liz. "How the Yemen conflict risks new chaos in the Middle East." *Washington Post*, March 27, 2015. Accessed March 27, 2015. http://www.washingtonpost.com/world/middle_east/how-the-yemen-conflict-risks-new-chaos-in-the-middle-east/2015/03/27/1c4e7b5c-d417-11e4-8b1e-274d670aa9c9_story.html.

79. "Yemen crisis: Who is fighting whom?" *BBC*, March 26, 2015. Accessed March 26, 2015. http://www.bbc.com/news/world-middle-east-29319423.

80. Ibid.

81. Wahab, Siraj. "Hezbollah 'Operating in Yemen' with Houthis." *Arab News*, March 28, 2015. Accessed March 29, 2015. http://www.arabnews.com/featured/news/724391.

82. Zelin, Aaron. "The Islamic State's First Colony in Libya" *The Washington Institute*, October 10, 2014. Accessed October 30, 2014. http://www.washingtoninstitute.org/policy-analysis/view/the-islamic-states-first-colony-in-libya. "Islamic State to launch Sat-TV station in Libya—Herald." *Libya Business Info*, October 15, 2014. Accessed October 30, 2014. http://www.libyabizinfo.com/story-z8641560.

83. Zelin, Aaron. "The Islamic State's First Colony in Libya" Washington Institute for Near East Policy, October 10, 2014. Accessed October 30, 2014. http://www.washingtoninstitute.org/policy-analysis/view/the-islamic-states-first-colony-in-libya.

84. "Ethiopia says Christians killed in Libya were its citizens." *Reuters*, April 20, 2015. Accessed April 20, 2015. http://news.yahoo.com/ethiopia-says-christians-killed-libya-were-citizens-125425132.html.

85. Sly, Liz "Attempted kidnapping in Turkey shows reach of the Islamic State" *Washington Post*, October 21, 2014. Accessed October 30, 2014. http://www.washingtonpost.com/world/middle_east/kidnapping-of-abu-issa-a-syrian-rebel-shows-islamic-states-reach-into-turkey/2014/10/21/aac04b3b-a0a7-4f34-a0b4-faf9c249ce5e_story.html?hpid=z1.

86. Ibid.

87. Scott, Alev and Christie-Miller, Alexander. "Exclusive: ISIS Starts Recruiting in Istanbul's Vulnerable Suburbs." *Newsweek*, September 12, 2014. Accessed October 30, 2014. http://www.newsweek.com/2014/09/19/exclusive-how-istanbul-became-recruiting-ground-islamic-state-269247.html.

88. "Huge amount of explosives 'that could destroy a city' seized in southeast Turkey." *Hurriyet Daily*, October 13, 2014. Accessed October 30, 2014. http://www.hurriyetdailynews.com/huge-amount-of-explosives-that-could-destroy-a-city-seized-in-southeast-turkey.aspx?pageID=238&nID=72894&NewsCatID=509.

89. Sly, Liz. "Attempted kidnapping in Turkey shows reach of the Islamic State." *Washington Post*, October 21, 2014. Accessed October 30, 2014. http://www.washingtonpost.com/world/middle_east/kidnapping-of-abu-issa-a-syrian-rebel-shows-islamic-states-reach-into-turkey/2014/10/21/aac04b3b-a0a7-4f34-a0b4-faf9c249ce5e_story.html?hpid=z1.

90. "Jihadi gift shop in Turkey sells Islamic State gear." *Toronto Sun*, August 9, 2014. Accessed October 30, 2014. http://www.torontosun.com/2014/08/09/jihadi-gift-shop-in-turkey-sells-islamic-state-gear.

91. Bilginsoy, Zeynep and Ivan Watson. "Pro-ISIS magazine in Istanbul is bombed." *CNN*, March 26, 2015. Accessed March 27, 2015. http://www.cnn.com/2015/03/26/europe/turkey-magazine-bombing/index.html.

92. Sly, Liz. "Turkey confronts policy missteps on Syria with rise of al-Qaeda across the border." *Washington Post*, November 16, 2013. Accessed October 30, 2014. http://www.washingtonpost.com/world/middle_east/turkey-confronts-policy-missteps-on-syria-with-rise-of-al-qaeda-across-the-border/2013/11/16/e6183f12-4e27-11e3-97f6-ed8e3053083b_story.html.

93. Ibid.

94. "Cops Foil First ISIS Terror Plot in U.K." *Daily Beast*, October 7, 2014. Accessed October 30, 2014. http://www.thedailybeast.com/cheats/2014/10/07/cops-foil-first-isis-terror-plot-in-u-k.html. National Security Division. "Rochester Man Indicted on Charges of Attempting to Provide Material Support to ISIS, Attempting to Kill U.S. Soldiers and Possession of Firearms and Silencers." *Department of Justice*. September 16, 2014. Accessed October 30, 2014. http://www.justice.gov/nsd/pr/rochester-man-indicted-charges-attempting-provide-material-support-isis-attempting-kill-us.

"Australia Raids Foil Alleged Beheading Plot in Support of ISIS." *NBC News*, September 18, 2014. Accessed October 30, 2014. http://www.nbcnews.com/storyline/isis-terror/australia-raids-foil-alleged-beheading-plot-support-isis-n205986.

95. Whitehead, Tom. "First alleged Isil terror plot on UK foiled amid growing fears of beheadings" *Telegraph*, October 7, 2014. Accessed October 30, 2014. http://www.telegraph.co.uk/news/uknews/terrorism-in-the-uk/11147495/First-alleged-Isil-terror-plot-on-UK-foiled-amid-growing-fears-of-beheadings.html.

96. Greenwood, Chris and Arthur Martin. "Dramatic moment anti-terror police arrested medical student dubbed The Surgeon over alleged ISIS-plot to attack Britain—in a flat just yards from scene of raid on 21/7 bombers" *Daily Mail*, October 7, 2014. Accessed October 30, 2014. http://www.dailymail.co.uk/news/article-2783689/Four-men-arrested-suspicion-terror-offences-series-raids-London.

97. "Police: Woman beheaded at Oklahoma workplace" *Yahoo*, September 26, 2014. Accessed October 30, 2014. http://news.yahoo.com/police-woman-beheaded-oklahoma-workplace-144459291.html. Ellis, Ralph and Joe Sutton. "Oklahoma beheading suspect regains consciousness, interviewed by police" *CNN*, September 28, 2014. Accessed October 30, 2014. http://www.cnn.com/2014/09/27/us/oklahoma-beheading/.

98. Gollom, Mark and Lindeman, Tracey. "Who is Martin Couture-Rouleau?" *CBC News*, October 22, 2014. Accessed October 30, 2014. http://www.cbc.ca/news/canada/who-is-martin-couture-rouleau-1.2807285. "Martin Couture-Rouleau, hit-and-run driver, arrested by RCMP

in July." *CBC News*, October 22, 2014. Accessed October 30, 2014. http://www.cbc.ca/news/canada/montreal/martin-couture-rouleau-hit-and-run-driver-arrested-by-rcmp-in-july-1.2807078.

"Canadian soldier dies after being run down by suspected militant." *Daily Times*, October 21, 2014. Accessed October 30, 2014. http://www.dailytimes.com.pk/foreign/21-Oct-2014/canadian-soldier-dies-after-being-run-down-by-suspected-militant.

99. Mayer, Andre. "Michael Zehaf-Bibeau and Martin Couture-Rouleau: How Canada tracks homegrown radicals." *CBC News*, October 27, 2014. Accessed October 30, 2014. http://www.cbc.ca/news/michael-zehaf-bibeau-and-martin-couture-rouleau-how-canada-tracks-homegrown-radicals-1.2807390. "Michael Zehaf-Bibeau threatened to act 'in the name of Allah in response to Canadian foreign policy': source." *National Post*, October 27, 2014. Accessed October 30, 2014. http://news.nationalpost.com/2014/10/27/police-investigating-whether-michael-zehaf-bibeau-told-anyone-about-his-plans-before-ottawa-shooting/.

100. "Spain Orders Detention of Alleged Member of ISIS." *Morocco World News*, September 29, 2014. Accessed October 30, 2014. http://www.moroccoworldnews.com/2014/09/140329/spain-orders-detention-of-alleged-member-of-isis/. Bilefsky, Dan. "Spain and Morocco Arrest 9 on Suspicion of Terrorism." *NY Times*, September 27, 2014. Accessed October 30, 2014. http://www.nytimes.com/2014/09/27/world/europe/spain-and-morocco-arrest-9-on-suspicion-of-terrorism.html?_r=1.

Moore, Jack "Leader of Isis-Linked Terror Cell in Spain and Morocco is the Brother of a Spanish Legion Soldier." *International Business Times*, September 26, 2014. Accessed October 30, 2014. http://www.ibtimes.co.uk/leader-isis-linked-terror-cell-spain-morocco-brother-spanish-legion-soldier-1467362.

101. Gall, Carlotta. "Spanish Police Target Cells Recruiting War Volunteers." *NY Times*, June 16, 2014. Accessed October 30, 2014. http://www.nytimes.com/2014/06/17/world/europe/spanish-police-target-cells-recruiting-war-volunteers-for-insurgencies-from-western-africa-syria-iraq.html.

102. Latza, Barbie. "Italy Steps Up Security Over Alleged ISIS Plot to Kill The Pope." *Daily Beast*, August 28, 2014. Accessed October 30, 2014. http://www.thedailybeast.com/articles/2014/08/28/italy-steps-up-security-over-alleged-isis-plot-against-the-pope.html.

103. "Belgian police launch probe into 'Jihadist training camp.'" *France 24*, October 6, 2014. Accessed October 30, 2014. http://www.france24.com/en/20141004-belgium-police-launch-probe-jihadist-training-camp-woods-ardennes/. "Key Figure Sharai4Belgium Killed in Syria." *Flanders News*, September 13, 2013. Accessed November 4, 2014. http://deredactie.be/cm/vrtnieuws.english/videozone_ENG/1.1728366.

Moreira, Enrique. "Les djihadistes s'entraînent dans les Ardennes belges." *L'Union*, October 3, 2014. Accessed November 4, 2014. http://www.lunion.presse.fr/accueil/les-djihadistes-s-entrainent-dans-les-ardennes-belges-ia0b0n417690.

104. Nolan, Markham and Gilad Shiloach. "ISIS Statement Urges Attacks, Announces Khorasan State." *Vocativ*, January 26, 2015. Accessed February 18, 2015. http://www.vocativ.com/world/isis-2/isis-khorasan/.

105. Ibid.

106. "Sunni rebels declare new 'Islamic caliphate.'" *Al-Jazeera*, June 30, 2014. Accessed October 30, 2014. http://www.aljazeera.com/news/middleeast/2014/06/isil-declares-new-islamic-caliphate-201462917326669749.html.

107. Hubbard, Ben. "Life in a Jihadist Capital: Order With a Darker Side." *NY Times*, July 24, 2014. Accessed October 30, 2014. http://www.nytimes.com/2014/07/24/world/middleeast/islamic-state-controls-raqqa-syria.html. Barfi, Barak and Zelin, Aaron. "Al Qaeda's Syrian Strategy." Washington Institute for Near East Policy, October 10, 2013. Accessed October 30, 2014. http://www.washingtoninstitute.org/policy-analysis/view/al-qaedas-syrian-strategy.

"Life Inside the ISIS Home Base of Raqqa, Syria." Video, 6:57. *Wall Street Journal*, September 15, 2014. Accessed November 4, 2014. http://www.wsj.com/video/life-inside-the-isis-home-base-of-raqqa-syria/AA8CB9E3-B6A9-49AB-A2C9-F8E843413B85.html.

"Scenes from Daily Life in the de Facto Capital of ISIS." *Vanity Fair*, October 6, 2014. Accessed October 30, 2014. http://www.vanityfair.com/politics/2014/10/raqqa-syria-isis-daily-life.

Ries, Brian. "Syrian Woman Wears Hidden Camera to Reveal Life Under ISIS Rule." *Mashable*, September 24, 2014. Accessed October 30, 2014. http://mashable.com/2014/09/24/syria-hidden-camera/.

108. Enders, David. "Islamist rebels consolidating hold in three northeast Syrian provinces" *McClatchy*, March 15, 2013. Accessed October 30, 2014. http://www.mcclatchydc.com/2013/03/15/186043_islamist-rebels-consolidating.html?rh=1. Borger, Julian. "Jihadists' control of Syrian oilfields signals a decisive moment in conflict" *Guardian*, May 19, 2013. Accessed October 30, 2014. http://www.theguardian.com/world/2013/may/19/jihadists-control-syrian-oilfields.

109. "How Syria's Islamists govern with guile and guns." Indian Express, June 20, 2013. Accessed October 30, 2014. http://indianexpress.com/article/news-archive/print/how-syrias-islamists-govern-with-guile-and-guns/99/.

110. Karouny, Mariam. "In northeast Syria, Islamic State builds a government." *Reuters*, September 4, 2014. Accessed October 30, 2014. http://www.reuters.com/article/2014/09/04/us-syria-crisis-raqqa-insight-idUSKBN0GZ0D120140904.

111. Caris, Charles C., and Samuel Reynolds. 2014. "ISIS governance in Syria." Institute for the Study of War: Online. Accessed November 4, 2014. http://www.understandingwar.org/report/isis-governance-syria#sthash.F757WmCi.dpuf.

112. Ibid.

113. Ibid.

114. al-Tamimi, Aymenn Jaweed. "The Dawn of the Islamic State of Iraq and Ash-Sham." *Hudson Institute*, March 11, 2014. Accessed October 30, 2014. http://www.hudson.org/research/10169-the-dawn-of-the-islamic-state-of-iraq-and-ash-sham.

115. Ibid.

116. Ibid.

117. Zelin, Aaron. "The Islamic State of Iraq and Syria Has a Consumer Protection Office." *Atlantic,* June 13, 2014. Accessed October 30, 2014. http://www.theatlantic.com/international/archive/2014/06/the-isis-guide-to-building-an-islamic-state/372769/.

118. Tran, Mark. "Who are Isis? A terror group too extreme even for al-Qaida." *Guardian,* June 11, 2014. Accessed October 30, 2014. http://www.theguardian.com/world/2014/jun/11/isis-too-extreme-al-qaida-terror-jihadi.

119. "Aleppo Vilayet: History, location, boundaries, space and fronts." Translated by @Wilaiat_Halab. June 26, 2014. Accessed October 30, 2014. http://translate.google.com/translate?hl=en&sl=ar&u=http://justpaste.it/halabreport&prev=/search%3Fq%3D:%2Bhttp://justpaste.it/HalabReport.%26client%3Dfirefox-a%26hs%3DBkj%26rls%3Dorg.mozilla:en-US:official%26channel%3Dfflb.

120. Ibid.

121. Ibid.

122. Ibid.

123. Ibid.

124. Sly, Liz. "Islam's Dysfunctional State: In Isis-controlled Syria and Iraq everyday life is falling apart." *Independent*. December 26, 2014. Accessed December 27, 2014. http://www.independent.co.uk/news/world/middle-east/islams-dysfunctional-state-in-isiscontrolled-syria-and-iraq-everyday-life-is-falling-apart-9945774.html.

125. Ibid.

126. Ibid.

127. Shiloach, Gilad. "ISIS Is Rebranding and Distributing Stolen U.N. Humanitarian Aid." *Vocativ*, February 1, 2015. Accessed February 4, 2015. http://www.vocativ.com/world/isis-2/isis-un-humanitarian-aid/.

128. Caris, Charles and Samuel Reynolds. "ISIS Governance in Syria." *Middle East Security Report 22,* Institute for the Study of War, July 2014. Accessed October 30, 2014. http://www.understandingwar.org/sites/default/files/ISIS_Governance.pdf.

129. "Islamic State creates police force in northwest Iraq." *Jerusalem Post,* September 19, 2014. Accessed October 30, 2014. http://www.jpost.com/International/Islamic-State-creates-police-force-in-northwest-Iraq-375825.

130. Ibid.

131. Ibid.

132. Ibid.

133. Seib, Gerald F. "Why the Islamic State Represents a Dangerous Turn in the Terror Threat." *Wall Street Journal,* August 18, 2014. Accessed October 30, 2014. http://online.wsj. com/articles/capital-journal-why-isis-represents-a-dangerous-threat-1408382052.

134. Hubbard, Ben. "Life in a Jihadist Capital: Order With a Darker Side." *NY Times,* July 23, 2014. Accessed October 30, 2014. http://www.nytimes.com/2014/07/24/world/middleeast/islamic-state-controls-raqqa-syria.html?_r=0.

135. Caris, Charles and Samuel Reynolds. "ISIS Governance in Syria." *Middle East Security Report 22,* Institute for the Study of War, July 2014. Accessed October 30, 2014. http://www.understandingwar.org/sites/default/files/ISIS_Governance.pdf.

136. Roggio, Bill. "ISIS video shows Zarqawi training camp in Syria." *Long War Journal,* May 8, 2014. Accessed October 30, 2014. http://www.longwarjournal.org/archives/2014/05/isis_video_shows_zar.php.

137. Ibid.

138. "Course Graduation at ISIS Training Camp in Iraq." MEMRI. Accessed October 11, 2014. http://www.memritv.org/clip/en/4547.htm. Duell, Mark. "ISIS releases chilling new video featuring 100 recruits at training camp in Iraq being kicked in stomach and shot at on the ground." *Daily Mail,* October 12, 2014. Accessed October 30, 2014. http://www.dailymail.co.uk/news/article-2790053/isis-releases-chilling-new-video-featuring-100-recruits-training-camp-iraq-kicked-stomach-shot-ground.html.

Evans, Zenon. "Watch: ISIS Releases Training Camp Propaganda Video." *Reason.com,* October 14, 2014. Accessed October 30, 2014. http://reason.com/blog/2014/10/14/watch-isis-releases-training-camp-propag.

139. Chulov, Martin. "Inside Isis: from border bootcamp to battle, jihad is run with ruthless skill." *Guardian,* September 5, 2014. Accessed October 30, 2014. http://www.theguardian.com/world/2014/sep/05/inside-isis-recruits-from-border-bootcamp-to-battle.

140. Warrick, Joby. "Extremist Syrian faction touts training camp for boys." *Washington Post,* December 16, 2013. Accessed October 30, 2014. http://www.washingtonpost.com/world/national-security/extremist-syrian-faction-touts-training-camp-for-boys/2013/12/16/e0b4cca4-628e-11e3-a373-0f9f2d1c2b61_story.html.

141. Abdullah, Omar. "ISIS Teaches Children How to Behead in Training Camps." *ABC,* September 6, 2014. Accessed October 30, 2014. http://abcnews.go.com/International/isis-teaches-children-behead-training-camps/story?id=25303940.

142. Newton, Jennifer. "Forced to watch crucifixions, stonings and beheadings and taught to fire machine guns as big as they are: How Islamic State training camps for children are swelling its ranks with junior jihadis." *Daily Mail,* August 30, 2014. Accessed October 30, 2014. http://www.dailymail.co.uk/news/article-2738469/Forced-watch-crucifixions-stonings-beheadings-taught-fire-machine-guns-big-How-Islamic-State-training-camps-children-swelling-ranks-junior-jihadis.html.

143. Hubbard, Ben. "Life in a Jihadist Capital: Order With a Darker Side." *NY Times,* July 23, 2014. Accessed October 30, 2014. http://www.nytimes.com/2014/07/24/world/middleeast/islamic-state-controls-raqqa-syria.html?_r=0.

144. Sherlock, Ruth. "Inside an Isil town: 'Raqqa is being slaughtered silently.'" *Telegraph,* August 23, 2014. Accessed October 30, 2014. http://www.telegraph.co.uk/news/worldnews/middleeast/syria/11052984/Inside-an-Isil-town-Raqqa-is-being-slaughtered-silently.html.

145. Masi, Alexandria. "ISIS Raqqa 'Governor' alledgedly executed, prompting wave of arrests for defection." International Business Times. February 2, 2015. Accessed February 4, 2015. http://www.ibtimes.com/isis-raqqa-governor-allegedly-executed-prompting-wave-arrests-defection-1802820.

146. Taylor, Adam. "The rules in ISIS' new state: Amputations for stealing and women to stay indoors." *Washington Post,* June 12, 2014. Accessed October 30, 2014. http://www.washingtonpost.com/blogs/worldviews/wp/2014/06/12/the-rules-in-isis-new-state-amputations-for-stealing-and-women-to-stay-indoors/.

147. Ibid.

148. Al-Abdeh, Malik. "Movement for Justice and Development in Syria," Terrorism Experts Conference, Centre of Excellence Defence Against Terrorism, Ankara, Turkey, October 16, 2014.

149. Ibid.

150. Ibid.

151. Pedley, Tim. "ISIS release shocking pictures of thief having hand cut off in public by Islamic extremists." *Daily Mirror*, December 20, 2014. Accessed December 27, 2014. http://www.mirror.co.uk/news/world-news/isis-release-shocking-pictures-thief-4846282.

152. Dark, Edward. "US strikes in Syria won't turn locals against Islamic State." *Al Monitor,* September 16, 2014. Accessed October 30, 2014. http://www.al-monitor.com/pulse/originals/2014/09/syrians-support-islamic-state-refuse-us-strike.html.

153. Ibid.

154. Al-Abdeh, Malik. "Movement for Justice and Development in Syria," Terrorism Experts Conference, Centre of Excellence Defence Against Terrorism, Ankara, Turkey, October 16, 2014.

155. Ibid.

156. "Expressions of Solidarity with ISIS in The West." *MEMRI,* June 30, 2014. Accessed October 30, 2014. http://www.memri.org/report/en/print8052.htm#_edn3.

157. Dark, Edward. "US strikes in Syria won't turn locals against Islamic State." *Al Monitor,* September 16, 2014. Accessed October 30, 2014. http://www.al-monitor.com/pulse/originals/2014/09/syrians-support-islamic-state-refuse-us-strike.html.

158. Ibid.

159. Gardner, Frank. "'Jihadistan': Can Isis militants rule seized territory?" *BBC,* July 8, 2014. Accessed October 30, 2014. http://www.bbc.com/news/world-middle-east-28222872.

Chapter Five

Foreign and Women Fighters

THE SCOPE OF THE PROBLEM

The destabilizing effects of foreign fighters globally were highlighted in a March 2015 UN report, noting the presence of over 25,000 foreign fighters originating from one hundred countries. From mid-2014 to March 2015, there was a 71 percent increase in amount of foreign fighters. The report projected that there were 20,000 foreign fighters in Iraq and Syria, while some 6,500 such individuals in Afghanistan. Additionally, "hundreds of foreigners are fighting in Yemen, Libya and Pakistan, around 100 in Somalia, and others in the Sahel countries in northern Africa, and in the Philippines."[1]

More narrowly, Syria is increasingly viewed as a hotbed and training ground for transnational (especially Sunni) jihadists. The multifaceted concerns about this emerging phenomenon include:

- The prospect that Syria comes under full or partial control of these jihadi forces.
- Syria becomes a failed state, with ungovernable areas, akin, in part, to areas of Pakistan, Afghanistan, and Iraq.
- Syria becomes a permanent terrorist training base for foreign fighters to learn their ways and return to their home countries, where they would wreak havoc, whether in neighboring states—Lebanon, Iraq, Jordan, Turkey, and Israel—or beyond, including the West.
- The gradual collapse occurring in Syria further undermines stability in the Middle East and elsewhere.

By 2014—if not earlier—the concerns noted above have largely come to pass in Syria. Likewise, it is arguable that the presence and activities of the Islamic State have contributed to Iraq reaching all troubling parameters noted above.

HISTORY REPEATS ITSELF

What is transpiring in Syria in relation to its serving as a magnet for foreign Sunni jihadi fighters is not novel. Foreign Sunni jihadi fighters joined Afghans in their quest to oust the Soviet Union following its invasion of Afghanistan in 1979.[2] Afterwards, Afghanistan came under Taliban control and became a base of terrorism, complete with training camps and a headquarters of al-Qa'ida, from which the latter planned the September 11th attacks.[3]

Subsequently, various other nations attracted transnational Sunni jihadists to train and wage war against their perceived oppressors. The Bosnian war in the early 1990s attracted such foreign mujahedeen.[4] So, too, did the Chechnya conflicts with Russia.[5] In 2001, following United States and International Security Assistance Forces (ISAF) efforts to depose the Taliban in Afghanistan and extricate al-Qa'ida, Afghanistan again became the land of destination for would-be mujahedeen.[6] In 2003, coalition forces, led by the United States, dethroned Iraqi dictator Saddam Hussein, which simultaneously made Iraq a location of interest for foreign jihadi fighters, both Sunni and Shia, and state interveners such as Iran.[7]

When Tunisia, Libya, Yemen, Bahrain, Egypt, and other countries experienced their versions of the Arab Spring, they too became sites of interest to international Sunni (and Shia) jihadi extremists, although to a far lesser degree than Syria.[8] It is worth noting that in the case of other nations not subject to the Arab Spring metamorphosis, such as Somalia and Mali, foreign jihadi fighters, including Westerners, also came to fight government forces there.[9]

In the past, U.S., Westerners, and other foreign fighters traveled to Yemen to join various terror groups, including al-Qa'ida in the Arabian Peninsula. Among them were France-based Kouachi brothers who traveled to Yemen, and later carried out the attack at the *Charlie Hebdo* office in 2015 on behalf of al-Qa'ida in the Arabian Peninsula. Carlos Bledsoe, an American, spent time in Yemen, allegedly training with the same group. In 2009, Bledsoe returned to the United States. That year Bledsoe killed one person and wounded another at a U.S. military recruiting station in Little Rock, Arkansas.

FOREIGN FIGHTERS IN SYRIA

Definition

According to UN Security Council Resolution 2178 (2014), the phrase "foreign terrorist fighters" refers to "individuals who travel to a state other than their states of residence or nationality for the purpose of the perpetration, planning, or preparation of, or participation in, terrorist acts or the providing or receiving of terrorist training, including in connection with armed conflict."[10] The terms "foreign terrorist fighters" and "foreign fighters" will be used interchangeably in this book, as the latter phrase has been used extensively in describing that phenomenon in Syria and Iraq.

The severity of the foreign fighter threat was recognized by the passage of UN Security Council Resolution 2178 (2014) in September 2014, which called on nations to assist in the prevention of recruitment, funding, assistance to, and travel of prospective foreign fighters.[11] More specifically, the difficulties that foreign fighters pose, the UN resolution articulates, are manifold: "foreign terrorist fighters increase the intensity, duration and intractability of conflicts, and also may pose a serious threat to their States of origin, the States they transit and the States to which they travel, as well as States neighbouring zones of armed conflict in which foreign terrorist fighters are active and that are affected by serious security burdens."[12] This international effort should aid in reducing the participation of foreign fighters in the Syrian conflict to some degree, if not in the short term, then later.

Foreign fighters frequently serve in units made up of people from their respective home countries, or as suicide bombers.[13] The majority of these newly recruited jihadists are young adults, 18–29 years old, who have felt socially, politically, or otherwise marginalized. Other triggers for participation in the conflict arise from the perception that their kindred—whether Sunni, Shiite, Kurd, or other groups—are being victimized and must be protected from rival religious, ethnic, or state powers. Some fighters seek involvement to aid in victimized populations, although the participant may not have any affinity with the apparently threatened group. Others want to fight due to the excitement or "Jihadi Cool" factor that is fueled by videos and other social media portraying the fighters as twenty-first century warriors. Many of the fighters are recruited through social media, although other methodologies to radicalize and garner recruits exist as well.[14]

How Many?

While most sources reference the destinations of Syria and Iraq when citing figures of the number of foreign fighters, sometimes only Syria is noted as the recipient country of such operatives although the exact same figures are used.

In January 2014, James Clapper, U.S. Director of National Intelligence, estimated that there were some 100,000 rebels fighting Assad's forces, of which about 25,000 were "extremists." Director Clapper further projected that foreign Sunni jihadi fighters traveling to and participating on behalf of disparate Syrian insurgent forces originated from over fifty countries, and numbered some 7,000 persons.[15] In August 2014, U.S. Secretary of State Deputy Spokesperson Marie Harf estimated that "there are approximately 12,000 fighters from at least 50 countries in Syria."[16] The following month, U.S. government sources projected foreign fighters in Syria to reach 15,000 from eighty nations.[17] These foreign fighters have come from across the globe (e.g., Tunisia, Saudi Arabia, Jordan, Pakistan, Chechnya, Kosovo, and Western Europe), although most are from the Middle East and North Africa.[18]

By December 2014, it was estimated that some 18,000 foreign fighters from ninety countries had traveled to Syria or Iraq to participate in the conflicts there, with some 10,000 of them joining the Islamic State.[19] In February 2015, it was projected that the number of foreign fighters to the region was over 20,000.[20]

While estimates vary, the leading sources of foreign fighters in Syria as of fall 2014 appear to be: Tunisia (3,000), Saudi Arabia (2,500), Jordan (2,089), Morocco (1,500), Lebanon (890), Russia (800), the United Kingdom (488), and Turkey (400).[21] Analogously, in terms of the highest contribution of foreign fighters to Syria per capita, the countries are: Kosovo, Albania, Belgium, Bosnia, Denmark, Macedonia, Australia, Netherlands, and Sweden.[22]

These figures suggest that there is worldwide interest among jihadis in traveling from their home countries to participate as fighters on behalf of the disparate warring parties in Syria and Iraq. Clearly, the threat and scope of the problem are immense, meriting a comprehensive, and collaborative counterterrorism effort.

Of note, the majority of the 3,000 Tunisians who have joined militants in Syria became affiliated with the Islamic State or Jabhat al-Nusra.[23] While Tunisia is the home of the inception of the Arab Spring, the country "has become fertile territory for extremist recruiters."[24] This phenomenon has occurred because Tunisia is "[l]acking the heavy-handed security apparatus of an authoritarian state, but [is] not yet strong or prosperous enough to offer its citizens a better life."[25]

Another explanation for the significant number of Tunisians becoming foreign fighters in Iraq-Syria is the fact that following the fall of dictator Zine el-Abidine Ben Ali in 2011, over 2,000 jihadists were released from prison.[26] Additionally, "Tunisia's immature post-revolutionary political culture hasn't helped" undermine the appeal of extremism.[27]

Besides the concern over Tunisians traveling to Syria to join Islamist groups, trepidation exists about some 400 Tunisians who were there and returned home. As of September 2014, the Tunisian government was crafting a response as to how to deal with such persons, in particular, distinguishing those returning home to integrate into a serene life, versus those seeking to recruit terrorists or conduct political violence at home (or elsewhere). [28]

As of 2013, over 1,200 European Muslims—mostly from Russia, France, the United Kingdom, Belgium, and Germany—were believed to have traveled to Syria, looking to fight on behalf of the rebels; most were Sunni-linked. [29] In September 2014, Gilles de Kerchove, the European Union's counterterrorism chief, said that over 3,000 Europeans had traveled to Iraq and Syria to fight with various militias. [30]

By January 2015, Europol chief Rob Wainwright said that up to 5,000 European Union nationals have joined jihadist groups in Iraq and Syria. A particular threat arising from these groups is their aggressive and imaginative use of the Internet. [31] The relative ease and low cost of reaching Syria through Turkey, Jordan, or Lebanon from Europe have contributed to the keen interest of European jihadis in fighting in Syria. [32]

British Fighters in Syria

In 2014, Theresa May, the United Kingdom Home Secretary, stated that at least 500 British citizens had traveled to Iraq and Syria to participate in the conflict. [33] She added that the majority of those fighters would return to the UK. [34]

By March 2015, *BBC* reported that at least 600 British nationals traveled to the region to participate in the conflicts in Iraq and Syria, the majority of whom joined the IS. Of that figure, about fifty are believed to have been killed, while thirty are presumed to be in Syria or Iraq. Thirteen British persons have been convicted of crimes connected with the Syrian or Iraqi conflicts. [35] Another source projects the number Britons who headed to fight in Syria as 700, with some 350 having returned to the UK. [36]

In September 2013, British brothers, Akram, 24, and Mohamed Sebah, 28, of Eritrean descent, were believed to have been killed while engaged with Sunni fighters against forces loyal to Assad. [37] In February 2014, Abdul Waheed Majeed conducted the first suicide bombing by a UK citizen in Syria, when he attacked a prison in Aleppo. [38] Majeed was the former driver of British Islamist group al-Muhajiroun co-founder, radical cleric Omar Bakri. Majeed carried out the attack on behalf of Jabhat al-Nusra. [39]

The IS militant who killed the American journalist James Foley in a video posted online on August 19, 2014, was immediately believed to be from Britain due to his London-accented English. [40] According to Didier Francois, a French former IS hostage who was held with Foley, the killer was one of a group of three British IS members that the hostages nicknamed "the Beatles" ("John," "George," and "Ringo"), who were in charge of guarding Western prisoners. Francois said he believed the killer was the one they called "John" while in captivity. The media began using the nickname "Jihadi John" to refer to the execution-style murderer.[41]

A London-based rapper named Abdel-Majed Abdel Bary (also known as L. Jinny) initially emerged as the key suspect for the identity of "Jihadi John" after being identified by British MI5 and MI6 officials.[42] He was presumed to have been the executioner of both James Foley and Steven Joel Sotloff.[43] However, the American FBI later denied that Bary had killed the two,[44] citing the results of recent investigations. The FBI refused to disclose the executioner's identity.[45] The current suspects for "Ringo" and "George" are (in no particular order) Aine Davis and Razul Islam.[46]

In February 2015, it was revealed that the true identity of "Jihadi John" is the dual Kuwaiti-British national, Mohammed Emwazi. Emwazi, aged in the mid-20s, earned an undergraduate degree in computers from the University of Westminster. He is believed to have carried out the execution of three Americans—James Foley, Steve Sotloff, and Peter (Abdul-Rahman) Kassig—and two British nationals—David Haines and Alan Henning—along with Japanese hostage Kenji Goto and a Syrian soldier. The executions were later released in ISIL-crafted videos.[47]

Emwazi claimed that he was harassed by British intelligence services. Emwazi alleged that the British government believed he was interested in participating in violent jihad in Somalia and possibly elsewhere. According to Emwazi, these pressures interfered with his capacity to travel abroad freely. These restrictions, he claimed, resulted in his losing nuptial and employment opportunities in his native Kuwait. In turn, Emwazi claimed he became increasingly antagonistic against the UK and West. Ultimately, he slipped out of the UK in 2013, reached Turkey, and then Syria. Once in Syria, Emwazi joined ISIS, which later became the Islamic State.[48]

A Briton of Bangladeshi descent, Ifthekar Jaman, also known as Abu Abd al-Rahman al-Briti, was raised and educated in the UK. He traveled to Turkey in May 2013, and then on to Syria. From there, he joined ISIS. Jaman documented his daily activities on Twitter and spoke of his training and meeting foreign fighters from many different Western nations. He was reportedly killed in battle in Syria in December 2013.[49]

In November 2014, Kabir Ahmed, a British national, was identified as the suicide bomber in an attack in Baiji, Iraq. Ahmed, a married father of two from Derby, is believed to be the second British citizen to serve as a suicide bomber in the Syrian-Iraq conflict. Initially, Ahmed traveled to Syria to join Jund al-Sham in Syria before switching to the Islamic State.[50]

American Fighters in Syria

Initially, one hundred U.S. citizens were estimated to be fighting in Syria on behalf of disparate rebel groups, including some dozen with the IS.[51] By March 2015, Director of National Intelligence, James Clapper said that 180 Americans had joined Islamic militants in Syria. Forty of them have apparently returned from Syria.[52]

A September 25, 2014, U.S. Army Threat Integration Center Special Assessment, states that U.S. government estimates have grown considerably with "300 Americans are fighting with ISIL; an increase from an initial estimate of 100."[53]

Others have attempted to travel to Syria or were involved in attempting (or providing) material support to terrorists, foreign terrorist organizations, or other entities there. In addition to providing material support, several individuals plotted to undertake attacks in the United States. A number of case studies relating to such activities are set out below.

U.S.-Linked Individuals Who Successfully Traveled to Syria and Joined a Fighting Force There

Eric Harroun

A former U.S. Army soldier, Eric Harroun, 30, was arrested in Virginia and charged in March 2013 with conspiring to use a rocket-propelled grenade while fighting with the Jabhat al-Nusra. More specifically, he was charged with conspiring to use a destructive device outside of the United States. Harroun apparently entered Syria in January 2013. He later trained and fought with the Jabhat al-Nusra. Ultimately, Harroun pled guilty to conspiracy to export defense articles and services in a September 2013 plea agreement. He was sentenced to time served in jail. In April 2014, he died of an apparent overdose.[54]

Amir Farouk Ibrahim

In July 2013, Amir Farouk Ibrahim's passport was found with the identification documents of other foreigners in Syria, at a base abandoned by ISIL. He is presumed to have been killed fighting Kurdish forces.[55] Ibrahim, 32, from Pittsburgh, Pennsylvania, received his undergraduate degree from Florida International University. Ibrahim was a dual U.S.-Egyptian citizen.[56]

Sinh Vinh Ngo Nguyen

In December 2013, Sinh Vinh Ngo Nguyen, 24, pled guilty to attempting to provide material support to Jabhat al-Nusra. In June 2014, he was sentenced to thirteen years in prison. Nguyen claimed that for several months he was in

Syria, fighting with Jabhat al-Nusra, and then returned to the United States. While in the United States, Nguyen interacted with a confidential informant, who he thought was an al-Qa'ida recruiter. Nguyen offered to travel to Pakistan, where he sought to train al-Qa'ida fighters for an attack against ISAF forces.[57]

Abu Dujana al-Amriki

Abu Dujana al-Amriki was reportedly an ISIS fighter whose *nom de guerre* implies he was American. Purportedly inspired by fiery online rhetoric, al-Amriki is said to have left the United States to fight against the Assad regime.[58] The Free Syrian Army killed him in Hama. His compatriots posted online his martyrdom video after his death.[59] The video threatens attacks against the U.S. homeland. There are some concerns that the video was a hoax perpetrated by the Assad regime to discredit U.S. support to Syrian rebels.[60]

Douglas McAuthur McCain

Douglas McAuthur McCain was born in the Chicago area and moved to Minnesota as a boy. Records show he attended two different high schools and did not graduate from either. While in the United States, McCain had run-ins with law enforcement.[61] McCain appeared to have multiple Twitter accounts under the name Duale Khalid, and another one, which was removed. Most of the content on his Facebook page was removed as well. In most of his Facebook and Twitter posts he mentioned his love for Islam and Allah.[62]

McCain retweeted a speech of the IS spokesperson. Eventually, he took a trip to Turkey, a common route to Syria. Comparing McCain's two mug shots with photos of dead IS fighters enabled authorities to identify McCain as having been killed in battle in Syria in August 2014.[63]

McCain was killed by Free Syrian Army members during an exchange with IS over a Syrian opposition checkpoint near Aleppo.[64] McCain's friend, Troy Kastigar, was killed in Somalia while fighting on behalf of al-Shabaab.[65]

Abdirahmaan Muhumed

Abdirahmaan Muhumed, a 29-year-old father of nine from Minneapolis, a Somali-American, was apparently killed in Syria in August 2014 while fighting on behalf of the IS. He was allegedly killed with McCain during an exchange with Free Syrian Army rebels near Aleppo.[66]

Ibn Zubayr

During an October 2014 interview with *CBS News*, a Somali-American from the Midwest admitted that he was a fighter with Jabhat al-Nusra in Syria. The man, who calls himself Ibn Zubayr, said U.S. officials are aware of his activities. Given that fact, he will not return to the United States. Although Ibn Zubayr stated that he would not undertake an attack in the United States, he expressed admiration for bin Laden and support for a terror attack there. It is estimated that more than twelve Somali-Americans are fighting in Syria. [67]

Moner Mohammad Abusalha

Three U.S. naturalized citizens of Somali descent undertook suicide bombings in Somalia on behalf of the Somali terror group al-Shabaab. [68] In July 2014, Moner Mohammad Abusalha, a U.S. citizen, conducted a suicide bombing in Syria on behalf of Jabhat al-Nusra. [69] The concern is that U.S.-origin individuals would fight in Syria or elsewhere overseas, return to the United States, and participate in terror attacks on U.S. soil. Abusalha's extensive martyr's video, in which he lauded jihad and denigrated the West, was disseminated widely. [70]

Ahmad Abousamra

The FBI is offering a reward of $50,000 for information on Ahmad Abousamra, a Massachusetts man who holds American and Syrian citizenships. He reportedly received jihadi training in Pakistan and Yemen before going to Iraq to try to kill U.S. soldiers. He last left the United States in 2006. Abousamra is presumed to reside in Aleppo. His co-conspirator, Tarek Mehanna, is serving a seventeen-and-a-half year prison sentence for providing material support to al-Qa'ida, among other crimes. [71]

Abousamra is believed to be running the Islamic State's social media operation. Born in France, raised in a Boston suburb, and educated at Northeastern University, Abousamra uses his European languages and American acculturation to craft a brutally viral online presence for the IS that has proved to be highly seductive to prospective jihadis. [72]

Mystery Man

In October 2014, the FBI issued a press release seeking information about a man who appeared in an IS propaganda video released on September 19, 2014. "In the video, a man whose face is obscured by a mask alternates seamlessly between English and Arabic in pro-ISIL pronouncements intended to appeal to a Western audience. Dressed in desert camouflage and wearing a shoulder holster, the masked man can be seen standing in front of purported prisoners as they dig their own graves and then later presiding over their executions."[73]

Abdirahman Sheik Mohamud

In April 2015, "Abdirahman Sheik Mohamud, 23, of Columbus, Ohio," was charged "with one count of attempting to provide and providing material support to terrorists, one count of attempting to provide and providing material support to a designated foreign terrorist organization, and one count of making false statements to the FBI."[74] Mohamud traveled to Syria in April 2014, where he joined Jabhat al-Nusra. He "obtained training from a group in shooting weapons, breaking into houses, explosives and hand-to-hand combat."[75] Upon completion of his training, a Jabhat al-Nusra cleric told him "to return to the United States and commit an act of terrorism."[76] Apparently, this would mark the first time where an American fighter in Syria traveled back to the United States with plans to conduct an attack on U.S. soil.[77]

Fighters on Behalf of YPG and Dwekh Nawsha

In October 2014, it was reported that three U.S. citizens, including Jordan Matson, were fighting with the Syrian-based Kurdish People's Protection Units (YPG) against the IS. Matson, originally from Wisconsin, is a former U.S. soldier. He was wounded during a battle with the IS. Matson disclosed that he sought to join a non-foreign terrorist organization that fights the IS. The identities of the two other U.S. fighters have not been disclosed.[78]

In February 2015, two Americans, Brett Royales (formerly with the U.S. Army) and Louis Park (previously with the U.S. Marines), told *Radio Free Iraq* that they joined the Assyrian Christian rebel group, Dwekh Nawsha, in order to fight the Islamic State. Royales explained his decision to join Dwekh Nawsha, "I can't sit home and watch what's going on here—the atrocities, crucifixions, rapes, sex slaves, people being driven out from their towns. It's unacceptable to me, so I'm here to do what I can to get people back in their homes and protect their way of life."[79] Park said, "I'm here to kill Daesh, but in the Marine Corps we learned about small unit leadership; I'm going to help them train as a small unit as well, and that way we can all be more effective."[80]

Neither Park nor Royales are paid for their services. "I'm not being paid at all, I'm being fed and I'm being armed and clothed and everything, but any gear that I need, I'm paying out of pocket. This is all money that I saved for this effort myself, because I believe in the cause a lot, so I'm willing to finance everything," Park said.[81] Royales concurred and elaborated, "If I wanted to fight for money, I'd have joined a mercenary group, the YPG [Syrian Kurdish People's Protection Units]."[82]

U.S.-Linked Individuals Who Attempted to Travel to Syria in Order to Provide Material Support to a Group There

Abdella Ahmad Tounisi

In April 2013, Abdella Ahmad Tounisi, an 18-year-old high school student from Illinois, was arrested as he attempted to board a flight from Chicago to Istanbul, on his way ultimately to Gaziantep, on the Turkish-Syrian border, and then to Syria. Tounisi, who interacted online with an undercover FBI employee, was charged with attempting to provide material support to Jabhat al-Nusra. A trial is expected in 2015, although Tounisi's lawyer, Molly Armor, indicated that her client was in the preliminary stage of plea negotiations. [83]

Nicholas Michael Teausant

In October 2014, Nicholas Michael Teausant, 20, was arrested for attempting to provide material support to the IS. Teausant came to the attention of U.S. law enforcement through his anti-U.S. and pro-jihadists rants on various social media sites. Subsequently, Teausant interacted with a confidential informant and an undercover FBI agent. The three discussed Teausant's plans to travel to Syria and fight with the IS. Teausant was arrested as he commenced his travels abroad. A trial is expected in 2015. [84]

Basit Javed Sheikh

In November 2013, Basit Javed Sheikh, 29, was arrested as he attempted to board a flight from North Carolina with a final destination to Lebanon. Sheikh believed that an individual—who turned out to be an FBI covert employee—could smuggle him into Syria. Sheikh was charged with attempting to provide material support and resources to Jabhat al-Nusra. Sheikh told the FBI covert employee that he was ready to fight and be a martyr there. In 2012, Sheikh spent several weeks in Turkey, while attempting to enter Syria to fight with Jabhat al-Nusra. A trial is expected in 2015. [85]

Michael Todd Wolfe

In June 2014, Texas-based Michael Todd Wolfe was charged with attempting to provide material support to terrorists in Syria. Wolfe, who was unknowingly in contact with undercover FBI agents, purchased airline tickets to Denmark on Iceland Air for himself, his wife (Jordan Nicole Furr, also known as Jordan Wolfe), and their two children, with the goal of subsequently entering Syria from Turkey. Wolfe explained that this route was cheaper than trying to fly directly to Turkey. Wolfe had concerns about joining Jabhat al-Nusra, and preferred aligning with the Islamic State. In June 2014, Wolfe and his family entered Houston's George Bush International Airport, attempting to board a flight to Toronto. From there, the family was supposed to travel to Iceland and then Denmark. In Denmark, Wolfe was supposed to meet with the undercover FBI agent, who was to assist the family to travel to Turkey and then Syria. Wolfe was arrested as he tried to board the Toronto-bound flight.[86] A trial is expected in 2015.

Avin Marsalis Brown and Akba Jihad Jordan

In August 2014, Raleigh, North Carolina-based Avin Marsalis Brown pleaded guilty to conspiracy to provide material to ISIL. Two months later, his co-conspirator, Akba Jihad Jordan, pleaded guilty to similar charges. They both await sentencing. Brown reached out online for assistance with the goal to travel abroad to join a jihadist terrorist group. His online interactions included contact to an undercover FBI employee. Subsequently, Brown and Jordan had "numerous discussions with an FBI confidential source in which they expressed a desire to travel overseas to join certain groups in fighting the 'kuffar' (non-Muslims) and 'munafiq' (Muslims considered to be hypocrites), primarily in either Syria or Yemen." Besides discussing "weapons and the use of weapons in fighting the kuffar, both overseas and in the United States … Jordan showed Brown how to break down the AK-47."[87]

The two agreed that Brown would travel to Turkey, and then make way to Syria, while reaching out to an ISIL contact he made online. Afterwards, with the assistance of Brown, Jordan would travel to Syria after obtaining a passport and adequate funds for travel. Brown was arrested on March 19, 2014, as he tried to board a flight from Raleigh Durham International Airport to Turkey. Jordan was arrested the same day.[88]

Donald Ray Morgan

Donald Ray Morgan was arraigned in September 2014 in North Carolina for being a convicted felon in possession of a firearm. In January 2014, Morgan traveled to Lebanon, and later to Turkey, seeking to enter Syria from there and join ISIS. However, Morgan claimed that he was unable to enter Syria. Morgan, a former sheriff's deputy, was a convert to Islam from Catholicism.[89] In tweets and interviews with the media, Morgan "expressed sympathy and support for the militant terror group ISIS."[90]

Morgan failed U.S. Army boot camp, was fired from a law enforcement job, became a bodybuilder, later married, then divorced and converted to Islam, and ultimately became radicalized in jihadi tenets before embarking on the travel outlined above. In October 2014, Morgan was charged with attempting to provide material support to ISIL. He pleaded guilty to that charge the same month and awaits sentencing in 2015.[91]

Mohammed Hamzah Khan

Mohammed Hamzah Khan, 19, a U.S. citizen from Bolingbrook, Illinois, was arrested in October 2014 as he tried to board an Austrian Airline flight from Chicago to Vienna, Austria, on his way to Turkey. Khan's two younger siblings were stopped with him at the airport. From Turkey, Khan planned to enter Syria to fight with ISIS. Khan interacted online with an undercover FBI agent, who Khan considered to be a recruiter for ISIS. If convicted of the alleged crime, Khan could spend up to fifteen years in prison and pay a $250,000 fine. [92]

Abdi Nur and Abdullah Yusuf

In November 2014, Abdi Nur and Abdullah Yusuf were charged with conspiracy to provide material support to a foreign terrorist organization (ISIL). Nur is also charged with providing material support to ISIL. Both men are of Somali descent and from the Minnesota area. Yusuf is associated with several men who traveled to Syria to join ISIL. Yusuf was arrested at the Minneapolis-St. Paul Airport, as he tried to commence travel from Minnesota to Turkey (and ultimately to Syria). In February 2015, Yusuf pleaded guilty to the conspiracy to provide material support charge. In a shift from other cases, Yusuf was placed in a half-way house, where he is expected to receive counseling. [93]

In May 2014, Nur managed to fly from Minnesota to Turkey, and later reached Syria, where he apparently joined ISIL. Both Nur and Yusuf paid for their flights using the same debit card associated with a checking account. They each replenished the accounts with some $1,500 in cash, both using ATMs for those transactions. [94]

Both obtained expedited passports for their travels overseas. Yusuf's interaction with the passport specialist at the Minneapolis Passport Office raised suspicions as to how Yusuf could afford the flight, where he would be staying in Turkey, among other matters. Because of this, the passport specialist contacted his supervisor, who then informed the FBI. Yusuf was subsequently placed under surveillance. [95]

Abdurasul Hasanovich Juraboev, Akhror Saidakhmetov, and Abror Habibov

In February 2015, Abdurasul Hasanovich Juraboev (an Uzbek national), 24, Akhror Saidakhmetov (a Kazakh national), 19, and Abror Habibov (an Uzbek national), 30, were charged in relation to attempting and conspiring to provide material support to a foreign terrorist organization, ISIL. Juraboev and Saidakhmetov had planned to travel to Turkey, and then make their way to Syria, where they intended to join ISIL. Juraboev was arrested while trying to board a plane to Turkey. Saidakhmetov had planned to travel to

Syria (via Turkey) in March 2015. Habibov assisted in funding Saidakhmetov's travel plans and goal of joining ISIL. "Juraboev was also prepared to engage in an act of terrorism in the United States if ordered to do so by ISIL, and Saidakhmetov intended to commit such an act if unable to travel abroad to join ISIL."[96] More specifically, Juraboev offered to kill President Obama, while Saidakhmetov considered acquiring "a machine gun and shoot[ing] police officers and FBI agents if thwarted in his plan to join ISIL in Syria."[97] The cabal was discovered following an initial lead arising from monitoring an Uzbek-language, pro-ISIL website. If convicted, each defendant faces up to fifteen years in prison.[98]

Tairod Nathan Webster Pugh

In March 2015, Tairod Nathan Webster Pugh, a U.S. citizen and former member of the U.S. Air Force, was indicted in relation to attempting to provide material support to a foreign terrorist organization (ISIL) as well as obstructing justice and attempting to obstruct justice. Pugh, who served as an avionics instrument system specialist while in the U.S. military, subsequently worked in similar roles in the private sector, including in the Middle East. In January 2015, Pugh traveled from Egypt—where he had been fired as an aviation mechanic—to Turkey, with the goal of traveling from there to Syria. Once in Syria, he had planned to join ISIL. Pugh was denied entry into Turkey, was returned to Egypt, and afterwards deported to the United States. A search of Pugh's electronics yielded ISIL-related data, and information on crossing into Syria from Turkey. He faces up to thirty-five years in prison.[99]

Hasan and Jonas Edmonds

In March 2015, a pair of cousins from Aurora, Illinois—"Army National Guard Specialist Hasan Edmonds, 22," and "Jonas Edmonds, 29,"—both U.S. citizens, were arrested and charged with conspiracy to provide material support to a foreign terrorist organization, ISIL. They devised a plan by which Hasan would travel to Syria, where he would join ISIL and fight on its behalf. Meanwhile, Jonas had planned to use Hasan's military identification to access a military installation in northern Illinois where Hasan worked. Once there, Jonas planned to undertake an attack, hoping to kill between 100 and 150 persons. Fortunately, Hasan was arrested while trying to fly from Chicago's Midway Airport to Egypt, while Jonas was taken into custody at his home. The Edmondses met and discussed the plot with an FBI undercover employee, who they believed was an ISIL operative. The pair faces penalties of 15 years in prison and a fine of $250,000.[100]

Zacharia Yusuf Abdurahman, Adnan Farah, Hanad Mustafe Musse, Guled Ali Omar, Abdirahman Yasin Daud, and Mohamed Abdihamid Farah

In April 2015, the U.S. government charged "Zacharia Yusuf Abdurahman, 19, Adnan Farah, 19, Hanad Mustafe Musse, 19, and Guled Ali Omar, 20," as well as "Abdirahman Yasin Daud, 21, and Mohamed Abdihamid Farah, 21," with "conspiracy and attempt to provide material support to a designated foreign terrorist organization," ISIL.[101] The Minnesota-based individuals of Somali descent were arrested following U.S. authorities' investigating links between that community and travel abroad to join terrorist groups, such as ISIL, Jabhat al-Nusra, and al-Shabaab.[102] "At least nine Minnesotans have now been charged as part of this conspiracy to provide material support to ISIL. The men are all alleged associates and friends of one another."[103]

U.S.-Linked Individuals who Provided Material Support to Those Seeking to Participate in Syrian Conflict and Other Terrorist Activities

Gufran Ahmed Mohammed and Mohamed Hussein Said

In August 2013, Gufran Ahmed Mohammed, 30, a naturalized U.S. citizen and resident of Saudi Arabia, and Mohamed Hussein Said, 25, from Kenya, were charged with conspiring to provide money and recruits to al-Qa'ida, al-Qa'ida in Iraq/Jabhat al-Nusra (in Syria), and al-Shabaab (in Somalia). Mohammed sent wire transfers to a person he believed was a fundraiser, recruiter, and supplier for al-Qa'ida and al-Qa'ida in Iraq/Jabhat al-Nusra with the goal of supporting those organizations. Also, Mohammed and Said agreed to aid al-Qa'ida and al-Qa'ida in Iraq/Jabhat al-Nusra by recruiting and transferring experienced al-Shabaab fighters to Syria. A trial is expected in 2015.[104]

Mufid A. Elfgeeh

In September 2014, Mufid A. Elfgeeh, of Rochester, New York, was indicted for the following crimes: three counts of providing material support to a foreign terrorist organization (ISIS), and "one count of attempted murder of current and former members of the United States military, one count of possessing firearms equipped with silencers in furtherance of a crime of violence, and two counts of receipt and possession of unregistered firearm silencers."[105] More specifically, Elfgeeh sought to assist three people to travel to Syria, where they would join and fight on behalf of the IS. Two of these individuals were confidential informants. Elfgeeh sent the third individual, who was based in Yemen, $600 to facilitate the Yemini's travel to Syria, where he would join and fight for the IS. "Elfgeeh also plotted to shoot and kill members of the United States military who had returned from Iraq. As part of the plan to kill soldiers, Elfgeeh purchased two handguns equipped with firearm silencers and ammunition from a confidential source."[106] The maximum sentence for these alleged crimes is 105 years in prison.[107] A trial is expected in 2015.

Elfgeeh, a naturalized U.S. citizen from Yemen, managed a convenience store, MoJoe's, in Rochester.[108] He used Twitter to articulate his animus towards the United States and his support for al-Qa'ida. In one tweet, Elfgeeh wrote, "al-Qaeda said it loud and clear; we are fighting the American invasion and their hegemony over the earth and the people."[109]

Bosnian-linked Cabal

In February 2015, six individuals of Bosnian descent—"Ramiz Zijad Hodzic, 40, his wife Sedina Unkic Hodzic, 35, and Armin Harcevic, 37, all of St. Louis County, Missouri; Nihad Rosic, 26, of Utica, New York; Mediha Medy Salkicevic, 34 of Schiller Park, Illinois; and Jasminka Ramic, 42, of Rockford, Illinois"—were charged with "conspiring to provide material support and resources to terrorists, and with providing material support to terrorists. Ramiz Zijad Hodzic and Nihad Rosic are also charged with conspiring to kill and maim persons in a foreign country."[110] A seventh individual, who was not charged, "Abdullah Ramo Pazara, a Bosnian native who at one time emigrated to the U.S., became a naturalized citizen, and then left the United States in 2013 to fight in Syria, Iraq and elsewhere in support of Al-Qaida and ISIS."[111]

The group transferred funds to Pazara and "shipped him boxes upon boxes filled with U.S. military surplus equipment—uniforms, combat boots, tactical gear and clothing, firearms accessories, optical equipment and range finders, rifle scopes, and other items bought in St. Louis, Mo.—to be used in carrying out terrorist acts."[112] Additionally, they "helped identify supporters and other conspirators in the U.S. and elsewhere from whom they could solicit money that was wired to various financial accounts, then transferred overseas, usually to Turkey or Saudi Arabia, headed to Pazara and others in Syria and Iraq."[113] A trial is expected in 2015.

High School Student

In March 2015, a 17-year-old in Woodbridge, Virginia, at Osbourn Park High School was arrested in relation to assisting an 18-year-old to travel to Syria and join the Islamic State. Also, it is reported that the teen attempted to recruit others in his high school to enlist in the group.[114] A trial is expected in 2015.

Foreign Fighters from Selected Countries

Turkey

By fall 2014, the number of Turkish fighters joining the IS was estimated to have reached 1,000 people. Some Turkish recruits have joined for ideological reasons. For instance, some consider Turkey as not being Islamic enough. Others seek participation with the Islamic State for financial reasons. After all, IS fighters can earn $150 per day. There are IS recruiting centers in Turkey, especially in a poor section of the capital, Ankara, called Hacibayram. From that district some one hundred residents left Turkey for Syria to fight on behalf of the IS.[115] In January 2015, Turkish Foreign Minister Mevlüt Çavuşoğlu expressed concern about the return of those foreign fighters to their home country: "What will happen when they return to their countries?"[116]

France

Mehdi Nemmouche has been in custody in France since his arrest for a May 2014 shooting at the Jewish Museum of Belgium in Brussels. Nemmouche left the IS after serving as a captor and torturer of IS hostages, as he sought to conduct attacks in Western Europe. In Brussels, he opened fire, killing four people, and fled the crime scene. After four French hostages were released from captivity, they spoke about Nemmouche's behavior. He had bought gloves just to beat the hostages, and made sure they knew that these gloves were made for them. Nemmouche is described as having a "violent and provocative personality."[117] The audio recordings that had been recovered from the videos that the ISIS had sent out allowed for a direct match to be made to between the Brussels attacker and Nemmouche.

Nemmouche tortured Nicolas Henin, a French reporter. Henin had been held in captivity with American journalists James Foley and Steven Sotloff, both of whom were beheaded by the IS in 2014.[118] Henin and other French journalists released in April 2014 described being held in about 10 underground places of captivity, mostly with other people.

Finland

In January 2015, Jari Taponen, Police Chief Inspector of Helsinki, said that about fifty people from Finland—including nearly twenty ethnic Finns—traveled to IS-controlled areas in Iraq and Syria to fight on behalf of the group. Eight were killed while abroad. In light of that threat, Finnish security officials are making efforts to reduce radicalization and integrate returning foreign fighters into society.[119]

A 22-year-old man of Somali extraction, "Muhammad," lived in Finland since the age of two. Apparently, he was an admirer of Anwar al-Awlaki. In December 2012, "Muhammad" traveled to Syria by way of Turkey. His social media feed contained photos of an IS attack in Hama, suggesting that he joined the group.[120]

Sweden

In January 2015, Swedish security service (Sapo) head Anders Thornberg stated that one hundred Swedes joined the Islamic State. In one instance, two individuals based in Sweden purchased a car and drove to Syria to participate in the conflict. The pair included an ethnic Swede, Abu Khattab al-Swedi, and an ethnic Afghan, Abu Uthman al-Afghani.[121]

Germany

Abu Osama al-Almani ("The German") appeared in a video that surfaced in November 2013. Al-Almani claimed that he went to Syria from Germany to spread the word of Allah and justice. Al-Almani called upon Muslim and non-Muslim Germans to join the jihad in Syria, although he urged non-Muslims to convert.[122]

Denis Mamadou Cuspert was once a popular rapper in Germany using the stage name Deso Dogg. After a near-death car accident turned him toward Islam, his already activist anti-American politics suddenly grew in intensity. Cuspert soon became an inflammatory Islamist singer and orator. He is thought to have inspired, if not encouraged, the killing of two U.S. airmen at Frankfurt Airport in March 2011. Also, Cuspert swore allegiance to Mullah Muhammad Omar, leader of the Taliban.[123]

Cuspert was thought to have left Germany in 2012, to join jihadist groups in Syria. Videos and photos posted online show him posing and with weapons in Syria.[124] Cuspert pledged allegiance to Abu Bakr al-Baghdadi in a video released in April 2014.[125] Later that month, Cuspert apparently died in a Jabhat al-Nusra Front suicide attack on IS forces, although reports are unconfirmed.[126] Nevertheless, in February 2015, the U.S. State Department designated him "as a Specially Designated Global Terrorist under Executive Order (E.O.) 13224, which targets terrorists and those providing support to terrorists or acts of terrorism."[127]

India

In November 2014, Areeb Majeed was arrested in Turkey, and subsequently transferred to Indian authorities. Majeed is an Indian member of the Islamic State, who apparently killed about fifty-five people while fighting for the group in Iraq. Majeed claimed that he was self-radicalized in the tenets of IS in Kalyan, India, after viewing many jihadi websites. He was then contacted by IS recruiters, who paid for his travel to Iraq, under the guise of a pilgrimage there. Majeed and three of his colleagues from India then took a taxi to Fallujah, before ultimately making their way to training camp near Mosul. At the training camp, they received ideological and weapons training, including using explosives and AK-47s. There are varying accounts as to why Majeed left Iraq. The reasons range from that he was wounded and sought medical treatment in Turkey, to leaving the group due to not receiving payment (or enough funds) for his services. Alternatively, he returned to India in order to undertake an attack there. [128]

Palestinians

Some one hundred Gazans have joined the Islamic State, with another 1,000 interested in joining the group. Gaza-based Palestinian Salafist jihadist leader, Abu Anas al-Maqdisi, stated, "The applicants (for joining ISIS) are subjected to comprehensive security research and coordination between the Salafist groups in Gaza, Iraq and Syria." [129]

Other Foreign Fighters

Other nations are sources of fighters to the IS. In July 2014, 5,000 Syrians and 1,000 foreigners joined IS. [130] By one account, about 1,000 Egyptians have traveled to join IS, while Egyptian security sources claim the figure of Egyptians fighting abroad with diverse jihadi groups is 8,000. [131]

In October 2014, the Belgian government released a report that 350 of its citizens traveled to Syria to join other jihadists, and 20 percent returned home. [132] In January 2015, it was reported that Malaysian men and women had taken out loans from banks and moneylenders to finance their travels to join the Islamic State. Other Malaysians seek to travel there in order to live in an Islamic caliphate. [133]

In January 2015, Saudi Interior Ministry spokesman Maj. Gen. Mansour al-Turki said that some 2,200 Saudi joined rebel groups in Syria, during the previous years, with 630 returning to the Kingdom. [134] The allure of fighting in Syria has even reached Australian shores. In 2014, Australia's Attorney General, George Brandis, stated that between 120–150 Australians traveled to Syria to participate in the conflict. [135]

Shiite Foreign Fighters

Concurrently, some 6,500 Shiite foreign fighters have fought to buttress the position of the Assad regime, affiliating themselves with the Shiite Lebanese-based terror group, Hezbollah; Iranian soldiers; and Iraqi volunteers. [136] While the majority of the Americans who travel to Syria are presumed to aspire to fight with Sunni jihadist groups there, some Americans fight in support of Syrian government forces, including Hezbollah forces. An example of the latter is Mohamad Anas Haitham Soueid, 48. In March 2012, Soueid was convicted of unlawfully acting as an agent of Syria. He was convicted of collecting videos and audio recordings and other information about individuals based in Syria and the United States who were protesting the Syrian government. Soueid provided this content to Syrian intelligence agencies, in order to intimidate and target the protesters. In July 2012, Soueid was sentenced to eighteen months in prison. [137]

In March 2014, Mohammad Hassan Hamdan was charged with attempting to provide material support to Hezbollah. [138] Hamdan, a Lebanese immigrant to the United States, was a Hezbollah member when he lived in Lebanon, including fighting with Hezbollah against Israel in 2006. In 2014, Hamdan was arrested at Detroit Airport before boarding a flight to Beirut. In Beirut, Hamdan planned to rejoin Hezbollah, get paid between $500 and $1,000 a month, and fight with Hezbollah members in Syria against various insurgent forces. [139]

In March 2014, a video was released showing pro-Assad Los Angeles gang members, "Creeper" from the Surenos or Sur-13 ("a group loosely affiliated with Mexican-mafia-linked southern California gangs")[140] and "Wino," Nerses Kilajyan of Westside Armenian Power. One, if not both of these gang members, were deported from the United States. [141]

Also, Kilajyan was photographed wearing Hezbollah clothing and with Hezbollah operatives. According to his Facebook page, Kilajyan has been in Aleppo since December 2012. [142] Armenian Christians have largely been supportive of the Assad regime. [143]

Other Foreign Fighters in Syria

The diversity of foreign fighters entering the fray in the Syrian and Iraq conflicts is exemplified by reports that German and Dutch motorcycle gang members have joined rebel groups to fight the IS. More particularly, three Dutchmen, apparently from Amsterdam, Breda, and Rotterdam, and members of the motorcycle gang No Surrender, are fighting alongside Kurds in Iraq. The Dutchmen are former members of the Dutch military, including marines and army. [144] Under Dutch law, fighting on behalf of a foreign armed force is permissible, as long as the group is not a terrorist organization nor at war with the Netherlands. [145] Also, several ethnically Kurdish Germans from the motorcycle gang Median Empire have joined Kurdish fighters in Syria against the IS. [146]

Similarly, individuals from the United States, Canada, the UK, Netherlands, Germany, and other Western countries, including some with military backgrounds, have traveled to Iraq and Syria to fight against the Islamic State while joining groups such as the Kurdish People's Protection Units, the YPG. Among the fighters are various veterans including: Jordan Matson and Jeremy Woodard from the United States, James Hughes from the UK, and Jamie Read from France. [147]

Additionally, in November 2014, it was reported that a Canadian-Israeli woman, Gil Rosenberg, joined Kurdish militants, YPG, to fight against the IS. Rosenberg's military experience includes previously serving in the Israeli army. [148] A German woman, Ivana Hoffman, also fought on behalf of YPG in Syria. She was killed while fighting against the IS in March 2015 in northeastern Syria. Hoffman claimed she was fighting in Syria to "fight for humanity and freedom." [149]

In January 2015, John McGuire, a former University of Ottawa student who joined ISIS in 2013, was killed in Kobani. Additionally, three Canadian cousins of Somali descent—Mahad, Hamsa, and Hersi Kariye—along with another cousin, Hanad Abdullahi Mohallim, from Minnesota, were killed in Syria during fall 2014, while fighting on behalf of the Islamic State. [150]

WOMEN IN IS

In Iraq and Syria, some women join the IS to ensure their freedom to practice their religion and traditions as well as avoid the daily dangers which are prevalent in war zones, such as rape, bombings, and lack of resources. For these women, such issues outweigh the organization's brutal tactics and patriarchy. [151] Additionally, the Islamic State's narrative to those outside the caliphate is along the following: "it has established a haven where Muslims, including young women, can enjoy the kind of excitement and purity they could not find in their Western homes, and directly contribute to breeding a new generation of believers." [152]

The IS actively radicalizes and recruits young women to join the jihad, marry IS fighters, and parent the next generation of warriors. [153] These radicalization and recruitment activities are largely conducted through a social media campaign. The IS propaganda focuses on how fulfilling private life can be when it is enveloped in jihad. In contrast, radicalization and recruitment activities geared to men largely feature violence and the rewards of martyrdom. Too, women are frequently responsible for cooking for IS fighters and distributing meals to the masses as a means of increasing support for the IS. [154]

Women are not generally used as combatants by the IS, although they are being utilized against IS enemies such as the Kurds. Kurdish forces had large numbers of female fighters, including several all-women units, participate in their operation to retake the Mosul Dam. [155] Female fighters appeal to the

IS's opponents, as some IS fighters believe that if they are killed by a woman they will not attain the benefits of martyrdom.

When the IS militants attacked the Yazidi communities, they separated the Yazidi women based on age. The IS militants sought to marry the younger Yazidi women if they converted to Islam.[156] According to one account, Yazidi women and girls "were sent to slave warehouses along with hundreds of other women. There, they were lined up in groups of 50 and displayed for ISIS fighters to choose among them, some for marriage, others for sexual slavery."[157]

Additionally, Human Rights Watch determined that the Islamic State has committed war crimes and perhaps crimes against humanity by establishing "a system of organized rape and sexual assault, sexual slavery, and forced marriage by ISIS forces."[158] In relation to forced marriages, the families of the prospective brides support the marriage to avoid hostilities with the fighters or to achieve better relations with them.[159] Many of the marriages involve abuse and only last for a few months, as the militants either die or abandon their wives in favor of new women.[160]

The Khansaa Brigade[161]

In the Islamic State, women have formed their own brigades, such as the Khansaa Brigade in Raqqa, Syria. This brigade acts as a type of morality police for women, arresting and sometimes beating women who do not have male escorts in public, wear veils that are too thin, or are otherwise not properly covered.[162] According to one Syrian teenager, "One of the women in the brigade came over, pointing her firearm at me. She then tested my knowledge of prayer, fasting and hijab."[163]

This women-focused morality enforcer group was created shortly after the IS gained control of Raqqa. The brigade is mostly comprised of the wives of foreign fighters in Syria.[164] According to another source, the females "must be single and aged between 18 and 25."[165]

The Khansaa Brigade was originally created to help at checkpoints where some men who opposed the IS would use burqas as disguises to evade detection. Decency rules prevented men from checking whether people wearing burqas were indeed women. So, the IS recruited women to do so. The Khansaa Brigade was named to commemorate a Muslim woman who lost several sons during fighting in Persia in the era of Mohammed.[166] Also, an IS official, Abu Ahmad, noted, "We have established the brigade to raise awareness of our religion among women, and to punish women who do not abide by the law." After all, he explained, "Jihad is not a man-only duty. Women must do their part as well."[167]

Al-Khansaa women patrol cities to pursue women and enforce legal marriages to mujahideen. Some women are recruited for marriage purposes, and thereby, serve as an incentive for young men to join the IS.[168] Khansaa Battalion women have raided local schools. There, they arrested women and young girls for perceived infractions of Islamic law. These morality enforcers take them to IS detention centers, where they are whipped.[169]

Umm Al-Rayan Battalion[170]

In February 2014, ISIS announced the formation of a second all-female brigade, the Umm al-Rayan Battalion. Its goal is to expose males who dress as women in order to bypass scrutiny at IS checkpoints. Currently, the brigade is not fighting or engaging in terror acts. For these duties, the women are paid a monthly salary of $200. Also, they must agree not to work for other groups.

Foreign Women

As of January 2015, approximately 500 Western women have traveled to IS-controlled territory to join the group. Their experiences there vary, but often consist of domestic and menial tasks, and having families. Some are quite ardent in their embracing of the strict precepts of the IS.[171]

British Women

Increasingly, some female British converts to Islam women and Muslim-born women are advocating on behalf of the Islamic State through social networks. In doing so, they have managed to persuade girls and women to join the cause, including moving to the Islamic State.[172]

In December 2014, British police stopped a 15-year-old girl from east London as she boarded a plane from London Heathrow Airport to Turkey, with an ultimate goal of joining the Islamic State. Another British female teenage eluded authorities and believed to have made it to Syria-Iraq to join the Islamic State.[173]

Aqsa Mahmood[174]

Using the alias, Umm Layth, a woman named Aqsa Mahmood established a Tumblr blog, "Diary of a Muhajirah."[175] In it, she discusses her life as a female member of the IS. The blog was last updated on September 11, 2014. Aqsa was born in Glasgow, Scotland, to a successful Pakistani immigrant businessman and his wife. Aqsa was educated in a top private school in the city, Craigholme School.[176] Friends remember her as being a Westernized girl. She later became more interested in Islam, when she wore a hijab, bought religious books, took classes on Islam, and chatted about Islamist ideology with people over the Internet.

Aqsa was not accepted at a university but, instead, went to study at Shawlands Academy. Subsequently, Aqsa took a course in diagnostic radiography at Glasgow Caledonian University. She left her studies in 2013. Afterwards, she reached Syria, joined the IS, and married an IS fighter.

Aqsa tweeted messages calling on others to repeat incidents like the murder of soldier Lee Rigby, the massacre at Fort Hood U.S. Army Base in Texas, and the Boston Marathon bombing. She is believed to be one of the leaders of the Khansaa Battalion.[177]

Sally Jones

Sally Jones (aka Umm Hussain Al-Britani, Sakinah Hussain) is a 45-year-old mother of two from Chatham, Kent, in the UK.[178] She was a musician of some renown in the early 1990s.[179] Jones married Junaid Hussain (also known as Abu Hussain Al-Britani), a 20-year-old computer hacker from Birmingham, UK. She and Hussain moved to Raqqa with her youngest son,[180] when Hussain went to fight for the IS.[181] Jones has denounced the United States and UK as terrorist nations. Also, she threatened to behead Christians.[182] Her husband is one of the suspects in the beheadings of American and British hostages. Jones herself has recently expressed concern that she will never be allowed back into the UK.[183]

Khadija Dare[184]

Khadija Dare is a 22-year-old mother of two from South London. The true identity of Khadija Dare is still unknown. She also goes by Umma Isa, Muhajirah Fil Sham, and Maryam.[185]

Dare grew up in Lewisham, South London. She converted to Islam at age 18. She went to local college to study media studies, film studies, psychology, and sociology. Dare began worshipping at Lewisham Islamic Centre. This location is viewed as a key concern for British intelligence services. She is married to Swedish jihadi Abu Bakr, whom she met online. The pair moved to Syria in 2012. Bakr is a fighter with the Sunni jihadi militia Katibat Al-Muhajireen, the Battalion of Immigrants, which pledged allegiance to the IS.[186]

In a video interview, Dare fired a Kalashnikov rifle, stated that she would like to fight and become a martyr. She also admonished British Muslims to "stop being selfish" and to give up their families and studies and join ISIS's fight.[187]

Hours after a British jihadist beheaded James Foley, Dare gloated about his execution on social media. She vowed to be the first British woman to kill a UK or U.S. "terrorist." She has become a celebrity recruitment personality for women in ISIS, claiming that she does not want to return to Britain, even if her husband is killed. "I will stay here [in Syria] because I didn't come here for him. I wouldn't like to go back to the UK. I'll stay here, raise my children, focus on the Arabic language to communicate with the Syrian people."[188]

Salma and Zahra Halane[189]

Salma and Zahra Halane (also known as the "Terror Twins") are 16-year-old twins, daughters of Somali refugees in the UK. Mohammad Shafiq, of the Ramadan Foundation, described the family as moderate Muslims,[190] although neighbors characterized them as "quite strict."[191] The girls grew up in Chorlton, Manchester, in the UK. They were excellent students who planned on becoming doctors before becoming radicalized over the Internet.[192]

The Halane sisters left their home on June 26, 2014. They are thought to have married jihadis, who likely funded their travel. Police sources say their brother had traveled to Somalia, where he linked up with Al-Shabaab. Apparently, the girls were inspired by his transformation. Salma and Zahra are currently based in Raqqa.[193]

American Women

Nichole Lynn Mansfield

In May 2013, Nicole Lynn Mansfield, 33, was killed with two men by Syrian government forces. According to Syrian government media reports, she was fighting with Ahrar al-Sham, the "Free Men of Syria." Mansfield's family claims that she was media coordinator to one of the Islamist rebel groups. According to some reports, Mansfield was introduced to extremist tenets by her second husband, a Saudi, whom she met online. A subsequent marriage to a man from the United Arab Emirates, whom she also met online, ended in divorce as well. In any case, Mansfield is believed to be the first American killed in the conflict.[194]

Unfortunately, Mansfield was far from the last American female enticed by the jihadist message. For example, in October 2014, three girls of Somali descent based in Colorado were detained in Germany and sent back to the United States, following the revelation of their plans to ultimately travel to Turkey (and then Syria) with the goal of joining the Islamic State.[195]

Shannon Maureen Conley[196]

A 19-year-old from Arvada, Colorado, Shannon is the daughter of a university professor and an employee in the computer industry. She enrolled in honors courses in high school. She did not have disciplinary problems there. According to a classmate at Regis University, Shannon tried several different religions in a period of six months before adopting Islam.

While online she made contact with a self-professed member of the ISIS. Shannon pledged to marry a fighter in Syria, provide tactical support to the organization, and even engage in combat if necessary. Through the Internet, Shannon met a Tunisian man thirteen years her senior who promised to marry her and help her engage in jihad. He was already in Syria, fighting on behalf of ISIS. She communicated with him through Skype.

Shannon joined the U.S. Army Explorers, a career program offered under the umbrella of the Boy Scouts of America. The program provides training in armed combat, military tactics, and the use of firearms. Shannon planned to use these skills and wage jihad abroad. In case she was unable to fight, she intended to help the jihadi fighters while serving as a nurse.

In April 2014, she was arrested at Denver International Airport while attempting to board a flight to Turkey. From there, she intended to continue to Syria and support ISIS fighters. In September 2014, she pleaded guilty to conspiracy to provide material support to a foreign terrorist group (ISIS). In January 2015, Conley was sentenced to four years in prison and subsequently "three years on supervised release."[197]

Those who knew Shannon described her transformation as the result of being essentially a "bright teenager lost in middle-class suburbia" searching for "love and purpose."[198] Following her arrest, authorities say they found CDs by U.S.-born radical cleric Anwar Al-Awlaki among her belongings.[199] On her Facebook page Shannon referred to herself as Halima, and described her work as "a slave to Allah." She told the FBI she sought to defend Muslims against their oppressors.[200]

Noelle Velentzas and Asia Siddiqui

In April 2015, two Queens, New York-based women and former roommates, Noelle Velentzas, 28, and Asia Siddiqui, 31, were arrested on charges of conspiracy to use weapons of mass destruction against persons or property in the United States.[201] From August 2014 until their arrest, the two plotted to detonate an explosive device in the United States, having considered using pressure cooker bombs, fertilizer bombs, and propane tanks. They interacted often with an undercover officer, discussing their interest in jihad, support of the Islamic State, and plans to conduct an attack in the United States. In particular, Siddiqui showed the law enforcement operative component parts for explosives, including propane tanks, as well as articulating that she knew how to produce explosive devices. Previously, Siddiqui published a poem in a predecessor of al-Qa'ida in the Arabian Peninsula's magazine, *Inspire*, extolling martyrdom. Velentzas said that there was no need to travel abroad to do jihad, as numerous targets were available in the United States.[202] A trial is expected in 2015.

Keonna Thomas

In April 2015, a 30-year-old woman from Philadelphia, Pennsylvania, Keonna Thomas—also known as the "Young Lioness," and "Fatayat Al Khilafah" meaning girls of the caliphate)—was charged with attempting to provide material support to a foreign terrorist organization, ISIL.[203] Thomas embraced the possibility of traveling to Syria, and becoming a martyr for the group. In late March 2015 she purchased an airplane ticket from Philadelphia to Barcelona, Spain. From there, she intended to take a bus to Turkey, and then on to Syria. Thomas was very active on Twitter, providing pro-ISIL and jihadi messages. She tweeted, "When you're a mujahid [jihadi fighter], your death becomes a wedding."[204] Additionally, she communicated with jihadi fighters in Somalia and Syria as well as "a radical Islamic cleric located in Jamaica."[205] These online interactions underscore the connectedness of individuals who embrace jihadi tenets and their ease of articulating these messages on the Internet.[206] A trial is expected in 2015.

Other Female Jihadis

In April 2014, Samra Kesinovic, 16, and Sabina Selimovic, 15, left their homes in Vienna, Austria, and embarked on travels to Syria.[207] There, they hoped to become brides to jihadi fighters. The two girls of Bosnian descent were apparently radicalized by Vienna-based Chechen youths. The pair posted photos of themselves with jihadi fighters. They have inspired other teenage girls to join the jihad in Syria. Reports that at least one of them has been killed or became pregnant have not been substantiated.[208] Subsequently, claims have surfaced that the girls have since written to friends on WhatsApp confirming that they are alive and well. "Neither of us is dead," Selimovic wrote.[209]

In November 2014, Hungary intercepted a 16-year-old Dutch girl at a Budapest train station using forged travel documents with plans to travel to Serbia, and eventually to Syria. She hoped to join the IS upon arriving in Syria. The girl was very active on jihadi websites that disseminate propaganda and recruit individuals to the cause.[210] Interest by Dutch youth in jihad is high, as demonstrated by the fact that "100 Dutch youngsters have left the country to take part in jihadist missions."[211]

A 15-year-old French girl of Moroccan descent, Assia Saidi, was stopped by her parents in November 2014, as she planned to travel to go to Syria and undertake jihad. In France, there are "at least 60 women, [who] are thought to be either actively engaged in jihad in Iraq and Syria or planning to go."[212]

In late November 2014, the ex-wife of Abu Bakr Al-Baghdadi, Saja al-Dulaimi, and her child were arrested in Lebanon, as they entered the country from neighboring Syria. The woman is believed to have used Lebanon to funnel money to the IS. She is the daughter of Hamid al-Dulaimi from a prominent tribe in Anbar province in Iraq. Hamid pledged allegiance to the Islamic State, and was killed in Homs, Syria, in 2014. Saja, who lived in Homs, eventually moved to the Lebanese border town of Arsal, as did many family members of Syrian militants. Al-Baghdadi married al-Dulaimi in about 2009, and divorced her after three months of marriage.[213]

PLANS AND CAPABILITIES OF PROSPECTIVE FOREIGN FIGHTERS

Among the factors that will affect the likelihood of violent actions by foreign fighters—including women—upon return to their native (or other) countries include:

- Why they chose to fight in Syria and/or Iraq in the first place (e.g., religious fervor, secular interests, to gain terrorist training)?
- What was their experience in Syria and/or Iraq? Did they gain terrorist training? Did they engage in combat? What was their perception of the group(s) they served with, the group's effectiveness, and ideologies? Did they become more extremist in their views than before their trip to Syria or Iraq?
- Did they acquire a heightened animus towards their home country?
- Did they view their experience in a positive manner or were they disheartened?
- Did they make helpful contacts as well as gaining skills and resources that could be used in their home countries and elsewhere?
- Will they continue their interest in supporting one side or another in the Syrian (and/or Iraqi) conflict(s) by raising money or recruiting others for the cause?
- Are law enforcement and the intelligence community in their home countries aware of their travel abroad, and awaiting their return for questioning and/or arrest?
- Will family, friends, or community members inform police about their participation as fighters in the Syrian (and/or Iraqi) conflict(s)?[214]

Also, selected foreign fighters become disillusioned or die while fighting in Syria or Iraq. Some foreign fighters may not necessarily seek violent jihad upon return to their home countries.

To no avail, the Islamic State has stepped up its attempts to dissuade Western countries from attacking its members in Iraq and Syria. Its main method of doing so is by inspiring unaffiliated adherents to its cause and activating its supporters abroad to carry out attacks in the West and elsewhere. In doing so, it is hoped that members of the coalition will change course and refrain from intervening in IS's region. Also, attacks in other countries will spur the coalescing of an IS affiliate or strengthen its cause.

COMBATING THE PARTICIPATION OF FOREIGN FIGHTERS

There are various characteristics and parameters that can be analyzed in relation to who ultimately serves as a foreign fighter (or provides assistance in that regard) on behalf of a faction in Syria (and/or Iraq). Among the factors that can be reviewed are:

- Race, ethnicity, national origin
- Gender
- Religion (including non-Muslims who have served as foreign fighters in Syria)
- Born Muslim or converted to Islam, other religions
- Criminal record
- Former/current military or law enforcement
- The status of the individual: dead, arrested, known but free, unknown and free/dead
- The groups they joined or attempted to join: IS, Jabhat al-Nusra, Hezbollah, Syrian government, YPG, Ahrar al-Sham (Free Men of Syria), etc.
- What role did they play/seek to undertake? Fighter, propagandist, recruiter, financier, or other
- Were these operatives/prospective terrorists aspirational or the "real deal"
- Discovery by law enforcement: informant, uncovered agent, tip from public, open source, online activity, other intelligence source (including foreign), or other
- Manner of recruitment: friend, family, from propagandist, online/offline activities, or other
- Did they go abroad (other than Syria and/or Iraq) to get training?
- Is this the first time they were involved with terrorist activity or with a particular group?
- Prospective targets of foreign fighters: Western countries, Muslim countries with secular regimes, other countries, Assad regime, other rebel/terror groups
- Foreign fighters killed by Assad regime, rebel/terror groups, or others
- Returned home after being abroad?

In addition to understanding the dispositions and goals of prospective foreign fighters, it behooves governments to take steps to reduce the frequency and negative ramifications of fighters leaving faraway lands for Syria—the most likely destination for IS foreign fighters. Government measures that can be pursued include:

- Outlawing travel to Syria except for limited reasons (e.g., media, humanitarian, or religious activities) and requiring notice to government officials of travels to neighboring countries.
- Enacting (or enforcing existing) legislation prohibiting citizens from fighting on behalf of a sovereign state or a sub-state group, including rebel organizations.
- Expanding enforcement against attempts by individuals, groups, and organizations to provide material support to foreign terrorist organizations and rebel groups.
- Heightening prosecution of incitement to violence, sedition, and conspiracies to commit terrorism (including providing material support) against those involved with recruiting terrorists.
- Increasing intelligence sharing domestically and internationally in this regard.
- Raising efforts on information-driven and community policing fronts in order to gain tips about individuals who plan on participating in the Syrian conflict—whether through fighting, recruiting, raising money, or acquiring weapons and supplies.
- Accelerating outreach to the public as to terrorism indicators so that terrorist activities can be recognized and undermined.
- Continuing the use of sting operations online and offline to ferret out prospective terrorists.
- Strengthening local communities in their struggle against radicalization.
- Undertaking de-radicalization activities among returning fighters and others who have embraced extremist tenets.
- Expanding counter-narratives against the alluring pitch of terror-themed recruiters. The U.S. State Department hosts the interagency Center for Strategic Counterterrorism Communications to counter recruitment and radicalization through counter-messaging, especially against Syrian and Iraq-based terrorists' online messaging. Also, during spring 2014, a Senior Advisor for Partner Engagement on Syria Foreign Fighters, Ambassador Robert Bradtke, was appointed.[215]
- Accelerating inquiry into non-profit entities and charities that have a nexus with Syria, as they may serve as terrorist abettors, including terror funding fronts.
- Increasing the training of law enforcement, intelligence community, military, and the private sector in relation to terrorists' profiles, terrorist indicators, suspicious activities, and suspicious financial transactions.[216]

Under U.S. federal law, 8 U.S. Code sec. 1481, an American-born or naturalized citizen may lose his citizenship if he: (3) enters or serves in a foreign army and that entity is engaged in hostilities against the United States or the person serves as a commissioned or non-commissioned officer in that fighting force; or (7) engages in a conspiracy to destroy the U.S. government or levy war against it.[217] As such, U.S. citizens who participate in fighting abroad or at home against the United States are subject to losing their citizenship, among other sanctions.

As has been witnessed in relation to some of the case studies outlined above, there are additional U.S. federal laws that can be used very effectively against foreign fighters and terrorists. Of particular utility is the material support statute, 18 U.S.C. 2339 (A-D) (2014), which prohibits individuals from providing material support, including financing, to terrorists, terrorist groups, and foreign terrorist groups.[218]

More specifically, under 18 USC sec. 2339A (2014) dealing with providing material support to terrorists, it is impermissible to: attempt, conspire, provide, or conceal "material support to an organization or person that is involved in preparing, carrying out, concealing, attempting, or conspiring to undertake a terrorist act." Material support or resources are defined as "any property, tangible or intangible, or service, including currency or monetary instruments or financial securities, financial services, lodging, training, expert advice or assistance, safehouses, false documentation or identification, communications equipment, facilities, weapons, lethal substances, explosives, personnel (one or more individuals who may be or include oneself), and transportation, except medicine or religious materials."[219] The penalties attaching to such conduct includes: fines, imprisonment (up to fifteen years), or both. Should a terror incident result in a death, any term of sentence, including a life sentence, may attach.[220]

With regard to outlawing the provision of material support or resources to designated foreign terrorist organizations (FTO), 18 USC sec. 2339B (2014) prohibits attempting or providing material support to an organization knowing that the organization is an FTO, has/is engaged in terrorism, or has/is engaged in terrorist activity. The penalties attaching to such activities are: fines, imprisonment (up to fifteen years), or both. Should a terror incident result in a death, any term of sentence, including a life sentence, may apply.[221] This has been used against various U.S.-based individuals who have attempted to travel to Syria and Iraq to assist a U.S.-designated foreign terrorist organization.

Under 18 U.S.C. sec. 2339B (2014), financial institutions that are aware of FTO assets should attach them and contact the U.S. government. If a financial institution fails to do so, it is penalized $50,000 per transaction. The U.S. government may assert jurisdiction whether defendant undertakes the material support in the United States or abroad. Also, no liability for providing "personnel" services will occur if the person acts entirely independently of the FTO even if he acts to advance the goals and objectives of FTO.[222]

Prohibitions on the financing of terrorism are discussed in 18 U.S.C. sec. 2339C (2014). Namely, it is impermissible for anyone to willfully provide, attempt to provide, undertake a conspiracy, or conceal the intent to raise funds, knowing that the funds will be used in full or in part to carry out a terrorist act. For purposes of the statute, funds means "assets of every kind, whether tangible or intangible, movable or immovable, however acquired, and legal documents or instruments in any form, including electronic or digital, evidencing title to, or interest in, such assets, including coin, currency, bank credits, travelers checks, bank checks, money orders, shares, securities, bonds, drafts, and letters of credit."[223] The U.S. government may assert jurisdiction whether defendant offers the material support in the United States or abroad.[224]

Also, violators of 18 U.S.C. sec. 2339C may be fined and sentenced up to twenty years in prison for providing, attempting to provide, or conspiring to, funding terrorism. For concealing such activity the penalties are only ten years in prison. In addition, a $10,000 penalty will be imposed on a U.S. organized entity if a person in a management or administrative role is involved in providing, attempting to provide, or conspiring to provide terror financing.[225]

Under post-9/11 legislation—the Intelligence Reform and Terrorism Prevention Act of 2004 (Public Law 108-458, Dec. 17, 2014)—the material support statute was revised to prohibit receiving military training from an FTO.[226] More specifically, under 18 U.S.C. sec. 2339D, whoever knowingly receives military-type training from or on behalf of an FTO, an organization that is/has engaged in terrorist activity, or an organization that is/has engaged in terrorism, may be fined, serve up to ten years in prison, or both. Military-type training includes "training in means or methods that can cause death or serious bodily injury, destroy or damage property, or disrupt services to critical infrastructure, or training on the use, storage, production, assembly of" explosives, firearms, and weapons of mass destruction.[227] The U.S. government may assert jurisdiction whether defendant does the military-type training arises in the United States or abroad.[228] Thus, if a foreign fighter receives military-type training whether in the United States or elsewhere on behalf of an FTO, he is subject to criminal liability.

There is greater appreciation that the foreign terrorist phenomenon merits a global response. UN Security Council Resolution 2178 (2014) demonstrated that the world community understands this threat. More specifically, it enunciated that combating "foreign terrorist fighters requires comprehensively addressing underlying factors, including by preventing radicalization to terrorism, stemming recruitment, inhibiting foreign terrorist fighter travel, disrupting financial support to foreign terrorist fighters, countering violent extremism, which can be conducive to terrorism, countering incitement to terrorist acts motivated by extremism or intolerance, promoting political and religious tolerance, economic development and social cohesion and inclusiveness, ending and resolving armed conflicts, and facilitating reintegration and rehabilitation."[229]

Another international response to this threat includes the Global Counterterrorism Forum (GCTF), which adopted a set of good practices to address the foreign terrorist fighter (FTF) phenomenon. More specifically, the GCTF's September 2014 "Hague-Marrakech Memorandum of Good Practices for a More Effective Response to the FTF Phenomenon" centers on the following broad efforts: "detecting and intervening against violent extremism"; "preventing, detecting, and intervening against recruitment and facilitation"; "detecting and intervening against travel and fighting"; and "detecting and intervening upon return."[230]

Also, in March 2015, the UN Office on Drugs and Crime announced that it was launching a new four-year initiative that will "assist Member States in criminalizing the FTF [foreign terrorist fighter] phenomenon, in areas such as terrorist recruitment, incitement to terrorism, terrorism financing, and terrorist training, among others."[231] Additionally, "UNODC's global initiative covers both foreign cooperation and domestic assistance: the former is critical given the transnational dimension of FTFs which makes a purely national approach insufficient, the latter meanwhile is central to efforts needed to strengthen national legislation against this emerging trend in terrorist operations and to enhance domestic capacities of criminal justice and law enforcement officials."[232]

Internationally, efforts to undermine the flow of foreign fighters to Iraq and Syria have yielded some positive results, particularly in 2015. For instance, between August 2014 and March 2015, 230 persons suspected of traveling to join armed factions in Iraq and Syria, including the IS, were prevented from leaving Australia.[233]

Additionally, Turkey created a foreign fighter watchlist of 12,500 people. As such, Turkey has been increasingly vigilante—particularly since 2015—to prevent individuals with suspicious intentions, such as traveling to Syria to join the IS, to enter Turkey.[234] In March 2015, Turkey detained and later deported foreigners who sought to enter Syria through Turkey. In the case of nine Britons—including four children—from Rochdale (Manchester area) who were captured in southern Turkey.[235]

NOTES

1. Lederer, Edith. "UN report: More than 25,000 foreigners fight with terrorists." *AP*, April 1, 2015. Accessed April 1, 2015. http://bigstory.ap.org/article/cec52a0dbfab4c00b89 bc543badf6c20/un-report-more-25000-foreigners-fight-terrorists.

2. Farivar, Massod. "The Foreign Fighters and Me." *NY Times,* April 1, 2014. Accessed October 28, 2014. http://www.nytimes.com/2014/04/02/opinion/the-foreign-fighters-and-me. html?_r=0.

Ganji, Akbar. "U.S.-Jihadist Relations (Part 1): Creating the Mujahedin in Afghanistan." *Huffington Post,* August 31, 2014. Accessed October 28, 2014. http://www.huffingtonpost. com/akbar-ganji/us-jihadist-relations_b_5542757.html.

Bakker, Edwin and Jeanine de Roy van Zuijdewijn. "Returning Western foreign fighters: The case of Afghanistan, Bosnia and Somalia." *International Center for Counter-Terrorism,* June, 2014. Accessed October 28, 2014. http://www.icct.nl/download/file/ICCT-De-Roy-van-Zuijdewijn-Bakker-Returning-Western-Foreign-Fighters-June-2014.pdf.

Tarabay, Jamie. "How the Afghan jihad went global." *Al Jazeera America*, November 12, 2013. Accessed October 28, 2014. http://america.aljazeera.com/articles/2013/11/12/how-afghan-jihadwentglobal.html.

3. "The 9/11 Commission Report." *National Commission of Terrorist Attacks Upon the United States*, August 21, 2004. Accessed October 28, 2014. http://www.9-11commission.gov/ report/911Report_Exec.htm.

"Milestones: 1977–1980; The Soviet Invasion of Afghanistan and the US Response, 1978–1980." *U.S. Department of State; Office of the Historian*, October 31, 2013. Accessed October 28, 2014. https://history.state.gov/milestones/1977-1980/soviet-invasion-afghanistan.

4. Wood, Nicholas. "Bosnia Plans to Expel Arabs Who Fought in Its War." *NY Times,* August 2, 2007. Accessed October 28, 2014. http://www.nytimes.com/2007/08/02/world/ europe/02bosnia.html?pagewanted=all.

Pyes, Craig, William C. Rempel, and Josh Meyer. "Bosnia Seen as Hospitable Base and Sanctuary for Terrorists." *LA Times,* October 7, 2001. Accessed October 28, 2014. http:// articles.latimes.com/2001/oct/07/news/mn-54505.

Kaletovic, Damir and Anes Alic. "Al-Qaida's Bosnian war move." *International Relations and Security Network,* October 3, 2008. Accessed October 28, 2014. http://www.isn.ethz.ch/ Digital-Library/Articles/Detail/?id=92320.

5. Tumelty, Paul. "The Rise and Fall of Foreign Fighters in Chechnya." Jamestown Foundation, January 31, 2006. Accessed October 27, 2014. http://www.jamestown.org/single/?no_ cache=1&tx_ttnews[tt_news]=658#.VC2AW-fXFe4.

Vidino, Lorenzo. "How Chechnya Became a Breeding Ground for Terror." *Middle East Quarterly*, Summer 2005. Accessed October 28, 2014. http://www.meforum.org/744/how-chechnya-became-a-breeding-ground-for-terror.

6. Williams, Brian Glyn. "On the Trail of the 'Lions of Islam': Foreign Fighters in Afghanistan and Pakistan, 1980–2010." Foreign Policy Research Institute, Spring, 2011. Accessed October 28, 2014. https://www.fpri.org/articles/2012/11/trail-lions-islam-foreign-fighters-afghanistan-and-pakistan-1980-2010.

7. Murphy, Dan. "Iraq's foreign fighters: few but deadly." *Christian Science Monitor*, September 27, 2005. Accessed October 28, 2014. http://www.csmonitor.com/2005/0927/ p01s03-woiq.html.

8. "Bahrain accuses Iran of training rebels." *Al Jazeera,* January 4, 2014. Accessed October 28, 2014. http://www.aljazeera.com/news/middleeast/2014/01/bahrain-accuses-iran-training-rebels-201413144049814960.html.

Roggio, Bill and Oren Adaki. "Pakistani, Algerian, French al Qaeda fighters killed or captured during Yemeni operation." *Long War Journal,* May 10, 2014. Accessed October 28, 2014. http://www.longwarjournal.org/archives/2014/05/pakistani_algerian_f.php.

Baron, Adam. "Yemeni leader says al Qaida fighters there include Brazilians, Europeans." *McClatchy DC,* April 29, 2014. Accessed October 28, 2014. http://www.mcclatchydc.com/ 2014/04/29/225982_yemeni-leader-says-al-qaida-fighters.html?rh=1.

9. Raghavan, Sudarsan. "Foreign fighters gain influence in Somalia's Islamist al-Shabab militia." *Washington Post,* June 8, 2010. Accessed October 28, 2014. http://www. washingtonpost.com/wp-dyn/content/article/2010/06/07/AR2010060704667.html.

Herridge, Catherine. "Ranks of Somali Terror Group Swelling With Foreign Fighters, Including Americans, Official Says." *Fox*, November 17, 2011. Accessed October 28, 2014.

http://www.foxnews.com/world/2011/11/17/ranks-somali-terror-group-swelling-with-foreign-fighters-including-americans/.

"Mali crisis: 'Foreign fighters come to help Islamists.'" *BBC*, October 23, 2012. Accessed October 28, 2014. http://www.bbc.com/news/world-africa-20050713.

Dreazen, Yochi. "The New Terrorist Training Ground." *Atlantic*, October 2013. Accessed October 28, 2014. http://www.theatlantic.com/magazine/archive/2013/10/the-new-terrorist-training-ground/309446/.

10. "Security Council Unanimously Adopts Resolution Condemning Violent Extremism, Underscoring Need to Prevent Travel, Support for Foreign Terrorist Fighters." *UNSC Meetings Coverage,* September 24, 2014. Accessed October 28, 2014. http://www.un.org/press/en/2014/sc11580.doc.htm.

11. "Resolution 2178." *UN Security Council*, September 24, 2014. Accessed October 28, 2014. http://www.un.org/en/ga/search/view_doc.asp?symbol=S/RES/2178%20%282014%29.

12. "Security Council Unanimously Adopts Resolution Condemning Violent Extremism, Underscoring Need to Prevent Travel, Support for Foreign Terrorist Fighters." *UNSC Meetings Coverage and Press Releases,* September 24, 2014. Accessed October 28, 2014. http://www.un.org/press/en/2014/sc11580.doc.htm.

13. Cockburn, Patrick. "Battle to establish Islamic state across Iraq and Syria." *Independent,* June 9, 2014. Accessed October 28, 2014. http://www.independent.co.uk/news/world/middle-east/battle-to-establish-islamic-state-across-iraq-and-syria-9510044.html.

14. Gomis, Benoit. "Growing Threat of European Fighters in Syria Highlights Need for EU Cooperation." *World Politics Review,* June 10, 2014. Accessed October 28, 2014. http://www.worldpoliticsreview.com/articles/13915/growing-threat-of-european-fighters-in-syria-highlights-need-for-eu-cooperation. "The Jihadist Pipeline." *NY Times,* March 4, 2014. Accessed October 28, 2014. http://www.nytimes.com/2014/03/05/opinion/the-jihadist-pipeline.html.

15. Dozier, Kimberly. "James Clapper Says Syrian Al-Qaida Group Aspires To Attack U.S." *Huffington Post,* January 29, 2014. Accessed October 28, 2014. http://www.huffingtonpost.com/2014/01/29/james-clapper-syria-al-qaida_n_4688266.html. Clapper, James R. "Remarks as delivered by James R. Clapper, Director of National Intelligence; Worldwide Threat Assessment to the Senate Select Committee on Intelligence." *Office of the Director of National Intelligence; Public Affairs Office,* January 29, 2014. Accessed October 28, 2014. http://www.dni.gov/files/documents/WWTA%20Opening%20Remarks%20as%20Delivered%20to%20SSCI_29_Jan_2014.pdf.

16. "Americans among 12,000 foreign fighters in Syria: US." *AFP,* August 21, 2014. Accessed October 28, 2014. http://news.yahoo.com/americans-among-12-000-foreign-fighters-syria-us-225059981.html.

17. "U.N. Security Council passes resolution on foreign jihadists." *AFP,* September 24, 2014. Accessed October 28, 2014. http://news.yahoo.com/un-security-council-passes-binding-resolution-jihadists-191829842.html.

18. Barrett, Richard. "Foreign Fighters In Syria." Soufan Group, June, 2014. Accessed October 28, 2014. http://soufangroup.com/wp-content/uploads/2014/06/TSG-Foreign-Fighters-in-Syria.pdf.

"The Phenomenon of Foreign Fighters from the Arab World in the Syrian Civil War, Most of Them Fighting in the Ranks of Organizations Affiliated with Al-Qaeda and the Global Jihad." The Meir Amit Intelligence and Terrorism Information Center, May, 2014. Accessed October 28, 2014. http://www.terrorism-info.org.il/Data/articles/Art_20646/E_013_14_873825825_830074808.pdf.

"Tunisian youths at forefront of Syria militant fighters." *Channel News Asia,* October 1, 2014. Accessed October 28, 2014. http://www.channelnewsasia.com/news/world/tunisian-youths-at/1392012.html.

Zelin, Aaron Y. "ICSR Insight: European Foreign Fighters in Syria." International Center for the Study of Radicalization and Political Violence, April 2, 2013. Accessed October 28, 2014. http://icsr.info/2013/04/icsr-insight-european-foreign-fighters-in-syria-2/.

19. Allen, Joseph. "Inside the war against the Islamic State." *Wall Street Journal*, December 26, 2014. Accessed December 27, 2014. http://www.wsj.com/articles/joe-rago-inside-the-war-against-islamic-state-1419636790.

"Two Minnesotans Charged with Conspiracy to Provide Material Support to the Islamic State of Iraq and the Levant." FBI, November 24, 2014. Accessed February 18, 2015. http://www.fbi.gov/minneapolis/press-releases/2014/two-minnesotans-charged-with-conspiracy-to-provide-material-support-to-the-islamic-state-of-iraq-and-the-levant.

20. "20,000 foreign fighters flock to Syria, Iraq to join terrorists." *CBS News*, February 10, 2015. Accessed February 11, 2015. http://www.cbsnews.com/news/ap-20000-foreign-fighters-flock-to-syria-iraq-to-join-terrorists/.

21. Tate, Julie, Gene Thorp and Swati Sharma. "Foreign fighters flow to Syria." *Washington Post,* October 11, 2014. Accessed October 28, 2014. http://www.washingtonpost.com/world/foreign-fighters-flow-to-syria/2014/10/11/3d2549fa-5195-11e4-8c24-487e92bc997b_graphic.html.

22. Safi, Michael and Nick Evershed. "Australians fighting in Syria: how many have joined the conflict?" *Data Blog; The Guardian,* April 9, 2014. Accessed October 28, 2014. http://www.theguardian.com/world/datablog/2014/apr/09/australians-fighting-in-syria-how-many-have-joined-the-conflict.

23. Ghribi, Asma. "Tunisia struggles to cope with returnees from Syrian jihad." *Foreign Policy*, September 12, 2014. Accessed September 28, 2014. http://foreignpolicy.com/2014/09/12/tunisia-struggles-to-cope-with-returnees-from-syrian-jihad/.

24. Petre, Christine. "The Jihadi Factory." *Foreign Policy*. March 20, 2015. Accessed March 27, 2015. http://foreignpolicy.com/2015/03/20/the-jihadi-factory-tunisia-isis-islamic-state-terrorism/.

25. Ibid.

26. Ibid.

27. Ibid.

28. Ghribi, Asma. "Tunisia struggles to cope with returnees from Syrian jihad." *Foreign Policy*, September 12, 2014. Accessed September 28, 2014. http://foreignpolicy.com/2014/09/12/tunisia-struggles-to-cope-with-returnees-from-syrian-jihad/.

29. Hegghammer, Thomas. "Number of foreign fighters from Europe in Syria is historically unprecedented. Who should be worried?" *Washington Post,* November 27, 2013. Accessed October 28, 2014. http://www.washingtonpost.com/blogs/monkey-cage/wp/2013/11/27/number-of-foreign-fighters-from-europe-in-syria-is-historically-unprecedented-who-should-be-worried/.

30. "Islamic State crisis: '3,000 European jihadists join fight.'" *BBC,* September 26, 2014. Accessed October 28, 2014. http://www.bbc.com/news/world-middle-east-29372494.

31. "European police agency says up to 5,000 EU nationals in Jihadist ranks, pose terror threat." *DNA*, January 14, 2015. Accessed February 19, 2015. http://www.dnaindia.com/world/report-european-police-agency-says-up-to-5000-eu-nationals-in-jihadist-ranks-pose-terror-threat-2052347.

32. "Returning Fighters from Syrian Conflict Cause Concern in the EU." *Europol,* May 29, 2014. Accessed October 28, 2014. https://www.europol.europa.eu/content/returning-fighters-syrian-conflict-cause-concern-eu. "It ain't half hot here, mum." *Economist,* August 30, 2014. Accessed October 28, 2014. http://www.economist.com/news/middle-east-and-africa/21614226-why-and-how-westerners-go-fight-syria-and-iraq-it-aint-half-hot-here-mum.

33. Erlanger, Steven. "Europe Tries to Stop Flow of Citizens Joining Jihad." *NY Times,* September 30, 2014. Accessed October 28, 2014. http://www.nytimes.com/2014/10/01/world/europe/isis-europe-muslim-radicalization.html.

34. Ibid.

35. "Tracking Britain's jihadists." *BBC News*, March 25, 2015. Accessed March 26, 2015. http://www.bbc.com/news/uk-32026985.

36. "Syria's trio London school linked to more girls trying to join IS." *AFP*, March 28, 2015. Accessed March 28, 2015. http://news.yahoo.com/syria-trios-london-school-linked-more-girls-trying-052300031.html.

37. Collins, David and Martin Bagot. "The face of British 'terror tourism': Estate agent and his brother who died in Syria fighting with al-Qaeda." *Mirror,* January 27, 2014. Accessed October 28, 2014. http://www.mirror.co.uk/news/uk-news/face-british-terror-tourism-estate-3065286.

38. "UK 'suicide bomber' Abdul Waheed Majid video posted online." *BBC,* February 14, 2014. Accessed October 28, 2014. http://www.bbc.com/news/uk-england-26187400. Evans, Natalie. "Pictured: British suspected suicide bomber in Syria—wearing MICKEY MOUSE ears in family snaps." *Mirror,* February 14, 2014. Accessed October 28, 2014. http://www.mirror.co.uk/news/uk-news/abdul-waheed-majeed-british-suicide-3145170.

"Married father is believed to be second British jihadi to carry out suicide blast." *Guardian,* November 9, 2014. Accessed November 20, 2014. http://www.theguardian.com/world/2014/nov/09/kabir-ahmed-iraq-suicide-blast-second-british-jihadi-reports.

"Briton Kabir Ahmed 'among Iraq suicide bombing dead.'" *BBC News,* November 10, 2014. Accessed November 21, 2014. http://www.bbc.com/news/uk-29974766.

39. "Married father is believed to be second British jihadi to carry out suicide blast." *Guardian,* November 9, 2014. Accessed November 20, 2014. http://www.theguardian.com/world/2014/nov/09/kabir-ahmed-iraq-suicide-blast-second-british-jihadi-reports. "Briton Kabir Ahmed 'among Iraq suicide bombing dead.'" *BBC News,* November 10, 2014. Accessed November 21, 2014. http://www.bbc.com/news/uk-29974766.

"British jihadist who died driving truck full of explosives into Syrian prison is revealed to be former driver for hate cleric Omar Bakri as footage of his suicide assault emerges." *Daily Mail,* February 13, 2014. Accessed January 22, 2015. http://www.dailymail.co.uk/news/article-2558463/Driving-doom-Rebels-release-footage-British-jihadist-driving-truck-explosives-suicide-assault-Syrian-prison.html.

"UK suicide bomber in Syria named as Abdul Waheed Majid." *BBC,* February 12, 2014. Accessed October 28, 2014. http://www.bbc.com/news/uk-26156533.

40. Allen, Nick and Philip Sherwell. "Hunt for 'British' Islamic State killer of US journalist James Foley." *Telegraph,* August 20, 2014. Accessed October 28, 2014. http://www.telegraph.co.uk/news/worldnews/middleeast/iraq/11044977/Hunt-for-British-Islamic-State-killer-of-US-journalist-James-Foley.html.

41. Robinson, Martin and Peter Allen. "'I know ISIS butcher known as John the Jailer': French former hostage says he has a 'rough' idea who masked British jihadi is." *Daily Mail,* August 21, 2014. Accessed October 28, 2014. http://www.dailymail.co.uk/news/article-2730336/Find-British-butcher-mask-Jihadi. Levy, Megan. "How London rapper L Jinny became Jihadi John, suspected of beheading James Foley." *Sydney Morning Herald,* August 25, 2014. Accessed October 28, 2014. http://www.smh.com.au/world/how-london-rapper-l-jinny-became-jihadi-john-suspected-of-beheading-james-foley-20140825-107zdz.html.

42. Phillips, Jack. "L. Jinny Update: Abdel-Majed Abdel Bary Suspected as Syria Terrorist 'Jihadi John' in James Wright Foley Case." *Epoch Times,* August 29, 2014. Accessed October 28, 2014. http://www.theepochtimes.com/n3/922507-l-jinny-update-abdel-majed-abdel-bary-suspected-as-jihadi-john-in-james-wright-foley-case/.

43. Levy, Megan. "How London rapper L Jinny became Jihadi John, suspected of beheading James Foley." *Sydney Morning Herald,* August 25, 2014. Accessed October 28, 2014. http://www.smh.com.au/world/how-london-rapper-l-jinny-became-jihadi-john-suspected-of-beheading-james-foley-20140825-107zdz.html.

44. Dearden, Lizzie. "'Jihadi John': Identity of Isis militant who beheaded Steven Sotloff and James Foley remains a mystery." *Independent,* September 3, 2014. Accessed October 28, 2014. http://www.independent.co.uk/news/world/middle-east/jihadi-john-identity-of-isis-militant-who-beheaded-steven-sotloff-and-james-foley-still-a-mystery-9708001.html.

45. Crompton, Paul. "FBI: U.S. identifies ISIS hostage executioner." *Al Arabiya,* September 25, 2014. Accessed October 28, 2014. http://english.alarabiya.net/en/News/middle-east/2014/09/25/U-S-identifies-ISIS-hostage-executioner.html.

46. Levy, Megan. "How London rapper L Jinny became Jihadi John, suspected of beheading James Foley." *Sydney Morning Herald,* August 25, 2014. Accessed October 28, 2014. http://www.smh.com.au/world/how-london-rapper-l-jinny-became-jihadi-john-suspected-of-beheading-james-foley-20140825-107zdz.html.

47. "'Jihadi John' named as Mohammed Emwazi of London." *BBC News*, February 26, 2015. Accessed February 27, 2015. http://www.bbc.com/news/uk-31637090.

48. "'Jihadi John' UK harassment claims revealed in emails." *BBC News*, February 26, 2015. Accessed February 27, 2015. http://www.bbc.com/news/uk-31647271.

49. Al-Abdo, Malik. "Foreign fighters from Western countries in the ranks of the rebel organizations affiliated with Al-Qaeda and the global jihad in Syria." *The Meir Amit Intelligence and Terrorism Information Center,* December, 2013. Accessed October 28, 2014. http://www.terrorism-info.org.il/en/article/20616.

50. "Married father is believed to be second British jihadi to carry out suicide blast." *Guardian*, November 9, 2014. Accessed November 20, 2014. http://www.theguardian.com/world/2014/nov/09/kabir-ahmed-iraq-suicide-blast-second-british-jihadi-reports. "Briton Kabir Ahmed 'among Iraq suicide bombing dead.'" *BBC News*, November 10, 2014. Accessed November 21, 2014. http://www.bbc.com/news/uk-29974766.

51. "'A dozen' Americans fighting with ISIS: Pentagon." *Daily Star*, September 5, 2014. Accessed October 28, 2014. http://www.dailystar.com.lb/News/Middle-East/2014/Sep-05/269640-a-dozen-americans-fighting-with-isis-pentagon.ashx#axzz3F1fdUxjv.

"Pentagon claims only a dozen Americans are fighting alongside ISIS amid thousands of foreigners that have come to Syria to join rebel factions." *Daily Mail,* September 5, 2014. Accessed   October 28, 2014. http://www.dailymail.co.uk/news/article-2745506/Pentagon-confirms-dozen-Americans-fighting-alongside-ISIS-fraction-hundreds-joined-rebel-groups-Syria.html.

52. "180 Americans have joined Islamic militants in Syria, 40 have already come home." *Newsweek*, March 2, 2015. Accessed March 5, 2015. http://www.newsweek.com/180-americans-joined-islamic-militants-syria-40-have-already-come-home-310789.

53. "(U) Special Assessment: ISIL Threats Against the Homeland." *Army Threat Integration Center (ARTIC)*, September 23, 2014. Accessed February 19, 2015. https://info.publicintelligence.net/ARTIC-HomelandThreatsISIL.pdf.

54. Pelton, Robert Young. "The All-American Life and Death of Eric Harroun." *Vice,* April 11, 2014. Accessed October 28, 2014. https://news.vice.com/article/the-all-american-life-and-death-of-eric-harroun. Bruer, Wes and Anna Therese Day. "Eric Harroun—accused of fighting with terrorists in Syria—has died, family says." *CNN,* April 10, 2014. Accessed October 27, 2014. http://www.cnn.com/2014/04/10/us/eric-harroun-death/.

55. Roggio, Bill. "American passport found at al Qaeda base in northern Syria." *Long War Journal*, July 23, 2013. Accessed October 27, 2014. http://www.longwarjournal.org/archives/2013/07/american_passport_fo.php.

56. Hiel, Betsy and Carl Prine. "Pittsburgh man reportedly dead in Syria." *WPXI*, July 26, 2013. Accessed October 28, 2014. http://www.wpxi.com/news/news/local/pittsburgh-man-reportedly-dead-syria/nY4rk/. Roggio, Bill. "American passport found at al Qaeda base in northern Syria." *Long War Journal*, July 23, 2013. Accessed October 27, 2014. http://www.longwarjournal.org/archives/2013/07/american_passport_fo.php.

"ISIS Succeeds Al Shaabab as Foremost Recruiter of American Militants." *Anti-Defamation League,* August 29, 2014. Accessed October 28, 2014. http://blog.adl.org/tags/amir-farouk-ibrahim.

57. Hamilton, Matt. "Sinh Vinh Ngo Nguyen sentenced to 13 years for trying to aid al Qaeda." *Christian Science Monitor,* June 30, 2014. Accessed October 28, 2014. http://www.csmonitor.com/USA/Latest-News-Wires/2014/0630/Sinh-Vinh-Ngo-Nguyen-sentenced-to-13-years-for-trying-to-aid-al-Qaeda. "'I'm literally having a blast': What Californian Muslim convert posted on Facebook from Syria before being arrested for aiding Al-Qaeda." *Daily Mail,* October 12, 2013. Accessed October 28, 2014. http://www.dailymail.co.uk/news/article-2457191/Im-literally-having-blast-What-Californian-Muslim-convert-posted-Facebook-Syria-arrested-aiding-Al-Qaeda.html.

58. Ward, Clarissa. "U.S. cleric inspiring jihadists in Syria?" *CBS,* April 15, 2014. Accessed October 28, 2014. http://www.cbsnews.com/news/fiery-speeches-lure-americans-to-fight-in-syria/.

59. "A message to the West from an American foreign fighter killed in Syria." The Meir Amit Intelligence and Terrorism Information Center, March 2, 2014. Accessed October 28, 2014. http://www.terrorism-info.org.il/en/article/20616.

60. Meek, James Gordon. "From Syria to Stateside: New Al Qaeda Threat to US Homeland." *ABC,* January 10, 2014. Accessed October 28, 2014. http://abcnews.go.com/Blotter/syria-stateside-al-qaeda-threat-us-homeland/story?id=21487394.

61. Bacon, John and Doug Stanglin. "American dies fighting for Islamic State." *Washington Post,* August 27, 2014. Accessed October 28, 2014. "http://www.washingtonpost.com/national/religion/american-dies-fighting-for-islamic-state/2014/08/27/45123dd0-2df5-11e4-bc9c-60cc44c01e7f_story.html. Vinograd, Cassandra and Ammar Cheikh Omar. "American Douglas McAuthur McCain Dies Fighting for ISIS in Syria." *NBC,* August 26, 2014. Accessed October 28, 2014. http://www.nbcnews.com/storyline/isis-terror/american-douglas-mcauthur-mccain-dies-fighting-isis-syria-n189081.

62. Beattie, Victor, Mike Eckel and Carol Guensburg. "Details Emerge About Douglas McCain, American Jihadist Killed in Syria." *Voice of America News,* August 27, 2014. Accessed October 28, 2014. http://www.voanews.com/content/us-man-suspected-of-fighting-alongside-militants-killed-in-syria/2429355.html. Moran, Rick. "American jihadist dies in Syria fighting for Islamic State." *American Thinker,* August 27, 2014. Accessed October 28, 2014. http://www.americanthinker.com/blog/2014/08/american_jihadist_dies_in_syria_fighting_for_islamic_state.html.

63. Vinograd, Cassandra and Ammar Cheikh Omar. "American Douglas McAuthur McCain Dies Fighting for ISIS in Syria." *NBC,* August 26, 2014. Accessed October 28, 2014. http://www.nbcnews.com/storyline/isis-terror/american-douglas-mcauthur-mccain-dies-fighting-isis-syria-n189081.

64. Vinograd, Cassandra. "ISIS' Douglas McCain, Best Friend Troy Kastigar Both Waged Jihad." *NBC,* August 27, 2014. Accessed October 28, 2014. http://www.nbcnews.com/storyline/isis-terror/isis-douglas-mccain-best-friend-troy-kastigar-both-waged-jihad-n190001.

Beattie, Victor et al. "Details Emerge About Douglas McCain, American Jihadist Killed in Syria." *Voice of America News,* August 27, 2014. Accessed October 28, 2014. http://www.voanews.com/content/us-man-suspected-of-fighting-alongside-militants-killed-in-syria/2429355.html.

65. Vinograd, Cassandra. "ISIS' Douglas McCain, Best Friend Troy Kastigar Both Waged Jihad." *NBC,* August 27, 2014. Accessed October 28, 2014. http://www.nbcnews.com/storyline/isis-terror/isis-douglas-mccain-best-friend-troy-kastigar-both-waged-jihad-n190001.

66. Wagner, Meg. "Minnesota dad-of-nine Abdirahmaan Muhumed killed fighting for ISIS in Syria: report." *NY Daily News,* August 28, 2014. Accessed October 27, 2014. http://www.nydailynews.com/news/national/american-isis-terrorist-killed-syria-id-report-article-1.1919877. Mathis-Lilley, Ben. "Minnesota Father of Nine Killed Fighting for ISIS in Syria." *Slate,* August 28, 2014. Accessed October 28, 2014. http://www.slate.com/blogs/the_slatest/2014/08/28/minnesota_isis_abdirahmaan_muhumed_killed_in_syria.html.

Lyden, Tom. "EXCLUSIVE: ISIS fighter worked at Minneapolis airport." *Fox,* September 30, 2014. Accessed October 28, 2014. http://www.myfoxtwincities.com/story/26432205/exclusive-isis-fighter-worked-at-minneapolis-airport.

67. Ward, Clarissa. "American Jihadist Talks to CBS News in Syria." *CBS News,* October 8, 2014. Accessed October 30, 2014. http://www.cbsnews.com/news/american-jihadist-in-syria-talks-to-cbs-news-clarissa-ward/. "Ibn Zubayr the American-born militant speaks out about fighting for al Qaeda in Syria." *Georgia Newsday,* October 9, 2014. Accessed October 28, 2014. http://www.georgianewsday.com/news/regional/294100-ibn-zubayr-the-american-born-militant-speaks-out-about-fighting-for-al-qaeda-in-syria.html#sthash.VqQKlY3H.dpuf.

68. Serwer, Adam. "Third American Suicide Bomber Ever Dies In Mogadishu Attack." *Mother Jones,* October 31, 2011. Accessed October 28, 2014. http://www.motherjones.com/mojo/2011/10/third-american-suicide-bomber-ever-dies-mogadishu-attack.

69. Wagner, Meg. "'We are coming for you': American suicide bomber who threatened U.S., burned passport returned to U.S. for months before Syria attack." *Daily Mail,* July 30, 2014. Accessed October 28, 2014. http://www.nydailynews.com/news/world/american-suicide-bomber-syria-threatens-video-article-1.1885341. Thompson, Paul "Parents' torment after 'all-

American' basketball-loving son from Florida turned suicide bomber in Syria—amid claims he was recruited by Texas terror cell." *Daily Mail,* June 1, 2014. Accessed October 28, 2014. http://www.dailymail.co.uk/news/article-2645784/He-American-son-parents-tormented-basketball-playing-son-turned-suicide-bomber.html.

70. Ibid.

71. "Help Us Catch a Terrorist U.S. Citizen Wanted for Supporting al Qaeda." *FBI Stories,* October 3, 2014. Accessed October 28, 2014. http://www.fbi.gov/news/stories/2012/october/help-us-catch-a-terrorist.

72. Zennie, Michael. "The American computer wiz running brutally effective ISIS social media campaign: College-educated son of top Boston doctor is on FBI Most Wanted list." *Daily Mail,* September 4, 2014. Accessed October 28, 2014. http://www.dailymail.co.uk/news/article-2743737/The-American-computer-wiz-running-ISIS-brutally-effective-social-media-campaign-College-educated-son-Boston-doctor-FBI-Most-Wanted-list.html.

73. Department of Justice. Federal Bureau of Investigation. "Seeking Information: Help Identify Individuals Traveling Overseas for Combat," October 7, 2014. Accessed October 30, 2014. http://www.fbi.gov/news/stories/2014/october/help-identify-individuals-traveling-overseas-for-combat/image/isil-unknown-subject.

74. "Columbus, Ohio, man charged with providing material support to terrorists." Office of Public Affairs. U.S. Department of Justice, April 16, 2015. Accessed April 16, 2015. http://www.justice.gov/opa/pr/columbus-ohio-man-charged-providing-material-support-terrorists.

75. Ibid.

76. Ibid.

77. Ibid.

78. Cousins, Sophie. "What Happened When Wisconsin Man Jordan Matson Decided To Take On ISIS." *Huffington Post,* October 8, 2014. Accessed October 28, 2014. http://www.huffingtonpost.com/2014/10/08/jordan-matson-isis_n_5952786.html. Walker, Hunter. "An American Has Joined A Kurdish Militia To Fight ISIS In Syria—And His Friends Are Cheering Him On With Memes." *Business Insider,* October 3, 2014. Accessed October 28, 2014. http://www.businessinsider.com/jordan-matson-joined-kurdish-militia-to-fight-isis-in-syria-2014-10.

"Jordan Matson An American Citizen Joined Ypg To Fight Against Isis." *Kurdish AGIT,* October 3, 2014. Accessed October 28, 2014. https://www.youtube.com/watch?v=Q8a-v9sACXk.

79. Coleman, Luke. "US veterans fighting IS with Assyrian Christian militia." *Basnews,* February 21, 2015. Accessed February 22, 2015. http://basnews.com/en/news/2015/02/21/us-veterans-fighting-is-with-assyrian-christian-militia/.

80. Ibid.

81. Ibid.

82. Ibid.

83. Hyde, Joan. "FBI Arrests Suburban Chicago Man on Charge of Supporting Terrorism Overseas." FBI, April 20, 2013. Accessed October 28, 2014. http://www.fbi.gov/chicago/press-releases/2013/fbi-arrests-suburban-chicago-man-on-charge-of-supporting-terrorism-overseas.

"Aurora Teen In Court On Naperville Nightclub Plot Charges." *ABC,* April 23, 2013. Accessed October 28, 2014. http://abc7chicago.com/archive/9075721/.

Goudie, Chuck. "Aurora teen, Abdella Tounisi, talking plea deal with federal prosecutors." *ABC7ChicagoNews.com,* January 8, 2015. Accessed March 26, 2015. http://abc7chicago.com/news/aurora-teen-abdella-tounisi-talking-plea-deal-with-feds/466816/.

84. Walsh, Denny and Sam Stanton. "San Joaquin County man indicted on terrorist charge." *Sacramento Bee,* March 26, 2014. Accessed October 28, 2014. http://www.sacbee.com/2014/03/26/6271828/san-joaquin-county-man-indicted.html. Department of Justice. Offices of the United States Attorneys. Eastern District of California. *United States of America vs. Nicholas Michael Teausant. Criminal Complaint,* Docket #: 2:14-cr-00087 JAM. March 17, 2014. Accessed August 20, 2014. http://www.justice.gov/usao/cae/news/docs/2014/2014_03/Teausant%20Complaint%20.pdf.

85. Mears, Bill. "North Carolina man allegedly tried to help Syrian jihadist group." *CNN,* November 12, 2013. Accessed October 28, 2014. http://security.blogs.cnn.com/2013/11/12/

north-carolina-man-allegedly-tried-to-help-syrian-jihadist-group/. "NC man arrested at airport, charged with trying to join al Qaeda-linked terrorist group." *NBC,* November 11, 2013. Accessed October 28, 2014. http://www.nbcnews.com/news/other/nc-man-arrested-airport-charged-trying-join-al-qaeda-linked-f2D11579411.

86. Brumfield, Ben. "Texas man pleads guilty to attempting to join ISIS' jihad in Syria." *CNN,* June 28, 2014. Accessed October 28, 2014. http://www.cnn.com/2014/06/28/justice/texas-terror-arrests/.

87. "Raleigh Man Pleads Guilty to Conspiring to Provide Material Support for Terrorism." U.S. Department of Justice, October 16, 2014. Accessed February 23, 2015. http://www.justice.gov/opa/pr/raleigh-man-pleads-guilty-conspiring-provide-material-support-terrorism.

88. Ibid.

89. Daly, Michael. "The Mystery of Donald Ray Morgan, the 44-Year-Old American Who Loved ISIS." *Daily Beast,* August 12, 2014. Accessed October 28, 2014. http://www.thedailybeast.com/articles/2014/08/12/the-mystery-of-donald-ray-morgan-the-44-year-old-american-who-loved-isis.html.

90. Mollerus, Meghann. "Suspected NC ISIS Supporter Pleads Not Guilty To Firearm Charge." *WFMY News,* September 4, 2014. Accessed October 28, 2014. http://www.wfmynews2.com/story/news/local/2014/09/04/isis-supporter-nc-man-federal-court-firearm-charge-donald-ray-morgan/15067635/.

91. "North Carolina man pleads guilty to attempting to aid international terrorist group." FBI Charlotte Division, October 30, 2014. Accessed November 15, 2014. http://www.fbi.gov/charlotte/press-releases/2014/north-carolina-man-pleads-guilty-to-attempting-to-aid-international-terrorist-organization. "Suspected American Islamic State member arrested at JFK airport amid fears he may be running guns for terror group or preparing for jihad." *Daily Mail,* August 11, 2014. Accessed October 28, 2014. http://www.dailymail.co.uk/news/article-2721812/Suspected-American-IS-member-caught-JFK-amid-fears-running-guns-terror-group-preparing-Jihad.

92. "FBI Arrests Suburban Chicago Man for Allegedly Attempting to Support Terrorism Overseas." FBI, October 6, 2014. Accessed October 27, 2014. http://www.fbi.gov/chicago/press-releases/2014/fbi-arrests-suburban-chicago-man-for-allegedly-attempting-to-support-terrorism-overseas.

Department of Justice. Offices of the United States Attorneys. Northern District of Illinois, Eastern Division. *United States V. Mohammed Hamzah Khan. Criminal Complaint,* October 6, 2014. http://www.justice.gov/sites/default/files/press-releases/attachments/2014/10/06/hamzah_complaint.pdf.

Walsh, Michael, et al. "llinois man busted trying to join ISIS left letter behind for parents: FBI." *NY Daily News*, October 7, 2014. Accessed October 28, 2014. http://nydailynews.com/news/national/illinois-man-charged-join-isis-overseas-fbi-article-1.1964946.

93. "Two Minnesotans Charged with Conspiracy to Provide Material Support to the Islamic State of Iraq and the Levant." FBI, November 24, 2014. Accessed February 18, 2015. http://www.fbi.gov/minneapolis/press-releases/2014/two-minnesotans-charged-with-conspiracy-to-provide-material-support-to-the-islamic-state-of-iraq-and-the-levant. "U.S. v. Abdullah Yusuf, Abdi Nur," Criminal Complaint, November 24, 2014. Accessed February 23, 2015. http://www.justice.gov/usao/mn/downloads/Yusuf%20and%20Nur%20Complaint.pdf.

Yuen, Laura. "Minnesotan charged with trying to join ISIS pleads guilty." *MPRNews,* February 26, 2015. Accessed April 3, 2015. http://www.mprnews.org/story/2015/02/26/abdullahi-yusuf.

94. Ibid.

95. Ibid.

96. "Three Brooklyn, New York, residents charged with attempt and conspiracy to provide material support to ISIL." Office of Public Affairs, Department of Justice, February 25, 2015. Accessed February 27, 2015. http://www.justice.gov/opa/pr/three-brooklyn-new-york-residents-charged-attempt-and-conspiracy-provide-material-support.

97. Ibid.

98. Ibid.

99. "US Air Force veteran charged with attempting to provide material support to ISIL." Office of Public Affairs, U.S. Department of Justice, March 17, 2015. Accessed March 19, 2015. http://www.justice.gov/opa/pr/us-air-force-veteran-charged-attempting-provide-material-support-isil.

100. "US Army National Guard soldier and his cousin arrested for conspiring to support terrorism (ISIL)." Office of U.S. Public Affairs, U.S. Department of Justice, March 26, 2015. Accessed March 26, 2015. http://www.justice.gov/opa/pr/us-army-national-guard-soldier-and-his-cousin-arrested-conspiring-support-terrorism-isil.

101. "Six Minnesota Men Charged with Conspiracy to Provide Material Support to the Islamic State of Iraq and the Levant." Office of Public Affairs, U.S. Department of Justice, April 20, 2015. Accessed April 22, 2015. http://www.justice.gov/opa/pr/six-minnesota-men-charged-conspiracy-provide-material-support-islamic-state-iraq-and-levant.

102. Ibid.

103. Ibid.

104. "Indian-American pleads guilty to funding al-Qaeda groups." *IBN Live,* July 13, 2014. Accessed October 28, 2014. http://ibnlive.in.com/news/indianamerican-pleads-guilty-to-funding-alqaeda-groups/485660-2.html. "American pleads guilty in Al-Qaeda sting operation." *AFP,* July 11, 2014. Accessed October 28, 2014. http://news.yahoo.com/american-pleads-guilty-al-qaeda-sting-operation-233931797.html.

105. Carlin, John P. "Rochester Man Indicted on Charges of Attempting to Provide Material Support to ISIS, Attempting to Kill U.S. Soldiers and Possession of Firearms and Silencers." Department of Justice, September 16, 2014. Accessed October 28, 2014. http://www.justice.gov/nsd/pr/rochester-man-indicted-charges-attempting-provide-material-support-isis-attempting-kill-us.

106. Ibid.

107. Ibid.

108. Craig, Gary. "FBI: Terror suspect wanted to kill returning soldiers." *USA Today,* June 2, 2014. Accessed October 28, 2014. http://www.usatoday.com/story/news/nation/2014/06/02/man-supportive-terrorist-groups-plot-kill-returning-soldiers/9884573/.

109. Ibid.

110. "Six defendants charged with conspiracy and providing materials support to terrorists." FBI, February 6, 2015. Accessed February 15, 2015. http://www.fbi.gov/stlouis/press-releases/2015/six-defendants-charged-with-conspiracy-and-providing-material-support-to-terrorists.

111. Ihejirika, Maudlyne. "Two Illinois residents among six accused of helping Islamic State, al-Qaida." *Chicago Sun-Times*, February 6, 2015. Accessed February 15, 2015. http://chicago.suntimes.com/news-chicago/7/71/351402/two-illinois-men-among-six-bosnian-immigrants-accused-helping-islamic-state-al-qaida.

112. Ibid.

113. Ibid.

114. "Va. teen accused of helping man join ISIS." *Fox 5*, March 4, 2015. Accessed March 15, 2015. http://www.myfoxdc.com/story/28264618/report-va-teen-accused-of-helping-man-join-isis. "Virginia teen accused of helping another join ISIS." *NBC Washington*, March 5, 2015. Accessed March 15, 2015. http://www.nbcwashington.com/news/local/Virginia-Teen-Accused-of-Helping-Another-Join-ISIS-295067761.html.

115. Yeginsu, Ceylan. "ISIS Draws a Steady Stream of Recruits From Turkey." *NY Times*, September 15, 2014. Accessed October 21, 2014. http://www.nytimes.com/2014/09/16/world/europe/turkey-is-a-steady-source-of-isis-recruits.html.

116. Zeyrek, Deniz. "Turkey concerned by return of Turkish ISIL fighters." *Hürriyet Daily News*, January 15, 2015. Accessed February 18, 2015. http://www.hurriyetdailynews.com/turkey-concerned-by-return-of-turkish-isil-fighters-.aspx?pageID=238&nID=76945&NewsCatID=338

117. "Brussels Jewish museum massacre suspect Mehdi-Nemmouche is Syrian captor, claims kidnapped journalist." *Independent*, September 6, 2014. Accessed October 27, 2014. http://www.independent.co.uk/news/world/europe/brussels-jewish-museum-massacre-suspect-mehdinemmouche-is-syrian-captor-claims-kidnapped-journalist-9716473.html.

118. "'Brussels Jewish Museum killer was IS torturer.'" *Times of Israel*, September 6, 2014. Accessed October 27, 2014. http://www.timesofisrael.com/brussels-jewish-museum-shooter-was-member-of-islamic-state/.

119. Paraszczuk, Joanna. "Dozens Of Finns, Swedes Fighting For IS." *Radio Free Europe Radio Liberty*, January 23, 2015. Accessed February 18, 2015. http://www.rferl.org/content/islamic-state-finland-sweden-isis-fighters/26809973.html.

120. "Foreign fighters from Western countries in the ranks of the rebel organizations affiliated with Al-Qaeda and the global jihad in Syria." The Meir Amit Intelligence and Terrorism Information Center, March 2, 2014. Accessed October 27, 2014. http://www.terrorism-info.org.il/cn/article/20616.

121. Paraszczuk, Joanna. "Dozens Of Finns, Swedes Fighting For IS." *Radio Free Europe Radio Liberty*, January 23, 2015. Accessed February 18, 2015. http://www.rferl.org/content/islamic-state-finland-sweden-isis-fighters/26809973.html.

122. "Foreign fighters from Western countries in the ranks of the rebel organizations affiliated with Al-Qaeda and the global jihad in Syria." The Meir Amit Intelligence and Terrorism Information Center, March 2, 2014. Accessed October 27, 2014. http://www.terrorism-info.org.il/en/article/20616.

123. Mekhennet, Souad. "Osama's name flows in our blood: Ex-rapper." *Indian Express*, September 2, 2011. Accessed October 27, 2014. http://archive.indianexpress.com/news/osama-s-name-flows-in-our-blood-exrapper/840441/0.

124. Lister, Charles. Twitter Post. August 30, 2013 12:25 AM. Accessed October 27, 2014. https://twitter.com/Charles_Lister/status/373345727637766145/photo/1. "Famous German Rap Singer converts to Islam, and goes off to Jihad in Syria." YouTube video, 1:29. Posted by "Muhajer Alrafidain." Accessed October 30, 2014. https://www.youtube.com/watch?v=yAMi8WI2duo.

Armstrong, Martin. "The Search for Deso Dogg, The German Rapper Turned Jihadi Poster Boy." *Vice*, September 20, 2013. Accessed October 27, 2014. http://www.vice.com/en_uk/read/the-search-for-deso-dogg-german-rapper-turned jihadi poster-boy.

125. "German Rapper Turned Jihadist Ruben Cupert (Deso Dogg) Pledges to ISIL." *Site*, April 11, 2014. Accessed October 27, 2014. http://ent.siteintelgroup.com/Jihadist-News/german-rapper-turned-jihadist-ruben-cuspert-deso-dogg-pledges-to-isil.html.

126. "German rapper turned jihadist killed in Syria." *Al Akhbar*, April 22, 2014. Accessed October 27, 2014. http://english.al-akhbar.com/content/german-rapper-turned-jihadist-killed-syria.

127. "Designation of Denis Cuspert." Office of the Spokesperson, U.S. State Department, February 9, 2015. Accessed February 19, 2015. http://www.state.gov/r/pa/prs/ps/2015/02/237324.htm.

128. "Indian jihadist 'kills 55 for ISIS, quits because no pay.'" *RT*, November 30, 2014. Accessed December 20, 2014. http://rt.com/news/210091-isis-india-recruit-quit-arrested/.

129. "More than 100 Palestinians join the Islamic State." *Aranews*, December 23, 2014. Accessed December 25, 2014. http://aranews.net/2014/12/100-palestinians-join-islamic-state/.

130. "ISIS recruits at record pace in Syria." *Al-Arabiya*, August 19, 2014. Accessed October 21, 2014. http://english.alarabiya.net/en/News/middle-east/2014/08/19/ISIS-recruits-at-record-pace-in-Syria-.html.

131. "The path to jihad and the Islamic State." *Jerusalem Post*, September 6, 2014. Accessed October 21, 2014. http://www.jpost.com/Middle-East/The-path-to-jihad-374571.

132. Higgins, Andrew. "Belgium Confronts the Jihadist Danger Within." *NY Times*, January 24, 2015. Accessed February 18, 2015. http://www.nytimes.com/2015/01/25/world/europe/belgium-confronts-the-jihadist-danger-within.html?_r=0.

133. "Some Malaysians borrowing cash to join ISIS." *AsiaOne*, January 14, 2015. Accessed February 18, 2015. http://news.asiaone.com/news/malaysia/some-malaysians-borrowing-cash-join-isis.

134. Gubash, Charlene and Alexander Smith. "ISIS Beheadings and Saudi Punishments: 'Difference Is Clear.'" *NBC News*, February 2, 2015. Accessed February 18, 2015. http://www.nbcnews.com/news/world/isis-beheadings-saudi-punishments-difference-clear-n296876.

135. Safi, Michael and Nick Evershed. "Australians fighting in Syria: how many have joined the conflict?" *Guardian; Data Blog,* April 9, 2014. Accessed October 28, 2014. http://www.theguardian.com/world/datablog/2014/apr/09/australians-fighting-in-syria-how-many-have-joined-the-conflict.

136. "Shi'ite Foreign Fighters in Syria." The Meir Amit Intelligence and Terrorism Information Center, March 18, 2014. Accessed October 28, 2014. http://www.terrorism-info.org.il/en/article/20631.

137. "Virginia Man Sentenced to 18 Months in Prison for Acting as Unregistered Agent for Syrian Government." FBI, July 20, 2012. Accessed October 28, 2014. http://www.fbi.gov/washingtondc/press-releases/2012/virginia-man-sentenced-to-18-months-in-prison-for-acting-as-unregistered-agent-for-syrian-government.

138. "Dearborn Resident Charged with Attempting to Support a Foreign Terrorist Organization." FBI. March 17, 2014. Accessed October 28, 2014. http://www.fbi.gov/detroit/press-releases/2014/dearborn-resident-charged-with-attempting-to-support-a-foreign-terrorist-organization.

139. "US v. Mohammad Hassan Hamdan." Department of Justice. Offices of the United States Attorneys. Eastern District of Michigan. Criminal Complaint. March 17, 2014. Accessed October 27, 2014. http://www.investigativeproject.org/documents/case_docs/2328.pdf.

140. Gander, Kashmira. "Syria: video shows pro-Assad LA gang members fighting in the civil war." *Independent*, March 4, 2014. Accessed October 27, 2014. http://www.independent.co.uk/news/world/americas/syria-video-shows-proassad-la-gang-members-fighting-in-the-civil-war-9169127.html.

141. Ibid.

142. "Video: Los Angeles gang member fighting in Syria." *Al Arabiya*, March 4, 2014. Accessed October 27, 2014. http://english.alarabiya.net/en/News/middle-east/2014/03/04/Video-Los-Angeles-gang-members-fighting-in-Syria.html#slide=4.

143. Gander, Kashmira. "Syria: video shows pro-Assad LA gang members fighting in the civil war." *Independent*, March 4, 2014. Accessed October 27, 2014. http://www.independent.co.uk/news/world/americas/syria-video-shows-proassad-la-gang-members-fighting-in-the-civil-war-9169127.html. Martinez, Michael. "Syria civil war: Video claims L.A. gang members are fighting for Assad." *CNN*, March 6, 2014. Accessed October 27, 2014. http://www.cnn.com/2014/03/05/world/meast/syria-los-angeles-gang-members-video/.

144. "Dutch bikers join fight against Islamic State in Iraq." *BBC*, October 15, 2014. Accessed October 27, 2014. http://www.bbc.com/news/world-middle-east-29635394. "German bikers unite with Dutch comrades in fight against ISIS." *RT*, October 17, 2014. Accessed October 27, 2014. http://rt.com/news/196864-germany-bikers-fight-isis/.

145. "Dutch bikers join fight against Islamic State in Iraq." *BBC*, October 15, 2014. Accessed October 27, 2014. http://www.bbc.com/news/world-middle-east-29635394.

146. "German bikers unite with Dutch comrades in fight against ISIS." *RT*, October 17, 2014. Accessed October 27, 2014. http://rt.com/news/196864-germany-bikers-fight-isis/.

147. "Int'l anti-ISIS brigade: Westerners flock to fight for Kurds." *RT*, November 24, 2014. Accessed December 11, 2014. http://rt.com/news/208083-westerners-isis-kurds-syria/.

148. Williams, Dan, et al. "Canadian-Israeli woman joins Kurds fighting Islamic State: radio." *Reuters,* November 10, 2014. Accessed November 20, 2014. http://www.reuters.com/article/2014/11/10/us-mideast-crisis-kurds-israeli-idUSKCN0IU1NY20141110.   Walkom, Thomas. "Gill Rosenberg, the Kurds and the complex politics of terror: Walkom." *Star*, December 2, 2014. Accessed December 9, 2014. http://www.thestar.com/news/canada/2014/12/02/gill_rosenberg_the_kurds_and_the_complex_politics_of_terror_walkom.html.

149. "German woman, 19, dies fighting the Islamic State in Syria." *BBC*, March 9, 2015. Accessed March 12, 2015. http://m.bbc.com/news/world-middle-east-31796228.

150. "Five Canadians killed in Syria fighting with IS." *Zeenews*, January 15, 2015. Accessed January 18, 2015. http://zeenews.india.com/news/world/five-canadians-killed-in-syria-fighting-with-is_1530493.html.

151. Gowrinathan, Nimmi. "The Women of ISIS." *Foreign Affairs*, August 21, 2014. Accessed October 27, 2014. http://www.foreignaffairs.com/articles/141926/nimmi-gowrinathan/the-women-of-isis.

152. Shinkman, Paul. "ISIS ability to recruit women baffles West, strengthens cause." *US News and World Report*, March 2, 2015. Accessed March 5, 2015. http://www.usnews.com/news/articles/2015/03/02/isis-ability-to-recruit-women-baffles-west-strengthens-cause.

153. Dettmer, Jamie. "The ISIS Online Campaign Luring Western Girls to Jihad." *Daily Beast*, August, 6, 2014. Accessed October 27, 2014. http://www.thedailybeast.com/articles/2014/08/06/the-isis-online-campaign-luring-western-girls-to-jihad.html.

154. Stoller, Amy. "Syria's ISIS recruits female brigades, hinting at changing role for women." *Foreign Policy Today*, February 10, 2014. Accessed October 27, 2014. http://www.fptoday.org/syrias-isis-recruits-female-brigades-hinting-at-changing-role-for-women/.

155. Parkinson, Joe. "Iraq crisis: Kurds push to take Mosul Dam as U.S. gains controversial guerrilla ally." *Wall Street Journal*, August 18, 2014. Accessed October 27, 2014. http://online.wsj.com/articles/kurds-with-u-s-aid-push-to-take-mosul-dam-1408322338.

156. Urquhart, Conal. "Iraq crisis: Isis militants plan to 'marry' captured Yazidi women." *Independent*, August 17, 2014. Accessed October 27, 2014. http://www.independent.co.uk/news/world/middle-east/iraq-crisis-isis-militants-plan-to-marry-captured-yazidi-women-9674922.html. Su, Reissa. "ISIS kidnaps, sells women as 'sex slaves' while Obama declares U.S. mission not over yet." *International Business Times*, August 18, 2014. Accessed October 27, 2014. http://au.ibtimes.com/articles/562953/20140818/isis-christians-obama-iraq-islamic-militants.htm#.VE5rvb5N3zJ.

157. Ghitis, Frida. "Ghitis: What jihadis plan for women." *WSBT.com*, April 16, 2015. Accessed April 17, 2015. http://www.wsbt.com/news/nationworld/ghitis-what-jihadis-plan-for-women/32405536.

158. Ibid.

159. Hanna, Asaad. "Syrian girls forced to marry ISIS fighters." *Al Monitor*, May 13, 2014. Accessed October 27, 2014. http://www.al-monitor.com/pulse/originals/2014/05/syria-girls-marriage-isis-raqqa.html#.

160. Ibid.

161. Smith, Lydia. "Islamic State's Women Warriors: How Feared Al-Khansa Battalion was Borne Out of Repression." *International Business Times*, August 13, 2014. Accessed October 27, 2014. http://www.ibtimes.co.uk/islamic-states-women-warriors-how-fierce-al-khansa-battalion-was-borne-out-repression-1461016.

162. Gilsinan, Kathy. "The ISIS Crackdown on Women, by Women." *Atlantic*, July 25, 2014. Accessed October 27, 2014. http://www.theatlantic.com/international/archive/2014/07/the-women-of-isis/375047/. Ernst, Douglas. "ISIL creates all-female brigade to terrorize women into following Sharia law." *Washington Times*, July 25, 2014. Accessed October 27, 2014. http://www.washingtontimes.com/news/2014/jul/25/isil-has-created-all-female-bridgade-terrorize-wom/.

163. Ernst, Douglas. "ISIL creates all-female brigade to terrorize women into following Sharia law." *Washington Times*, July 25, 2014. Accessed October 27, 2014. http://www.washingtontimes.com/news/2014/jul/25/isil-has-created-all-female-bridgade-terrorize-wom/.

164. Al Fares, Zaid. "Frontline Isis: Meet the Women, Children, and Britons at the Core of the Islamic State." *International Business Times*, August 12, 2014. Accessed October 27, 2014. http://www.ibtimes.co.uk/frontline-isis-meet-men-children-britons-core-islamic-state-1460888.

165. "Al-Qaeda in Syria forms female brigades." *Al Arabiya*, February 2, 2014. Accessed October 27, 2014. http://english.alarabiya.net/en/News/middle-east/2014/02/02/Syria-jihadist-group-ISIS-forms-women-only-battalions.html.

166. Stoller, Amy. "Syria's ISIS recruits female brigades, hinting at changing role for women." *Foreign Policy Today*, February 10, 2014. Accessed October 27, 2014. http://www.fptoday.org/syrias-isis-recruits-female-brigades-hinting-at-changing-role-for-women/. Smith, Lydia. "Islami State's Women Warriors: How Feared Al-Khansa Battalion was Borne Out of Repression." *International Business Times*, August 13, 2014. Accessed October 27, 2014. http://www.ibtimes.co.uk/islamic-states-women-warriors-how-fierce-al-khansa-battalion-was-borne-out-repression-1461016.

167. Al-Bahri, Ahmad. "All-Female ISIS Brigade Cracks Down on Women in Raqqa." *ABC News*, July 20, 2014. Accessed October 27, 2014. http://abcnews.go.com/International/female-isis-brigade-cracks-women-raqqa/story?id=24622389.

168. "Al-Qaeda in Syria forms female brigades." *Al Arabiya*, February 2, 2014. Accessed October 27, 2014. http://english.alarabiya.net/en/News/middle-east/2014/02/02/Syria-jihadist-group-ISIS-forms-women-only-battalions.html.

169. Al-Bahri, Ahmad. "All Female ISIS brigade cracks down on women in Raqqa." *ABC News*, July 20, 2014. Accessed October 26, 2014. http://abcnews.go.com/International/female-isis-brigade-cracks-women-raqqa/story?id=24622389.

170. "Umm Al-Rayan." Terrorism Research and Analysis Consortium. Accessed October 30, 2014. http://www.trackingterrorism.org/group/umm-al-rayan.

171. Sanghani, Radhika. "Hipster jihadis, cheesecake and miscarriages: Life inside Isil for Western women." *Telegraph*, January 28, 2015. Accessed February 4, 2015. http://www.telegraph.co.uk/women/womens-politics/11374818/Isil-for-women-Hipster-jihadis-cheesecake-and-miscarriages.html. "Western women joining IS militants 'cheerleaders, not victims." *I24News*, January 28, 2015. Accessed February 4, 2015. http://www.i24news.tv/en/news/international/59265-150128-women-joining-is-militants-cheerleaders-not-victims.

172. Longman, James. "Female Muslim converts drawn to Islamic State." *BBC*, January 29, 2015. Accessed February 3, 2015. http://www.bbc.com/news/uk-31027457.

173. Wellman, Alex. "Terror cops pull teen girl travelling to Syria from plane seconds before take off." *Daily Mirror*, December 17, 2014. Accessed December 24, 2014. http://www.mirror.co.uk/news/uk-news/terror-cops-pull-teen-girl-4827311.

174. Rahman, Khaleda and Victoria Allen. "The private school jihadist: As PM unveils new terror crackdown, a Scots girl incites bloody massacre on British streets." *Daily Mail*, September 1, 2014. Accessed October 27, 2014. http://www.dailymail.co.uk/news/article-2740268/The-private-school-jihadist-As-PM-unveils-new-terror-crackdown-Scots-girl-incites-bloody-massacre-British-streets.html.

175. Layth, Umm. Tumblr. Accessed October 30, 2014. http://fa-tubalilghuraba.tumblr.com/.

176. "UK-born private school girl joins Syria militants." *Al Arabiya*, September 2, 2014. Accessed October 27, 2014. http://english.alarabiya.net/en/News/middle-east/2014/09/02/Scottish-private-school-girl-joins-Syria-militants.html.

177. Yeatman, Dominic. "Meet the British women jihadis fighting for IS." *Metro*, September 7, 2014. Accessed October 27, 2014. http://metro.co.uk/2014/09/07/meet-the-british-women-jihadis-fighting-for-is-4860074/.

178. Ibid.

179. "British rocker mom joins ISIS, vows to 'behead Christians with blunt knife.'" *RT*, September 1, 2014. Accessed October 27, 2014. http://rt.com/uk/184212-british-mother-isis-christians/.

180. Gillman, Ollie. "New picture merges of British jihadist Sally Jones with partner and new-born baby taken ten years before she joined ISIS." *Daily Mail*, September 12, 2014. Accessed October 27, 2014. http://www.dailymail.co.uk/news/article-2753864/New-picture-emerges-British-jihadist-Sally-Jones-partner-new-born-baby-taken-ten-years-joined-ISIS.html. Hunter, Chris. "'Why I joined Islamic State': Chatham mum Sally Jones speaks of jihadist mission after moving to Syria with husband Junaid Hussain." *Kent Online*, September 8, 2014. Accessed October 27, 2014. http://www.kentonline.co.uk/medway/news/jihadist-sally-jones-23110/.

181. Gillman, Ollie. "New picture emerges of British jihadist Sally Jones with partner and new-born baby taken ten years before she joined ISIS." *Daily Mail*, September 12, 2014. Accessed October 27, 2014. http://www.dailymail.co.uk/news/article-2753864/New-picture-emerges-British-jihadist-Sally-Jones-partner-new-born-baby-taken-ten-years-joined-ISIS.html.

182. Ibid.

183. Gadher, Dipesh. "'My son and I love life with the beheaders.'" *Sunday Times*, September 7, 2014. Accessed October 27, 2014. http://www.thesundaytimes.co.uk/sto/news/uk_news/National/Terrorism/article1455900.ece.

184. "White British girl who's now a 'celebrity jihadi': Mother-of-two a 'top priority' for MI6 and she calls on Muslims to join the terror group." *Daily Mail*, September 1, 2014. Accessed October 27, 2014. http://www.dailymail.co.uk/news/article-2739705/White-British-girl-s-celebrity-jihadi-Mother-two-priority-MI6-calls-Muslims-join-terror-group.html.

185. Herrmann, Joshi. "INVESTIGATION: the chilling tale of how a typical Lewisham teen became an Isis bride in Syria." *London Evening Standard*, July 25, 2014. Accessed October 27, 2014. http://www.standard.co.uk/lifestyle/london-life/investigation-the-chilling-tale-of-how-a-typical-lewisham-teen-became-an-isis-bride-in-syria-9628523.html.

186. Morris, Kyle, et al. "How British women are joining the jihad in Syria." *Channel 4 News*, July 23, 2014. Accessed October 27, 2014. http://www.channel4.com/news/syria-rebels-jihad-british-foreign-assad.

187. Ibid.

188. Dearden, Lizzie. "James Foley beheading: 'I want to be the first UK woman to kill a Westerner,' says British jihadist in Syria." *Independent*, August 22, 2014. Accessed October 27, 2014. http://www.independent.co.uk/news/world/middle-east/james-foley-beheading-i-want-to-be-the-first-uk-woman-to-kill-a-westerner-says-british-jihadist-in-syria-9684908.html.

189. Reilly, Jill. "Twin Manchester schoolgirls who ran away to Syria 'have married ISIS fighters and mainly stay indoors and read the Qur'an unless their jihadi husbands take them out.'" *Daily Mail*, July 24, 2014. Accessed October 27, 2014. http://www.dailymail.co.uk/news/article-2703792/Twin-Manchester-schoolgirls-ran-away-Syria-married-ISIS-fighters-mainly-stay-indoors-read-Quran-unless-jihadi-husbands-out.html.

Glendinning, Amy. "Twin girls who ran away to Syria were star pupils with 28 GCSEs between them." *Manchester Evening News*, July 9, 2014. Accessed October 27, 2014. http://www.manchestereveningnews.co.uk/news/greater-manchester-news/salma-zahra-halane-twin-girls-7394173.

Robinson, Martin. "'I love the name Terror Twin . . . I sound scary.' What schoolgirl who fled to Syria and married an Isis fighter said after hearing her nickname." *Daily Mail*, August 7, 2014. Accessed October 27, 2014. http://www.dailymail.co.uk/news/article-2718746/I-love-Terror-Twin-I-sound-scary-What-schoolgirl-fled-Syria-married-Isis-fighter-said-hearing-nickname.html.

190. Reilly, Jill. "Twin Manchester schoolgirls who ran away to Syria 'have married ISIS fighters and mainly stay indoors and read the Qur'an unless their Jihadi husbands take them out.'" *Daily Mail*, July 24, 2014. Accessed October 27, 2014. http://www.dailymail.co.uk/news/article-2703792/Twin-Manchester-schoolgirls-ran-away-Syria-married-ISIS-fighters-mainly-stay-indoors-read-Quran-unless-jihadi-husbands-out.html.

191. "Zahra and Salma Halane: Missing twins 'now in Syria'." *BBC*, July 9, 2014. Accessed October 27, 2014. http://www.bbc.com/news/uk-england-manchester-28230931.

192. "Runaway British schoolgirl Zahra Halane tweets anger at Islamic State husband over missing kitten." *News.com.au*, September 12, 2014. Accessed October 27, 2014. http://www.news.com.au/world/middle-east/runaway-british-schoolgirl-zahra-halane-tweets-anger-at-islamic-state-husband-over-missing-kitten/story-fnh81ifq-1227055973013.

193. Ibid.

194. Bates, Daniel. "American woman killed in Syria 'was converted to Islam by her Saudi Arabian husband who hated the West.'" *Daily Mail*, June 3, 2013. Accessed October 28, 2014. http://www.dailymail.co.uk/news/article-2334767/Nicole-Lynn-Mansfield-American-woman-killed-Syria-converted-Islam-Saudi-Arabian-husband.html. Preston, Jennifer. "Michigan Woman Killed in Syria War, Reports Say." *NY Times*, May 31, 2013. Accessed October 28, 2014. http://www.nytimes.com/2013/06/01/us/syria-fighting-touches-a-family-in-michigan.html.

Hausmann, Joanna. "Nicole Lynn Mansfield: 5 Fast Facts You Need to Know." *Heavy*, May 30, 2013. Accessed October 28, 2014. http://heavy.com/news/2013/05/nicole-lynn-mansfield-flint-us-citizen-killed-syria/.

Sheasley, Chelsea. "Who was Nicole Mansfield and what was she doing in Syria?" *Christian Science Monitor*, May 31, 2013. Accessed October 28, 2014. http://www.csmonitor.com/USA/USA-Update/2013/0531/Who-was-Nicole-Mansfield-and-what-was-she-doing-in-Syria.

195. Brumfield, Ben. "Officials: 3 Denver girls played hooky from school and tried to join ISIS." *CNN*, October 22, 2014. Accessed November 20, 2014. http://www.cnn.com/2014/10/22/us/colorado-teens-syria-odyssey/.

196. Kedmey, Dan. "Colorado teenager pleads guilty of conspiracy to support ISIS." *Time*, September 10, 2014. Accessed October 27, 2014. http://time.com/3319092/isis-colorado-woman-shannon-conley/. "Arvada teen, Shannon Conley, pleads guilty to helping foreign ter-

rorist organization ISIS." *Denver Channel 7 News*, September 10, 2014. Accessed October 27, 2014. http://www.thedenverchannel.com/news/local-news/arvada-teen-shannon-conley-pleads-guilty-to-helping-foreign-terrorist-organization-isis.

"Shannon Conley, accused of helping ISIS in terrorism case, plans guilty plea." *Denver Channel 7 News*, August 11, 2014. Accessed October 27, 2014. http://www.thedenverchannel.com/news/local-news/shannon-conley-accused-of-helping-isis-in-terrorism-case-plans-guilty-plea.

"Shannon Conley, 19-Year-Old American Jihadist, Pleads Guilty To Aiding ISIS." *Huffington Post*, September 10, 2014. Accessed October 27, 2014. http://www.huffingtonpost.com/2014/09/10/shannon-conley-guilty_n_5799242.html.

197. "Arvada Woman Sentenced for Conspiracy to Provide Material Support to a Designated Foreign Terrorist Organization." FBI, January 23, 2015. Accessed February 18, 2015. http://www.fbi.gov/denver/press-releases/2015/arvada-woman-sentenced-for-conspiracy-to-provide-material-support-to-a-designated-foreign-terrorist-organization.

198. Deam, Jenny. "Colorado woman's quest for jihad baffles neighbors." *Los Angeles Times*, July 25, 2014. Accessed October 27, 2014. http://www.latimes.com/nation/la-na-high-school-jihadi-20140726-story.html#page=1. "Judge won't release Arvada woman in terror case; Shannon Conley to remain in jail until sentencing." *Denver Channel 7 News*, September 17, 2014. Accessed October 27, 2014. http://www.thedenverchannel.com/news/local-news/judge-wont-release-arvada-woman-in-terror-case-shannon-conley-to-remain-in-jail-until-sentencing09172014.

"Arvada teen, Shannon Conley, pleads guilty to helping foreign terrorist organization ISIS." *Denver Channel 7 News*, September 10, 2014. Accessed October 27, 2014. http://www.thedenverchannel.com/news/local-news/arvada-teen-shannon-conley-pleads-guilty-to-helping-foreign-terrorist-organization-isis.

"Sharnnon Conley, accused of helping ISIS in terrorism case, plans guilty plea." *Denver Channel 7 News*, August 11, 2014. Accessed October 27, 2014. http://www.thedenverchannel.com/news/local-news/shannon-conley-accused-of-helping-isis-in-terrorism-case-plans-guilty-plea.

"Shannon Conley, 19-year-old American jihadist, pleads guilty to aiding ISIS." *Huffington Post*, September 10, 2014. Accessed October 27, 2014. http://www.huffingtonpost.com/2014/09/10/shannon-conley-guilty_n_5799242.html.

199. "American teen wears hijab in court as she pleads guilty to charges she tried to join ISIS in Syria." *Daily Mail*, September 10, 2014. Accessed October 27, 2014. http://www.dailymail.co.uk/news/article-2750264/Colorado-woman-set-plead-guilty-terror-case.html.

200. Deam, Jenny. "Colorado woman's quest for jihad baffles neighbors." *LA Times*, July 25, 2014. Accessed October 27, 2014. http://www.latimes.com/nation/la-na-high-school-jihadi-20140726-story.html#page=1.

201. "U.S. v. Noelle Velentzas and Asia Sidiqqui." Complaint and affidavit in support of arrest warrants. U.S. District Court for the Eastern District of Pennsylvania, April 1, 2015. Accessed April 2, 2015. http://www.justice.gov/sites/default/files/opa/press-releases/attachments/2015/04/02/velentzas-siddiqui-complaint.pdf.

202. Ibid.

203. "U.S. v. Keonna Thomas." Criminal Complaint, U.S. District Court for the Eastern District of Pennsylvania, April 3, 2015. Accessed April 4, 2015. http://media.philly.com/documents/KeonnaThomasComplaint.pdf.

204. Ibid.

205. Ibid.

206. Ibid.

207. "Teenage girl jihadists hunted by Interpol inspire first copycats as two more Austrian children try to run away to Syria to join ISIS." *Daily Mail*, September 10, 2014. Accessed October 27, 2014. http://www.dailymail.co.uk/news/article-2750637/Teenage-girl-jihadists-inspire-copycats-try-run-away-Syria-join-ISIS.html.

208. Squires, Nick. "Austrian teenage girl jihadist 'killed in Syria.'" *Telegraph*, September 15, 2014. Accessed October 27, 2014. http://www.telegraph.co.uk/news/worldnews/europe/austria/11098039/Austrian-teenage-girl-jihadist-killed-in-Syria.html.

209. Bacchi, Umberto. "Austrian teenage jihadi brides Samra Kesinovic and Sabrina Selimovic 'alive.'" *International Business Times*, September 16, 2014. Accessed October 27, 2014. http://www.ibtimes.co.uk/austrian-teenage-jihadi-brides-samra-kesinovic-sabina-selimovic-alive-1465725.

210. "Hungary intercepts Dutch girl, 16, on way to join ISIS." *Al Arabiya,* November 5, 2014. Accessed November 20, 2014. http://english.alarabiya.net/en/News/middle-east/2014/11/05/Hungary-intercepts-Dutch-girl-16-on-way-to-join-ISIS-.html.

211. "Two arrested after 15-year-old girl heads for Syria." *Dutch News*, January 15, 2014. Accessed November 23, 2014. http://www.dutchnews.nl/news/archives/2014/01/two_arrested_after_15-year-old.php/.

212. "French girl Assia Saidi, 15, stopped while 'on the way to Syria to wage jihad.'" News.Com.Au, October 6, 2014. Accessed November 23, 2014. http://www.news.com.au/world/french-girl-assia-saidi-15-stopped-while-on-the-way-to-syria-to-wage-jihad/story-fndir2ev-1227080841372.

213. Naylor, Hugh and Suzan Haidamous. "Arrest in Lebanon lifts veil on life of Islamic State leader's ex-wife, Saja al-Dulaimi." *Washington Post*, January 28, 2015. Accessed February 3, 2015. http://www.washingtonpost.com/world/middle_east/an-arrest-in-lebanon-lifts-the-veil-on-the-life-of-islamic-state-leaders-ex-wife/2015/01/26/081820b4-86d5-11e4-abcf-5a3d7b3b20b8_story.html?tid=pm_world_pop.

214. Bakker, Edwin, Christophe Paulussen, and Eva Entenmann. "Dealing with European Foreign Fighters in Syria: Governance: Challenges & Legal Implications." *International Centre for Counterterrorism*, December 2013. Accessed October 30, 2014. http://www.icct.nl/download/file/ICCT-Bakker-Paulussen-Entenmann-Dealing-With-European-Foreign-Fighters-in-Syria.pdf.

"Report Cities Conference on Foreign Fighters to Syria." *Radicalisation Awareness Network*, January 30, 2014. Accessed October 30, 2014. http://ec.europa.eu/dgs/home-affairs/what-we-do/networks/radicalisation_awareness_network/cities-conference/docs/report_cities_conference_on_foreign_fighters_en.pdf.

"Returning fighters from Syrian conflict cause concern in the EU." *Europol*, May 29, 2014. Accessed October 27, 2014. https://www.europol.europa.eu/content/returning-fighters-syrian-conflict-cause-concern-eu.

215. "FACT SHEET: Comprehensive U.S. Government Approach to Foreign Terrorist Fighters in Syria and the Broader Region." Office of the Press Secretary, September 24, 2014. Accessed October 27, 2014. http://www.whitehouse.gov/the-press-office/2014/09/24/fact-sheet-comprehensive-us-government-approach-foreign-terrorist-fighte.

216. Ibid.

217. Department of Justice. Office of Legal Counsel. *Selected Memorandum and Opinions Advising the President of the United States of America.* Volume 26. 2002. Accessed October 30, 2014. http://www.justice.gov/sites/default/files/olc/legacy/2013/07/26/op-olc-26.pdf.

218. 18 U.S. Code § 2339A—Providing material support to terrorists. http://www.law.cornell.edu/uscode/text/18/2339A.18 U.S. Code § 2339B—Providing material support or resources to designated foreign terrorist organizations. http://www.law.cornell.edu/uscode/text/18/2339B.

18 U.S. Code § 2339C—Prohibitions against the financing of terrorism. http://www.law.cornell.edu/uscode/text/18/2339C.

18 U.S. Code § 2339D—Receiving military-type training from a foreign terrorist organization. http://www.law.cornell.edu/uscode/text/18/2339D.

219. 18 U.S. Code § 2339A—Providing material support to terrorists. http://www.law.cornell.edu/uscode/text/18/2339A.

220. Ibid.

221. U.S. Code § 2339B—Providing material support or resources to designated foreign terrorist organizations. http://www.law.cornell.edu/uscode/text/18/2339B.

222. Ibid.

223. 18 U.S. Code § 2339C—Prohibitions against the financing of terrorism. http://www.law.cornell.edu/uscode/text/18/2339C.

224. Ibid.

225. Ibid.

226. PUBLIC LAW 108–458—DEC. 17, 2004. http://www.gpo.gov/fdsys/pkg/PLAW-108publ458/pdf/PLAW-108publ458.pdf.

227. 18 U.S. Code § 2339D—Receiving military-type training from a foreign terrorist organization. http://www.law.cornell.edu/uscode/text/18/2339D.

228. Ibid.

229. "Security Council unanimously adopts resolution condemning violent extremism, underscoring need to prevent travel, support for foreign terrorist fighters." *United Nations Newsroom*, September 24, 2014. Accessed October 27, 2014. http://www.un.org/press/en/2014/sc11580.doc.htm.

230. "Marrakech Memorandum on Good Practices for a More Effective Response to the FTF Phenomenon." *Global Counterterrorism Forum,* September 19, 2014. Accessed October 30, 2014. https://www.thegctf.org/documents/10162/140201/14Sept19_The+Hague-Marrakech+FTF+Memorandum.pdf.

231. "UNDOC launches new global initiative to boost criminal justice responses to foreign terrorist fighters." Press Release. *UN Office on Drugs and Crime*, March 25, 2015. Accessed March 26, 2015. http://www.unodc.org/unodc/en/press/releases/2015/March/unodc-launches-new-global-initiative-to-boost-criminal-justice-responses-to-foreign-terrorist-fighters.html.

232. Ibid.

233. McGuirk, Rod. "230 suspected jihadis prevented from leaving Australia." *Washington Post*, March 25, 2015. Accessed March 25, 2015. http://www.washingtonpost.com/world/middle_east/200-suspected-jihadists-prevented-from-leaving-australia/2015/03/24/388c785c-d294-11e4-8b1e-274d670aa9c9_story.html.

234. "UN: Number of foreign fighters joining militants skyrockets to 25,000." *DW*, April 2, 2015. Accessed April 2, 2015. http://www.dw.de/un-number-of-foreign-fighters-joining-militants-skyrockets-to-25000/a-18357629.

235. "Briton Held On Syria Border Is Councillor's Son." *Sky News*. April 2, 2015. Accessed April 2, 2015. http://news.sky.com/story/1457674/briton-held-on-syria-border-is-councillors-son.

Chapter Six

Combating the Islamic State

National, Regional, and Global Responses

The chapter addresses the national, regional, and global responses to the Islamic State. These themes are covered as follows: The efforts of the principal parties in the Middle East are discussed, followed by a review of the smaller Middle Eastern countries. Then the responses of world powers—the United States, Russia, and China—and European countries are addressed. Other national as well as international and regional responses are noted. Lastly, the efforts of ethnic and religious organizations are delineated.

By fall 2014, a U.S.-led coalition of over sixty countries with various contributions was aligned against the IS. The coalition partners have centered their focus on "five common purposes—the military campaign, disrupting the flow of foreign fighters, counterfinance, humanitarian relief and ideological delegitimization."[1]

As to air power, between September 23 and late December 2014, some 10,000 sorties were flown by coalition members, about three-quarters by U.S. military. As of December 15, 2014, non-U.S. members of the coalition have flown 14 percent of the 1,287 airstrikes that have been waged in Iraq and Syria.[2] As of December 2014, "[c]oalition nations conducting airstrikes in Iraq include the United States, Australia, Belgium, Canada, Denmark, France, Netherlands and the United Kingdom. Coalition nations conducting airstrikes in Syria include the United States, Bahrain, Jordan, Saudi Arabia and the United Arab Emirates."[3]

By late 2014, "Iraqi security forces are being rebuilt with a counteroffensive being planned to retake and hold terrain such as Mosul, Haditha and Beiji" and hundreds of Yazidis "were rescued from a long mountaintop

217

siege."[4] Although improving, other data suggests that the Iraqi military may need several more years before it is an effective military force.

More specifically, by the end of December 2014, coalition airstrikes against the Islamic State "helped reverse or stall Isis offensives on numerous fronts, from the town of Kobani in northern Syria to the farmland south of Baghdad."[5] These developments, coupled with invigorated efforts of Iraqi security forces, Shiite militias, and Kurdish fighters, provide greater evidence that the IS is not invincible.

By February 2015, the number of coalition airstrikes reached over 2,800.[6] As of March 29, 2015, "Coalition nations conducting airstrikes in Iraq include the United States, Australia, Belgium, Canada, Denmark, France, Jordan, the Netherlands, and the United Kingdom. Coalition nations conducting airstrikes in Syria include the United States, Bahrain, Jordan, Saudi Arabia, and the United Arab Emirates."[7] By March 12, 2015, "the total cost of operations related to ISIL since kinetic operations started on Aug. 8, 2014, is $1.83 billion and the average daily cost is $8.5 million."[8]

According to U.S. Central Command, from August 2014 to March 2015, ISIL lost between 20–25 percent of populated areas in Iraq that it once controlled. That area translates to about 4,100–5,200 square miles.[9] The Islamic State's control in Syria as of March 2015 is mostly the same as in August 2014 except for "its withdrawal from 'Ayn al 'Arab [Kobani] and Tall Hamis."[10]

Also, as of March 18, 2015, coalition forces have damaged or destroyed 5,314 ISIL targets, including:

- Tanks 73
- Humvees 282
- Staging areas 408
- Buildings 1,652
- Fighting positions 1,003
- Oil collection points and refineries 151
- Other targets 1,745[11]

Still, it is unlikely that IS will be defeated quickly barring some substantial shift of resources and efforts against the entity.[12] After all, it has been estimated that IS forces garnered enough weaponry in 2014 to last at least another two years. An expanded discussion of efforts against IS and other jihadist forces in Iraq and Syria is set out below.

PRINCIPAL MIDDLE EAST PARTIES

Iraq

Despite having numerous times as many troops as the Islamic State,[13] Iraqi forces had little success countering the militants during their initial push in summer 2014. The Iraqi Security Force (ISF) suffers from poor morale and a lack of national unity. It is not immune from the sectarian divisions that plague Iraqi society. Its weakness manifested itself in the mass desertion and retreat of Iraqi troops from Mosul in the face of a numerically smaller IS force.[14]

The ISF has attempted to retake some of the lost ground, such as in Fallujah and Ramadi, but its efforts have been largely unsuccessful.[15] Recapturing the Mosul Dam had arguably been its greatest success, although this was due more to the efforts of the Kurdish Peshmerga forces than to the Iraqi military.[16]

For instance, in December 2014, Iraqi Prime Minister Haider al-Abadi congratulated Kurdish Region President Masoud Barzani for the successes of the Kurdish Peshmerga in battling the Islamic State in northern Iraq. This reconciliation marks an important step towards future cooperation and relations between the Iraqi central government and Kurdish regional government. Also, the two leaders pledged to cooperate on various issues.[17] After all, Kurdish Peshmerga forces freed a large part of the Sinjar in northern Iraq from Islamic State control. Aided by U.S. air support, the Kurds were able to provide a safe haven to several hundred Yazidis who were under threat from the IS. This marked a significant achievement against the Islamic State. In their offensive, the Kurds also liberated the towns of Zumar and Sunoni.[18] "The peshmerga have liberated around 70 percent of the areas around Mount Sinjar, but the southern part of the Sinjar region is still under ISIS control."[19]

Additionally, in December 2014, Kurdish Democratic Union Party (PYD) claimed that Syrian-Kurdish militiamen also were able to open up another corridor between their region of northeastern Syria and Mt. Sinjar in neighboring Iraq. The Syrian-Kurdish fighters also captured nine villages from ISIS militants."[20]

In addition to the Kurds, the ISF has also been coordinating with Shiite militias and tribal groups for the past year to bolster their forces.[21] In June 2014, Iraq's leading Shiite religious figure, Grand Ayatollah Ali al-Sistani, called upon Shiites to join the fight against the IS. As a result, during summer 2014 there were thousands of new recruits to these Shiite militias. If Shiite holy sites continue to be threatened, there will likely be even greater Shiite mobilization, probably acting in the forms of Iranian government troops, Iraqi Shiite militias, mercenaries, and unaffiliated groups. Following the capture of Mosul by the IS in June 2014, Prime Minister Nouri al-Maliki visited

Samarra where the al-Askari shrine is located. In doing so, he made clear to the public the importance of Shiite shrines to his administration. [22]

As recently as February 2015, Abu Deraa, a leading figure as a Shiite fighter against Iraqi Sunnis during Iraq's 2006–2007 civil war, explained the role of Shiite militias as such, "How would you feel if your family was slaughtered? How would you act and where would you go? Those who have killed and committed crimes should be punished. If you aren't capable of doing it yourself, we are here for you. We will give you back your rights."[23] To fully comprehend the deep and historical context of the Shiite-Sunni divide, Deraa's other comments speak volumes, "For 1,400 years we have been living under injustice, since the death of the prophet."[24]

Deraa's brutality against Sunni civilians during the conflict led him to be viewed as the Shiite answer to Abu-Musab al-Zarqawi. [25] Not surprisingly, Deraa is loyal to influential Shiite cleric Muqtada al-Sadr. So much so that in February 2015, Deraa said, "If [Sadr] wants us to stand up and rise, we will. If he says stand down, we will. We'll do whatever he says."[26] In a January 2015 meeting with Iraq's Minister of Defense, Deraa pledged his support, and the support of his followers, for the Iraqi army's fight against the IS. [27] Some expect Deraa and his men to be enlisted for support.

Too, the Iraqi government is "increasingly reliant on the powerful militias and a massive Shiite volunteer force, which together may now equal the size of Iraq's security forces."[28] For instance, "Sheikh Jassim al-Saidi, a commander with [Shiite] Kataib Hezbollah, said his group has more than tripled in size since June [2014], now boasting more than 30,000 combatants."[29] More broadly, some Shiite militias are organized under the Iraqi government-run Popular Mobilization Committee. [30]

Some of the U.S. military supplies that are allocated to the Iraqi government end up in the control of Iranian-aligned Shiite militias in Iraq. Gen. Mike Flynn, former director of the Defense Intelligence Agency, said that, "the accountability of weapons systems, once turned over to any Iraqi, is at best weak and it may be nonexistent."[31] Furthermore, in January 2015, an American official said that Iraqi government forces need the support of Iran's Revolutionary Guard to fight the IS. Also, the official contended that were the United States to stop providing weapons, the situation would deteriorate. [32]

In January 2015, Iraqi security personnel and government-aligned Shiite militias allegedly executed seventy-two unarmed Sunni civilians during an offensive in Barwana, in eastern Iraq. Others contend that the killings were conducted by IS fighters. [33]

In late December 2014, U.S. envoy General John Allen provided a complimentary tone, "the Iraqi government also demonstrated its commitment to becoming a more proactive partner in the fight against ISIL." Also, General Allen asserted, "Iraq's continued progress toward reform and inclusiveness will be imperative to the coalition's success."[34] For instance, in December 2014, "Iraqi security forces and pro-government militias took control of large parts of the Tigris River town of Dhuluiya north of Baghdad" from IS militants.[35]

At the March 2015 meeting of the coalition's stabilization working group, General Allen underscored the need to synchronize military operations against the IS with civilian stabilization. Along those lines, he outlined a four-pronged approach that should be followed:

> First, there is the clearing component, when the Iraqi Army and/or the Popular Mobilization Committee remove Daesh from a town or city.
>
> Second is the security and policing component that deals with crime and provides general security so life can begin to return to normal. This will likely come from a combination of PMC units, local tribes, and police.
>
> Third is the restoration of local governance, which will be difficult because many officials are in exile, were killed, or cooperated with Daesh.
>
> Fourth is the provision of essential services. This includes immediate humanitarian assistance to address life-threatening issues, as well as short-term restoration of services such as health, water, electricity, and rebuilding critical infrastructure.[36]

In April 2015, the ISF, backed by Shiite militias and U.S. airstrikes, was able to regain control of Tikrit from IS forces, another key milestone. It is doubtful that this would have been achieved had the ISF carried out its efforts against the IS by itself.[37]

Unfortunately, in April 2015, IS forces made advances on Ramadi, the capital of Anbar province. As a consequence, thousands of Ramadi residents fled to Baghdad to escape the expected wrath of IS militants. The loss of Ramadi, at the heart of the Sunni triangle, was a devastating loss to the Iraqi government and anti-IS coalition.[38]

Additionally, in April 2015, IS fighters launched large-scale attacks against Iraq's largest oil refinery in Baiji. Iraqi armed forces responded by surrounding the site, and then entered it to presumably guard the location.[39] Also, that month a suicide car bomb attack outside the U.S. Consulate in Erbil killed four people and injured eighteen.[40]

Syria

Assad's regime purposely allowed ISIS and other jihadists to grow and develop more fully in order to portray Assad as a stabilizing force, worthy of keeping his post. In doing so, the regime could argue that, like the West's efforts against al-Qa'ida (and then the Islamic State), he, too, was combating Sunni-inspired terrorists.

Following the U.S. invasion of Iraq in 2003, the Assad regime allowed foreign fighters to transverse Syria into Iraq, where many would serve as suicide bombers. In 2013–2014, the Assad regime collaborated with ISIS, often bombing rebel forces fighting ISIS. After all, Assad assumed, the West's distaste for jihadists was greater than its aversion to his regime. By allowing ISIS to emerge untouched from his regime—for a time—the group would be strengthened. In turn, the West would keep itself busy with ISIS rather than on Assad's reign. Following the fall of Mosul to ISIS in June 2014. ISIS fighters turned their efforts against the Assad regime, attacking and conquering various Syrian government assets and sites.[41] Although there were periodic fights between Syrian forces and IS militants, Syrian airstrikes against the group commenced on August 17, 2014, marking an end to an unofficial truce between the combatants.[42]

Jabhat al-Nusra fighters captured two Assad regime military posts, Wadi al-Deif and Hamidiyeh, in northwest Syria. During the fight between the parties, over one hundred Syrian soldiers were killed and "at least 120 soldiers [were taken] prisoner, while another 100 fled south towards the town of Morek in the neighbouring province of Hama."[43] Meanwhile, eighty Jabhat al-Nusra forces were killed during the attacks.[44] Jabhat al-Nusra's efforts underscored that there are various jihadi groups battling Assad regime forces.

In December 2014, Kurdish People's Protection Units (YPG) killed thirty IS fighters in the Syrian town of Qassiab and another fourteen in Kobani. During the clashes, YPG regained control of Qassiab from IS control.[45] And so, efforts against the Assad regime span many groups and interests. In February 2015, IS militants and regime forces continued to clash for control over the Dayr az-Zawr airbase.[46] Seven IS fighters were reportedly killed.[47]

In mid-September 2014, over 200,000 people left the areas surrounding Kobani, Syria, amid Islamic State attacks. At least 130,000 took refuge in Turkey as Kurdish forces attempted to fight off IS militants.[48] From the inception of the Syrian conflict through March 2015, the Assad regime tortured to death 2,751 people in Syrian prisons, the Syrian Observatory for Human Rights alleged.[49]

Turkey

Turkey has taken the brunt of the refugee flow from the Syrian conflict, currently hosting over 1.3 million displaced persons.[50] It also faces the difficult problem of individuals moving in the other direction, from Turkey to Syria, to fight for IS, the Kurdish Peshmerga, or other groups.[51] To stem this tide, the Turkish government created a "no-entry" list of persons who are suspected of traveling to Iraq and Syria to join extremist groups.[52]

Concurrently, Turkish officials argue that part of the onus of stopping foreign fighters' use of Turkey as a gateway to the Iraqi and Syrian conflicts should rest with the home countries of the participants. In other words, the Turkish government stresses that foreign terrorists should be prevented from traveling abroad in the first place.

Turkish military assistance and involvement in the coalition was limited while the IS held forty-six Turkish nationals, including diplomats and children, as hostages. During this period, the Turkish government would not allow its territory to be used as a base for airstrikes.[53] Part of this reticence stemmed from fear that threats against the IS would endanger the lives of Turkey's citizens who were kidnapped in Mosul. Other contributing factors in limiting Turkish action against the Islamic State is Turkey's position that such assistance will indirectly aid the cause of Kurdish independence in Turkey and Syria. Additionally, Turkey fears that the West's resolve and staying power in the Syrian and Iraqi crises are short-lived, essentially leaving Turkey alone to deal with the aftermath of the campaign.

By September 20, 2014, the IS freed the Turkish hostages, likely in a negotiated prisoner exchange.[54] A week later, President Recep Tayyip Erdogan indicated that Turkey would start to play a military role in the coalition saying, "It's wrong to say that Turkey will not take any kind of military position. Turkey will do whatever is its duty to do." He also expressed his support for the use of ground troops in combating the IS stating, "You are not going to be able to finish off a terrorist group just with air strikes, at some point ground forces will be fundamental. Of course, I am not a soldier, but air (forces) are about logistics. If ground troops do not go, then nothing is going to be permanent."[55] During the fight over Kobani, President Erdogan once again voiced his opinion that airstrikes alone would not suffice to halt the advance of the IS.

Nonetheless, Turkey has yet to commit any of its troops to the coalition action against the IS. Turkey is seemingly holding out regarding troops until broader international intervention takes place or it views its national interest's meriting such a decision. Prime Minister Ahmet Davutoglu expressed the reasons for Turkey's reluctance to join in the coalition in early fall 2014, saying, "We are ready to do everything if there is a clear strategy and if we can be sure that our border can be protected after (Islamic State is gone). We don't want the regime on our border pushing people towards Turkey. We don't want other terrorist organization. If Assad stays in Damascus with this brutal policy, if (the Islamic State) goes, another radical organization may come."[56] Moreover, the Turkish government argued that Assad is as much a risk to the region as is the IS.

Turkish tanks were on the Turkish-Syrian border by September 29, 2014, and the Turkish Parliament approved the military's buffer zone plan a day later.[57] On October 4th, President Erdogan stated that if IS forces attack Turkey's enclave inside Syria—the Tomb of Süleyman Şah and Memorial Outpost—then Turkey would not hesitate to strike back.[58] In February 2015,

Turkish troops moved the tomb and outpost to a "new site within Syria, corresponding to the acreage of the previous one, in the north of Suriye Eşmesi village close to the Turkish borders."[59]

As the Syrian conflict has evolved, there have been some cross-border shelling exchanges between Turkey and Syria (including rebel forces), although those interactions quickly dissipated.[60] Furthermore, Turkey and Syria each downed the other's military aircraft on at least one occasion.[61] In addition, Turkey's predominately Shiite border town of Reyhanli experienced two car bombings that killed and injured over forty and one hundred, respectively.[62]

Noteworthy, too, in January 2014, the Turkish Air Force destroyed several ISIS vehicles during a bombing raid in Syria.[63] In 2013, Turkey received Patriot missile batteries from the North Atlantic Treaty Organization (NATO) to defend itself from the Syrian regime.[64]

Turkey's government continues to be apprehensive that weapons supplied to Syrian or Iraqi Kurds would end up in the hands of the Kurdistan Workers' Party (PKK), which is a designated terrorist group in Turkey and the United States.[65] By September 29, 2014, Turkey reaffirmed its support for (the Iraqi) Kurdistan Regional Government, promising to help in the fight against the IS and deal with the humanitarian crisis.[66]

However, Turkey's actions vis-à-vis Syrian Kurds was dramatically different. As local Kurdish forces fought the IS for control of the border town of Kobani in Syria, Turkish security forces effectively prevented their reinforcement, out of mistrust for the PKK. They barred Turkish Kurds from crossing the border into Kobani to assist their brethren and prevented Iraqi Kurdish supply convoys from using Turkish territory to reach the besieged town. PKK fighters then attacked a Turkish military outpost in Hakkari province, near the border with Iraq. The government responded with airstrikes on Kurdish positions, and PKK leadership set a deadline for aid to their fighters in Syria.[67]

This policy was suddenly reversed, however, once the IS started to lose ground to sustained Kurdish resistance and increased American air support and supply drops in October 2014. On October 20, 2014, Turkey announced it would allow Iraqi Kurdish Peshmerga forces to cross into Syria through its territory.[68]

Also, Turkey has delivered several hundred tons of humanitarian supplies to Iraq, including food, water, tents, and medical supplies, as well as having pledged $1.8 million in aid.[69] At the UN General Assembly debate on September 29, 2014, President Erdogan argued Islam should not be associated with terrorism. He also called upon other countries to contribute more to help Syrian refugees, stressing that it is important to protect those who oppose civilian killings in Iraq and Syria.[70]

Iran

According to Australian defense analyst Peter Jennings, "Iran is the only Middle Eastern country that clearly wins from a fragmented Iraq and a devastated Syria."[71] Analogously, Ali Khedery, a Dubai-based analyst who advised the U.S. government on Iraq, said "ISIS will be defeated. The problem is that afterwards, there will still be a dozen militias, hardened by decades of battle experience, funded by Iraqi oil, and commanded or at least strongly influenced by [Iran's Revolutionary Guard Corps]. And they will be the last ones standing."[72]

Sheikh Hassan Abboud, the now deceased leader of Ahrar al-Sham, accused the Iran Revolutionary Guard of training top IS leadership. He also suggested that Iran was brokering a deal to unite the various rebel groups in Syria.[73] However, this seems unlikely as Iran has always supported the Assad regime in the conflict.

At the end of June 2014, Iran announced it would support Iraq's fight against the IS using the same strategy with which it has backed the Syrian government, although it did not provide any further details.[74]

There have been some reports of Iranian troops operating against the IS in Iraq. Yet, despite strong evidence to that effect, the Iranian government has denied this assertion.[75] Iran does admit to conducting air operations against the IS in Iraq near its border with Iran.[76] However, Iran did admit its support for military intervention against IS.[77] In reality, between June-December 2014, Iran has sent over 1,000 military advisers to Iraq and provided the country with $1 billion in military assistance.[78]

On September 15, 2014, Ayatollah Ali Hosseini Khamenei, Iran's Supreme Leader, said Iran would not help the United States in its mission against the IS, claiming that the "U.S. has corrupted its hands in this issue."[79] Iran supports the idea of fighting the IS in Iraq, but Iranian President Hassan Rouhani has said the airstrikes in Syria are illegal since they are done without the Syrian government's consent.[80]

Iran is committed to protecting Shiite holy sites in Iraq. It would likely be motivated to become even more directly and openly involved in the conflict if such shrines were threatened further.[81] Meanwhile, Iran has supplied weapons and ammunition to Iraqi Kurds to combat the IS threat.[82]

In December 2014 in Samarra, Iraq, an IS sniper shot and killed Brigadier General Hamid Taqavi of the Iranian Revolutionary Guard. Indeed, "Unspecified numbers of Iranian advisors and combatants are defending holy Shi'ite sites in Iraq and Syria against raids by Sunni Jihadi fighters. Iran sent reinforcements to Iraq to help stave off an advance on Baghdad by IS militants this year at the request of Iraqi government and Shi'ite leaders."[83] In January 2015, Iran's military publicly stated that it would attack IS militants in Iraq if they traveled within forty kilometers of the Iranian border.[84]

OTHER MIDDLE EASTERN PARTIES

Saudi Arabia

Saudi Arabia is participating in airstrikes in Syria against the IS and collaborating with the U.S.-led coalition. Saudi Arabia is also training Syrian opposition fighters, who are simultaneously engaged in fighting the IS and Assad regime.[85] Additionally, Saudi Arabia has contributed $500 million to UN humanitarian missions in Iraq.[86] Despite accusations that the government has provided funds directly or indirectly to the IS, Foreign Minister Prince Saud al-Faisal expressed that the Kingdom does not support the IS in any manner whatsoever.

In April 2015, the Saudi Arabian government arrested ninety-three suspected IS terrorists, seventy-seven of whom are Saudi, in relation to fundraising and plans to establish bases on behalf of the group and a plot to attack the U.S. Embassy in Riyadh.[87]

Analysts have recommended that Saudi Arabia could contribute to the fight against IS financially by using its "oil weapon." Saudi Arabia has used its oil market power to drive down the price of oil, which the IS relies upon heavily to fund its fighters and buy weapons.[88]

Qatar

Qatar does not have pilots participating directly in the airstrikes in Syria, but it has provided support to the U.S.-led coalition.[89] For instance, Qatar provides ancillary aircraft and allows other U.S. allies to use air bases in Qatar.[90] Also, Qatar has delivered about 300 tons of humanitarian aid to Iraq.[91]

At the UN General Assembly debate on September 29, 2014, Sheikh Tamim bin Hamad al-Thani, the Emir of Qatar, argued that the UN's principles of human rights should be the basis of achieving world peace. He also criticized the UN response to the IS, warning that the international community is too slow in its response to extremist groups in the Middle East.[92]

Bahrain

Bahrain claims that dealing with the IS is a top concern.[93] Bahrain participated in the Paris Conference,[94] an anti-IS coalition meeting that took place in September 2014 to formulate a battle plan. Also, Bahrain is taking part in U.S.-led airstrikes.[95] Bahrain's foreign minister said there are reports of several of its citizens fighting with the IS in both Iraq and Syria. He said they were being monitored, and would be arrested if they return to the kingdom.[96] Bahrain pledged $100 million in aid to the people of Iraq and Syria.[97] Also, Bahrain granted the UK and other Western powers permission to use its territory to establish military bases.[98]

United Arab Emirates

The UAE has taken part in the airstrikes in Iraq and Syria against the IS.[99] The country's first-ever female pilot participated in airstrikes, drawing both derision and praise.[100]

Jordan

Former Jordanian Foreign Minister Marwan Muasher initially said Jordan's primary role against the IS would be providing intelligence to Western allies.[101] In an interview on *60 Minutes*, King Abdullah II of Jordan said that his country's army had retaliated against "contacts" with militants on the border.

The Islamic State has threatened the kingdom, and Jordan's army has responded forcefully. "We have retaliated [against] several contacts over the past several months to those who have come across our borders or tried to come across our borders," King Abdullah said. He also remarked that the unique danger that the IS poses is its funding capabilities.[102] Later, Jordan joined U.S. led airstrikes in Syria, destroying several undisclosed targets.[103]

At the UN General Assembly debate on September 29, 2014, King Abdullah II suggested that one approach to fighting the IS would be to designate crimes against religious groups, like those committed against the Yazidis, as crimes against humanity. He also called for support for taking care of displaced Syrians.[104]

In December 2014, IS fighters captured a Jordanian F-16 pilot, Moaz al-Kasasbeh, after he crashed near Raqqa. The U.S. government refutes claims by the IS that it shot down the military aircraft. He was the first coalition fighter captured by IS forces.[105] While al-Kasasbeh's family appeared in the media to plead for their family member's life, the IS released an interview with the pilot, in which he predicted he would be killed. Subsequently, IS supporters began Twitter hashtags suggesting ways to kill al-Kasasbeh.[106]

The immolation of al-Kasasbeh, which was videotaped and distributed globally, accelerated Jordanian efforts, including airstrikes, against the IS. So too, the burning of al-Kasasbeh, and worsening conditions, led Jordan to deploy thousands of soldiers to the Iraqi border to guard against infiltration by IS fighters.[107]

Egypt

Egyptian President Abdel Fattah al-Sisi stated that Egypt will not send troops to Iraq.[108] Meanwhile, Egyptian religious leaders have declared that IS actions are not representative of the Muslim faith.[109] The United States has asked Saudi Arabia, Egypt, and Qatar to broadcast anti-IS messages on television.[110]

At the UN General Assembly debate on September 29, 2014, President al-Sisi emphasized the need to create a political framework in Syria that would neither compromise with terrorists nor replicate the Assad regime. He also argued that Iraq's political stability was key to retaking territory from the IS and ending the bloodshed.[111]

In late January 2015, more than a dozen army and police targets were struck in the Sinai Peninsula by IS-linked militants. The simultaneous attacks involved a car bomb and mortar rounds, killing thirty security officers and wounding at least sixty.[112]

Egypt's President al-Sisi stated that the ongoing struggle against insurgents in the Sinai Peninsula would be a long-term operation. His remarks came two days after the IS-linked Ansar Beit al-Maqdis killed thirty security personnel in four simultaneous attacks. Egypt also banned the armed wing of Hamas, claiming that the group was supporting the Sinai insurgency.[113]

Israel

On August 3, 2014, Israel officially banned the IS and any association with it.[114] The ban outlaws meetings of any kind between IS members, calling it an illegal organization. Israel can now take action against individuals raising funds for or associating in any way with the terror group. Likewise, the Israeli government will prosecute any person who expresses sympathy or allegiance to the IS.[115]

Prime Minister Benjamin Netanyahu stated at the UN that he fully endorses President Obama and the coalition against the IS, stating "these groups must be fought, they must be rolled back, and they must ultimately be defeated."[116] Israel has supported the U.S.-led campaign with satellite intelligence.[117] It has also shared information from travel databases recording Westerners who went to the Middle East to fight for the terror group.[118]

Prime Minister Netanyahu tried to refocus the world attention on the threat posed by Iran. Echoing statements made by U.S. policy makers,[119] Netanyahu stated that the idea of easing sanctions on Iran in exchange for the Islamic Republic's aiding in the fight against the Islamic State is absurd.[120]

In January 2015, Israel undertook airstrikes on the Syrian-controlled side of the Golan Heights, killing six people. Among those killed were Iranian Gen. Mohammad Ali Allahdadi, who was advising the Assad regime, as well as "Jihad Mughniyeh—the son of Imad Mughniyeh, a top Hezbollah operative assassinated in 2008 in Damascus."[121] Later that month, two Israeli soldiers and a Spanish UN peacekeeper were killed by Hezbollah during a missile strike on Sheeba Farms, an area where Israel, Syria, and Lebanon meet.[122] So far, those exchanges have not precipitated an escalation in clashes between Israel and Hezbollah to the same degree as their war during

2006. Also in January 2015, Israeli officials announced that they had broken up the first IS cell, comprised of seven individuals, in the country. [123]

WORLD POWERS

United States of America

The U.S. government began to respond against the IS in earnest publicly after the fall of Mosul in June 2014. The Islamic State's victory in Iraq's second-largest city made clear deficiencies in the Iraqi military and government that only had been hinted at during the election crisis earlier in 2014.

In June 2014, the U.S.S. George H.W. Bush and its carrier strike group were deployed to the Persian Gulf. It has since been used to launch airstrikes in Iraq. [124] In mid-August, American forces conducted thirty-five airstrikes to aid the Kurdish forces fighting for control of the Mosul Dam, hitting over ninety targets. [125] The United States also launched airstrikes to protect the Haditha Dam in conjunction with an Iraqi offensive on September 6–7. [126] Between August 8 and early November 2014, the coalition airstrikes in Iraq and Syria numbered 506 and 406 respectively. During August 8–October 8, 2014, the coalition targeted nearly 300 armed vehicles (including tanks), some seventy-five firing positions/weapons, with the remainder being bases (including training camps and garrisons), checkpoints/observation posts/airfields, Islamic State fighters, and refineries. [127]

According to a Pentagon spokesman Commander Bill Urban, "As of Dec. 11, 2014, the total cost of operations related to ISIL since kinetic operations started on August 8, 2014 is $1.02 billion and the average daily cost is $8.1 million." [128] Moreover, "U.S and its coalition partners had flown 1,371 airstrikes in both countries—799 in Iraq and 572 in Syria." [129]

Through December 15, 2014, the U.S. military carried out 488 airstrikes in Syria, killing some 1,119 IS members and fifty-two civilians. [130] By March 12, 2015, "the total cost of operations related to ISIL since kinetic operations started on Aug. 8, 2014, is $1.83 billion and the average daily cost is $8.5 million." [131]

In October 2014, the White House indicated that it will not be applying its new drone strike rules, meant to temper civilian death tolls, to airstrikes in Iraq and Syria. Unlike the areas such as Yemen and Pakistan where drone strikes are regularly carried out, Iraq and Syria are not "outside areas of active hostility." The heightened standard for drone strikes required "near certainty that non-combatants will not be injured or killed," [132] before the attack could be ordered. It also called for confirmation of the terrorist target's presence and certification that capture was not a feasible option.

The White House clarified that the United States will still abide by the strict standards demanded by the Geneva Conventions to prevent Iraqi and

Syrian civilians from dying, but not by the heightened standard used in drone strikes. Rear Adm. John Kirby, the Pentagon's spokesman, explained this stance:

> While we continue to hit [IS] where they are, it doesn't mean we can or even that we should hit them everywhere they are at every moment. . . . We must choose. We must discriminate between targets that matter more to us in space and time than others, and between those that run higher risks of collateral damage or civilian casualties. [133]

On September 22, 2014, the United States attacked the IS in Syria for the first time, with fourteen airstrikes carried out with the help of allied Arab nations Bahrain, Qatar, Saudi Arabia, the United Arab Emirates, and Jordan.[134] The airstrikes against the Islamic State took out oil rigs, headquarters, and weapon stations, to stymie IS's momentum. The United States also attacked the Khorasan Group, which has been a concern of the United States for some time, given its desire to attack Western targets.[135] Some seventy IS fighters were killed, and 300 injured in initial attacks in Syria.[136]

In the fight for Kobani, the U.S. undertook over 135 airstrikes against IS forces, as the situation became more desperate. These efforts were accompanied by American supply drops, including weapons, ammunition, and medical supplies, that circumvented Turkish obstruction of Kurdish reinforcements.[137]

After a new Iraqi prime minister was chosen to replace al-Maliki, the United States sent 130 military advisors to Iraq to help the Iraqi and Kurdish forces with strategic decisions.[138] In addition, President Obama ordered 350 additional troops to protect the U.S. Embassy in Baghdad.[139]

In September 2014, the U.S. Congress supported $500 million in funding to help train and equip some 5,000 of the National Coalition for Syrian Revolutionary and Opposition Forces, led by Ahmad Jarba, as the more moderate Syrian rebel group to counter the IS. President Obama assented to congressional approval shortly thereafter. Jarba is a member of the Shammar tribe, as are many members of his rebel organization. The United States and Saudi Arabia backed the group.[140] On September 12, 2014, Secretary of State John Kerry announced that the United States donated $500 million in humanitarian aid to Syria.[141]

Even before airstrikes, U.S. manned planes and drones conducted extensive surveillance missions in Iraq.[142] Also, American planes dropped humanitarian supplies on Sinjar Mountain where tens of thousands of Yazidis were trapped in early August 2014.[143] Over the weekend of October 17, U.S. forces dropped weapons, ammunition, and medical supplies to Kurdish fighters in Kobani, who had been blocked from receiving support by Turkey.[144]

While one report estimated that over one hundred American citizens have joined IS, U.S. government officials claim that the correct figure is about ten persons.[145] The U.S. government has started to warn its citizens that anyone joining a terrorist group could forfeit his or her American citizenship. The U.S. State Department has created a counter-propaganda video, which displays the flaws of IS ideology and outlines that joining that group will most likely result in death. Additionally, returning to the United States would be almost impossible without facing arrest.[146]

On September 6, 2014, the United States and some NATO allies announced a coalition to stop the IS and the flow of foreign fighters. The UK, France, Australia, Germany, Canada, Turkey, Italy, Poland, and Denmark all vowed to provide monetary/military support for the fight against the IS.[147] Following the supply drops for Kurdish resistance in Kobani, Secretary of State John Kerry assured Turkish allies that the support was a "momentary effort" in a "crisis moment."[148]

At the September 29, 2014, UN General Assembly debate on the IS, President Obama argued that defeating the IS would result from reform in the Muslim world. He continued, the young Muslim generation needs to accept change, not at the expense of tradition and faith, but to preserve the values of education, innovation, and the dignity of life.[149]

In December 2014, the Pentagon's spokesman announced, "Up to 1,300 more U.S. troops, including approximately 1,000 soldiers from the Army's 82nd Airborne Division, will begin to deploy to Iraq in late January" 2015.[150]

Also, in December 2014, U.S. troops engaged Islamic State fighters for the first time, while aiding the Iraqi army to protect an attack on the Ein al-Asad military base. American officials characterized these activities as self-defense measures.[151] As Kurdish and Iraqi government forces receive instruction from U.S. forces, it is probable that U.S. troops will expand their interactions with IS forces, whether initially planned or as an unavoidable fact of conflict, following future ensuing support operations.

While initially, U.S. troops "are protecting U.S. facilities and assisting the Iraqi military in Baghdad and Kurdish fighters in Erbil in the north,"[152] that will change as the conflict ensues.

In December 2014, U.S. Secretary of State John Kerry called for the U.S. Congress to authorize the Obama administration to use military force against ISIL without geographical limitation.[153]

In January 2015, the U.S. deployed search and rescue teams to northern Iraq after the UAE, which pulled out of conducting airstrikes, demanded better rescue capabilities.[154] Also that month, the Pentagon announced that up to 1,000 U.S. troops—comprising "trainers as well as support personnel, and forces would range from special operations to conventional"—would be used to train Syrian opposition fighters. The training is expected to commence in spring 2015 and last several months.[155]

It is anticipated that the vetted Syrian fighters will be ready to fight the Islamic State by the end of 2015. The purpose of this training is to "get them ready to defend their own citizens and communities, to eventually go on the defensive against ISIL inside Syria, and to help them work with political opposition leaders toward a political solution in Syria."[156]

President Obama's mentioned the issue of IS and the region during his State of the Union address in January 2015, namely:

> In Iraq and Syria, American leadership—including our military power—is stopping ISIL's advance. Instead of getting dragged into another ground war in the Middle East, we are leading a broad coalition, including Arab nations, to degrade and ultimately destroy this terrorist group. We're also supporting a moderate opposition in Syria that can help us in this effort, and assisting people everywhere who stand up to the bankrupt ideology of violent extremism. Now, this effort will take time. It will require focus. But we will succeed. And tonight, I call on this Congress to show the world that we are united in this mission by passing a resolution to authorize the use of force against ISIL. We need that authority.[157]

In February 2015, President Obama formally requested authorization of the use of force against the IS. According to the White House, the main elements of the proposal are:

- A three-year limit on the AUMF so that the next President, Congress, and the American people can assess the progress we have made against ISIL and review these authorities again
- A repeal of the 2002 Iraq AUMF which authorized the 2003 Iraq invasion under President George W. Bush.

President Obama's proposal on the authorization of use of material force would not authorize long-term, large-scale ground combat operations like those the United States conducted in Iraq and Afghanistan. Rather, his proposal seeks the flexibility to conduct ground operations in other, more limited circumstances, including:

- Rescue operations involving U.S. or coalition personnel
- Special Operations missions against ISIL leadership
- Intelligence collection and assistance to partner forces.[158]

Russia

Russia sent military planes and possibly pilots to Iraq to fly under Iraqi markings.[159] Also, Russia provided military experts to aid the Iraqi army.[160]

President Vladimir Putin said Russia would carry out airstrikes on the IS in Syria if Assad's government, a Moscow ally, provided consent.[161]

In September 2014 President Putin discussed with his advisors how Russia would approach the growing cooperation globally against the IS. Russia's strained ties with Washington (and NATO) over the crisis in Ukraine have prevented Putin from officially joining the U.S.-sponsored coalition to destroy IS. Still, the Kremlin's spokesman Dmitry Peskov stated that Russia was in talks with the UN Security Council about "possible forms of cooperation . . . to counter [the] Islamic state in the framework of international law."[162] In winter 2015, Russia hosted peace negotiations among some of the parties in the Syrian conflict, to no avail.

China

China remains ambivalent on participating in the anti-Islamic State coalition.[163] Chinese officials have expressed concern about its citizens traveling to the Middle East to join IS and other militant groups.[164] They claim the majority of Chinese nationals fighting for the IS are Muslim Uighur minorities from Xinjiang province.[165]

EUROPEAN COUNTRIES

United Kingdom

In September 2014, the British Parliament authorized airstrikes in Iraq, but not in Syria.[166] The authorization ruled out the possibility of ground troops,[167] a point underlined by Prime Minster David Cameron.[168] However, Britain has sent military supplies, including heavy machine guns, ammunition, and ten tons of helmets and body armor to Kurdish fighters.[169] The UK deployed six RAF Tornados for reconnaissance and bombing runs, as well as several large transport planes and helicopters for support. Also, the British government provided seventy-five tons of humanitarian aid.[170]

After the video execution of British aid worker David Haines, Prime Minister Cameron outlined a plan to continue supporting the fight against the IS with increased resolve. This plan included arming Kurdish and Iraqi forces, contributing to U.S. military action, working with the UN to build a broader coalition, and increasing counterterrorism efforts at home.[171]

The prime minister raised concerns that if the IS is not defeated, its militants will attack the UK.[172] In late September 2014, UK security forces arrested eleven persons suspected of belonging to the banned extremist group al-Muhajiroun.[173] In mid-October 2014, the British government arrested six people on the charge of being "concerned in the commission, preparation, or instigation of acts of terrorism."[174]

After the IS released the beheading video of British aid worker Alan Henning, Prime Minister Cameron called the attacks repulsive and barbaric, meriting punishment for the perpetrators of the attack.[175] On October 21, 2014, British Defense Minister Michael Fallon said Britain had authorized surveillance drones and aircraft to fly over Syria. He also made clear that weapons would not be employed in Syria, since that would require permission from British Parliament.[176]

Speaking at the September 29, 2014, UN General Assembly debate, Prime Minister Cameron said that the extremism in the Middle East affects everyone, so a broad coalition should work to resolve this matter. He proposed that the UN establish a Special Representative on Extremism.[177]

France

France carried out multiple rounds of airstrikes on IS positions in Iraq in conjunction with the United States.[178] France flew reconnaissance missions over Iraq and delivered fifty-nine tons of aid.[179] It also supplied the Kurdish forces with weapons,[180] while openly encouraging other nations to help them.[181]

At the UN General Assembly debate on September 29, 2014, President Hollande expressed support for the democratic Syrian opposition, saying that democratically inclined rebels are the only legitimate representatives of the Syrian people.[182] After the January 2015 terrorist attacks in Paris, including by Amedy Coulibaly who claimed allegiance to the IS, France resolved to expand its efforts against transnational jihad and the IS.

Germany

As of April 2015, Germany was not planning to participate in airstrikes or send troops to Iraq or Syria.[183] However, Germany sent aid to the Kurdish Peshmerga forces,[184] including defense equipment and humanitarian support such as night vision goggles, vehicles, bomb detectors, blankets, and food.[185] Forty German paratroopers have been deployed to conduct weapons training with Kurdish troops, while thirty elite Peshmerga forces are being trained in Germany. Also, Chancellor Angela Merkel's government sent 16,000 assault rifles and hundreds of hand grenades and antitank missiles to Kurdish forces fighting IS militants.[186] Germany flew over thirty-six tons of humanitarian aid into the area around Ebril, Iraq. Also, Germany contributed $57 million for UNICEF to aid Iraqis.[187]

Domestically, Germany announced a ban on activities that support the IS, including any displays of the black flag used by it and other jihadi groups. The purpose of this step was to suppress the terrorist group's propaganda and recruitment work among Germans. Other displays of support for the IS and efforts aimed at enticing Germans to join the group are likewise prohibited. Interior Minister Thomas de Maiziere referred to the IS as a terror organization, which had no place in Germany. Wolfgang Bosbach, a senior member of Chancellor Angela Merkel's ruling conservative Christian Democratic Union, said that the move was aimed at "smashing an organizational structure, to rob members of grass-roots support for their activities."[188]

Belgium

Belgium has been dealing with IS and its supporters at home and abroad. In May 2014, Mehdi Nemmouche, a Frenchmen who guarded Western hostages while affiliated with ISIS in Syria, attacked the Jewish Museum of Belgium, killing four. He was subsequently captured in France.[189]

On September 21, 2014, Belgium foiled a potential terror plot of a couple returning from fighting in Syria.[190] Just over a week later, the government began the trial of forty-six people linked to the organization Sharia4Beligum, which has been working to recruit and train Belgian youths to join the overseas jihad and fight with IS.[191]

On September 26, 2014, Belgium voted to send six F-16 fighter jets and 120 military personnel to join the anti-IS campaign in Iraq.[192] Also, Belgium sent at least thirteen tons of humanitarian assistance.[193] In January 2015, Belgium became the object of an IS-linked plot to attack Belgian police as punishment for the country's participation in the anti-IS coalition.

Denmark

On August 27, 2014, the Danish Parliament voted to commit one Hercules C-130J to aiding anti-IS relief efforts in northern Iraq.[194] This commitment was expanded on September 26, 2014, when Prime Minister Helle Thorning-Schmidt announced that Denmark would be joining the international coalition against IS. In turn, Denmark dispatched seven F-16 fighter jets along with two hundred and fifty pilots and support staff, saying, "No one should be ducking in this case. Everyone should contribute."[195] In addition, Denmark contributed about $360,000 to relief efforts.[196]

Following the EU vote on efforts against the IS, a Danish jihadist stated that the group declared Denmark as an enemy.[197] This seemed to be borne out in a new IS propaganda video released in September 2014 that specifically mentioned Denmark as a target. In February 2015, a lone wolf jihadi, Omar el-Hussein, apparently inspired by IS and the previous month's terror attacks in Paris, killed two people during attacks at a Copenhagen café and synagogue.[198]

Aarhus, Denmark's second largest city, began offering rehabilitation to returning jihadists. This rehabilitation framework includes physical and psychological treatment for them as well as assistance with job placement and education.[199] In contrast, an Aarhus mosque has lent its open support and allegiance to the IS.[200]

The Netherlands

The Netherlands sent eight F-16s and 380 military personnel to aid in coalition airstrikes. Also, the Dutch provided 1,000 helmets and armor for Kurdish soldiers. They participated in the aid drops on Sinjar Mountain and pledged $8 million in aid.[201]

Interestingly, hundreds of Dutch citizens are fighting in Syria and Iraq, both for the IS and against them, including with Kurdish forces.[202] The Dutch cabinet is planning to introduce legislation to revoke the citizenship of individuals who leave the Netherlands to fight for terrorist groups.[203] The U.S. State Department has praised the Netherlands for implementing measures to help stop the influx of foreign fighters into the region.[204]

Italy

Italian Foreign Minister Federica Mogherini said on September 15, 2014, that Italy will not take part in U.S.-led airstrikes.[205] However, the Italian government sent 600 machine guns, mortars, and 2,000 rockets, and provided training for the Kurdish Peshmerga.[206] This was complemented by about fifty tons of humanitarian aid, including food, water, tents, and sleeping bags.[207]

Defense Minister Roberta Pinotti underscored the need to use all possible means to contain the IS. Also, she said that the assistance of countries like Turkey in the fight against the Islamic State was critical.[208] Meanwhile, the Vatican disclosed that it was not concerned about threats made by the Islamic State against Vatican City.[209]

Sweden

The Swedish government contributed $16 million in aid to Iraq.[210] Swedish Security Police (SAPO) estimated that about 150 Swedish Muslims have traveled to Iraq and Syria to become Islamic State fighters. Anders Kassman, SAPO's Chief Operating Officer, said ninety cases had been confirmed and twenty-three of those had been killed in action.[211]

OTHER STATES

Australia

Australia sent eight Royal Australian Air Force F/A-18s, an E-7A Wedgetail AWACS, and a KC-30A tanker/transport to the UAE to support the coalition airstrike campaign.[212] Australia also pre-deployed 600 Australian Defense Force members to the region. The foreign ministry further indicated that a second proposal will be submitted to approve action in Syria.[213]

Australia provided humanitarian aid to refugees, including Yazidis trapped on Mount Sinjar. Also, the nation absorbed about 4,400 refugees from Iraq and Syria combined.[214]

On October 20, 2014, Foreign Minister Julie Bishop confirmed that Australia had reached an agreed legal framework with the government of Iraq to allow Australian Special Forces legal protection in Iraq. According to Prime Minister Tony Abbot, 200 troops had been delayed in the UAE while waiting for this clearance. These troops include elite joint terminal attack controllers, who work with the Royal Australian Air Force to coordinate pinpoint airstrikes from the ground.[215]

India

The Indian government is looking to crack down on the IS after reports of Indians joining the terrorist organization. There are attempts by the National Investigation Agency to move towards formally banning the organization in India.[216] Home Minister Rajnath Singh played down concerns over Indian Muslim youth joining the IS and fighting in Iraq and Syria, saying India's Muslims are fiercely opposed to the terrorist organization.[217]

Congress leader Manish Tewari urged all democratic governments to unite in fighting the IS. In addition, he advised the BJP-led NDA government to reflect on what was causing a number of Indian youth to join IS.[218] Meanwhile, eighty Indian Muslims representing many organizations from across India, including intellectuals, community and religious leaders, and scholars and academics, released a joint statement condemning the IS.[219]

Japan

Japanese Press Secretary Takako Ito declared continued support and coordination with the United States and its allies against the IS. The Abe administration pledged $7.8 million in humanitarian aid to Iraqi refugees.[220] Chief Cabinet Secretary Yoshihide Suga said Japan does not plan to offer military assistance to the coalition, as it is prohibited under the country's pacifist-minded constitution.[221]

Morocco

About 1,200 Moroccans are estimated to be fighting with extremists in Syria and Iraq. On July 16, 2014, the Moroccan government announced an elevated alert there. It deployed anti-aircraft missiles around key infrastructure.[222] The Interior Ministry has been working to dismantle IS recruitment cells, mostly in Fez.[223]

Nigeria

Boko Haram leader Abubakar Shekau praised Abu Bakr al-Baghdadi. Shekau declared that he would be governing territory under his control as a caliphate.[224] At the September 29, 2014, UN General Assembly discussion on the IS, Nigerian President Goodluck Jonathan criticized the lack of UN Security Council action with regards to Iraq and Syria. He stressed the need to reform the council.[225]

Pakistan

Top Pakistani clerics rejected the Islamic State's claim of a caliphate, calling it a "mockery of Islam."[226]

Brazil

President Dilma Rousseff criticized the American-led campaign against the IS. At the UN General Assembly debate, she argued the use of force will only further alienate opposing sides and make a negotiated settlement less likely. Furthermore, she stated that military intervention does not lead to peace.[227]

Canada

Canada has taken part in the U.S.-led effort against the IS, sending 69 Canadian Special Forces as advisors for a 30-day mission.[228] Canada also provided about $10 million in equipment and ammunition to the overall effort as well as $5 million in humanitarian aid.[229]

INTERNATIONAL ORGANIZATIONS

Arab League

Nabil Elaraby, head of the Arab League, called on its member states to confront the IS militarily and politically. He expressed frustration at the lack of assistance against terrorist groups among Arab nations in the past.[230] The

Arab League agreed upon measures to combat the Islamic State on political, defense, security, and legal levels. The organization's measures, however, did not explicitly back the American military campaign against the IS. The draft resolution backed the UN resolution that imposed sanctions on terrorist foreign fighters.[231] Furthermore, the Arab League urged nations to suppress the flow of extremists leaving their homelands for Iraq and Syria.[232]

European Union

The EU originally responded to the Islamic State by condemning the actions of the terror group and increasing humanitarian funding for Iraq to €12 million in 2014.[233] At a meeting of European Union foreign ministers on August 15, 2014, the EU authorized member states to send weapons to Kurdish forces as long as the Iraqi government supports such actions.[234] Additionally, EU foreign ministers vowed to provide more humanitarian assistance to Iraqi Kurds.[235]

As of September 24, 2014, an estimated 3,000 Europeans had joined Islamist groups in Iraq and Syria.[236] Twenty to 30 percent of those people returned to their home countries in Europe since traveling to the Middle East.[237] As such, Europe faces a significant threat of terrorist attacks within its own borders from its nationals who return to home after fighting on behalf of terrorists in Iraq and Syria.

On October 20, 2014, the EU instituted additional sanctions against the Assad regime. Two entities and two individuals were added to the list of travel bans and asset freezes, bringing the total to sixty-three entities and 211 individuals for involvement in violent repression of civilians and "practical support to the Syrian regime."[238]

The EU has reached an agreement to launch new anti-terrorism projects with Muslim countries and to increase its intelligence sharing in the aftermath of deadly attacks in France and violent confrontations in Belgium. After a meeting with the Arab League's Secretary General, Nabil Elaraby, EU Foreign Affairs Chief Federica Mogherini announced that the EU will also be sharing information on suspected terrorists and possible attacks with many countries throughout the Arab world, Africa, and Asia.[239]

United Nations

In early August 2014, the UN declared the situation in Iraq a level three humanitarian emergency, meaning it is "the most severe, large-scale humanitarian crises."[240] Other instances of such classifications include Syria, the Central African Republic, and South Sudan.[241]

The UN has approached the IS issue with both security and humanitarian concerns in mind. For instance, the UN Security Council blacklisted the IS, subjecting it to the same sanctions that target al-Qa'ida.[242] A unanimous UN Security Council resolution, passed in August 2014, demanded that the IS disband, although the council provided no means of enforcement.[243]

Additionally, the UN Security Council blacklisted six people associated with the IS and Jabhat al-Nusra. Also, the UN Security Council threatened sanctions against anyone who helps foreign fighters in Syria or trades with the IS.[244] The UN Security Council demanded that countries "prevent and suppress" the recruitment and travel of foreign fighters to join Islamic militant groups like the IS.[245]

From a human rights perspective, the UN Refugee Agency and the UN Children's Fund[246] have committed to large humanitarian aid missions to help the hundreds of thousands of people displaced throughout Iraq.[247] The UN also considers the executions that were carried out in the northern Iraqi city of Tikrit to be war crimes.[248]

In September 2014, U.S. President Barack Obama delivered a speech to UN General Assembly, in which he vowed to fight the "network of death."[249] President Obama also mentioned that the United States was considering the training of moderate Syrian rebels to fight the IS.[250]

On September 29, 2014, the UN Security Council held a general debate in which the IS was the main topic. What follows is a summary of remarks for each nation that has not been mentioned in the foregoing section.[251]

Sam Kahamba Kutesa— President of the 69th session of the General Assembly	The President of the General Assembly underscored the importance of improving cooperation between the United Nations and regional organizations in order to solve violent conflicts.
Spain—Don Felipe VI, King	Spain is willing to make a contribution towards stability in the Middle East. He observed that peace in the Middle East is necessary to achieve world peace.
Mauritania—Mohamed Ould Abdel Aziz, President	The fight against terrorism is an international responsibility. Collaboration is necessary in order to solve conflict in the world.
Korea—Park Geun-hye, President	The unrest in Iraq and Syria poses a threat to all regions around the world.
Mexico—His Excellency Enrique Peña Nieto, President	While he did not address the issues of Syria or Iraq directly, the president did confirm his support of UN peacekeeping operations.

Indonesia—His Excellency Susilo Bambang Yudhoyono, President	He stated that the IS is not a proper representation of Islam. Instead, Indonesia is an example of Islam working alongside modernity and democracy.
Switzerland—His Excellency Didier Burkhalter, President	He emphasized the need to focus on legal responses over the use of force when dealing with such issues.
Chad—His Excellency Idriss Déby Itno, President	He called for a peaceful resolution of the Syrian crisis.
Sri Lanka—His Excellency Mahinda Rajapaksa, President	He expressed support for multilateral efforts against international terrorism.

NATO

Many NATO members are part of the U.S.-led coalition formed to combat the IS.[252] At this point, the group includes: the United States, Great Britain, Canada, Denmark, France, Germany, Italy, Poland, and Turkey. Former NATO Secretary General Anders Fogh Rasmussen stated that he supports NATO military force against the IS.[253] Rasmussen also welcomed the approval of the new Iraqi government instituted by Iraqi Parliament.[254] Jens Stoltenberg, the new NATO Secretary General as of September 30, 2014, vowed NATO would respond if Turkey's territorial sovereignty came under attack from the IS.[255]

Shanghai Cooperation Organization

At its annual summit in Dushanbe, Tajikistan, in September 2014, the Shanghai Cooperation Organization focused on expanding its membership and responding to the possible terrorist threats coming out of Afghanistan in the post-NATO era.[256] During the summit, members shared the same fear as Western countries that their citizens would return from fighting with the IS and inflict damage within their own borders.[257]

International Atomic Energy Agency

When the IS took over Mosul, it seized nuclear material from Mosul University. In light of this development, International Atomic Energy Agency (IAEA) commented, "The material involved is low-grade and would not present a significant safety, security, or nuclear proliferation risk. Nevertheless, any loss of regulatory control over nuclear and other radioactive materials is a cause for concern."[258]

ETHNIC AND RELIGIOUS GROUPS

The Kurds

The Kurdish Peshmerga has been on the front lines against the IS since its expansion in Syria. By various measures, it has shown competence, unity, and bravery, while a portion of the Iraqi national security forces crumbled and deserted.

The Peshmerga, which is the official name for the armed forces of Iraqi Kurdistan, has also been used to refer to Kurdish fighters more broadly. Turkey-based Kurdistan Workers' Party (PKK) fighters have traveled to the region and helped their Syrian Kurdish brethren. These reinforcements have caused some controversy and diplomatic difficulties, as PKK is considered to be a terrorist organization by both Turkey and the United States.[259] Kurdish forces spread their influence, training hundreds of Yazidi men to fight against the IS to defend their homes.[260]

As of March 2015, over 1,000 Peshmerga have been killed fighting the Islamic State in Iraq. Additionally, several hundred Kurds are believed to have joined the IS. The result is that there are Kurds fighting on both sides of the conflict associated with the IS.[261]

After the IS made its initial advance on Mosul, the Iraqi Kurds took advantage of the situation. As the Iraqi army was in full retreat, the Peshmerga were able to capture Kirkuk. This town and the oil-rich province of Tamim have been disputed between Iraq and the KRG (Kurdish Regional Government) for some time.[262] The KRG and Peshmerga gained full control of oil fields in Kirkuk and Bai Hassan, claiming they intended to protect those areas from the IS where the Iraqi army could not. Iraqi Prime Minister Nuri al-Maliki was furious, accusing the KRG of harboring Islamic State fighters in Erbil. Kurdish representatives left the government in protest. Kurdish President Masoud Barzani urged al-Maliki to step down. [263]

Many Iraqi refugees sought refuge in Kurdish-controlled areas, as the Peshmerga tended to offer better protection against IS than did the Iraqi army. Despite IS terror attacks in Kirkuk, Peshmerga forces were more effective in slowing down the advance of the IS militia than the national army. Additionally, the KRG announced plans to hold a referendum on the independence of its newly acquired regions.[264]

It was Kurdish forces that defended Mosul Dam until it was taken by the IS in August 2014. American airstrikes supported and reinforced Kurdish positions until the Peshmerga were able to retake the dam later that month.[265]

In addition, Kurdish forces have taken the brunt of the fighting in Syria, holding the IS at bay in increasingly desperate fighting[266] in Kobani while both Turkey[267] and the United States[268] initially demurred. Kurdish parties are demanding more assistance and even threatening to torpedo 2-year-old peace negotiations with Turkey if they are not aided.[269]

Failing to find adequate support from Turkey for their defense of Kobani, Syrian Kurds turned to Iraqi Kurds for supplies. Due to its battlefield successes and discipline, the semi-autonomous KRG has become the proxy of choice for Western powers. It has collected military supplies and/or received training from the United States, Germany, France, the UK, the Netherlands, Italy, and Iran.[270]

However, Turkey initially blocked aid convoys from Iraqi Kurdistan from reaching Kobani. Turkey was still concerned that arming Kurdish militias that it has been fighting for decades might backfire. [271] Despite this, reports in mid-October 2014 indicated that Kurdish forces retook strategic positions in Kobani, with the help of American airstrikes. This success was achieved after a month of fighting in which the IS advanced to the center of the town.[272] By January 2015, IS forces were mostly ousted from Kobani, although the city was left devastated.

Muslim Diaspora

Muslim governments throughout the world vehemently condemned the group, calling for clergy leadership in their nations to denounce it. Due to the outrage and many disagreements with the actions of the Islamic State, 125 Muslim clerics and experts signed an anti-IS letter claiming the extremist group's actions do not represent the principles of Islam.[273] Likewise, other clerics claim that IS fighters are not true Muslims.[274]

The International Union of Muslim Scholars stated that the IS claim to have established a caliphate is "null and void."[275] Several Indonesian Muslim groups have publicly denounced the IS.[276]Imam Sheikh Dr. Ahmed A. Nabhan from the Colorado Muslim Society and Catholic Archbishop Samuel J. Aquila issued a joint statement condemning the IS and requesting further U.S. action to stop the organization.[277]

Globally, numerous mainstream Muslim organizations also decried the activities of the IS. Concurrently, there was a recognition that significant efforts must be made to eradicate those elements within their communities which disseminate extremist tenets and misinterpretations of Islam. Ultimately, it is understood that significant, sustained, and effective counternarratives provided principally by the Muslim community will be paramount to weakening the potency of IS and other extremist ideologies.

About 200 Shiite and Sunni Muslims gathered in Calgary, Canada, to protest the IS's reign of terror in June 2014.[278] At this rally, one of the most prominent Shiite imams in Great Britain, Fadhil al-Milani, posted a video online asking Muslims not to join the IS and to support those fighting the group.[279]

Several protests have been held across Europe condemning the IS attacks on Christians. While the protests are generally not exclusively Muslim, there have been many Muslims in attendance.[280] The Assyrian American National Federation held a protest against the IS in Chicago in August 2014.[281] A "Burn IS Flag Challenge" has spread through social media. From the United States to Lebanon, Muslims around the world are burning the IS flag and posting it on sites such as Twitter, Facebook, and YouTube. This propaganda effort comes after the beheadings of two U.S. journalists outraged many people globally.[282]

Muslims Targeted in Response to IS Violence

In the aftermath of the January 2015 Paris jihadist attacks, European countries are increasingly concerned about the marginalization and discord among some of their young male Muslim populations. So, too, there is serious apprehension about the growing strength of far-right groups and political parties in Europe. In addition, there is fear of possible violent attacks against Muslims—whether group-affiliated or lone wolves. In Belgium, for instance, Muslim "children are taunted at school, anti-Muslim graffiti has been scrawled near mosques, and lawmakers are debating rules that could strip citizenship from Belgians who take up arms in Syria."[283]

Additionally, "anti-immigrant nationalists have been soaring in polls from Britain to Hungary, France to Greece."[284] In Germany, the support of the Pegida movement—with a similar ideological bent—may exacerbate Muslim-non-Muslim tensions, particularly in light of the January 2015 terror attacks in Paris, and counterterror operations across Europe.[285]

There is also uneasiness in the United States that graphic and well-exposed killings by the IS, in particular, of non-Muslims may spur an increase in hate crimes against Muslims and persons of Arab and South Asian descents. In February 2015, Craig Stephen Hicks was charged with three counts of first-degree murder in relation to the execution-style slaying of Deah Shaddy Barakat, his wife Yusor Abu-Salha, and her sister, Razan Abu-Salha in Chapel Hill, North Carolina.[286] While according to some accounts, Hicks had a dispute with the three over parking spaces at the condominium where they lived, the FBI is investigating whether the murders were a hate crime, as the victims were Muslims and Hicks had articulated anti-Muslim sentiments online.[287]

CONCLUSION

A review of the aforementioned efforts on international, regional, and national levels against the Islamic State demonstrates that there is a substantial community of interest in this regard. Sadly, words often ring hollow. Rather, the defeat of the Islamic State will necessitate more than lofty discussions. Instead, it will require strategic, forceful, and effective actions. Some of these activities have already commenced against the Islamic State, with more, hopefully, to come.

NOTES

1. Rago, Joseph. "Inside the war against the Islamic State." *Wall Street Journal*, December 26, 2014. Accessed December 27, 2014. http://www.wsj.com/articles/joe-rago-inside-the-war-against-islamic-state-1419636790.

2. Thompson, Mark. "Jordanian pilot captured by ISIS militants." *Time*, December 24, 2014. Accessed December 26, 2014. http://time.com/3646645/jordan-pilot-isis/.

3. "Inherent resolve airstrikes continue against ISIL." *DOD News*, December 18, 2014. Accessed December 20, 2014. http://www.defense.gov/news/newsarticle.aspx?id=123860.

4. Rago, Joseph. "Inside the war against the Islamic State." *Wall Street Journal*, December 26, 2014. Accessed December 27, 2014. http://www.wsj.com/articles/joe-rago-inside-the-war-against-islamic-state-1419636790.

5. Sly, Liz. "Islam's dysfunctional state: In Isis-controlled Syria and Iraq everyday life is falling apart." *Independent*. December 26, 2014. Accessed December 27, 2014. http://www.independent.co.uk/news/world/middle-east/islams-dysfunctional-state-in-isiscontrolled-syria-and-iraq-everyday-life-is-falling-apart-9945774.html.

6. Redfield, John. "ISIL strategy is working, but will take time, admiral says." U.S. Central Command Public Affairs, March 13, 2015. Accessed March 14, 2015. http://www.centcom.mil/en/news/articles/isil-strategy-working-but-will-take-time-admiral-says.

7. "Airstrikes hit ISIL in Syria, Iraq." *CJTF—Operation Inherent Resolve News Release*, March 29, 2015. Accessed March 29, 2015. http://www.defense.gov/news/newsarticle.aspx?id=128485.

8. "Airstrikes in Iraq and Syria." U.S. Department of Defense, undated. Accessed March 25, 2015. http://www.defense.gov/home/features/2014/0814_iraq/.

9. "Iraq and Syria: ISIL's reduced operating areas as of March 2015." U.S. Department of Defense, undated. Accessed March 28, 2015. http://www.defense.gov/home/features/2014/0814_iraq/ReducedOperatingAreas0315.pdf.

10. Ibid.

11. "Targets damaged/destroyed as of March 2015." *Department of Defense*, March 18, 2015. Accessed March 21, 2015. http://www.defense.gov/home/features/2014/0814_iraq/.

12. Nicholson, Brendan. "'Stalemate' in war on jihadis." *Australian*, December 27, 2014. Accessed December 27, 2014. http://www.theaustralian.com.au/in-depth/terror/stalemate-in-war-on-jihadis/story-fnpdbcmu-1227167497754.

13. Sky, Emma. "Iraq crisis needs a regional diplomatic response." *NY Times*, August 7, 2014. Accessed October 9, 2014. http://www.nytimes.com/roomfordebate/2014/06/15/how-to-stabilize-iraq-and-stop-the-march-of-isis/iraq-crisis-needs-a-regional-diplomatic-response.

14. Mintz, Zoe. "Iraq IS incursion presents dilemma for Sunni Muslims." *International Business Times*, June 13, 2014. Accessed October 9, 2014. http://www.ibtimes.com/iraq-isis-incursion-presents-dilemma-sunni-muslims-1600822.

15. "Iraqi Security Forces battle militants in Ramadi." *Radio Free Europe/Radio Liberty*. 1:13. May 27, 2014. Accessed April 21, 2015. http://www.rferl.org/media/video/iraq-ramadi-fighting/25400231.html.

16. "Iraqi and Kurdish forces recapture Mosul dam." *Al Jazeera*, August 19, 2014. Accessed October 9, 2014. http://www.aljazeera.com/news/middleeast/2014/08/kurdish-forces-claim-control-mosul-dam-2014818174534291467.html.

17. Hawrami, Karzan Sabah. "Abadi acknowledges Peshmerga success." *Basnews*, December 20, 2014. Accessed December 22, 2014. http://basnews.com/en/news/2014/12/20/abadi-acknowledges-peshmerga-success/.

18. "Kurds free large part of Iraq's Sinjar town from IS." *IANS*, December 22, 2014. Accessed December 24, 2014. https://in.news.yahoo.com/kurds-free-large-part-iraqs-sinjar-town-202403593.html. "Peshmerga Fighters Free Yazidis Besieged by ISIS on Iraq's Sinjar Mountain." *NBC News*, December 19, 2014. Accessed December 22, 2014. http://www.nbcnews.com/storyline/isis-terror/peshmerga-fighters-free-yazidis-besieged-isis-iraqs-sinjar-mountain-n271536.

19. Zebari, Abdelhamid. "Iraq Kurds press fightback as top jihadi reported killed." *Daily Star*, December 19, 2014. Accessed December 22, 2014. http://www.dailystar.com.lb/News/Middle-East/2014/Dec-19/281651-iraq-kurds-press-fightback-as-top-jihadi-reported-killed.ashx#sthash.Z1CbDZAP.dpuf.

20. "Killing top ISIS leaders won't cripple group: experts." *Daily Star*, December 20, 2014. Accessed December 24, 2014. http://www.dailystar.com.lb/News/Middle-East/2014/Dec-20/281742-killing-top-isis-leaders-wont-cripple-group-experts.ashx#sthash.Z3q55qc4.dpuf.

21. Ali, Ahmed and Kimberly Kagan. "The Iraqi Shi'a Mobilization to Counter the IS Offensive." *Institute for the Study of War*, June 14, 2014. Accessed October 9, 2014. http://www.understandingwar.org/backgrounder/iraqi-shi%E2%80%99-mobilization-counter-isis-offensive.

22. Ibid.

23. Parker, Ned. "Iraq civil war leader rallies Shi'ite fighters against the Islamic State." *Reuters*, February 18, 2015. Accessed February 21, 2015. http://www.reuters.com/article/2015/02/18/us-mideast-crisis-iraq-militias-idUSKBN0LM15920150218.

24. Ibid.

25. Ibid.

26. Ibid.

27. Hussein, Ahmed. "Sadr confirms his support to Iraqi Army." *Iraqi-News*, January 19, 2015. Accessed February 23, 2015. http://www.iraqinews.com/features/sadr-confirms-his-support-to-iraqi-army/.

28. Nicholson, Brendan. "'Stalemate' in war on jihadis." *Australian*, December 27, 2014. Accessed December 27, 2014. http://www.theaustralian.com.au/in-depth/terror/stalemate-in-war-on-jihadis/story-fnpdbcmu-1227167497754.

29. Ryan, Missy and Loveday Morris, "The U.S. and Iran are aligned in Iraq against the Islamic State—for Now." *Washington Post,* December 27, 2014. Accessed December 27, 2014. http://www.washingtonpost.com/world/national-security/the-us-and-iran-are-aligned-in-iraq-against-the-islamic-state--for-now/2014/12/27/353a748c-8d0d-11e4-a085-34e9b9f09a58_story.html?hpid=z1.

30. Parker, Ned. "Iraq civil war leader rallies Shi'ite fighters against the Islamic State." *Reuters*, February 18, 2015. Accessed February 21, 2015. http://www.reuters.com/article/2015/02/18/us-mideast-crisis-iraq-militias-idUSKBN0LM15920150218.

31. Rogin, Josh and Eli Lake. "Iran-Backed Militias Are Getting U.S. Weapons." *Bloomberg View*, January 8, 2015. Accessed April 30, 2015. http://www.bloombergview.com/articles/2015-01-08/iranbacked-militias-are-getting-us-weapons-in-iraq.

32. Ibid.

33. Rasheed, Ahmed, Ned Parker, and Stephen Kalin. "Survivors say Iraqi forces watched as Shi'ite militias executed 72 Sunnis." *Yahoo News,* January 28, 2015. Accessed February 3, 2015. http://news.yahoo.com/survivors-iraqi-forces-watched-shiite-militias-executed-72-193441145.html.

34. Allen, John. "Degrading and defeating ISIL." *Defense News*, December 29, 2014. Accessed December 31, 2014. http://www.state.gov/s/seci/235545.htm.

35. "Iraqi security forces make gains against Islamic State." *Reuters*, December 27, 2014. Accessed December 28, 2014. http://www.newsweek.com/iraqi-security-forces-make-gains-against-islamic-state-295531?piano_t=1.

36. Allen, John. Special Presidential Envoy for the Global Coalition to Counter ISIL. "Inaugural meeting of the coalition stabilization working group." Department of State, March 18, 2015. Accessed March 21, 2015. http://www.state.gov/s/seci/239446.htm.

37. "Islamic State conflict: Iraq declares Tikrit 'victory.'" *BBC*, April 1, 2015. Accessed April 1, 2015. http://www.bbc.com/news/world-middle-east-32153836.

38. Morris, Loveday. "Thousands of Iraqis flee as Islamic State makes gains in Sunni heartland." *Washington Post*, April 17, 2015. Accessed April 18, 2015. http://www.washingtonpost.com/world/middle_east/thousands-of-iraqis-flee-as-islamic-state-makes-gains-in-sunni-heartland/2015/04/17/b143d9aa-e44d-11e4-ae0f-f8c46aa8c3a4_story.html?.

39. Abdul-Zahra, Qassim and Sameer Yacoub. "Iraqi soldiers enter refinery amidst Islamic State attacks." *AP*, April 18, 2015. Accessed April 18, 2015. http://news.yahoo.com/iraqi-official-ground-forces-enter-iraqs-biggest-refinery-104922287.html. "Islamic State group attacks Iraq's largest oil refinery." *France24*, April 12, 2015. Accessed April 17, 2015. http://www.france24.com/en/20150412-islamic-state-group-attacks-iraq-largest-oil-refinery/.

40. Alkhshali, Hamdi. "ISIS claims blast near U.S. Consulate in Irbil, Iraq." *CNN*, April 17, 2015. Accessed April 18, 2015. http://www.cnn.com/2015/04/17/middleeast/iraq-violence/index.html.

41. Reuter, Christoph. "The terror strategist: Secret files reveal the structure of the Islamic State." *Der Spiegel,* April 18, 2015. Accessed April 19, 2015. http://www.spiegel.de/international/world/islamic-state-files-show-structure-of-islamist-terror-group-a-1029274.html.

42. "Syrian jets hammer Islamic State stronghold." *Al Jazeera,* August 17, 2014. Accessed October, 11, 2014. http://www.aljazeera.com/news/middleeast/2014/08/syrian-jets-hammer-islamic-state-stronghold-2014817193245769730.html.

43. "Nearly 200 dead as Syria bases lost to Qaeda: monitor." *AFP*, December 16, 2014. Accessed December 18, 2014. http://news.yahoo.com/nearly-200-dead-syria-bases-lost-qaeda-monitors-092339489.html.

44. Ibid.

45. "More than 40 militants killed in Syrian Kurdistan." *Basnews*, December 25, 2014. Accessed December 26, 2014. http://basnews.com/en/news/2014/12/25/more-than-40-militants-killed-in-syrian-kurdistan/.

46. "Clashes continue between the IS and regime forces around Der-Ezzor military airport." *Syrian Observatory for Human Rights,* February 3, 2015. Accessed February 23, 2015. http://syriahr.com/en/2015/02/clashes-continue-between-the-is-and-regime-forces-around-der-ezzor-military-airport/.

47. "7 ISIS killed around Der-Ezzor military airport." Syrian Observatory for Human Rights, February 4, 2015. Accessed February 23, 2015. http://syriahr.com/en/2015/02/7-isis-killed-around-der-ezzor-military-airport/.

48. Brumfield, Ben and Gul Tuysuz. "200,000 flee in biggest displacement of Syrian conflict, monitor says." *CNN,* September 23, 2014. Accessed October, 11, 2014. http://www.cnn.com/2014/09/22/world/meast/syria-civil-war/.

49. "About 13,000 detainees tortured to death inside Bashar al-Assad's jails." Syrian Observatory for Human Rights, March 13, 2015. Accessed March 16, 2015. http://syriahr.com/en/2015/03/about-13000-detainees-tortured-to-death-inside-bashar-al-assads-jails/.

50. Zalewski, Piotr, "Turkey grapples with an unprecedented flood of refugees fleeing IS." *Time*, September 23, 2014. Accessed October, 11, 2014. http://time.com/3423522/turkey-syria-isis-isil-refugees/.

51. Smith-Spark, Laura, Salma Abdelaziz, and Yousuf Basil. "Kurdish fighters from Turkey join battle to save Syrian Kurdish town from IS." *CNN*, September 21, 2014. Accessed October, 11, 2014. http://www.cnn.com/2014/09/20/world/meast/syria-turkey-kurdish-fighters/.

52. Nichols, Michelle. "U.N. Security Council plans to suppress foreign extremist fighters." *Reuters,* September 9, 2014. Accessed October, 11, 2014. http://www.reuters.com/article/2014/09/09/us-iraq-crisis-un-idUSKBN0H408E20140909.

53. Williams, Lauren. "Turkey shuns key role in fighting Islamic State." *USA Today,* September 18, 2014. Accessed October, 11, 2014. http://www.usatoday.com/story/news/world/2014/09/17/turkey-coalition-against-islamic-state/15668093/.

54. Graham-Harrison, Emma. "Turkey celebrates return of hostages and opens border to Kurds fleeing Isis." *Guardian,* September 20, 2014. Accessed October, 11, 2014. http://www.theguardian.com/world/2014/sep/20/turkey-hostages-syria-kurds-isis.

55. "New air strikes on IS, Turkey hints at military role." *Al Arabiya,* September 27, 2014. Accessed October, 11, 2014. http://english.alarabiya.net/en/News/middle-east/2014/09/27/U-S-renews-air-strikes-against-IS.html.

56. Butler, Daren and Oliver Holmes. "Erdogan: Kobani about to fall to Islamic State, ground operation needed." *Haaretz,* October 7, 2014. Accessed November 3, 2014. http://www.haaretz.com/news/middle-east/1.619622.

57. "Turkish tanks take up position on Syrian border next to besieged Kurdish town." *Hurriyet Daily News,* September 29, 2014. Accessed October, 11, 2014. http://www.hurriyetdailynews.com/turkish-tanks-take-up-position-on-syrian-border-next-to-besieged-kurdish-town.aspx?pageID=238&nID=72319&NewsCatID=352. "Islamic State: Turkish MPs back Iraq-Syria deployment." *BBC,* October 2, 2014. Accessed October, 11, 2014. http://www.bbc.com/news/world-middle-east-29455204.

58. "Turkey warns will hit back if IS attacks Syria exclave." *Al Arabiya,* October 4, 2014. Accessed October, 11, 2014. http://english.alarabiya.net/en/News/middle-east/2014/10/04/Turkey-warns-will-hit-back-if-IS-attacks-Syria-exclave-.html.

59. "No: 70, 22 February 2015, press release regarding the temporary location of the Tomb of Süleyman Şah and Memorial Outpost." Ministry of Foreign Affairs, Republic of Turkey, February 22, 2015. Accessed March 15, 2015. http://www.mfa.gov.tr/no_-70_-22-february-2015_-press-release-regarding-the-temporary-relocation-of-the-tomb-of-s%C3%BCleyman-%C5%9Fah-and-memorial-outpost.en.mfa

60. "Turkey returns artillery fire at Syria for 5th day." *CBC News*, October 7, 2012. Accessed November 5, 2014. http://www.cbc.ca/news/world/turkey-returns-artillery-fire-at-syria-for-5th-day-1.1145085.

61. Tawfiq, Saif. "Turkish warplanes shoot down Syrian helicopter." *Reuters,* September 16, 2013. Accessed November 5, 2014. http://www.reuters.com/article/2013/09/16/us-syria-crisis-turkey-idUSBRE98F0K920130916. Butler, Desmond and Albert Aji. "Turkish jet downs Syrian warplane near border." *Associated Press,* March 23, 2014. Accessed November 5, 2014. http://bigstory.ap.org/article/heavy-clashes-syria-near-turkish-border.

"Turkey downs Syria warplane on border." *Al-Arabiya,* March 23, 2014. Accessed November 5, 2014. http://english.alarabiya.net/en/News/middle-east/2014/03/23/Turkey-downs-Syria-warplane-on-border.html.

62. "Blasts kill dozens in Turkish town Reyhanli on Syria border." *BBC News*, May 11, 2013. Accessed November 5, 2014. http://www.bbc.com/news/world-middle-east-22494128.

63. "Turkey launches air strike on Al Qaida convoy in N. Syria." *World Tribune,* January 30, 2014. Accessed November 5, 2014. http://www.worldtribune.com/2014/01/30/turkey-launches-air-strike-on-al-qaida-convoy-in-n-syria/.

64. "NATO promises to protect Turkey against ISIS threat." *RT*, October 6, 2014. Accessed November 5, 2014. http://rt.com/news/193584-nato-turkey-isis-syria/.

65. Cooper, Helene. "Turkey is courted by U.S. to help fight IS." *NY Times,* September 8, 2014. Accessed October 11, 2014. http://www.nytimes.com/2014/09/09/world/europe/turkey-is-courted-by-us-to-help-fight-isis.html.

66. "Turkey vows to help Erbil in the war against IS." *Rudaw,* September 9, 2014. Accessed October, 11, 2014. http://rudaw.net/english/middleeast/29092014.

67. Pamuk, Humeyra and Daren Butler. "U.S.-led air strikes intensify as Syria conflict destabilizes Turkey." *Reuters,* October 14, 2014. Accessed November 3, 2014. http://mobile.reuters.com/article/idUSKCN0I30ZI20141014?irpc=932.

68. "Islamic State: Turkey to let Iraq Kurds join Kobane fight." *BBC News,* October 20, 2014. Accessed November 3, 2014. http://www.bbc.com/news/world-middle-east-29685830.

69. Ritzen, Yarno and Mohsin Ali. "Interactive: Countries countering ISIL." *Al Jazeera,* October 15, 2014. Accessed November 3, 2014. http://www.aljazeera.com/indepth/interactive/2014/10/isil-us-syria-airstrike-coalition-uae-saudi-2014101142731382476.html.

70. "General Debate: 24–30 September 2014." *United Nations,* September 24–30. Accessed October 10, 2014. http://www.un.org/en/ga/69/meetings/gadebate/24sep/.

71. Nicholson, Brendan. "'Stalemate' in war on jihadis." *Australian*, December 27, 2014. Accessed December 27, 2014. http://www.theaustralian.com.au/in-depth/terror/stalemate-in-war-on-jihadis/story-fnpdbcmu-1227167497754.

72. Ryan, Missy and Loveday Morris, "The U.S. and Iran are aligned in Iraq against the Islamic State—for Now." *Washington Post,* December 27, 2014. Accessed December 27, 2014. http://www.washingtonpost.com/world/national-security/the-us-and-iran-are-aligned-in-iraq-

against-the-islamic-state--for-now/2014/12/27/353a748c-8d0d-11e4-a085-34e9b9f09a58_
story.html?hpid=z1.

73. Ridley, Yvonne. "Shaikh Hassan Abboud's final interview." *Middle East Monitor,* September 22, 2014. Accessed October, 10, 2014. https://www.middleeastmonitor.com/resources/
interviews/14279-exclusive-shaikh-hassan-abbouds-final-interview.

74. "Iraq crisis: Iran pledges military help against Isis as battle for Tikrit escalates." *Telegraph,* June 29, 2014. Accessed October, 10, 2014. http://www.telegraph.co.uk/news/
worldnews/middleeast/iraq/10933934/Iraq-crisis-Iran-pledges-military-help-against-Isis-as-battle-for-Tikrit-escalates.html.

75. Ali, Ahmed and Kimberly Kagan. "The Iraqi Shi'a mobilization to counter the IS offensive." Institute for the Study of War, June 14, 2014. Accessed October, 10, 2014. http://www.understandingwar.org/backgrounder/iraqi-shi%E2%80%99-mobilization-counter-isis-offensive.

76. Evans, Michael. "Russia and Iran attack IS jihadists." *CNN,* August 11, 2014. Accessed October, 10, 2014. http://ireport.cnn.com/docs/DOC-1160609.

77. "Many Iranians want military to intervene against Isis." *Guardian,* June 27, 2014. Accessed October, 10, 2014. http://www.theguardian.com/world/iran-blog/2014/jun/27/iran-isis-military-intervention.

78. Ryan, Missy and Loveday Morris, "The U.S. and Iran are aligned in Iraq against the Islamic State—for Now." *Washington Post,* December 27, 2014. Accessed December 27, 2014. http://www.washingtonpost.com/world/national-security/the-us-and-iran-are-aligned-in-iraq-against-the-islamic-state--for-now/2014/12/27/353a748c-8d0d-11e4-a085-34e9b9f09a58_
story.html?hpid=z1.

79. "Who is doing what in the coalition battle against IS?" *CNN,* September 17, 2014. Accessed October, 10, 2014. http://www.cnn.com/2014/09/14/world/meast/isis-coalition-nations/.

80. "Iran's Rouhani: U.S. Strikes In Syria Illegal." *Huffington Post,* September 23, 2014. Accessed October, 10, 2014. http://www.huffingtonpost.com/2014/09/23/iran-rouhani-syria-strike_n_5868780.html.

81. Ali, Ahmed and Kimberly Kagan. "The Iraqi Shi'a mobilization to counter the IS offensive." Institute for the Study of War, June 14, 2014. Accessed October, 10, 2014. http://www.understandingwar.org/backgrounder/iraqi-shi%E2%80%99-mobilization-counter-isis-offensive. "Iraq crisis: Iran pledges military help against Isis as battle for Tikrit escalates." *Telegraph,* June 29, 2014 Accessed October, 10, 2014. http://www.telegraph.co.uk/news/
worldnews/middleeast/iraq/10933934/Iraq-crisis-Iran-pledges-military-help-against-Isis-as-battle-for-Tikrit-escalates.html.

82. Coles, Isabel. "Iran supplied weapons to Iraqi Kurds; Baghdad bomb kills 12." *Reuters,* August 28, 2014. Accessed October, 10, 2014. http://www.reuters.com/article/2014/08/26/us-iraq-security-kurds-idUSKBN0GQ11P20140826.

83. Balali, Mehrdad. "Iranian general killed by sniper bullet in embattled Iraqi city." *Reuters,* December 28, 2014. Accessed December 29, 2014. http://www.reuters.com/article/2014/
12/28/us-mideast-crisis-iran-idUSKBN0K60F020141228.

84. Hussein, Ahmed. "Iran marks 40-km red zone inside Iraq to stop IS: commander." *Iraqi News,* January 9, 2015. Accessed February 23, 2015. http://www.iraqinews.com/features/iran-marks-0-km-red-zone-inside-iraq-to-stop-is-commander/.

85. McClam, Erin and Abigail Williams. "Which countries are doing what in the IS coalition?" *NBC News,* September 26, 2014. Accessed October 13, 2014. http://www.nbcnews.com/
storyline/isis-terror/which-countries-are-doing-what-isis-coalition-n212596.

86. Fantz, Ashley. "Who is doing what in the coalition battle against IS?" *CNN,* September 17, 2014. Accessed October 10, 2014. http://www.cnn.com/2014/09/14/world/meast/isis-coalition-nations/.

87. Wahab, Siraj. "Kingdom slams IS as destructive terror group." *Arab News,* June 19, 2014. Accessed October 13, 2014. http://www.arabnews.com/news/588971. "Ninety-three suspected ISIS terrorists arrested in Saudi Arabia after 'authorities uncover plot to car-bomb U.S. Embassy." *Daily Mail,* April 28, 2015. Accessed April 29, 2015. http://www.dailymail.co.uk/

news/article-3059200/Saudi-says-arrests-93-Islamic-State-suspects-foils-U-S-embassy-attack. html.

88. Hussain, Yadullah. "Saudi Arabia could fight ISIS with oil—if it can bear the price." *Financial Post*, September 11, 2014. Accessed November 5, 2014. http://business.fin ancialpost.com/2014/09/11/saudi-arabia-could-fight-isis-with-oil-if-they-can-bear-the-price/?_ _lsa=9e6b-d0b9.

89. McClam, Erin and Abigail Williams. "Which countries are doing what in the IS coalition?" *NBC News*, September 26, 2014. Accessed October 13, 2014. http://www.nbcnews.com/ storyline/isis-terror/which-countries-are-doing-what-isis-coalition-n212596.

90. Whitlock, Craig. "U.S. military leaders: Strikes in Syria are just the start of a prolonged campaign." *Washington Post*, September 23, 2014. Accessed October 13, 2014. http://www. washingtonpost.com/world/us-attacks-islamic-state-in-syria-with-five-middle-east-partners/ 2014/09/23/b78ad7e8-c8f2-4aa8-aaa7-ec92572f6716_story.html.

91. Ritzen, Yarno and Mohsin Ali. "Interactive: Countries countering ISIL." *Al Jazeera,* October 15, 2014. Accessed November 3, 2014. http://www.aljazeera.com/indepth/interactive/ 2014/10/isil-us-syria-airstrike-coalition-uae-saudi-2014101142731382476.html.

92. "General Debate: 24–30 September 2014." *United Nations*, September 24–30. Accessed October 10, 2014. http://www.un.org/en/ga/69/meetings/gadebate/24sep/.

93. Khalid bin Hamad Al Khalifa. Interviewed by *Morning Joe*. "Bahrain official: Dealing with IS top concern." *MSNBC* video. 3:52. September 29, 2014. http://www.msnbc.com/ morning-joe/watch/bahrain-official--dealing-with-isis-top-concern-334840899895.

94. Tran, Mark. "Isis: world leaders give strong backing for Iraq at Paris conference—as it happened." *Guardian*, September 15, 2014. Accessed October 10, 2014. http://www. theguardian.com/world/live/2014/sep/15/isis-leaders-hold-crisis-meeting-on-isis-in-paris-live-coverage.

95. McClam, Erin and Abigail Williams. "Which countries are doing what in the IS coalition?" *NBC News*, September 26, 2014. Accessed October 10, 2014. http://www.nbcnews.com/ storyline/isis-terror/which-countries-are-doing-what-isis-coalition-n212596.

96. "Bahrain's role in U.S.-led raids on IS 'not symbolic:' FM." *Al Arabiya*, September 26, 2014. Accessed October 10, 2014. http://english.alarabiya.net/en/News/middle-east/2014/09/ 26/Bahrain-s-role-in-U-S-led-raids-on-IS-not-symbolic-FM.html.

97. Ritzen, Yarno and Mohsin Ali. "Interactive: Countries countering ISIL." *Al Jazeera,* October 15, 2014. Accessed November 3, 2014. http://www.aljazeera.com/indepth/interactive/ 2014/10/isil-us-syria-airstrike-coalition-uae-saudi-2014101142731382476.html.

98. Johnston, Ian. "Isis response: UK military planning to set up new bases in Middle East." *Independent*, September 10, 2014. Accessed November 3, 2014. http://www.independent.co. uk/news/world/middle-east/isis-response-uk-military-planning-to-set-up-new-bases-in-middle-east-9722545.html.

99. McClam, Erin and Abigail Williams. "Which countries are doing what in the IS coalition?" *NBC News,* September 26, 2014. Accessed October, 13, 2014. http://www.nbcnews. com/storyline/isis-terror/which-countries-are-doing-what-isis-coalition-n212596.

100. "Islamic State crisis: UAE female pilot in air strikes." *BBC,* September 25, 2014. Accessed October, 13, 2014. http://www.bbc.com/news/world-middle-east-29367214.

101. Fantz, Ashley. "Who is doing what in the coalition battle against IS?" *CNN,* September 17, 2014. Accessed October, 13, 2014. http://www.cnn.com/2014/09/14/world/meast/isis-coalition-nations/.

102. "King Abdullah says Jordan successfully fended off Islamic State and secured its borders." *Jerusalem Post,* September 22, 2014. Accessed October, 13, 2014. http://www.jpost. com/Middle-East/King-Abdullah-says-Jordan-successfully-fended-off-Islamic-State-and-secured-its-borders-376014.

103. Cooper, Helene and Michael R. Gordon. "U.S. Is Carrying Out Vast Majority of Strikes on IS, Military Officials Say." *NY Times,* September 23, 2014. Accessed October, 13, 2014. http://www.nytimes.com/2014/09/24/world/middleeast/us-is-carrying-out-vast-majority-of-strikes-on-isis-military-officials-say.html?_r=0.

104. "General Debate: 24–30 September 2014." *United Nations*, September 24–30. Accessed October 10, 2014. http://www.un.org/en/ga/69/meetings/gadebate/24sep/.

105. Jha, Supriya. "US says ISIS didn't down Jordan aircraft after Islamic State captures pilot." *ZeeNews.com*, December 25, 2014. Accessed December 26, 2014. http://zeenews.india.com/news/world/us-says-isis-didnt-down-jordan-aircraft-after-islamic-state-captures-pilot_1520046.html. Thompson, Mark. "Jordanian pilot captured by ISIS militants." *Time*, December 24, 2014. Accessed December 26, 2014. http://time.com/3646645/jordan-pilot-isis/.

106. Pestano, Andrew. "Islamic State publishes interview with captured pilot, asks Twitter followers how to kill him." *UPI*, December 30, 2014. Accessed December 31, 2014. http://www.upi.com/Top_News/World-News/2014/12/30/Islamic-State-publishes-interview-with-captured-pilot-asks-Twitter-followers-how-to-kill-him/3101419960006/. "Captured pilot's family urge IS to release him." *ITV News*, December 25, 2014. Accessed December 27, 2014. http://www.itv.com/news/story/2014-12-25/captured-pilots-family-urge-is-to-release-him/.

107. Sarhan, Amre. "Jordan deploys 'thousands' of troops at its border with Iraq." *Iraqi News*, February 10, 2015. Accessed February 23, 2015. http://www.iraqinews.com/iraq-war/jordan-deploys-thousands-troops-border-iraq/

108. Hussein, Ahmed. "Sissi rules out sending Egyptian troops to Iraq, assures Iraqi Army's ability to defeat ISIL." *Iraqi News*, September 21, 2014. Accessed October, 10, 2014. http://www.iraqinews.com/baghdad-politics/sissi-rules-out-sending-egyptian-troops-to-iraq-assures-iraqi-army-s-ability-to-defeat-isil/.

109. Glatz, Kyle. "Muslim leaders condemn Isis, call them 'Crazy Criminals.'" *World Religion News,* August 29, 2014. Accessed October, 10, 2014. http://www.worldreligionnews.com/issues/muslim-leaders-condemn-isis-call-crazy-criminals.

110. Fantz, Ashley. "Who is doing what in the coalition battle against IS?." *CNN,* September 17, 2014. Accessed October, 10, 2014. http://www.cnn.com/2014/09/14/world/meast/isis-coalition-nations/.

111. "General Debate: 24–30 September 2014." *United Nations,* September 24–30. Accessed October 10, 2014. http://www.un.org/en/ga/69/meetings/gadebate/24sep/.

112. "Simultaneous attacks in Egypt kill scores." *Al Jazeera,* January 29, 2015. Accessed February 5, 2015. http://america.aljazeera.com/articles/2015/1/29/simultaneous-attacks-in-egypt-kill-25.html.

113. "Egypt's battle against jihadists will be a long one: Sisi." *Daily Mail,* January 31, 2015. Accessed February 4, 2015. http://www.dailymail.co.uk/wires/afp/article-2934515/Egypts-Sisi-says-battle-against-jihadists-tough-one.html. Sweilam, Ashraf. "President: Egypt faces long fight to defeat Sinai militants." *Charlotte Observer,* January 31, 2015. Accessed February 4, 2015. http://www.charlotteobserver.com/2015/01/31/5484675/president-egypt-faces-long-fight.html -.VNJFVGTF84R.

114. Grossman, Michelle Malka. "Islamic State officially outlawed in Israel." *Jerusalem Post,* September 3, 2014. Accessed October 10, 2014. http://www.jpost.com/Arab-Israeli-Conflict/Islamic-State-officially-outlawed-in-Israel-374348.

115. Levi, Yaakov. "Israel's top cop: We'll throw the book at IS supporters." *Israel National News*, September 8, 2014. Accessed October 10, 2014. http://www.israelnationalnews.com/News/News.aspx/184884#.VA9FrEv4vwI.

116. Payne, Sebastian. "What the 60-plus members of the anti-Islamic State coalition are doing." *Washington Post,* September 25, 2014. Accessed October 10, 2014. http://www.washingtonpost.com/news/checkpoint/wp/2014/09/25/what-the-60-members-of-the-anti-islamic-state-coalition-are-doing/.

117. "'Israel provides satellite imagery, other intelligence for US-led campaign against IS.'" *Jerusalem Post,* September 8, 2014. Accessed October 10, 2014. http://www.jpost.com/Middle-East/Israel-provides-satellite-imagery-other-intelligence-for-US-led-campaign-against-IS-374790.

118. Ibid.

119. Edelman, Eric, Dennis Ross, and Ray Takeyh. "Iran remains America's biggest challenge." *Washington Post,* September 18, 2014. Accessed October 10, 2014. http://www.washingtonpost.com/opinions/2014/09/18/f786fd1c-3f56-11e4-9587-5dafd96295f0_story.html. "'Israel provides satellite imagery, other intelligence for US-led campaign against IS.'" *Jerusalem Post,* September 8, 2014. Accessed October 10, 2014. http://www.jpost.com/

Middle-East/Israel-provides-satellite-imagery-other-intelligence-for-US-led-campaign-against-IS-374790.

120. Speyer, Lea. "Netanyahu: Easing Iranian sanctions for help against IS 'absurd.'" *Breaking Israel News*, September 22, 2014. Accessed October 10, 2014. http://www.breakingisraelnews.com/21935/netanyahu-easing-iranian-sanctions-help-isis-absurd/?utm_source=rss&utm_medium=rss&utm_campaign=netanyahu-easing-iranian-sanctions-help-isis-absurd#RVWj3y5IZvMbkRyT.97.

121. Karam, Zeina and Nasser Karimi. "Iranian General Mohammad Ali Allahdadi killed alongside Hezbollah fighters in Israeli air strike, Tehran says." *National Post*, January 24, 2015. Accessed February 18, 2015. http://news.nationalpost.com/2015/01/19/iranian-general-mohammad-ali-allahdadi-kiled-alongside-hezbollah-fighters-in-israeli-airstrike-tehran-says/.

122. "Three killed as Israel and Hezbollah clash on Lebanese border." *BBC*, January 28, 2015. Accessed February 18, 2015. http://www.bbc.com/news/world-middle-east-31015862.

123. Williams, Dan. "Israel says cracks first local Islamic State cell." *Reuters*, January 18, 2015. February 23, 2015. http://www.reuters.com/article/2015/01/18/us-mideast-crisis-israel-idUSKBN0KR0EP20150118.

124. Lynch, Dennis. "Iraq crisis: Pentagon confirms USS George H.W. Bush is en route to Persian Gulf in response to IS activity." *International Business Times*, June 14, 2014. Accessed October 10, 2014. http://www.ibtimes.com/iraq-crisis-pentagon-confirms-uss-george-hw-bush-en-route-persian-gulf-response-isis-1601456. Lamothe, Dan. "USS George H.W. Bush and its Super Hornet fighters strike in Iraq." *Washington Post*, August 8, 2014. Accessed October 10, 2014. http://www.washingtonpost.com/news/checkpoint/wp/2014/08/08/uss-george-h-w-bush-and-its-super-hornet-fighters-strike-in-iraq/.

125. Weaver. Matthew. "US hails recapture of Mosul dam as symbol of united battle against Isis." *Guardian,* August 19, 2014. Accessed October 10, 2014. http://www.theguardian.com/world/2014/aug/19/us-mosul-dam-isis-iraq-kurd-pentagon-obama.

126. Cooper, Helene, Kareem Fahim, and C.J. Chivers. "U.S. launches new airstrikes on IS to protect dam in Iraq." *NY Times*, September 7, 2014. Accessed October 10, 2014. http://www.nytimes.com/2014/09/08/world/middleeast/iraq.html.

127. "Battle for Iraq and Syria in maps." *BBC*, November 21, 2014. Accessed November 22, 2014. http://www.bbc.com/news/world-middle-east-27838034.

128. Martinez, Luis. "U.S. airstrikes in Iraq and Syria have cost $1 Billion." *ABCNews.com*, December 19, 2014. Accessed December 20, 2014. http://abcnews.go.com/Politics/us-airstrikes-iraq-syria-cost-billion/story?id=27728260.

129. Ibid.

130. "Over 1,000 Islamist militants killed in U.S.-led strikes in Syria: Report." *Reuters*, December 23, 2014. Accessed December 25, 2014. http://www.huffingtonpost.com/2014/12/23/syria-strikes_n_6371624.html?cps=gravity_2684_-5081708203998889793.

131. "Airstrikes in Iraq and Syria." U.S. Department of Defense, Undated. Accessed March 25, 2015. http://www.defense.gov/home/features/2014/0814_iraq/.

132. Acosta, Jim and Kevin Liptak. "White House exempts IS strikes from civilian casualty guidelines." *CNN,* October 2, 2014. Accessed October 10, 2014. http://www.cnn.com/2014/10/01/politics/wh-isis-civilians/index.html?hpt=hp_t1.

133. Ibid.

134. Chulov, Martin, Spencer Ackerman, and Paul Lewis. "US confirms 14 air strikes against IS in Syria." *Guardian,* September 23, 2014. Accessed October 10, 2014. http://www.theguardian.com/world/2014/sep/23/us-launches-air-strikes-against-isis-targets-in-syria.

135. Cooper, Helene and Michael R. Gordon. "U.S. is carrying out vast majority of strikes on IS, Military Officials Say." *NY Times*, September 23, 2014. Accessed October 10, 2014. http://www.nytimes.com/2014/09/24/world/middleeast/us-is-carrying-out-vast-majority-of-strikes-on-isis-military-officials-say.html?_r=0.

136. "Some 70 Islamic State fighters said killed in U.S.-led air strikes on Syria." *Haaretz,* September 23, 2014. Accessed October 10, 2014. http://www.haaretz.com/news/middle-east/1.617310.

137. United States Central Command, 2014. "U.S. military conducts aerial resupply of Kurdish forces fighting ISIL." October 19, 2014. Accessed November 3, 2014. http://www.centcom. mil/en/news/articles/u.s.-military-conducts-aerial-resupply-of-kurdish-forces-fighting-isil.

138. "United States sends another 130 military personnel to Iraq" *Reuters,* August 13, 2014. Accessed October 10, 2014. http://www.reuters.com/article/2014/08/13/us-iraq-security-usa-advisers-idUSKBN0GC25820140813.

139. Dunham, Will. "Obama increases U.S. force protecting embassy in Baghdad." *Reuters,* September 2, 2014. Accessed October 13, 2014. http://www.reuters.com/article/2014/09/03/us-iraq-crisis-usa-idUSKBN0GY01F20140903.

140. Al Omran, Ahmed. "John Kerry meets with Saudi King Abdullah, Syrian opposition leader Jarba." *Wall Street Journal,* June 27, 2014. Accessed October 10, 2014. http://online. wsj.com/articles/john-kerry-meets-with-saudi-king-abdullah-1403888673. Queally, John. US Senate approves $500 million to arm Syrian militants." *Common Dreams News Organization,* September 19, 2014. Accessed November 4, 2014. http://www.commondreams.org/news/2014/ 09/19/us-senate-approves-500-million-arm-syrian-militants.

"U.S. approves $500 million to fund and arm moderate Syrian rebels against ISIS." *ABC News,* September 19, 2014. Accessed November 4, 2014. http://abcnews.go.com/International/ video/us-approves-500-million-fund-arm-moderate-syrian-25633715.

"Profile: Ahmad Jarba, Syrian opposition leader." *BBC,* July 8, 2014. Accessed October 10, 2014. http://www.bbc.com/news/world-middle-east-23229258.

141. "Syria." *USA Aid,* September 12, 2014. Accessed October 10, 2014. http://www.usaid. gov/crisis/syria.

142. Wong, Kristina. "Hagel: US knows Iran, Russia aiding Iraq in fight against IS." *Hill,* July 11, 2014. Accessed October 10, 2014. http://thehill.com/policy/defense/212024-hagel-us-knows-iran-russia-aiding-iraq-in-fight-against-isis.

143. "U.S. military aircraft drop food, water to Iraqis for second night." *Reuters,* August 8, 2014. Accessed October 10, 2014. http://www.reuters.com/article/2014/08/09/us-iraq-security-usa-drop-idUSKBN0G902R20140809.

144. "U.S. military conducts aerial resupply of Kurdish forces fighting ISIL." United States Central Command, 2014. October 19, 2014. Accessed November 3, 2014. http://www.centcom. mil/en/news/articles/u.s.-military-conducts-aerial-resupply-of-kurdish-forces-fighting-isil.

145. Fitzgerald, Sandy. "Report: Hundreds of Americans may be fighting for IS." *Newsmax,* August 27, 2014. Accessed October 10, 2014. http://www.newsmax.com/Newsfront/IS-Iraq-Douglas-McAuthur-McCain.

146. "U.S. releases graphic anti-IS video: 'Welcome to the Islamic State Land.'" *Q13 Fox,* September 5, 2014. Accessed October 10, 2014. http://q13fox.com/2014/09/05/state-dept-releases-graphic-anti-isis-video-aimed-at-potential-recruits-think-again-turn-away/.

147. Tate, Amethyst. "US, NATO allies form coalition against IS, vow to stop flow of foreign fighters." *International Business Times,* September 5, 2014. Accessed October 10, 2014. http://www.ibtimes.com/us-nato-allies-form-coalition-against-isis-vow-stop-flow-foreign-fighters-1679796.

148. "Remarks With Philippine Foreign Secretary Del Rosario Before Their Meeting." U.S. Department of State, 2014. http://www.state.gov/secretary/remarks/2014/10/233148.htm.

149. "General Debate: 24–30 September 2014." United Nations, September 24–30, 2014. Accessed October 10, 2014. http://www.un.org/en/ga/69/meetings/gadebate/24sep/.

150. Richmond, Jake. "Hagel authorizes up to 1,300 additional troops to deploy to Iraq." *DOD News,* December 19, 2014. Accessed January 1, 2014. http://www.defense.gov/news/ newsarticle.aspx?id=123863.

151. Charlton, Corey. "American troops battle ISIS for the first time as they see off attempted attack by militants on Iraqi base." *Daily Mail.* December 18, 2014. Accessed December 19, 2014. http://www.dailymail.co.uk/news/article-2878897/American-troops-battle-ISIS-time-attempted-attack-militants-Iraqi-base.html.

152. Fattah, Zainab and Aziz Alwan. "U.S. soldiers fight Islamic State in Iraq, Kurds advance." *Bloomberg,* December 20, 2014. Accessed January 22, 2015. http://www.bloomberg. com/news/2014-12-20/u-s-troops-fight-islamic-state-in-western-iraq-al-jazeera-says.html.

153. "Authorization for the use of military force against ISIL." U.S. Department of State, 2014. http://www.state.gov/secretary/remarks/2014/12/234876.htm.

154. Stewart, Phil and Mark Hosenball. "U.S. moves rescue assets to Iraq in fight against Islamic State." *Reuters*, February 5, 2015. Accessed March 31, 2015. http://www.reuters.com/article/2015/02/05/us-mideast-iraq-usa-idUSKBN0L92VT20150205.

155. Moon Cronk, Terri. "U.S. troops to train Syrian opposition could number 1,000." *DoD News*, January 16, 2015. Accessed February 18, 2015. http://www.defense.gov/news/newsarticle.aspx?id=123989.

156. Ibid.

157. "Remarks by the President in State of the Union Address January 20, 2015." *White House*, January 20, 2015. Accessed February 18, 2015. http://www.whitehouse.gov/the-press-office/2015/01/20/remarks-president-state-union-address-january-20-2015.

158. "The authorization of military force against ISIL terrorists: What you need to know." *White House*, February 11, 2015. Accessed February 16, 2015. http://www.whitehouse.gov/blog/2015/02/11/authorization-military-force-against-isil-terrorists-what-you-need-know.

159. Evans, Michael. "Russia and Iran attack IS jihadists." *CNN*, August 11, 2014. Accessed October 13, 2014. http://ireport.cnn.com/docs/DOC-1160609.

160. Spence, Katie. "Move over, America: Russia responds to IS by sending warplanes to Iraq." *Motley Fool*, July 5, 2014. Accessed October 13, 2014. http://www.fool.com/investing/general/2014/07/05/move-over-america-russia-responds-to-isis-by-sendi.aspx.

161. Smith, Alexander. "Russia tells Iraq it's 'ready' to support fight against IS." *NBC News*, September 26, 2014. Accessed October 13, 2014. http://www.nbcnews.com/storyline/isis-terror/coalition-airstrikes-pound-isis-target-syria-n224571.

162. "Putin looking at cooperatoin to fight Islamic State." *Jerusalem Post*, September 22, 2014. Accessed October 13, 2014. http://www.jpost.com/Breaking-News/Putin-looking-at-cooperation-to-fight-Islamic-State-376025.

163. Wan, William. "U.S. urges China to help with Islamic State in Iraq." *Washington Post*, September 9, 2014. Accessed October 10, 2014. http://www.washingtonpost.com/world/us-urges-china-to-help-with-islamic-state-in-iraq/2014/09/09/4f73ac90-3823-11e4-9c9f-ebb47272e40e_story.html.

164. Wong, Edward. "Iraqis identify prisoner as Chinese Islamist fighter." *NY Times*, September 4, 2014. Accessed October 10, 2014. http://www.nytimes.com/2014/09/05/world/middleeast/iraqis-identify-prisoner-as-chinese-islamist-fighter.html.

165. Ibid.

166. Smith-Spark, Laura. "UK: Warplanes are set to strike in Iraq, but are gathering intel for now." *CNN,* September 28, 2014. Accessed October, 13, 2014. http://www.cnn.com/2014/09/27/world/meast/uk-isis-iraq/.

167. Ibid.

168. Young, Sarah. "British role in Iraq will not involve ground forces: Cameron." *Reuters,* August 18, 2014. Accessed October, 13, 2014. http://www.reuters.com/article/2014/08/18/us-iraq-security-britain-idUSKBN0GI0JH20140818. Swinford, Steven and Ben Farmer. "UK jets deployed to stop advance of Islamic State in Iraq." *Telegraph*, August 18, 2014, 13, 2014. http://www.telegraph.co.uk/news/worldnews/middleeast/iraq/11040290/UK-jets-deployed-to-stop-advance-of-Islamic-State-in-Iraq.html.

169. Ritzen, Yarno and Mohsin Ali. "Interactive: Countries countering ISIL." *Al Jazeera,* October 15, 2014. Accessed November 3, 2014. http://www.aljazeera.com/indepth/interactive/2014/10/isil-us-syria-airstrike-coalition-uae-saudi-2014101142731382476.html.

170. Swinford, Steven and Ben Farmer. "UK jets deployed to stop advance of Islamic State in Iraq." *Telegraph*, August 18, 2014, 13, 2014. http://www.telegraph.co.uk/news/worldnews/middleeast/iraq/11040290/UK-jets-deployed-to-stop-advance-of-Islamic-State-in-Iraq.html Ritzen, Yarno and Mohsin Ali. "Interactive: Countries countering ISIL." *Al Jazeera,* October 15, 2014. Accessed November 3, 2014. http://www.aljazeera.com/indepth/interactive/2014/10/isil-us-syria-airstrike-coalition-uae-saudi-2014101142731382476.html.

171. Levis, John and Jetrho Mullen. "Britain vows to 'confront' the IS 'menace' after killing of David Haines." *CNN,* September 14, 2014. Accessed October, 13, 2014. http://www.cnn.com/2014/09/14/world/meast/isis-david-haines-beheading/index.html?hpt=hp_t1.

172. Mason, Rowena. "David Cameron: IS is planning to attack UK." *Reuters*, June 18, 2014. Accessed October 10, 2014. http://www.theguardian.com/politics/2014/jun/18/david-cameron-iraq-crisis-not-dismissed.

173. "Radical preacher Anjem Choudary released after terror arrest." *ITV*, September 26, 2014. Accessed November 3, 2014. http://www.itv.com/news/story/2014-09-26/radical-preacher-anjem-choudary-released-after-terror-arrest/.

174. "Six arrested by anti-terror police." *BBC News*, October 14, 2014. Accessed November 3, 2014. http://www.bbc.com/news/uk-29610742.

175. "IS releases video showing beheading of Alan Henning." *NBC News*, October 3, 2014. Accessed October 10, 2014. http://www.nbcnews.com/storyline/isis-terror/isis-releases-video-showing-beheading-alan-henning-n208816.

176. James, William and Andrew Osborn. "Britain sends drones to fly surveillance missions over Syria." *Reuters*, October 21, 2014. Accessed November 3, 2014. http://www.reuters.com/article/2014/10/21/us-mideast-crisis-britain-idUSKCN0IA0WI20141021.

177. "General Debate: 24–30 September 2014." *United Nations*, September 24–30. Accessed October 10, 2014. http://www.un.org/en/ga/69/meetings/gadebate/24sep/.

178. "France carries out fresh round of air strikes in Iraq." *Al Arabiya*, September 25, 2014. Accessed October, 10, 2014. http://english.alarabiya.net/en/News/middle-east/2014/09/25/Cameron.

179. Fantz, Ashley. "Who is doing what in the coalition battle against IS?" *CNN*, September 17, 2014. Accessed October, 10, 2014 http://www.cnn.com/2014/09/14/world/meast/isis-coalition-nations/.Ritzen, Yarno and Mohsin Ali. "Interactive: Countries countering ISIL." *Al Jazeera*, October 15, 2014. Accessed November 3, 2014. http://www.aljazeera.com/indepth/interactive/2014/10/isil-us-syria-airstrike-coalition-uae-saudi-2014101142731382476.html.

180. "France to send arms to Iraqi Kurds." *Al Jazeera*, August 13, 2014. Accessed October, 10, 2014. http://www.aljazeera.com/news/middleeast/2014/08/france-supply-weapons-iraqi-kurdistan-2014813143856260983.html.

181. Ward, Jillian and Gregory Viscusi. "France urges Europe to arm Kurds to battle Islamic State." *Bloomberg*, August 12, 2014. Accessed October, 10, 2014. http://www.bloomberg.com/news/2014-08-12/france-urges-europe-to-arm-kurds-to-battle-islamic-state.html.

182. "General Debate: 24–30 September 2014." *United Nations*, September 24–30. Accessed October 10, 2014. http://www.un.org/en/ga/69/meetings/gadebate/24sep/.

183. "Germany supplies arms and ammunition to Kurdish forces in Iraq." *Economic Times*, September 27, 2014. Accessed October, 10, 2014. http://articles.economictimes.indiatimes.com/2014-09-27/news/54377054_1_kurdish-forces-kurdish-peshmerga-arms-and-ammunition.

184. "German lawmakers want debate on supplying arms to Kurds." *DW*, August 21, 2014. Accessed October, 10, 2014. http://www.dw.de/german-lawmakers-want-debate-on-supplying-arms-to-kurds/a-17868904.

185. "Germany debates arms shipments for Kurdish fighters." *DW*, August 12, 2014. Accessed October, 10, 2014. http://www.dw.de/germany-debates-arms-shipments-for-kurdish-fighters/a-17846758. Martin, Michelle. "Germany sends first plane carrying aid to northern Iraq." *Reuters*, August 15, 2014. Accessed October, 10, 2014. http://www.reuters.com/article/2014/08/15/us-iraq-security-germany-idUSKBN0GF0JT20140815.

186. Smale, Alison. "Germany steps up its response to global security crises." *NY Times*, August 31, 2014. Accessed October, 10, 2014. http://www.nytimes.com/2014/09/01/world/europe/germany-steps-up-its-response-to-global-security-crises.html. Ritzen, Yarno and Mohsin Ali. "Interactive: Countries countering ISIL." *Al Jazeera*, October 15, 2014. Accessed November 3, 2014. http://www.aljazeera.com/indepth/interactive/2014/10/isil-us-syria-airstrike-coalition-uae-saudi-2014101142731382476.html.

187. Ritzen, Yarno and Mohsin Ali. "Interactive: Countries countering ISIL." *Al Jazeera*, October 15, 2014. Accessed November 3, 2014. http://www.aljazeera.com/indepth/interactive/2014/10/isil-us-syria-airstrike-coalition-uae-saudi-2014101142731382476.html.

188. Eddy, Melissa. "Germany bans support for IS." *NY Times*, September 12, 2014. Accessed October, 10, 2014. http://www.nytimes.com/2014/09/13/world/europe/germany-bans-support-of-isis.html.

189. "Brussels Jewish Museum killer was IS torturer." *Times of Israel*, September 6, 2014. Accessed October 27, 2014. http://www.timesofisrael.com/brussels-jewish-museum-shooter-was-member-of-islamic-state/.

190. Traynor, Ian. "Couple returning from Syria 'were plotting assault on EU Brussels office.'" *Guardian*, September 21, 2014. Accessed October 10, 2014. http://www.theguardian.com/world/2014/sep/21/couple-returning-belgium-syria-plotted-assault-eu-berlaymont-building-brussels.

191. "Belgium takes action to bring down IS recruiting network." *Daily Sabah*, September 30, 2014. Accessed October 10, 2014. http://www.dailysabah.com/europe/2014/09/30/belgium-takes-action-to-bring-down-isis-recruiting-network.

192. "Belgium joins US-led coalition to fight IS." *Daily Star*, September 26, 2014. Accessed October 10, 2014. http://www.dailystar.com.lb/News/Middle-East/2014/Sep-26/272115-belgium-joins-us-led-coalition-to-fight-isis.ashx#axzz3EocXKVRI.

193. Ritzen, Yarno and Mohsin Ali. "Interactive: Countries countering ISIL." *Al Jazeera*, October 15, 2014. Accessed November 3, 2014. http://www.aljazeera.com/indepth/interactive/2014/10/isil-us-syria-airstrike-coalition-uae-saudi-2014101142731382476.html.

194. "Danish Parliament approves military contribution to Iraq." Ministry of Foreign Affairs of Denmark, August 27, 2014. Accessed October 10, 2014. http://um.dk/en/news/newsdisplaypage/?newsid=03254085-63a8-4df6-ab0f-d396b7c7ffba.

195. "Denmark joins coalition against Islamic State group." *Fox News*, September 26, 2014. Accessed October 10, 2014. http://www.foxnews.com/world/2014/09/26/denmark-joins-coalition-against-islamic-state-group/.

196. Ritzen, Yarno and Mohsin Ali. "Interactive: Countries countering ISIL." *Al Jazeera*, October 15, 2014. Accessed November 3, 2014. http://www.aljazeera.com/indepth/interactive/2014/10/isil-us-syria-airstrike-coalition-uae-saudi-2014101142731382476.html.

197. "IS sets sights on Denmark as EU nation wades into Iraq crisis." *RT*, August 29, 2014. Accessed October 10, 2014. http://rt.com/news/183732-isis-denmark-jihad-security/.

198. "Pictured: Danish lone wolf 'jihadi' who was gunned down by police." *Daily Mail*, February 14, 2015. Accessed February 15, 2015. http://www.dailymail.co.uk/news/article-2953594/Shots-fired-Copenhagen-cafe-free-speech-event.html. "Denmark named in new Isis propaganda video." *Local*, September 23, 2014. Accessed October 10, 2014. http://www.thelocal.dk/20140923/denmark-named-in-new-isis-propaganda-video/.

199. Hooper, Simon. "Denmark introduces rehab for Syrian fighters." *Al Jazeera*, September 7, 2014. Accessed October 10, 2014. http://www.aljazeera.com/indepth/features/2014/09/denmark-introduces-rehab-syrian-fighters-201496125229948625.html.

200. "Danish mosque openly backs Islamic State's campaign of terror." *RT*, September 2, 2014. Accessed October, 10, 2014. http://rt.com/news/184600-isis-denmark-support-mosque/.

201. Ritzen, Yarno and Mohsin Ali. "Interactive: Countries countering ISIL." *Al Jazeera*, October 15, 2014. Accessed November 3, 2014. http://www.aljazeera.com/indepth/interactive/2014/10/isil-us-syria-airstrike-coalition-uae-saudi-2014101142731382476.html.

202. Lageman, Thessa. "Islamic State fears take hold in Netherlands." *Al Jazeera*, September 5, 2014. Accessed October, 13, 2014. http://www.aljazeera.com/indepth/features/2014/09/islamic-state-fears-take-hold-netherlands-201492131426326526.html.

203. Sengupta, Somini. "Nations trying to stop their citizens from going to Middle East to fight for IS." *NY Times*, September 12, 2014. Accessed October, 13, 2014. http://www.nytimes.com/2014/09/13/world/middleeast/isis-recruits-prompt-laws-against-foreign-fighters.html.

204. Fantz, Ashley. "Who is doing what in the coalition battle against IS?" *CNN*, September 17, 2014. Accessed October, 13, 2014. http://www.cnn.com/2014/09/14/world/meast/isis-coalition-nations/.

205. "Italy will not take part in air strikes against Isis." *The Local*, September 15, 2014. Accessed October, 10, 2014. http://www.thelocal.it/20140915/italy-will-not-take-part-in-air-strikes-against-isis.

206. "U.S hits IS with airstrike in Syria." *CBS News*, September 22, 2014. Accessed October, 10, 2014. http://www.cbsnews.com/news/u-s-launches-first-airstrikes-against-isis-in-syria/.

207. Ritzen, Yarno and Mohsin Ali. "Interactive: Countries countering ISIL." *Al Jazeera,* October 15, 2014. Accessed November 3, 2014. http://www.aljazeera.com/indepth/interactive/2014/10/isil-us-syria-airstrike-coalition-uae-saudi-2014101142731382476.html.

208. "IS targeting Rome and Italy says Italian minister Alfano." *Ansa Med,* September 9, 2014. Accessed October, 10, 2014. http://www.ansamed.info/ansamed/en/news/sections/generalnews/2014/09/09/isis-targeting-rome-and-italy-says-italian-minister-alfano_4a5b0df9-c76d-438b-a243-37c50c2bb962.html.

209. Grant, Madeline. "IS threat against Pope 'Nothing Serious,' says Vatican." *Newsweek,* August 29, 2014. Accessed October, 10, 2014. http://www.newsweek.com/isis-threat-against-pope-nothing-serious-says-vatican-267583.

210. Freeman, Colin. "Who is in the anti-Islamic State coalition and what are they contributing." *Telegraph,* September 26, 2014. Accessed November 3, 2014. http://www.telegraph.co.uk/news/worldnews/middleeast/syria/11124070/Who-is-in-the-anti-Islamic-State-coalition-and-what-they-are-contributing.html.

211. "Sweden raises estimate of citizens joining Islamic State." *Ynet News,* October 22, 2014. Accessed November 3, 2014. http://www.ynetnews.com/articles/0,7340,L-4583000,00.html.

212. Fantz, Ashley. "Who is doing what in the coalition battle against IS?" *CNN,* September 17, 2014. Accessed October 10, 2014. http://www.cnn.com/2014/09/14/world/meast/isis-coalition-nations/.

213. Hurst, Daniel. "Australian cabinet to sign off on military action in Iraq within days, Julie Bishop says." *Guardian,* September 28, 2014. Accessed October 10, 2014. http://www.theguardian.com/world/2014/sep/28/cabinet-to-sign-off-on-military-action-in-iraq-within-days-julie-bishop-says.

214. Ritzen, Yarno and Mohsin Ali. "Interactive: Countries countering ISIL." *Al Jazeera,* October 15, 2014. Accessed November 3, 2014. http://www.aljazeera.com/indepth/interactive/2014/10/isil-us-syria-airstrike-coalition-uae-saudi-2014101142731382476.html.

215. "Foreign Minister Julie Bishop confirms Australian special forces will be deployed in Iraq." *Sydney Morning Herald,* October 20, 2014. Accessed November 3, 2014. http://www.smh.com.au/federal-politics/political-news/foreign-minister-julie-bishop-confirms-australian-special-forces-will-be-deployed-in-iraq-20141020-118iql.html.

216. "Indian government looking to crack down on IS sympathisers." *DNA India,* August 28, 2014. Accessed October, 10, 2014. http://www.dnaindia.com/india/report-indian-government-looking-to-crack-down-on-isis-sympathisers-2014541.

217. "Indian Muslims unequivocally condemn brutal atrocities of IS." *Two Circles,* August 19, 2014. Accessed October, 10, 2014. http://twocircles.net/2014aug19/indian_muslims_unequivocally_condemn_brutal_atrocities_isis.html#.VBiCgy55Mgp.

218. "Government should reflect on what is leading some Indian youths to join IS: Manish Tewari." *DNA India,* September 14, 2014. Accessed October 10, 2014. http://www.dnaindia.com/india/report-government-should-reflect-on-what-is-leading-some-indian-youths-to-join-isis-manish-tewari-2018560.

219. "Indian Muslims unequivocally condemn brutal atrocities of IS." *Two Circles,* August 19, 2014. Accessed October 10, 2014. http://twocircles.net/2014aug19/indian_muslims_unequivocally_condemn_brutal_atrocities_isis.html#.VBiCgy55Mgp.

220. Taylor, Rob, Alexander Martin, and Te-Ping Chen. "Obama gets backing on plan to beat back Islamic State." *Wall Street Journal,* September 11, 2014. Accessed October 10, 2014. http://online.wsj.com/articles/obama-gets-backing-on-plan-to-beat-back-islamic-state-1410410994.

221. Kyodo, Jiji. "Japan rules out military support as U.S.-led coalition takes fight to Islamic State group." *Japan Times,* September 16, 2014. Accessed October 10, 2014. http://www.japantimes.co.jp/news/2014/09/16/national/japan-rules-out-military-support-as-u-s-led-coalition-takes-fight-to-islamic-state-group/#.VDf_Rr5N3zJ.

222. Schemm, Paul. "Morocco police announce arrest of 2 suspected members of Islamic State group amid terror alert." *U.S. News,* August 22, 2014. Accessed October 13, 2014. http://www.usnews.com/news/world/articles/2014/08/22/morocco-arrests-suspected-islamic-state-members.

223. "Morocco dismantles IS recruitment cell." *Times of Israel*, September 12, 2014. Accessed October 13, 2014. http://www.timesofisrael.com/morocco-dismantles-is-recruitment-cell/.

224. Grant, Madeline. "Boko Haram Seek to Imitate 'Inspirational' Islamic State and Establish African Caliphate." *Newsweek,* September 11, 2014. Accessed October 13, 2014. http://www.newsweek.com/boko-haram-seek-imitate-inspirational-islamic-state-and-establish-north-african-269884.

225. "General Debate: 24–30 September 2014." *United Nations*, September 24–30. Accessed October 10, 2014. http://www.un.org/en/ga/69/meetings/gadebate/24sep/.

226. Khan, Hasan. "Pakistanis, Afghans reject ISIL 'caliphate' as anti-Islam." *Al-Shorfa*, July 10, 2014. Accessed October 13, 2014. http://al-shorfa.com/en_GB/articles/meii/features/2014/07/10/feature-02.

227. "General Debate: 24–30 September 2014." *United Nations*, September 24–30. Accessed October 10, 2014. http://www.un.org/en/ga/69/meetings/gadebate/24sep/.

228. Kapelos, Vassy and Laura Stone. "EXCLUSIVE: U.S. says Canada offered to help in Iraq—not the other way around." *Global News*, September 25, 2014. Accessed October 10, 2014. http://globalnews.ca/news/1583315/exclusive-u-s-says-canada-offered-to-help-in-iraq-not-the-other-way-around/.

229. Fantz, Ashley. "Who is doing what in the coalition battle against IS?" *CNN*, September 17, 2014. Accessed October 10, 2014. http://www.cnn.com/2014/09/14/world/meast/isis-coalition-nations/. Ritzen, Yarno and Mohsin Ali. "Interactive: Countries countering ISIL." *Al-Jazeera,* October 15, 2014. Accessed November 3, 2014. http://www.aljazeera.com/indepth/interactive/2014/10/isil-us-syria-airstrike-coalition-uae-saudi-2014101142731382476.html.

230. "Arab League chief: Confront Islamic State group." *Washington Post,* September 7, 2014. Accessed October 10, 2014. http://www.washingtonpost.com/world/middle_east/iraqi-governor-wounded-during-islamic-state-clash/2014/09/07/5bd68192-368e-11e4-a023-1d61f7f31a05_story.html.

231. "Arab League agrees to combat Islamic State group." *Washington Post,* September 8, 2014. Accessed October 14, 2014. http://www.washingtonpost.com/world/middle_east/arab-league-agrees-to-combat-islamic-state-group/2014/09/08/f804a064-374f-11e4-a023-1d61f7f31a05_story.html.

232. "Arab League pledges to tackle Islamic State." *Al Jazeera,* September 7, 2014. Accessed October 10, 2014. http://www.aljazeera.com/news/middleeast/2014/09/arab-league-islamic-state-201497164726900705.html.

233. "Council of the European Union." *Consilium.Europa,* June 23, 2014. Accessed October 10, 2014. http://www.consilium.europa.eu/uedocs/cms_data/docs/pressdata/EN/foraff/143347.pdf.

234. Croft, Adrian and Barbara Lewis. "EU gives European governments go-ahead to arm Iraqi Kurds." *Reuters,* August 15, 2014. Accessed October 10, 2014. http://www.reuters.com/article/2014/08/15/us-iraq-security-arms-idUSKBN0GF1CY20140815.

235. "EU pledges aid, arms to Iraqi Kurds as Islamic State militants continue advance." *Japan Times,* August 16, 2014. Accessed October 10, 2014. http://www.japantimes.co.jp/news/2014/08/16/world/eu-pledges-aid-arms-to-iraqi-kurds-as-islamic-state-militants-continue-advance/#.U_Ni9PldWSo.

236. "EU Counter-Terrorism Chief: Flow of Europeans to IS 'Isn't Drying Up.'" *Business Insider*, September 24, 2014. Accessed October 10, 2014. http://www.businessinsider.com/eu-counter-terrorism-chief-flow-of-europeans-to-isis-isnt-drying-up-2014-9.

237. Ibid.

238. "EU steps-up sanctions against Assad's regime." *Dow Jones Business News,* October 20, 2014. Accessed November 3, 2014. http://www.nasdaq.com/article/eu-stepsup-sanctions-against-assads-regime-20141020-00888.

239. Beattie, Victor and Selah Hennessy. "EU launches anti-terrorism projects with Muslim countries." *Voice of America*, January 19, 2015. Accessed February 5, 2015. http://www.voanews.com/content/terrorism-threat-to-dominate-eu-talks/2604206.html.

240. "UN declares highest level of emergency in Iraq over IS advance." *RT,* August 13, 2014. Accessed October 10, 2014. http://rt.com/news/180160-un-highest-emergency-isis-iraq/.

241. "Emergencies | OCHA." Unocha.org. 2014. Accessed November 3 2014. http://www. unocha.org/where-we-work/emergencies.

242. "UN moves to rein in Islamic State group." *Al Jazeera,* August 16, 2014. Accessed October 10, 2014. http://www.aljazeera.com/news/middleeast/2014/08/un-moves-rein-islamic-state-group-2014815191831901897.html.

243. Lederer, Edith M. "Security Council orders Islamic State to disband." *Times of Israel,* August 16, 2014. Accessed October 10, 2014. http://www.timesofisrael.com/security-council-orders-islamic-state-to-disband/.

244. "UN moves to rein in Islamic State group." *Al Jazeera,* August 16, 2014. Accessed October 10, 2014. http://www.aljazeera.com/news/middleeast/2014/08/un-moves-rein-islamic-state-group-2014815191831901897.html.

245. Nichols, Michelle. "U.N. Security Council plans to suppress foreign extremist fighters." *Reuters,* September 9, 2014. Accessed October 10, 2014. http://www.reuters.com/article/2014/09/09/us-iraq-crisis-un-idUSKBN0H408E20140909.

246. Ibid.

247. "U.N. sends aid to half a million fleeing violence in Iraq." *Reuters,* August 19, 2014. Accessed October 10, 2014. http://www.reuters.com/article/2014/08/19/us-iraq-un-aid-idUSKBN0GJ0OS20140819.

248. Spencer, Richard. "Iraq crisis: UN condemns 'war crimes' as another town falls to Isis." *Telegraph,* June 16, 2014. Accessed October 10, 2014. http://www.telegraph.co.uk/news/worldnews/middleeast/iraq/10904414/Iraq-crisis-UN-condemns-war-crimes-as-another-town-falls-to-Isis.html.

249. Landler, Mark. "In U.N. Speech, Obama vows to fight IS 'Network of Death.'" *NY Times.* September 25, 2014. Accessed October 25, 2014. http://www.nytimes.com/2014/09/25/world/middleeast/obama-syria-un-isis.html?_r=0.

250. Szep, Jason. "U.S. courts skeptical Arab allies in Islamic State fight." *Reuters,* September 9, 2014. Accessed October 10, 2014. http://www.reuters.com/article/2014/09/09/us-usa-kerry-mideast-idUSKBN0H32DV20140909.

251. "General Debate: 24–30 September 2014." United Nations, September 24–30. Accessed October 10, 2014. http://www.un.org/en/ga/69/meetings/gadebate/24sep/.

252. Masi, Alessandria. "NATO Coalition Against IS: Turkey Role Mostly Symbolic." *International Business Times,* September 7, 2014. Accessed October 10, 2014. http://www.ibtimes.com/nato-coalition-against-isis-turkey-role-mostly-symbolic-1680708.

253. Dahlburg, John-Thor. "NATO: We must confront threats from Russia, IS." *Daily Star,* September 15, 2014. Accessed October 10, 2014. http://www.dailystar.com.lb/News/Middle-East/2014/Sep-15/270740-nato-we-must-confront-threats-from-russia-isis.ashx.

254. Ibid.

255. Sobczyk, Marcin. "NATO ready to defend Turkey from violence in Syria." *Wall Street Journal,* October 6, 2014. Accessed October 10, 2014. http://online.wsj.com/articles/nato-ready-to-defend-turkey-from-violence-in-syria-1412602876.

256. Tiezzi, Shannon. "The new, improved Shanghai Cooperation Organization." *Diplomat,* September 13, 2014. Accessed October 10, 2014. http://thediplomat.com/2014/09/the-new-improved-shanghai-cooperation-organization/.

257. Sands, Gary. "China and the IS threat." *Diplomat,* September 26, 2014. Accessed October 10, 2014. http://thediplomat.com/2014/09/china-and-the-isis-threat/.

258. "IAEA statement on seized nuclear material in Iraq." International Atomic Energy Agency, July 10, 2014. Accessed October 10, 2014. http://www.iaea.org/press/?p=4644.

259. Coles, Isabel. "'Terrorists' help U.S. in battle against Islamic State in Iraq." *Reuters,* August 21, 2014. Accessed October 9, 2014. http://www.reuters.com/article/2014/08/21/us-iraq-security-pkk-insight-idUSKBN0GL1H420140821.

260. Boudlal, Youssef. "Kurdish militants train hundreds of Yazidis to fight Islamic State." *Reuters,* August 18, 2014. Accessed October 9, 2014. http://www.reuters.com/article/2014/08/18/us-syria-crisis-yazidis-idUSKBN0GH0G220140818.

261. "Islamic State video purports to show Kurdish peshmerga forces." *Reuters,* March 20, 2015. Accessed March 23, 2015. http://www.reuters.com/article/2015/03/20/us-mideast-crisis-islamicstate-beheading-idUSKBN0MG0VH20150320.

262. "Iraqi Kurds 'fully control Kirkuk' as army flees." *BBC News*, June 12, 2014. Access November 3, 2014. http://www.bbc.com/news/world-middle-east-27809051.

263. "Iraq conflict: Kurds seize two oilfields in north." *BBC News*, July 12, 2014. Accessed November 3, 2014. http://www.bbc.com/news/world-middle-east-28265064.

264. Ibid.

265. Rasheed, Ahmed and Raheem Salman. "Islamic State grabs Iraqi dam and oil field in victory over Kurds." *Reuters,* August 3, 2014. Accessed November 3, 2014. http://www.reuters.com/article/2014/08/03/us-iraq-security-idUSKBN0G20FU20140803. "US air strikes helping Kurdish, Iraqi forces retake Mosul dam from Islamic State." *Fox News,* August 17, 2014. Accessed November 3, 2014. http://www.foxnews.com/politics/2014/08/17/us-air-strikes-helping-kurdish-iraqi-forces-retake-mosul-dam-for-islamic-state/.

Rasheed, Ahmed and Michael Georgy. "Backed by U.S. strikes, Iraq Kurds retake strategic dam: officials." *Reuters,* August 18, 2014. Accessed November 5, 2014. http://www.reuters.com/article/2014/08/18/us-iraq-security-idUSKBN0GH0JL20140818.

266. Eleftheriou-Smith, Loulla-Mae. "Kurdish female suicide bomber attacks Isis in fight for Kobani." *Independent,* October 6, 2014. Accessed October, 11, 2014. http://www.independent.co.uk/news/world/middle-east/kurdish-female-suicide-bomber-attacks-isis-in-fight-for-kobani-9776779.html.

267. Rasheed, Ahmed and Michael Georgy. "Backed by U.S. strikes, Iraq Kurds retake strategic dam: officials." *Reuters*, August 18, 2014. Accessed November 3, 2014. http://www.reuters.com/article/2014/10/12/us-mideast-crisis-idUSKCN0I10SR20141012.

268. "Kerry: Saving Kobane not part of strategy." *Al Jazeera,* October 12, 2014. Accessed November 3, 2014. http://www.aljazeera.com/news/middleeast/2014/10/kerry-saving-kobane-not-part-strategy-2014101223481559892.html.

269. Semple, Kirk and Tim Arango. "Kurdish rebels assail Turkish inaction on IS as peril to peace talks." *International NY Times,* October 12, 2014. Accessed November 3, 2014. http://www.nytimes.com/2014/10/13/world/middleeast/kurdish-rebels-assail-turkish-inaction-on-isis-as-peril-to-peace-talks.html.

270. "Germany to send rifles, tank busters to aid Kurds fighting Islamic extremists in Iraq." *570 News,* August 31, 2014. Accessed November 3, 2014. http://www.570news.com/2014/08/31/germany-to-send-rifles-tank-busters-to-aid-kurds-fighting-islamic-extremists-in-iraq/.

271. Perry, Tom and Alison Williams. "Syrian Kurds get arms from Iraq, but cannot send them to Kobani." *Reuters,* October 14, 2014. Accessed November 3, 2014. http://mobile.reuters.com/article/idUSKCN0I30U420141014?irpc=932.

272. "Islamic State crisis: Kurds 'recapture key Kobane hill.'" *BBC News*, October 14, 2014. Accessed November 3, 2014. http://www.bbc.com/news/world-middle-east-29611673.

273. "In the fight against IS, Islam is part of the Solution." *Daily Beast*, September 28, 2014. Accessed October 10, 2014. http://www.thedailybeast.com/articles/2014/09/28/in-the-fight-against-isis-islam-is-part-of-the-solution.html.

274. "U.S., World Muslim Leaders' open letter refutes IS's ideology, urges supporters to 'Repent,' 'Return to the Religion of Mercy.'" Council on American-Islamic Relations, September 24, 2014. Accessed October 10, 2014. http://www.cair.com/press-center/press-releases/12663-muslim-leaders-open-letter-refutes-isis-ideology.html.

275. "Prominent scholars declare IS caliphate 'null and void.'" *Middle East Monitor*, July 5, 2014. Accessed October 10, 2014. https://www.middleeastmonitor.com/news/middle-east/12567-prominent-scholars-declare-isis-caliphate-null-and-void.

276. "Indonesian Muslims denounce IS ideology." *Jakarta Globe*, August 3, 2014. Accessed October 10, 2014. http://thejakartaglobe.beritasatu.com/news/indonesian-muslims-denounce-isis-ideology/.

277. Ryan, Tim. "Denver religious leaders want IS stopped." *9 News*, August 11, 2014. Accessed, October 13, 2014. http://www.9news.com/story/news/local/2014/08/11/denver-religious-leaders-want-isis-stopped/13915891/.

278. "Hundreds of Calgary Muslims protest IS violence in Iraq." *CBC News*, June 21, 2014. Accessed October 10, 2014. http://www.cbc.ca/news/canada/calgary/hundreds-of-calgary-muslims-protest-isis-violence-in-iraq-1.2683589.

279. Malik, Shiv. "Shia cleric tells British Muslims not to join fight against Isis in Iraq." *Guardian*, June 15, 2014. Accessed October 10, 2014. http://www.theguardian.com/world/2014/jun/15/shia-british-muslims-fight-isis-iraq.

280. Serinci, Deniz. "Global protests against IS attack on Christians." *Rudaw*, August 2, 2014. Accessed October 10, 2014. http://rudaw.net/english/world/020820141.

281. Rodgriguez, Meredith. "Chicago-area Assyrians march against IS, others protest airstrikes." *Chicago Tribune*, August 8, 2014. Accessed October 10, 2014. http://www.chicagotribune.com/news/local/breaking/chi-chicagoarea-assyrians-march-against-isis-others-protest-airstrikes-20140808-story.html.

282. Tomlinson, Simon. "The burn IS Flag Challenge: Outraged Muslims flood web with their version of the Ice Bucket Challenge in protest against Islamic State barbarism." *Dailymail*, September 8, 2014. Accessed October 10, 2014. http://www.dailymail.co.uk/news/article-2747644/The-Burn-IS-Flag-Challenge-Outraged-Muslims-flood-web-version-Ice-Bucket-Challenge-protest-against-Islamic-State-barbarism.html.

283. Birnbaum, Michael. "Belgian Muslims face renewed anger, alienation after attacks in Paris." *Washington Post*, January 15, 2015. Accessed February 18, 2015. http://www.washingtonpost.com/world/europe/after-paris-attacks-belgian-muslims-face-renewed-fight/2015/01/14/823d8f40-9b62-11e4-96cc-e858eba91ced_story.html?hpid=z9.

284. Faiola, Anthony. "New far-right anti-immigrant sentiment hits German streets." *Washington Post*, January 24, 2015. Accessed February 18, 2015. http://www.washingtonpost.com/world/europe/new-far-right-anti-immigrant-sentiment-hits-german-streets/2015/01/23/dd23ec5c-a282-11e4-9f89-561284a573f8_story.html?tid=pm_world_pop.

285. Ibid.

286. Fantz, Ashley. "Slain North Carolina couple and sister remembered as generous, loving." *CNN*, February 11, 2015. Accessed February 13, 2015. http://www.cnn.com/2015/02/11/us/chapel-hill-shooting-victims/index.html.

287. Saeed, Ahmed and Catherine Shoichet. "3 students shot to death in apartment near UNC Chapel Hill." *CNN*, February 11, 2015. Accessed February 13, 2015. http://www.cnn.com/2015/02/11/us/chapel-hill-shooting/index.html.

Chapter Seven

Conclusions and Recommendations

This chapter provides conclusions and recommendations about the Islamic State and related topics, including the quasi-state's effects of instability on the region. Also discussed are the unprecedented regional and global alliances that have been forged in order to combat the challenges of the IS. In addition, we review the costs involved, security implications drawn, and the lessons learned of what works and what does not when combating terror groups.

INSTABILITY FOR THE REGION

Civil wars, as are occurring in Iraq and Syria, often have manifold destructive spillover consequences. Among the five principal effects of civil wars are the following:

- *Humanitarian crisis* (refugees, whether traversing areas within or outside their territory, are victimized)
- *Terrorism* (civil wars can serve as breeding grounds of terrorism, creating power vacuums that enable terror groups to prosper)
- *Secessionism* (subgroups within countries—whether religious, ethnic, or otherwise—often seek independence)
- *Radicalization* (the nature of civil wars often instills a process of embracing extremist ideologies against the state, opposing parties, or groups), and
- *Intervention* (regional and international powers often participate in the conflict in their quest to influence outcomes and establish stability).[1]

HUMANITARIAN CRISIS: FLOOD OF REFUGEES

More specifically, the ramifications of millions of Iraqi and Syrian refugees pouring into Turkey, Lebanon, and Jordan, coupled with internal displacement, are complex, variegated, and serious for refugees and recipient countries alike. The source nations also lose the important contributions that these refugees could otherwise provide in their roles as consumers, workers, businessmen, technologists, artisans, and in other walks of life.[2] In a region full of precarious power-sharing structures, demographic shifts brought on by refugee flows can have dire implications, including the destabilizing of sovereign states with influxes of otherwise ideologically or politically aligned persons.

In October 2014, the UN High Commissioner for Refugees (UNHCR) reported that there were 3,024,494 registered Syrian refugees, about one-seventh of a population of twenty-three million.[3] These persons have been displaced to five principal countries: Lebanon (1,133,834), Turkey (1,065,902), Jordan (619,376), Iraq (222,468), and Egypt (140,130).[4] The newly arrived Syrian refugees have vast and stark needs that must be met by host nations, international organizations, and donors. Among such requirements are "food, rent, and basic items (blankets, clothes, kitchen utensils, plastic buckets/jerry cans)."[5]

Of note as well, "the most vulnerable [refugee] families include those whose household expenditures exceed the identified average minimum expenditure basket and those families with large family size, large number of children or who live in crowded conditions."[6] Also, "Winter will add additional concerns for families including the need for heating fuel, warm clothes, reinforced winterized shelters and additional blankets."[7]

By March 2015, the UN estimated that about half the Syrian population had been displaced. "Of the displaced, nearly 4 million have been forced to flee to the nearby countries of Lebanon, Turkey, Jordan, Iraq and Egypt."[8] In light of the situation, international donors pledged $3.8 billion in humanitarian aid to the Syrian crisis, including to countries that are hosting Syrian refugees.[9]

With regard to another acute humanitarian impact, Iraq "is not only receiving large numbers of Syrian refugees, but is also seeing the return of many Iraqi refugees, particularly from Syria. Often these returnees cannot go back to their places of origin, leading to new secondary displacement inside Iraq."[10] As of January 2014, there were 954,128 internally displaced people in Iraq, while 350,000 Syrian refugees had that same status in December 2013.[11] During 2014, more than two million Iraqis left their homes in anticipation of advances by IS forces. Also, nearly "half of the Iraqis fleeing their communities this year have crowded into Iraqi Kurdistan, already home to more than 200,000 Syrian refugees."[12]

TERRORISM: ENDEMIC

Within the contexts of the Syrian and Iraqi civil wars, terrorism has become endemic. A full array of modi operandi—bombings, suicide bombings, kidnappings, and gunfire, to name a few—and a wide range of targets (government, business, non-profits, non-governmental organizations, and civilians) have been put at risk.

Whether undertaken by Shiite- or Sunni-connected terror groups, including state actors such as the governments of Iran, Iraq, Syria, and the Islamic State—through their operatives or linked militias—or others, this form of political violence permeates Iraq and Syria, with profound consequences for the victims and stability in the region.

Secession: Redrawing Borders

The creation of the Islamic State from portions of Iraq and Syria is an example of civil wars triggering, broadly speaking, secessionism. Also, the government of the autonomous Kurdish region in northern Iraq sent its troops to capture Kirkuk from the control of the Iraqi central government, and in doing so, expanded its territory. This move alienated the central Iraqi government as well as many non-Kurdish Iraqis.

RADICALIZATION: RAMPANT AND VIOLENT

Unfortunately, radicalization is alive and well throughout Syria and Iraq, fueled by oppressive regimes—to a lesser extent in Iraq—and by sectarianism, principally Shiite-Sunni, although there are also other religious (Christian), ethnic, and nationalist groups in the mix. The embrace of extremism exhibits itself in virulent opposition and violence against outcast and opposing groups, including bombings of their religious sites and gatherings. The Islamic State is especially adroit at attracting individuals of all ages online and offline, in Iraq-Syria and abroad. Whether a majority or minority group in Iraq and Syria, each paints itself as victim of another, making it easy to persuade individuals to believe this worldview.

Intervention: Long History, Toxic Mix

Intervention in Syria and Iraq predates the civil wars there. Currently, intervention in Syria consists of: Iran and Hezbollah's supporting the Assad regime with fighters, weapons, and funding; Russia's assisting the government by providing weapons and political-backing (especially in the UN Security Council); China's assisting the Assad regime politically (including in the UN Security Council); the U.S.-led coalition of over sixty countries participating in efforts to defeat the Islamic State in Iraq and Syria;[13] the anti-Assad role of selected Arab countries (Saudi Arabia, Qatar, United Arab Emirates, Jordan, and others); and the interference of Iran and the West in Iraq.

IRAQ

The political crisis in Iraq, which predated the IS crisis, is ongoing, although—at least on the surface—less volatile than previously. Although Prime Minister al-Abadi managed to take office with relatively broad support, he had difficulty filling high-level cabinet positions over the opposition of the Iraqi Parliament. His harshest critics, however, come from his own Shiite-majority party.

Former Prime Minister Nouri al-Maliki, now relegated to one of three vice presidential positions, and his allies, seek to undermine al-Abadi. Al-Maliki refused to vacate the Prime Ministerial offices in one of the former Saddam Hussein palaces.[14]

Nevertheless, al-Abadi did manage to win the support of opposition parties early in his tenure. His conciliatory moves towards Sunnis and Kurds brought them back into the government, although these actions also had the effect of alienating some in his own party. However, if al-Abadi proves unable to keep his political allies in line and al-Maliki's influence in check, the Iraqi military is unlikely to be able to drastically reverse its fortunes.[15]

Some 50,000 Iraqi soldiers get paid but in fact do not serve in the army. Rather, they are "ghost" employees, who provide part of their salary to their superiors as kickbacks, but do not participate in military activities.[16] "Most of those ghost elements of the Ministry of Interior are sons, relatives, guards of senior officers."[17] This revelation by the Iraqi government in late 2014 provided additional pessimism about the Iraqi army's capacity to combat the Islamic State.

In October 2014, al-Abadi said, "No ground forces from any superpower, international coalition or regional power will fight here [against ISIS]."[18] In reality, Iraq already permits another foreign power's security services and military to operate in Iraq—namely Iran's. As long as Sunni Iraqis feel that the Iraqi regime unfairly supports and assists Shiite Iraqis at their expense, the Islamic State benefits.[19]

Another discordant element in Iraq is the rebel group, Jaysh Rijal al-Tariqa al-Naqshbandia (JRTN). "They're Sunni nationalists, many of whom are former members of Saddam Hussein's Baath party loyalists. Its leader is Izzat Ibrahim al-Duri, a former Saddam deputy."[20] In contrast to an Islamic caliphate as with IS, JRTN seeks to create a secular dictatorship.[21]

For most of 2014, the Iraqi army performed poorly while fighting the IS. Most troubling, in Mosul "Thirty-thousand Iraqi troops ran from 800 ISIS fighters."[22] Desertions in the Iraqi army were quite frequent.[23] However, in 2015, the Iraqi army potency improved, partly due to the contributions of Shiite militias, Iranian advisors, U.S. advisors and U.S.-coalition airstrikes, such as in the defeat of Tikrit.

SYRIA

The Syrian government opposes the Islamic State because it is a direct threat to the survival of the Assad regime. Damascus views all other opposition efforts—including by "moderate" rebels, which the U.S. and some allies support—as anathema. It is worth noting that the Assad regime and the rulers of Iran have as an intense disdain toward the Islamic State as do Western countries. At the same time, a strong Islamic State focuses allied attention on that entity and less on trying to remove Assad from power, thus creating a kind of triangular struggle in Syria.

The rise of the Islamic State, occurring in part as a result of Damascus's mostly hands-off approach against the IS until fall 2014, assists Assad to a great extent. First, he contends that Syria would become a base for anti-West Sunni jihadists if the Islamic State is not defeated. Second, Assad argues that for "stability" in Syria and the region, his regime must remain in power. After all, Assad asserts, Western notions of democracy have led to civil war and the disintegration of Syria. Third, the Islamic State's territorial gains and growing viciousness have compelled the West to use air power and other instrumentalities of war against the IS, although not against Assad. Along those lines, while the moderate Free Syrian Army (FSA) applauded Western and Arab efforts against the IS, it fears that these actions will aid the regime by creating stronger efforts against its opponents.[24]

"The [Assad] regime has employed artillery, air power, bulldozers, sectarian massacres, and even ballistic missiles to force Syrian populations out of insurgent held areas."[25] Some of these attacks can be characterized as war crimes, crimes against humanity, and genocide. Also, the regime has used chemical weapons and "highly destructive barrel bombs"[26] against opponents.

To a great degree, pro-Assad militias have reinforced the Syrian army. The Assad-linked, principally-Alawite Shabiha mafias, have applied harsh measures to the Syrian opposition. The local Popular Committees are comprised of armed minorities who defend their communities from rebels. The Assad regime assists these militias. Also, the Iranian government and Hezbollah provide assistance to these fighters.[27]

From spring 2014 onward, the tide in the civil war turned militarily in favor of the Assad regime—aside, of course, from Islamic State gains—with the dictator's forces succeeding against rebels in Homs and near the Lebanese border. [28] In practice, U.S. coalition efforts against the Islamic State lessen the need for the Assad regime to exert extensive forces against that adversary. For instance, in September and October 2014, the Assad regime mounted attacks against the rebellious areas in Saraqeb, Bdama, and the northern province of Aleppo. [29] Also, "the core territories of non-Islamic State insurgents, such as Idlib, Aleppo and the Damascus suburbs" [30] have witnessed more far-reaching assaults by Syrian aircraft since foreign efforts against Islamic State targets commenced. [31]

TURKEY AND KURDISH FORCES

Some Syrian opposition forces and other parties in the region, including Turkey, are incredulous that coalition offensive efforts against the Islamic State have not been paired with simultaneous attacks on the Assad regime. In October 2014, Turkish Prime Minister Ahmet Davutoğlu argued that any comprehensive effort against the Islamic State should include a strategy to remove President Assad, a no-fly zone in Syria, and a safe-zone along the Turkish border. [32]

Prime Minister Davutoğlu added that the Assad regime is at least as significant a threat to the region as the Islamic State. After all, he said, the Assad regime enabled the Islamic State to gain potency. [33] Moreover, the Turkish parliament approved a measure that "allows military incursions into Syria and Iraq against a threat to Turkey and allows foreign forces to use Turkish territory for possible operations against" the Islamic State. [34]

Much of the transnational refugee flow from the Syrian conflict has spread to neighboring Turkey. The nation is host to an estimated 1.3 million Syrians, 220,000 of them in camps along the Turkish-Syrian border. In mid-September 2014, gains by Islamist militants in northern Syria (near Kobani) forced up to 130,000 refugees across the border during several days. Many of these were Kurds, creating a volatile situation that may threaten the ongoing peace process between the Erdogan government and Kurdish parties in Turkey. [35]

Although they seemingly cooperated during the initial stages of the conflict, relations between the Turkish government and the Kurds of Iraq and Syria began to deteriorate markedly in mid-October 2014. Turkey is home to some fifteen million Kurds whose leaders have supported secession for several decades. These self-determination efforts have been marked by widespread terrorism that has cost 40,000 lives. The fragile détente and peace process between the Turkish government and its Kurdish population seems set to crumble. [36] Indeed, the rise of the Islamic State changed the calculus in the region. [37]

As the IS garnered territory and victories over Iraqi and Syrian forces, including other rebel groups, Kurdish forces in Syria and Iraq became, to a degree, the West's proxy in the fight against the IS. Still, Kurdish forces and political leadership maintain their own interests, namely greater autonomy, and ultimately, an independent state(s) carved out of Turkey, Syria, and Iraq.

Despite generations of conflict and distrust of its own Kurdish population, Turkey has become a valuable ally of the Iraqi Kurdish government based in Erbil. Turkey is Kurdistan's largest trading partner, largely due to an oil pipeline that runs from Kurdish oil fields to the Mediterranean Sea, politically bypassing the Iraqi government. Turkish President Recep Tayyip Erdogan has declared his support for Erbil against the IS. Also, Turkey has promised to aid Kurdistan's humanitarian crisis, brought on by the influx of Iraqi refugees fleeing from the IS.[38]

Turkey's relationship with other Kurdish enclaves is more complicated. Turkey has become the de facto safe haven for Kurdish forces fighting in northern Syria, particularly in Kobani. The Kurdish town became a focal point and test case for the international coalition's resolve and capabilities, as the Islamic State's siege of it began in September 2014. Although Turkish forces prevented Kurdish protesters from crossing over to aid their Syrian allies, they did allow 2,000 refugees and ambulances across the border.[39] By late October 2014, Turkey permitted Iraqi Kurdish Peshmerga fighters and Free Syrian Army members to cross into Syria.[40] Following U.S. airdrops of weapons and ammunition to Kurdish fighters in Kobani, Turkey modified its position, allowing 200 Iraqi Peshmerga Kurdish fighters to travel across the border into Kobani.[41]

Meanwhile, Turkey has been hesitant to arm Kurdish fighters who might turn on their government. Concurrently, during October 2014, at least thirty-five died in riots as Kurds in Turkey protested the Erdogan government's refusal to intervene in the defense of Kobani. Elsewhere, PKK fighters attacked a Turkish military outpost in Hakkari province, near the Turkish-Iraqi border. The Turkish government responded with airstrikes on Kurdish positions, while imprisoned PKK leader Abdullah Ocalan set a deadline for aid to their fighters in Syria.[42]

Notably, Kurdish forces in Syria and Iraq have included female units, which have served important roles in fighting against the Islamic State. All-female units were created in April 2014 and now number 10,000 women. In turn, Islamic State militants fear that being killed by Kurdish women would remove from the fighters the rewards of a *shaheed* or *shahid* (holy martyr).[43] Nevertheless, that reticence did not prevent IS members from beheading three Kurdish women fighters in October 2014.[44]

In a statement that has since been walked back, U.S. Vice President Joseph Biden criticized Turkey, the UAE, and Saudi Arabia for allowing and abetting the Islamic State's success. According to Vice President Biden, the

UAE's and Saudi Arabia's funding of Syrian rebels inadvertently landed in the coffers of al-Qa'ida and the IS. Meanwhile, he argued, Turkey was unable or unwilling to close the border with Syria, allowing foreign and Turkish fighters to join the Islamic State. These three nations emerged as some of America's key allies in the campaign against the IS. Needless to say, Mr. Biden's remarks caused a considerable diplomatic flap.[45]

Turkey was initially not amenable to joining the U.S.-led coalition against the IS because the terrorist group was holding forty-six Turkish citizens as hostages, including a consul, diplomats and their families, and elite forces. President Erdogan secured the release of all of the hostages, in addition to three Iraqis, in a prisoner exchange in September 2014. Among those released by Turkey in the prisoner exchange were two known British jihadists.[46]

Getting the hostages back allowed Turkey to become more engaged in the conflict, authorizing a buffer zone and issuing sweeping statements on the protection of its border.[47] However, at this point Turkey proved unwilling to cooperate broadly with American-allied Kurdish forces on the ground[48] and pushed back against claims that it would be allowing the U.S.-led coalition to use its air bases without further discussion.[49] Subsequently, Turkey offered to host Syrian rebels to receive military training.

LEBANON

The rise of the IS has caused difficulties for Lebanon's already precarious political, military, and social dynamic. The Islamic State's invasion of Arsal, Lebanon, highlighted and exacerbated tensions between Lebanon's Sunnis and Shiites. It put on display the inability of the Lebanese army to effectively confront the IS, given the: limitations of its training, inadequacy of its weapons and arsenal, and sectarianism penetrating Lebanese society, even in the army. Even some non-Shiite Lebanese backed Hezbollah as it is viewed as the only group that can defend the country from the IS onslaught.[50] In a mirror image, some Sunnis in Iraq and Syria believe that only the Islamic State can protect their interests from Shiite attacks.

The efforts of Jabhat al-Nusra and the Islamic State against Hezbollah—and the Sunni jihadi groups' capacity to carve away some territory along Lebanon's eastern border with Syria—in 2014 pushed Lebanon closer to civil war. This development is due in part to the political stalemate among Lebanese political parties that has ensued for months.

In January 2015, two Jabhat al-Nusra members from Lebanon, "Taha Samir al-Khayal, 22, and Bilal Mohammad al-Mariyan, 29,"[51] conducted suicide attacks at the Omran café in an Alawite-majority neighborhood, Jabal Mohsen, in Tripoli, Lebanon. Apparently, the perpetrators "received their training in the mountainous region of Syria's Qalamoun on the border with Lebanon"[52] prior to returning to Lebanon to undertake the attacks.[53]

The Islamic State has been able to garner support among some segments of the Lebanese Sunni population, particularly among impoverished populations in northern Lebanon. In fact, in Tripoli tensions have run high between the city's predominantly Sunni and mainly Shiite areas, with the former increasingly supportive of the IS, while the latter align themselves with President Assad and Hezbollah.[54] While there is some support for Jabhat al-Nusra in Tripoli, Sunni recruits tend to flock to the IS "because the group is much better funded."[55] Moreover, a segment of Tripoli's Christian population is fearful of the IS's advances in nearby Syria. The Christians there cite a January 2014 incident when a Christian bookstore was set afire.[56]

Lebanon, to some degree, seems likely to be the next country to become a target of the Islamic State.[57] In particular, "[t]he Islamic State wants access to Lebanon's second city, Tripoli, which would give it a crucial outlet to the sea."[58] In January 2015, Major General Abbas Ibrahim, Lebanon's Security Chief, stated that the IS was actively seeking to create bases within Lebanon.[59]

In fact, in January 2015, the IS appointed extremist Lebanese cleric Ahmad al-Assir as an emir there. In 2014, "a Lebanese military judge sought the death penalty for Assir after he was charged with the murder and attempted murder of soldiers and civilians during the clashes in the Lebanese southern city of Sidon in July 2013. Assir remains at large."[60] "According to Ahmad Moussalli, Professor of Political Science at the American University of Beirut (AUB), Assir was financed by Gulf states to help and entice people against the regime of Bashar al-Assad."[61]

While a portion of the Sunni population in Lebanon opposes the Islamic State, there was support for the demise of the Iraqi al-Maliki regime among Sunni Lebanese who thought Sunni interests there suffered under him. The former president of the Muslim Scholars Association, Salem al-Rafii, said that the al-Maliki regime was infused with anti-Sunni sectarianism and treated Sunnis unfairly.[62]

Lebanon's problems are worsened by the presence of, officially, 1.5 million Syrian refugees in the country,[63] the majority of whom are Sunni. In certain instances, these refugees have not only expressed support for the IS, but also have actively joined its ranks in the fight against the Lebanese army, as occurred in Arsal.[64] Sectarian tensions coupled with attempts by Hezbollah and the Assad regime to have Lebanon refrain from participation in the U.S. coalition—although unsuccessful—have threatened to weaken Lebanon's already fragile government and army. Further pressures on these institutions could prove disastrous for Lebanon and beyond.

JORDAN

Jordan has already paid a heavy price for the Syrian civil war, accepting about 20 percent of its population in refugees, some 1.4 million people.[65] Additionally, two million Iraqis and 600,000 Egyptian refugees have come to Jordan in the past few years.[66] In January 2015, Jordanian authorities confirmed that there were 1.4 million Syrians living in the country, with some 637,000 of that number registered as refugees. The Jordanian government announced $2.87 billion in funding to address this matter.[67] This influx has created mostly negative political, social, and economic effects, straining finances and undermining stability in Jordan.[68]

The Islamic State's designs on Jordan and their implications merit discussion. In videos and elsewhere, Islamic State members have threatened Jordan while Jordanians who joined the group burned their Jordanian passports.[69] In June 2014, the Hashemite Kingdom reinforced its border with Iraq, as it was reported that IS forces gained control of Treibel, Iraq, a border crossing.[70]

In October 2014, a trial commenced for twelve Jordanians charged with being members of the Islamic State and promoting its tenets in Jordan. Some one hundred other individuals were arrested for suspicions of connections with the Islamic State.[71] More than 2,000 Jordanians have traveled to fight in Syria, demonstrating a strong desire to participate in the conflict. In the rebellious southern Jordanian town of Ma'an, concerns about poverty, unemployment, and dissatisfaction with the monarchy, have fueled some interest in the Islamic State.[72]

Besides Ma'an, the Islamic State may also be finding support in the town of Zarqa (where al-Zarqawi hailed from). After all, the two municipalities have a long history of alignment with Salafist ideology.[73] Prior to the Islamic State's formation, there were jihadist groups in the region, including some conducting terror attacks, such as the October 2002 assassination of U.S. Agency for International Development representative Laurence Foley in Amman, and three nearly simultaneous suicide bombings against Western hotels in Amman in November 2005, undertaken by al-Qa'ida in Iraq.[74]

King Abdullah II of Jordan claims that the Islamic State's success rests with its ability to self-finance, relying on oil in the territory it has seized. The cash-rich organization has been able to buy weapons and attract foreign fighters.[75]

Jordanian military and security forces are strong and loyal to the monarchy.[76] Also, Jordanian and Israeli security cooperation has expanded with the Jewish state likely to intervene should the Hashemite Kingdom be at substantial risk. In addition, U.S.-Jordanian military cooperation has been extensive over decades.[77] As noted earlier, the Islamic State's execution of a Jordanian pilot by burning him to death spurred a zealous patriotism in Jordan and calls for revenge against the group, which came quickly in the form of increased airstrikes and the possible insertion of Jordanian special forces.[78]

UNPRECEDENTED ALLIANCES

As aptly put by U.S. envoy General John Allen in December 2014, "ISIL is not solely an Iraqi problem. Nor is it solely a Syrian problem. ISIL is an international problem and demands a sustained international response."[79] Against that backdrop, there have been a number of instances of cooperation, both publicly declared and "under the table," among Middle Eastern nations and Western countries against the IS threat. The most prominent and politically risky of these involve the U.S.-led airstrikes against the IS targets in Iraq, which began on August 8, 2014, and in Syria, which started on September 23, 2014.

When the strikes against Syria commenced, U.S. President Barack Obama praised the Arab nations agreeing to take part in the operations: Saudi Arabia, the UAE, Jordan, Bahrain, and Qatar. Of these, all but Qatar flew sorties in the bombings (Qatar played a support role). All of these nations except Bahrain are majority Sunni. The publicity about their cooperation was likely meant to solidify the bona fides of the coalition and shore up support for the majority-Shiite Iraqi government among Iraqi Sunnis. U.S. Secretary of State John Kerry also declared that Turkey would increase its cooperation as a NATO member against the Islamic State.[80]

Despite its stated objective of removing the Assad government, the United States still notified Damascus regarding its upcoming airstrikes in Syria. However, this notice to the Syrian regime was likely undertaken primarily to avoid the possibility of interference by Syrian military air defenses. [81] American officials have repeatedly asserted they would not be cooperating with the regime in Damascus. The Islamic State's success in Syria is partly due to the Assad regime's minimal efforts against the group, unlike the Syrian state's brutal and enthusiastic actions against other opposition elements.

Overall, by early December 2014, some 1,200 airstrikes had been conducted against the IS targets in Iraq and Syria. The Islamic State's momentum has been undermined to some degree in Iraq, as have "ISIL's command-and-control nodes, supply lines, fighters and leaders, and military and economic infrastructure and resources in Syria."[82] Despite some signs of progress against the group, that same month, Lieutenant General James Terry, who leads U.S. forces against IS in Syria and Iraq, predicted defeating IS would "take a minimum of three years."[83]

By February 2015, the number of coalition airstrikes reached over 2,800.[84] A more upbeat assessment of efforts against ISIL was articulated in

March 2015 by Rear Adm. Jim Malloy, deputy director of operations for U.S. Central Command. Rear Adm. Malloy said that anti-ISIS steps are "tailorable and scalable and [are] being applied in different ways and along different timelines in Iraq, Syria and the region. It will take some time, [but] our strategy is collaborative, and we are leveraging the support and skill of partners and allies."[85]

As of March 15, 2015, "Coalition nations which have conducted airstrikes in Iraq include Australia, Belgium, Canada, Denmark, France, Jordan, Netherlands, United Kingdom and U.S. Coalition nations which have conducted airstrikes in Syria include Bahrain, Jordan, Saudi Arabia, United Arab Emirates and U.S."[86] It was reported in January 2015 that following the capture of the Jordanian pilot in Syria the previous month, the United Arab Emirates (UAE) suspended its participation in airstrikes, apparently citing insufficient rescue resources in the coalition.[87] After the IS burned the pilot to death, both Jordan and UAE resumed participation in coalition airstrikes.

As of March 2015, the IS "can no longer do what he did at the outset, which is to seize and to hold new territory. He has assumed a defense crouch in Iraq," said U.S. Central Command Commander Gen. Lloyd J. Austin III.[88] Likewise, General John Allen asserted that coalition forces have "achieved the first phase of our campaign: we have blunted ISIL's organization's strategic, operational, and tactical momentum in Iraq."[89]

In April 2015, U.S. Defense Secretary Ashton Carter predicted that, ultimately, the Islamic State would be defeated. Even so, he projected, U.S. forces would be needed in Iraq "to train, advise and assist the Iraqi Security Forces so that they can be the force that sustained the defeat of ISIL after ISIL is defeated, which it will be."[90] Ultimately, as U.S. Air Force Secretary Deborah Lee James noted in December 2014, "This is not just a military thing. This has got to be a political solution, and ultimately, there needs to be various accommodations."[91]

IRAN

Iran, as a Shiite Islamic republic, continues to play a major role in Syria and Iraq, including providing considerable support to those governments. Iran is reported to have sent various forces to fight in Iraq (to protect Shiite interests) and Syria (to assist against the IS and other groups). Iran buttressed the Maliki regime and helped suppress Sunni initiatives and advances in Iraq. Maj. Gen. Qassem Suleimani of the Quds Force, Iran's Revolutionary Guards Corps paramilitary unit, is aiding Iraqi forces against the Islamic State. Prior to the Syrian civil war and as now, Iran has been the principal sponsor of the Assad regime.[92]

Relations between Iran and the U.S. have been strained for several decades. The two nations have not had diplomatic relations since 1979. The interactions between the two countries include difficult negotiations over Iran's nuclear program, which arrived at a framework for an agreement in spring 2015.

Washington prefers that both nations work independently to undermine the IS when coordination is not possible. Such moves would have to take place through back channels and intermediaries to avoid escalating ethnic tensions between Shiites and Sunnis, alienating the Gulf allies, and courting domestic political disaster on both sides.[93] While the United States has made some public overtures to collaborate with Iran against the IS, Iranian leadership has publicly strongly denied any sort of cooperation.[94] In 2015, U.S. airstrikes targeting IS strongholds in Tikrit did not take place until Iranian military leadership that advised the Iraqi forces left the area.

Prior to that, in June 2014, some 500 members of the Iranian Revolutionary Guard traveled to Iraq, in order to protect Shiite sites and interests from the IS.[95] Since that time, Iranian Revolutionary Guard members have been killed fighting against Islamic State members.[96] Too, while coalition efforts are focusing on combating the Sunni-inspired Islamic State, Iran is making advances in supporting Shiite leadership in Iraq and Syria (Alawite) and aiding Shiite rebels in Yemen and Bahrain.[97]

ISRAEL

Cooperation between coalition forces and Israel faces similar issues. Anti-IS coalition members are largely loathe to having a public partnership with Israel. For most of the sixty-plus coalition, any apparent collaboration with Israel would be deemed domestic political suicide. Israel has particular strength in mapping imagery and other intelligence on Syria and Iraq. Israel and the United States have signed a military agreement codifying possible coordination in Syrian airspace.[98]

For its part, Israel is concerned about the Islamic State's gaining territory in Syria and in neighboring countries, such as Jordan, Lebanon, and Egypt (Sinai), which could serve as launching pads against the Jewish state. Moreover, Israel and the United States would seriously consider military intervention if the Islamic State threatened the survival of the Jordanian monarchy.[99]

SAUDI ARABIA

On September 22, 2014, Saudi Arabia and Iran held their first foreign minister-level meeting since the election of Iranian President Hassan Rouhani. Those countries represent divergent sides in the Syrian conflict—Saudi Arabia supporting Sunni jihadists, although recently condemning the IS, and Iran supporting the Assad regime and Shiite/Alawite interests there. Also, the nations have an extended competition for leadership in the Islamic world—Saudi Arabia's Wahhabi Sunnis and Iran's Khomeini-Khamenei Shiism.

Now, both fear the Sunni-based Islamic State, even as Saudi Arabia views itself as heading the Muslim—in particular, the Sunni—world. Saudi Foreign Minister Saud Al-Faisal, referencing the advance of the IS in Iraq and Syria, said, "We believe that by using this precious opportunity and avoid[ing] the mistakes of the past, we can deal with this crisis successfully."[100]

Also, in September 2014, Saudi Arabia initiated construction on a 600-mile border barrier between itself and Iraq. The barrier, which will include chain link fences with razor wire, sand berms, and underground movement sensors, was initially contemplated in 2006, but was perceived as urgent with the Islamic State's advances in summer 2014.[101]

In January 2015, two attacks at a Saudi Suweif border outpost, believed to be directed (or inspired) by the IS, killed "General Oudah al-Belawi, commander of border operations in Saudi Arabia's northern zone," and a Saudi guard.[102] The attackers, including a suicide bomber, were also killed in the operation.[103]

COSTS OF COMBATING THE ISLAMIC STATE

U.S. Central Command (CentCom)—the unified combatant command (Co-Com) responsible for Central Asia and the Middle East—put the financial costs of the American campaign against the IS as of early October 2014 at about $1.1 billion. The daily cost increased as the conflict escalated and airstrikes expanded into Syria, but averaged between $7 million and $10 million per day. This paid for forty-seven Tomahawk cruise missiles,[104] and over 4,100 air sorties, including surveillance,[105] refueling, and bombing.

By March 12, 2015, "the total cost of operations related to ISIL since kinetic operations started on Aug. 8, 2014, is $1.83 billion and the average daily cost is $8.5 million."[106] In 2014, coalition forces flew 6,981 air sorties with 1,411 air sorties involving the release of at least one weapon. During January–February 2015, coalition forces flew 3,740 air sorties with 937 air sorties involving the release of at least one weapon, an escalation in efforts against the IS.[107]

A United Nations High Commission on Refugees (UNHCR) report released in September 2014 estimates that 4,692 Iraqi civilians were killed and 6,467 were wounded during summer 2014. Also, the UNHCR puts the number of displaced persons at 1.8 million. The report also detailed Islamic State abuses against ethnic and religious communities such as Christians, Yazidis, Failis, Kurds, and Shiites. According to the UN, the Islamic State's persecution of these groups includes attempts at destruction and ethnic cleansing, war crimes, and crimes against humanity.[108] According to the UN, between January–June 2014 "at least 5,576 civilians were killed and another 11,665 wounded" during the conflict in Iraq.[109]

Fighting around Kobani, on the border between Syria and Turkey, claimed at least 400 lives during the initial weeks of siege.[110] More than 160,000 residents, mostly Kurds, fled the fighting.[111] Between September 23 and October 22, 2014, U.S.-led air strikes in Syria killed 553 persons, including 464 IS members, fifty-seven al-Nusra Front fighters, and thirty-two civilians, the Syrian Observatory for Human Rights reported.[112]

As of April 8, 2015, there have been no American combat deaths in the conflict with the Islamic State. Due to the Islamic State's success in taking Mosul in June 2014, oil prices rose precipitously until their subsequent decline later that summer.[113] By spring 2015, oil prices hovered around $60 per barrel.

CONSEQUENCES

Afghanistan

The rise of the Islamic State also has direct implications for the planned U.S. withdrawal from Afghanistan. The resolution of the 2014 Afghan elections was delayed due to allegations of fraud. In September 2014, Afghan President Ashraf Ghani was finally sworn into office. President Ghani signed a Bilateral Security Agreement with the United States; his predecessor, Hamid Karzai, had refused such an accord. The agreement stipulates that 12,000 U.S. troops will be permanently stationed in the country. The arrangement also exempts American forces from the Afghan legal system. In light of the rise of the Islamic State and its advances in Iraq, the Afghans viewed the bilateral pact with the United States as necessary. In contrast, then Iraqi Prime Minister Nouri al-Maliki refused to enter into such a status of forces agreement (SOFA) with America.[114] For the record, many believe that he would have done so if the United States had pressured him more than it did, but that the United States itself was eager to pull out of Iraq at the time.

SHIITE MILITIAS

After the Islamic State's capture of Mosul, Shiite militias aided the Iraqi government with increased fervor. Over fifty of them are actively recruiting new adherents while fighting with vigor against the Islamic State. For example, they have been instrumental in the liberation of some towns which were besieged by the IS. However, many of these militias, such as the U.S.

designated terrorist group Kataib Hezbollah, have extensive or even direct ties to Iran. Also, some of these groups fought against U.S. forces during the Iraqi insurgency.

These Shiite militias are employing American military armor, vehicles, and weapons provided to them by the Iraqi army. (We now have Shiite militias and Sunni insurgents—the Islamic State—both using U.S. weapons that were initially allocated to the Iraqi army!) In turn, the Iraqi army has become more reliant on Shiite militias to enforce order. Some militia leaders are exploiting the Iraqi army to gain political power. The ensuing Shiite political power grab has increased the sectarian tensions within the Iraqi government, as Sunnis view this as another indicator of Sunni marginalization.[115]

There is also growing evidence that these Shiite militias are out of control. They have been accused of war crimes against Sunni civilians in Baghdad, Samarra, Kirkuk, and Tikrit. The previous Iraqi government seemed unwilling or unable to control the militias it sanctioned and called into action, despite the fact that in many ways they mirrored the Islamic State's tactics of executions and kidnapping for ransom.[116] The existence of violent rebel groups on both sides of the Sunni-Shiite divide in Iraq and Syria, which sometimes violate the norms of the rules of armed conflict and decency, severely undermines the prospects of unity and collaboration there for the coming years.

According to Amnesty International's Donatella Rovera, AI's Senior Crisis Response Adviser, "By granting its blessing to militias who routinely commit such abhorrent abuses, the Iraqi government is sanctioning war crimes and fuelling a dangerous cycle of sectarian violence that is tearing the country apart. Iraqi government support for militia rule must end now."[117] Moreover, Amnesty International's October 2014 report, *Absolute Impunity: Militia Rule in Iraq*, found that, "Scores of unidentified bodies have been discovered across the country handcuffed and with gunshot wounds to the head, indicating a pattern of deliberate execution-style killings."[118]

Two examples are illustrative of the fierce sectarianism exacerbated by the Shiite militias in Iraq. A fighter affiliated with one of the strongest Shiite militias, Asaib Ahl al-Haq (the League of the Righteous), said, "We break into an area and kill the ones who are threatening people."[119] Another Asaib Ahl al-Haq member manning a checkpoint near Baghdad said, "If we catch 'those dogs' [Sunnis] coming down from the Tikrit area we execute them. . . . They come to Baghdad to commit terrorist crimes, so we have to stop them."[120]

Indeed, the Shiite militias have been further stoking religious and ethnic tensions—broadly speaking, tribalism—endemic to Iraqi society. Those same pressures are widely held responsible for the complete abdication of the Iraqi army in Mosul, as well as the street celebrations by Sunnis that greeted the Islamic State. To put it another way, the continued belligerency of Shiite militias against Sunnis, and the Islamic State's violence against Shiites (and others), will ensure that violent sectarianism in Iraq will likely escalate further, influencing—as it already has—Sunni-Shiite relations in Syria, and elsewhere.

Analogously, in March 2015, former CIA director and commander of U.S. forces in Iraq during the surge, General David Petraeus, argued,

> The most significant long term threat is that posed by the Iranian-backed Shiite militias. If Daesh is driven from Iraq and the consequence is that Iranian-backed militias emerge as the most powerful force in the country—eclipsing the Iraqi Security Forces, much as Hezbollah does in Lebanon—that would be a very harmful outcome for Iraqi stability and sovereignty, not to mention our own national interests in the region. [121]

WEAPONS OF MASS DESTRUCTION (WMD)

The specter of WMD has haunted the Levant region since the Iran-Iraq war. Iraqi President Saddam Hussein used mustard gas and tabun against Iran in 1983 and 1984, [122] allegedly utilizing American intelligence to further his attacks. [123] Hussein again used chemical weapons to put down a Kurdish rebellion in Halabja in 1988. [124]

After the Gulf War, the 1990s saw back-and-forth negotiations, UN resolutions, sanctions, and WMD inspections in Iraq, culminating in the Operation Desert Fox bombing campaign in 1998 that destroyed much of what was left of Hussein's WMD infrastructure. [125] During the run-up to the Iraq War in 2002–2003, weapons inspectors did not find any active chemical, biological, or nuclear weapons. However, Hussein's regime was unwilling or unable to provide evidence that Iraq had dismantled its holdings that remained after Operation Desert Fox. [126]

Some Iraqi chemical arms, apparently destroyed in the 1990s or during the American military presence, remained. Between 2003 and 2011, these weapons were found in buried caches and even in roadside bombs by American troops sometimes unprepared and ill equipped to handle corroding chemical agents. Many of these old munitions, all produced before 1991, were embarrassingly based on American and European designs. Insurgents used these weapons to ambush American soldiers. Some were found leaking in shoddy hidden munitions deposits from the Hussein era. Over 4,500 sarin, mustard gas, and other chemical rounds were found. Most of these incidents were not initially reported by the U.S. Department of Defense. After the American withdrawal in December 2011, the Iraqi government was left to deal with the dangerously loose stockpiles. One of these complexes, al-Muthanna, fell into the hands of the Islamic State before the complex could be destroyed. [127]

Also, the IS could have obtained chemical weapons from one of the Syrian bases it has captured. [128] The use of sarin [129] and chlorine gas [130] by the Assad regime in 2013 nearly drew the United States further into the conflict. The Organisation for the Prohibition of Chemical Weapons (OPCW) concluded at the end of its initial disarmament mission in Syria on August 28, 2014, that Assad's government had destroyed 94 percent of its declared category-one chemical weapons. [131] As a dual-use chemical, chlorine is not required to be declared, but using it or storing it for military purposes is against the Chemical Weapons Convention. [132]

In May 2014, the OPCW reported that the Assad regime used chlorine gas as a weapon on the villages of Talmanes, al Tamanah, and Kafr Zeta, all located in northern Syria. [133] U.S. Secretary of State John Kerry declared Syria to have breached its commitments and condemned its actions, promising the United States was discussing ways to further punish Assad. [134] Moreover, Assad has continuously violated international norms by painfully slaughtering thousands by other means throughout the conflict. These atrocities include targeting civilians and using barrel bombs.

It is hardly surprising, then, that evidence has surfaced indicating that the Islamic State has used chemical weapons against Kurdish forces. The Islamic State apparently employed mustard gas or some other blistering agent— likely recovered from one of Saddam Hussein's hidden stockpiles—in its attack on the Iraqi village of Avdiko in July 2014. [135] The Islamic State is thought to be storing its chemical capacities in Raqqa. [136] The Pentagon, for its part, declared that it has not yet found any indications that the Islamic State possesses chemical weapons. [137] Yet, in September 2014, the Islamic State used chlorine gas on the battlefield in Balad, Iraq, some fifty miles north of Baghdad. [138]

In addition, the Islamic State's access to nuclear materials has raised concerns. In early July 2014, Iraq reported to the UN that the Islamic State had seized eighty-eight pounds of nuclear material from Mosul University. [139] Luckily, according to the IAEA: "The material involved is low-grade and would not present a significant safety, security or nuclear proliferation risk." [140] "Nevertheless," the organization's statement continued, "any loss of regulatory control over nuclear and other radioactive materials is a cause for concern." [141]

The capture and control of any weapon of mass destruction by the Islamic State (or other extremist groups in the conflict) could cause a deadly escalation in the tactics of the various warring sides. Use of such weapons may accelerate the introduction of ground troops by coalition forces. President Obama stated recently that the Islamic State's possession of nuclear weaponry would be a reason for expanding U.S. use of ground forces in the area.

The Islamic State benefits by having its territory straddle the border between Syria and Iraq. As such, in case of pressure by opposing armies or rebels in one country, it could retreat to the other nation. However, U.S.-led coalition efforts attacking the IS in both countries essentially eliminates the concept of safe zones.[142] Still, since airstrikes against IS positions in Iraq, and then Syria, began, the IS has modified its military formations and tactics. Whenever possible, IS groups travel in smaller vehicles or even motorcycles with fewer operatives traveling together. The modification reduces the prospects of mass casualties of IS fighters as well as of the destruction of their weaponry and other assets.

OTHER EFFECTS

Additional ramifications worthy of mention include the negative effects of the IS-spurred conflicts on the fates of women and children. They are brutalized and abused in their exploitation by the IS, whether in the form of forced participation as combatants, their serving as slaves and objects of sexual deviancy, or, sometimes, ultimately, being subjugated to painful deaths. Likewise, traditional concepts like the rule of law and good governance are shattered in both theory and practice under the iron fist of the Islamic State. Also, corruption and inequities continue to resonate within the IS and elsewhere in Iraq and Syria.

U.S. POLICY TOWARDS THE ISLAMIC STATE

The Obama administration's interpretation of the risk the Islamic State poses has evolved, with growing recognition of its potency and destabilizing effects. For instance, during a January 2014 interview with *The New Yorker* magazine President Obama surprisingly said, "The analogy we use around here sometimes, and I think is accurate, is if a jayvee team puts on Lakers uniforms that doesn't make them Kobe Bryant." Moreover, he added, "I think there is a distinction between the capacity and reach of a bin Laden and a network that is actively planning major terrorist plots against the homeland versus jihadists who are engaged in various local power struggles and disputes, often sectarian."[143]

In a June 13, 2014 statement, President Obama acknowledged the threat of ISIL, namely, "Over the last several days, we've seen significant gains made by ISIL, a terrorist organization that operates in both Iraq and in Syria. In the face of a terrorist offensive, Iraqi security forces have proven unable to defend a number of cities, which has allowed the terrorists to overrun a part of Iraq's territory. And this poses a danger to Iraq and its people. And given the nature of these terrorists, it could pose a threat eventually to American interests as well."[144]

Six days later, President Obama announced that in light of the ISIL threat, the U.S. government:

- was "working to secure our embassy and personnel operating inside of Iraq"
- "significantly increased our intelligence, surveillance, and reconnaissance assets so that we've got a better picture of what's taking place inside of Iraq. And this will give us a greater understanding of what ISIL is doing, where it's located, and how we might support efforts to counter this threat."
- "will continue to increase our support to Iraqi security forces. We're prepared to create joint operation centers in Baghdad and northern Iraq to share intelligence and coordinate planning to confront the terrorist threat of ISIL. Through our new Counterterrorism Partnership Fund, we're prepared to work with Congress to provide additional equipment. We have had advisors in Iraq through our embassy, and we're prepared to send a small number of additional American military advisors—up to 300—to assess how we can best train, advise, and support Iraqi security forces going forward. American forces will not be returning to combat in Iraq, but we will help Iraqis as they take the fight to terrorists who threaten the Iraqi people, the region, and American interests as well."
- "positioned additional U.S. military assets in the region. Because of our increased intelligence resources, we're developing more information about potential targets associated with ISIL. And going forward, we will be prepared to take targeted and precise military action, if and when we determine that the situation on the ground requires it. If we do, I will consult closely with Congress and leaders in Iraq and in the region."[145]

The U.S. government's initial public step towards using force against the Islamic State was President Barack Obama's announcement on August 7, 2014, that he "authorized the U.S. Armed Forces to conduct targeted airstrikes in Iraq. These military operations will be limited in their scope and duration as necessary to protect American personnel in Iraq by stopping the current advance on Erbil by the terrorist group Islamic State of Iraq and the Levant and to help forces in Iraq as they fight to break the siege of Mount Sinjar and protect the civilians trapped there."[146] In addition, he "authorized U.S. Armed Forces to provide humanitarian assistance in Iraq in an operation that commenced on August 7, 2014. These operations will also be limited to supporting the civilians trapped on Mount Sinjar."[147]

It is worth noting that on August 28, 2014, President Obama said, "I don't want to put the cart before the horse. We don't have a strategy yet."[148]

Almost immediately, White House press secretary Josh Earnest tried to clarify the statement: "What's clear is: We have a comprehensive strategy for dealing with ISIL. . . . He was referring to military options for striking ISIL in Syria. Those options are still being developed by the Pentagon."[149]

On September 10, 2014, President Obama enunciated his administration's revised strategy against the Islamic State.[150] The four-pronged elements of the new strategy sought "to degrade, and ultimately destroy, ISIL [Islamic State]."[151] More specifically, President Obama outlined the strategy as such:

> First, we will conduct a systematic campaign of airstrikes against these terrorists. Working with the Iraqi government, we will expand our efforts beyond protecting our own people and humanitarian missions, so that we're hitting ISIL targets as Iraqi forces go on offense. Moreover, I have made it clear that we will hunt down terrorists who threaten our country, wherever they are. That means I will not hesitate to take action against ISIL in Syria, as well as Iraq. This is a core principle of my presidency: If you threaten America, you will find no safe haven.
>
> Second, we will increase our support to forces fighting these terrorists on the ground. In June, I deployed several hundred American service members to Iraq to assess how we can best support Iraqi security forces. Now that those teams have completed their work—and Iraq has formed a government—we will send an additional 475 service members to Iraq. As I have said before, these American forces will not have a combat mission—we will not get dragged into another ground war in Iraq. But they are needed to support Iraqi and Kurdish forces with training, intelligence and equipment. We'll also support Iraq's efforts to stand up National Guard Units to help Sunni communities secure their own freedom from ISIL's control.
>
> Across the border, in Syria, we have ramped up our military assistance to the Syrian opposition. Tonight, I call on Congress again to give us additional authorities and resources to train and equip these fighters. In the fight against ISIL, we cannot rely on an Assad regime that terrorizes its own people—a regime that will never regain the legitimacy it has lost. Instead, we must strengthen the opposition as the best counterweight to extremists like ISIL, while pursuing the political solution necessary to solve Syria's crisis once and for all.
>
> Third, we will continue to draw on our substantial counterterrorism capabilities to prevent ISIL attacks. Working with our partners, we will redouble our efforts to cut off its funding; improve our intelligence; strengthen our defenses; counter its warped ideology; and stem the flow of foreign fighters into and out of the Middle East. And in two weeks, I will chair a meeting of the U.N. Security Council to further mobilize the international community around this effort.
>
> Fourth, we will continue to provide humanitarian assistance to innocent civilians who have been displaced by this terrorist organization. This includes Sunni and Shia Muslims who are at grave risk, as well as tens of thousands of Christians and other religious minorities. We cannot allow these communities to be driven from their ancient homelands.[152]

American commitment to undermine and destroy the Islamic State grew in early November 2014. More specifically, on November 7, 2014, the Obama administration revised and expanded its strategy to confront the Islamic State, with nine key features: supporting effective governance in Iraq, denying ISIL safe-haven, building partner capacity, enhancing intelligence collection on ISIL, disrupting ISIL's finances, exposing ISIL's true nature, disrupting the flow of foreign fighters, protecting the homeland, and humanitarian support. Also, that day, the Obama administration proposed $5.6 billion for Fiscal Year 2015 Overseas Contingency Operations to weaken and eliminate ISIL. In support of Operation Inherent Resolve, "$5.0 billion [would be made available] for DOD to conduct a range of military operations against ISIL in the Middle East region, which includes the $1.6 billion Iraq Train and Equip Fund. These operations directly support the components of the Administration's strategy that aim to deny ISIL a safe-haven and expand intelligence collection against ISIL."[153]

> More specifically, on November 7, 2014, President Obama announced, . . . authorized the deployment of up to 1,500 additional U.S. military personnel in a non-combat role to train, advise, and assist Iraqi Security Forces, including Kurdish forces. The President further authorized U.S. personnel to conduct these integral missions at Iraqi military facilities located outside Baghdad and Erbil. U.S. troops will not be in combat, but they will be better positioned to support Iraqi Security Forces as they take the fight to ISIL.[154]

That same day, Pentagon Press Secretary Rear Admiral John Kirby provided more specifics about this expanded undertaking:

> U.S. Central Command will establish two expeditionary advise and assist operations centers, in locations outside of Baghdad and Erbil, to provide support for the Iraqis at the brigade headquarters level and above. These centers will be supported by an appropriate array of force protection capabilities. U.S. Central Command will establish several sites across Iraq that will accommodate the training of 12 Iraqi brigades, specifically nine Iraqi army and three Peshmerga brigades. These sites will be located in northern, western, and southern Iraq. Coalition partners will join U.S. personnel at these locations to help build Iraqi capacity and capability. The training will be funded through the request for an Iraq Train and Equip Fund that the administration will submit to Congress as well as from the Government of Iraq.[155]

By November 2014, coalition airstrikes escalated, and increasingly targeted other Sunni jihadist groups besides the Islamic State. These actions, coupled with U.S. plans to authorize additional military trainers and allocate more funding to combating the Islamic State, are steps in the right direction.

On one level, the deterioration of the situation in Iraq, particularly the rapid expansion of the Islamic State there, rests in part on the Obama Administration's inability to negotiate a status of forces agreement with the Iraqi government. Without such an agreement, U.S. combat troops left Iraq in 2011.[156] The lack of a physical presence of the U.S military in Iraq—the thought goes—enabled the IS to overrun Iraqi territory. Yet, while that may have contributed to the disintegration of Iraq, it is critical to note that the U.S. government spent nearly a decade in Iraq, a significant time during which it trained and supported the Iraqi military and security forces. The U.S. government provided Iraq with billions of dollars worth of military and civilian aid. Also, the U.S. paid a high human toll in the war in Iraq, with 4,488 U.S. soldiers killed and tens of thousands injured.[157] Non-U.S. coalition forces experienced 318 deaths in Iraq.[158]

The Iraqi army's largely poor record in the face of the IS—until 2015—suggests that a major part of problem rests in Iraq, as some Sunni soldiers perceived the Iraqi government as failing to support Sunni interests, while other Shiite soldiers were unmotivated and unprepared.[159] Meanwhile, some Shiite generals had simply purchased their positions to engage in graft and corruption, and provided limited leadership when the time came. Along those lines, significant U.S. military and other equipment that was provided to the Iraqi army was lost due to corruption or in battle with the IS and other militants.

On October 23, 2014, U.S. Central Command announced that Iraqi forces might not be ready to fight a sustained ground war against the IS for several months.[160] Troubling, too, is the fact that "Iraq's main military divisions in Anbar—the seventh, eighth, ninth, 10th and 12th—have been badly damaged. At least 6,000 Iraqi soldiers were killed through June 2014 and double that number have deserted."[161] Thus, to believe that additional training for the Iraqi military will enable it to defeat the Islamic State without a substantial presence of U.S. and coalition ground troops in Iraq (and ultimately, in Syria, too), or expanded use of Shiite militias (and Iranian advisers)—which create other challenges—is unrealistic.

Still, there are some glimmers of hope, particularly with anti-ISIL efforts during the spring 2015. ISIL "can no longer do what he did at the outset, which is to seize and to hold new territory. He has assumed a defense crouch in Iraq," said U.S. Central Command Commander Gen. Lloyd J. Austin III.[162] Whether these successes can be sustained without aggravating sectarian tensions as Sunni-aligned IS suffers defeats, only time will tell. The declining fortunes of IS fighters in Iraq, particularly since 2015, seem to be based more on coalition airstrikes and advisers, Kurdish fighters contributions, Shiite militias, and Iranian support than on the Iraqi army.

In relation to Syria, General David Petraeus argued in March 2015 that, "here are legitimate questions that can be raised about the sufficiency of the present scale, scope, speed, and resourcing," about American efforts to establish anti-IS Syrian rebel forces. Also, he asserted that the United States will not be able "to establish a headquarters inside Syria to provide command and control of the forces we help train and equip as long as barrel bombs are dropped on it on a regular basis."[163]

U.S. policy in relation to Syria includes: support for the removal of the Assad regime, offering training and equipment to "moderate" Syrian opposition fighters, undermining IS capabilities through coalition airstrikes and support to Kurdish and other forces, and clandestine operations. The removal of the Assad regime, as justifiable as it is, will nonetheless lead to a power vacuum, which must—from a U.S. perspective—be filled by entities other than factions of the IS, Jabhat al-Nusra, and other jihadi elements, Shiite interests such as Hezbollah and Iran, and other entities with objectives antithetical to those of the United States.

LESSONS LEARNED AND RECOMMENDATIONS

Characteristics of the Islamic State

Although the Islamic State is hierarchical in many respects, the entity has features of networked groups as well. Also, by spreading its message globally and recruiting individuals to travel to the Islamic State or to act locally, the entity has a modicum of decentralization. Its expansive and rising use of technology and virtualization affords the IS opportunities for growth in a rapid and relatively inexpensive manner. The IS has exhibited other powers of statehood, including the issuance of passports and declarations that it will establish a national currency.

As gatekeeper, the IS can determine which individuals can join the group. It is open to individuals who self-select, and to cabals. The Islamic State's fighters include Iraqis, Syrians, and a multitude of foreign fighters. In September 2014, a CIA spokesman estimated that it "can muster between 20,000 and 31,500 fighters across Iraq and Syria."[164] That same month, U.S. government sources projected foreign fighters in Syria and Iraq to include 15,000 persons from eighty nations.[165] By February 2015, that figure had reached over 20,000 persons from ninety countries.

The adversaries that the Islamic State encounters locally are the fragile states of Iraq and Syria, various rebel groups, dissenters, and other segments of the populace. Also, the Islamic State has made adversaries of Iran, which aids the Syrian and Iraqi governments as well as the West, and some sixty countries in the U.S.-led coalition. As with other Islamist groups, Israel is a natural enemy of the Islamic State.

Through the growth and transformation that the IS has undertaken—from its origins as Jama'at al Tawhid wal Jihad in 1999 to its caliphate status from 2014—the entity has been characterized by fluid and non-linear traits. Presently, the Islamic State and its antecedents are on various terrorist-designation lists, including those of the United States, European Union, and UN.

Globally, civilized countries and the vast majority of their citizenry view the Islamic State as an abhorrent deviant threat that merits elimination in the swiftest manner possible. Yet, unfortunately, the entity claims significant support from adherents in Syria, Iraq, the Middle East, and worldwide. The international outreach and character of the Islamic State's message is akin, in a way, to the characteristics of al-Qa'ida, particularly at its height.

Ultimately, a determinant as to the future success of the Islamic State rests with the battle of ideas: whether its hate-based messages are more attractive to the citizenry than multi-pronged counter-narratives. The counter-narratives will mostly have to emanate from the Muslim world, as other messaging will not be deemed as credible in the region. Nevertheless, non-Muslim-majority countries also have a role in crafting and disseminating counter-narratives and alternatives to the Islamic State's message. Other initiatives, such as military campaigns, interference with the flow of foreign fighters, and counter-terror financial moves, will also be indispensable in combating the group.

Various countries, such as Saudi Arabia, the United Arab Emirates, Qatar, and Kuwait, have been accused of supporting or allowing their citizenry to aid Sunni jihadist fighters against the Assad regime. Inevitably, some of this assistance is believed to have reached the Islamic State or its precursors. By 2014, these countries were members of the anti-IS coalition.

State sponsorship or pseudo-state assistance has clearly aided the Islamic State. However, this type of aid has lessened precipitously since summer 2014. The Islamic State is in a weaker financial position because of that. Although, this loss has been offset to a considerable degree by IS's ability to garner substantial funds through oil sales, extortion, kidnapping for ransom, smuggling, and organized crime, among other sources. These funding activities, too, have suffered under coalition airstrikes and anti-IS efforts by Kurdish and Iraqi forces.

At its core, it is arguable that the Islamic State is partly a sovereign state and provider of services to its constituents, however brutally. The organization also clearly acts as a terrorist entity as it utilizes violence for a political objective and aims at military and civilian targets alike, with indiscriminate severity. Islamic State fighters have at times acted as insurgents, although they appear to have focused very extensively on targeting civilians, which is not "typical" during insurgencies. To some degree, the Islamic State also acts like an organized criminal entity, since a portion of its funding and activities arises from coordinated illicit activities where monetary gains predominate. It can thereby be characterized as a hybrid entity with terror group, organized criminal enterprise, and pseudo-state attributes.

The activities of the Islamic State are producing profound political, social, and economic implications in the Middle East and beyond. To weaken and ultimately defeat the IS will require extensive energy, time, funds, and manpower. Still, some elements of the IS may remain after its demise, although of less potential. It is possible that one of its affiliates abroad may expand, and, depending on where it is based geographically, may pose a significant threat to its respective region, and perhaps beyond.

The removal of its leadership may severely weaken the IS, although as we have seen after the death of al-Qa'ida's bin Laden, it is easier to kill a man than an idea. At the same time, the death, imprisonment, and other efforts aimed at al-Qa'ida senior leadership have weakened that organization. Reports that IS leader al-Baghdadi may have been killed in U.S. airstrikes during 2014 and spring 2015 were not substantiated. Even al-Baghdadi's death, however, when it occurs, would not decimate the Islamic State, as it has developed a hierarchical governing framework with other seasoned leaders to take his place. Still, the elimination of several levels of IS leadership would be very helpful, particularly if such individuals would not be replaced with operatives of at least equal capabilities.

Like other "sovereigns" and terror groups, the Islamic State does not operate in a vacuum. It connects and interacts with non-state and state actors that are found locally and globally. As with any organization, the Islamic State has vulnerabilities and inefficiencies that affect its capacity to govern, fight, and undertake strategic communications, though it has managed to excel at the latter, despite some recent challenges. As it evolves, the IS likely will experience additional cohesion and fragmentation as an entity, which must be confronted and exploited.

While this assessment offers a glimpse of current and likely developments of the Islamic State, there are additional aspects that deserve consideration and clarification. The following are some core questions and responses:

First, how are terror groups defeated, and what are the implications for the Islamic State?

Terror groups lose their effectiveness and crumble under various scenarios:[166]

- They are defeated militarily.
- Their leadership and operatives are killed or imprisoned.
- Police and intelligence communities infiltrate and eliminate them.
- Circumstances or facts on the ground change so that the terror group, through its activities and messaging, is no longer relevant or attractive.
- They lose support, political and financial, from their domestic or international backers, so much so that they cannot sustain themselves.

- Alternative terror, rebel, or other groups arise so that the terror group loses its appeal or sustainability.
- It reaches a compromise with the government or other entity with which it has a grievance.
- It determines that its violent tactics no longer work, so it decides to use non-violent actions.
- It achieves its goals and withers.
- The terror group reaches its objective and transitions into the political process, including governing.

Appreciating these alternatives can provide an insight as to how to combat the Islamic State. One could suggest that several—rather than one—of these available options might be implemented against the Islamic State, such as: defeating the group militarily, using repressive measures to kill or arrest relevant Islamic State leadership and operatives, infiltrating and undermining it from within, impeding its capacity to garner support and funding, supporting political and social alternatives in the areas that the IS controls so that its support dwindles, and changing the circumstances on the ground so that the IS is not viewed favorably. Given the Islamic State's current worldview, it is highly unlikely that a political compromise would be feasible. However, broad and extensive counternarratives to the Islamic State—by government and other entities—could well prove effective.

During late 2014 and early 2015, there was an escalation of some rifts within the Islamic State's ranks, as exemplified by the following developments:

- Islamic State military police in Raqqa killed more than one hundred foreign fighters who sought to leave the group. That same force arrested 400 other fighters for other perceived threats to the IS.[167] Overall, the Islamic State is believed to have killed 120 of its members, including those seeking to abandon the group.[168] Among those killed were three Chinese nationals who had joined the group and then deserted.[169]
- Tensions and disillusionment exist among local fighters who believe that they face higher risks than foreign fighters, who receive better conditions, including wages and female slaves. Also, rifts exist among IS fighters of disparate ethnicities and nationalities, with some IS members continuing to have alliances and allegiances to groups in their respective home countries.[170]
- Some individuals abandon the group due to the Islamic State's savagery, endless and arbitrary killing including women, children, and other jihadist and opposition groups from Jabhat al-Nusra to the Free Syrian Army. Also, conditions for some fighters can appear to be difficult, particularly if led by Libyan IS commanders.[171]

- The IS released a video in December 2014 showing the confession of four Raqqa-based IS members who were planning a coup against IS leadership and sought to undermine IS interests in Islamic State territory. Amazingly, the plotters alleged that IS was not radical enough, and that its leader, Abu Bakr al-Baghdadi, is an infidel.[172]
- Tensions between some IS fighters of Chechen descent with IS leadership over strategy and loyalty issues, including how to deal with the Jordanian pilot captured in December 2014 and whether Latakia, Syria-based Chechen fighters should declare allegiance to the IS.[173]

Second, should the IS be viewed as a threat equal to or greater than al-Qa'ida for the United States and the international community?

The IS should be deemed a greater threat to the United States and the international community than al-Qa'ida, for a number of reasons. The Islamic State, unlike al-Qa'ida, is on an upward trajectory. The IS has amassed and controls sizeable territory in its own right, while al-Qa'ida merely has had sanctuary at different times in Sudan and Afghanistan, and de facto currently in northwest Pakistan. The IS has exhibited sovereign state-like governance, providing services and enforcing its own policies with inhabitant populations. In contrast, al-Qa'ida never participated in formal governance, but rather was successful in training terrorists, killing people, propagating its message, and raising funds.

The Islamic State has gathered support and affinity from groups and individuals worldwide, particularly due to its broad and sophisticated use of social media in multiple languages. Al-Qa'ida has been involved in such efforts, although to a lesser extent in 2014. Still, the group and its affiliates have also engaged in some innovative modes of strategic communications, such as the online publications *Inspire* (geared to prospective jihadists) and *al Shamikha* (aimed at females and spouses of jihadists).

Al-Qa'ida spawned several named formal entities, including a precursor to the IS—al-Qa'ida in Iraq—as well as al-Qa'ida in the Arabian Peninsula, and al-Qa'ida in the Islamic Maghreb. In September 2014, al-Qa'ida in the Indian Subcontinent was launched. Other Sunni jihadist groups, such as al-Shabaab in Somalia, and others have, at times, pledged allegiance to al-Qa'ida.

While al-Qa'ida has been responsible for various large-scale terrorist incidents, its successful recent terrorist attacks have been few and far between.[174] Among the most spectacular al-Qa'ida attacks were the 1998 suicide bombings of the U.S. embassies in Kenya and Tanzania, which killed some 300 people, and the September 11, 2001, attacks that killed some 3,000 persons in New York City; Washington, DC; and in Pennsylvania.[175] Still, al-Qa'ida has attempted various other large-scale incidents in the United States and elsewhere, including three simultaneous suicide bombings at New York City subway stations in 2009 and a 2006 UK–linked plot to conduct nine simultaneous bombings of commercial airplanes using liquid explosives.[176] Also, al-Qa'ida has inspired numerous individuals globally to undertake additional terror attacks in their home countries, travel abroad to participate in a conflict, and join other Sunni jihadi groups, including the other al-Qa'ida-named groups and al-Qa'ida affiliates.[177]

While the IS has conducted numerous targeted attacks against civilian and military targets, such as suicide bombings in Iraq and Syria, the extent of their carnage has been much more extensive than al-Qa'ida, including mass executions of Syrian and Iraqi soldiers who should have been treated as prisoners of war, and indiscriminate widespread murder of civilians. The extent and toll of IS's deadly violence is such that its actions have been characterized as genocide, crimes against humanity, and war crimes, by the international community.

At its zenith, al-Qa'ida did not possess the array of advanced conventional weapons, including tanks and aircraft fighters, that the Islamic State has been able to acquire through its battles with Syrian and Iraqi armies. In October 2014, for instance, the Islamic State was able to gain possession of "seven American M1 Abrams tanks from three Iraqi army bases in Anbar province."[178]

The Islamic State has also reportedly obtained radiological materials, though apparently not of weapons grade, in its seizure of the Iraqi city of Mosul. The group has obtained and used chlorine-infused explosives. In addition, IS apparently is interested in bio-warfare capabilities. The Islamic State has a self-proclaimed Hacking Division, so some cyber attacks and cyber-terror incidents are expected besides hacking the Pentagon's Twitter account, among other activities.

Third, will the IS and its foreign fighters export terrorism to their home countries?

Unfortunately, as the world has already witnessed, the answer is clearly yes. The Islamic State's capacity to promote terrorism abroad is a threat on several levels. The movement is able to radicalize and recruit individuals globally, and they then are able to plan and undertake attacks domestically. Also, its operatives can travel to their home countries or third countries to recruit others and undertake local attacks. Often these incidents are smaller-scale operations, using easily accessible tactics (e.g., using cars to run over targets, or legally-acquired rifles) against landmarks and soft targets. Selected illustrations of such activities during 2014 include the following plots and incidents:

- In April and June, Malaysian authorities arrested nineteen jihadists, including two women, who planned to travel to Turkey, and then Syria, to join the IS. Additionally, the group pursued a plot to undertake a terror attack in Putrajaya, Malaysia's administrative capital.[179] In June, Ahmad Tarmimi Maliki became the first Malaysian to conduct a suicide bombing on behalf of the IS, when he attacked the military target in Iraq's Anbar province, killing 25 elite Iraqi soldiers.[180]
- An attack on the Jewish Museum of Belgium in Brussels in May by Mehdi Nemmouche (who spent time with the IS, including guarding foreign hostages in Syria) killed four people.
- In August, it was reported that the Islamic State planned to kill Pope Francis for "bearing false witness against Islam."[181]
- Two IS-inspired attacks in October in Quebec and Ottawa, Canada, by Martin Couture-Rouleau and Michael Zehaf-Bibeau, respectively, resulted in the death of one Canadian soldier at each location.[182] In October, Michel Coulombe, head of the Canadian Security Intelligence Service, reported that there were between 120 and 135 Canadians who went abroad to participate in terrorist-related activities and eighty individuals residing in Canada who had terror-related training overseas.[183]
- In September, Alton Nolen perpetrated an IS-inspired beheading of a female co-worker and stabbing of another in Oklahoma.[184] An IS-linked plot in September called for its operatives in Australia to videotape a beheading to be conducted in public. Australian police arrested fifteen people in the planned incident.[185] During the same month two Australian police officers were attacked by knife-wielding, IS adherent, Abdul Numan Haider, who was subsequently killed by police.[186]
- Authorities in Spain and Morocco in September arrested nine men believed to be linked with the Islamic State who were planning to undertake a terror attack in Spain. The cabal included eight Moroccans and one Spaniard.[187]
- In September, Belgium foiled a potential terror plot by a couple returning from fighting in Syria.[188] The next month, a Sunni jihadist-linked terror training camp was discovered in the Ardennes region in Belgium.[189]
- British authorities in October arrested four men in London, believed to be planning an IS-linked terror attack, such as a public beheading or other public killing, in the UK.[190]
- On October 11, a U.S. Department of Homeland Security and FBI "Joint Intelligence Bulletin" warned that U.S.-based individuals aligned with or inspired by the IS might attack U.S. law enforcement as "ISIL [ISIS] and its supporters continue to issue threats online."[191] As such, the bulletin sought "to remind all law enforcement personnel to remain vigilant in matters of personal safety given an increase in recent attacks against and plots targeting law enforcement personnel overseas."[192] In addition, the

bulletin referenced various messages by the IS spokesman, Abu-Muhammad al-Adana, and others, advocating lone-wolf attacks in the West against soldiers, police, security, and intelligence personnel. [193]

- In November, the FBI issued a warning of IS-linked individuals in the United States planning attacks against U.S. military personnel or their families in America. Given these facts, the bulletin asks "members of the military review their online social media presence for any information that might attract the attention of violent extremists" as well as advising that they should "use caution and practice operational security when posting." [194]

- In December, a French national born in Burundi, Bertrand Nzohabonayo, stabbed three French police officers at a police station in Joue-les-Tours, near Tours, injuring them. The perpetrator screamed "Allahu Akbar" (God is great, in Arabic) during the attacks. French police shot and killed him. Nzohabonayo is suspected to have been inspired by the Islamic State's calls to attack law enforcement worldwide, as he had an ISIL flag on his Facebook page. [195]

Unfortunately, IS-inspired or connected terrorism outside the Islamic State continued in 2015. Among such instances are:

- In January, al-Qa'ida in the Arabian Peninsula and an IS-inspired terrorist launched attacks at the offices of the satirical magazine, *Charlie Hebdo*, and a kosher supermarket, respectively, in Paris. The three perpetrators— including two brothers, Said and Cherif Kouachi, and Amedy Coulibaly— killed seventeen people. [196] There is growing evidence that the two sets of operatives knew each other, as information has come to light about some 500 phone calls between the wife of Coulibaly, Hayat Boumeddiene, and the wife of Cherif Kouachi. [197] Additionally, Cherif and Amedy are believed to have met in prison, and "became devoted followers of Djamel Beghal, a French-Algerian man with ties to al-Qaeda who was convicted of plotting in 2001 to blow up the U.S. Embassy in Paris." [198] In a video recording found at his apartment, Coulibaly said that he undertook the attack on behalf of the Islamic State. As French Prime Minister Manuel Valls remarked after the attacks, "We must not lower our guard, at any time," as "serious and very high risks remain." [199]

- In January, two terrorists with the Libyan branch of IS—Abu Ibraheem Al-Tunsi and Abu Sulaiman Al-Sudani—used gunfire and a car bomb to attack the Corinthia Hotel in Tripoli, Libya. At least ten persons, including five foreigners—among them an American security contactor, David Berry—were killed during the attack. The group claiming responsibility for the attack said it was undertaken to honor Abu Anas al-Libi, an al-Qa'ida member who died in U.S. custody while awaiting trial for involvement in the 1998 terror attacks against U.S. embassies in Kenya and Tanzania. The hotel is popular with foreigners and government officials. Also, the head of the self-declared Libyan government, Omar al-Hassi, resided at the hotel.[200]

- In February, an IS-inspired, former gang member, Omar Abdel Hamid el-Hussein, undertook two attacks in Copenhagen, Denmark: at a café that was sponsoring a free speech seminar featuring Lars Vilks—the Danish cartoonist who drew the controversial cartoon featuring the Prophet Mohammed as a dog—and synagogue. The incidents resulted in two deaths and five injuries. The same day as the attacks, el-Hussein was shot and killed outside his home following an exchange of gunfire with Danish police. El-Hussein's attacks appeared to mimic the January 2015 attacks in Paris against the media and Jewish targets.[201]
- In March, Brusthom Ziamani, a 19-year-old from south London, was sentenced to twenty-two years in prison for his plan to undertake a terrorist act. In particular, Ziamani intended to behead a soldier in the UK, similar to the 2013 murder of Lee Rigby. At the time of his arrest, Ziamani possessed a ten-inch kitchen knife, hammer, and black flag used by jihadi groups worldwide.[202]

If Islamic State operatives or IS-inspired individuals succeed in carrying out a large-scale terror attack in the West, it is likely that efforts against the IS will escalate, including the possibility of the use of ground troops. It is imaginable that the IS will outsource some terrorist efforts to other groups, although its current falling out with al-Qa'ida makes such an arrangement more unlikely with that group or its affiliates. Still, there have been some signs of an Islamic State-Jabhat al-Nusra truce since U.S.-led airstrikes took place, such as cooperation in Yarmouk, Syria, in April 2015.

An increasingly common practice among jihadist terrorists is to attack different parts of a large city, shopping mall, or educational institution, to cause mass murder and mayhem. The precedent for such types of attacks include: the Laskar-e-Taiba's multi-site attacks in Mumbai in 2008, al-Shabaab's Nairobi Westgate shopping mall attack in 2013, Pakistani Taliban's attack at the Army Public School in Peshawar, Pakistan in 2014, and al-Shabaab's attack at Garissa University in 2015.[203] Other such instances, although on a smaller scale, were the January 2015 Paris attacks against *Charlie Hebdo* office and the kosher supermarket.

In September 2014, senior European Union officials predicted that a large-scale IS-connected terror attack in Europe was almost inevitable. This is particularly so as foreign IS fighters return to the continent after spending time in Iraq and Syria,[204] while lone wolves and cabals inspired by the Islamic State proliferate worldwide.

Fourth, is the assistance of Assad's regime and Iran needed to defeat the IS, and what are the implications of an approach to these governments?

As to whether the participation of the Assad regime or Iran is necessary to help defeat the IS, the dynamics are very convoluted. But the answer appears to be no on both accounts. Still, were the Assad regime and Iran to undertake extensive efforts against the IS, its defeat would naturally occur more rapidly than otherwise.

Until fall 2014, the Assad regime had mostly avoided confrontation with Sunni jihadist groups, including the Islamic State and its antecedents. This was due, in part, to the limited assets and manpower of the Assad regime. Also, the Assad regime calculated—correctly—that the only thing the West feared and hated more than his rule was the prospect of Syria's becoming a base for Sunni jihadists. It took the Islamic State's successes in Iraq and Syria during summer 2014, along with the well-publicized IS beheadings of U.S. and UK citizens, to finally convince the West that the immediate threat was, in fact, the Islamic State, and not the Assad regime.

Iran, which considers itself the protector of Shiite Muslims worldwide, has long supported Iraq's Shiite-led government following the fall of Iraqi President Saddam Hussein in 2003. But Iran also had very close relations with Syria on many levels and practically turned Damascus into Tehran's proxy. As it grew in strength, the IS severely aggravated sectarian conflict between Sunnis and Shiites in Iraq and Syria. In doing so, the IS has presented an increasing threat to Iran by undermining the Persian regime's projection of power in those two countries.

Iran has military advisors and fighters in both Syria and Iraq, while it assists the Alawite regime in Syria and Shiite-led rulers in Iraq. As the Islamic State targets those two regimes, and Shiites in general in Syria and Iraq, it is in the interest of Iran to actively work to weaken or defeat the IS. Depending on how such a scenario unfolds, Iran again could be in a very strong position to influence strategic trends in the region. After all, one should recall that Iran was a principal beneficiary of the defeat of Saddam Hussein's regime.

Fifth, would military support, including airstrikes, by the United States and its allies against the IS in Syria strengthen Assad's regime, and, if this is unavoidable, what can the United States do to undermine the Syrian government as well?

Any efforts against the IS by the United States, its allies, Iran, Hezbollah, or other forces, naturally strengthen the Syrian regime, as one of its major opponents would be weakened. Ultimately, the Syrian regime would also focus its efforts on defeating the IS. Alternatively, the Syrian regime could decide to allow the IS to hold whatever territorial gains the terrorist group made, until Assad could turn on the IS when it suited him best.

To be sure, the United States can perform an important strategic and tactical leadership role in combating the IS and other like-minded groups. To achieve a successful military defeat of the Islamic State, the United States will most likely need to use U.S. ground troops, as Iraqi forces and, to a lesser degree, Kurdish fighters have to date proven inconsistent, although both are performing better in 2015.

Still, while the United States has the ability to defeat the Islamic State on the battlefield, it is likely that the IS would respond by scattering and re-grouping for a subsequent fight against the United States or another interven-ing force, should one appear. Thus, the efforts required will need to be extensive and multi-year in scope, especially after an initial "military victo-ry" is achieved. The proverbial quandary of when to leave a former unstable region—if at all—will be applicable in any long-term quest against the IS.

The United States is still in Germany, Japan, and Korea many decades after the end of World War II and the Korean War. American presence there has in fact strongly aided stability throughout those regions. Yet, the dynam-ics of those conflicts and regions, as well as other geopolitical aspects, are distinct from those of the IS threat and ever-expanding Middle East crises, including aggravating situations in Libya and Yemen.

Sixth, will non-Islamic countries such as Russia and China join the international coalition fighting the IS?

Western, Sunni, and Shiite interventions in the Syrian and Iraqi conflicts raise tensions with superpowers such as China and Russia, as those nations—despite their own Sunni jihadist threats—prefer to see the Assad regime remain in power. After all, Russia provided economic and military assistance to the Assad regime, while China was a leading trading partner of Syria. [205]

Seventh, can the IS be destroyed or will its successes on and off the battlefields in the Middle East ultimately expand its influence into other regions, particularly Europe and North America, at least in the form of terrorist incidents?

The future of the Islamic State in Syria and Iraq will depend on the level of effort that the sixty-country coalition and other nations sustain against the group. The support that the IS has acquired both in the region and beyond will also affect its sustainability. Unless counterbalanced, the Islamic State's well-developed social media instruments and strategic communications will likely enable it to continue to gain new adherents, both direct operatives and those inspired by the regime.

As a consequence, the ultimate military defeat of the IS in Syria and Iraq is clearly needed, to put a stop to the threat that the IS poses today and in the future. This is all the more evident given the Islamic State's possession of tanks and other weaponry generally available only to *de jure* nation-states. Once it achieves a military defeat of the IS, the international coalition will then need to create some semblance of stability so that traditional elements of civil society can function.

Recommendations: "Best-Practices" Roadmaps

At this point, for the West, defeating a transnational Sunni jihadist group that has seized large swaths of territory in Syria and Iraq is more important than defeating the bloody dictator of Syria, President Assad, an Alawite. Countries will only contribute to a cause when it is viable politically and considered to be in their national interest. The longer a terror group operates, the more difficult it is to undermine its activities.

Despite commitments from several dozen countries, the defeat of the IS will be very difficult and take years even if coalition ground troops are used. The additional training of Iraqi troops and moderate Syrian rebels, while important, is unlikely to achieve the desired results. Further instruction and arming of both, which is supposed to take months—if not years—will be insufficient. Realistically, to effectively reverse the Islamic State threat will necessitate an immediate effort of a higher caliber.

More bluntly, if previous training of Iraqi troops has proven less than ideal, why would a new round of instruction produce a different result? This is not a defeatist perspective, but rather, it highlights an important concern so as not to repeat an attempted remedy that—used alone—is likely to be ineffective. So, ultimately, the use of proven reliable ground troops, including coalition forces, will be needed.

Alternatively, in relation to Iraq, Iranian interests and Shiite militias can be permitted to have free reign in their efforts against the IS (it is arguable that is already the reality). Under such a scenario, a defeat of IS in Iraq would be suspect, if not a highly lengthy ordeal. Also, the regime in conquered IS lands might resemble Iran or be its proxy. So, too, Western and Sunni interests in Iraq would be severely undermined.

The Islamic State did not arise overnight nor without extensive resolve and resources. The solutions to undermining, and ultimately, defeating this quasi-state will be lengthy, arduous, multifaceted, and no doubt entail some risk. But the risk of not acting is clearly greater. Ideally, the introduction of such concepts as inclusion and pluralism would also be beneficial, so that a multitude of interests can be considered. Sadly though, this is most unlikely, at least in the short term, given the Islamic State's disdain for accommodation and its bloody record of extremism and brutal governance. So too, compromise is hard to come by in post-conflict areas.

The coalition against the IS should be more comprehensive, in terms of commitment and resources dedicated by a diverse group of countries. The aftermath of a defeat of the Islamic State, should it occur, does not guarantee a particular outcome. References to stability in Germany and Japan post-World War II as examples for Iraq and Syria are somewhat misguided. Such analysis does not fully appreciate the regional dynamics, history, and cultural aspects involved, particularly if coalition forces do not remain in the region for decades.

Also worth factoring in is who will be among the beneficiaries in the region of a defeated Islamic State: the Assad regime, Shiite interests in Iraq, Iran, and Lebanon, including Hezbollah, and whatever rebel groups remain in Syria, including former rival Sunni jihadist groups such as Jabhat al-Nusra. Depending on the shape of the outcome, other nations and parties would benefit from having differing combinations of interests and powers governing Syria and Iraq.

As the Islamic State continues to call for its operatives and new adherents to attack Western and other targets, efforts must be made to undermine plots against the United States or Western homeland. While often traditional law enforcement and intelligence efforts have proven helpful in preventing terror attacks, encouraging the public to forewarn law enforcement about alleged suspicious activities, including actions that appear out of line with normal conditions, is critical. Among pre-terror incident indicators the public should report to authorities include: terrorists conducting surveillance, gathering information, testing security, acquiring supplies and funds, acting suspiciously, undertaking dry runs, and getting into position to undertake an attack.[206] Also, there is the unforgettable one-liner, "If you see something, say something."

More broadly, recommendations regarding the defeat of the Islamic State will be divided into two categories: the responses of national governments (gaining control over the flow of foreign fighters, establishing reliable ground forces, promoting and hastening political inclusion and non-sectarianism, and anticipating externalities) and non-governmental organizations' (NGOs') efforts.

Gain Control over the Flow of Returning Fighters

The most important goal of all countries is to protect their citizens from attack at home and abroad. Governments are increasingly focused on confronting the problem of jihadist fighters returning from Syria or Iraq. Nations must also prevent their citizens from becoming radicalized/recruited and leaving their home countries in the first place.

Europe has experienced thousands of radicalized Muslims becoming members of the Islamic State (and other groups) while taking part in combat operations in Syria and Iraq. These individuals can pose threats to security while abroad as well as after returning. For example, they can use their social media presence as recruitment and incitement tools for future jihadists, reveal intelligence about targets to the IS, and serve as fighters. The case of Mehdi Nemmouche—a Frenchmen who guarded foreign hostages for IS and undertook an attack in 2014 at the Jewish Museum of Brussels in Brussels—illustrates how such fighters can be equally dangerous when they return or travel to target third countries. Likewise, Cherif and Said Kouachi undertook weapons training with al Qa'ida in the Arabian Peninsula in Yemen, before returning to France, and subsequently attacked the office of *Charlie Hebdo* in Paris in 2015.[207]

Interestingly enough, in its rigid brutality, the Islamic State may prove to be the best weapon to undermine allegiance to its own cause. The burning alive of Jordanian pilot by the IS in February 2015 galvanized zealous opposition to IS by Jordan and other Muslim countries, together with a grim determination to defeat the group.

There are two general categories of people who return from fighting for organizations like the Islamic State: those who seek to continue the fight and commit acts of violence, and others who grow disillusioned with the lofty promises of the jihadi extremism and wish to return to normalcy. The former should be countered by using the instrumentalities of the state and civil society. The latter should be tasked to work against radicalization, such as conducting outreach in vulnerable communities, or serving as confidential informants.

Some nations, like the UK, have often barred the re-entry of all suspected fighters. This may displace the problem (to some other country), rather than solve it. It denies the opportunity to turn disillusioned jihadists into something more positive. But governments can hardly be blamed for electing to protect their people above all else. In the United States, those individuals who return from fighting abroad or attempt to join a foreign terrorist organization are prosecuted. Other nations, like Denmark, have instituted a type of probationary period for foreign fighters, offering them counseling and even career placement.

At this point, it is difficult to conclude which systems produce the best results. However, the relative infrequency of successful jihadist attacks on U.S. soil since 9/11 implies the benefits of using the American approach. Still, the possibility of quickly incorporating foreign fighters as informants, assuming they are "turned" and vetted, lends credence to some elements of the Danish program as well.

Several British jihadists originally traveled to Syria to fight against the Assad regime. Once there, they joined the IS simply because the organization had more English speakers than other groups. However, after the Islamic State began attacking civilians and conquering territory in Iraq, some fighters tried to leave, only to be threatened with death.[208] These disillusioned jihadis could provide valuable intelligence and counter-radicalization support. Lastly, the UN Security Council's September 2014 resolution on foreign fighters demonstrates how reducing this contributing factor to the Islamic State's success requires a global solution.

Establish Reliable Forces on the Ground

The declared strategy of the United States and its coalition allies has been to degrade and destroy the Islamic State's capabilities. To date, this has been pursued primarily through airstrikes and limited coordination with Kurdish and Iraqi fighters armed, supplied, and trained by coalition militaries and contractors. On November 7, 2014, the U.S. government announced an expansion of its commitment to the conflict by tasking an additional 1,500 forces to train the Iraqi army and Kurdish forces. Also, the Obama administration proposed $5.6 billion to further fund anti-IS efforts.

Coalition airstrikes have focused on rolling back the Islamic State's advances from key positions such as the Mosul Dam, Kobani, and important IS assets. Also, in September 2014 cruise missiles were launched on Jabhat al-Nusra and the Khorasan group targets. In early November 2014, airstrikes in Syria accelerated against the Islamic State, Jabhat al-Nusra, and the Khorasan Group, while also targeting Ahrar al Sham, another jihadist group in Syria.[209] That same month Khorasan's French bomb-maker David Drugeon was believed killed in a drone strike.[210]There has been limited coordination between coalition airstrikes and the Free Syrian Army.[211]

Moderate Syrian rebel forces are not viewed as the sole solution to defeating the IS and Assad in Syria. While a portion of these forces have received arms and training, they are too few. Also, they mostly lack strong central leadership and public support to take the fight to the IS and Assad regime. In addition, some rebels are expressing disappointment in the seeming ambivalence—in practical military terms—the United States and coalition forces have shown vis-à-vis the Assad regime, which the Free Syrian Army (FSA) and other opponents (including Turkey) see as the ultimate enemy. Incidentally, the FSA is "a term used to describe dozens of armed groups fighting to overthrow Assad but with little or no central command."[212]

General John Allen, the Special Presidential Envoy for the Global Coalition to Counter ISIL,[213] claimed that the FSA is to be supplied and trained until it is strong enough for the Assad regime to acknowledge the entity and give it a seat at any negotiations.[214] Prior to his appointment in forging alliances against the IS, General Allen wrote in August 2014 that the Islamic State is a "clear and present danger to the U.S."[215]

By late October 2014, General Allen remarked, "The outcome that we seek in Syria is akin to the [anti-Islamic State] strategy that fits into a much larger regional strategy and that outcome is a political outcome that does not include Assad."[216] To balance keeping the rebels strong enough to defeat the IS and resist eradication by the Assad regime, yet weak enough to maintain the ultimate prospect of a democratic Syria, is an arduous prospect.

One way forward is to establish stronger ties and effective cooperation on the ground with militaries that already have the support and respect of their constituents. Although improving, the Iraqi army is not that force, given its earlier failures, sectarian tinges, and politics-suffused nature. The military, like Iraqi political society itself, is simply too divided by years of sectarian strife to form a reliable bedrock for martial stability. Prime Minister al-Abadi's plan for an Iraqi National Guard may yet create a viable defense force. But, if his difficulties in the first few months of governing are any indication,[217] al-Abadi has a tough road ahead. Of particular concerns for the West are the expansive use of Shiite militias and influences of Iran on the Iraqi regime.

Meanwhile, Iraqi Shiite militias, aligned ideologically and otherwise with Iran, appear to be more effective than the Iraqi army. However, their loyalty to a pluralistic Iraq—shunning sectarian attacks against Sunnis while concurrently defeating IS fighters in Tikrit and other majority-Sunni cities—needs to be seen. Moreover, allegations that the Shiite militias are merely proxies of Iran further complicate the balance of power in the region. Ultimately, the Shiite militias may aid in defeating the IS, but, concomitantly, will further divide Iraqi society and increasingly entrench Iran as the puppeteer in Iraq.

The Kurdish Peshmerga are more in line with the requirements of a strongly supported military. They have the loyalty of their constituents and the Kurdistan Regional Government. Furthermore, the Peshmerga have proven willing and capable of holding strategic positions and pursuing combat operations against the Islamic State. They are more professional and motivated than is the Iraqi army. Despite their sectarian underpinnings, the Peshmerga demonstrated a willingness to aid other groups in humanitarian interventions such as with the Iraqi Yazidis trapped on Mount Sinjar as well as elsewhere. If the American strategy relies on finding reliable partners on the ground, the Peshmerga are currently the best option.

Duplicating moderate Iraqi Sunni contributions to combating the Islamic State, as occurred during the 2007 Anbar Awakening, is unlikely to take root with a large number of Sunni operatives—at least in the short-term. Political mistrust arising from unfulfilled promises continues to reign. Additionally, there is concern that any foreign intervention that would ensure protection of Sunni interests would be short-lived, as proved to be the case when U.S. troops left Iraq in December 2011. Also, the IS has instituted a bloody campaign against some Sunni tribes and Sunni leaders to dissuade them from any cooperation with the U.S.-led coalition. As recently as February 2015, IS militants abducted thirty members of the al-Obeidi clan in western Iraq.[218]

A substantial international force led by U.S. troops could defeat the Islamic State militarily, assuming that IS fighters do not simply blend into civilian populations or find alternatives to sustain their viability. Still, this option would also likely come with the hazard that such an international force would remain in the region for decades, for fear of a re-emergence of the IS or a similar threat.

President Obama's February 2015 request for authorization of military force against the IS marks a new stage in the conflict. More specifically, it may result in shifting U.S. participation in the form of troops engaged in direct combat on the ground rather than being limited to training or supportive activities. Time will tell, but the precedent of military engagements is that they often expand from small beginnings to complex and lengthy wars. Lest we forget, the United States has been engaged in airstrikes against IS interests since August 2014.

Promoting Political Inclusion and Non-Sectarianism

Promoting political inclusion, non-sectarianism, and incorporation of differing perspectives, particularly regarding governance, are critical to provide some semblance of long-term stability and functionality in both Syria and Iraq. Such accommodating policies would be a refreshing and needed alternatives to the myopic totalitarianism of both the Assad and Islamic State regimes. If these political goals are unachievable, then belligerency involving all parties in the conflicts is likely to endure for decades.

Anticipate Externalities

Although it is impossible to predict the timing of a defeat for the IS— assuming an appropriate international effort—some points are worth mentioning. The ramifications of the demise of the IS will rest partly on which groups or interests are positioned as victors. Some power vacuums will be created, at least in the short term. Externalities will likely play a role in the future of the Islamic State, be they drought, economic degradation, political upheavals, other military incursions, large-scale terror acts, or disdain for further intervention by foreign powers. One need only look at the optimistic predictions about a stable democratic Iraq after the removal of Saddam Hussein to see how unintended consequences are well ingrained in the Middle East.

Importance of Moderate Muslim Leaders

Moderate Muslim leaders in the West and in the Muslim world itself can play a vital role in combating the IS and its ability to radicalize and recruit individuals. Muslim religious leaders can help limit the Islamic State's success in the region by preaching moderation, tolerance, and peace, and against the violent extremism that distorts Islam's true tenets. Muslim religious leaders can serve the Muslim community and the rest of the world by continuing to distance themselves and Islam from IS's extremist ideology.

Efforts to debunk the IS as profoundly un-Islamic are crucial. Such activities are being conducted with increasing urgency, both globally and with the support of governments across the Middle East. These actions should be expanded, intensified, and echoed as appropriate by inter-faith voices. After all, ideological struggles and counter-messaging take time to show fruition.

It is noteworthy that most of victims of the Islamic State, as well as other jihadist groups, are themselves Muslims. As such, they have the biggest stake in stopping the IS. Too, as Abbas Barzegar, professor of religious studies at Georgia State University, explained, "Muslim leaders and lay practitioners the world over continue to condemn ISIS and find its alien interpretation of Islam grotesque and abhorrent. Unfortunately, in the context of failed states and civil wars most sane voices are often the most drowned out."[219]

Developing cogent and convincing responses to the Islamic State is absolutely vital for Muslim and global communities. Such activities greatly contribute to the international effort to combat this terrorist group, which has attempted to usurp the soul of Islam. It is also vital that this religious counter-messaging be conducted by Muslim leaders, without excessive input or influence from the non-Muslim world, which could undermine its credibility.

That being said, non-Muslim governments can and have taken effective steps through counter-radicalization programs and counter-violent extremism measures, with some successes. Western programs should be continued where they have yielded gains in respective communities.

In December 2014, Rashad Husain, U.S. Envoy Special Envoy to the Organization of Islamic Cooperation, suggested initiatives that government and other entities can undertake to combat violent extremism and online recruiting within the Muslim community. For instance, undermining online jihadi recruitment efforts should include:

- "Amplifying the Islamic response to extremists to stem recruiting"
- "'De-glamorizing' Daesh"
- "Highlighting former radicals and Muslim victims of terrorism"
- "Maintaining a more constant and creative online presence"
- "Highlighting positive narratives."[220]

Additionally, Husain states that the international community should "support the creation and dissemination of credible content and positive alternatives to extremist narratives":[221]

- "Support for Messaging Centers and Initiatives"
- "Content Creation Grants"
- "Regional Conferences"
- "Online Competitions"
- "Amplification of Messages within Muslim-Majority Countries"
- "Amplifying and Mobilizing Religious Leaders"
- "Supporting Effective De-radicalization Programs."[222]

As General Martin Dempsey, Chairman of the Joint Chiefs of Staff, aptly put it, the Islamic State would "ultimately be defeated when their cloak of religious legitimacy is stripped away and the population on which they have imposed themselves reject them."[223] So too, this path will have to be repeated among other jihadist terrorists and other religiously motivated terrorists worldwide.

In doing so, the world community must undermine the Islamic State and like-minded extremists rather than malign followers of Islam. This approach was encapsulated by U.S. Secretary of State John Kerry in January 2015:

> Obviously, the biggest error that we could make would be to blame Muslims collectively for crimes not committed by Muslims alone—crimes that the overwhelming majority of Muslims oppose, crimes that their faith utterly rejects, and that Muslim leaders themselves have the greatest ability to address. Religions don't require adherence to raze villages and blow up people. It's individuals with a distorted and an even ignorant interpretation of religion who do that, abetted by networks of individuals who have a different agenda and who incite and finance those actions. And we will certainly not defeat our foes by vilifying potential partners or by suppressing the very freedoms that terrorists try to destroy. Unless we direct our energies in the right direction, we may very well fuel the very fires that we want to put out.[224]

Countering Violent Extremism

In February 2015, the White House organized an international summit Countering Violent Extremism (CVE). Its goal was

> . . . to bring together local, federal, and international leaders—including President Obama and foreign ministers—to discuss concrete steps the United States and its partners can take to develop community-oriented approaches to counter hateful extremist ideologies that radicalize, recruit or incite to violence. Violent extremist threats can come from a range of groups and individuals, including domestic terrorists and homegrown violent extremists in the United States, as well as terrorist groups like al-Qaeda and ISIL.[225]

In order to undermine such radicalism, the summit advocated:

- *Building awareness*—including briefings on the drivers and indicators of radicalization and recruitment to violence;
- *Countering extremist narratives*—directly addressing and countering violent extremist recruitment narratives, such as encouraging civil society-led counter narratives online; and
- *Emphasizing Community Led Intervention*—empowering community efforts to disrupt the radicalization process before an individual engages in criminal activity. [226]

Within that context, the U.S. government will launch in three cities—Los Angeles, Greater Boston, and the Twin Cities—"pilot programs to foster partnerships between local government, law enforcement, mayor's offices, the private sector, local service providers, academia, and many others who can help prevent violent extremism." [227]

Other efforts include:

> . . . the appointment of a "CVE Coordinator at the Department of Homeland Security"; seeking additional funding for supporting "community-led efforts to build resilience and counter violent extremism"; supporting workshops and symposium on CVE; and collaborating with Canadian and British researchers "to deliver practical, timely and plainspoken results to practitioners. This international compilation will ensure the best results are validated and shared with those who need them most." [228]

Besides calling for the United Nations to continue its efforts to take "concrete steps taken to address 'the underlying grievances and conflicts that feed extremism,'" the Summit emphasized the threat arising from foreign fighters—as articulated in UN Security Council Resolution 2178 and the Global Counterterrorism Forum's Foreign Terrorist Fighter Working Group's activities. [229] In relation to widening the global base of CVE stakeholders, social media efforts, religious leaders and faith engagement, supporting civil society, and youth engagement were advocated. [230]

Good over Evil

In January 2015, IS militants entered the Central Library of Mosul and removed all books not pertaining to Islam, including materials on sports, health, culture, and science. Those books were subsequently loaded onto trucks and hauled away for burning. [231] The burning of the texts is reminiscent of the 1821 Heinrich Heine play, *Almansor*, pointing out that "Where they burn books, they will ultimately burn people." [232] The following month, the IS burned to death a captured Jordanian pilot in Syria, and paraded twenty-one captured Kurdish fighters in cages, while threatening to burn them as well.[233]

While such savagery instills fear globally, more so, it demonstrates that nihilistic and apocalyptic perspectives, exemplified by cruelty, have no place in modern society. Such violence—as with Nazism—is ultimately bound to fail as coherent and strong forces increasingly align to defeat the Islamic State, as the alternative is too horrific to imagine.

In sum, as the foregoing materials illustrated, and as General John Allen warned in March 2015, the Islamic State "is a threat that is real; a threat that is here; and a threat that demands both our urgent and, assuredly, our enduring attention."[234]

NOTES

1. Byman, Daniel and Kenneth Pollack. "The Syrian spillover." *Foreign Policy*, August 10, 2012. Accessed November 12, 2014. http://www.foreignpolicy.com/articles/2012/08/10/the_syrian_spillover.

2. Shafy, Samiha. "The wave from Syria: Flow of refugees destabilizes Lebanon." *Der Spiegel Online International,* October 2, 2013. Accessed November 12, 2014. http://www.spiegel.de/international/world/lebanon-faced-with-refugee-crisis-and-hezbollah-conflict-a-925767.html. UN High Commission for Refugees. *The state of the world's refugees 2006: Human displacement in the new millennium.* Oxford: Oxford University Press, 2006. Chapter 3. Available at http://www.unhcr.org/4a4dc1a89.html.

3. UN High Comission for Refugees. "UNHCR Syria regional refugee response." *Unhcr.org.* Accessed November 12 2014. http://data.unhcr.org/syrianrefugees/regional.php.

4. Ibid.

5. RRP6 Monthly Update—August, Basic Needs (Regional Dashboard), UN High Commissioner for Refugees, August 2014.

6. Ibid.

7. Ibid.

8. "International donors pledge $3.8 billion in aid for Syrians." *Daily Star*, April 1, 2015. Accessed April 1, 2015. http://www.dailystar.com.lb/News/Lebanon-News/2015/Apr-01/292903-international-donors-pledge-38b-in-aid-for-syrians.ashx.

9. Ibid.

10. UN High Comission for Refugees. "2014 UNHCR country operations profile Iraq." *Unhcr.org.* Accessed November 12, 2014. http://www.unhcr.org/pages/49e486426.html.

11. Ibid.

12. Morris, Loveday. "Iraq faces new crisis as winter descends on millions uprooted by Islamic State." *Washington Post*, December 26, 2014. Accessed December 30, 2014. http://www.washingtonpost.com/world/middle_east/iraq-faces-new-crisis-as-islamic-state-forces-millions-from-their-homes/2014/12/26/9956a666-8227-11e4-9f38-95a187e4c1f7_story.html.

13. U.S. Department of State. "Special Presidential Envoy for the Global Coalition to Counter ISIL." *State.gov.* Accessed November 12, 2014. http://www.state.gov/s/seci/.

14. Semple, Kirk. "At War against ISIS, Iraqi Premier is Facing Battles Closer to Home." *International NY Times*, October 15, 2014. Accessed November 12, 2014. http://www.nytimes.com/2014/10/16/world/middleeast/at-war-against-isis-iraqi-premier-is-facing-battles-closer-to-home.html?ref=world.

15. Ibid.

16. "Iraq Says It Found 50,000 'Ghost Soldiers' on Payroll." *NBC News*, December 1, 2014. Accessed December 5, 2014. http://www.nbcnews.com/storyline/isis-terror/iraq-says-it-found-50-000-ghost-soldiers-payroll-n259096.

17. Smith, Alexander, "Not Fighting ISIS: How Iraq's 50,000 'Ghost Soldiers' Run Their Scam." December 29, 2014. Accessed December 30, 2014. http://www.nbcnews.com/storyline/isis-terror/not-fighting-isis-how-iraqs-50-000-ghost-soldiers-run-n267261.

18. "Iraq PM rules out foreign boots on the ground." *Times of India,* October 20, 2014. Accessed November 12, 2014. http://timesofindia.indiatimes.com/world/middle-east/Iraq-PM-rules-out-foreign-boots-on-the-ground/articleshow/44889829.cms.

19. Beauchamp, Zack. "17 things about ISIS and Iraq you need to know." *Vox,* October 9, 2014. Accessed November 12, 2014. http://www.vox.com/cards/things-about-isis-you-need-to-know/what-is-isis.

20. Ibid.

21. Ibid.

22. Ibid.

23. Ibid.

24. Amost, Deborah. "Syrian Rebels Fear Assad Will Benefit From ISIS Airstrikes." *NPR,* September 29, 2014. Accessed November 12, 2014. http://www.npr.org/2014/09/29/352538345/syrian-rebels-fear-assad-will-benefit-from-isis-airstrikes.

25. Holliday, Joseph. "The Assad Regime: From Counterinsurgency to Civil War." Middle East Security Report. March 2013. Accessed November 12, 2014. http://www.understandingwar.org/report/assad-regime#sthash.eXyufPQL.dpuf.

26. "Syrian president Bashar al-Assad says civil war is turning in regime's favour." *Guardian,* April 13, 2014. Accessed November 12, 2014. http://www.theguardian.com/world/2014/apr/14/syrian-al-assad-war-turning-regimes-favour.

27. Holliday, Joseph. "The Assad Regime: From Counterinsurgency to Civil War." Middle East Security Report. March 2013. Accessed November 12, 2014. http://www.understandingwar.org/report/assad-regime#sthash.eXyufPQL.dpuf.

28. "Syrian president Bashar al-Assad says civil war is turning in regime's favour." *Guardian,* April 13, 2014. Accessed November 12, 2014. http://www.theguardian.com/world/2014/apr/14/syrian-al-assad-war-turning-regimes-favour.

29. Barnard, Anne, and Eric Schmitt. "U.S. Focus on ISIS Frees Syria to Battle Rebels." *International NY Times,* October 8, 2014. Accessed November 12, 2014. http://www.nytimes.com/2014/10/09/world/middleeast/us-focus-on-isis-frees-syria-to-battle-rebels.html?_r=0.

30. Ibid.

31. Ibid.

32. "Turkey insists 'Assad must go' while US focuses on ISIL." *Today's Zaman,* October 7, 2014. Accessed November 12, 2014. http://www.todayszaman.com/anasayfa_turkey-insists-assad-must-go-while-us-focuses-on-isil_360924.html.

33. "Davutoglu: Assad's removal pre-condition for Turkish boots in Syria." *Middle East Monitor,* October 7, 2014. Accessed November 12, 2014. https://www.middleeastmonitor.com/news/europe/14538-davutoglu-assads-removal-pre-condition-for-turkish-boots-in-syria.

34. Ibid.

35. Zalewski, Piotr. "Turkey Grapples With an Unprecedented Flood of Refugees Fleeing ISIS." *Time,* September 23, 2014. Accessed November 12, 2014. http://time.com/3423522/turkey-syria-isis-isil-refugees/.

36. Pamuck, Humeyra and Daren Butler. "U.S.-led air strikes intensify as Syria conflict destabilizes Turkey." *Reuters,* October 14, 2014. Accessed November 12, 2014. http://mobile.reuters.com/article/idUSKCN0I30ZI20141014?irpc=932.

37. Hacaoglu, Selcan. "Kurd Rebels Fighting Islamic State Boost Hand for Turk Talks." *Bloomberg,* September 1, 2014. Accessed November 12, 2014. http://www.bloomberg.com/news/2014-08-31/kurd-rebels-fighting-islamic-state-boost-hand-for-turkey-talks.html.

38. "Turkey Vows to Help Erbil in the War Against ISIS." *Rudaw,* September 29, 2014. Accessed November 12, 2014. http://rudaw.net/english/middleeast/29092014.

39. Butler, Daren and Oliver Holmes. "Turkey says Syria town about to fall as Islamic State advances." *Reuters,* October 7, 2014. Accessed October 8, 2014. http://www.reuters.com/article/2014/10/07/us-mideast-crisis-idUSKCN0IIW0G320141007.

40. Nueman, Scott. "Kurdish Fighters Begin Using Turkish Crossing to Reach Kobani." *NPR*, October 29, 2014. Accessed November 12, 2014. http://www.npr.org/blogs/thetwo-way/2014/10/29/359775623/kurdish-fighters-begin-using-turkish-crossing-to-reach-kobani.

41. "Turkey says help coming for Kurds battling ISIS." *CBS News*. October 23, 2014. Accessed November 12, 2014. http://www.cbsnews.com/news/turkey-iraqi-kurdish-peshmerga-to-cross-into-syria-for-kobani-battle/.

42. Pamuck, Humeyra and Daren Butler. "U.S.-led air strikes intensify as Syria conflict destbilizes Turkey." *Reuters*, October 14, 2014. Accessed November 12, 2014. http://mobile.reuters.com/article/idUSKCN0I30ZI20141014?irpc=932.

43. Earle, Geoff. "ISIS fighters terrified of being killed by female troops." *NY Post*, September 19, 2014. Accessed November 12, 2014. http://nypost.com/2014/09/19/isis-fighters-terrified-of-being-killed-by-female-troops/.

44. "Women fight on front lines of battle against ISIS in Syria, Iraq." *Fox News*, October 26, 2014. Accessed November 12, 2014. http://www.foxnews.com/world/2014/10/26/women-fight-on-front-lines-battle-against-islamic-state-militants-in-syria-iraq/.

45. Ratnam, Gopal. "Joe Biden is the only honest man in Washington." *Foreign Policy,* October 6, 2014. Accessed October 8, 2014. http://www.foreignpolicy.com/articles/2014/10/06/joe_biden_is_the_only_honest_man_in_washington?utm_content=bufferbdf42&utm_medium=social&utm_source=twitter.com&utm_campaign=buffer.

46. Simpson, John and Alex Christie-Miller. "UK Jihadists were traded by Turkey for hostages." *Times,* October 6, 2014. Accessed October 8, 2014. http://www.thetimes.co.uk/tto/news/uk/article4227988.ece. "UK jihadist prisoner swap reports 'credible.'" *BBC*, October 6, 2014. Accessed October 8, 2014. http://www.bbc.com/news/uk-29504924.

47. "Ankara 'won't let Kobani fall.'" *Arab News*, October 4, 2014. Accessed October 8, 2014. http://www.arabnews.com/middle-east/news/639516.

48. Perry, Tom. "Syrian Kurds get arms from Iraq, but cannot send them to Kobani." *Reuters,* October 14, 2014. Accessed November 12, 2014. http://mobile.reuters.com/article/idUSKCN0I30U420141014?irpc=932.

49. "No deal on İncirlik yet but talks continuing, Turkey says." *Hurriyet Daily News,* October 13, 2014. Accessed November 12, 2014. http://www.hurriyetdailynews.com/no-deal-on-incirlik-yet-but-talks-continuing-turkey-says.aspx?pageID=238&nID=72906&NewsCatID=

510. Sly, Liz and Craig Whitlock. "Turkey denies reaching accord with U.S. on use of air base against Islamic State." *Washington Post*, October 13, 2014. Accessed November 12, 2014. http://www.washingtonpost.com/world/national-security/turkey-denies-reaching-accord-with-us-on-use-of-air-base-against-islamic-state/2014/10/13/9f705cd0-52da-11e4-809b-8cc0a295c773_story.html.

50. Blanford, Nicholas. "Hezbollah, warily, lines up with 'Great Satan' to fight against IS." *Christian Science Monitor*, September 17, 2014. Accessed October 8, 2014. http://www.csmonitor.com/World/2014/0917/Hezbollah-warily-lines-up-with-Great-Satan-to-fight-against-IS.

51. Al-Ali, Misbah. "North Lebanon suicide bomber 'acted normal' before attack: residents." *Daily Star*, January 11, 2015. Accessed February 18, 2015. http://www.dailystar.com.lb/Article.aspx?id=283686&link=News/Lebanon-News/2015/Jan-11/283686-lebanon-army-confirms-2-suicide-bombers-behind-tripoli-attack.ashx#sthash.EY1WnLdG.dpuf.

52. Ibid.

53. Ibid.

54. Anderson, Sulome. "In Northern Lebanon, Life Under ISIS's Shadow." *NY Magazine*, September 15, 2014. Accessed November 12, 2014. http://nymag.com/daily/intelligencer/2014/09/northern-lebanon-life-under-isis-shadow.html.

55. Ibid.

56. Ibid.

57. "ISIS in Lebanon: Stoking Sunni-Shia tensions." *CBC News*, October 18, 2014. Accessed November 12, 2014. http://www.cbc.ca/news/world/isis-in-lebanon-stoking-sunni-shia-tensions-1.2804508.

58. Winsor, Morgan. "Islamic State Update: ISIS Militants Spread to Lebanon, Eye Tripoli." *International Business Times,* October 21, 2014. Accessed November 12, 2014. http://www.ibtimes.com/islamic-state-update-isis-militants-spread-lebanon-eye-tripoli-1708576.

59. Bassam, Laila. "Islamic State seeking bases inside Lebanon: Lebanon security chief." *Reuters*, January 3, 2015. Accessed January 10, 2015. http://www.reuters.com/article/2015/01/03/us-mideast-crisis-lebanon-syria-idUSKBN0KC0AM20150103.

60. "ISIS to appoint Ahmad al-Assir as Emir in Lebanon, claims local newspaper." *Al Arabiya*, January 28, 2015. Accessed February 18, 2015. http://english.alarabiya.net/en/News/middle-east/2015/01/28/Radical-cleric-to-soon-become-ISIS-emir-in-Lebanon-.html .

61. Moukhallati, Dana. "Breaking down Ahmad al-Assir: the man behind the beard." *Al Arabiya*, June 25, 2013. Accessed February 18, 2015. http://english.alarabiya.net/en/perspective/profiles/2013/06/25/Breaking-down-Ahmad-al-Assir-the-man-behind-the-beard.html.

62. Rifi, Ghassan. "Lebanese Salafists don't support ISIS." *Al-Monitor*, June 6, 2014. Accessed November 12, 2014. http://www.al-monitor.com/pulse/tr/security/2014/06/lebanon-salafist-do-not-support-isis-iraq.html#ixzz3HGsMZgxA.

63. Abou Zeid, Mario. "A time bomb in Lebanon: The Syrian refugee crisis." Carnegie Endowment for International Peace, October 6, 2014. Acessed October 8, 2014. http://carnegieendowment.org/syriaincrisis/?fa=56657.

64. Moore, Jack. "Isis flag raised by Syrian refugees at Arsal camp in Lebanon." *International Business Times*, September 25, 2014. Accessed October 8, 2014. http://www.ibtimes.co.uk/isis-flag-raised-by-syrian-refugees-arsal-camp-lebanon-1467209.

65. Pelly, Scott. "The Islamic State: Repercussions." *CBS News*, September 21, 2014. Accessed November 12, 2014. http://www.cbsnews.com/news/isis-islamic-state-repercussion-leon-panetta-king-abdullah-jordan/.

66. Al-Sharif, Osama. "Jordan shaken by threats from ISIS, Iraq, Syria." *Al-Monitor*, June 25, 2014. Accessed November 12, 2014. http://www.al-monitor.com/pulse/originals/2014/06/jordan-isis-anbar-iraq-salafi-jihadist-maan.html.

67. "Number of registered Syrian refugees reaches 637,000—gov't." *Jordan Times,* January 28, 2015. Accessed February 3, 2015. http://jordantimes.com/number-of-registered-syrian-refugees-reaches-637000----govt.

68. Pelly, Scott. "The Islamic State: Repercussions." *CBS News*, September 21, 2014. Accessed November 12, 2014. http://www.cbsnews.com/news/isis-islamic-state-repercussion-leon-panetta-king-abdullah-jordan/.

69. Al-Sharif, Osama. "Jordan shaken by threats from ISIS, Iraq, Syria." *Al-Monitor*, June 25, 2014. Accessed November 12, 2014. http://www.al-monitor.com/pulse/originals/2014/06/jordan-isis-anbar-iraq-salafi-jihadist-maan.html.

70. Ibid.

71. Ben-Gedalyahu. Tzvi. "Jordan Trying 12 ISIS Terrorists." *Jewish Press*, October 28, 2014. Accessed November 12, 2014. http://www.jewishpress.com/news/breaking-news/jordan-trying-12-isis-terrorists/2014/10/28/.

72. Said, Samira, Jomana Karadsheh, and Laura Smith-Spark. "Pro-ISIS sympathies simmer in Jordanian city." *CNN*, September 30, 2014. Accessed November 12, 2014. http://www.cnn.com/2014/09/30/world/meast/jordan-isis-supporters/.

73. Beaumont, Peter. "Abu Qatada verdict illustrates Jordan's logic in fight against Islamic State. *Guardian*, September 24, 2014. Accessed November 12, 2014. http://www.theguardian.com/world/2014/sep/24/abu-qatada-verdict-jordan-logic-islamic-state.

74. "U.S. diplomat killed in Jordan." *CNN*, December 14, 2002. Accessed November 12, 2014. http://edition.cnn.com/2002/WORLD/meast/10/28/jordan.shooting/. Finer, Jonathan and Naseer Mehdawi. "Bombings Kill Over 50 at 3 Hotels in Jordan." *Washington Post,* November 10, 2005. Accessed November 12, 2014. http://www.washingtonpost.com/wp-dyn/content/article/2005/11/09/AR2005110901185.html.

75. Pelly, Scott. "The Islamic State: Repercussions." *CBS News*, September 21, 2014. Accessed November 12, 2014. http://www.cbsnews.com/news/isis-islamic-state-repercussion-leon-panetta-king-abdullah-jordan/.

76. Schenker, David. "Countering the ISIS threat to Jordan." *Wall Street Journal*, July 13, 2014. Accessed November 12, 2014. http://online.wsj.com/articles/david-schenker-countering-the-isis-threat-to-jordan-1405290956.

77. Ibid. Kais, Roi. "Jordan, Israel cooperate in face of ISIS threat." *Ynet News*, June 25, 2014. Accessed November 12, 2014. http://www.ynetnews.com/articles/0,7340,L-4534226,00.html.

78. "Jordan vows 'earth-shaking' response to pilot's killing." *Reuters*, February 3, 2015. Accessed February 21, 2015. http://news.yahoo.com/jordan-vows-earth-shaking-response-pilots-killing-191933825.html. Harress, Christopher. "Jordan's 'Relentless War' after ISIS burns pilot alive may include Special Forces, more airstrikes." *International Business Times*, February 4, 2015. Accessed February 21, 2015. http://www.ibtimes.com/jordans-relentless-war-after-isis-burns-pilot-alive-may-include-special-forces-more-1805500.

79. Rago, Joseph. "Inside the war against the Islamic State." *Wall Street Journal*, December 26, 2014. Accessed December 27, 2014. http://www.wsj.com/articles/joe-rago-inside-the-war-against-islamic-state-1419636790.

80. Baldor, Lolita and Bassem Mroue. "Airstrikes in Syria and Iraq are just the start." *Associated Press,* September 23, 2014. Accessed October 8, 2014. http://bigstory.ap.org/article/e404649613d7467f8ff7a1a5c4a75561/pentagon-us-partners-begin-airstrikes-syria.

81. Karouny, Mariam and Laila Bassam. "Syria says U.S. informed it of planned attack on Islamists hours before air strikes." *Reuters*, September 23, 2014. Accessed October 8, 2014. http://www.reuters.com/article/2014/09/23/us-syria-crisis-kerry-idUSKCN0HI11Q20140923.

82. Allen, John. "Degrading and defeating ISIL." Defense News, December 29, 2014. Accessed December 31, 2014. http://www.state.gov/s/seci/235545.htm.

83. Stewart, Philip and David Alexander, "Islamic State fight to take at least 3 years, U.S. general says." *Huffington Post*, December 18, 2014. Accessed December 20, 2014. http://www.huffingtonpost.com/2014/12/18/james-terry-islamic-state-fight_n_6348282.html?ncid=txtlnkusaolp00000592.

84. Redfield, John. "ISIL strategy is working, but will take time, admiral says." U.S. Central Command Public Affairs, March 13, 2015. Accessed March 14, 2015. http://www.centcom.mil/en/news/articles/isil-strategy-working-but-will-take-time-admiral-says.

85. Ibid.

86. "Mar. 15: Military airstrikes continue against ISIL in Syria and Iraq." *CJTF—Operation Inherent Resolve News Release*, March 15, 2015. Accessed March 20, 2015. http://www.centcom.mil/en/news/articles/mar.-15-military-airstrikes-continue-against-isil-in-syria-and-iraq.

87. Miklaszewski, Jim. "UAE Suspends Syrian Airstrikes Over Lack of Rescue Resources." *NBC News*, February 4, 2015. Accessed February 18, 2015. http://www.nbcnews.com/storyline/isis-terror/uae-suspends-syrian-airstrikes-over-lack-rescue-resources-n300381.

88. Ibid.

89. Allen, John. Special Presidential Envoy for the Global Coalition to Counter ISIL. "Remarks at the Atlantic Council." U.S. Department of State, March 2, 2015. Accessed March 9, 2015. http://www.state.gov/s/seci/238108.htm.

90. Scarborough, Rowan. "Iraq war planners urge U.S. military presence once the Islamic State is defeated." *Washington Times*, April 1, 2015. Accessed April 2, 2015. http://www.washingtontimes.com/news/2015/apr/1/iraq-war-planners-urge-us-military-presence-once-i/.

91. Lyle, Amaani. "AF Secretary: ISIL fight requires comprehensive approach." *DoDNews*, December 10, 2014, accessed January 1, 2015. http://www.defense.gov/news/newsarticle.aspx?id=123809.

92. Gertz, Bill. "ISIL Moving Seized U.S. Tanks, Humvees to Syria." *Free Beacon,* June 17, 2014. Accessed November 12, 2014. http://freebeacon.com/national-security/isil-moving-seized-u-s-tanks-humvees-to-syria/.

93. Spetalnick, Matt and Peter Apps. "U.S., Iran seek common ground against militants, but doubts persist." *Reuters*, September 23, 2014. Accessed October 8, 2014. http://www.reuters.com/article/2014/09/23/us-iraq-crisis-usa-iran-idUSKCN0HI08G20140923.

94. "Iran rejects American request for cooperation against ISIS." *CBS News,* September 15, 2014. Accessed November 12, 2014. http://www.cbsnews.com/news/iran-rejects-american-request-for-cooperation-against-isis/.

95. "Iran's elite Revolutionary Guards fighting in Iraq to push back Islamic State." *Jordan Tmes,* August 3, 2014. Accessed November 12, 2014. http://jordantimes.com/irans-elite-revolutionary-guards-fighting-in-iraq-to-push-back-islamic-state. Tawfeeq, Mohammed et. al. "Terrifying execution images in Iraq; U.S. Embassy in Baghdad relocates some staff." *CNN,* June 17, 2014. Accessed November 12, 2014. http://www.cnn.com/2014/06/15/world/meast/iraq-photos-isis/.

96. "Iran's elite Revolutionary Guards fighting in Iraq to push back Islamic State." *Jordan Times,* August 3, 2014. Accessed November 12, 2014. http://jordantimes.com/irans-elite-revolutionary-guards-fighting-in-iraq-to-push-back-islamic-state.

97. "Peters: Iran Is building a new empire in the Middle East." *Fox News,* January 22, 2015. Accessed February 18, 2015. http://insider.foxnews.com/2015/01/22/peters-iran-building-new-empire-middle-east.

98. Williams, Dan. "Israel provides intelligence on Islamic State: Western diplomat." *Reuters,* September 8, 2014. Accessed October 8, 2014. http://www.reuters.com/article/2014/09/08/us-mideast-islamicstate-israel-idUSKBN0H31UE20140908. Opall-Rome, Barbara. "US-Israel Accord to support coordinated air ops in Syria." *Defense News,* September 16, 2014. Accessed October 8, 2014. http://www.defensenews.com/article/20140916/DEFREG04/309160023/US-Israel-Accord-Support-Coordinated-Air-Ops-Syria.

99. Lake, Eli. "Israel could get dragged into ISIS's war, Obama admin warns." *Daily Beast,* June 27, 2014. Accessed November 12, 2014. http://www.thedailybeast.com/articles/2014/06/27/israel-could-get-dragged-into-isis-s-war-obama-admin-warns.html.

100. Maclean, William and Michelle Moghtader. "Iran foreign minister hails "new chapter" in Saudi ties—IRNA." *Reuters,* September 22, 2014. Accessed October 8, 2014. http://in.reuters.com/article/2014/09/22/iran-saudi-relations-idINKCN0HH13I20140922.

101. Spencer, Richard. "Revealed: Saudi Arabia's 'Great Wall' to keep out Isil." *Telegraph,* January 14, 2015. Accessed February 18, 2015. http://www.telegraph.co.uk/news/worldnews/middleeast/saudiarabia/11344116/Revealed-Saudi-Arabias-Great-Wall-to-keep-out-Isil.html.

102. Spencer, Richard. "Saudi general 'killed in attack on border with Isil-held Iraq'." *Telegraph,* January 5, 2015. Accessed February 18, 2015. http://www.telegraph.co.uk/news/worldnews/middleeast/saudiarabia/11325032/Saudi-general-killed-in-attack-on-border-with-Isil-held-Iraq.html.

103. Ibid.

104. "Pentagon: Up to $1.1 billion cost for Iraq, Syria." *Washington Post,* October 6, 2014. Accessed October 8, 2014. http://www.washingtonpost.com/world/national-security/pentagon-up-to-11-billion-cost-for-iraq-syria/2014/10/06/3a20344a-4dad-11e4-877c-335b53ffe736_story.html.

105. "Thousands of U.S. sorties flown in Iraq, Syria war." *Al-Arabiya,* September 30, 2014. Accessed October 8, 2014. http://english.alarabiya.net/en/News/middle-east/2014/09/30/-Thousands-of-U-S-sorties-flown-in-ISIS-war.html.

106. "Airstrikes in Iraq and Syria." U.S. Department of Defense, Undated. Accessed March 25, 2015. http://www.defense.gov/home/features/2014/0814_iraq/.

107. "Operation Inherent Resolve." Combined Forces Air Component Commander 2010–2015 Airpower Statistics, Pentagon, February 28, 2015. Accessed March 13, 2015. http://www.defense.gov/home/features/2014/0814_iraq/Airpower_28_February_2015.pdf.

108. *Report on the Protection of Civilians in Armed Conflict in Iraq: 6 July–10 September 2014.* Office of the High Commissioner for Human Rights. UN Assistance Mission for Iraq Human Rights Office. http://www.ohchr.org/Documents/Countries/IQ/UNAMI_OHCHR_POC_Report_FINAL_6July_10September2014.pdf.

109. "Iraqi civilian death toll passes 5,500 in wake of Isis offensive." *Guardian,* July 18, 2014. Accessed November 12, 2014. http://www.theguardian.com/world/2014/jul/18/iraqi-civilian-death-toll-5500-2014-isis.

110. Karouny, Mariam. "At least 400 people killed in battle for Syria's Kobani—monitoring group." *Reuters*, October 7, 2014. Accessed October 8, 2014. http://uk.reuters.com/article/2014/10/07/uk-mideast-crisis-kobani-deathcount-idUKKCN0HW0XF20141007.

111. Adams, Paul. "Kobane: Civilians flee IS street-to-street fighting." *BBC*, October 7, 2014. Accessed October 8, 2014. http://www.bbc.com/news/world-middle-east-29515431.

112. "US-led air strikes on Syria have killed more than 500 Isis and al-Nusra fighters." *The Guardian*, October 23, 2014. Accessed November 12, 2014. http://www.theguardian.com/world/2014/oct/23/kobani-death-us-air-strikes-550-isis-syria.

113. Plumer, Brad. "This map shows how violence in Iraq could threaten the oil supply." *Vox*, June 12, 2014. Accessed November 12, 2014. http://www.vox.com/2014/6/12/5805282/this-map-shows-how-violence-in-iraq-could-threaten-the-oil-supply/in/5568955. Beauchamp, Zack. "17 things about ISIS and Iraq you need to know." *Vox*, October 9, 2014. Accessed November 12, 2014. http://www.vox.com/cards/things-about-isis-you-need-to-know/what-is-isis.

114. Owen, Gary. "The Islamic State in Iraq is altering US plans for withdrawal from Afghanistan." *Vice News*, August 31, 2014. Accessed October 6, 2014. https://news.vice.com/article/the-islamic-state-in-iraq-is-altering-us-plans-for-withdrawal-from-afghanistan.

115. Smyth, Phillip. "All the Ayatollah's Men." *Foreign Policy*, September 18, 2014. Accessed October 8, 2014. http://www.foreignpolicy.com/articles/2014/09/18/all_the_ayatollahs_men_shiite_militias_iran_iraq_islamic_state.

116. "Iraq: Evidence of war crimes by government-backed Shi'a militias." *Amnesty International News*, October 14, 2014. Accessed November 12, 2014. http://www.amnesty.org/en/news/iraq-evidence-war-crimes-government-backed-shi-militias-2014-10-14.

117. Ibid.

118. Ibid.

119. Kirkpatrick, David D. "Shiite Militias Pose Challenge for U.S. in Iraq." *International NY Times*, September 16, 2014. Accessed November 12, 2014. http://www.nytimes.com/2014/09/17/world/middleeast/shiite-militias-pose-challenge-for-us-in-iraq.html?_r=0.

120. "Iraq: Evidence of war crimes by government-backed Shi'a militias." *Amnesty International News*, October 14, 2014. Accessed November 12, 2014. http://www.amnesty.org/en/news/iraq-evidence-war-crimes-government-backed-shi-militias-2014-10-14.

121. Sly, Liz. "Petraeus: The Islamic State isn't our biggest problem in Iraq." *Washington Post*, March 20, 2015. Accessed March 21, 2015. http://www.washingtonpost.com/blogs/worldviews/wp/2015/03/20/petraeus-the-islamic-state-isnt-our-biggest-problem-in-iraq/.

122. "Iraq WMD timeline: How the mystery unraveled." *NPR*, November 15, 2014. Accessed November 16, 2014. http://www.npr.org/templates/story/story.php?storyId=4996218.

123. Harris, Shane and Matthew M. Aid. "Exclusive: CIA files prove America helped Saddam as he gassed Iran." *Foreign Policy*, August 26, 2013. Accessed November 12, 2014. http://www.foreignpolicy.com/articles/2013/08/25/secret_cia_files_prove_america_helped_saddam_as_he_gassed_iran?page=0,2.

124. "Iraq WMD timeline: How the mystery unraveled." *NPR*, November 15, 2014. Accessed November 16, 2014. http://www.npr.org/templates/story/story.php?storyId=4996218.

125. Ibid.

126. Ibid.

127. Chivers, C.J. "The secret casualties of Iraq's abandoned chemical weapons." *International NY Times*, October 14, 2014. Accessed November 13, 2014. http://www.nytimes.com/interactive/2014/10/14/world/middleeast/us-casualties-of-iraq-chemical-weapons.html?smid=tw-nytimes. Barnes, Julian E. "Sunni Extremists in Iraq Occupy Hussein's Chemical Weapons Facility." *Wall Street Journal*, June 19, 2014. Accessed November 13, 2014. http://online.wsj.com/articles/sunni-extremists-in-iraq-occupy-saddams-chemical-weapons-facility-1403190600.

128. Ahronheim, Annie. "IS used chemical weapons against Kurds in Syria." *i24 News*, October 14, 2014. Accessed November 13, 2014. http://www.i24news.tv/en/news/international/middle-east/47223-141014-turkey-bombs-kurdish-rebel-targets-in-southeast.

129. "Bodies still being found after alleged Syria chemical attack: opposition." *Daily Star*, August 22, 2013. Accessed November 13, 2014. http://www.dailystar.com.lb/News/Middle-

East/2013/Aug-22/228268-bodies-still-being-found-after-alleged-syria-chemical-attack-opposition.ashx#axzz2chzutFua.

130. Sherlock, Ruth. "Syria chemical weapons: the proof that Assad regime launching chlorine attacks on children." *Telegraph,* April 29, 2014. Accessed November 13, 2014. http://www.telegraph.co.uk/news/worldnews/middleeast/syria/10796175/Syria-chemical-weapons-the-proof-that-Assad-regime-launching-chlorine-attacks-on-children.html.

131. "OPCW: All Category 1 chemicals declared by Syria now destroyed." *OPCW News,* August 28, 2014. Accessed November 13, 2014. https://www.opcw.org/news/article/opcw-all-category-1-chemicals-declared-by-syria-now-destroyed/.

132. Patel, Faiza. "It's time to do something about Syria's other chemical weapons." *Just Security,* October 13, 2014. Accessed November 13, 2014. http://justsecurity.org/16325/time-syrias-chemical-weapons/.

133. "OPCW Fact Finding Mission: 'Compelling Confirmation' that chlorine gas used as weapon in Syria." *OPCW News,* September 10, 2014. Accessed November 13, 2014. https://www.opcw.org/news/article/opcw-fact-finding-mission-compelling-confirmation-that-chlorine-gas-used-as-weapon-in-syria/.

134. McElroy, Damien. "John Kerry declares Syria regime has broken chemical weapons deal." *Telegraph,* September 18, 2014. Accessed November 13, 2014. http://www.telegraph.co.uk/news/worldnews/middleeast/syria/11107389/John-Kerry-declares-Syria-regime-has-broken-chemical-weapons-deal.html.

135. Alster, Paul. "Gruesom photos may show ISIS using chemical weapons on Kurds, report says." *Fox News,* October 13, 2014. Accessed November 13, 2014. http://www.foxnews.com/world/2014/10/13/gruesome-photos-may-show-isis-using-chemical-weapons-on-kurds-says-report/.Spyer, Jonathan. "Meria special report: did ISIS use chemical weapons against the Kurds in Kobani?" GLORIA Center, October 12, 2014. Accessed November 13, 2014. http://www.gloria-center.org/2014/10/meria-special-report-did-isis-use-chemical-weapons-against-the-kurds-in-kobani-warning-graphic-content/.

136. Spyer, Jonathan. "Meria special report: did ISIS use chemical weapons against the Kurds in Kobani?" GLORIA Center, October 12, 2014. Accessed November 13, 2014. http://www.gloria-center.org/2014/10/meria-special-report-did-isis-use-chemical-weapons-against-the-kurds-in-kobani-warning-graphic-content/.

137. Ryan, Missy. "Islamic State militants do not appear to have seized any chemical weapons." *Washington Post,* October 15, 2014. Accessed November 13, 2014. http://www.washingtonpost.com/world/national-security/islamic-state-militants-do-not-appear-to-have-seized-any-chemical-weapons/2014/10/15/65f4bf86-54b1-11e4-ba4b-f6333e2c0453_story.html.

138. Morris, Loveday. "Islamic State militants allegedly used chlorine gas against Iraqi security forces." *Washington Post,* October 23, 2014. Accessed November 13, 2014. http://www.washingtonpost.com/world/middle_east/islamic-state-militants-allegedly-used-chlorine-gas-against-iraqi-security-forces/2014/10/23/c865c943-1c93-4ac0-a7ed-033218f15cbb_story.html?tid=pm_world_pop.

139. Nichols, Michelle. "Exclusive: Iraq tells U.N. that 'terrorist groups' seized nuclear materials." *Reuters,* July 9, 2014. Accessed October, 8, 2014. http://www.reuters.com/article/2014/07/09/us-iraq-security-nuclear-idUSKBN0FE2KT20140709.

140. "IAEA statement on seized nuclear material in Iraq." International Atomic Energy Agency, July 10, 2014. Accessed October 10, 2014. http://www.iaea.org/press/?p=4644. Dahl, Fredrick. "UPDATE 4-Seized nuclear material in Iraq 'low grade'—UN agency." *Reuters,* July 10, 2014. Accessed November 13, 2014. http://uk.reuters.com/article/2014/07/10/iraq-security-iaea-idUKL6N0PL1RM20140710.

141. "IAEA statement on seized nuclear material in Iraq." International Atomic Energy Agency, July 10, 2014. Accessed October 10, 2014. http://www.iaea.org/press/?p=4644.

142. Beauchamp, Zack. "17 things about ISIS and Iraq you need to know." *Vox,* October 9, 2014. Accessed November 12, 2014. http://www.vox.com/cards/things-about-isis-you-need-to-know/what-is-isis.

143. Remnick, David. "Going the distance." *New Yorker,* January 27, 2014. Accessed June 14, 2014. http://www.newyorker.com/magazine/2014/01/27/going-the-distance-2.

144. "Statement by the President on Iraq." Office of the Press Secretary, The White House, June 13, 2014. Accessed June 14, 2014. http://www.whitehouse.gov/the-press-office/2014/06/13/statement-president-iraq.

145. "Remarks by the President on the Situation in Iraq." Office of the Press Secretary, The White House, June 19, 2014. Accessed June 20, 2014. http://www.whitehouse.gov/the-press-office/2014/06/19/remarks-president-situation-iraq.

146. Letter from the President—War Powers Resolution Regarding Iraq. Office of the Press Secretary, The White House, August 8, 2014. Accessed November 13, 2014. http://www.whitehouse.gov/the-press-office/2014/08/08/letter-president-war-powers-resolution-regarding-iraq.

147. Ibid.

148. Parkinson, John and Erin Dooley. "President Obama Says 'We Don't Have a Strategy Yet' to bomb ISIS in Syria." *ABC News*, August 28, 2014. Accessed November 13, 2014. http://abcnews.go.com/Politics/president-obama-strategy-fight-isis/story?id=25164105.

149. Gerstein, Josh. "Obama's 'strategy' misfire." *Politico,* August 28, 2014. Accessed November 13, 2014. http://www.politico.com/story/2014/08/obama-no-strategy-isil-110435.html#ixzz3HZ8J71Oo.

150. "Statement by the President on ISIL." Office of the Press Secretary, White House. September 10, 2014. Accessed September 12, 2014. http://www.whitehouse.gov/the-press-office/2014/09/10/statement-president-isil-1.

151. Ibid.

152. Ibid.

153. FACT SHEET: The Administration's Strategy to Counter the Islamic State of Iraq and the Levant (ISIL) and the Updated FY 2015 Overseas Contingency Operations Request. Office of the Press Secretary, The White House. November 7, 2014. Accessed November 13, 2014. http://www.whitehouse.gov/the-press-office/2014/11/07/fact-sheet-administration-s-strategy-counter-islamic-state-iraq-and-leva.

154. Statement by the Press Secretary on the Deployment of Additional U.S. Military Personnel to Iraq. Office of the Press Secretary, U.S. Department of Defense. November 7, 2014. Accessed November 13, 2014. http://www.whitehouse.gov/the-press-office/2014/11/07/statement-press-secretary-deployment-additional-us-military-personnel-ir.

155. Ibid.

156. Beauchamp, Zack. "17 things about ISIS and Iraq you need to know." *Vox,* October 9, 2014. Accessed November 12, 2014. http://www.vox.com/cards/things-about-isis-you-need-to-know/what-is-isis.

157. iCasualties. *iCasualties.org.* http://icasualties.org/

158. iCasualties. "US Casualties by State." *iCasualties.org.* http://www.icasualties.org/Iraq/USCasualtiesByState.aspx.

159. Beauchamp, Zack. "Why the Iraqi army can't defeat ISIS." *Vox*, June 20, 2014. Accessed November 13, 2014. http://www.vox.com/2014/6/20/5824480/why-the-iraqi-army-cant-defeat-isis.

160. "Iraqi forces 'months away' from sustained offensive against Isis." *Guardian*, October 24, 2014. Accessed November 13, 2014. http://www.theguardian.com/world/2014/oct/24/iraqi-forces-months-away-from-sustained-offensive-against-isis.

161. Ibid.

162. Redfield, John. "With ISIL in 'defensive crouch,' Iraqi forces re-take town from terrorist control." U.S. Central Command Public Affairs, March 6, 2015. Accessed March 15, 2015. http://www.centcom.mil/en/news/articles/mar.-10-anti-isil-fighters-retake-key-terrainhttp://www.centcom.mil/en/news/articles/with-isil-in-defensive-crouch-iraqi-forces-re-take-town-from-terrorist-cont.

163. Sly, Liz. "Petraeus: The Islamic State isn't our biggest problem in Iraq." *Washington Post*, March 20, 2015. Accessed March 21, 2015. http://www.washingtonpost.com/blogs/worldviews/wp/2015/03/20/petraeus-the-islamic-state-isnt-our-biggest-problem-in-iraq/.

164. Sciutto, Jim, Jamie Crawford, and Chealsea J. Carter. "ISIS can 'muster' between 20,000 and 31,500 fighters, CIA says." *CNN*, September 12, 2014. Accessed November 13, 2014. http://www.cnn.com/2014/09/11/world/meast/isis-syria-iraq/.

165. "U.N. Security Council passes resolution on foreign jihadists." *Yahoo News*, September 24, 2014. Accessed November 13, 2014. http://news.yahoo.com/un-security-council-passes-binding-resolution-jihadists-191829842.html.

166. Kurth Cronin, Audrey. How Terrorism Ends: Understanding the Decline and Demise of Terrorist Campaigns. Princeton: Princeton University Press, 2009. Alexander, Yonah. ed. *Combating Terrorism: Strategies of Ten Countries*. Ann Arbor: University of Michigan Press, 2002.

Alexander, Yonah. ed. Counterterrorism Strategies: Successes and Failures of Six Nations. Arlington: Potomac Books, Inc., 2006.

Rand Corp. "How Terrorist Groups End." Research Briefs, RB-9351. Accessed November 13, 2014. http://www.rand.org/pubs/research_briefs/RB9351/index1.html.

Gaibulloev, Khusrav and Todd Sandler. "Determinants of the Demise of Terrorist Organizations." Dallas, TX: University of Texas at Dallas, 2012. http://www.utdallas.edu/~tms063000/website/Demise%20of%20Terrorist%20Organizations.pdf.

167. "100 Foreign fighters executed by ISIS trying to quit—report." *RT*, December 22, 2014. Accessed December 26, 2014. http://rt.com/news/216339-isis-fighters-executed-report/.

168. "About 2000 people killed by Islamic State since the establishment of 'Caliphate.'" Syrian Observatory for Human Rights. December 28, 2014. Accessed December 29, 2014. http://syriahr.com/en/2014/12/about-2000-people-killed-by-islamic-state-since-the-establishment-of-caliphate/.

169. "Islamic State executes three of its Chinese militants: China paper." *Reuters*, February 5, 2015. Accessed February 23, 2015. http://www.reuters.com/article/2015/02/05/us-mideast-crisis-china-idUSKBN0L90T620150205.

170. "100 Foreign fighters executed by ISIS trying to quit report." *RT*, December 22, 2014. Accessed December 26, 2014. http://rt.com/news/216339-isis-fighters-executed-report/.

171. Hall, Benjamin. "'You want to kill': ISIS deserter recounts training, torture and terror." *Foxnews.com*, November 6, 2014. Accessed November 26, 2014. http://www.foxnews.com/world/2014/11/06/want-to-kill-isis-deserter-recounts-training-torture-and-terror/.

172. "Rifts emerge among ISIS militants." *Aranews*, December 23, 2014. Accessed December 26, 2014. http://aranews.net/2014/12/rifts-emerge-among-isis-militants/.

173. Bar'el, Zvi. Haaretz. "Cracks within ISIS: Rivalries and internal disputes could lead to small breakaway militias." *Haaretz*, December 24, 2014. Accessed December 26, 2014. http://www.haaretz.com/mobile/.premium-1.633648?v=08C96B6B4769F36E3170F3485BDA5934.

174. "Chapter 6. Foreign Terrorist Organizations." In *Country Reports on Terrorism 2013*. U.S. Department of State Bureau of Counterterrorism. http://www.state.gov/j/ct/rls/crt/2013/224829.htm.

175. Ibid.

176. Ibid. Robertson, Nic, Paul Cruickshank, and Tim Lister. "Document shows origins of 2006 plot for liquid bombs on planes." *CNN*, April 30, 2012. Accessed November 13, 2014. http://www.cnn.com/2012/04/30/world/al-qaeda-documents/.

177. "Chapter 6. Foreign Terrorist Organizations." In *Country Reports on Terrorism 2013*. U.S. Department of State Bureau of Counterterrorism. http://www.state.gov/j/ct/rls/crt/2013/224829.htm.

178. MacAskill, Ewen and Martin Chulov. "Isis apparently takes control of US weapons airdrop intended for Kurds." *Guardian*, October 22, 2014. Accessed November 13, 2014. http://www.theguardian.com/world/2014/oct/22/isis-us-airdrop-weapons-pentagon.

179. Leong, Chan Kok. "Malaysian police: Planned militant attacks not ISIS but similar ideology." *CNN*, August 20, 2014. Accessed November 13, 2014. http://www.cnn.com/2014/08/20/world/asia/malaysia-terror-arrests/.

180. "ISIS and the first Malaysian suicide bomber." *Star Online*, June 14, 2014. Accessed November 13, 2014. http://www.thestar.com.my/News/Nation/2014/06/14/ISIS-and-the-first-Malaysian-suicide-bomber/. "Malaysia's first ISIL bomber blew up 25 soldiers in Iraq, says report." *Straits Times*, June 14, 2014. Accessed November 13, 2014. http://www.straitstimes.com/news/asia/south-east-asia/story/malaysias-first-isil-bomber-blew-25-soldiers-iraq-says-report-201406.

181. Latza Nadeau, Barbie. "Italy steps up security over alleged ISIS plot to kill the Pope." *Daily Beast,* August 28, 2014. Accessed November 13, 2014. http://www.thedailybeast.com/articles/2014/08/28/italy-steps-up-security-over-alleged-isis-plot-against-the-pope.html.

182. MacCharles, Tonda and Allan Woods. "Quebec attacker gave no hint of deadly plan, say RCMP, family, friends." *The Star,* October 21 2014. Accessed November 13, 2014. http://www.thestar.com/news/canada/2014/10/21/attack_on_soldiers_linked_to_terrorist_ideology.html. Farrell, Paul. "Martin Couture-Rouleau Facebook posts: Pics you need to see." *Heavy,* October 21, 2014. Accessed November 13, 2014. http://heavy.com/news/2014/10/martin-couture-rouleau-facebook-posts-page-allah-lone-wolf-isis-patrice-vincent/.

Gollom, Mark and Tracey Lindeman. "Who is Martin Couture-Rouleau?" *CBC News*, October 21, 2014. Accessed November 13, 2014. http://www.cbc.ca/news/canada/who-is-martin-couture-rouleau-1.2807285.

Ahmed, Saeed and Greg Botelho. "Who is Michael Zehaf-Bibeau, the man behind the deadly Ottawa attack?" *CNN,* October 23, 2014. Accessed November 13, 2014. http://www.cnn.com/2014/10/22/world/canada-shooter/index.html.

Perraudin, Frances and Lauren Gambino. "Ottawa shooting suspect Michael Zehaf-Bibeau: What do we know?" *Guardian*, October 23, 2014. Accessed November 13, 2014. http://www.theguardian.com/world/2014/oct/23/ottawa-shooting-suspect-michael-zehaf-bibeau-canada-parliament.

White, Patrick and Les Perreaux. "Ottawa gunman was drug addict, acquaintances at shelters say." *Globe and Mail,* October 23, 2014. Accessed November 13, 2014. http://www.theglobeandmail.com/news/national/ottawa-gunman-was-drug-addict-acquaintances-at-shelters-say/article21273168/.

Freeze, Colin and Les Perreaux. "Suspected killer in Ottawa shootings had religious awakening." *Globe and Mail,* October 22, 2014. Accessed November 13, 2014. http://www.theglobeandmail.com/news/national/suspected-killer-in-ottawa-shootings-had-a-disturbing-side/article21252419/.

183. Payton, Laura and Louise Elliot. "ISIS threat to Canada not imminent but real, CSIS director warns." *CBC News,* October 8, 2014. Accessed November 13, 2014. http://www.cbc.ca/news/politics/isis-threat-to-canada-not-imminent-but-real-csis-director-warns-1.2792121.

184. "Oklahoma beheading suspect described as 'a little odd.'" *CBS News*, September 27, 2014. Accessed November 13, 2014. http://www.cbsnews.com/news/alton-nolen-oklahoma-beheading-suspect-described-as-a-little-odd/. Pearson, Michael. "Who is Oklahoma beheading suspect Alton Nolen?" *CNN,* September 30, 2014. Accessed November 13, 2014. http://www.cnn.com/2014/09/29/justice/oklahoma-beheading-suspect/.

"Oklahoma Beheading: Alton Nolen idolized ISIS." *Inquisitr*, September 27, 2014. Accessed November 13, 2014. http://www.inquisitr.com/1504078/oklahoma-beheading-alton-nolen-idolized-isis/.

185. Siegel, Matt. "Australian PM says police raids follow IS linked beheading plot." *Reuters*, September 18, 2014. Accessed November 13, 2014. http://www.reuters.com/article/2014/09/18/us-australia-security-raids-idUSKBN0HC2FJ20140918. "Australia raids foil reported ISIS beheading plots." *Fox News,* September 18, 2014. Accessed November 13, 2014. http://www.foxnews.com/world/2014/09/18/australia-terror-raid-prompted-by-isis-plans-for-public-killing-pm-says/.

186. "Neubauer, Ian Lloyd. "A teenage terrorism suspect is shot dead in Australia after attacking police." *Time*, September 24, 2014. Accessed November 13, 2014. http://time.com/3423975/isis-australia-melbourne-police-terrorism-suspect-abdul-numan-haider/.

187. "Spain orders detention of alleged member of ISIS." *Morocco World News,* September 29, 2014. Accessed November 13, 2014. http://www.moroccoworldnews.com/2014/09/140329/spain-orders-detention-of-alleged-member-of-isis/. Bilefsky, Dan. "Spain and Morocco Arrest 9 on suspicion of terrorism." *NY Times*, September 26, 2014. Accessed November 13, 2014. http://www.nytimes.com/2014/09/27/world/europe/spain-and-morocco-arrest-9-on-suspicion-of-terrorism.html.

Moore, Jack. "Leader of Isis-linked terror cell in Spain and Morocco is the brother of a Spanish Legion soldier." *International Business Times*, September 26, 2014. Accessed November 13, 2014. http://www.ibtimes.co.uk/leader-isis-linked-terror-cell-spain-morocco-brother-spanish-legion-soldier-1467362.

188. Traynor, Ian. "Couple returning from Syria 'were plotting assault on EU Brussels office.'" *Guardian*, September 21, 2014. Accessed October 10, 2014. http://www.theguardian.com/world/2014/sep/21/couple-returning-belgium-syria-plotted-assault-eu-berlaymont-building-brussels.

189. "Belgian police launch probe into 'jihadist training camp.'" *France 24,* October 6, 2014. Accessed November 13, 2014. http://www.france24.com/en/20141004-belgium-police-launch-probe-jihadist-training-camp-woods-ardennes/.

190. Whitehead, Tom. "First alleged Isil terror plot on UK foiled amid growing fears of beheadings." *Telegraph,* October 7, 2014. Accessed November 13, 2014. http://www.telegraph.co.uk/news/uknews/terrorism-in-the-uk/11147495/First-alleged-Isil-terror-plot-on-UK-foiled-amid-growing-fears-of-beheadings.html.

191. Darby, Brandon. "Exclusive Leak: FBI report warns of potential homegrown ISIS attacks against law enforcement in US." *Breitbart,* October 23, 2014. Accessed November 13, 2014. http://www.breitbart.com/Breitbart-Texas/2014/10/23/FBI-Report-Warns-of-Potential-Homegrown-ISIS-Attacks-Against-Law-Enforcement-in-US.

192. Ibid.

193. Ibid.

194. Brown, Pamela and Jim Scuitto, "FBI warns military of ISIS threat." December 1, 2014. Accessed December 2, 2014. http://www.cnn.com/2014/12/01/politics/fbi-warns-military-of-isis-threat/index.html?iid=article_sidebar.

195. "French police shooting linked to calls for jihadist attacks." *France24,* December 21, 2014. Accessed December 30, 2014. http://www.france24.com/en/20141221-police-shooting-allahu-akbar-joue-tours-jihad-islamic-state/.

196. Witte, Griff. "In a kosher grocery store in Paris, terror takes a deadly toll." *Washington Post,* January 9, 2015. Accessed February 18, 2015. http://www.washingtonpost.com/world/europe/paris-kosher-market-seized-in-second-hostage-drama-in-nervous-france/2015/01/09/f171b97e-97ff-11e4-8005-1924ede3e54a_story.html.

197. Birnbaum, Michael. "Hayat Boumeddiene, wife of Paris attacker, becomes France's most-wanted woman." *Washington Post,* February 2, 2015. Accessed February 18, 2015. http://www.washingtonpost.com/world/europe/wife-of-paris-attacker-now-frances-most-wanted-woman/2015/02/02/b03c6950-a7da-11e4-a162-121d06ca77f1_story.html.

198. Birnbaum, Michael."Who is kosher market suspect Amedy Coulibaly?" *Washington Post,* January 9, 2015. Accessed February 18, 2015. http://www.washingtonpost.com/blogs/worldviews/wp/2015/01/09/who-is-kosher-market-suspect-amedy-coulibaly/.

199. "France: Terror funding, attack weapons came from abroad." *Daily Mail,* January 13, 2015. Accessed March 16, 2015. http://www.dailymail.co.uk/wires/ap/article-2907904/Charlie-Hebdo-plans-unprecedented-3-million-run-new-issue.html.

200. "Gunmen attack Corinthia Hotel in Libya." *WDSU.com,* January 28. 2015. Accessed February 4, 2015. http://www.wdsu.com/national/gunmen-attack-corinthia-hotel-in-libya/30938752. "Father of American killed in Libya speaks out." *CNN,* January 28, 2015. Accessed February 3, 2015. http://www.cnn.com/videos/us/2015/01/28/lead-intv-berry-father-american-killed-libya.cnn.

Lamothe, Dan. "Security contractor David Berry, killed in Libya, leaves a legacy of U.S. military service." *Washington Post,* January 28, 2015. Accessed February 3, 2015. http://www.washingtonpost.com/news/checkpoint/wp/2015/01/28/security-contractor-david-berry-killed-in-libya-leaves-a-legacy-of-u-s-military-service/.

"Nine dead in Libya hotel attack." *iAfrica,* January 28, 2015. Accessed February 9, 2015. http://news.iafrica.com/worldnews/980374.html.

Jha, Supriya. "Islamic State raid on luxury Libya hotel: American among 10 killed, FBI to investigate." ZNews, January 28, 2015. Accessed February 4, 2015. http://zeenews.india.com/news/world/islamic-state-raid-on-luxury-libya-hotel-american-among-10-killed-fbi-to-investigate_1537514.html.

201. Olsen, Jan. "Denmark shooting highlight links between gangs and radicals." *AP,* February 21, 2015. Accessed February 25, 2015. http://news.yahoo.com/denmark-shooting-

highlight-links-between-gangs-radicals-101057480.html. Chrisafis, Angelique. "Copenhagen shooting suspect Omar el-Hussein—a past full of contradictions." *Guardian*, February 16, 2015. Accessed February 18, 2015. http://www.theguardian.com/world/2015/feb/16/copenhagen-shooting-suspect-omar-el-hussein-a-past-full-of-contradictions.

202. "Soldier beheading plan teenager Brusthom Ziamani jailed." *BBC News*, March 20, 2015. Accessed March 23, 2015. http://m.bbc.com/news/uk-31987242.

203. Nelson, Dean. "Pakistan details how Lashkar-e-Taiba 2008 Mumbai attack gunmen were trained." *Telegraph*, November 12, 2012. Accessed November 13, 2014. http://www.telegraph.co.uk/news/worldnews/asia/pakistan/9672494/Pakistan-details-how-Lashkar-e-Taiba-2008-Mumbai-attack-gunmen-were-trained.html. "Mumbai attack gunman Ajmal Qasab executed." *BBC News*, November 21, 2012. Accessed November 13, 2014. http://www.bbc.com/news/world-asia-india-20422265.

Howden, Daniel. "Terror in Nairobi: the full story behind al-Shabaab's mall attack." *Guadian*, October 4, 2013. Accessed November 13, 2014. http://www.theguardian.com/world/2013/oct/04/westgate-mall-attacks-kenya.

Cruickshank, Paul and Tim Lister. "Al-Shabaab breaks new ground with complex Nairobi attack." *CNN*, September 23, 2013. Accessed November 13, 2014. http://www.cnn.com/2013/09/22/world/meast/kenya-mall-al-shabaab-analysis/.

204. Traynor, Ian. "Major terrorist attack is 'inevitable' as Isis fighters return, say EU officials." *Guardian*, September 25, 2014. Accessed November 13, 2014. http://www.theguardian.com/world/2014/sep/25/major-terrorist-attack-inevitable-isis-eu.

205. Carpenter, Ted Galen. "The Syrian civil war's global implications." Cato Institute, 2012. http://www.cato.org/publications/commentary/syrian-civil-wars-global-implications.

206. Learn how to spot suspicious activity." New York State Division of Homeland Security and Emergency Services, undated. http://www.dhses.ny.gov/oct/safeguardNY/8signs.cfm.

207. Bayoumy, Yara and Mohammed Ghobari, "Both brothers behind Paris attack had weapons training in Yemen: sources." *Reuters*, January 11, 2015. Accessed January 13, 2015. http://www.reuters.com/article/2015/01/11/us-france-shooting-yemen-idUSKBN0KK0F620150111.

208. Townsend, Mark. Isis threatens to kill British jihadis wanting to come home." *Guardian*, October 25, 2014. Accessed November 13, 2014. http://www.theguardian.com/world/2014/oct/25/isis-threatens-kill-british-jihadis-wanting-to-come-home.

209. Cruickshank, Paul. "Killing Khorasan bomb-maker a big win—but at what cost?" *CNN*, November 6, 2014. Accessed November 13, 2014. http://www.cnn.com/2014/11/06/world/meast/syria-strike-bomb-maker/index.html.

210. "US airstrikes 'kill French Khorasan bombmaker' in Syria." *Telegraph*, November 7, 2014. Accessed November 13, 2014. http://www.telegraph.co.uk/news/worldnews/islamic-state/11215196/US-airstrikes-kill-French-Khorasan-bombmaker-in-Syria.html.

211. Rogin, Josh. "Exclusive: America's allies almost bombed in Syrian airstrikes." *Daily Beast*, September 30, 2014. Accessed November 13, 2014. http://www.thedailybeast.com/articles/2014/09/30/exclusive-america-s-allies-almost-bombed-in-syrian-airstrikes.html.

212. "General John Allen sees FSA role in political, not military solution." *Al-Arabiya*, October 27, 2014. Accessed November 13, 2014. http://english.alarabiya.net/en/News/middle-east/2014/10/27/John-Allen-sees-FSA-role-in-political-not-military-solution.html.

213. "Special Presidential Envoy for the Global Coalition to Counter ISIL." U.S. Department of State. http://www.state.gov/s/seci/.

214. Westall, Sylvia. "U.S. sees Syria rebels in political, not military solution: Asharq al-Awsat newspaper." *Reuters*, October 27, 2014. Accessed November 13, 2014. http://www.reuters.com/article/2014/10/27/us-mideast-crisis-syria-rebels-idUSKBN0IG0PV20141027.

215. Gordon, Michael R. "Retired Gen. John R. Allen in line to lead effort vs. ISIS." *NY Times*, September 11, 2014. Accessed November 13, 2014. http://www.nytimes.com/2014/09/12/us/retired-general-is-picked-to-lead-effort-vs-isis.html?_r=0.

216. "General John Allen sees FSA role in political, not military solution." *Al-Arabiya*, October 27, 2014. Accessed November 13, 2014. http://english.alarabiya.net/en/News/middle-east/2014/10/27/John-Allen-sees-FSA-role-in-political-not-military-solution.html.

217. Al-Laythi, Nidal. "Iraqi Prime Minister Abadi's government finally complete." *Al-Monitor*, October 23, 2014. Accessed November 13, 2014. http://www.al-monitor.com/pulse/politics/2014/10/iraq-appoint-ministers-defense-interior.html.

218. Sarhan, Amre. "ISIS kidnaps 30 people from Obeidi clan in Anbar." *Iraqi News*, February 15, 2015. Accessed February 23, 2015. http://www.iraqinews.com/iraq-war/isis-kidnaps-30-people-obeidi-clan-anbar/.

219. Botelho, Greg. "ISIS: Enslaving, having sex with 'unbelieving' women, girls is OK." *CNN*, December 13, 2014. Accessed December 15, 2014. http://www.cnn.com/2014/12/12/world/meast/isis-justification-female-slaves/.

220. Hussain, Rashad. Special Envoy to the Organization of Islamic Cooperation, Hedayah CVE Expo, Abu Dhabi, DC, United Arab Emirates, December 9, 2014. Accessed December 11, 2014. http://www.state.gov/p/io/rm/2014/234988.htm.

221. Ibid.

222. Ibid.

223. "Killing top ISIS leaders won't cripple group: experts." *Daily Star*, December 20, 2014. Accessed December 24, 2014. http://www.dailystar.com.lb/News/Middle-East/2014/Dec-20/281742-killing-top-isis-leaders-wont-cripple-group-experts.ashx#sthash.Z3q55qc4.dpuf.

224. "Remarks at the World Economic Forum." Secretary of State, U.S. Department of State, January 23, 2015. Accessed February 18, 2015. http://www.state.gov/secretary/remarks/2015/01/236254.htm.

225. "Fact Sheet: The White House Summit on countering violent extremism." Office of the Press Secretary, The White House, February 18, 2015. Accessed February 19, 2015. http://www.whitehouse.gov/the-press-office/2015/02/18/fact-sheet-white-house-summit-countering-violent-extremism.

226. Ibid.

227. Ibid.

228. Ibid.

229. Ibid.

230. Ibid.

231. Salaheddin, Sinan and Sameer Yacoub. "Iraqi Libraries Ransacked By Islamic State Group In Mosul." *Associated Press,* January 31, 2015. Accessed February 5, 2015. http://www.seattlepi.com/news/world/article/Iraqi-libraries-ransacked-by-Islamic-State-group-6053105.php.

232. "Where they burn books, they will ultimately burn people." *OneJerusalem.com*, May 20, 2008. Accessed February 15, 2015. http://www.onejerusalem.com/2008/05/20/where-they-burn-books-they-will-ultimately-also-burn-people/.

233. Harress, Christopher. "Jordan's 'Relentless War' after ISIS burns pilot alive may include Special Forces, more airstrikes." *International Business Times*. February 4, 2015. Accessed February 21, 2015. http://www.ibtimes.com/jordans-relentless-war-after-isis-burns-pilot-alive-may-include-special-forces-more-1805500."Paraded in cages 'to be burned alive' like Jordanian pilot: ISIS releases video claiming to show 17 Kurdish fighters in humiliating procession through Iraqi city." *Daily Mail*, February 14, 2015. Accessed February 18, 2015. http://www.dailymail.co.uk/news/article-2952924/ISIS-releases-video-claiming-17-Kurdish-fighters-humiliating-caged-procession-Iraqi-city-Kirkuk.html.

234. "Remarks at the Atlantic Council." Allen, John. Special Presidential Envoy for the Global Coalition to Counter ISIL. U.S. Department of State, March 2, 2015. Accessed March 9, 2015. http://www.state.gov/s/seci/238108.htm.

Selected Bibliography

The purpose of the following selected bibliography is to provide interested readers with a broader context that supplements our documented work on the Islamic State.

Ajami, Fouad. *The Foreigner's Gift: The Americans, the Arabs, and the Iraqis in Iraq.* New York: Free Press, 2007.
———. *The Syrian Rebellion.* Palo Alto: Hoover Institution Press, 2012.
Alexander, Dean C. *Business Confronts Terrorism: Risks and Responses.* Madison: University of Wisconsin Press, 2004.
Alexander, Dean C. and Yonah Alexander, *Terrorism and Business: The Impact of September 11, 2001.* Ardsley: Transnational Publishers, 2002.
Alexander, Matthew. *Kill or Capture: How a Special Operations Task Force Took Down a Notorious Al-Qaeda Terrorist.* New York: St. Martin's Press, 2011.
Alexander, Yonah, ed. *Combating Terrorism: Strategies of Ten Countries.* Ann Arbor: University of Michigan Press, 2002.
———. *Counterterrorism Strategies: Successes and Failures of Six Nations.* Dulles: Potomac Books, 2006.
———. *Middle East Terrorism: Current Threats and Future Prospects.* New York: G.K. Hall, 1994.
———. *Terrorists in Our Midst: Combating Foreign-Affinity Terrorism in America.* New York: Praeger, 2010.
———. *The Role of Communication in the Middle East Conflict: Ideological and Religious Aspects.* New York: Praeger Publishers, 1973.
Alexander, Yonah, Edgar H. Brenner, and Serhat Tutuncuoglu Krause, eds. *Turkey: Terrorism, Civil Rights, and the European Union.* London: Cavendish, Taylor & Francis, 2008.
Alexander, Yonah, Edgar H. Brenner, and Don Wallace, Jr., eds. *Perspectives on Detention, Prosecution, and Punishment of Terrorists: Implications for Future Policy and Conduct.* Arlington: Potomac Institute Press, 2011.
Alexander, Yonah and Milton Hoenig. *The New Iranian Leadership: Ahmadinejad, Terrorism, Nuclear Ambition, and the Middle East Conflict Implications for Future Policy and Conduct.* New York: Praeger, 2008.
Alexander, Yonah and Michael B. Kraft, eds. *Evolution of U.S. Counterterrorism Policy (Volumes I–III).* Westport: Praeger, 2008.
Alexander, Yonah and Tyler B. Richardson, eds. *Terror on the High Seas: From Piracy to Strategic Challenge.* Santa Barbara: Praeger, 2009.

Alexander, Yonah and Michael S. Swetnam. *Al-Qa'ida: Ten Years After 9/11 and Beyond.* Arlington: Potomac Institute Press, 2012.

———. *Cyber Terrorism and Information Warfare: Threats and Responses.* Ardsley: Transnational Publishers, 2001.

———. *Usama bin Laden's al-Qaida: Profile of a Terrorist Network.* Ardsley: Transnational Publishers, 2001.

Andress, Carter and Malcolm McConnell. *Victory Undone: The Defeat of Al-Qaeda in Iraq and Its Resurrection as ISIS.* Washington, D.C.: Regnery, 2014.

Armstrong, Karen. *Fields of Blood: Religion and the History of Violence.* New York: A.A. Knopf, 2014.

Art, Robert J. and Louise Richardson. (eds.) *Democracy and Counterterrorism: Lessons from the Past.* Washington, D.C.: United States Institute of Peace Press, 2007.

Azani, Eitan. *Hezbollah.* New York: Palgrave Macmillan, 2009.

Bengio, Ofra and Meir Litvak. *The Sunna and Shi'a In History.* New York: Palgrave Macmillan, 2011.

Bennoune, Karima. *Your Fatwa Does Not Apply Here: Untold Stories from the Fight Against Muslim Fundamentalism.* New York: W.W. Norton & Company, 2013.

Bergen, Peter L. *Manhunt: The Ten-Year Search for Bin Laden—from 9/11 to Abbottabad.* New York: Crown Publishers, 2012.

———. *The Longest War.* New York: Free Press, 2011.

Berntsen, Gary and Ralph Pezzullo. *Jawbreaker: The Attack on Bin Laden and Al Qaeda: A Personal Account by the CIA's Key Field Commander.* New York: Three Rivers Press, 2006.

Bigo, Didier and Anastassia Tsoukala. *Terror, Insecurity and Liberty.* New York: Routledge, 2008.

Blin, Arnaud and Gerard Chaliand. *The History of Terrorism: From Antiquity to al Qaeda.* Berkeley: University of California Press, 2007.

Bolger, Daniel. *Why We Lost: A General's Inside Account of the Iraq and Afghanistan Wars.* Boston/New York: Eamon Dolan/Houghton Mifflin Harcourt, 2014.

Bowden, Mark. *The Finish: The Killing of Osama bin Laden.* New York: Atlantic Monthly Press, 2012.

Brachman, Jarret M. *Global Jihadism: Theory and Practice.* New York: Routledge, 2009.

Burgat, Francois and Patrick Hutchinson. *Islamism in the Shadow of Al-Qaeda.* Austin: University of Texas Press, 2008.

Bush, George W. *Decision Points.* New York: Crown Publishers, 2010.

Calvert, John. *Sayyid Qutb and The Origins Of Radical Islamism.* New York: Columbia University Press, 2010.

Chandrasekaran, Rajiv. *Imperial Life in the Emerald City: Inside Iraq's Green Zone.* New York: Vintage Books, 2007.

Coll, Steve. *Ghost Wars: The Secret History of the CIA, Afghanistan, and Bin Laden, from the Soviet Invasion to September 10, 2001.* New York: Penguin Books, 2004.

Crouch, Cameron I. *Managing Terrorism and Insurgency: Regeneration, Recruitment and Attrition.* New York: Routledge, 2009.

Crews, Robert D. and Amin Tarzi. *The Taliban and the Crisis of Afghanistan.* Cambridge: Harvard University Press, 2009.

Cronin, Audrey Kurth. *How Terrorism Ends.* Princeton: Princeton University Press, 2009.

Crumpton, Henry A. *The Art of Intelligence: Lessons from a Life in the CIA's Clandestine Service.* New York: Penguin Press, 2012

El Fadl, Khaled Abou. *The Great Theft: Wrestling Islam from Extremists.* New York: HarperOne, 2007.

Euben, Roxanne Leslie and Muhammad Qasim Zaman. *Princeton Readings In Islamist Thought.* Princeton: Princeton University Press, 2009.

Filkins, Dexter. *The Forever War.* New York: Vintage Books, 2009.

Gall, Carlotta. *The Wrong Enemy: America in Afghanistan, 2001–2014.* New York: Houghton Mifflin Harcourt, 2014.

Gates, Robert M. *Duty: Memoirs of a Secretary of War.* New York: A.A. Knopf, 2014.

Gerges, Fawaz A. *The Rise and Fall of Al Qaeda*. Oxford: Oxford University Press, 2011.

Gordon, Michael and Bernard Trainor. *Cobra II: Inside Story of the Invasion and Occupation of Iraq*. New York: Vintage, 2007.

Greenwald, Glenn. *No Place to Hide: Edward Snowden, the NSA, and the U.S. Surveillance State*. New York: Metropolitan Books, 2014.

Gunter, Michael. *Out of Nowhere: The Kurds of Syria in Peace and War*. London: Hurst, 2014.

Halverson, Jeffry R. *Theology and Creed In Sunni Islam*. New York: Palgrave Macmillan, 2010.

Hegghammer, Thomas. *Jihad In Saudi Arabia*. Cambridge: Cambridge University Press, 2010.

Hoffman, Bruce, and Fernando Reinares. *The Evolution of the Global Terrorist Threat*. New York: Columbia University Press, 2014.

Hokayem, Emile. *Syria's Uprising and the Fracturing of the Levant*. London: Routledge 2013.

Humphreys, Stephen. *Problems of Political Cohesion in Early Islam*. Farnham: Ashgate Publishing, 2009.

Hutchinson, Patrick and François Burgat. *Islamism in the Shadow of al-Qaeda*. Austin: University of Texas Press, 2010.

Ibrahim, Raymond. *The Al-Qaeda Reader*. New York: Broadway Books, 2007.

Isikoff, Michael and David Corn. *Hubris: The Inside of Spin, Scandal, and Selling of the Iraq War*. New York: Broadway Books, 2007.

Jarvis, Lee, and Michael Lister. *Critical Perspectives on Counter-terrorism*. London: Routledge, 2014.

Jones, Seth G. *In the Graveyard of Empires: America's War in Afghanistan*. New York: W.W. Norton & Company, 2010.

Kandil, Hazem. *Inside The Brotherhood*. Cambridge: Polity, 2014.

Kaplan, Fred. *The Insurgents: David Petraeus and the Plot to Change the American Way of War*. New York: Simon & Schuster, 2013.

Kaplan, Jeffrey. *Terrorist Groups and the New Tribalism: The Fifth Wave of Terrorism*. New York: Routledge, 2010.

Kepel, Gilles. *Jihad: The Trail of Political Islam*. Boston: Harvard University Press, 2002.

Khatab, Sayed. *The Political Thought of Sayyid Qutb*. London: Routledge, 2006.

Krämer, Gudrun. *Hasan Al-Banna*. Oxford: Oneworld, 2010.

Lang Jr., Anthony F. *War, Torture, and Terrorism*. New York: Routledge, 2008.

Laqueur, Walter and Yonah Alexander. *The Terrorism Reader: A Historical Anthology*. New York: American Library Penguin, 1987.

Lawrence, Quil. *Invisible Nation: How the Kurds' Quest for Statehood Is Shaping Iraq and the Middle East*. London: Walker & Company, 2009.

Lesch, David. *Syria: The Fall of the House of Assad*. New Haven: Yale University Press, 2013.

Levanthal, Paul and Yonah Alexander, eds. *Preventing Nuclear Terrorism*. Lexington: Lexington Books, 1987.

Levitt, Matthew. *Hezbollah: The Global Footprint of Lebanon's Party of God*. Washington, D.C.: Georgetown University Press, 2013.

Lewis, Bernard. *The Crisis of Islam: Holy War and Unholy Terror*. New York: Modern Library, 2003.

Lia, Brynjar. *Architect of Global Jihad: The Life of Al-Qaeda Strategist Abu Mus'ab Al-Suri*. London: Hurst, 2009.

Lynch, Mark. *The Arab Uprising: The Unfinished Revolution of the New Middle East*. New York: Public Affairs, 2013.

Mackey, Chris and Greg Miller. *The Interrogators: Task Force 500 and America's Secret War Against Al Qaeda*. New York: Little, Brown, and Company, 2005.

Mandaville, Peter. *Global Political Islam*. New York: Routledge, 2007.

Mansfield, Stephen. *The Miracle of the Kurds: A Remarkable Story of Hope Reborn in Northern Iraq*, Brentwood: Worthy Publishing, 2014.

Mansoor, Peter. *Surge: My Journey with General David Petraeus and the Remaking of the Iraq War*. New Haven: Yale University Press, 2014.

Mastors, Elena. *Breaking Al-Qaeda: Psychological and Operational Techniques*. Boca Raton: CRC Press, 2014.

Mazzetti, Mark. *The Way of the Knife: The CIA, A Secret Army, and a War at the Ends of the Earth*. New York: Penguin Press, 2013.

McChrystal, Stanley. *My Share of the Task: A Memoir*. New York: Portfolio, 2014.

McDermott, Terry and Josh Meyer. *The Hunt for KSM: Inside the Pursuit and Takedown of the Real 9/11 Mastermind, Khalid Sheikh Mohammed*. New York: Little, Brown and Company, 2012.

Meiselas, Susan. *Kurdistan: In the Shadow of History*. Chicago: University of Chicago Press, 2008.

Miniter, Richard. *Mastermind: The Many Faces of the 9/11 Architect, Khalid Shaikh Mohammed*. New York: Sentinel HC, 2011.

Moghadam, Assaf. *The Globalization of Martydom: Al Qaeda, Salafi Jihad, and the Diffusion of Suicide Attacks*. Baltimore: Johns Hopkins University Press, 2011.

Mueller, John. *Atomic Obsession: Nuclear Alarmism from Hiroshima to Al-Qaeda*. Oxford: Oxford University Press, 2009.

Nance, Malcolm W. *Terrorists Of Iraq*. Boca Raton: CRC Press, 2014.

Napoleoni, Loretta. *Insurgent Iraq: Al Zarqawi and the New Generation*. New York: Seven Stories Press, 2005.

Nasr, Vali, *The Shia Revival: How Conflicts within Islam Will Shape the Future*. New York: W. W. Norton & Company, 2007.

Neal, Andrew W. *Exceptionalism and the Politics of Counter-Terrorism: Liberty, Security, and the War on Terror*. New York: Routledge, 2008.

Neep, Daniel. *Occupying Syria under the French Mandate: Insurgency, Space and State Formation*. Cambridge: Cambridge University Press, 2014.

Neumann, Peter R. *Joining Al-Qaeda: Jihadist Recruitment in Europe*. London: Routledge, 2009.

Owen, Mark and Kevin Maurer. *No Easy Day: The Autobiography of a Navy Seal: The Firsthand Account of the Mission That Killed Osama bin Laden*. New York: Dutton, 2012.

Packer, George. *The Assassins' Gate: America in Iraq*. New York: Farrar, Straus and Giroux, 2006.

Pankhurst, Reza. *The Inevitable Caliphate? A History of the Struggle for Global Islamic Union, 1924 to the Present*. London: Hurst, 2013.

Panetta, Leon and Jim Newton, *Worthy Fights: A Memoir of Leadership in War and Peace*. New York: Penguin Press, 2014.

Peskes, Esther. *Wahhabism—Doctrine And Development*. Berlin: Gerlach Press Islamic Studies, 2014.

Peter, Frank, and Rafael Ortega. *Islamic Movements of Europe*. London: I.B. Tauris, 2014.

Peters, Gretchen. *Seeds of Terror: How Heroin is Bankrolling the Taliban and Al Qaeda*. Oxford: Oneworld Publications, 2011.

Phares, Walid. *Future Jihad*. New York: Palgrave Macmillan, 2005.

Pope, Hugh. *Dining with al-Qaeda: Three Decades Exploring the Many Worlds of the Middle East*. New York: Thomas Dunne Books, 2010.

Qutb, Sayyid. *Milestones*. Damascus: Dar al-Ilm, 1990.

Qutb, Sayyid and Albert Bergesen. *The Sayyid Qutb Reader*. New York: Routledge, 2008.

Rabil, Robert G. *Salafism In Lebanon: From Apoliticism to Transnational Jihadism*. Washington, D.C.: Georgetown University Press, 2014.

Rapoport, David C. and Yonah Alexander, eds. *The Morality of Terrorism: Religious and Secular Justifications*. Revised Edition. New York: Columbia University Press, 1989.

Rashid, Ahmed. *Descent into Chaos: The U.S. and the Disaster in Pakistan, Afghanistan, and Central Asia*. New York: Penguin Books, 2009.

————. *Taliban: Militant Islam, Oil and Fundamentalism in Central Asia*. New Haven. Yale University Press, 2010.

Rice, Condoleezza. *No Higher Honor: A Memoir of my Years in Washington*. New York: Crown Publishers, 2011.

Ricks, Thomas. *Fiasco: The American Military Adventure in Iraq 2003–2005*. New York: Penguin Books, 2007.

_____. *The Gamble: General Petraeus and the American Military Adventure in Iraq*. New York: Penguin Books, 2010.

Riedel, Bruce. *Deadly Embrace: Pakistan, America, and the Future of Global Jihad*. Washington, DC: Brookings Institution, 2011.

_____. *The Search for Al Qaeda: Its Leadership, Ideology, and Future*. Washington, DC. Brookings Institution, 2011.

Risen, James. *Pay Any Price: Greed, Power, and Endless War*. New York: Houghton Mifflin Harcourt, 2014.

Rumsfeld, Donald. *Known and Unknown: A Memoir*. New York: Sentinel, 2011.

Sahner, Christian. *Among the Ruins: Syria Past and Present*. Oxford: Oxford University Press, 2014.

Sayyid, S. *Recalling the Caliphate: Decolonization and New World Order*. London: Hurst, 2014.

Scahill, Jeremy. *Dirty Wars: The World is a Battlefield*. New York: Nation Books, 2013.

Silber, Mitchell D. *The Al Qaeda Factor: Plots Against the West*. Philadelphia: University of Pennsylvania, 2011.

Soufan, Ali. *The Black Banners: Inside the Hunt for Al Qaeda*. New York: W.W. Norton & Company, 2011.

Stephens, Bret. *American in Retreat: The New Isolationism and the Coming Disorder*. New York: Sentinel, 2014.

Tomsen, Peter. *The Wars of Afghanistan: Messianic Terrorism, Tribal Conflicts, and the Failure of Great Powers*. New York: PublicAffairs, 2013.

Tucker, Jonathan. *War of Nerves: Chemical Warfare from the World War I to Al-Qaeda*. New York: Anchor Books, 2007.

Toth, James. *Sayyid Qutb*. Oxford: Oxford University Press, 2013.

Turner, John A. *Religious Ideology and the Roots of the Global Jihad: Salafi Jihadism and International Order*. New York: Palgrave Macmillan, 2014.

Warrick, Joby. *The Triple Agent: The al-Qaeda Mole who Infiltrated the CIA*. New York: Doubleday, 2011.

Woodward, Bob. *Bush at War*. New York: Simon and Schuster, 2002.

_____. *Plan of Attack*. New York. Simon and Schuster, 2004.

_____. *Obama's Wars*. New York: Simon and Schuster, 2010.

Wright, Lawrence. *The Looming Tower: Al Qaeda and the Road to 9/11*. New York: A.A. Knopf, 2006.

Zarate, Juan. *Treasury's War: The Unleashing of a New Era of Financial Warfare*. New York: PublicAffairs, 2013.

Index

About the Authors

Yonah Alexander is director of the Inter-University Center for Terrorism Studies (at the Potomac Institute for Policy Studies) and the Inter-University Center for Legal Studies (at the International Law Institute).

Educated at Columbia University (PhD), the University of Chicago (MA), and Roosevelt University of Chicago (BA), Professor Alexander is a former Professor of International Affairs and Director of Terrorism Studies at the State University of New York and the George Washington University. He also held academic appointments at American University, Catholic University of America, University of Chicago, Columbia University, Georgetown University, and elsewhere.

Additionally, Professor Alexander has lectured throughout the world, including in Ankara, Beijing, Brussels, Cairo, Geneva, Jerusalem, Lima, London, Moscow, New Delhi, Sydney, and Tokyo. He founded and served as editor-in-chief of five international journals: *Terrorism, Political Communication and Persuasion, Minorities and Group Rights, NATO's Partnership for Peace Review*, and *Terrorism: An Electronic Journal & Knowledge Base.*

Professor Alexander has published over one hundred books, such as *Al-Qa'ida: Ten Years After 9/11 and Beyond* (2012) and *NATO: From Regional to Global Security Provider* (2015). His works have been translated into more than twenty-five languages and his personal collections are housed at the Hoover Institution Library and Archives at Stanford University.

Dean Alexander is professor and director of the Homeland Security Research Program at Western Illinois University. His teaching, research, and speaking activities encompass terrorism, security, and legal issues. He has lectured in ten countries, including to law enforcement and military officials

335

at North Atlantic Treaty Organization (NATO), U.S. State Department, and National Intelligence University events. His professional experience includes executive, business development, and legal positions in the United States and abroad. He worked as a consultant to the World Bank, Organization of American States, law enforcement agencies, homeland security firms, and investment companies.

Since publishing his first work on terrorism in 1991, Professor Alexander has published several books on the subject, including *Business Confronts Terrorism: Risks and Responses* (University of Wisconsin Press, 2004) and *Terrorism and Business: The Impact of September 11, 2001* (Transnational, 2002). His numerous peer-reviewed and other articles have addressed terrorism, security, business, and legal issues. He was a founding Advisory Council member of the Marsh Center for Risk Insights and a Research Fellow at the Chesapeake Innovation Center (the first business incubator focused on homeland security), and served on the Anti-Terrorism Advisory Council executive board for the Central District of Illinois.

He earned law degrees from Georgetown University Law Center (LL.M.) and American University, Washington College of Law (J.D.). He received his undergraduate degree from Georgetown University and attended the Graduate Institute of International Studies (Geneva).